The Queen Mother

THE UNTOLD STORY OF
ELIZABETH BOWES LYON,
WHO BECAME
QUEEN ELIZABETH THE QUEEN MOTHER

The Queen Mother

LADY COLIN CAMPBELL

St. Martin's Press ✦ New York

www.stmartins.com

ISBN 978-1-250-01897-7

First published in Great Britain by Dynasty Press Ltd. under the title *The Untold Life of Queen Elizabeth The Queen Mother*

First U.S. Edition: April 2012

10 9 8 7 6 5 4 3 2 1

Contents

This book is dedicated to my beloved sons,
Dima and Misha

Acknowledgements

This book would not have been possible without inadvertent as well as intentional contributions from people over a lifetime that is now in its seventh decade. I freely admit I never had any intention of writing it, and would not have done so had it not been for my English publishers, who convinced me that it would be a shame to waste knowledge that I had acquired, often serendipitously, in the course of a varied life. They took the view that, since I had been fortunate enough to know or be related to people who knew Queen Elizabeth The Queen Mother well, and since that knowledge would disappear unless it was recorded, it would be historically irresponsible not to put pen to paper.

I wish to emphasise that many of the insights I acquired came from people who had no idea that their comments would ever see the light of day. Had they known that their views would ultimately form the basis of a biography, they might well have tailored their remarks somewhat. The fact that they did not is all to the good, for Queen Elizabeth The Queen Mother is a major historical figure, and it is about time the extraordinary woman behind the mythological façade is revealed in her glorious and sometimes conflicting complexity.

The people to whom I owe debts are Margaret, Duchess of Argyll; the 3rd Lord Glenconner; the Revd. Philip Hart; Lady Jean Campbell; the 6th Viscount Hardinge of Lahore; Michael Thornton; Lady Lindsay of Dowhill; Percy Savage; Lord Charteris of Amisfield; the Hon. John Pringle; Homan Potterton; Charles du Cane; Ned Ryan; the Hon. Shaun Plunket; the Duchess of Leeds, Dowager Lady Hobart; Lady Diana Cooper; Dr Etienne Dunnett; Donald Douglas; Emma, Lady Temple; Anna, Lady Brocklebank; the Marquesa de Casa Maury; Clare, Duchess of Sutherland; Rene Silvin;

Parker Ladd; Lady Sarah Spencer-Churchill; Burnet Pavitt; Princess Olga of Russia; Frederick Fox; Richard Adeney; Michael Ziadie; Julian (Lord) Fellowes (of West Stafford) and E. Charles Hanna.

I would also like to thank Buckingham Palace for the photograph they provided for inclusion in the photographic section of the book; the celebrated portrait painter Basia Kaczmarowska Hamilton for allowing us to use her excellent portrait of Queen Elizabeth The Queen Mother on the back cover; the gifted photographer David Chambers for the author photograph as well as for photographing Sir Gerald Kelly's sketch of King George VI's State Portrait; my English publishers Dynasty Press and especially Roger Day, Dean Rockett, Darren Strudwick, and Nigel Mitchell; my American publishers St Martin's Press and especially Hope Dellon, Sally Richardson, John Murphy and Stephen Lee; Diana Colbert and Ailsa Macalister of Colbert Macalister, who provided invaluable PR advice, and last but not least my two sons Dima and Misha, who were wonderfully patient as only the children of authors observing deadlines can be.

The following photographs appear by kind permission of the copyright holders:

Glamis Castle © Vittoriano Rastelli/Corbis.

Elizabeth and her younger brother © Underwood and Underwood/Corbis.

St. Paul's Walden Bury © Country Life/A.E.Henson.

The Duke and Duchess of York © Hulton-Deutsch Collection/Corbis.

Elizabeth's Wedding © Hulton-Deutsch Collection/Corbis.

Marion Crawford and the little princesses © Bettman/Corbis.

The Duke and Duchess of Kent © Bettman/Corbis.

Thelma Furness and Gloria Vanderbilt © Bettman/Corbis.

Official Coronation © Bettman/Corbis.

The Windsors © Hulton-Deutsch Collection/Corbis.

Norman Hartnell © Hulton-Deutsch Collection/Corbis.

The Glamourous Elizabeth © Hulton-Deutsch Collection/Corbis.

King George VI and the Roosevelts © Hulton-Deutsch Collection/Corbis.

King George VI and Elizabeth enjoy tea at Royal Lodge © Hulton-Deutsch Collection/Corbis.

Elizabeth at the Castle of Mey © Bettman/Corbis.

Elizabeth with the young Prince Charles © Lisa Sheridan/Studio Lisa/Getty Images.

Princess Anne's Christening © Hulton-Deutsch Collection/Corbis.

The vanity of Elizabeth © Norman Parkinson/Sygma/Corbis.

The Snowdons dancing © AFP/Getty Images.

Elizabeth and Lady Diana Spencer © Hulton-Deutsch Collection/Corbis.

Elizabeth and the Princes © Russell Boyce/Reuters/Corbis.

Introduction

At 3.15 pm on Holy Saturday, 30th March, 2002, Queen Elizabeth The Queen Mother slipped peacefully away at the grand old age of 101. With her at Royal Lodge in Windsor Great Park were her daughter, Queen Elizabeth II, her grandson David, Viscount Linley, her granddaughter Lady Sarah Chatto, her niece Margaret, the Honourable Mrs. Rhodes, and the Chaplain of St. George's Chapel, Canon John Ovendon, who had held her hand as she lapsed into unconsciousness ten minutes before her death, praying aloud and uttering the Highland lament:

I am going now into the sleep,
Be it that I in health shall awake;
If death be to me a deathly sleep,
Be it that in thine own arms keep,
Oh God of Grace, to new life I wake;
Oh be it in thy dear arms keep,
Oh God of Grace that I shall awake.

As so often had occurred during her life, the occasion was almost perfectly staged. Her death was peaceful and painless. It had been expected, not least by the old lady herself, who had spent the previous week ringing up old and trusted friends and retainers, saying goodbye and distributing tokens of her regard.

In death as in life, however, perfection is elusive, and so it proved this Saturday afternoon between the two most holy days in the Christian calendar: Good Friday and Easter Sunday. Her favourite grandchild Charles, Prince of Wales, had been informed too late that she was fading faster than anticipated. He was therefore unable to return from Klosters in Switzerland, where he had taken his sons for their annual skiing trip.

And yet, while everyone who knew Charles and his grandmother felt that he would have dearly loved to be there with her, many who knew her believed that she actually would have preferred that he was not there at all.

All her life, whether in the guise of the Honourable Elizabeth Bowes Lyon, Lady Elizabeth Bowes Lyon, the Duchess of York, Queen and Empress Consort Elizabeth, or Queen Elizabeth The Queen Mother, Elizabeth had recoiled from unpleasantness. Distressing scenes were more than anathema to her; she had spent her whole life actively avoiding them. Departing this life in the presence of the person she loved above all others on this earth would certainly have been distressing for both of them, and many people who knew her and the Prince of Wales well expressed the view that it had been merciful that he was absent. Indeed, in his excellent 2005 biography *Elizabeth The Queen Mother*, the Old Etonian author Hugo Vickers, who did know her and had good contacts with the Palace, even forwards the view that she might well have elected to die on the day she did, knowing that in doing so she would be sparing her grandson pain and others trouble.

Fanciful though that view might seem, Elizabeth was such a determined woman that, if anyone could have elected her time of death, it would have been her. She was a truly remarkable human being, with an awe-inspiring strength of character and indomitability of will. By her own admission she was 'not as nice' as people believed, which does not mean that she could not be, and frequently wasn't, very nice indeed. But there was steel beneath the velvet glove, as she herself acknowledged, and in the course of her long and eventful life she would have the scope to indulge all the aspects of her character, from the kindliest to the harshest. In so doing, she made herself into one of the most popular and, for a time, influential, characters on the 20th century world stage.

Although no one has ever said it before, the truth is: seldom in history has there been a public personage whose virtues and failings so perfectly suited the role she was called upon to play. And seldom in history has someone handled her role as effectively as Elizabeth did.

Fortunately for her, and for the British monarchy, Elizabeth had a unique set of attributes which meant that she became, when the occasion demanded it, an almost perfect evocation of the role of the idealised queen she strove to be. But beneath that exterior lay the human being, with the unique mixture of virtues and failings which each of us possesses. No rendering of her story can be justly deemed complete without an examination of both her virtues and her failings, which have hitherto been either ignored entirely, or then hinted at so obtusely that only those 'in the know' can get even the obscurest hint of what the author is getting at.

Elizabeth and the public both deserve better, especially now that she and many of the participants in her story have died. 'Character is destiny', as the Ancient Greek philosopher Heraclitus observed, and the only way for any biographer to do justice to the life of a subject is to present a well-rounded picture of that individual.

Elizabeth was undoubtedly a fascinating woman who lived an amazing life. While she was unquestionably a force for good much of the time, and while she made significant contributions not only to British national life during the nearly seventy-nine years she occupied a public position, but also to the Western world during her glory days during the Second World War, both her life and her character were far more complex than her public image suggested. How she dealt with its demands, how her strengths and weaknesses affected her destiny and those surrounding her, is not the stuff of fairy tales, but of life. Though inevitably with royalty there is a fairy tale element to a fate so far removed from ordinary mankind, it does not behove anyone ever to think that royalty is anything but human. Prick their veins and the blood invariably flows red. They are human just like everyone else, and their lives only become genuinely interesting when one can inspect them in their entirety.

I hope that by examining Elizabeth's character and some of the hitherto unknown issues which shaped her, the reader will come to a fuller appreciation of her as a living, breathing individual who sought to shape her destiny, and succeeded so brilliantly that she has gone down in history as one of the central characters of the 20th century.

The Much Wanted Angel

Chapter One

The world into which Elizabeth Bowes Lyon was born on 4th August, 1900, was dramatically different in structure from the one in which she would live as an adult. It was a world of superficial certainties, with the rich man in his castle and the poor man at the gate. With the exception of France, all the major European powers were monarchies. The aristocracy held sway throughout that continent, even in Republican France, and certainly in England, where her father was the proud owner of a comfortable house called St. Paul's Walden Bury in Hertfordshire, and in Scotland, where her grandfather, the 13th Earl of Strathmore and Kinghorne, occupied the ancient position of Thane of Glamis, the historic castle mentioned by Shakespeare in *Macbeth*. Across the water in America, the old and new elite also held sway, though there was more fluidity in society than there was in the Old World.

Certainly, some things would remain the same throughout her life. The English weather was as variable then as it is now. In July 1900 the South East of England experienced a heatwave that left London's Hyde Park as scorched and dusty as it would become in 1976 and at the turn of the 21st century. Then, at the end of the month, the heatwave broke, and cooler, more English weather returned to the parched environment, much to the relief of the citizens of London and the farmers in nearby Hertfordshire, where Elizabeth's main childhood home was situated.

Beneath the apparent certainties, however, modernity, with all its impending, sometimes violent, changes, was already asserting itself, and nowhere more so than amongst the heads of state and royals who would, one day, be such a feature of the adult Elizabeth's world. On 29th July, King Umberto I of Italy became the first of a series of monarchs and their heirs to be assassinated in the new century, when he was shot four times at Monza by the Italian-

American anarchist Gaetano Bresci.

The ancient Romans, with their belief in omens, would doubtless have thought, erroneously as it turned out, that the week of Elizabeth's birth was so unlucky for royalty that no marriage should ever be countenanced between her and a royal. The day after Umberto's assassination, on 30th July, 1900, Queen Victoria's second son Alfred, firstly Duke of Edinburgh, latterly Duke of Coburg, succumbed to throat cancer at the relatively early age of 55 at Schloss Rosenau, his castle in his duchy of Coburg.

This death would have a long-standing impact upon Elizabeth's adult life, partly because his namesake son and heir had died following a suicide attempt the year before, leaving the duchy with no direct heir. Coburg was a hallowed place in Queen Victoria's eyes, and the aged queen was still very much the matriarch of Europe. Her beloved consort Albert had been a Coburg prince, as indeed had been her uncle King Leopold of the Belgians and her own mother, all of whom had been brought up at Rosenau. She therefore viewed the role of Duke of Coburg with rather more importance than it warranted.

When her third son the Duke of Connaught and his heir Prince Arthur declined the dubious honour of becoming Coburg's ruler, Victoria foisted it upon her fatherless, sixteen-year-old grandson Charles Edward, Duke of Albany. This unfortunate young man did not want to leave his mother, sister and country. He had never known his father, Victoria's fourth and youngest son Prince Leopold, who had died of haemophilia prior to his birth, with the result that Charles Edward had the distinction of being born a royal duke instead of a mere prince. Lacking the more necessary protection of a father would prove to be a disadvantage throughout his life which was, off any interpretation, unfortunate for someone who had been born a British prince and royal duke. How Elizabeth would cope with this cousin of her husband's when she became queen says much about her character and the forces that drove it, but all of this was still in the future when Coburg found itself without a reigning duke in the week of her birth.

What was very much in the present was the third adverse royal omen within a week. Days after the death of the Duke of Coburg, the Qajar Shah of Persia, Mozzafar ad-Din, who was visiting Paris for the 1900 World Expo trade fair, narrowly escaped death at the hands of an anarchist. It is interesting to speculate to what extent Elizabeth's future life would have been different if Salson had succeeded in his attempted regicide. Certainly it would have been poorer, for the Shah's demise would have prevented him from signing the Concession with William Knox D'Arcy in 1901, which proved to be so advantageous to British financial interests but so economically disastrous to the Persians.

If Elizabeth was born in a week of tumult, her birth itself would prove to be rather more multi-faceted than it appeared to be on its face. The official version, which remained static for eighty years, was straightforward enough. In it, she was born at St. Paul's Walden Bury in Hertfordshire, England, on the 4th August, 1900, the ninth child and fourth daughter of Lord and Lady Glamis. Her father Claude was, as we have seen, the heir to the 13th Earl of Strathmore and Kinghorne, while his wife Cecilia had been born a Cavendish-Bentinck, with all that implied to the cognoscenti. Despite being untitled, and with a father who was a mere Reverend, Cecilia was undoubtedly of illustrious lineage, Cavendish-Bentinck being the surname of the Dukes of Portland. Her great-grandfather had been Prime Minister twice during George III's reign and had the doubtful distinction of being the only Prime Minister of England never to have spoken in Parliament. But for the rule of primogeniture, which prevented females from succeeding to most English titles, she would have succeeded her uncle, who inherited the dukedom sideways and became the fifth duke. Instead of which all but one of the following dukes failed to have male heirs, and the title died out with the 9th and last duke, Victor, in 1990, his son having predeceased him.

By then, the Portland dukedom was somewhat remote from Elizabeth, who is not on record as having expressed any regret at the termination of such an illustrious ducal house. While purists might have looked to Victor's divorce from his first wife Clothilde as the reason for her apparent disinterest, those who knew Elizabeth well understood that his divorced status had nothing to do with her attitude, which, contrary to popular belief, was remarkably tolerant of divorce within her social circle. Lurking in her family cupboard, however, was a secret so dark and damaging, that it provides an easy answer to her indifference to the fate of the dukedom of Portland, while also explaining why she spent her whole life ignoring the circumstances of her birth when she could, and, when she could not, succumbed to such pathological hatred that her normal equanimity and serenity were replaced with a cold and dreadful vengeance.

The first, and least significant, mystery of Elizabeth's birth is her birthplace. This in itself was unusual, indeed extraordinary, for, in the ordinary course of events, aristocratic ladies of that time invariably gave birth at home. Had a Caesarean been necessary, there might have been justification for an expectant mother to be transported, by one of the horse-drawn ambulances then prevalent, to a hospital, though even such a step was highly unusual. Lady Glamis, however, produced all her children naturally. Certainly all the children born before Elizabeth entered the world, in true aristocratic fashion, at home.

Elizabeth, however, was not born at home. Indeed, no one has ever been able to determine with certainty where she actually entered the world. If she herself knew, she made sure she obfuscated to such an extent that the only conclusion one could come to was that she was wilfully sowing seeds of confusion. To one lady-in-waiting, she said, 'I might have been born in the back of a taxi,' a truly preposterous notion, for there were no circumstances which could justify Lady Glamis delivering an infant in a taxi, as any well-bred person knew only too well. To her page, William Tallon, Elizabeth provided the slightly more plausible hypothesis of being born in the back of a horse-drawn ambulance. However, neither of these versions made much sense, for her birth was not an emergency; it was not treated as such; it was never stated to be such; nor was Lady Glamis laid up after it, as she would have been for an extensive period, in keeping with contemporaneous medical custom.

Despite filling out papers for her passport in 1921 stating that she had been born in London, in 1937 Elizabeth herself unveiled a plaque which categorically commemorated her birthplace and christening as having taken place in the parish of All Saints Parish Church, St. Paul's Walden. Her official biographer, William Shawcross, observes, with some merit, that 'no comment by her seems to have survived as to why St. Paul's Walden was officially listed as her birthplace, or why she willingly unveiled a plaque containing wrong information.' The reason, as he might well have known (and if he did not, he ought to have), was a concerted and fully understandable attempt by the lady in question to keep her darkest secret out of the public domain.

The matter of Elizabeth's birthplace was, in fact, only one of the questions relating to her birth. The actual date of her birth was also open to question. Kindly biographers such as Hugo Vickers have forwarded the theory that she took care to adhere to the official date of 4th August in an attempt to limit the damage an alteration would have caused. The prospect of a queen consort of the United Kingdom of Great Britain and Northern Ireland admitting that her official birth date was in fact incorrect would have caused havoc, not just amongst the many official bodies whose functions overlapped or intersected with hers, and would consequently necessitate changing not only records but also dates of celebration and the host of other paraphernalia which go along with being royal. The fact that it would also have opened up awkward questions as to why someone, whose lineage was as eminent as Elizabeth's, could possibly have been given the wrong birth date was, of course, glossed over. And for good reason, as the simple fact is that such questions would have driven the whole wretched question into the discomfiting territory of truthfulness.

In July 1980, in the run up to the official celebrations for Elizabeth's eightieth birthday, the issue seemed in danger of erupting embarrassingly. According to the fable which was promulgated at the time, preparations for the celebrations the following month were well in hand when a parishioner at All Saints, the parish church for St. Paul's Walden Bury, noticed that her birthplace had been omitted from the relevant literature despite the presence of the plaque. In the fifty-seven years since Elizabeth had become royal, no one had ever publicly questioned the anomalies surrounding her birth. Now an enquiry of her Household, as to why St. Paul's Walden Bury had been omitted, presented them with the possibility that the circumstances surrounding her birth were in danger of being made public. Realising that the submerged part of the iceberg was infinitely more damaging than the tip, and knowing only too well that there was every possibility that the main story had reached the ears of the press, who had concocted the tale of the sharp-eyed parishioner as a cover for deeper ferreting out of the facts, Queen Elizabeth The Queen Mother's Household wisely decided to divert the press's attention away from the embarrassing underbelly of the berg by dishing up the news of its tip. Rather than issuing a repetition of the fiction, which had been purveyed to the public since 1923, that she had been born at St. Paul's Walden Bury, Clarence House therefore issued an announcement to the effect that Her Majesty had been born in London, and not in Hertfordshire as the official line had been for the previous decades.

As anyone with any knowledge of the media knows, an admission of this magnitude is sure to create enough of a splash to satisfy those who require coverage, while silencing those who theorise that there might well have been more to the iceberg than met the eye.

Although there was never much likelihood of the average reporter in Britain, or anywhere else for that matter, having heard the stories about Elizabeth's birth, there were one or two well-born or well-married journalists who had to have known of them. However, such was Queen Elizabeth The Queen Mother's popularity that, even had they been tempted to take the matter further, their editors, all of whom enjoyed lunches at the Palace with the Queen, would never have jeopardised the cordiality of their relations with their sovereign by publishing such incendiary news about her mother.

For the fact is, royal and aristocratic circles had been alight for decades with the story that Elizabeth Bowes Lyon, while undoubtedly the daughter of the 14th Earl of Strathmore and Kinghorne, was not the child of his wife Cecilia, nor was her younger brother David, born nearly two years after her on 2nd May, 1902. The two Benjamins, as they were known in the Bowes

Lyon family (in a Biblical allusion to the brother of Joseph, who was himself the product of a coupling between his father and his mother's maid), were supposedly the children of Marguerite Rodiere, an attractive and pleasant Frenchwoman who had been the cook at St. Paul's Walden Bury and is meant to have provided Lord and Lady Glamis with the two children they so yearned for after Cecilia was forbidden by her doctors from producing any more progeny. Hence the nickname of Cookie, which the Duke and Duchess of Windsor took care to promulgate throughout international Society once Elizabeth proved herself to be their most formidable enemy.

This early version of surrogacy, if surrogacy it was, might have been unusual, but there was nothing extraordinary or unheard of about it in aristocratic circles. In 1900, adoption was not a regulated practice, but primarily a personal arrangement pursued by those who wanted children, and those who did not. There was none of the bureaucracy which exists today. If you wanted to adopt a child, and its parents agreed, you drew up documents, signed them, and that child was legally yours.

In many of the European monarchies, titles could be passed down from adoptive parents to adopted children. For instance, in 1847 Elzear, 1ˢᵗ Duc de Sabran, adopted the child of his wife's second cousin, Count Marc de Pontevès-Bargème. One of his descendants is the present Duchesse d'Orléans, a member of the French Royal Family. The late Maharajah of Jaipur was adopted by his heirless predecessor, and Prince Jonathan Doria Pamphilj was adopted by his mother, Princess Orietta Doria Pamphilj, and her husband, Commander Frank Pogson, as late as 1963.

In Britain, however, adopted children, like illegitimate children, could not, and still cannot, succeed to peerages. Worse still, they were prevented from using the courtesy titles that ordinarily devolved upon the younger children of a peer. There were some notable anomalies which caused much distress to the individuals involved. The writer Anthony Haden-Guest, despite being the elder son of the 4ᵗʰ Lord Haden-Guest, was subjected to the constant reminder that his birth had preceded his parents' marriage by being denied the honorific of The Honourable. In a world where titles counted and everyone knew who did and did not have one, this was an unnecessary humiliation to inflict upon anyone. What made it even worse, however, was the fact that his younger brother Christopher, the husband of the movie star Jamie Lee Curtis, was an Honourable from birth, their parents having married by this time, and would ultimately succeed to the barony.

This was a humiliation shared by the actress Nimmy March, the adopted daughter of the Duke and Duchess of Richmond and Gordon, who remained in private life Miss Naomi Gordon-Lennox. The four children of the 4ᵗʰ

Marquess and Marchioness of Aberdeen and Temair fared no better. Subjected to perpetual reminders of their adoptive status by remaining the Misses Mary and Sarah Gordon and Messrs. Andrew and James Gordon while all their relations had titles, their mother June became increasingly vociferous in her condemnation of a practice that remained a thorn in all adoptive children's sides. It was one thing for adopted children to elect to inform others of their adoptive status, and quite another to have that fact declared at all times to all and sundry whether they wished it to be or not. Being the founder and musical director of the famed Haddo House Choral and Operatic Society and something of a powerhouse, June Aberdeen was in an ideal position to make her voice heard, and heard she made it. She lived to see the fruit of her labours rewarded when, on 30th April, 2004, Queen Elizabeth II issued a Royal Warrant giving all adoptive children the right to use the same courtesy titles as the natural children of peers.

Prior to the issuing of that Royal Warrant, adoptive children were forced to live as second-class citizens in a first-class world. Of course their parents usually minded as much as the children themselves, for adoptive parents often love their adopted children at least as much as, and often more than, the children whom nature has imposed upon them, as I know from my own personal experience.

It is hardly surprising, therefore, that aristocrats who wanted children (or more children, as is supposed to have been the case with Claude and Cecilia Glamis) sometimes went to extreme lengths to ensure that their offspring were born without the stigma of inequality. The legal principle of presumption of legitimacy worked in the favour of such couples, because a child who was born within a valid marriage was deemed to be the legitimate product of both parties to that union. As long as the child was acknowledged officially by both parents as their natural-born issue, it automatically assumed the rank, style and title that was the due of all legitimate children of peers.

This practice worked, not only for adopted children whose parents were intent on ensuring that they went through life with the privileges of legitimate issue, but also to the benefit of philandering wives, or wives whose husbands could not produce children but wanted them.

The aristocracy was rife with these children, and the way Elizabeth would treat them throughout her years as queen consort and queen mother, often in direct contradiction of her espoused values and the way she treated everyone else, goes some way to confirming the rumours about her birth. For instance, the 8th Duke of Rutland's sculptress wife Violet gave birth in 1892 to a beautiful little girl who was known from birth as Lady Diana Manners, despite being Mr. Henry (Harry) Cust's daughter. Her actual paternity made no difference to her status, and she would go down in history as the fabled Lady Diana Cooper, wife of the British Ambassador to France, Duff Cooper, and one of the few people who could curtsey to the Duchess of Windsor and remain on cordial terms with Elizabeth.

Another notable 'jacket', as such babies were known in the circles which had need of them, whose life interwove with Elizabeth's, was the 7th Earl of Carnarvon. His ancestral home, Highclere Castle, was famous for the Tutankhamun treasures it had housed since the time of his birth in 1924, and is now even more famous for being the setting for the hit television series, *Downton Abbey*. His father Henry (always known as Porchy after his courtesy title Lord Porchester) was a famous roué and raconteur who entertained both Society and the masses with two volumes of memoirs and countless television and radio interviews, which might have been embarrassing to his family, but were a study in hilarity for everyone else. I knew him slightly, albeit to my regret when he talked me out of backing Ile de Bourbon during Royal Ascot in the 1970s and it romped home, while Porchy's 'certainty' lagged sadly behind. Short, and rather attractive in an ugly sort of way, because his captivating personality more than made up for the irregularity of his features, he was supposedly sterile. His son and heir, another Henry (also known as Porchy except to his father's friends, who then had to make the distinction between Big Porchy and Little Porchy), was his physical antithesis. Little Porchy was tall and strapping, indisputably handsome with regular features, and a gravity of manner that was sorely at odds with Big Porchy's levity. There was also a daughter, Lady Anne Penelope Herbert, born in 1925 to his American first wife Anne Wendell, after which there were no further children, even though the marriage lasted until 1936.

This in itself was noteworthy. In a day and age before antibiotics, when children frequently died in childhood from minor infections, and sole heirs stood a sufficiently great chance of being killed in a war to necessitate at least a spare or two, couples who had only one or two children often delivered the message that there was a problem within the marriage. This might be that the wife did not like sex, or that the husband was infertile, or that something had gone wrong with her childbearing capacity. The grander the couple, the more likely that there was a serious problem, for great estates were entailed upon the title, meaning that a peer could not leave his property to whom he pleased. It had to be inherited by the next holder of the title, irrespective of whether that was his eldest son or third cousin twice removed (as often happened), so there was a strong incentive for a couple to produce enough children for the title not to go sideways to some distant cousin. The aristocracy was filled with horror stories about widows and daughters of great peers living in penury while some distant cousin was lording it over them in more ways than one.

This paucity of children indicating a problem was certainly true in the case of the Carnarvons, and their situation is worthy of examination if only because it was redolent of so much in Elizabeth's circumstances. Three years after the American countess divorced the earl in 1936, Big Porchy married Tilly Losch, the celebrated Austrian dancer, actress and artist whose first husband had been the Anglo-American multi-millionaire art patron, Edward James. Marrying her was indicative of Porchy's strength of character, for by then King George VI and Queen Elizabeth sat on the English throne. Following the abdication of King Edward VIII, divorce, which had been steadily gaining acceptance in all social circles, once more resulted in ostracism, especially when the wife was deemed to be the guilty party. And Tilly Losch had been ascribed guilt in the most scandalous divorce case of its day, Edward James having divorced her for adultery citing Tsar Alexander II's tall and handsome son-in-law Prince Serge Obolensky, after she had thrown over the lover of whom he approved, the Hon. Thomas (Tom) Mitford, brother of the famous Mitford girls and heir to Lord Ribblesdale. But what made the James divorce particularly scandalous was that Tilly had cross-petitioned, alleging that her husband was a homosexual (which he was well known to be within trans-Atlantic Society) at a time when homosexuality was illegal on both sides of the Atlantic. When her petition failed, she had a serious nervous breakdown, and had to be hospitalised in Switzerland, whence she was rescued by the charming and deliciously unorthodox Porchy.

There was no progeny from this marriage, a fact which Tilly Losch made no bones about. She matter-of-factly stated on many an occasion that her husband was sterile and had always been, following a bout of post-puberty mumps. Although she was occasionally warned by friends to tone down her comments, lest she call into question the legitimacy of the heir, she seems never to have done so, nor to have thought that she was endangering the future of the Carnarvon earldom with what, on the face of it, seemed to be blatant indiscretion. In that regard, she was correct, for Society was littered with children whose legitimacy owed everything to presumption and nothing to genetics, and there was no prospect at all of anyone challenging Little Porchy's right to the Carnarvon title and estates.

There was an unexpected postscript which shows how accommodating Elizabeth was behind what became her professed veneer of rectitude. Although Porchy and Tilly were somewhat racy and deemed to be that bit too openly scandalous to be embraced by Bertie and herself once they were the king and queen, his son and heir was accepted unreservedly. As he grew towards adulthood, Little Porchy became rather chummy with Lilibet, as Princess Elizabeth, the heiress to the throne, was known within her family circle. Towards the end of the Second World War, while she was writing to Prince Philip of Greece as a prospective beau but nothing had been agreed between them either formally or informally, Lilibet began to see rather a lot of Porchy. Highclere Castle was relatively near to Windsor Castle, where the young princesses spent most of the war. Queen Elizabeth, who much preferred British aristocrats to royals of any persuasion, liked Porchy and had nothing against a prospective union between him and her elder daughter. On the other hand, she made it clear that she disliked the possibility of a marriage between her daughter and Philip, to whom she referred disparagingly as 'the Hun'. King George VI, however, watched the budding friendship with growing horror, and when it became apparent that it was in danger of blossoming into a fully-fledged romance, took active steps to discourage it. 'She cannot marry a man when no one knows who his father is,' he is alleged to have said to one relation, while to another he said, 'Young Porchester is charming but there is no possibility of my condoning a union between a daughter of mine and a butler's son.'

George VI was giving voice to the methods adopted by a trio of Society doctors whose success had been much enhanced by their talent for 'assisting' childless peeresses to produce the heirs their husbands needed. Doctors Abrahams, Aarons and Zimmerman were fashionable obstetricians and gynaecologists who had an infallible technique for providing peeresses with these much-needed miracles. The ladies in question would attend their surgeries in Harley Street. In an adjoining room would be one of the handsome, strapping butlers who were on the doctors' payroll as sperm donors. After these men had ejaculated, their semen was taken next door and injected into the lady in question, who was spread-eagled with a speculum awaiting her chance of a miracle. Lady and donor would never meet. No one but the doctor would know who the natural father was. But what 'everyone' in Society knew was that, his good looks aside, the butler in question would be of superior genetic stock, the proud possessor of intelligence and organisational skills without which he could never have risen to such a responsible position.

While nowadays people might think of butlers as being servants who were unctuous twits gliding around large houses opening doors and serving drinks, the reality was different. Butlers were, in effect, the managing directors of households at a time when many were larger than most companies. To function in their allotted role, they had to possess native intelligence, organisational skills, management abilities, discipline, a steady temperament, and the social aptitude to deal ably with their superiors, equals and inferiors. In other words, they were the top flight executives of their day. While they undoubtedly came from more disadvantaged backgrounds than their masters, they were often their human equals, and sometimes their human superiors, not, of course, that either side would have been foolhardy enough to acknowledge such a reality. Many of them were also handsome, for some were hired as much for their good looks as for their other abilities. Moreover, because of their inferior social status, they would never have the means or the prestige to cause future problems for the women impregnated with their semen.

This proved to be a brilliant solution to the problems of many childless aristocrats, especially in a world where inbreeding had sometimes created unfortunate physical or personal characteristics. Claude Glamis, however, had no problem fathering children, as his wife Cecilia had proven eight times over. Nor did she have problems producing healthy, happy, good-looking and charming children. However, one of those tragedies which periodically happened in those pre-antibiotic days, might well have been at the root of the problem. On 17th October, 1893, Claude and Cecilia Glamis's eldest child Violet died of heart failure following a bout of diphtheria. Cecilia had given birth to her youngest son Michael less than three weeks before, on 1st October, 1893. According to all sources, Lady Glamis was an exceptionally loving mother who lived primarily for her children. Already emotionally vulnerable following the latest birth, she was devastated by the death of this child whom she always said was 'beautiful' and admitted till her dying day to missing.

In *Queen Elizabeth The Queen Mother: The Official Biography,* William Shawcross euphemistically states that 'Lady Glamis bore her daughter's loss with as much courage as she could muster'. The fact is, she suffered a severe nervous breakdown from which she never entirely recovered. She would always remain fragile, both physically and personally, and while she recovered sufficiently to resume her role in Society, she was prone to nervous attacks which incapacitated her for the remainder of her life. At times like these, she would withdraw, not from family life, but from everything else. During the First World War, after the death of one son and the loss of another (who would turn out to have been captured), her health became so precarious that the teenage Elizabeth often had to step into her mother's shoes and fill the role of chatelaine of Glamis Castle for her. She would also rather touchingly wake up early and intercept the post in case it contained bad news for which she would then need to prepare her mother.

One cannot help but sympathise with a woman who so loves her children that she cannot fully come to terms with the loss of one. Whether Cecilia went on to have two more children, as the official sources state, or whether she was so damaged by the loss of her firstborn that she was not allowed to put herself through the trauma of giving birth yet again, one fact is indisputable: For seven years, St. Paul's Walden Bury saw no more births.

According to the rumours that were so prolific that it is almost miraculous they remained within the narrow confines of aristocratic circles for so long, as more and more time elapsed after the death of Violet, both Claude and Cecilia Glamis wanted more children. In those days, however, doctors were even more convinced than they would be today, that a woman whose health was fragile, should not expose herself to the biological and emotional changes pregnancy inevitably brings in its wake.

This view had a degree of merit, for the hormonal changes of pregnancy can induce post-partum depression in even a healthy woman. For someone like Cecilia Glamis, who had failed to recover fully from the grief of losing a child, the risks of pregnancy were adjudged to be too great. According to the Duke of Windsor, who had access to all the reports when he was king, and had moreover known of the background while Prince of Wales through his brother Bertie, Claude and Cecilia resorted to a primitive form of surrogacy, whose existence is as old as civilisation itself. This method had the merit of possessing the Bible's stamp of approval. Cecilia, it must be remembered, was the daughter of an Anglican minister of religion, her father having been the Reverend Charles Cavendish-Bentinck. She was schooled and steeped in the Bible, and would ensure that all her children were too. In that, more God-fearing age, when Scripture lessons were an integral part of all children's education, and Biblical stories were far more commonly known than they are today, both she and Claude would have known from Genesis about Sara saying to Abraham about her maid Hagar, 'Sleep with my maidservant; perhaps I can build a family through her,' and of Rachel saying to Jacob, 'Here is Bilah, my maidservant. Sleep with her so that she can bear children for me and that through her I too can build a family.' Joseph, the product of that surrogacy, enjoys fame to this day, if only through the musical *Joseph and his Amazing Technicolour Dreamcoat*, though people like Claude and Cecilia Glamis would not have needed Andrew Lloyd Webber to be aware that the arrangement was such a success that Joseph became his father's favourite child.

This Biblical stamp of approval cannot be exaggerated, especially with people like Claude and Cecilia, who were devout Christians. When a man lay with his wife's maidservant for the purposes of providing them with a child, he was not having an affair, nor was he being unfaithful. He was implanting his seed in the finest tradition of Abraham and Jacob. As such, his actions had been sanctioned by God, for *Genesis* makes it clear that neither Abraham nor Jacob was breaking the commandment against adultery while lying with Hagar and Bilah.

Moreover, the family had form and relatively recent form at that, with an Earl of Strathmore having issue with a maid. Claude's great-uncle John Lyon Bowes, the 10th earl, had met Mary Milner, the daughter of a local gardener, while staying at a hunting lodge near Streatlam, one of the two large County Durham estates in northern England which had come into the family when his father John Lyon, the 9th earl, had married one of the greatest heiresses in England, Mary Eleanor Bowes. After that he and the family were known as Lyon Bowes for the next two generations, before switching the order of the names to the more familiar Bowes Lyon. Mary Eleanor Bowes was one of the richest women in the 18th century, having been left the immense fortune of £1,000,000 as a little girl by her father, with the proviso that whoever married her had to adopt the name Bowes to share in her wealth.

Mary Eleanor's son John Lyon Bowes, being one of the richest young men in the kingdom, as well as the possessor of the great and ancient Scottish titles of Strathmore and Glamis, was in the position to do as he pleased, and prior to meeting Mary Milner, the woman who pleased him was the wild, captivating and equally rich, but decidedly married, Sarah, Countess of Tyrconnel. She ran off with him to Gibside Hall, the magnificent Jacobean stately home in County Durham which his mother had inherited from her father. This caused a major scandal which was widely reported in the newspapers at the time, though by then the English public was used to scandals concerning the family, for his mother had also been the subject of a major scandal which is better recounted elsewhere, while Sarah had achieved celebrity status when her affair with Prince Frederick, Duke of York hit the tabloids. Although she and John loved each other, theirs was a star-crossed union, for she died of consumption aged thirty-seven at Gibside Hall.

It was during the period that John was grieving for Sarah that the darkly attractive Mary Milner caught his eye. Notwithstanding that she was uneducated and unacceptable in the social circles in which the Bowes and Lyon families moved, he struck up a relationship with her that quickly deepened into something so profound that, against all the odds, he set her up in a house in London. There they lived in connubial if unmarried bliss. She produced a son whom they named John Milner Bowes, itself shocking for the time, as earls simply did not live openly with servant girls or name their bastards after themselves. This action, however, was an indication of the depth of feeling John Senior had for John Junior as well as for the boy's mother. Soon he took another unprecedented step, settling a large sum of money upon the son of whom he 'was inordinately fond'.[1]

When John Junior was nine, John Senior, realising that he was dying, took yet more unprecedented steps to ensure the boy's future. He left him all his English and Scottish estates, and, despite having to go to elaborate lengths to execute his objective, married Mary. He was plainly hoping that by doing so he would not only secure his beloved Mary's future, but also that of their son. He had to be held up during the marriage ceremony, and died the following day, fully intending that John Junior would succeed him as the 11th Earl of Strathmore.

His younger brother, Thomas, Claude's grandfather, was having none of it however. As far as he was concerned, he was the only rightful heir to the earldom, thanage, and all the estates and property entailed upon them. He promptly laid claim to the lot.

After protracted legal proceedings, Thomas was found to be the rightful heir to the title, illegitimate children, as we have previously seen, not being able to inherit titles even after their legitimisation. All the property that was entailed upon the earldom of Strathmore – the Scottish, Lyon, part of the family's heritage – went to him, while all the English, Bowes, property, which John Senior had been legally free to dispose of as he wished, went to John Junior.

This separation of the Bowes and Lyon parts of the family's patrimony meant that the earls had overnight ceased to be immensely rich, for the lion's share of their fortune had been Bowes, not Lyon. Fortunately for the family, however, John Milner Bowes did not have any children. When he died in 1885, all his properties united once more under the umbrella of the earldom, which by then was held by Elizabeth's grandfather. However, John had spent much of his money amassing a vast art collection, which he left, together with a museum to house it, to the public, so Elizabeth's family would never be as rich again as they had been before the Scottish and English properties had been split in two.

If ever a family had had a lesson in the importance of keeping on the right side of the legal divide where illegitimacy, legitimisation, and congress between earls and servant girls were concerned, the Strathmores had. The fact that all had ended relatively well did not obviate the need to remember the lessons of the past, chief amongst which was the need for discretion. In Victorian England even more so than in the more liberal Georgian times, it was not what you did, but what you admitted to, that made the difference between a smooth, socially acceptable life, or a bumpy, unacceptable one. Although John Bowes had been a fine and very rich gentleman, even his legitimisation had not rendered him the equal of his significantly poorer Lyon relations.

'Jackets' of any description, whether the issue of a peeress and her lover or the illegitimate issue of a lord and his surrogate, must be passed off as legitimate progeny. The alternative, of an open declaration of illegitimacy, was unthinkable. The illegitimate children of aristocrats did not enjoy the status of aristocrats, even if both their parents were aristocrats. They endured the status of a lower class of person, even if they were well off financially. Caught somewhere between the lower classes and the impoverished gentry, they belonged to no world at a time when social position was a point fixed at birth and unchangeable till death.

The progeny of an aristocrat and a servant were in an even more invidious position, for they were perceived to be of the rank of their non-aristocratic parent. The only exceptions to this rule were officially recognised royal bastards, but since Lord and Lady Glamis were not royal, and there was no prospect of their elevating any bastard the way Charles II had created the Dukes of St. Albans, Grafton, and Monmouth, or the way King William IV had successfully ennobled Mrs. Jordan's FitzClarence brood, there was only one solution: Elizabeth had to be seen to be legitimate.

The solution was simple enough. In a day and age when women withdrew from social life once they started to 'show', it was relatively easy for surrogacies to proceed without remark, for few people would see a woman as she approached her term. Without the need to pad or otherwise indulge in straightforward deception, the main hurdle to discovery would be at the birth itself. Because babies were customarily born at home, it would be difficult to dupe a midwife or doctor when of course she or he would know exactly what the mistress of the house looked like. On the other hand, if the midwife or doctor were complicit, there was the possibility, no matter how remote, of trust being violated in the future. It therefore reduced the possibilities for vulnerability, and made more sense, for the baby to be born away from home, delivered preferably by someone who did not know either the birth or putative mother. In such a situation, a midwife would be preferable to a doctor. She was a lower class than a doctor, and as such, a lesser threat for the future. Furthermore, midwives usually performed a specific function, namely assisting at a birth, and only at the birth, while doctors had more all-encompassing relationships with their patients. And in such a situation, the more involved the relationship, the more likelihood of word getting out, Hippocratic Oath or none.

What militated in favour of the anonymous midwife over the known doctor was that there was nothing suspicious about a midwife being called to attend upon a woman whom she did not know, and who had been taken in labour suddenly. Midwives were well used to being called out at all hours of the day and night to women they knew well, slightly, or not at all. There was nothing suspicious about a woman going into labour unexpectedly when she was far away from home. In such a situation, the midwife would be as quickly in and out as the birth required. Her job did not involve checking on the mother afterwards, or attesting to the birth, or in any other way assuming the vigilance that contemporary midwives adopt. They really were delivery merchants, pure and simple, and for that reason, it made good sense that babies born to one woman but passed off as the fruit of another womb should be delivered by someone without the resources to check upon the mother in the future, or indeed necessarily to know who the mother actually was.

Human nature being what it is, however, the trusting will trust. And who better to trust than your own doctor? Dr. Bernard Thomas, a General Practitioner in Welwyn, which was the town nearest to St. Paul's Walden, is alleged to have claimed to have been present at the birth, although there is no proof one way or the other that he actually did make this claim.[2]

Canon Dendle French, the chaplain at Glamis Castle who was previously the vicar at All Saints, St. Paul's Walden, took it upon himself to launch his own investigations in the hope of arriving at the truth. Aware that there were sufficient claims from locals at St. Paul's Walden to rule out London as the likely birthplace, he contacted a *compos mentis* and youthful ninety-one-year-old spinster, Miss Margaret Valentine, whose father, the Revd. Henry Valentine, had been the vicar who christened Elizabeth in September 1900. She recollected that she had been practising the piano at the vicarage when a maid came over from the Bury, as the big house was known locally, to say that Lady Glamis had given birth to a baby girl. She claimed to have asked her if this had been at the Bury, and the maid confirmed that that was where the birth had taken place.[3]

Without intending in any way to disparage Miss Valentine's veracity, one has to wonder how likely it was that a young girl would have found it necessary to nail down the place of birth so pointedly by asking if it had specifically taken place at the house. That is the sort of question one asks only if one knows that one has not been provided with full or accurate information. It is not the sort of question a young girl asks a maid who has just informed her that the birth did indeed take place at the very place she is now cross-examining her about. In a court of law, this is the sort of detail which would raise a huge red flag for a competent attorney or judge, and there is no reason for the reader to view Miss Valentine's account as anything but an elderly lady's clumsy but understandable attempt to lay the ghosts of the past to rest before they come back to haunt the living (for Elizabeth was still very much alive at that time). While it is entirely credible that the maid did indeed walk over to the vicarage to announce the birth of the baby, and while it is even more likely that she would have informed them that Lady Glamis was the mother, this does not actually prove that the birth took place at the Bury, or indeed that Cecilia was the individual who gave birth. All it proves is that the maid was sent over to the vicarage to give the Valentines the good news of Elizabeth's birth, which, if it was a surrogacy, would certainly have required the family to provide disinformation for the staff to spread.

Bad as Canon French's investigations were proving to be, worse was to follow. He uncovered the existence of quite a lot of gossip in the village, all of which both he and William Shawcross neglect to recount in the official biography, save for 'the rumour that Lady Glamis had actually been en route from London when the contractions began and that the birth had taken place in or near Welwyn. One story passed down, but acknowledged as only hearsay, was that the baby started to arrive en route from London and that Lady Glamis was taken to Dr. Thomas's home, Bridge House, Welwyn, where the infant was delivered. At the same time, one of Canon French's elderly parishioners told him that her aunt had been in charge of the laundry at the Bury and her work made her certain that the birth had taken place there.'[4]

These conflicting versions present difficulties for the rational. Firstly, Lady Glamis had produced eight children prior to 1900. It was therefore extremely unlikely that she would have been travelling between London and St. Paul's Walden on or near her due date. This is not the sort of behaviour anyone with considerable experience of childbirth would have indulged in, especially someone who was as devoted to her family as Cecilia Glamis. Remember, in 1900 there were no luxurious automobiles to ferry even the aristocracy between London and the country. There were trains and there were carriages. The former were comfortable, the latter far less so. No woman in her right mind would have been subjecting herself to the danger of a bumpy ride in even a well-sprung carriage, nor would she have been boarding a train at that late stage of her pregnancy. On the other hand, if the objective was to conceal the truth of what had actually taken place, obfuscation in the form of various and conflicting versions of the same event was singularly sensible. By tying up everyone in knots so that no one knew what to believe, the secret could be, if not exactly kept, then certainly retained sufficiently so that no one would know quite where the truth lay.

However, some people did know the truth. Chief amongst these was Elizabeth's brother-in-law, David, the man who, as Prince of Wales, was one of her closest friends and greatest supporters, and who always paved the way for her and his younger brother Bertie. As King Edward VIII, David had access to all the information about Elizabeth's secret which was not so secret in aristocratic and royal circles. When he discovered, to his horror, that Elizabeth was actively scheming with his own courtiers to undermine his position as king and prevent him from marrying the woman he loved, he used the wealth of access at his disposal to circumvent his own private and deputy private secretaries and obtain sight of the documents, which confirmed that Elizabeth had been born, not on 4th August as supposed, but on 3rd August at St. Paul's Walden Bury to Marguerite Rodiere. Unfortunately for all concerned, she arrived slightly earlier than anticipated. Lady Glamis was still in London, and had to hightail it down to St. Paul's Walden Bury. She did indeed stop off at Dr. Thomas's house in Welwyn, after which she was taken to the Bury, where she met her youngest daughter for the first time.

Both Strathmores had faith in their doctors, for later, when he was dying, Claude confided in Dr. Ayles, who was attending to him in Scotland that Elizabeth and David had indeed been born to the cook, though the sentiments he conveyed are best left for later in this work. Meanwhile, as Cecilia was familiarising herself with her latest daughter, her husband was in Scotland preparing for the Glorious Twelfth, the opening of the grouse season. He would not come down south for some weeks thereafter.

The Duke of Windsor always maintained that he would never have revealed Elizabeth's secret had he not discovered at the time of the Abdication Crisis, through Lord Beaverbrook, that Elizabeth was behind the scurrilous and utterly untrue rumour that Wallis had learnt secret sexual techniques in a bordello in China, and it was this which was the secret hold she had over King Edward VIII. Once he knew this to be true, however, he felt justified in rumbling the sister-in-law who had a secret of her own, and one, moreover, which had, in his view, more merit than the one she had invented about his beloved.

Thereafter, Elizabeth was known as Cookie. For those who asked, as I did when I was a late teenager, why she was being called by that nickname, there was always a member of the Windsor circle willing and able to recount how the High and Mighty Princess Elizabeth, Queen of the United Kingdom and Northern Ireland, Empress of India, Queen of Canada, Australia, etc. etc., was not even legitimate, but the daughter of the 13th Earl of Strathmore and Kinghorne and St. Paul's Walden Bury's cook, Mademoiselle Marguerite Rodiere.

Whether this was indeed the case, none of us will ever know definitively unless DNA studies are done on Elizabeth and Cecilia to establish whether they shared a genetic link. In the absence of them, however, the behaviour of Elizabeth tends to support the claims of the Duke of Windsor and Dr. Ayles. Why else would she assert that she was born in London, as she did consistently in latter years? The answer is simple. She knew that she was born at St. Paul's Walden Bury. Even if she did not know about the laundress's claim to have washed the sheets, she would have known that the laundress would have seen bloodied sheets, and would, in the nature of things, have reported on the state of the linen to the other servants. Anyone who has had servants knows they gossip. It is easier to conceal a secret from a spouse than a servant, and no amount of aristocratic rising-above-the-gossip silences the inevitable garrulousness.

Elizabeth must also have known that the local village was awash with gossip to the effect that she and her brother David were not born to Lady Glamis, but to Marguerite Rodiere, and moreover, that changing her birth date from the 4th to the 3rd of August would have rendered it impossible for Cecilia to have given birth to her. It is unlikely that she would have welcomed the intervention of Dr. Thomas, who, tellingly, is meant to have maintained that he was present at her birth, without actually stating who the mother was. All this meant that the only way to keep her secret was to maintain that she had been born in London. In a horse-drawn ambulance. Or even in a London taxi. Anywhere anonymous, as long as it wasn't in the family flat at Grosvenor Gardens opposite Buckingham Palace, which is where she would have been born, had she been born to Lady Glamis in London.

In 1937, when Elizabeth was newly ascended to the throne of England as consort, she had allowed her birthplace to be declared in that plaque at All Saints Parish Church as St. Paul's Walden Bury, but time had shown her that this was a tactical error. And the reason why she made it? Because, in 1937, when she unveiled the plaque, she was not yet alert to the danger that admitting her birthplace would place her in. She did not yet know that the Windsors were already disseminating the truth about her birth to all and sundry.

Thereafter, she was assiduous in asserting that she had been born anywhere but at St. Paul's Walden Bury. Nor was she alone in doing so. She enlisted the support of the one person whom she could trust above all others: the other Benjamin, her indisputable full-brother, by then the Hon. Sir David Bowes Lyon.

According to the author Hugo Vickers in his 2005 biography, *Elizabeth The Queen Mother*, David Bowes Lyon told the author Dorothy Laird, whose 1966 biography was written with the co-operation of Elizabeth, 'that she had not been born at St. Paul's.' There is no doubt that this assertion cannot have been made without the connivance of Elizabeth. This placed the author in something of a quandary, for until then, St. Paul's Walden had been the official birthplace. Publish David Bowes Lyon's disclaimer and open up both author and subject to the prospect of cataclysmic controversy. Or remain silent and continue to enjoy the co-operation of Her Majesty Queen Elizabeth The Queen Mother. So Laird chose a path unique in the annals of biography, and wrote a book that omits to mention any place of birth whatsoever.

Thereafter, until her death, Elizabeth sowed confusion the way a Biblical farmer scattered seeds, and she was able to live out the remainder of her life with her secret safe from the knowledge of the general public.

An Enchanted Childhood

Chapter Two

Irrespective of who produced her, Elizabeth Bowes Lyon's birth was registered by her father Claude at the register office in Hitchin, where he paid a fine of 7/6d (seven shillings and six pence) for his tardiness, on Friday, 21st September, 1900. Her mother was listed as Lady Glamis, and hereafter Cecilia will be referred to as her mother.

The arrival of a ninth child, even a much longed-for one, is never quite as momentous as the arrival of the first, second, or third, but even so, Elizabeth's christening was almost as noteworthy as her birth because of the bizarre features surrounding it.

The first issue was the godparents. All Christians understand the importance of godparents, and no one more so than an aristocrat, who chooses his or her child's godparents with a view to what help or use they will be to the child in future. Devout Christians like Claude and Cecilia also understand that the role of godparent consists of a spiritual element. They are meant to look out for the spiritual as well as the earthly well-being of their godchildren. The result is that even the most casual Christians invariably manage to provide the requisite number of godparents for their offspring, choosing the cream of the crop from amongst their friends, relations and social connections. Elizabeth, however, might well have had no godparents, which would be truly extraordinary.

Normally, the church registers the identity of the godparents and provides the parents with a Baptismal Certificate listing the names of the child, the officiating clergyman or clergymen, the parents, and the godparents. But this was not done, either because there were no godparents, or because the Revd. Tristram Valentine was lax beyond all belief, which seems unlikely.

Later on, once Elizabeth was a royal duchess and questions were raised as to who her godparents were, the family managed to remember two godmothers, though they never did summon up even one godfather, no matter how obscure or insignificant. This was also extraordinary, for all children of practising Christians had at least one godfather if they were a girl, and one godmother if they were a boy, as well as two or more godparents of the same sex. And amongst the aristocracy, four, five, or even six godparents of both sexes was the norm rather than the exception, as indeed my own children can attest to. Yet the best the Strathmore family could come up with was the sum total of two godmothers, both of whom were safely members of the family: Claude's spinster sister Lady Maud Bowes Lyon, and Cecilia's decidedly rackety but nevertheless royally-connected second cousin Mrs. Arthur James.

If these ladies were contemporaneous choices in September 1900, two more unpromising godmothers could hardly have been found for an infant who would presumably need as much assistance as any other well-born girl required as she grew into adulthood. A retiring spinster aunt would hardly be in a position to endow the infant with worldly goods or useful direction as she grew up, nor would a scandal-ridden, albeit broadminded, miser, although both fitted the bill nicely if they stepped into the breach anachronistically.

Whether Venetia James accepted becoming a godmother in 1900, when she was a still-beautiful, sixteen-inch waisted thirty-nine-year-old who had once captivated the then Prince of Wales, or whether she did so later, one thing is certain. She was the ideal nominee for godmother if there were difficulties attached to the birth, for she had survived ostracism from the royal circle, and would therefore be attuned to the nuances necessary for Elizabeth to be navigated safely through Society.

As a young woman, Venetia had been a luminous presence in the Marlborough House Set, as the Prince and Princess of Wales's social circle was known. A great friend of his acknowledged mistress, Alice Keppel, despite having enjoyed HRH's attentions herself, she then committed the cardinal error of embarrassing Bertie and Alexandra by popping out of a huge Easter egg with whoops of delight and a decorous curtsey in front of a host of other people. This was a solecism which neither the heir to the throne nor his wife could tolerate, for they lived by the inflexible rule that no matter what you did in private, in public you preserved decorum. And such public over-familiarity, though intended good-naturedly, was a decided breach of protocol which, if allowed to pass unpunished, might well open the floodgates to public acknowledgement of Bertie's promiscuous private life, and the attendant humiliations it heaped upon his beautiful but deaf wife. After this solecism, Venetia was therefore banished from the royal circle, and ended up a stern, miserly, severe old woman whom people took care to avoid as much as possible.

Another bizarre element of the christening was the Revd. Tristram Valentine's conduct when it came time to name Elizabeth. Rather than baptise the infant with the mixture of seriousness and joyousness which are supposed to be features of all Christian baptisms, this deeply traditional clergyman failed to name the child in keeping with his instructions. Whether he misheard, misunderstood, or deliberately resisted the choice of names he was given for this latest scion of the Bowes Lyon family, he made such a hash of the naming, both during the ceremony and afterwards, when he filled out the Baptismal Certificate incorrectly, that it can only have been the insistence of the parents that caused him to scratch about on the certificate to rectify matters and provide her with their chosen names: Elizabeth Angela Marguerite.

The choice of names might well have added to the problem. While Elizabeth was uncontroversial and Angela, though unaristocratic, was touching – she was her parents' angel – the inclusion of the name Marguerite might well have caused the clergyman to resort to covert resistance. For Elizabeth had also been named after the cook at St. Paul's Walden Bury, whom the local vicar will have known, and that was more than unusual. It was unthinkable.

To a late Victorian clergyman, functioning in a world where there was a vast chasm between the upper and lower classes, it was literally unheard of for an aristocratic infant to be called after a servant, and while that reverberates positively with us in the 21st century – especially if Lord and Lady Glamis were being decent enough to acknowledge, albeit subtly, the part Marguerite Rodiere had played in their daughter's existence – such conduct would not have been favourably received by a clergyman. Especially one who, like Mr. Valentine, was a leading light in a small community, and would undoubtedly have already heard the gossip which was even then flourishing about the strange circumstances of Elizabeth's birth. It is likely that he would have resented being implicated in an arrangement he did not particularly approve of. Nevertheless, he would have felt powerless to oppose the Lord of the Manor openly, for clergymen were even more dependent then than they are now upon the benevolence of the owners of the local Big House. As such, Lord Glamis was not someone whom Mr. Valentine could afford to fall out with openly.

On the other hand, he would also have been reluctant to sully his reputation with his flock, which he definitely would have done had he been perceived to be colluding too willingly with passing the infant off as legitimate when local gossip already had her labelled illegitimate. So he took the only course open to him. He botched the job just enough for his congregation to know that he had not been a willing participant, but not so much that the Lord of the Manor did not get what he wanted. Which he did, for neither Claude nor Cecilia left All Saints until their youngest daughter had been given her full allotment of names.

Fortunately for baby Elizabeth, once this hurdle had been overcome, life settled down to the agreeable tenor it would thereafter have for her. She was, indeed, a much longed-for baby, and in many ways she cannot have been born into a better family. Claude, Cecilia and their eight other children were exceptional in many ways, not because they were one of the richest or grandest or best-connected families in the land – they were solidly of middling rank and importance amongst the aristocracy – but because they were unusually happy. This was in large measure due to Cecilia's personality, though Claude's sensible, down-to-earth values contributed to this state of being. Although desirous of his children's welfare and keen that they make good matches, he was also remarkably unambitious for their advancement at Court. Having been attached briefly to the Palace in his youth, he had seen enough of the jockeying for position and the prostitution of values to hold the view thereafter that the one thing he did NOT wish for any of his children was a position at Court.

In a day and age when few aristocratic marriages were genuinely happy, Claude and Cecilia's was an oasis of fulfilment which highlighted the desert their peers were often forced to endure. They seem to have been the ideal foil for each other. Both of them enjoyed social life, and were constantly giving or attending parties. Like all Earls of Strathmore and Lords Glamis, he was quiet, somewhat taciturn, and reserved, while she was outgoing, amusing, and fun-loving. Both of them were kind-hearted, though she was the more charismatic personality of the two. Where she glittered as a personality, he was quietly but good-naturedly solid. The 27th Earl of Crawford and Balcarres described him in a diary entry for 2nd October, 1905, as a 'delightful man', a sentiment everyone who crossed paths with him seemed to share, including his estate workers and tenants. Keenly interested in his estates, he rode out each day on his pony, in an old mackintosh tied with twine at the waist[1] to inspect the multitude of small-holdings which he owned. Benevolence as a landlord was something of a tradition in the Strathmore family (in 1865 the tenants of Glamis had presented Claude's father with a silver ship 'in appreciation of his liberal conduct as a landlord'), and when Claude wasn't checking to see that his tenants were happy, he was making innovations like importing larch from Norway to renew his forests.

Something of a character, 'he liked to bowl food down the length of the dining table to his wife (who, apparently, was a dab hand at fielding whatever came flying)'², and enjoyed regaling his friends with 'how an outraged minister of the Kirk was scandalised that he would let a hired hand clear a storm drain on the Sabbath'. The labourer, of course, was the earl himself. Still, he politely wrote back, promising '"such a despicable act" would never happen again.'³ Whenever he suffered from insomnia, rather than while away the hours reading or resting, he would chop logs he kept at the end of his bed for that purpose. He was convinced that eggs were dangerous, and was constantly warning anyone who would listen, 'Poison, my dear, poison.'⁴

A man of fixed habits, he would make his own cocoa every morning in a stab at self-sufficiency that was remarkable at a time when most aristocrats did not even know how to dress themselves. Liking plum pudding and failing to see why he should limit himself to it during the Christmas season only, the way everyone else did, he had it at luncheon every day of his life. In yet another stab at independence, his place at table was always set with its own jug of water which he himself used to dilute his wine. This practice was not only admirable for what it implied about Claude's character, but says a lot about his prescience, for alcoholism ran in his family, and this was a way of controlling his intake. An avid cricketer, he used to enjoy nothing better than playing with his sons, his butler, and his valet when he wasn't blasting the grouse, partridge, pheasant, woodcock and mallard during their respective seasons from August to February. Nowadays, people might classify Claude as having been eccentric, but at the time, when individuality was more prevalent than it is nowadays, he was perceived merely as robustly individual.

Like her husband, Cecilia was both physically active and robustly individualistic. If her conduct would now be regarded as less eccentric than his, in that she had no defining peculiarities like eating Christmas pudding all year round, she was nevertheless very much her own person. William Shawcross states that she 'dominated her family and household,'⁵ and one need look no further than Cecilia to see who became the role model for the dominating but loving Elizabeth when the time came to be matriarch of her own family. One daughter described Cecilia as 'a very wonderful woman, very talented, very go-ahead, and so upright. She had a terrific sympathy; the young used to pour their troubles out to her and ask for advice, often when they would not go to their own parents.'⁶ She was 'the pivot of the family,' as Elizabeth confirmed to the Archbishop of Canterbury following her death in 1938. Devoid of snobbery, she had real *joie de vivre* and was always finding new things to be enthusiastic about, such as creating the Italian Garden at Glamis between 1907 and 1911. As this involved the felling of some four acres of trees and the levelling and draining of the ground, it was not a simple task, but she set the men of the estate to work on it, and to this day it stands as a testament to the artistic side of her nature. Aside from gardening, Cecilia also gave full vent to these sensibilities by creating and executing elaborate embroidery and crewel work, often while conversing in the evening after dinner.

Possibly where she excelled above all else was as a story-teller. With her vivacity and imagination, qualities which Elizabeth absorbed in full, she used to entertain the children with stories about what life at Glamis had been like in centuries past. In doing so, she managed to impart to them a love of history and tradition in an entertaining, socialising way.

Cecilia did not believe that her children's enjoyment should be spoilt by too much learning, and since it was she who set the tone of family life, the children's lives were turned over to pleasures, albeit innocent ones. This idyll Elizabeth tried to recreate for her own two daughters when their turn came to be educated, but the attempt backfired spectacularly, especially where Princess Margaret was concerned. She never forgave her mother for preventing her from having the education her intelligence and rank required.

In other respects, however, Margaret replicated features of her mother's upbringing that owed everything to Cecilia and her strong belief that life should be as easy and pleasurable as possible. Cecilia was a practised pianist with a good singing voice, and one of her favourite activities was to gather her large brood and many guests around the piano after dinner. Sometimes they would have sing-alongs, a practice which Elizabeth and Margaret would perpetuate into the following two generations, even after the advent of television made self-generated entertainment effectively redundant. On other occasions, Cecilia would provide background music on the piano while her children and their guests played charades.

Cecilia seems to have been more intelligent, as well as more sophisticated, than Claude. This was in part due to her mother, Caroline Burnaby, who was widowed when Cecilia was only three. Five years later, in 1870, she married Harry Scott of Ancrum. They lived in some style at Forbes House in Ham near London until his death in 1889. After this, she spent most of her time in Italy, firstly at the Villa Capponi in Florence, thereafter at San Remo and Bordighera on the Italian Riviera. At a time when few people travelled extensively, Cecilia had to do so, if only to see her mother, and travel proved to be as broadening an experience as the maxim states it is.

Sophisticated as she was, Cecilia and her children nevertheless were as ignorant as her husband when it came to some of the most basic matters in their lives. The year after they became the Earl and Countess of Strathmore following his father's death in 1904, Lord Crawford had cause to say, 'I am amazed at the phenomenal ignorance of the castle and its contents, displayed by Lord and Lady Strathmore, and the two eldest sons. The second son asked his mother about the identity of a portrait which turned out to be a portrait of his own grandmother.'[7]

Although Cecilia was described as 'fey' in manner, she was anything but fuzzy where her values or beliefs were concerned. Like many another God-fearing vicar's daughter in post-Victorian Britain, Cecilia inculcated into her family a love of God, King and Country. This was no alien concept which they could put on and take off the way they did their overcoats, but was a living, breathing part of their everyday life. It was integral to what made British best, and both Claude and Cecilia genuinely lived by the Victorian ideal of the British Empire being a force for good which was elevating the rest of the world with a civilising example of how British values could improve other cultures through the dissemination of Christianity, English justice, and British technological advances. Although people today might mock such values, they were fundamental to many people at that time, and would prove to have a lasting impression upon Elizabeth, as did the centrality of Christian faith to Cecilia's life.[8] She taught her children to kneel beside their beds and say their prayers every night, a practice which Elizabeth is meant to have maintained through her nearly 102 years. She made sure that the family said daily prayers together in the chapel at Glamis or at St. Paul's Walden Bury, and of course they went to church every Sunday, another of Cecilia's practices to which Elizabeth adhered all her life.

Like many of her generation, Cecilia was a strong believer in duty. She set about instilling this concept in her children with the repetition of such maxims as 'work is the rent you pay for life' and 'life is for living and working at. If anything or anyone bores you, then the fault is in yourself.' These would stand her in good stead with the adult Elizabeth, but for the moment she limited herself to those maxims as well as the one which would ensure that her youngest daughter would have good posture: 'Never look at your feet.'

Cecilia was also a firm believer in the value of good manners, and she made sure that each of her children had the most exquisite manners. I have often said, over the years, that the people who have the best manners of anyone I have met are well-bred Arabs and the Japanese, with the exception of the Bowes Lyon family, who are on a par with them. The present Earl of Strathmore, for example, is as well-mannered and charming as his great-aunt Elizabeth used to be, so Cecilia's heritage resides in her Bowes Lyon descendants to this day.

Like many strong and upstanding but loving women who are fun to be around, Cecilia demanded harmoniousness in her houses. According to Shawcross, she was 'strict' without being 'harsh'. Although her sons were elsewhere described as being 'wild',[9] she plainly inspired such devotion in her large brood that none of her ten children is on record as having even once opposed her or rebelled against her standards. This is possibly because her rules were few and far between, her expectations limited, the boundaries laid down leaving so much scope for individual foibles that there was little to rebel against except her hardly-arduous concept of duty, which really involved being agreeable company and well-mannered while you enjoyed yourself.

There are countless stories, all substantiated, of the scamps the young Elizabeth and David were. 'At Glamis, they smoked on the stairs and, from a turret accessed by a 143-step spiral staircase, they poured cold water on the heads of well-dressed, unsuspecting guests....' pretending it was hot oil. 'They also once painted the lower rungs of a ladder with white paint, unbeknown to the painter standing several rungs above. Much to their pleasure, his white footprints covered the whole of the lawn.'[10] On another occasion, Elizabeth cut up a new set of sheets which had been put on her bed. When the plainly-astonished adult enquired of the naughty child what her mother would say when she found out, she replied jauntily, 'Oh, Elizabeth!', which turned out to be the case.[11] Elizabeth was even allowed to bring her Shetland pony, Bobs, into the house, and once even took it upstairs to her bedroom.

Such latitude might have been destructive had the Bowes Lyon brood been expected to make their own way in the world, but since they were not, it laid the foundations for a happy, freewheeling and delightfully entertaining family life. Elizabeth herself described her mother as being 'so vital and so loving and so marvellously loyal to those she loved, or the things she thought right – an Angel of goodness and fun.'[12] 'She had such a good perspective of life – everything was given its *true* importance. She had a young spirit, great courage & unending sympathy whenever or wherever it was needed, & such a heavenly sense of humour. We all used to laugh together and have such fun.'[13]

With personalities such as theirs, it is hardly surprising that Claude and Cecilia were a magnet, not only for their children, whom they loved devotedly and who all loved them in return, but also for their many friends. The death of Queen Victoria in January 1901 and the accession of her pleasure-seeking but politically astute son Bertie, Prince of Wales as King Edward VII, ushered in the Edwardian age. This was the apogee of the aristocratic way of life. To the adults in Elizabeth's world, life was effectively one long party broken up into balls, dances, dinners, luncheons, picnics, and hunting, shooting and fishing functions. No one, that is no one in the aristocracy, worked, but that is not to say that they were idle. They had a duty to maintain a full and active social life, and those who did not do so quickly lost their desirability along with their kudos.

During the London Season, aristocrats, including Claude and Cecilia, might attend three or four balls a night. Those of cultural bent would attend the opera, ballet, theatre or concerts, while those of artistic bent performed in their own houses and often publicly on stage in charity recitals for the poor. During the day they rode in Hyde Park or fenced when they weren't calling upon one another to drop off visiting cards or have tea. When the London Season came to a close, they adjourned to their country estates, where they stayed with each other in large house parties.

Then, more than now, country house visits revolved around two fixed points: the table and sport. Although some of the ladies might take their breakfast in their bedrooms, the gentlemen invariably congregated in the dining room for a full English breakfast. Both sexes gathered together for lunch, tea and dinner irrespective of which sport was on the calendar. The aristocracy was far more physically active then than its equivalent is today. Everyone rode, if not on a daily basis then frequently, for motor cars were a recent and unreliable invention and horses were an integral part of everyone's life. When people were not riding horses or ponies for pleasure, they would use them for transportation, either riding them or driving them in pony or horse-drawn traps. Everyone knew how to drive one of these conveyances, even children, for carriages were not used for everything, and only invalids did not customarily drive one of the small one-horse vehicles which everyone used for travelling short distances in the country. Elizabeth had her own pony from an early age, and by her own admission loved tending to the horses.

Fishing was another sport open to both sexes, and Elizabeth absorbed a love of that sport from both her parents. She also adopted their practice of going for long walks which were, and regrettably sometimes still are, one of the downsides of staying in country houses. All gentlemen and many ladies also fenced, and indeed, my predecessor Gertrude, Lady Colin Campbell was a fencing champion. Although Elizabeth never was, she did take fencing lessons, both with her brother and without, for when he was learning how to box, she pursued the more decorous art of *l'épée*.

People like Claude and Cecilia entertained constantly when they were not staying with friends or relations. Their houses were run on orderly and well-oiled lines, with what we would nowadays regard as a plethora of staff to keep the wheels revolving smoothly. While some of the greater houses like Blenheim Palace or Woburn Abbey had literally hundreds of servants, workmen and gardeners, Elizabeth's parents were not in that category. At the time of Elizabeth's birth, Claude had not yet succeeded to the earldom. His father was still very much in control of the family properties aside from St. Paul's Walden Bury which had been ceded over to his heir, so Elizabeth and her parents and siblings were really visitors in the many houses her grandfather owned. The two main houses the family had access to were Streatlam Castle, which functioned on a skeleton staff as no one lived there permanently, and Glamis Castle, which, being the primary residence of the Earls of Strathmore, was the most fully-staffed. Even so, it was hardly luxurious, and Queen Mary's unmarried equerry, Sir Richard Molyneux, who made something of a career out of staying in as many country houses as he could, dismissed it as 'an average picknicky place – parlourmaids and that sort of stuff.'[14] It had no creature comforts such as central heating or electricity, and indeed would not have the latter until 1929, while there is still scant evidence of the former throughout its many rooms. Torches, candles and roaring log fires provided not only warmth and light for this ancient castle but also atmosphere, and the Liberal Prime Minister H.H. Asquith's son Raymond 'was glad' that he had enough imagination 'to fancy myself in a distant century',[15] which was nothing but a polite way of saying that he found the whole thing pretty primitive.

Although St. Paul's Walden Bury was a pretty house with beautiful grounds encompassing some sixty acres of grounds and gardens, it too was hardly luxurious. It was what we would today call shabby chic – some good pieces of antique furniture with some good paintings intermingling with a quantity of attractive-looking but second-rate stuff. It also had a relatively modest number of staff: there was a twenty-four-year-old governess named Hedwig Walters for Elizabeth's elder siblings; Marguerite Rodiere, the cook; a lady's maid; a dairymaid; two footmen; a page; a housemaid, a kitchenmaid; a coachman who became the chauffeur when the family got its first motor car in 1908; and a livery groom, all of whom were local, except for the French Mademoiselle Rodiere. With Elizabeth's advent, the household would be swollen by two nursery additions: the nurse, as nannies were then known in aristocratic and royal circles, and the nursery maid, again both home-grown. The household was completed by Arthur Barson, the butler who had worked his way up from footman and still functioned as Claude's valet despite being accorded the respect due to all butlers, and therefore known by his surname alone. (This was a day and age when gentlemen often called their best friends by their surnames alone, and indeed Consuelo Vanderbilt always called her ducal husband Marlborough rather than using his Christian name or nicknames. On the other hand, tradesmen were known as Mister, so the exclusion of that prefix was a compliment rather than a putdown).

Glamis was also staffed primarily by locals. Elizabeth would subsequently tell Eton headmaster Eric Anderson during their conversations between 1994 and 1995 that her ancestral home 'was really like a little village.' This was actually typical of the time, for most of the employees in large houses were drawn from the local villages and farms. Being the family's main establishment, Glamis had more indoor and outdoor staff than the family's other houses, but even so, no one ever recalled the castle as being as sumptuously staffed as any of the great houses of the period, where liveried footmen standing behind chairs during dinner was one of the yardsticks used to measure whether a house was grand or merely typical.

Ironically, the very lack of luxuriousness was what helped to make all the Bowes Lyon family's houses so appealing to houseguests. There was none of the feeling that one was in a museum and had to be careful not to break anything, the way one felt at Luton Hoo or Wentworth Woodhouse. Life at St. Paul's Walden Bury and Glamis, once Claude succeeded his father in 1904, was very, very relaxed. Indeed ribald. Houseguest Prince Paul of Serbia, subsequently the Regent of Yugoslavia, recounts in his memoirs what fun it was to stay at Glamis before Elizabeth married Bertie and became the Duchess of York.

It is no exaggeration to say that one of the main things that attracted Bertie to Elizabeth was the great sense of fun she and her family possessed. After the constriction imposed upon him by his repressive father King George V and strait-laced mother Queen Mary, this was more than a breath of fresh air. It was oxygen to someone who had been living with toxicity his whole life.

Nor is it possible to exaggerate how important social life was to the aristocracy. From the days of the Stuarts, when the aristocratic way of life as we know it got underway with a real swing, until the 1990s, social life was of overriding importance to upper-class Britons. This was because socialising was not only about pleasure, though it was centred around pleasurable activities. It was primarily about confirming one's worth through the affirmation of one's stature, and enhancing one's status through one's connections and social activities. In other words, it was serious work posing as pleasure.

It has only been in the last two decades that there has been a diminution in the importance of aristocratic social life. As more and more members of the upper classes have joined the workforce, and wealth and celebrity have eclipsed Society in terms of national and international superstardom, the aristocracy as an entity has lost much of its cachet and no longer enjoys the prestige or influence it once did. This lessening of the aristocracy's importance, and the elevation of non-aristocrats to parity and sometimes superiority, has created a new social order, and this more than anything else has resulted in the aristocracy widening its horizons.

Nowadays, everybody appreciates the value of networking, and no one feels the need to dress it up as anything else. We live in an age where ambition and advancement are desirable goals in themselves, and materialism is accepted as a more valid yardstick for association than shared backgrounds. It is fair to say that in this, more egalitarian, age, class has lost much of its clout. Everyone is perceived to be entitled to a stake in the game of advancement, and succeeding in it is far more important than your antecedents. Indeed, Sir Donald Gosling has far more credit socially than most marquesses, and few are the ambitious Becky Sharps who would miscalculate how much more desirable one Stavros Niarchos is than a brace of Manchester dukes and Alexander earls.

A century ago, however, British life could not have been more different. Social acceptability did not automatically or immediately follow accomplishment. It usually came humiliatingly slowly. For instance, Sir Ernest Cassel, despite being enormously rich and a knight who helped to bankroll King Edward VII before and after he acceded to the throne, was never regarded as being socially acceptable, much less desirable, though his daughter would marry Lord Mountcastle and his granddaughter Edwina would underscore the family's arrival when she wed the king's cousin Lord Louis Mountbatten.

Although the most important element for inclusion in Society was entitlement by right of background, once you belonged, gradations of wealth and status were leavened only by the presence of outstanding physical beauty or supreme social skills. If you had good looks or were excellent company, or better still possessed a combination of the two, you would assuredly find yourself in the greatest demand. This is how Cecilia and her daughter Elizabeth became the successes that they did. Although neither woman was a great beauty, both of them were relatively pretty while young, and this, allied to their truly outstanding personalities, combined to attract a multitude of admirers. Both of them actually married 'up', and both had the charm and grace to accomplish the transition so successfully that their humbler origins were ignored.

Despite this, the Strathmores were of middling aristocratic rank, and even after Claude succeeded to the earldom and the family's elevation began in earnest, Cecilia was still not one of the leading hostesses of the day. They were not rich or grand enough to belong to the *Haute Monde* like the Marchioness of Londonderry or the Duchess of Devonshire, and no amount of social skill displayed by Cecilia could mask that fact.

Nevertheless, while Elizabeth was growing up, her mother had a well-deserved reputation as a good guest and superb hostess. When she was staying with others, her sparkling good humour was an asset, and when she was the hostess, this vibrant sense of fun was heightened by the warmth of her hospitality and the relaxed tone she set for everyone. Raymond Asquith and Lord Gage were only two of the many people, aside from Prince Paul of Serbia, who commented on what a superb hostess she was, and long before her daughter Elizabeth married into the Royal Family, important people in Society like Prince Paul and Queen Mary's lady-in-waiting (and Glamis neighbour) Mabell, Countess of Airlie, were observing that her daughter Elizabeth was as appealing a personality and enjoyable a companion as her mother. In a world where dullness was often allied to inertia, this was high praise indeed.

What was Cecilia and Elizabeth's secret? It seems to have been a genuine love of social life. Both mother and daughter would entertain throughout their long lives with relish, and both would provide for their guests with such gusto that an invitation to their table or house was always welcome.

While Elizabeth was growing up, staying with her parents was even more fun than staying with her would prove to be once she got married. Her royal status engulfed her in an invisible aura of unapproachability beyond which few strayed, and it would take time for her to come to terms with this once she got married. Until she did, she would question whether people liked her for herself or her royal status. Being royal, she discovered, like many another royal bride coming after her, was not all it was cooked up to be, but she persevered, and, with time, found the way to enjoy being royal without sacrificing her innate personality the way Queen Mary did.

As Elizabeth would replicate the atmosphere of her earlier life once she became royal, it is useful to explore what this early life really was like. Cecilia as a hostess had a sure touch born out of genuine commitment to fun and good manners intermingled with a true love of people. At her house parties, she ensured that there was lively conversation in a relaxed, convivial way by surrounding herself with the children she had trained to be entertaining, as well as by including as many of her scintillating friends to act as a counterweight to the dullards whom one had to endure. Conversational boundaries at St. Paul's Walden Bury, Glamis and Streatlam were delightfully lacking in delineation except where offensiveness or vulgarity was concerned.

Appreciating that conversation was only one part of the fun to be had, Cecilia and her brood organised entertaining, sometimes silly, games such as charades, blind man's buff, and *Are you there Moriarty?* Her descendants would perpetuate these long after she had died. The family would explore dungeons with their guests, and sometimes thrill and sometimes frighten them with ghost stories about Glamis. The castle was reputedly haunted, so this was a rich vein to explore, as were the many stories surrounding its bloodthirsty past. Although Shakespeare placed Duncan's demise there, it is more likely that it was Duncan's grandfather who died there. Irrespective of whose blood marked this hall or that floor, it was all a real link to the ages past, and few visitors failed to leave unmoved by the castle and its occupants.

Occasionally, the family would host balls, usually at Glamis, and these were also thoroughly enjoyable, the wildness of the Scottish setting adding atmosphere to the occasion, as Raymond Asquith recounted in his 1905 diary entry: 'The place is an enormous 10th century dungeon. It was full of torches and wild men in kilts and pretty women pattering on the stone stairs with satin slippers.'[16]

Elizabeth's parents were sufficiently well-connected and monied to live comfortable lives surrounded by their peers, but not being one of the pre-eminent aristocratic families in the land, and with no ambitions to join such hallowed ranks, they were free to behave as they saw fit. While such eminences as the Dukes of Argyll and Marlborough, and others of their ilk, had such constraints upon their conduct that personal and marital happiness were usually throttled at the umbilicus, Claude and Cecilia could, and did, dedicate themselves to rich and fulfilling lives within the bosom of their large family and amongst their many friends. Elizabeth and David profited from this even more than their older siblings, who had been raised before Claude succeeded to the earldom, for they were no longer guests in the family's houses but hosts themselves.

If life in Claude and Cecilia's family was more enjoyable than life within many of their peers' families, this was not the only feature that set the Strathmores apart. The family was unusually, indeed anachronistically, child-centred. There was none of the 'children are to be seen and not heard' dicta which were then characteristic of most well-bred households.[17] Whenever Elizabeth and David were taught a new dance by their dance master, Mr. Neill of Forfar, they were encouraged to show it off to the assembled adults, though they had to maintain decorum and remain in character until they had been applauded.[18] If they had an opinion, they were encouraged to deliver it, no matter how young they were, the only proviso being that they should do so politely and civilly. This combination of discipline and indulgence clearly brought out the best in Elizabeth, though whether it did not undermine the children's characters is open to question.

It was often commented upon by Elizabeth herself, as well as by David and everyone who knew them well, how very similar in character they were.

While majesty protected her reputation in later life, he did not have a similar shield. During the Second World War, when he was sent to New York to take over the political warfare and propaganda work of British security co-ordination, he not only fomented untold mischief for the Duke and Duchess of Windsor on behalf of his sister,[19] but proved to be such a disaster at the job – 'David has a poor mind and no knowledge of Europe,' wrote Sir Robert Bruce Lockhart, Director-General of the Political Warfare Executive, and as such, David's actual boss – that Minister of Information Brendan Bracken, who was Churchill's protégé, dismissed him as an 'intriguer' and wanted to be rid of him. But he enjoyed the protection of his sister the Queen and Lord Halifax, the British Ambassador in Washington who was her good friend, so he remained *en poste* as his infamy spread. Bruce Lockhart even went to the lengths of recording in his *Diaries* that 'he is quite incapable of "playing straight"', while John Wheeler-Bennett, King George VI's official biographer, regarded him as 'a bad man'[20] and had 'a low opinion of David's character and thinks that his capacity for intrigue and untruthfulness has no limit.'[21]

Because Elizabeth and David were acknowledged to be so similar, when all these individuals came to publish their works, they would do so in the knowledge that the cognoscenti would read the word David and include Elizabeth as well.

When they were youngsters, however, their characters had still not been formed. The three most important adult presences in their young lives were their parents and their nurse, Alah, whom Cecilia employed for Buffy, as Elizabeth was known in the family when she was a month old.

Born Clara Cooper Knight, Alah was the daughter of a tenant farmer on Claude's Hertfordshire estate. She stayed with the family throughout her working life, leaving the Strathmore household when Elizabeth was eleven to care for the children of the eldest living daughter May, by then Lady Elphinstone. She returned to Elizabeth's household in 1926 when she gave birth to the present Queen. Thereafter, Alah nursed both Lilibet and Margaret when she came along four years later. When the former married Prince Philip and produced Prince Charles in 1948, she joined the Edinburghs at Clarence House to take care of their infant son.

The way the adult Elizabeth spoke about the devoted Alah says much about both of them. Although Elizabeth remained fond of her nurse all her life, she always had a cool, detached eye, and was never one to miss the quip which summed up the person while ensuring that her audience had a good laugh. On 19th June, 1932, she informed Viscountess Astor[22] that their holiday at Rest Harrow in Sandwich was the first time she had ever known Alah to display enthusiasm for anything.

Whether Alah was as dour as Elizabeth remembered is a moot point. None of her other charges seemed to have found her so, and there is every reason to suppose that the unfortunate nurse simply had the task of restraining an ebullient child who was precocious and self-willed, and who would grow into an equally ebullient and strong-willed woman. Not for nothing was Elizabeth known within the family as Merry Mischief and The Imp.

Yet there was clearly affection on both sides. Alah remembered her first charge as being[23] 'an exceptionally happy, easy baby: crawling early, running at thirteen months and speaking very young'.

Although one always has to guard against exaggeration when people, especially employees, speak about the Great and the Good, royalty above all, her comments have the ring of truth. All the evidence points to the fact that Elizabeth was always bright, with a sunny disposition, and a captivating personality. Even her enemies in later life would always concede that she was intelligent, appeared to be easy to get along with, and was extraordinarily charming. This really was a case of the baby, then the little girl, foreshadowing the qualities the woman would possess.

Nor was the young Elizabeth's personality the only appealing thing about her. Although in adulthood she would run to fat and become 'dumpy' and, in so doing, lose whatever looks she might once have had, she was nevertheless an unusually pretty baby and little girl. All the photographs and portraits show a beautiful, angelic-looking child with huge blue eyes, a delicate nose, cute mouth, long, dark hair and a truly beautiful complexion which she would never lose.

As the family's letters make clear, Elizabeth was adored by both her parents and in turn she adored them, her mother even more so than her father. In adulthood she would express doubt as to whether she would survive her mother's ultimate demise, which shows the extent to which she was emotionally wrapped up with her.

Cocooned in this chrysalis of loving approval delineated only by the need to avoid offensiveness and overt aggression, Elizabeth grew into a delightful little girl whose precocity was endearing rather than off-putting. Once, when she was three years old, her mother came down to see her daughter holding forth as she poured tea for neighbours who had arrived early. Not only was she behaving more the way an adult would than a child of such tender age, but she had even ordered the tea herself.[24]

Her grandmother Caroline Scott also gives us a glimpse of what Elizabeth was like at that age. She was 'quite a companion'[25] and was already displaying signs of what Princess Margaret would acidly refer to as 'Mummy's irresistible persuasiveness', although Mrs. Scott found 'her coaxy little ways' delightful and relished her company.[26]

This bright little girl was already observant beyond her years. Once, she went into the kitchen and informed the staff, 'If you could make the pats of butter smaller, it would be much better. Persons leave some of the big pats on their plates and that is very waste.' (sic)[27]

One can readily imagine how amused the recipient of her order might have been, although, since this anecdote was deployed to illustrate how she would 'boss the kitchen staff',[28] it is possible that there were already people who found her extreme self-assertiveness off-putting rather than enchanting.

'We followed the birds,' Queen Elizabeth used to say of her parents' schedule, and this pithy comment was undeniably true. Out of the shooting season, St. Paul's Walden Bury was the family's main base. Between 1906 and 1920, they also had 20 St. James's Square, a large Adam house between the Board of Trade and the Cleveland Club off Pall Mall, which Claude leased. Their neighbours included some of England's greatest aristocrats, including the Duke of Norfolk, the Duchess of Buckingham, and the Earl of Derby. This was certainly a vast improvement on Belgrave Mansions, the apartment near to Victoria Station on Grosvenor Gardens behind Buckingham Palace which had been their London residence prior to Claude's accession to the earldom.

When the London Season was over, they would sometimes head to Streatlam Castle in County Durham, no longer as guests, but as hosts. This large and splendidly proportioned baroque historic house, sitting in 1,190 acres, had an estate of twenty farms. There was also the magnificent Jacobean stately home, Gibside Hall, in striking distance, but the family had never lived there or even visited, as it was rented out from 1908 to a Gateshead solicitor named Victor Crunhut, and after the Great War, during which time the Army Girls were billeted in the servants' quarters, Claude had this architectural gem dismantled rather than undertake the expense of restoring it to its former splendour. In 1920 he had all its treasures, including fixtures and fittings, carted off to Glamis. It was then blown up in 1959 as a part of a military exercise, so no trace of it remains.

There were two other valuable though less impressive properties nearby, Howick and Wemmengill, but these too were not occupied by the family.

To the young Elizabeth, however, only one place was home. As her younger brother David put it, both Benjamins thought of Glamis as a 'holiday place, Streatlam as a visit, and St. Paul's as "Home".'[29]

One can see why they felt like this. St. Paul's Walden Bury was a lovely Queen Anne house covered in honeysuckle and magnolia. Elizabeth's first biographer Lady Cynthia Asquith described it as having an atmosphere of a happy English home, possessing 'so many of the familiar delights of childhood – charades, schoolroom-tea, home-made toffee, Christmas Eve, hide-and-seek. Nowhere in this well-worn house, one feels, can there ever have been strict rules as to the shutting of doors, the wiping of boots or the putting away of toys. There was none of the Victorian and Edwardian edict that children must been seen, not heard.'[30]

Both Elizabeth and the closest companion of her childhood, her younger brother David, enjoyed the many benefits that beloved children of means do. While Glamis was fun in a gory sort of way when the Scottish mists parted and the Scottish rain declined to sog the summer's ground, it was St. Paul's Walden Bury which they truly loved. There were barns to explore, fields to tramp through, outbuildings which made for mysterious and wonderfully messy adventure. From an early age Elizabeth loved horses, and enjoyed polishing the bits which the stable boys gave her. 'Absolute bliss,'[31] was how she described this pastime. She delighted in playing in the gardens which were her mother's pride and joy. Designed originally by Geoffrey Jellicoe in the 18th century, then supplemented over the centuries by others including Cecilia, there were vistas ending in statues and a woodland beyond it where beech-hedges delineated long grassy avenues which were intersected by lateral rides. There were ponds to wade in and a vast oak tree which Elizabeth used to climb or use as a hiding place. There was a rock garden, but, above all, 'At the bottom of the garden, where the sun always seems to be shining, is THE WOOD – the haunt of fairies, with its anemones and ponds, and moss-grown statues, and THE BIG OAK.'[32]

At this stage of their lives, the two Benjamins functioned as a unit. 'We were never separated if we could avoid it,' David said.[33] They devised a hiding place in an old brewhouse where they stashed their haul of 'forbidden delicacies acquired by devious devices. This store consisted of apples, oranges, sugar, sweets, slabs of Chocolat Menier, matches and packets of Woodbines' (cigarettes).[34] The only way to gain access to this hiding place was a very rotten ladder which no adult could ascend. This was ideal for escaping morning lessons, which they often did, without ever once being punished for doing so.

Mrs. Thompson, the housekeeper, remembered Elizabeth and David as being 'the dearest little couple' and confirmed that Elizabeth 'always took the lead. She would come tripping down the stairs and it would be 'Mrs. Thompson, have you any of those nice creams left for us?' and she would herself open the cupboard and help herself to what she liked best.'[35]

Notwithstanding Cecilia's belief that civility came before academia, she was careful that all her children had the knowledge which they would need to see them through the aristocratic way of life. Cecilia herself taught Elizabeth and David the rudiments of writing, dancing, drawing and music, Elizabeth's first piano lesson being 'The Musical Pathway', and, as soon as they were old enough, she organised dancing, fencing, and piano lessons for them.

A well-bred person who could not dance well was regarded as a social liability, so it was important that Elizabeth even more than David should excel. Aristocratic girls needed every edge they could get in the marital rat race which began as they approached eighteen, and the younger they started dancing lessons, the better dancers they would become. Aside from Mr. Neill in Forfar, who taught Elizabeth and David when they were at nearby Glamis Castle, there was Madame d'Egville in London.

Fortunately for her parents, Elizabeth showed an early aptitude for dancing. Later on, she enjoyed a reputation amongst her peers as a superb dancer, and there are many photographs of the ancient Elizabeth reeling the night away as she approached a hundred years old.

As neither Elizabeth nor David would need to defend themselves socially with the sword, fencing was not regarded as anything but a minor though aristocratic accomplishment, but piano playing was altogether different. Once more, this was a skill which was more necessary for girls to master than for boys, because married men were not necessarily required to sit down and play a piano of an evening, but married women were, and a music-loving beau might just opt for the better pianist amongst the many girls who would form the marriage market they would all need to compete in. It was therefore perceived as essential that young ladies who were not inordinately rich in their own right played the piano well. Cecilia provided not only an example but also encouragement which, once more, was not lost on the young Elizabeth, who was sent to Madame Mathilde Verne's Pianoforte School at 194 Cromwell Road, South Kensington.

Mathilde Verne was no slouch. She was a well-regarded concert pianist who had been taught by the great Clara Wieck Schumann in Frankfurt for four years prior to embarking upon a successful career in England. After a brief stint as a piano teacher at the Royal College of Music, she set up her own piano school in 1909. Her star pupil, between 1910 and 1915, was the great English pianist Solomon, whom she discovered. She also discovered Dame Moura Lympany. During Elizabeth's tenure at the school, the former Miss Wurm played under Henry Wood at the Queen's Hall Promenade Concerts and thereafter at the Sunday afternoon concerts.

Although pupils like Elizabeth were the bread and butter which kept the school afloat, Madame Verne recognised early on that Elizabeth did not have the character to become an accomplished pianist, irrespective of how much innate talent she might have had. The young Elizabeth, unsurprisingly considering her mother's attitude to effort, was both workshy and unwilling to extend herself if something did not come easily. Madame Verne observed an incident in which one of Elizabeth's teachers was trying to get her to persevere with exercises which were causing her some trouble. 'I looked at the child. Though reverent in face, there was a warning gleam in her eyes as she said to the teacher, "Thank you very much. That was wonderful," and promptly slid off the music stool, holding out her tiny hand in polite farewell.'[36] Although Elizabeth was eventually persuaded to return to her lesson, Madame Verne had gained a real insight into the determined but infinitely polite way in which she ensured that she got her own way, irrespective of who or what was involved.

Even more revealing is the pride which Elizabeth took in her ability to get her own way. Time and again she would allude to it in the future, but Madame Verne's observations were written with Elizabeth's collusion in 1927, long before she had had the opportunity to establish just how determined a character she was. So she was clearly happy for others to make the point for her.

No education, not even one as lacking as Elizabeth's, could entirely ignore academe. By the time Elizabeth was old enough to enter the schoolroom at St. Paul's Walden Bury, Hedwig Walters had been replaced as governess by Miss Mary Wilkie. Lessons took place mostly in the mornings, hence why she and David often hid in the Flea House, where no adult could climb up the rickety, rotting steps to fetch them. Miss Wilkie agreed with Madame Verne's assessment of Elizabeth as being 'a very pretty, vivacious little girl', and stayed with the family for some nine years, teaching both the Benjamins. However, she did not travel with them, for when the children were at Glamis their governess was Miss Laurel Gray.

Miss Gray provided a vignette of the bright and sparky little girl Elizabeth was when she recounted their first meeting. 'I expect that you can spell quite long words,' she said, assessing her new pupil. 'Oh yes, I can spell capercailzie and ptarmigan,' she replied without a smidgen of bashfulness.[37]

Cecilia required the governess to keep a record of her pupils' progress. 'When they were good, a good mark and a penny. And of course a bad mark, that was shocking,' Miss Gray recalled. 'Elizabeth wasn't too good but she always had a good mark, she was naturally a good scholar. A bad mark made no difference to David. I was as strict as I could be, he was terrible.'[38]

There was also a French governess in the form of Mademoiselle Lang. Known to the children by the contraction Made, as were all their subsequent French governesses (Cecilia believed in 'holiday governesses' who would speak to the children in their national language, whether it was French or German), she worked with them from about 1901 till 1910. Unlike the regular governess, who did not travel with the family, Made Lang could be found with them whatever side of the border they were on.

The evidence suggests that while Elizabeth and David were taught full-time by governesses when they were in Hertfordshire or Scotland, in London their parents took a stab at sending them to kindergarten when they were approaching nine and seven respectively. They were sent to the Frobel-trained Miss Constance Goff's school in Marylebone. Joan Ackland, a fellow pupil, was impressed by their good manners and devotion to each other, while Elizabeth remembered the plays they performed in French and German and being called a show-off for starting an essay on the sea with the Greek version of that word. But the family's peregrinations came before education, and when it suited Claude and Cecilia, the youngsters were duly yanked out of school for their governesses to resume their hodgepodge of an education.

Grief, however, was about to tear a hole in the even tenor of the family's happy life, the way it had prior to Elizabeth's birth. By Easter 1911, Elizabeth's third brother Alec, who had suffered from increasingly bad headaches ever since he was hit on the head by a cricket ball at Eton, was visibly declining. That July his elder brother Jock, who was working in Boston for an American bank, responded to a letter their mother had written him alerting him to his younger brother's deteriorating health. 'What do the doctors say about the condition of his head? Poor Alec, what an awful long time it has been for him.'[39] Although the doctors could not yet say with certainty that he had a brain tumour, it was obvious he did even before he died in his sleep early on the morning of 19th October, 1911.

Although Cecilia had had warning of the death of this twenty-four-year-old son, who had been tall, good looking and charming, she was once more overcome by grief the way she had been when she had lost her firstborn child.

Even though Cecilia would finally recover sufficiently to function, her loved ones were all painfully aware that the loss of a second child had left her in an even more fragile state than she had been after Violet's death. Thereafter, the family in general, and Elizabeth in particular, became overtly watchful of Cecilia's well-being, and there are several contemporaneous accounts of the consideration Elizabeth and the other children paid their mother.

Time, however, is its own palliative. When the *Titanic* sank in April 1912, family life was already back on an even keel and preparations were being made for David to go away to school. All of Elizabeth's older brothers had been sent to Eton, and at the beginning of the school year in 1912, when David was ten, he was sent as a precursor to preparatory school at St. Peter's Court in Broadstairs, Kent. Prince Henry and Prince George, two of King George V and Queen Mary's three youngest sons, were also students there prior to going to Eton, though David seems never to have been particularly friendly with either of them.

'David went to school for the first time on Friday. I miss him horribly,' Elizabeth wrote in the diary she kept intermittently.[40] Although not a boarder like him, she now started at The Misses Birtwhistle's Academy at 30 Sloane Street, off Knightsbridge in London.

The Misses Dorothy and Irene Birtwhistle were two spinsters who ran what was, for its time, a superior educational establishment. Elizabeth was taught thirteen different subjects, including History, Geography, Geometry, Arithmetic, Natural History, Scripture, English Grammar, English Composition, English Literature, English Recitation, French History and French. Although she had no aptitude for Arithmetic, she showed ability in English, History and Scripture, three subjects which her mother had inculcated into her through story-telling and, in the case of the Scriptures, by reading a chapter in the Bible to her every afternoon during their rest.

In the late 1960s, when my brother Michael was sitting his dinners at Gray's Inn, he used to room with Dorothy Birtwhistle, who had long since retired from teaching and had opened up her house in Guildford, Surrey to law students as paying guests. Miss Birtwhistle was a game old bird who enjoyed reminiscing about her former students, Queen Elizabeth The Queen Mother included. She remembered Elizabeth well, and used to regale my brother with accounts of the bright, sweet, mischievous and lazy child she was. Charm she had in spades. Self-possession too. But she was also a wily little devil who could, and did, get away with all sorts of mischief. Even at that age, she had perfected the art of hiding behind an angelic exterior. But the glint of steely determination which Madame Verne discerned was also picked up by Miss Birtwhistle, who was nevertheless sad to see Elizabeth leave her Academy after the Easter term of 1913.

'I was not surprised with the life she ended up having,' Miss Birtwhistle told my brother Michael. 'I could see, even when she was twelve, that she would make her mark on the world if given a chance.' Miss Birtwhistle liked her, but she said she never trusted her. She found her too wily to be trustworthy.

Elizabeth said later that she did not think she learned anything at the Birtwhistles', though a 'little bit of poetry I certainly remember. So I'm afraid I'm uneducated on the whole.'[41] Her school reports tell another story.

Whether it was the lapse of time which made her memory fade, or she was reluctant to give credit where it was due to people whom she might not have liked because they had pressurised her into working harder than she wished to, is open to interpretation. What is not, however, is the fact that she misinformed Eric Anderson about the standard of education at the Misses Birtwhistle's Academy, where pupils were expected to apply themselves to their school work rather than flirt with knowledge while smiling angelically and doing the minimum.

Performing true to the dictum that pleasure came before formal education, but that civilisation was of paramount importance, Cecilia removed Elizabeth from The Misses Birtwhistle's Academy and took her, along with David, to visit her mother Caroline Scott in Bordighera. From there they moved to the Hotel Minerva in Florence, where they visited art galleries and churches and the nearby town of Fiesole.

When they returned to England, David went back to his prep school while, if Elizabeth's diary entries for the 2nd and 3rd June 1913 are to be believed, she was enrolled at Miss Wolff's Classes in South Audley Street, Mayfair. This establishment had two merits. It was closer to St. James's Square, so the walk to school with her nanny was shorter for Elizabeth, and it was easier academically. What it lacked in educational accomplishment it made up for with the quality of its students, who included the vastly rich Sir Alfred Mond's daughter Eva, (later the Marchioness of Reading and mother of Elizabeth's good friend in adulthood, Lady Zuckerman), and Earl Spencer's daughters Delia and Lavinia, both of whom would become great friends of hers in later life. 'In London I went to what was called classes. One terrifying person called Miss Wolff,'[42] she asserted, providing the reason why her mother now sought out yet another temporary governess prior to removing Elizabeth from yet another educational establishment. Clearly, Elizabeth and work were anathema to each other.

Käthe Kübler was the latest in this long line of temporary governesses. She later published her memoirs once Elizabeth was famous, so there is a written record of this period, including her first day at St. Paul's Walden Bury. She arrived on a wonderfully sunny spring afternoon to find the family having tea in the garden room overlooking the park. They greeted her warmly, and after they had all finished their tea, Elizabeth took her to look at the dogs and horses. Her dog Juno had recently given birth to five puppies, and Fraulein Kübler wrote, 'As soon as she noticed that I loved animals I knew that I had won her over.'

Fraulein Kübler had certainly made a hit with her charming if troublesome charge, and within two weeks Cecilia was offering her a permanent position if she was willing to undertake all of Elizabeth's education. As this included gymnastics, drawing, piano lessons and needlework as well as all the academic subjects, the prospect might have been a daunting one for a less strong character than this twenty-one-year-old daughter of a Prussian official from Erlangen, Bavaria. But Fraulein Kübler was not intimidated. In her own words, 'I was very willing to do so, and so we both set to work with zest. Hitherto Lady Elizabeth had had only French governesses, and she had been to school only for a very short time. A regular education, as we know it in Germany, was something quite unknown to her. With true German thoroughness I drew up a timetable for her lessons and a plan of study, both of which were approved by Lady Strathmore.'[43]

This timetable kicked off with a piano lesson before breakfast. After that meal, governess and charge would adjourn to the schoolroom, where the first lesson began at 9.30. The curriculum covered Literature, Mathematics, Geography, History, Science, French and German. Lessons, which stopped at 4.30 in the afternoon, were in English, though out of the schoolroom, Käthe Kübler spoke to Elizabeth only in German. After tea, they would go walking or play golf or tennis, and sometimes they would go for a picnic tea in the woods. On these occasions, they would load up the pony cart with a basket containing sandwiches and cake, and once they had chosen their spot for the picnic, they would build a fire and heat up the water for their tea. During the strawberry and gooseberry season, they would also decamp to the kitchen garden, where 'Lady Elizabeth was adept at crawling under the netting and filling herself with strawberries while lying on her stomach,' to quote Fraulein Kübler.

This rustic way of life suited Elizabeth better than the Birtwhistles' Academy or Miss Wolff's Classes. But the London Season meant that her parents had to base themselves during the week at 20 St. James's Square, and there was no question of them leaving 'darling Elizabeth', as they customarily referred to her, in the country. So Fraulein Kübler and Elizabeth would head up to town as well, where lessons took place at home. Afterwards, there would be walks in Hyde Park and ballet and dancing lessons interspersed with visits to the cinema to see the latest silent 'moving pictures' from America.

Käthe Kübler's memoirs confirm how social the Strathmores were. During the day, they would frequently host luncheons which both governess and charge attended. She proudly recounted having sat next to the former Prime Minister, the 5th Earl of Rosebery, and the former Viceroys of India the 1st Marquess Curzon of Kedleston and the 5th Marquess of Lansdowne. In the evening, like two characters out of a movie, Elizabeth and Käthe Kübler would watch from a vantage point on the landing upstairs as Claude and

Cecilia's guests arrived for one of the evening receptions which they frequently held.

No one stayed in London over the weekend, so the family would return to Hertfordshire. Here, Fraulein Kübler recalled, 'On Sunday morning we all went to the little village church together, and at 4 p.m. there was often a cricket match: Lord Strathmore and his four eldest sons would play with the village lads, and the butler and valet played too. Lady Rose [the elder, beautiful sister who would later become Countess Granville], Lady Elizabeth and I sat in the field and watched with the villagers.'

After celebrating Christmas that year in the relative comfort and warmth of Hertfordshire, the family headed north on the *Flying Scotsman* to Glamis for Hogmanay, the most important night in the Scottish calendar. When they returned, Elizabeth and Fraulein Kübler got down to the serious business of preparing her for the Oxford Local Preliminary Examination. The gaps in Elizabeth's education needed to be filled if she was to pass, and the governess recalled, 'We worked at such a pace that Lady Elizabeth grew pale and thin.' Elizabeth started to complain to her mother. ' I do hate my lessons sometimes, and (become) sicker every day of this beastly exam. I know less and less.' There is no surprise to how Cecilia reacted. 'Her mother made us stop,' Fraulein Kübler wrote, 'and said with a smile: "Health is more important than examinations."'

But Cecilia and Elizabeth had met their match in Käthe Kübler. With infinite charm and determination, she refused to give up until Elizabeth had learnt the lessons needed to pass the examination, which she did early that summer. In theory at least, Elizabeth was now ready for the next phase of her education which, Cecilia hoped, the German governess would oversee. She invited her to stay on for the next four years, not only to teach Elizabeth, but also to 'round her off' with travel abroad to such places as France, Germany, Italy and Austria.

Despite the difficulties Fraulein Kübler was having in getting Elizabeth and Cecilia to agree to work, she was genuinely fond of them, and they of her. Admitting in her memoirs that she came to love her pupil, she also confessed to loving Cecilia 'almost more than my pupil' because she was so gracious, so kind, so loving, and such a delight to be around. She has also left us an eyewitness account of Elizabeth's great, almost exaggerated, love for her mother which, while excessive, seems to have been well deserved. 'How often I heard her high, clear voice calling through the house: "Mother darling, where are you?" Every morning when she woke, she went to her mother's bedroom, where they would read a chapter of the Bible together.'

But each of us is a prisoner of the fate earthshattering events have in store for us, and around the time of Elizabeth's exam, the Archduke Franz Ferdinand was assassinated. Käthe Kübler recounted going down 'into the breakfast room in the morning I saw distraught faces. Lord Strathmore gave me the *Morning Post*. "Here, read this. It means war." I would not and could not believe it.'

Less than two weeks later, on 12th July, Fraulein Kübler left for her month's holiday and for the celebrations of her parents' silver wedding anniversary. Three weeks later, on Elizabeth's fourteenth birthday on 4th August, 1914, war was declared. The First World War, the Great War, had begun, trapping many loved ones on different sides of the divide.

There was now no question of Käthe Kübler returning to a country in which she had become an enemy alien. She therefore volunteered for the Red Cross in Erlangen, and was soon tending to a never-ending stream of wounded soldiers. Meanwhile, Elizabeth would head to Glamis, where she would learn at first-hand what tending to the emotional needs of injured soldiers involved.

Yet the civilities which are now unthinkable between warring sides had not yet disappeared from practice. Throughout the war, former governess and charge continued to correspond with each other through the British Consulate at The Hague.

The way all sides in the conflict pursued the Great War would change warfare as mankind had always known it for all time. No one yet understood that civilised warfare was a thing of the past and that total war was the order of the new day.

At the time of its declaration, the populaces on each side of the divide were exultant and enthusiastic. Elizabeth was with her mother and relations at the London Coliseum watching a vaudeville review by the Russian ballerina Sophie Federova, Charles Hawtrey, and G.P. Hartley when the announcement was made. She witnessed the packed auditorium erupting in exhilaration. 'I think they honestly thought it was going to be about a month and it would be finished.'[44]

As the first waves of troops on either side of the Channel left within days for the fronts on both sides of the Continent, one sentence above all was most frequently heard: 'It will all be over by Christmas.'

With such misguided optimism, and for no foreseeable reward on any side of this futile war, would the flower of a generation charge off to meet its Maker.

The Great War

Chapter 3

No other single event in history has changed civilisation as decisively as the First World War. When it began in 1914, Europe was ruled by a series of blood relations, all of whom were interconnected, if not each with the other, then one with another. The Russian Tsar, Nicholas II, was the first cousin of the British King, George V, whose sister Maud was the Queen of Norway, whose husband King Haakon VII was the younger brother of the King of Denmark, Christian X, a cousin of the King of Sweden, Gustav V, who was a cousin of the reigning Grand Duchess of Luxembourg, Marie-Adelaide, who was a cousin of the Dutch Queen, Wilhelmina, who was a cousin of the Bulgarian Tsar, Ferdinand I, who was the nephew of the Austrian Emperor, Franz Joseph, as well as the father-in-law of the daughter of the King of Italy, Victor Emmanuel III, whose heir would marry the daughter of the Belgian King, Albert I, who was a cousin of the German Emperor, Wilhelm II, who was the brother-in-law of the Greek King, Constantine II.

When the war ended four years later on 11th November, 1918, Russia was Communist, its Tsar and his family murdered at Ekaterinburg, and the German and Austro-Hungarian Empires were in the process of disintegrating literally overnight. In a forty-eight hour period, the only two remaining European emperors lost their thrones, Imperial Germany giving way to the Weimar Republic, and the Austrian Empire splintering into a quantity of republics such as Austria and Czechoslovakia, or regrouping as smaller monarchies such as the Kingdom of the Serbs, Croats and Slovenes. Although both Wilhelm II and the young Austrian Emperor, Karl, tried to remain in their countries, they were both forced into exile, the former to the safety of the Netherlands, where Queen Wilhelmina refused to extradite him to face trial as a war criminal, and the latter to Switzerland, where he would remain for two years until he tried to regain his Hungarian throne. At which point the Allies shipped him and his wife Zita off to Madeira, the small Portuguese island 400 kilometres off the European mainland, which became his place of exile for the few months remaining to him before he died of pneumonia.

Historians argue that the upper and middle classes enjoyed a higher standard of living in the run-up to the First World War than they have since war was declared on 4th August, 1914. There is much evidence to support this hypothesis. Inflation was virtually non-existent, so money not only kept its value, but everything else associated with it did too. Housing had improved to such an extent that the middle classes were living in sumptuous properties the like of which only multi-millionaires can afford nowadays. Indeed, many a bourgeois residence in London, Paris, New York, Berlin or Vienna from that epoch is nowadays either broken up into flats for the prosperous or used as houses for the extremely rich. The palatial properties which used to proliferate along such streets as Fifth Avenue in New York or Park Lane in London, to mention but two of the addresses which were the exclusive domain of the rich, no longer exist. They have long since been torn down to make way for apartment blocks, department stores, or hotels. More ordinary houses, such as the brownstones in New York's Upper East Side or the terraced houses in London's fashionable Chelsea squares, have now become upmarket areas, when once they were the province of the decidedly middle class. Slums like SoHo on the Lower East Side in Manhattan, or working-class areas like Oberkampf in the 11th *arrondissement* in Paris, are now chic. Prosperous artists, writers, authors, and musicians live cheek by jowl with the few remaining residents of the former servant class. Where a family of relatively modest means might have had three servants and a rich one would have had a multitude more, today even people who consider themselves relatively wealthy have to survive with either no live-in staff or so few that our equivalents from a century ago would have pitied us. Billionaires and movie stars are the only people who can muster a complement of staff commensurate with what the most minor aristocrat or insignificant gentleman from the gentry would have taken for granted prior to the Great War, which is when civilisation as they knew it ended. And this happened literally overnight, just like the collapse of the Hohenzollern and Hapsburg empires.

Elizabeth's family was no more immune than the lowliest worker to the sudden and dramatic changes which were taking place all over Britain and Europe as the armies of all the major powers, and several minor ones, mobilised. Three of her older brothers were already commissioned officers: Patrick and Jock with the 5th Battalion of the Black Watch, Fergus with the

8th Battalion of the same regiment. The fourth and youngest of these older brothers, Michael (Mike), volunteered with the 3rd Battalion of the Royal Scots, and as they prepared to ship out to France, frenzy and excitement replaced the orderliness and calm that had hitherto been a feature of the family's routine.

Even the unimaginative can imagine the anxiety that Cecilia was experiencing as her sons prepared for their departure, the drama being heightened by the two unmarried Bowes Lyon boys rushing to wed their sweethearts before they set off for the front and possible death. On 17th September Fergus married the 15th Earl of Portarlington's daughter Lady Christian Lawson-Damer in Sussex, and twelve days later Jock married the younger daughter of the 21st Lord Clinton, the Hon. Fenella Hepburn-Stuart-Forbes-Trefusis at Fasque, Kincardineshire. Elizabeth was a bridesmaid at both weddings, but this can have been scant compensation for the insecurity and disruption which impinged none-too-pleasantly upon her life. She was not only losing her four brothers but also the butler and her father's valet, who also volunteered.

Within a matter of weeks of the declaration of war, houses the length and breadth of the British Isles and the European continent were denuded of men. Many British landowners found a novel way to help the war effort. They encouraged their workers to volunteer, promising to keep their jobs open for their return, and offered in the meantime to allow their families to live rent free on their estates. Such was the war fever that youngsters of sixteen and seventeen were lying about their ages so that they too could enlist. This would have tragic consequences in several cases, for once the fighting started in earnest, some of them became so shell-shocked that they froze to the spot when ordered to advance. Deemed to be cowards, they were invariably court-martialled and shot at dawn, despite being too young to be in the army.

Elizabeth and her mother had been in London when war was declared. Claude and Cecilia took the decision to base themselves at Glamis, so Elizabeth and the family headed north to their 65,000-acre estate on the *Flying Scotsman*. This year, however, the convivial atmosphere which had always surrounded the family's move northwards was lacking. There were no shooting parties to celebrate the Glorious Twelfth, which no longer seemed so glorious now that the menfolk would be shooting the enemy instead of grouse. There were no jolly sing-alongs around the piano with a house full of guests who would sparkle and scintillate, or just be dull and worthy.

Although the family headed south again within weeks to attend the weddings of the two boys, once Elizabeth and her parents had done so, and said goodbye, they returned to Glamis. Claude was the Lord Lieutenant of

Forfarshire and chaired the local territorial defence associations, so he was busy liaising with the local farmers and landowners, instructing them what they should do in the event of an invasion.

For her part, Cecilia was also busy. The newly appointed Secretary of State for War, Field Marshal Earl Kitchener of Khartoum, had called for 100,000 volunteers, warning, to the irritation of his Cabinet colleagues, that the war might well be a long one. The response was overwhelming. The problem would not be the number of men, but how to kit out such a vast number before sending them abroad to fight.

The Government was having difficulty with all aspects of equipment, from guns and ammunition to clothing and bedding. With their customary generosity and public-spiritedness, Claude and Cecilia stepped into the breach and resolved to provide each of the thousand men in the local Black Watch battalion with a sheepskin coat in lieu of the greatcoats which were supposed to form part of the winter uniform, but which would not be ready in time for their departure for the front. The women also pitched in to make items of clothing for the soldiers. Elizabeth later reminisced, 'during these first few months we were so busy knitting, knitting, knitting and making shirts for the local battalion – the 5th Black Watch.'[1] There were socks and mufflers to fabricate in endless quantities, so needlepoint and embroidery were replaced with a more useful after-dinner activity. Her 'chief occupation was crumpling up tissue paper until it was so soft that it no longer crackled, to put into the lining of sleeping bags.'[2]

From Elizabeth's point of view, the war offered one boon above all else. Once Madeleine Girardot de Villiers, the French temporary governess who was substituting for the vacationing Käthe Kübler, had returned to France in September, there was no one to educate her. For the next two months, she was able to rush about, enjoying unparalleled release from the grind of the schoolroom.

But this happy interlude was about to come to an end. The outgoing temporary governess had suggested to an English friend of hers from the Maison d'Education de la Légion d'Honneur that she write to Cecilia proposing herself for the vacant position. This school was where the best French governesses had come from since the days of Napoleon, who had imperialised the Royalist school for impecunious young ladies established by Louis XIV's morganatic wife the Marquise de Maintenon at St. Cyr, so any graduate came armed with an impeccable pedigree. Beryl Poignand, having returned to England that summer from France, duly wrote to Cecilia.

Beryl was the daughter of an Indian Army officer, whose father had died recently. She was living with her mother in Farnham, Surrey. Not only was she excellently educated, but she also had just the right tinge of exotica to appeal to the Strathmore family, her father being descended from a physician at the Court of Louis XVI who had fled to England during the Revolution. Cecilia replied to the approach positively, offering this unknown governess the position for a few months.

It is interesting to note how much more trusting people were a hundred years ago. Nowadays, it would be regarded as the height of recklessness, or at least naïveté to apply for, or offer, such a responsible position to a total stranger, yet this was the norm at a time when people were expected to behave well, and usually did.

The way Cecilia responded to Beryl's acceptance of her offer gives an insight into her daughter's character. 'I do hope you will be happy here,' she said, the thought that she herself might be unhappy with this latest governess the furthest thing from her mind, 'Elizabeth is really a delightful companion – very old for her age – and very sensible. So that you will not have a <u>child</u> with you always.'[3]

While Cecilia had a very high opinion of her daughter, the same was not uniformly true of the governesses and staff. When Elizabeth died, Sally Kinnes wrote an interesting, well-informed article about her for *The Scotsman*. 'Though she evidently had plenty of charm,' this respected journalist asserted, 'Elizabeth had a mean streak. "Some governesses are nice and some are NOT," she confided to an exercise book', which, of course, would be read by this latest governess she was setting up for victimhood. 'Mademoiselle Madeleine...sent to teach the 14-year-old, had an especially hard time.' Kinnes goes on to catalogue a series of cruelties which the unfortunate Frenchwoman was subjected to as Elizabeth set out to torment her by frightening her with stories about 'the devil faced spider of Glamis.' She was also 'doing her best to have her shivering in her bed' with missives stating that 'it is now seven years since you left the Asylum; cured of your hallucinations...' She threatened that the 'unfortunate attacks are due to return 29 Dec! We are keeping a bed for you...Doctor Waring, the man you tried to murder with a carving knife, is not quite recovered and is awaiting your return with great eagerness.'[4]

Even if such conduct could have been interpreted as ghoulish humour, there is no mistaking the underlying and rather disturbing menace. Whether Cecilia knew about this is a moot point. It is likely she did not, for governesses did not complain about the petty acts of cruelty imposed upon them by the children in their charge; not unless they wanted to have dubious references. It is even less likely that Madeleine would have been complaining to Beryl Poignand, not when she was recommending that she apply for the job which the young woman needed. But Elizabeth's conduct is a matter of record, so even the governess's discretion and her mother's possible ignorance turned out to be no shield where posterity is concerned.

While letters were going back and forth between Cecilia and Beryl Poignand, Elizabeth's mother had other matters to deal with as well. She and Claude had decided to use Glamis as a convalescent home for wounded soldiers after they had been discharged from nearby Dundee Royal Infirmary, so they set about having the huge dining table, chairs, and sideboards moved out of the dining room. These were replaced with rows of beds, bedside tables, and chairs as well as all the paraphernalia a comfortable and well-equipped ward required. The billiard table was removed from the nearby games room, which was turned into a stock room for the winter clothes they were stockpiling in case the war lasted beyond Christmas.

Towards the end of November, Elizabeth's sabbatical ended with Beryl's arrival in the evening. She was assigned a large tower bedroom, where she found a roaring fire and supper laid on in the schoolroom. She liked 'the old place…all nooks & corners & stairs up & down & long passages – many floors of stone of course,' and more importantly, 'I like Elizabeth very much & I think we shall be great friends.'[5]

Although Elizabeth would be having only four hours of lessons a day rather than the more taxing regimen which Käthe Kübler had devised, Cecilia was still intent on ensuring that her little angel was not overburdened with too much work. 'I don't know if very advanced mathematics are required for Elizabeth's exam, but I do not wish her to take anything very advanced. I am not a believer in very high mathematics for girls.'[6]

Beryl found that 'it is not too easy teaching her. I have to make things as interesting as possible or she would easily get bored I think. She is intelligent – it is a wonder to me that she knows all she does – her education has been rather quaint.'[7]

Beryl patently understood her brief as well as her charge. Elizabeth would later on reminisce about 'those happy days', describing a regimen which seemed to involve far more food and fun than work. As Elizabeth described it, a typical day started at eight with a history lesson which was interrupted for breakfast. Upon rising from the table, there was arithmetic, but this too was suspended when Nurse Anderson interrupted it because she was in urgent need of a chat, which of course they were only too happy to oblige her with. This level of industriousness required a break for biscuits, hot chocolate and the exchange of jokes, following which governess and charge went for a walk through the pinetum rather than return to their lessons. All this exertion resulted in Elizabeth working up a huge appetite, which was just as well, for it was now time for lunch. By her own account, she ate 'an 'orrid amount', which of course required another walk rather than something sedentary like study. Even Beryl and Elizabeth, however, could not entirely escape the need to make a show of learning occasionally, so after this latest foray, it was 'back to the schoolroom for a bit.' So much exercise clearly drained her of all energy, so lessons were once more dispensed with for her to recharge her batteries by eating 'enormous quantities of Vida bread, at tea.' She was now so exhausted by everything but learning that 'I sleep before the fire while Medusa [her nickname for Beryl] reads about the Queens of England.' Refreshed by her rest, she and her governess, who clearly liked learning because she did not read trash for pleasure, did not resume her studies, as one would expect after such a workshy day. Instead, they headed towards the soldiers' ward to play the card game whist with some of the convalescents. This took them up to supper, at which time Elizabeth provided yet another brilliant display, not of anything she might have learnt during the day, but through the enormous amount of food she managed to pack away. Not surprisingly, she was now so stuffed full from a day of eating, eating, and more eating, with the occasional walk and gossip and some card games, that she was utterly exhausted and wandered 'bedwards, tired, but let us hope happy!!!'[8]

If the world around her was collapsing, Elizabeth was nevertheless having a pretty good war, as her reminiscences confirm. This was due in no small measure to the hub of activity which Glamis had become. The first convalescents arrived in December 1914. There were only two of the ten Bowes Lyon children living at home at this point: Elizabeth and Rose, the beautiful, unmarried daughter who returned to London in January 1915 to train as a nurse prior to coming back to her ancestral home to tend to the recuperating soldiers.

Being too young to nurse, Elizabeth's task was to make the injured young men feel at home. To jolly them along. To provide good cheer. To run errands for them, like going to the shops to buy cigarettes, tobacco and the chocolates which she already loved so much. She wrote letters home for them, read to them, and, as we have seen, played cards with them. In short, she did what she would always do best: she charmed them with her excellent company.

Whatever her failings, even Elizabeth's detractors never denied that she was superb company and possessed charm to an overwhelming degree. As her sister-in-law Wallis Windsor rather tartly put it in her autobiography, *The Heart Has Its Reasons*, Elizabeth had 'justly famous charm'.

You only needed to meet her glancingly, as I first did after the running of the King George VI and Queen Elizabeth Stakes at Ascot Races in summer

1973, to become aware of the force and charm of her personality. I was talking to my hostess, my good friend Mary Anne Innes Ker, and the Duke of Atholl when, who should stop to say hello but Queen Elizabeth The Queen Mother and the Queen. The elder Elizabeth was without a doubt one of the most dynamically charming and charismatic personalities I had met up to that point, or indeed have encountered since. Her daughter was charming in an entirely less overwhelming way, which is not to disparage the power of the monarch's personality, for what shone through was integrity. I did not pick up the same quality from her mother, however, which is not to say that I thought it did not exist. It was simply not in evidence. But her charm certainly was.

People who knew Elizabeth from childhood, like Lord David Cecil, confirmed that this aspect of her personality was already in evidence when she was very young. In 1980 he would recall meeting her during King Edward VII's reign (which ended in 1910) at a dance class at Lansdowne House, and being struck by her 'great sweetness and sense of fun; and a certain roguish quality. The personality which I see now was there already.'

Always intensely personable and something of an actress who liked nothing better than an audience to which she could display her wonderful personality, Elizabeth might have been too young to nurse the soldiers who now started to arrive at Glamis, but she was definitely mature enough to turn the full barrage of her charms upon them. Taking her cue from her mother, who treated the men as if they were houseguests rather than patients, she displayed just the right amount of levity to raise their spirits. Many of them were shell-shocked from warfare in the trenches, and this bright, endearing and mature fourteen-year-old, whose greatest joy appeared to be being appreciated by others, was in many ways the ideal balm for their needs. These were considerable, for those whose nerves were not shot often had bad wounds, such as a gunshot in the stomach or through the lungs. Those who were less severely injured would go for walks in the grounds, sometimes accompanied by Elizabeth. They would join the family for chapel. They would even dance with her and Rose and, when he was home from boarding school, their brother David. Elizabeth's good humour and her undoubted willingness to please helped to create a happy atmosphere, especially that first Christmas of the war, when people were finally beginning to realise that it might well turn out to be of longer duration than they had originally anticipated.

Doing their utmost to inject good cheer into a season which might otherwise become a cause for depression, the family had a huge tree decorated in the crypt. They gave each man a present. According to Elizabeth, everyone ate far too much, which of course she and David tried to work off by dancing with their 'houseguests'. She remembered, 'The fun was fast and furious' and it was 'a dandy Xmas, you bet your bottom dollar.'[9]

Elizabeth ensured that the jolly tone which her mother had set continued into the new year. She was constantly joking around with the soldiers. Above all, she chatted to them, her blend of impish charm and angelic sweetness, offset as they were with a strong streak of intelligent mischievousness, proving to be a welcome lift to their spirits. One convalescent said 'my three weeks at Glamis have been the happiest I ever struck. I love Lady Strathmore so very much on account of her being so very like my dear mother, as was, and as for Lady Elizabeth, why, she and my fiancay are as like as two peas.'[10]

Nor was this an isolated instance. Elizabeth struck up enduring relationships with many of the convalescents, some of whom she corresponded with after their departure, and in the occasional case, for years to come, such as Corporal Ernest Pearce of the Durham Light Infantry. He met Elizabeth three months after his shoulder was shattered at Ypres. He said that whenever their paths crossed during the weeks they were both in residence at Glamis 'she was always the same. "How is your shoulder?" "Do you sleep well?" "Does it pain you?" "Why are you not smoking your pipe?" "Have you no tobacco?" "You must tell me if you haven't and I'll get some for you."' He thought, 'For her fifteen years she was very womanly, kind-hearted and sympathetic.' He was 'often her partner in the boisterous games of whist they played in the evenings'[11] and, when he returned to service in 1916, they corresponded with each other.

When Corporal Pearce was making his recollections of the warm and wonderful teenager Elizabeth was, she had become the Duchess of York, but it is not possible that he could have been fabricating her qualities because it is these very qualities which extended their relationship beyond its ordinary parameters. She 'helped him in the post-war years' and when he ceased to work in a Sunderland shipyard, she employed him as a gardener: a job he kept for the remainder of his life.'[12]

Nor is that the end of the link between Elizabeth and the Pearce family. In 1946, she employed Corporal Pearce's niece Mary Ann Whitfield, promoting her until she became head cook at Royal Lodge, a job which lasted until 1986.

Such conduct gives an insight into Elizabeth's ability, maybe even her need, to maintain as many affectionate and enduring relationships as she could, even when they were with individuals who were out of her personal orbit.

But all that was in the future in January 1915. Now that it really did look as if everyone had to hunker down for a long war, in the middle of the month

Cecilia re-established her pre-war life to the extent that she could. Although there would no longer be large house parties at St. Paul's Walden Bury or the multitude of gracious receptions which had previously proliferated at St. James's Square, if only because everywhere houses were being run without the benefit of male servants, she nevertheless left Claude alone at Glamis and headed south with Elizabeth and David, and of course Beryl the governess, to resume the old routine of weeks in London and weekends in Hertfordshire. For her part, Elizabeth found it no sacrifice to give up tending to convalescent soldiers and head off most afternoons for tea with her friends or to the cinema in Regent Street or Marble Arch, following a morning of what passed for lessons with Beryl. Often she would be accompanied by her equally vivacious friend Lady Lavinia Spencer, who lived just down the road from her at Spencer House, overlooking Green Park.

Cecilia also established a home for convalescents at St. Paul's Walden Bury, so when Elizabeth returned there, a month after coming down to London, she was able to resume the enjoyable task of keeping up the men's spirits with her own blend of high spirits and charm. Later that February of 1915, her brother Patrick came home with a wounded foot. A month later it was Mike's turn. He had a head wound as well as shell shock, for which the cure was rest and lots of it. Beryl provided us with an insight into his mother's worry about keeping one of her wild sons tame: 'now Lady S. is worrying about how in the world she will manage to keep him at all quiet – he is so headstrong & will want to be going to the theatres etc. all the time.'[13]

Six weeks later an injured Jock had to be sent home in an overcrowded troop ship which was carrying over twice its complement of 400 soldiers. His left index finger had been shattered by a bullet and it had to be amputated, but this was one cloud which had a silver lining from his baby sister Elizabeth's point of view. Beryl recounted in her diary for 15th May, 1915, how Elizabeth, who unabashedly adored attention, was thrilled to be quoted in the *Daily Mail*, which had telephoned to ask about the injury. Another silver lining turned out to be the consequence of Jock's amputation. He was invalided out of the army, joined the Foreign Office and was sent to the indisputable safety of the American capital.

It is interesting to speculate how Elizabeth would have coped with life had she not married as well as she did. Would she have been happy as the wife of an untitled man? Or as a mere countess? Even as a little girl she had shown signs of having too big a personality for her circumstances. Like one of today's starstruck country girls who sees herself more suited for superstardom than ordinary living, even though she has never done anything to deserve it, and shows no particular talent in any of the fields which are a requirement for such a glittering life, being Lady Elizabeth Bowes Lyon seemed rather too modest for her self-image. She famously told one vicar who asked who she was enacting: I am the Princess Elizabeth. Now she and Lady Lavinia Spencer, who alternated between adoration of actors like Henry Ainley and Basil Hallam respectively, and handsome sailors (it is useful to remember that all the senior royal males went into the navy as a part of their royal training), started a silly, but humorous and telling, correspondence as Queen Mary and King George V. Soon they formed a triumvirate of sailor-loving acolytes with Lady Katie Hamilton, the Duke of Abercorn's daughter who would become another lifelong friend.

Elizabeth's burgeoning sexuality was not limited to interest in handsome sailors alone. She was already showing signs of the lifelong predilection she would have for attractive men, and, reading between the lines, was also showing signs of the flirtatiousness which would be such a feature of her adult personality.

Shawcross observes in his official biography, 'Handsome men in uniform did not have to be sailors to attract Elizabeth's attention. In London she and Beryl had taken to watching the Red Cross chauffeurs outside their headquarters in St. James's Square. Elizabeth dubbed one of these drivers "The Beautiful One". And he appears frequently in her letters of these years.'

The love of the theatre which she was already showing would remain another lifelong passion, and she celebrated her fifteenth birthday in London by going to the Hippodrome. The time was swiftly approaching for her annual move up north. The day of her departure, she went shopping, for, amongst other things, another of her lifelong passions, 'lots of chocs', and as she and David were departing 'alonio' to catch the night train to Scotland she got 'a wonderful last smile from The Beautiful One, we waved to each other for the <u>first and last</u> time, a fitting goodbye.'[14]

On the way up north she recounted sharing a carriage with 'two <u>most</u> beautiful sailors', whom she engaged in 'long conversations in the corridor in the morning.'[15]

When she and David arrived at Glamis, fortunately there was a former sailor to capture her interest. She wrote her vacationing governess, 'Dear Miss Poignand, you are missing something! One is a fisherman and Naval Reserve, he has been shipwrecked five times. Blue eyes, black hair, <u>so</u> nice. Reminds me of Henry.' (Ainley, the actor).[16]

But Elizabeth did not limit her attentions to only those men who caught her eye. She maintained her policy of treating one and all the convalescents as if they were treasured houseguests, and, according to Corporal Ernest Pearce, who met her at this time, everyone at Glamis 'worshipped' Elizabeth. Even accounting for the exuberance which her royal status would have engendered at the time of his recollections, there is an ample body of evidence which shows that she was indeed popular with the recovering men.

In September David started at Eton. This was only the first, and most pleasant, of the changes which were about to rock the family, for tragedy was lurking around the corner. Fergus came home for leave in August, in time to celebrate his first wedding anniversary and to see his daughter Rosemary, who was born on 18th July. After a short stay at Glamis, he rejoined his regiment in time for the Battle of Loos. This was to be one of the major carnages of World War One. The British commander of I Corps of the British Expeditionary Force, General Sir Douglas (later Field Marshal The Earl) Haig wrote in his diary, 'The greatest battle in the world's history begins today,' but it would have been more appropriate if he had written, 'the most pointless debacle', for the French commander, General Joffre, had determined, against the wisdom of Earl Kitchener of Khartoum, the British Minister for War, that the British forces must not be allowed to fight in the open countryside, but alongside the French in the constricted terrain of the devastated village of Loos.

On the night of 26th September, the Black Watch had captured the Hohenzollern Redoubt, but by the morning of the 27th, the Germans, who knew these trenches very well indeed, for they were their own, had retaken a trench nearby. So Fergus and his men, who had been fighting solidly for forty-eight hours, were ordered to clear them out just as they were preparing breakfast for themselves. Although they had only been relieved of duty shortly beforehand, at 4 a.m., he gathered up his men and led them out to follow his orders. No sooner was Fergus visible than a bomb blew off his right leg, shrapnel embedding itself in his chest. Bullets then tore into his chest and shoulder, fatally injuring him. He lingered, in considerable pain, for several hours, dying shortly before midday.

Another casualty of this exercise in futility was the only son of England's most popular author. Something of a jingoist, Rudyard Kipling had pulled strings to ensure that his son John, whose eyesight was so bad that he had been rejected for military service on medical grounds, was deemed fit for service. He never forgave himself for his interference, and wrote some beautiful poetry bemoaning the loss of so many flowers of the younger generation.

It took four days for the news of Fergus's death to reach Glamis. At first Cecilia was led to believe by Lieutenant G.B. Gilroy of the 8th Battalion Black Watch that his death had been painless, but later, after she had had time to accept the death of a third child, she discovered that it had been anything but. Even without that knowledge, however, she was devastated, and it is a mark of her strength of character that she nevertheless remained as gracious and considerate a hostess as she had always been. When the convalescents, who had sent her a letter of condolence, refrained from using the billiard room and playing music on the gramophone, or going outside onto the lawns, she thanked them for their consideration but expressed the wish that they continue using the facilities as they had done before. They were her guests, and must make themselves at home.

As for 'poor little Elizabeth', as Beryl described her charge, she too performed in character. She remained 'gay and bright'. But beneath the good cheer lay practical consideration for the mother she adored. She started to walk out every morning to intercept the mail, just in case there was more bad news Cecilia would need to be prepared for. This was an early sign of the solicitousness which she would display during her marriage, to marked effect.

Although Cecilia continued to worry about Mike and Jock, who were still fighting in France, at least she did not have to worry that Patrick would also be killed. Lady Mary Clayton would later describe her personable, charming and vivacious uncle as being so handsome he 'really looked as if he'd stepped down from Olympia', but no amount of charm or good looks could mend his broken mind once it was shattered by shell shock[17]. Although he had appeared at first to be making a good recovery from the wound he received in 1915, it gradually became evident that he was more badly shell-shocked than had at first been apparent. As his physical wounds healed, his mental ones worsened, until he was no longer able to eat. Although he was sent to a nursing home for treatment, and his anorexia did improve, he never fully recovered his health. He was compelled to resign his commission and was invalided out of active service, never to be the same personable, jolly man he had once been.

If Elizabeth's eldest brother was tremulous, the same could not be said of his youngest sister. A new and fearsome weapon, the Zeppelin, 'the H-bomb of its day, an awesome sword of Damocles to be held over the cowering heads of Germany's enemies,' to quote Martin Gilbert in *First World War*, had recently been raining terror on London and the Home Counties. Zeppelins, named after their founder Graf von Zeppelin, were massive airships which flew silently and had recently cascaded hundreds of bombs onto the terrified populace, killing scores of people. They inspired absolute terror in their targets on the ground, who, until that time, had never had to worry about being killed from the direction of the sky. Naturally, Elizabeth was not going to let something like a tiny little thousand-foot long Zeppelin packed with bombs intimidate her, not when she wanted to go to the theatre. So she and David went to see *The Scarlet Pimpernel*, Baroness Orczy's tale about the French Revolution, at the recently-bombed Strand Theatre. No one can summarise Elizabeth's attitude better than herself. On 30th October she wrote to Beryl saying, 'When the Zepps were last here, they dropped a bomb into the pit of the Strand and killed 6 people, so of course we went there.'

Only too soon, Christmas was rolling around again. Once more the family spent it up at Glamis. Once more there was an immense tree with presents for each soldier. Another good time was had by all. And, as Elizabeth herself recounted, they drank a toast 'To Hell with the bloody Kaiser.'

If her language was ripening along with everything else, she was about to be given another opportunity to be particularly fruity. The Junior Examination of the Oxford Local Examinations Board was looming in March. As we have seen, neither Cecilia nor Elizabeth had done anything so far to foster her prospects of passing. Failure, however, would not reflect well upon her governess, and Beryl, being aware of this, now tried to get her lazy charge to settle down to doing some work. Elizabeth admitted that Beryl was 'really in despair about my exam, you see I'm so frightfully stupid & don't know anything except what I've learnt with her about – Julius Caesar, Napoleon, French History, & a lot of little things about the Gods & Goddesses, Hades etc.'[18]

Of course, anyone who knew Elizabeth's history will have known that she was being unfair to the many previous governesses and teachers, including Dorothy Birtwhistle and Käthe Kübler, who had knocked themselves out trying to get her to work. Not only had she been well taught before, but she was no fool either, as this attempt to absolve the governess of responsibility for her recalcitrance, by laying the ground with a judicious mixture of manipulative falsehoods, showed. Trying to shut the stable door after the horse had bolted, Beryl attempted to cram her in the new year, but even though it was obvious how dire her educational situation was, Elizabeth could not resist the lure of pleasure, so when she and Beryl were not enjoying perambulations in the grounds at Glamis or playing cards with the convalescents, they were embarking upon activities such as a visit to the theatre in Dundee. 'I am hopelessly rotton (sic) at Arithmetic, Literature, Drawing, History, and Geography,' this young woman, whose best subject was English and who prided herself on her acumen in it, wrote to Beryl's mother. If Mrs. Poignand had any sense at all, that one spelling mistake alone would have alerted her that Elizabeth had scant chance of passing an examination in which no amount of charm and angelic sweetness could compensate for ignorance born of a cavalier disdain for work.

The first of the exams, a memory drawing paper, took place on the morning of 17th March, 1916, in Hackney in London's East End. This was an hour away from St. James's Square by bus and tram-car, but the journey back and forth did not deter Elizabeth from returning home for lunch, after which she had to head eastwards again to sit model drawing.

Between these exams and the forthcoming ones in Literature, Geography and Arithmetic, Elizabeth found time, not to bone up on those subjects, but to write to her heart-throb Henry Ainley to inform him that she was planning to come to see him in *Who is He?* She was jubilant when he responded, 'I shall myself look forward with keen pleasure to Friday evening.' She either did not realise, or then did not care, that he was politely brushing her off when he promised, 'at the end of the first act I shall raise my eyes to that part of the house where you & your friend will be seated, & may I hope to meet a smile of appreciation & pleasure.' Nevertheless, he was kind enough to offer her words of encouragement for the 'most difficult advanced examination' she was 'at present engaged on' which he was confident she would pass with 'flying colours'.[19]

The heart-throb's kindly encouragement could not have been more misplaced. Her ensuing Literature paper should have presented her with a decided advantage, had she ever opened up a book on Sir Walter Scott, or listened to her mother's tales about Glamis. Presuming of course that they had extended beyond the narrow confines of the castle itself, its traditions, terrors, and the Bowes Lyon family history. Scott had stayed there in the late 1770s, writing an account of the terror it engendered in him: 'I must own that when I heard door after door shut, after my conductor had retired, I began to consider myself as far too far from the living, and somewhat too near to the dead.'[20] So inspired was he by the castle and the family that he subsequently wrote about them in his novels *Waverley* and *The Antiquary*, but not even this link could shed light on Elizabeth's ignorance. Scott was too 'difficult', she declared, a sentiment carried through when she dismissed Geography and Arithmetic as being 'quite hopeless, much too complicated for me!'[21] She doubted that she would pass her exams, which at least shows that beneath all the laziness and pleasure-seeking was a head sufficiently well-screwed-on to recognise reality when it was staring her in the face.

Elizabeth's perspicacity proved prescient. A few weeks later, the Oxford Examination Board informed her that she was not 'entitled to a Certificate.' Her response was pure, unadulterated fury, a response she would have many times in later life when things did not go the way she wanted. 'All I can say is, DAMN THE EXAM!!' she informed Beryl, using language that was most definitely forbidden by her mother, though of course Cecilia did not believe in reprimanding Elizabeth any more than in allowing her to make too much of an effort, hence why she had reached this pass. 'I was good at poetry, wasn't I?!!' she asked, clearly perplexed that what she regarded as good hadn't made the grade. 'I'm not going to tell anyone about it anyhow, till they ask me!! Good heavens!' she said, expressing her frustration, 'What was the purpose of toiling down to that – er – place Hackney? None, I tell you none. It makes me <u>boil</u> with rage to think of that vile stuff, tapioca, eaten for – nothing? Oh, hell,' she continued in like vein, before admitting, 'I am very disappointed, but I daresay I shall get over it, if I go and see Henry.'[22]

The disproportionality of equating a night out at the theatre to see her heart-throb with being as important as failing a major examination might have been understandable considering her age, but it nevertheless showed a disquieting presence of over-confidence in what she herself would often dismiss throughout her life by reference to 'the *true i*mportance of things'.

Elizabeth duly went to see her beloved Henry Ainley and duly wrote about the evening to the one person who would share her joy in the pleasure it brought her: Cecilia, whose sense of the *true* importance of things also allowed her to dismiss academic failure as insignificant compared with the delights her angel would experience through an evening at the theatre in London looking at her heart-throb. 'I've seen old Henry in "Who is He" and simply <u>loved </u>it. He's so good looking (do tell Mike & Rosie, and make him as young and beautiful as you can) with BLUE eyes and BLACK hair, and quite THIN, not <u>too</u> thin, but just right. I <u>am </u>so triumphant, you'd love him, he's so funny.'[23]

Here was an insight into Elizabeth's real character: pleasure-loving and triumphalist, traits that would be much in evidence throughout her long life.

Of course, Cecilia's objective had never been to cultivate her daughters' minds, but to prepare them mentally, physically, socially, spiritually, and personally for life as a wife. In this, she would be brilliantly successful, especially with Elizabeth. But Elizabeth wasn't her only success. All her daughters got married suitably, the latest to do so being Rose (Rosie). Her engagement to the enormously fat, seventeen-stone and ironically-nicknamed 'Wisp' Leveson-Gower was announced around the time that her little sister's exam results were received.

A month afterwards, Rosie Bowes Lyon and the 2nd Earl Granville's second son were married at St. James's Piccadilly, with Elizabeth a bridesmaid yet again. Although only a minor scion of a minor peerage of the ducal house of Sutherland, Wisp nevertheless bore a properly aristocratic name, and though the marriage could not be deemed splendid, Wisp's prospects did improve with time, and ultimately he would succeed his childless brother as the 4th

Earl. He would also go on to have a successful naval career, helped no doubt by a combination of ability allied to the marital alliance between his wife's family and the Royal Family. He ended up a vice-admiral before retiring and becoming Governor of Northern Ireland from 1945 to 1952.

Around the time that Rosie's engagement was announced, Elizabeth's friend Lavinia Spencer helped her to move a step further in the direction of her own royal destiny by asking her to a tea party at Spencer House 'to meet Princess Mary and Prince Albert.'[24] She had met him once before, in 1905, when the Duchess of Buccleuch gave a party for her grandchildren at Montagu House, Whitehall, but Elizabeth made no more of an impression upon him this time than she had on the first occasion. Indeed, she wasn't even seated in the same room as he was, denoting her relative unimportance at an event where *placement* was all. She told her mother that she had found the tea party 'rather frightening – in fact, very' and though 'Prince Albert (was) next door, he's rather nice.'[25] He was also four years and nine months older than Elizabeth, which was a significant age difference at that point in their lives, rather more from his than hers, for she was already very attuned to the attractions of the male sex, as we have seen from the innumerable comments she made about sundry soldiers, sailors, and chauffeurs. Yet this sailor prince, who within weeks of this meeting would ship out to the North Sea and the Battle of Jutland on board the HMS *Collingwood,* was the one sailor she omitted to commend as handsome or even attractive. In the light of her friend Helen Hardinge's later comment that Elizabeth told her she found Bertie 'almost repellent',[26] this omission of his physical charms is worth noting.

At this juncture, the English and German navies were engaged in a monumental struggle for ascendency. German U-boats, as their submarines were known, were the scourge of the seas, inflicting huge losses on their British enemy, but after the Battle of Jutland, when England lost several of its most important ships, including the *Invincible*, the *Indefatigable*, and the *Queen Mary*, through a combination of tactical inefficiency and faulty design, two of the ships blowing up for no good reason with a loss of over three thousand lives, there was a shake-up in the naval high command. Admiral of the Fleet Earl Jellicoe was promoted to First Sea Lord and Vice-Admiral Sir David Beatty, who had commanded the battle cruisers during the Battle of Jutland, was promoted to Admiral as well as Commander of the Grand Fleet. Although the German fleet had fled the scene, in England the outcome was seen as a major defeat for Britain, because they did not pursue the Germans. Notwithstanding that the German fleet thereafter stayed close to port, and effectively knocked themselves out of the war by desisting from engaging the British, they inflicted so much damage on British shipping with their U-boats, which Jellicoe was convinced could not be defeated, that he was summarily dismissed thirteen months later.

These changes at sea shifted the onus for winning the war solely on to land. This proved disastrous to the armies of all the combatants, and within weeks they were fighting the greatest land battle of all time: the bloodbath known as the Battle of the Somme. On the first day alone, 1st July, 1916, the British Army's casualties were nearly 60,000, with more than a third of that number being fatalities. Virtually every man who had volunteered from the Dominion of Newfoundland, off the coast of North America, was dead. By the time the battle petered out in November, over one million men lay dead, yet the British and French armies had only managed to advance 6.6 miles into German-occupied territory. Not one of the Allied objectives had been met. The British Army remained some three miles from Bapaume and had not even managed to capture Le Transloy. The Germans remained deeply entrenched in France and were nowhere near as demoralised as the British and French had hoped they would be.

From the perspective of the German and French armies as well as the British, the Battle of the Somme was disastrous in terms of loss of life. But from the British viewpoint, there was another element to the disaster. As the British Army was primarily a volunteer force, consisting of battalions with a disproportionate number of officers over enlisted men, the officer class suffered a heavier percentage of casualties than the enlisted men. As Lady Diana Cooper later observed, 'The First World War was such a waste. We all lost most of our friends. A whole generation of wonderful young men, wiped out. And for what?'[27]

While the conflagration of all time was taking place on the banks of the Somme River in France, a conflagration of a different sort broke out at Glamis Castle. The afternoon of Saturday, 16th September, 1916, seemed like any other. Claude had gone shooting with the factor, Gavin Ralston, and his youngest son David, leaving Cecilia and Elizabeth to deal with the convalescents who had not gone to the local moving pictures theatre in Forfar. Suddenly, Sergeant Cowie, one of the men who had caught Elizabeth's appreciative eye – 'remarkably good looking. Very quiet and Scotch and huge'[28] – smelled smoke. No sooner did he cry out that the castle was on fire than Elizabeth showed her good sense and mettle by taking charge. First she rang up the fire brigades in nearby Forfar and in the larger town of Dundee further away, then she organised four soldiers and all the maids to form a chain and douse the fire, which was somewhere in the tower, with buckets of water. However, the 'more water, the more smoke, we absolutely could <u>not</u>

find the fire.'[29]

By this time, the alarm had been well and truly raised. As the villagers ran up to help, the fire continued spreading until flames were flickering through the roof. The Forfar fire brigade, which was impressively prompt, was nevertheless 'absolutely <u>no</u> use' as they only had a hand pump, so it is just as well she had had the presence of mind to telephone the more distant Dundee fire brigade as well. With their more powerful equipment, they were able to shoot water up to the roof of the tower and douse the flames. Unfortunately, there was a large metal cold-water storage tank in the attic beneath the roof. Already hot from the fire, the combination of fire and water caused it to explode.

Meanwhile, David had returned from shooting, so Elizabeth instructed him and some of the maids to sweep the water down the stairs with brooms, while she organised a line of some thirty people to remove all the pictures, furniture and objects from the rooms which were at risk from water damage, and to take them to safer quarters. Water continued 'pouring into the drawing room all night, and the Chapel is a wreck,'[30] Elizabeth confirmed, but she had nevertheless saved the day with her quick thinking and undoubted efficiency.

Writing about the fire, the *Dundee Courier* justifiably called her 'a veritable heroine in the salvage work she performed within the fire zone', and Cecilia informed Beryl that Elizabeth 'was wonderful – she worked without ceasing & long before I had time to think of anything <u>inside</u> the Castle, she had gathered up all the treasures & put them in safety – & then she <u>directed</u> & saved all the furniture possible. She really is a wonderful girl....'[31]

Elizabeth had indeed acquitted herself admirably. This was the first time in her life that she had displayed the unalloyed presence of mind, the innate good sense, the unflappable clear-sightedness required to solve a grave problem in a crisis situation, but it would not be the last. Cecilia was right. She was a wonderful girl: at least, most of the time, and certainly magnificent in a crisis.

With the excitement of the fire out of the way, life returned to an even sort of keel. Mercifully released from the arduousness of having to study since failing her exams, Elizabeth nevertheless now found herself obliged to take lessons of a different sort. She was being confirmed, a real rite of passage for any Protestant believer, for no Protestant could receive Holy Communion prior to Confirmation. This religious ceremony provided Elizabeth with another opportunity to show her mettle, albeit in a less attractive way, for she had resolved, even before the fire, that the service should be held at St. John's Parish Church in Forfar instead of in the chapel at Glamis. 'That's the one thing <u>I will not have</u>. I'm <u>quite</u> determined. I know exactly what it would be. <u>Rows</u> of gaping soldiers and domestics,' she wrote to Beryl on 5th September, 1916,[32] showing that beneath the charm and the sweetness and the displays of concern and consideration for the convalescents lay a discomfiting element of disdain, which rendered them unfit to be an audience at such an important occasion in her life.

As was her wont, Elizabeth got her way yet again.

Once she had been confirmed, Elizabeth and Cecilia headed south, to London and Hertfordshire, where the latter had devised another fun-filled way of contributing to the war effort. She started holding tea dances, the latest social occasion then in vogue, for officers at St. James's Square and St. Paul's Walden Bury. Elizabeth, naturally, was roped in to share in the fun, and she in turn encouraged Beryl, who had gone from being governess to confidante, to bring 'a hat & your best dress' and 'join the gory throng that goes fox trotting along.'[33]

Beneath the fun, however, the edifice of civilisation as Elizabeth and her contemporaries knew it was fracturing. By the new year of 1917, the Allies and Central Powers had both lost millions of men. While the British and French losses were vast, some 10,000,000 Russians were dead, wounded or missing in action/captured, which made the other members of the Entente's losses pale into insignificance – if that word can be applied to millions of men dead, injured, or captured. The Germans also had casualties of some 2,500,000, and their Austro-Hungarian allies were faring no better.

Desperate to find a way out of the bloodbath, the new Austrian Emperor Karl took desperate measures, instructing his brother-in-law Prince Sixte de Bourbon-Parme, an officer in the Belgian Army, to treat secretly with the French on his behalf to see if a separate peace could not be negotiated which would take the Austro-Hungarian Empire out of the war. Meanwhile, the Russian Empire was in turmoil and the Tsar abdicated later that month. Disappointed when the Provisional Government under Alexander Kerensky kept republican Russia in the war, the Kaiser decided to undermine the enemy on his eastern front from within. He had Vladimir Illych Lenin, the Bolshevik leader, smuggled in a sealed train into Russia from exile in Switzerland, confident that the ensuing political turmoil would knock Russia out of the war. Which it did, with devastating consequences not only for the Russian people, but for the rest of the world as well, for Lenin seized power in October 1917 and signed the Treaty of Brest-Litovsk with Germany the following April. This took the newly-constituted Union of Soviet Socialist States out of the war, and Lenin was now free to turn his attention to solidifying his hold on power.

Within weeks of the abdication of Nicholas II, the War Office telegraphed

Claude to tell him that his son was missing in action. He promptly sent a telegram to Rose in London: BAD NEWS. MICHAEL MISSING APRIL 28. WAR OFFICE WILL WIRE FURTHER NEWS. TELL MOTHER THEY SAY NOT MEAN NECESSSARILY KILLED OR WOUNDED.[34]

For the next nineteen days the family was in a state of dreadful anxiety. The news they received was so sketchy that they could never tell whether Michael had been taken prisoner without being wounded; wounded and captured; or killed. Cecilia was in a pathetic state, as Elizabeth wrote and told Beryl, and she herself did not 'know what to say, you know how we love Mike, and it would be so terrible if he is killed.'[35] Showing the extent to which Cecilia's diktats about good manners and consideration for others had been absorbed by her, she continued, 'It's horrid & selfish of me to write you a miserable letter, but I'm so unhappy, & added to that I can't help worrying about Mother in London.'[36] Then, on 22nd May Cox's Bank telephoned the house at St. James's Square to say that they had received a cheque written by Mike since he had gone missing. He was definitely a prisoner of war.

By this time, everyone on all sides of the conflict was exhausted by the interminableness of this war which was unlike any other in history. As 1917 ground on in its disruptive way, people everywhere began to despair of it ever ending. That September, General Sir Horace Smith-Dorrien, the commander of the Second Army on the Western Front in 1915, had lunch at Glamis. To Elizabeth's consternation, he said that 'he didn't think that there was any likelihood of the War ending for some time.'[37]

This dose of cold water had more than one effect. Elizabeth was coming of age. Although there were no Court balls for debutantes to be presented to the King and Queen the way there had been in peacetime, Society still had a social life of sorts. This was necessary not only to keep spirits up, but also for young ladies of marriageable age to find suitable husbands.

Claude and Cecilia now resumed their pre-war pattern. They spent Christmas at St. Paul's Walden Bury, and were in London two weeks later for Elizabeth to attend her first dance. This was for Margaret Sutton, the niece of the Hon. Edward Wood. Elizabeth dined with him and his wife, the former Lady Dorothy Onslow, beforehand, little realising that in future her path would cross this couple's in many a way. He became Viceroy of India as Lord Irwin when she was the newly-married Duchess of York, then 3rd Viscount Halifax, in which capacity he was appointed Foreign Secretary and elevated to an earldom while she was queen. He would also function as protector of her brother David when Sir Robert Bruce Lockhart and the Minister of Information Brendan (later 1st Viscount) Bracken wanted him recalled from the United States for being an intriguing nuisance rather than a help in promoting positive propaganda during the war.

Although Elizabeth claimed to have 'trembled all afternoon' before the dance,[38] she nevertheless 'enjoyed it very much', especially as how she 'danced every single dance.'[39] She could hardly believe it when her mother and brother David remonstrated with her 'that I ought to be more flirtatious. I nearly died of surprise. You know I daresay I've got rather quiet from having all those Australian and NZ (!!!) at Glamis as one simply <u>must</u> sit on them!'[40] It was one thing to discourage the attentions of soldiers by 'sitting on them', but quite another to dampen the ardour of prospective bridegrooms. Not when the true purpose of a debutante's first Season was to land herself as big a fish as she could catch.

There was a set formula to a 'gel's' season. She was asked out, and her parents reciprocated by throwing as large a dance as they could manage. According to Elizabeth (and we must remember that she always had a tendency to gild the lily), what started out as a 'tiny' party had grown like topsy because 'millions of people invited themselves.' A more likely scenario is that Claude and Cecilia, both intensely social, got carried away and asked so many people to Elizabeth's coming out dance that, when 7th February, 1918, dawned, 'nearly <u>everybody</u> is coming.' Then, covering a boast with grace, she stated, 'I really had no idea the Strathmore family was so popular, it's awful,'[41] when of course she meant how wonderful it was. Popular or not, her family was not of the first rank of the aristocracy, and no royals were in attendance, but this seems not to have dampened the success of the evening where Elizabeth and her parents were concerned. She had a wonderful time.

Now well and truly 'out', Elizabeth had two advantages over much of the competition: her native intelligence and her clear-sighted perspicacity, which allowed her to wield her charm and vivacity to devastating effect. She had always been popular with the boys, but now she started on her way to becoming one of the more popular girls in Society. Within a month, she had a beau: Charles, Lord Settrington, heir to the Earl of March who was himself heir to the Duke of Richmond and Gordon. This was like hitting bull's eye with your first dart. Settrington's grandfather was a duke three times over, and a very rich one at that. Goodwood House, with its adjoining Goodwood Racecourse nestling on the Goodwood Estate in Sussex, south-east of London, was infinitely grander and more valuable than all the Bowes Lyon properties put together. If Elizabeth managed to land him, she would one day be the wife of the 9th Duke of Richmond, the 9th Duke of Lennox, and the 4th Duke of Gordon. She would be chatelaine of one of the most valuable properties in all of England and the holder of one of the greatest titles to boot.

Not only would she have moved her family two rungs up the peerage, but the only degree which would outrank hers was the Royal Family.

Whether Elizabeth struck up a friendship with his sister, Lady Doris Gordon-Lennox, to ensure that she had access in case this new beau needed the occasional jolt, or whether she did so despite the obvious advantage it would be to her, she nevertheless became very friendly very quickly with the girl she hoped would become her sister-in-law. As with the majority of her relationships, this became lifelong, for Elizabeth was already the sort of individual who ensured that everyone who came into her orbit remained there, unless, as happened in the minority of instances, the relationship in question proved disadvantageous, at which point they were jettisoned without compunction, with no thought or care for all that had taken place in the past.

A contemporary of hers, the Hon. Stephen Tennant, whose brother Christopher, 2nd Lord Glenconner, became one of her beaus, grew to know her very well during this period. He regarded her as a hypocritical, calculating, ambitious opportunist of 'skill and tact.' He thought that behind the façade of someone who was 'gentle, gullible, tenderness mingled with dispassionate serenity, cool, well-bred, remote,' lay an individual who 'looked everything she was not.' He thought her 'hard as nails.' He believed that 'she picked her men with the skill of a chess player, snobbish, poised' and felt that she 'schooled her intentions like a detective, totting up her chances.'[42]

Evidently, Elizabeth had taken on board the advice her mother and brother had given her to flirt more, and was now sparkling in pursuit of a good marriage with a brightness which denoted ambition over sincerity, at least to those observant enough to spot the difference.

If ambition was her driving force, and she had a ducal coronet within her sights, there was very little that might be beyond her grasp. Others thought it, and she, who seems never in the whole of her life to have had a moment's self-doubt, must have too, for she set out to capture the Prince of Wales as soon as she met him.

The Duke of Windsor would later say that he realised from the very first time he met her, that Elizabeth was eager for him to press his suit. He claimed he took an instantaneous liking to her, for she was wonderful, easy company, but his interest never went beyond sociability. He did not then consider her to be insincere, but later he would come to view her as such.

They first met at a dance Viscountess Coke hosted in March 1918 on behalf of her husband, Thomas (married men did not send out or receive replies to invitations: this was the function of a wife). The viscount was an aide-de-camp, hence the presence of the heir to the throne. His family would remain established courtiers, and even after he became the 4th Earl of Leicester in

1941, his links with the Royal Family would continue to intertwine his and his descendants' lives with Elizabeth and her progeny. For instance, his granddaughter Anne became Princess Margaret's lifelong friend and lady-in-waiting. She would also marry Stephen Tennant's nephew Colin, ultimately 3rd Lord Glenconner, after Princess Margaret was compelled to refuse his proposal of marriage. That incident is best recounted elsewhere, however.

But Elizabeth's spectacular rise in the world was still in the future, and she had no more means of seeing what that would be than anyone else. She could hope; she could scheme; she could calculate; she could sparkle brightly in the hope of enticing subliminally; but those were the limits, beyond which she was powerless to determine her fate. No grandee would ask for her hand in marriage because of worldly advantage, the way they might have done had she been a great duke's daughter, the scion of a princely house, or a great heiress; but what she lacked in status she made up for in self-confidence.

The Prince of Wales, who was known as David within his family circle, was then a handsome, golden-haired twenty-four-year-old who was already known as a natty dresser. Stylish and glamorous, he was regarded as the most eligible bachelor in the world. Although prone to depression and privately tormented by the constant disapproval of his irascible father King George V, like Elizabeth he was a fun-loving, party-going sybarite who, on the face of it, seemed ideal husband material for any of the multitude of aristocratic girls who set their caps at him.

Until the First World War, there would have been no question of the heir to the throne marrying someone like Lady Elizabeth Bowes Lyon. The many German Protestant royal houses could provide, and had provided for the past two centuries, brides for English princes. But the war had changed all that. Even when it came to an end, there would be no prospect of a future Queen of England originating from one of the states currently warring with Britain. It was well known in aristocratic circles that Prime Minister David Lloyd George had advised the King against countenancing marriages between the newly-renamed House of Windsor and its enemies, even after hostilities ceased. After total war, he advised the King, the people of Britain would not tolerate a German princess of anything, much less of Wales.

Because the Act of Settlement of 1701 forbade marriages between royals in the line of succession to the British throne and Roman Catholics, that ruled out many of the princesses of the royal houses such as the Belgians and Italians who were presently fighting on the Allied side. The result was that the remaining pickings were, if not totally non-existent, then certainly very slim indeed. So the Prime Minister advised the King to solve the problem by allowing his sons to marry the daughters of British aristocrats.

Notwithstanding that no English prince had been granted permission by the Sovereign to do so since King Charles II allowed his younger brother the Duke of York (subsequently King James II) to remarry the 1st Earl of Clarendon's very pregnant daughter Anne Hyde in 1660, following a secret marriage when they had been in exile in 1659, the King, seeing the wisdom of this advice, accepted it.

There had actually been two valid marriages between royal princes and aristocratic girls since then. Prince William Henry, Duke of Gloucester and Edinburgh, had married the Dowager Countess Waldegrave, Maria Walpole, the illegitimate daughter of Sir Robert Walpole, in 1766, without his elder brother King George III's permission, and on 2nd October, 1771, their younger brother Prince Henry, Duke of Cumberland, married the widowed Anne Horton, daughter of Viscount (later 1st Earl of) Carhampton. Although both marriages were lawful, by this time marriages between royals and non-royals were deemed to be even more undesirable than they had been when the Duke of York had married the formidable Anne Hyde (whose father in any event was a senior courtier of the exiled King Charles II, and therefore too powerful to ignore), and George III expressed his disapproval by refusing to allow his nieces Princesses Sophia and Caroline or his nephew Prince William Frederick to be styled as Royal Highnesses. (There was no issue from the Cumberland marriage.) As the great-grandchildren of a monarch, King George II, they were Highnesses, but he did not elevate the two living siblings, Caroline having died in infancy, to Royal dignity, until Prince William Frederick married his cousin Princess Mary.

The second of those unequal marriages, however, resulted in George III creating the draconian Royal Marriages Act of 1772. This forbade anyone in the line of succession to the throne from marrying without the Sovereign's consent. Any marriage entered into without this was deemed to be invalid, which meant that the days of princes and princesses marrying whom they pleased had come to an end. The Act was still in force in 1918, which is what made George V's taking of Lloyd George's advice so important. In fact, it remains binding at the time of writing.

Inevitably in a Government where a goodly proportion of the politicians were Peers of the Realm, the news that their daughters, granddaughters, nieces or cousins were now deemed suitable consorts for English princes spread like wildfire through the stately homes of England, Scotland, Wales and Ireland.

Elizabeth would have been as aware of this upping of the stakes as all her competing debutantes were. And, like many a girl, she set her cap at the Prince of Wales. Although always much too canny to flaunt her ambitions openly, David nevertheless spotted them instantly. However, she was the antithesis of his type. Her aura bespoke the quaintness of the past, his the brisk modernity of the present. While she dressed in an antiquated, almost shambolic, way, and oozed *nostalgie d'hier* charm, he liked everything bang-up-to-the-minute, from his cars and his suits to his girls and their clothes. Though still relatively slender, she lacked the sleek lines he demanded of his women. She preferred to hide behind a veil of sweetness and femininity, by her own admission, while he was overt in all he did. Where she vacillated, he was decisive. While she 'schemed', to quote Stephen Tennant, he prized frankness to the degree that only someone who has been surrounded by yes-men all his life, and wants a measure of honesty, can appreciate. They did have two important things in common, however. Both liked a good time at a good party, though even there she was gregarious while he tended to taciturnity on occasion, and both were excellent dancers who loved to dance. So he danced with her twice at the Cokes'.

This was all it took for the Harcourts, their hosts at a dance a few nights later, to seat Elizabeth between David and the semi-royal Count Michael Torby, Grand Duke Michael of Russia's son, who might well have shared the fate of most of his father's relations had his immediate family been allowed to live in Russia. However, his mother was the product of another of those unions between royals and aristocrats which were so much frowned upon in those dynastic days, though, it has to be said, the Europeans had a far more tolerant approach to such unions than the British, allowing them under the convention of the morganatic marriage. This enabled a legitimate but unequal union, with the royal in question retaining his rank, but the non-royal wife and their children remaining non-royal and unable to become a part of the line of succession to the throne.

Because morganatic marriages were not an accepted English convention, people like Michael Torby and his mother were accorded semi-royal status here. But Elizabeth had no interest in this sprig of the Imperial family. The glamorous Prince of Wales was another matter entirely. He never forgot how she turned the full fusillade of her charms onto him, hoping to stimulate his interest. All Elizabeth's vivacity, however, could not stimulate anything but David's desire to dance with her, and though they opened the dancing together, and had two other dances later that evening, he took care thereafter figuratively to keep her at arms' length. She had made her interest, which he knew he could never share, sufficiently clear for him to be wary of leading her on.

Because Elizabeth was canny, playing her cards so close to her chest that she seldom left a visible trace of what she was scheming, or, as she put it, 'a clever woman uses her femininity to conceal her intentions', it was not always easy to discern what her objective was. The Duke of Windsor, however, believed that she had 'set her cap' at him, and was trying to play him off against Charlie Settrington, in the hope that she would land her prince, and failing that, hook her ducal heir. He concluded that she hoped to become a duchess, one way or another, and if she could not manage to become a royal one, she would settle for being a non-royal duchess instead.

Girls in those days had limited opportunities to 'close the deal'. If they could not interest a man sufficiently for him to pay them court, they would be marooned on the shelf once the dancing season was over. This one was due to end at the beginning of April 1918.

Elizabeth had played her cards well with Charlie Settrington, managing to encourage both him and his sister to become friends, which was always the cleverest way for a single girl to land a man, for then she had time on her side. However, the war was an ever-present sword of Damocles, as 'a lot of these boys are going out quite soon – in fact nearly everybody I know.' In her clear-sighted way, Elizabeth supposed 'they expect fearful casualties.'[43] They did, and she was relieved when Charlie Settrington, though he was captured by the enemy, turned out not to be a fatality, but a mere prisoner of war.

With no available suitor who could elevate her to the rank of royal or non-royal duchess, Elizabeth did what Stephen Tennant concluded she did best. She stimulated the interest of as many men as she could, keeping her options open, vacillating and calculating in the knowledge that the only future worth having was a marital one. She would have only one crack of the whip, unless, of course, death intervened to make her a young widow, which was always a possibility if she married during the war.

One woman who knew all about the pain of young widowhood was her grandmother, Caroline Scott, whom death claimed on 22nd June. Rather than bemoaning the passing of her exotic grandmother, or in any other way indicating that she actually *felt* the loss, Elizabeth complained about missing her mother. Cecilia had left her to run the house in London while she went to Devon to arrange the funeral. 'Oh dear! I do miss her so dreadfully. I never knew before how much I depended on her,' was Elizabeth's self-centred lament.[44]

Dependent though she was upon her mother, she was also hopeful that the war was coming to an end, now that the Americans were fighting alongside the Allies. Until 1917, the Americans had adhered to a strictly neutral policy. The Germans were largely responsible for provoking them to abandon isolationism. The first act of provocation resulted from a change in the German practice of warning passenger and freight-carrying vessels that they were about to be torpedoed, thereby giving the passengers a chance to disembark before the vessel was sunk. This change led to the sinking of the luxury liner the *Lusitania* off the coast of Ireland in 1915, with the loss of 120 American lives. The following year they sank the *Sussex*, with a similar loss of American life, causing the American Government to threaten to sever diplomatic relations unless Germany respected the rights of its citizens to sail the high seas without threat. Although the Germans then suspended these U-boat attacks, by 1917 the Central Powers were even more desperate than the Allies to end the war, so the German Ambassador Count von Berstorff announced the Empire's intention to continue submarine warfare on the high seas without warning, and severed diplomatic relations with Washington.

Fearful that the United States would enter the war against his country, the German Foreign Minister Dr. Alfred Zimmerman now moved against America even before trying to knock Russia out as a belligerent by sneaking Lenin into the Russian capital. He sent top secret cables to Mexico and Japan, encouraging those two countries to attack America, and promised to come to their aid once Germany had won the war against its enemies in Europe. Mexico, he envisaged, would attack the United States in the south-west in an attempt to recover its former territories such as California, while Japan would threaten the western coast while harrying American overseas dependencies. The British, however, intercepted these communications and handed them on to the Americans, whom they had been hoping to induce to enter the Great War on their side. Which the United States now did, declaring war upon the German Empire on 6th April, 1917.

With its raw energy and raw materials, America would prove to be a decisive factor in breaking the stalemate between the Central Powers and the Allies. It also made another inadvertent and wholly accidental contribution, whose effects are only now being given the recognition it deserves. In January 1918, in Haskell County, Kansas, the first case of a disease, which would come to be known as Spanish Influenza, was recorded. On 4th March, 1918, Albert Gitchell, the company cook at Fort Riley, Kansas, reported sick. Within days, 522 men at the camp had come down with this mystery illness. By the 11th of the month, the virus had spread halfway across the country, to the borough of Queens in New York.

It was only when the world was threatened recently with the Avian Flu pandemic that the medical profession began to take an interest in the earlier and far more devastating Spanish Influenza epidemic of 1918–1920. This was the greatest natural disaster of all time. It killed more people than the First World War and the Bubonic Plague combined. Current estimates are that fifty to one hundred million people worldwide died. In the United States, 28% of the population were infected and between 500,000 and 675,000 people died. In Britain, 250,000 died, and in France over 400,000. The Austrians and Germans were even more badly affected, which proved decisive in undercutting their ability to fight. Whole platoons and battalions on both sides of the war were rendered incapable of action, though the Allied losses were not as significant.

The Pasteur Institute's Dr. C. Hannoun believes that the virus originated in China, mutated in the United States, then spread to Europe. The historian Alfred W. Crosby considers that the virus originated in Kansas, while the popular writer John Barry echoes Crosby and narrows down the point of origin to Haskell County, Kansas. There is little doubt that a significant cause of the pandemic's intensity was the vaccination programme being undertaken by the American Army and Navy. Vaccinations were then given by needle. Had they been given orally, the body would have had some chance to fight off much of its exposure to the various diseases, largely through vomiting, but by giving the vaccinations directly into the body, the soldiers and sailors were being assailed with direct doses of diseases without the possibility of their bodies expelling intolerable excesses.

Vaccinations work on the principle of mild exposure to the disease being vaccinated against, but when you provide a cocktail of vaccines, the body's immune system is already stimulated to cope with an unnatural combination which would not ordinarily occur in nature. If you are then exposed to a new form of infectious disease, such as occurred with the Spanish Influenza strain, there is a chance of the disease mutating to such an extent that it becomes lethal. It would appear that this is what most likely happened at Fort Riley in March 1918, when the recently-vaccinated men, whose immune systems were already in overdrive, came down with this new form of flu. Not only did the Spanish Flu virus intensify exponentially as it tore through the troops at Fort Riley, but thereafter it was most lethal when caught by people with strong immune systems, namely young men and women. Until this bizarre occurrence, those most vulnerable to influenza's lethal qualities had been the aged, the infirm, or the very young – precisely the groups which now proved most resistant to the enhanced strain of Spanish Influenza.

Within a week, from the 4th to 11th March, the virus had spread across the American continent. As the Spanish Influenza epidemic took hold in the United States, troops were being shipped across the Atlantic along with war materiel. So too was the Spanish Influenza virus, which rampaged throughout Europe within weeks, and had killed millions before the end of the year.

It took a while for the armies on all sides to realise that they were facing a new and deadly disease whose impact would be more devastating than any weapon man could invent. By the time Elizabeth turned 18 on 4ᵗʰ August, 1918, there was reserved but definite hope that the war could not continue much longer, if only because the troops everywhere were ill. A month later, the Austro-Hungarian Empire, whose troops had been even more badly affected than the others, made decisive moves to terminate their involvement as belligerents. The Germans, also disproportionately infirm, started to withdraw their troops from the Western Front which they had been occupying so tenaciously for four years. Influenza had succeeded in crippling the armies where nothing else had, and this is no fanciful premise, as more American soldiers died during the First World War from influenza than in action.

The end of the war, when it came, was sudden, possibly because none of the belligerents actually appreciated to what extent the Spanish Influenza epidemic was affecting the outcome of the war. Hitler would famously blame a 'stab in the back', but history and medical research are now showing that it was something far more basic than human treachery: disease.

By the beginning of November both the Austrian and German Emperors were feeling the pressure to abdicate, and though the former never did so, and the latter only after his Chancellor, Prince Max of Baden, had taken it upon himself to 'end the war' by announcing an abdication which had not yet taken place, the end was inexorable.

On 11ᵗʰ November, 1918, at 11 a.m. the Great War ended. The total number of military and civilian casualties was some 37,000,000. Of those, 17,000,000 were mortalities and 20,000,000 wounded. Some 10,000,000 were military personnel and 7,000,000 were civilian. Of the military deaths, two-thirds were from fighting over a four and a quarter year period, but a third were from disease, primarily Spanish Influenza, which had been unheard of before March of that year.

The war which should have ended by Christmas 1914 had introduced many new and various elements into society, and these were changes which Elizabeth and her generation would have to cope with for the remainder of their lives. Theirs was the generation that would straddle the age of the horse and buggy, and man walking on the moon. And Elizabeth would play a decisive role upon the world stage, and make contributions which would affect many of our lives.

Love and Marriage

Chapter Four

Peace brought with it many new and exciting prospects for people every-where, and Elizabeth was no exception to that rule.

In the first week of 1919, her brother Mike returned from his prisoner of war camp. Charlie Settrington also came back home. Everyone, from former prisoners and soldiers, to those left behind to take care of the home fronts, tried to readjust to life in peacetime.

For Elizabeth, this was an exciting period. She and Charlie started going out, usually in groups of friends, such as in April 1919, when they went to see George Robey perform in *Joybells*, though she also snuck out of St. James's Square to spend the day *à deux* in the country. After lunching at Walton and taking an extended walk on Box Hill, they had tea at what she described as an 'extraordinary place.' The waiter winked at them and informed them that he 'also came from London,'[1] in so doing making it obvious that he had picked up the clandestine nature of their date.

Charlie was due to ship out to Russia, where civil war raged following the murder of the Tsar, the downfall of the Kerensky Provisional Government, and the creation of the Bolshevik state under Vladimir Illych Lenin. The White Army (the Royalists) had been pitted against the Red Army (the Bolsheviks) for over a year, and had made significant gains, for the greater part of the former Russian Empire had not even known what Communism was, and had no desire to live under a dictatorship of the proletariat. The peasantry especially was devoted to the Tsar and supportive of a restoration of the monarchy, as were most landowners, though the middle classes were more open-minded about retaining a republican form of government. Like many idealistic young men, including Winston Churchill, Charlie Settrington felt that it was in Britain's interest to support the Whites against the Reds, and while in battle-weary England there was little stomach for yet another war, individuals like Charlie did volunteer, little appreciating the rabid fanaticism of the Soviet leadership under men like Lenin, Trotsky, and Stalin.

Undermanned and facing an enemy who would sooner die than give ground, Charlie Settrington and his ilk headed off to add their number to the White Army. Meanwhile, the Allies were concluding the negotiations which would redefine the map of Europe and penalise Germany for starting a war which it had not actually started. On 28th June, 1919, the Treaty of Versailles was signed with Germany, officially ending the conflict which had resulted from the assassination of the Archduke Franz Ferdinand of Austria five years before to the very day.

To say that the Allies were unfair is to make one of the biggest understatements of all time. The Inter-Allied Reparations Committee originally demanded that Germany pay reparations of the vastly overinflated sum of 226 billion Marks. The French were harkening back to the reparations the Germans had made them pay following the conclusion of the 1871 Franco-Prussian War which caused the collapse of the French Second Empire under the Emperor Napoleon III, and the creation of the German Empire under Kaiser Wilhelm II's grandfather Kaiser Wilhelm I. Those reparations had themselves been payback for the ones the great Napoleon I had forced the Prussians to make to the First French Empire in 1807. But the preposterousness of such historical tit-for-tatting weighed sufficiently heavily upon the other Allies, especially the Americans, for a slight sense of proportion to be introduced. The reparations were recalculated as being 132 billion Marks, which was US$31.4 billion or £6.6 billion Sterling at 1919 exchange rates. Economists such as John Maynard Keynes warned that these were excessive, unwarranted and unjust, and would ultimately lead to trouble, but the Allies, scenting the financial advantages of vengeance and the possibility of destroying German might for all time while filling their own coffers, pressed ahead, even as they were being warned that it would take until 1988 for the Germans to pay off such vast reparations.

The world knows that this injustice created the political climate for Nazism to flourish, but what is less well known is that the German state only finished paying off the Great War reparations on 4th October, 2010.

Between signature of the Treaty of Versailles and the Treaty of St. Germaine-en-Laye, which was signed on 10th September, 1919, Elizabeth experienced the first major setback of her adult life. Eight weeks after the Allies forced the Weimar Republic of Germany to sign the treaty which would create a peace which inevitably led to another war, Elizabeth was up at Glamis when she received horrifying news. Her beloved Charlie Settrington had been badly injured. She promptly wrote to Beryl on 22ⁿᵈ August, pouring out her heart. Two days later, on 24ᵗʰ August, 1919, Lord Settrington, heir to the Earl of March, future Duke of Richmond and Gordon as well as Lennox, died.

According to Shawcross, Elizabeth was 'inconsolable'. This is a fair estimate by all accounts. She had not only lost a man of whom she was fond, but the possibility of a way of life to which she aspired. Nor was this loss limited to being a great and grand duchess. He had other rare, almost unique, qualities which appealed to her. 'He is my only real friend & one feels one can never have another like him,' she told Beryl, indicating for the first time how intense her feelings were. 'I think I must have been fonder of him than I realised, because now there seems a kind of blank – if you understand what I mean?' Admitting that she 'wasn't shy of him, and he was so delightful,' she then provided the clue to what made their relationship particularly desirable to her: 'I liked him specially because he never tried to flirt, or make love or anything like that – which always spoils friendships. Even that day spent down at Box Hill.'[2]

This antipathy to the carnal side of the man/woman relationship would arise time and again in Elizabeth's life, but this is the only instance when she actually spells out so clearly how distasteful she found the sexual element. Since her attitude would be key to many of the relationships she would subsequently have with men, it is helpful to remember her own statement on the subject. It is also important to bear in mind that when she used the words 'make love' she was not referring to sexual intercourse as we understand it, but to what could be termed mild 'making out': kissing, cuddling, touching, maybe even the stroking of the cheek or the hair. If the expression making love had more limited connotations then than it does now, the word friendship was the absolute opposite. Boys and girls remained friends until they were engaged. Even when they were 'making out', they were friends, the catch-all word which described every degree of acquaintanceship between stranger and sexual partner, covering such contemporary distinctions as acquaintance, chum, mate, boyfriend, girlfriend, sweetheart and lover.

With Charlie Settrington dead and the Prince of Wales decisively against any friendship that would lead to matrimony, Elizabeth must have felt like the shepherd who was given a bag of gold valuable enough to procure all his worldly desires, and, running to share the good news with his cronies, dropped it off a high bridge into a deep ravine. Would Elizabeth have to lower her sights? Would the dearth of available ducal heirs force her to cast a wider net over lower rank than she had hitherto been doing?

According to the Duke of Windsor, she 'covered all the bases'. She continued to flash him green lights every time their paths crossed. Although he remained as friendly in manner as he had always been, he also kept his feet planted firmly on his side of the Rubicon. Only years later would he come to realise that she had been deeply frustrated by his personal disinterest, and that her frustration was accompanied by a simmering rage. This, however, did not prevent her from twinkling brightly for his benefit, as well as that of all other prospective grooms right in front of him.

She had clearly taken her mother and brother's advice to heart about flirting, for she was gaining a reputation as something of a flirt, though one who kept things well within the bounds of chaste decorum. Such 'come hither' conduct inspired many a young man to fancy that he had a chance with her, including Stephen Tennant's brother the Hon. Christopher Tennant, heir to the 1st Lord Glenconner. Although Lord Lieutenant of Peeblesshire and the brother-in-law of the previous Prime Minister, H.H. Asquith, whose wife Margot was his sister, Lord Glenconner was very new money. And girls like Elizabeth set their sights far higher than the heir to a 1st Baron, whose grandfather hadn't even had a title.

The surest way to meet and marry a desirable man was to take part in the social parade. This Elizabeth did with relish. She was as sociable and social as both her parents, and now that the war was over, the aristocracy tried to pick back up its pre-1914 way of life. Although replicating it would ultimately prove to be impossible, no one knew that yet as they partook of the old routines. Court balls, levees, garden parties and the myriad other forms of entertainment which formed part of royal life were being revived, and, that June of 1919, Royal Ascot resumed for the first time since 1914. Though Charlie Settrington's absence, then death, would have been expected to put a damper on the many dinners and dances which Elizabeth attended that first summer of peace with her friends, no engagement was yet forthcoming. Ever the realist, she once more displayed the resilience she had shown when Fergus was killed. She bravely soldiered on with apparent good cheer and admirable tenacity to her true purpose, which was enjoying herself while hunting for the most suitable spouse she could find.

Once Charlie Settrington was dead, what also seems to have helped keep her spirits buoyant was the interest she took in one of her brother Mike's brother officers. Elizabeth had met Captain the Hon. James Stuart when she attended a musical soirée at Tivoli Gardens with Mike. Whether she asked him to invite the handsome third and youngest son of the 17th Earl of Moray for a house party in the September following Charlie's death, or whether Mike did it in an attempt to divert his baby sister and keep her spirits up, we will never know. But we do know that Mike asked him up to Glamis. He came and, by the time he left, Elizabeth had fallen in love for the first, and possibly the last, time in her life. Charlie Settrington had been dead for only a month.

It is said that the course of true love never runs smoothly. Whatever the merits of that maxim are, what is undeniable is that Elizabeth was considerably more taken with James Stuart than he was with her. Three and a half years older, and considerably more experienced as a result of his wartime exploits – he had survived the traumas of three of the bloodiest battles, at Somme, Arras and Ypres – he was a decorated officer, with the Military Cross and Bar to his credit. He counted himself fortunate to have survived the fighting without injury when so many of his brother officers and men had been wounded or killed. While away, his sweetheart had been Elfie Findlayson, whose family lived at Coldoch near to his at Doune Lodge, and when he returned after the war, he had proposed and she had accepted him. Previously, his elder brother Lord Doune had also asked for her hand in marriage, but had been rejected. Their father had also conducted a somewhat racy correspondence with the young lady, leading to the conclusion that these descendants of an illegitimate son of King James V of Scotland had decidedly flexible attitudes to possessiveness, jealousy, and sexual attraction. That July of 1919, James was to be found with Elfie at Coldoch, but two months later he appeared on his own for a ten-day stay at Glamis, which is when he solidified his hold over Elizabeth's heart.

James Stuart seems to have been one of those men whom women found irresistible. Men were painfully aware of this, as Captain the Hon. Alexander Hardinge, heir to the 1st Viscount Hardinge of Penshurst and later Private Secretary to Kings Edward VIII and George VI, demonstrated when he wrote to his fiancée Helen Cecil, saying, 'You won't let James cut me out, will you Helen? He is so attractive that there would be every justification for it.'[3]

James, now no longer engaged, was reading law at Edinburgh University, which was conveniently close to Glamis. In October of that year he was appointed an equerry to the King's second son, Prince Albert, who was studying up at Cambridge with his younger brother Prince Henry. This meant that James was often with Bertie throughout the autumn and winter and into the spring of 1920, at Cambridge, which was not so accessible to Glamis, nor indeed to St. Paul's Walden Bury when Elizabeth moved south with her mother in keeping with the routine Cecilia had established.

If absence made the heart fonder for Elizabeth, out of sight seemed to have put her out of James's mind. Or possibly her discouragement of the carnal presented a problem for this lusty young man, who soon embarked upon an affair with one of her friends, Mollie Lascelles.

Vreda Esther Mary Lascelles was Elizabeth's contemporary, being six weeks younger. A beautiful, racy young woman whose background gave her the confidence to do as she pleased, she was the elder daughter of Major William Lascelles, a descendant of the immensely rich Earls of Harewood, whose money had come from their business interests in the great Jamaican trading company, Lascelles de Mercado, and of Lady Sybil Beauclerk, a daughter of the 10th Duke of St. Albans. That dukedom had come about when his ancestress, Nell Gwynn, known even by herself as the 'Protestant Whore', had threatened King Charles II with dropping their infant son out of the window unless the child were ennobled. This had inspired the King to respond, 'Pray, Madame, spare a thought for our beloved Duke of St. Albans,' since when the royal origins of this ducal family had placed them in the first rank of the aristocracy along with other royal bastards such as the Dukes of Grafton.

Despite being in love with James Stuart, Elizabeth understood where her duty lay. It did not lie in pining after sexy swains who were having romances elsewhere, but in flirting so decorously that a suitable man would propose marriage. And if that man should be the one she was in love with, so much the better. In quest of that, she continued to gather herself a reputation as an engaging and popular girl whom all the boys wanted. She was exultant at being asked to join the Marchioness of Salisbury's house party at Hatfield House for the Hertford Ball, which was conveniently close to St. Paul's Walden Bury. According to Stephen Tennant, she was afraid of meeting the wrong people at parties, which really meant that she hated wasting her time charming people whom it was not in her interest to cultivate. However, she was commensurately delighted when she succeeded with the right ones. These included Walter (Earl of) Dalkeith, heir to the 7th Duke of Buccleuch and Queensberry, whose interest Elizabeth is meant to have tried to peak. He did drop her home after the weekend, but this seems to have been an unnerving rather than a romantic experience, for this latest ducal heir to capture her interest had barely driven before, and kept on running into ditches. He managed to issue a rather unexpected *coup de grâce* at the journey's end, when he crashed his 'motor', as cars were then called, into the gate at St. Paul's Walden Bury, causing Elizabeth to remark, 'I wonder that I am alive.'[4]

James Stuart's dearth of interest would have been crushing to a girl who was less popular and determined than Elizabeth, but she was clever, resourceful and wise. By sticking to the policy of trying to captivate every man who crossed her path, she would ultimately prove that there wasn't only safety in numbers, but increased choice as well. A prize that others want is always more valued than one which is unique to one individual alone, and she was already well on the way to getting a reputation of being a girl with whom many men were in love. This, of course, only had the effect of making her even more desirable to those who might not yet know her, or knew her but were unsure of how they felt. And when she ran across someone upon whom her magic did not work, as happened with Walter Dalkeith, she was canny enough to make sure that he too remained one of her many friends. This showed a wisdom and maturity beyond her years, for it left the possibility open for a change of heart on the one hand, and if there was not one, the disinterested friend could on the other hand easily be confused by onlookers as nevertheless being a suitor, which could only enhance her reputation. The line between friend, sweetheart, swain, and prospective suitor being often so blurred as to be indecipherable, she was surrounding herself with an aura of success and desirability which could only be to her credit, as indeed proved to be the case.

Two months after the weekend at Hatfield House, Elizabeth was taken to Buckingham Palace for the first time. She should not actually have been there at all, for her elder sister May and a group of Scottish ladies were presenting Queen Mary with a set of covers which they had embroidered for chairs at the Palace of Holyroodhouse in Edinburgh. But the third Bowes Lyon sister Rosie being unable to attend, Elizabeth was infiltrated as a replacement for her. Queen Mary was none the wiser as to the substitution, and Elizabeth was delighted by her first glimpse of the palace which she would not only occupy one day, but leave with the greatest reluctance when it came time to do so.

That summer, Elizabeth was formally presented for the first time when the Sovereign and Court moved north, to Edinburgh. Then as now, the whole Court moved into Holyroodhouse for a series of official functions including investitures, garden parties, balls, dances, dinners, presentations and receptions. Arriving on Saturday 3rd July, King George V and Queen Mary hosted a dinner on the Monday evening for forty; consisting primarily of Edinburgh dignitaries leavened with a dash of Scottish aristocrats including Claude and Cecilia, their daughter May and her husband Lord Elphinstone, as well as Elizabeth. She was one of only two unmarried females present, the other being the monarch's only daughter, Princess Mary. Although Elizabeth had met her briefly, they were hardly friends, but such was the way with royalty that even the most distant of acquaintances was adjudged to be desirable company as long as they were deemed to be suitable socially.

The following day, the King and Queen held an afternoon presentation at the Palace. Elizabeth was presented along with 150 other young ladies. This was nowhere near as grand as a presentation at Buckingham Palace as a debutante would have been, for these 'select young ladies' shared the honours with nearly a thousand other presentees, instead of decorously taking their bows in white dresses while Their Majesties sat on their thrones in the Throne Room, tiaras asparkle all around them. But there had been a war, and there was a bottleneck of young ladies who needed to be presented if they were not to be deprived of the privilege, so honour was served all round with this non-glamorous but nevertheless practical solution. The following afternoon there was another of these large gatherings when the King and Queen held a garden party at Holyroodhouse running well into four figures yet again, with Elizabeth and her parents in attendance once more. Patently, Claude had no objection to being entertained by his sovereign, even if he did not want his children to hold positions at Court.

No sooner was the garden party over than Elizabeth and her mother boarded the night train to London, where Elizabeth was due to attend the Royal Air Force Ball at the Ritz on the evening of Thursday 8th July. James Stuart was also going to be there, and she was eager to pursue her 'friendship' with him in the hope that it would lead to something more conclusive. Instead, she was about to meet her destiny in the most unexpected manner.

Elizabeth was dancing with James Stuart, doubtlessly as vivaciously and flirtatiously as only a girl in love can do. Although her wiles did not move the object of her desire to the conclusion she was hoping for, they did catch the eye of the newly-created Duke of York, upon whom James Stuart was in attendance as equerry that evening. In his memoirs, *Within the Fringe*[5] , Stuart recounted how Prince Albert asked him 'who was that girl with whom I had just been dancing. I told him that her name was Lady Elizabeth Bowes Lyon and he asked me if I would introduce him, which I did.'

Bertie then asked Elizabeth to dance. Contrary to popular belief, there was no real click between them. His mother's lady-in-waiting Mabell, Countess of Airlie, would later claim that he told her subsequently that 'he had fallen in love that evening, although he didn't realise it until later,' but the later was so much later that this can only be another case of fanciful revisionism inspired by royal rank. Falling in love, even for princes, is not akin to a thief sneaking upon one in the night, but something altogether more moving, and Bertie was actually in love with someone else at the time. And she was the antithesis of the ostensibly demure and petite Elizabeth.

Significantly taller at 5 foot 6, with the slender figure of a model, this brown-eyed, auburn-haired stunner was a sophisticated member of the Prince of Wales's set and the same age as Bertie. The wife of the heir to the 5th Earl of Rosslyn, she was known to be exciting, exotic, and great fun. Born Margaret Sheila MacKellar Chisholm in Sydney in 1895, but known as Sheila, she had met Bertie through his elder brother David. They had embarked upon a loving and comfortable romance, of which his father finally got wind. By May of 1920 the King, worried where a relationship with a married woman would lead, was demanding that Bertie give up his inamorata. Bertie was sufficiently distressed to write three 'long, sad' letters to his elder brother David, who was away at sea. In them, he complained that he was 'getting it in the neck about his friendship with poor little Sheilie' from their father.[6] She was indeed poor little Sheilie, not only metaphorically, but literally. Both her husband and his father had huge gambling problems. The popular song *The Man Who Broke the Bank at Monte Carlo* had been written about Lord Rosslyn, but no gambler ever wins for long, and Sheila's life was already being adversely affected by the gaming and drinking addictions of both her father-in-law and husband.

Although the Prince of Wales's relationship with his father was sufficiently antipathetic for him to give up trying to win approval that was never forthcoming from his perpetually disapproving father, Bertie's was different. Ultimately, he wanted to please his father, and when King George V made it clear that an ongoing affair with Lady Loughborough would be an impediment to his continuing approval, while terminating it would result in paternal approbation in the form of 'that fine old title of Duke of York which I bore for more than 9 years & is the oldest Dukedom in the country,'[7] Bertie agreed to swap love for the dukedom. His reward was immediate. On George V's fifty-fifth birthday on 3rd June, 1920, he created his second son Duke of York, commending him for having 'done what I asked you to do' and having 'behaved very well, in a difficult situation for a young man' when his son pointed out that he hoped he would live up to the title and 'I can tell you that I fulfilled your conditions to the letter, and that nothing more will come of it.'[8]

Although the newly-created Duke of York was sufficiently recovered from the loss of the divine Sheila, (who would subsequently become not only royal but imperial as well when she married the last Tsar of Russia's nephew, Prince Dimitri), to notice Elizabeth at The RAF Ball, he was still nevertheless pining for his Australian *exotique*. And Elizabeth had eyes only for James Stuart, to such an extent that she wrote Beryl the day after the ball, stating, 'I danced with Prince Albert, who I hadn't known before, he is quite a nice youth.' Either her memory was playing tricks on her, and she had forgotten meeting him at that tea party in 1916 when she was seated in the room adjoining his, or then she had not met him on that occasion as she had claimed to Beryl, but had been too humiliated to admit not being introduced. Either way, she had definitely met him finally, and had actually danced with him as well, though her description of him as a 'youth' shrieked disinterest as well as disdain, considering that he was over four years older.

As the London Season continued on its way, Elizabeth was finding James Stuart tantalisingly difficult to land. She had two other suitors up her sleeve, however, both of whom shared a flat in London with her brother Mike. One was Henry Rainald, 6th Viscount Gage, known to his friends as Grubby, the other Prince Paul of Serbia, whose uncle was King Peter I of the Serbs, Croats and Slovenes. Neither of these supposed suitors were actually suitable husband material for Elizabeth. The Gages had a tradition of earthiness and lustiness, as is evinced by the present Viscount who recently married a woman young enough to be his granddaughter, and then proceeded to father a child in his late seventies. Such lustiness would not have appealed to Elizabeth, and Henry 'Chips' Channon summarised the dilemma well in his *Diaries* when he wrote, 'Poor Gage is desperately fond of her – in vain, for he is far too heavy, too Tudor and squirearchal for so rare and patrician a creature as Elizabeth.' Plainly, someone as ethereal as Elizabeth could never abide a man like Henry, also known for some reason as George, who would require her to endure the lustiness and earthiness of a Tudor squire.

Although Prince Paul's predilections were more to Elizabeth's taste – he was a renowned 'aesthete' which was then code for gentlemen who preferred the company of other gentlemen, and was supposed to be the special friend of Chips Channon – there was no question of his being tempted into what would have been a misalliance. His uncle King Peter had been awarded the throne of Serbia in 1903 when a *coup d'état* overthrew King Alexander, of the opposing royal house of Obrenovic. Aside from the newness of their occupancy of the throne, which made suitable marriages with other royals of overriding importance, the Karageorgevic dynasty had few heirs. There was Paul and his father Prince Arsene before him, and before them King Peter's second son Alexander, who had been appointed Crown Prince in 1909 when his elder brother George, in a fit of rage, kicked a servant to death. Forced to renounce his rights of succession to the throne after this episode, he remained at liberty until his brother became king. In 1925 he was then declared insane and committed to an asylum in Nis, where he remained until the Germans liberated him during the Second World War. When Tito took control of Yugoslavia and the other members of the Royal Family were declared to be enemies of the state, the former Crown Prince was excluded from that interdict, and was the only member of the Karageorgevic dynasty allowed to live in Communist Yugoslavia, marrying an ordinary Yugoslav named Radmila Radonjic in 1947 and dying on 17th October, 1972.

With a history like that, it was obvious that there was no possibility of a marriage between any scion of the house of Karageorgevic and Elizabeth.

But even if there had been, it is extremely unlikely that she would have opted for marriage to any man who took her out of a British orbit.

Arthur Penn, fourteen years older than Elizabeth and a contemporary at Eton of her brother Jock, was another suitor who would have kept her within the desired orbit, and, though he was charming and witty and not the sort of man who would make lusty Tudor demands upon any wife, he was simply not grand enough for her. But he was fond of her, and she of him, and he would prove to be one of those people who, once in her life, were never to leave it.

Another contemporary who also claimed to be a suitor was the 3rd Lord Gorell. He would later profess to Elizabeth's biographer Elizabeth Longford that he was 'madly in love with her. Everything at Glamis was beautiful, perfect. Being there was like living in a Van Dyck picture.' He claimed that 'the magic gripped us all. I fell *madly* in love. They all did.'[9] One suspects that a healthy amount of scepticism is required here, but even if he did fall in love with Elizabeth as he claimed they all did, there is no doubt that she did not even consider him as a possibility for her hand. He simply wasn't grand enough. His father, Sir (John) Gorell Barnes, had been president of the Probate, Divorce and Admiralty Division of the High Court of Justice until he was ennobled as the 1st Lord in 1909. If the Glenconners, with all their money, were not grand enough because they were such *arrivistes,* there was no likelihood of a virtually penniless legal practitioner's son being considered as anything but window dressing.

That June of 1920, while Elizabeth was trying to be as dazzling as she could be, or, to put it like Stephen Tennant, weighing up her options, a house move gave her cause to consider how much more life-enhancing permanent security was than transience. The lease on the house in St. James's Square having come to an end, the Strathmores had to move across Hyde Park Corner to the rather less desirable area of Belgravia, where Claude took a house in Eaton Square. Elizabeth, whom Stephen Tennant noted was always weighing up things and people with snobbish prescience, disliked the area, which was nowhere near as chic as Mayfair in those inter-war years. She was mightily relieved when the family moved back across the magical circle that was Hyde Park Corner to Bruton Street in Mayfair.

Although Elizabeth was torn between the incompatible objectives of envisaging herself as a bride for the Prince of Wales and the Hon. James Stuart, and was not having much success with either, her mother's friend Lady Nina Balfour was, unbeknownst to her, stepping in to give fate a helping hand. She asked Elizabeth and Bertie down to Bisham, her house on the Thames near Henley, for the weekend of 17th July. Although Bertie was still lovesick enough about Sheila to write to David complaining about her loss, and reproached both him and their mother for suggesting marriage to someone else as an antidote, he still managed to hold Elizabeth's hand in front of their hostess while they were being driven in her motor boat. 'Elizabeth says it was quite worth it just to see Nina's face,' her friend Helen Cecil wrote and told her fiancé, the King's recently-appointed Assistant Private Secretary.[10] Yet again Elizabeth's disdain and disinterest are evident.

Shortly afterwards, Elizabeth and the rest of the family headed north for yet another Glorious Twelfth. This summer would prove to be anything but glorious for her, however, when Helen Cecil informed Elizabeth that the affair of their mutual friend Mollie Lascelles and James Stuart, which had petered out, had not only been revived, but was proceeding intensely. In a rage, the proprietary Elizabeth severed all contact with Mollie despite the fact that she had no more right to his attentions than her friend did. Then she set about getting all their girlfriends to gang up against Mollie. Mollie in turn blamed Helen for having leaked the news, which, of course, Helen denied, though there was no one else from whom it could have emanated. All three young women now found themselves in the eye of a hurricane, all of Elizabeth's making, by the end of which Mollie and James had gone their separate ways; Mollie's friendship with Elizabeth was irretrievably destroyed; and the hapless Helen, who continued to be friends with both, had Elizabeth's ostensible gratitude. This, Helen would come to realise in later years, was illusory rather than real, for Elizabeth would repay her loyalty with a deviousness and ruthlessness that her friend might have found harder to accept had she not already seen how such skills came naturally to the young Elizabeth.

While Elizabeth 'schemed' and 'intrigued' as any other young woman would have done to attract the attention of the man with whom she was in love, Mollie went from strength to strength. Walter Dalkeith turned the interest, which Elizabeth had not been able to stimulate in him, to Mollie, who married him a few months later, on 21st April, 1921. As Countess of Dalkeith and future Duchess of Buccleuch and Queensberry, she had not only bagged a ducal heir of royal descent, but she was now one of the richest women in the land, because he was the heir to the largest landowner in the United Kingdom. She was the future chatelaine to Drumlanrig Castle and its 90,000-acre Queensberry Estate, as well as Dalkeith Palace and Boughton and Bowhill stately homes, all with their vast estates in the hundreds of thousands of acres north and south of the border. Compared to the Buccleuchs, the Strathmores were penniless and decidedly of the third rank, which of course they were both literally and metaphorically.

The Duke of Windsor said Elizabeth was 'pathologically jealous' and 'virulent when crossed, with a vengefulness that was awesome to behold. She had to be the centre of attention at all times, and could not bear to be outshone by anyone.'[11]   One does not need much imagination to envisage how infuriated someone of her intense nature must have been when the girl she had set about freezing out of their circle not only managed to hook one of the biggest catches in Christendom, and one moreover who had eluded her, but who was now so grand that all the girlfriends whom she thought she had managed to get to ostracise Mollie turned up at the Lascelles/Dalkeith wedding. Everyone but Elizabeth, who had not been asked. Matters will not have been helped when, nine months less one day after the grandest Society wedding of the year, Mollie produced a beautiful baby girl, and eighteen months after that a son and heir to the dukedom who was named after his father Walter. There would be a gap of five years before she produced her third and final child, Lady Caroline Montagu Douglas Scott, which was itself an indication of the fact that the fleet-footed Mollie had returned to her roving ways. Nothing, however, could induce Elizabeth to forgive her erstwhile friend for having romanced the man Elizabeth herself had wanted, but who had not wanted her in return.

Mollie could not have cared less about Elizabeth's ongoing vendetta against her, but Elizabeth clearly did, for she pursued it with the 'vengeance' David gave her credit for. She hugged her loathing of her former friend to her bosom the way she would with others in the future who fell foul of her. But this resulted in no discomfort for the new Lady Dalkeith or her family. Rather, Mollie was wryly amused by the turn events had taken. She told another Scottish duchess, Argyll,[12] that she knew only too well that Elizabeth might have forgiven her for the supposed solecism of romancing James Stuart, had she been forced to marry badly or not at all, but such a 'paen to vanity as Elizabeth' could never forgive her flourishing despite Elizabeth's best endeavours to spoil things for her. And flourish Mollie and the family did. She was the current Duchess of Buccleuch and Queensberry when her husband's sister Alice married Bertie and David's younger brother Prince Henry on 6th November, 1935, becoming in the process Her Royal Highness The Duchess of Gloucester and the royal lady who ranked in precedence immediately after Elizabeth herself. Mollie also had the pleasure of seeing her elder daughter, named Elizabeth but definitely not after her former friend, become the 10th Duchess of Northumberland. In so doing, this Elizabeth linked two of the greatest dukedoms in the land, and herself became chatelaine of two of the nation's greatest historic houses, Alnwick Castle in Northumberland and Syon House in Middlesex, near Richmond outside London. This was where Elizabeth's grandmother had lived in what the Strathmore family supposed was sumptuousness, but was near-poverty compared with Syon's splendour. Mollie's younger daughter Caroline also married relatively well – 'better than Elizabeth's own second daughter', Mollie observed – when she wed the baronet Sir Ian Gilmour, whose family was both more eminent and richer than Tony Armstrong-Jones's. But above all, Mollie had the pleasure of witnessing Elizabeth's discomfiture as she helped to bear the canopy at the coronation of the former friend, who still would not speak to her, even at this moment of her supreme elevation. 'She delighted in recounting how she had been Elizabeth's rival for James Stuart's affections,' Margaret Argyll told me. She also thoroughly enjoyed flaunting her affair with Prince George, before he became Duke of Kent, under Elizabeth's 'sanctimonious nose', amused and bemused by Elizabeth's ongoing hostility towards her, 'notwithstanding that she had no more right to him (James Stuart) than I did'.[13]

It was against this backdrop of incipient but feverish feminine competitiveness that Elizabeth prepared for the Forfar Ball on the first day of the second week of September 1920. Naturally, she had asked all of her 'suitors' such as Paul of Serbia and Lord Gage, as well as the man on whom she had her eye. James Stuart came, but frustratingly went right back to Balmoral and the charms of the luscious Mollie, without displaying the level of interest that Elizabeth had sought from him.

Shortly thereafter, however, Bertie came to her rescue, or so she thought, when he invited himself and his equerry to stay at Glamis. His sister Mary was staying at nearby Airlie Castle with their mother's lady-in-waiting Mabell Airlie and her children, who were good friends of the Bowes Lyon brood. To Bertie, the prospect of a lively time as the two house parties linked up and swapped visits with each other seemed a welcome break from the tedium of Balmoral, where the King and Queen were, as usual, stolidly entertaining as many dullards as they could find, to paraphrase the criticism each of their children in turn made of time spent with their parents.

Year in, year out, George V would invite the same worthies to stay at the same time. If it was the Archbishop of Canterbury's weekend, the Archbishop of York could never be considered, not when he had not been a part of the 'tradition' before. Spontaneity and fun were to be avoided at all costs, and Princess Victoria, the King's favourite (and only maiden) sister whom her nephew David called 'a complete bitch' was usually only too painfully visible, to refresh the damper the King and Queen put on all proceedings by maintaining the most rigid and dull of Courts. George V's aunt, Princess Louise, Duchess of Argyll, used to say that 'Georgie and May ensured that no amusement was ever allowed to amuse', and, preferring the company of her artistic friends and even the solitude of her apartment in Kensington Palace to any occasion with them, would only accept invitations when she could no longer find excuses for not doing so.

Entertaining royalty always required a host and hostess to pull out all the stops, and this the whole Strathmore family now did. Elizabeth called upon her circle of girlfriends, including Lord Edward Cecil's daughter Helen, the 3rd Duke of Abercorn's daughter Katie Hamilton, the 1st Viscount Hardinge of Penshurst's daughter Diamond Hardinge, and Charlie Settrington's sister Lady Doris Gordon-Lennox, to provide background foliage. Naturally, James Stuart would be accompanying the prince as his equerry, and his elder brother Lord Doune was also asked, to plump out the house party with as many young and appealing people as possible. Cecilia even roped in Elizabeth's putative godmother Venetia James, who had once so scandalised Society when she had embarrassed the present king's grandfather, with whom she was having an affair, by making her familiarity too apparent in the presence of his grandmother, the aged but still beautiful Queen Alexandra, who was very much in evidence at Balmoral, deaf as a post and impossible to converse with.

On the day of Bertie's arrival, Helen wrote to her fiancé Alec Hardinge, who was on duty at staid old Balmoral with all the staid old fogeys, informing him, 'There is a <u>fearful</u> fuss over tonight & the week-end in general. We are to have reels & all sorts of wild things tonight which will be awful.'[14]

Fearful as the fuss was, and awful though the wild Scottish dances might have been for those who did not know them, Bertie and his sister Mary enjoyed themselves thoroughly. The following day, he and Elizabeth both played tennis, and after a service in the castle chapel, 'I showed her and the Duke the castle, & terrified them with ghost stories! We also played ridiculous games like hide & seek, they really are babies! She didn't leave till 6.30, & then we all played General Post & Flags etc. till dinner time.'[15] After dinner, they gathered round the piano and sang lustily 'the most appalling songs' which Bertie sang 'with more gusto than anyone else.'[16] At midnight, Elizabeth and her friends apple-pied the beds of her brother David and James, who was still being frustratingly elusive.

The following morning after breakfast, everyone in the house party went for a walk. The others discreetly hung back while Bertie and Elizabeth walked on ahead *à deux*. While they were enjoying a *tête-à-tête* in the garden, Elizabeth at her most charming, the others ran about boisterously, the men pelting the girls with mud in their version of good, clean, innocent fun. Only too soon, it was time for the prince and his equerry to depart, leaving Elizabeth to provide an account of the weekend to Beryl. 'Poor P.

Mary,' she wrote ostensibly kindly but with a discomfiting underbelly of the disdain which Stephen Tennant had picked up, 'she really did enjoy herself.' Tellingly, she refrained from passing any comment whatsoever about Bertie, and concluded that Princess Mary was 'most awfully nice.'[17] One suspects that even if she had not been – and according to those who knew her, she genuinely was – Elizabeth, like most other socially ambitious aristocrats, would have found something nice to say about the king's only daughter, at the precise moment that she was leavening the loaf with a dash of contempt.

Elizabeth's autumn now looked up with a bit of help from her father and brothers, who had James Stuart over to Glamis for a week's shooting in October. She even repeated the *risqué* mode of behaviour she and Charlie Settrington had indulged in when she had snuck out of St. James's Square with him to go for that lingering lunch in the country followed by the long walk at Box Hill. They drove over unchaperoned to Sir Stuart and Lady Coat's at Ballathie House near Perth, which caused Elizabeth sufficient anxiety, lest she would be perceived as 'fast', to write to her friend Doris Lennox-Gordon wondering if she had committed too clear a breach of the rules. 'Of course we didn't think anything of you & James coming! No one thought it a bit funny. I think everyone here now realises how fashionable it is to tour round Perthshire & Forfarshire with "Les frères Stuart" & I assure you it was quite alright.'[18]

Elizabeth would have been better advised to heat up the ardour of her hot-blooded 'friend' with a bit less anxiety about decorum and a bit more sensuality, but 'she had no sex appeal whatsoever,' the Duke of Windsor said, and this assessment seems to have been one which James Stuart shared. While he liked Elizabeth enough to respond to her flirtatiousness, he was patently more interested in girls like Mollie than in Elizabeth. Nor was he alone in finding that her appeal was too limited. Few of her beaus actually proposed marriage. Despite the fact that men and women alike said lovely things about her, such as that she was 'just the most perfect person that ever was' (Helen) and an 'angel' (from convalescent soldiers to friends of both sexes) whom everyone 'adored', a disquieting sense of her being too good for men to want to settle down with was emerging. This is touched upon subtly in the 1927 biography of Elizabeth which her sister May's friend Lady Cynthia Asquith wrote with Elizabeth's approval. By then she was the Duchess of York. In authorised biographies, royalty is seldom allowed to be anything but remarkably spectacular, no matter how ordinary they actually are. It simply would not have done for Asquith to say that Elizabeth lacked sex appeal; that many men initially found her attractive because she was such good fun, but upon getting to know her better, found it frustrating that she could never change gears from being wonderful, angelic, effervescent Elizabeth to something rather less sociable and more sensual. It was not enough that Elizabeth was genuinely popular with her friends – these friends had to be suitors, all of whom were competing for her hand in marriage. And of course all these fantastically desirable men had been trounced by her royal prince, who, by implication, was therefore far more attractive and appealing than any of the fantastic men she had not considered worthy of her hand.

On the other hand, Asquith could not have written such tosh without coating it in a protective layer of tactful truthfulness. Too many people in the world – her world, Elizabeth's world, the royal world – knew that many a man who was purported to have jostled for her hand in marriage had actually turned elsewhere when it actually came to the crunch. Christopher Glenconner, for instance, was supposed to have even bought a ring with a view to proposing marriage, but when the moment came to do so, kept his mouth tightly shut and the ring firmly in his pocket. So Asquith promoted the myth of Elizabeth's desirability at the very moment that she was shooting it down in code, saying that Elizabeth is meant to have 'found it difficult to decide upon which of them to bestow her ultimate favour' but that indecision 'on her part was countered by similar changes of front among many of the young men of her acquaintance.' In other words, when the men got tired of all that ethereality, they took their interest elsewhere.

By November of 1920, Elizabeth was back in London. Disappointingly for her, James Stuart's royal boss, not the handsome Scotsman himself, dropped in uninvited to see her one afternoon. She had been expecting Beryl and wrote to enquire why her former governess had stood her up. Then she said, 'As a matter of fact, our <u>Bert</u> stayed till 7, talking 100 to 20, or even 200 to the dozen.'[19] Once more her disdain for the younger brother she had no interest in is eloquent, but all that practised charm had hit its mark with our Bert, whose interest had recently intensified significantly.

To the extent that anyone can decipher why one person falls in love with another, Bertie's interest in Elizabeth was explicable by his past experiences as well as by his character. He was one of those figures of pathos who seem fated to be foils. Born in 1895, a year after his elder brother David, the two brothers were almost caricature opposites of each other. Because they were so close in age, they were brought up as a unit, to the advantage of the elder and the misfortune of the younger.

From the time they were toddlers, David radiated ease, Bertie awkwardness. While the former grew into a bright and beautiful golden-haired child, with the face of an angel and a captivating manner, the latter developed into an ungainly, unattractive, mousey-haired boy who people thought mouselike as well as imbecilic. The 2nd Viscount Esher, who was Deputy Constable and Lieutenant-Governor of Windsor Castle while the boys were youngsters, and knew them well, 'found David clever and composed. He had thought of a riddle in bed, and it was really quite witty for a child. Prince Edward (as David was known officially) develops every day fresh qualities, and is a most charming boy: very direct, dignified, and clever.' Lord Esher could find nothing positive to say about Bertie, so he damned not with faint praise, but with eloquent silence.[20]

The boys' childhoods were the source of their problems. In her excellent biography of King Edward VIII, Frances Donaldson paints a grim picture of their youthful lives. They seldom saw their parents, and when they did, the experience was one of anguish rather than pleasure. King George V quite deliberately brought his children up to be in terror of him, as he himself admitted. And Queen Mary, who had grave communication difficulties, found it impossible to shield her children from their father's cruelty or to provide them with a mother's love and warmth. She used to acknowledge that she could never forget that their father and her husband was also their *king*, which meant that they had to defer to him in all things. The product of a morganatic marriage between King George III's granddaughter Princess Mary Adelaide of Cambridge (known as 'Fat Mary' because of her enormous girth) and the Duke of Teck, who was himself the product of another morganatic union between Duke Alexander of Wurttemberg and an attractive Hungarian noblewoman named Countess Claudine Rhédey von Kis-Rhéde, Queen Mary had a massive inferiority complex. Her granddaughter Princess Margaret, who could not abide her because she made it plain that she was of no consequence since she would not ascend the throne like the Mary's pet Lilibet, used to say that Queen Mary was obsessed with the throne and royalty because of her humble par-royal antecedents. May, as she was known within the family, could never forget that she had not been born of royal rank; that she had been a mere Serene Highness until her marriage rescued her from the ignominy of being second-class in a first-class world. She often suffered slights during family holidays with her German relations, who were all obsessed with rank and purity. This was especially true at Darmstadt, the Hesse family home, where her cousin Princess Alix (Queen Victoria's granddaughter through her daughter Alice, the Grand Duchess of Hesse) never failed to rub in May's inferiority.

Such petty cruelty had an effect on both women's future lives, for May, despite being a lively, intelligent and well-educated young woman, developed into a living, breathing automaton who crushed all human responses in favour of enacting the majestic role she believed her husband wanted her to live out. Meanwhile, spoilt, silly, self-indulgent Alix became the adored wife of the Emperor of All the Russias and proceeded to create havoc with her inept political interference and reliance upon spiritual guidance from phoney religious mystics such as Rasputin, with the result that her husband Nicky, George V's first cousin and double, who deferred to her in all things, was forced to abdicate. Nicky turned to Georgie for refuge, to which the Prime Minister of the Provisional Government, Alexander Kerensky, agreed and which Georgie's Prime Minister, David Lloyd George and the Cabinet, granted. It was May who talked her husband into withdrawing the offer of sanctuary to the Russian Imperial Family, playing upon his fears of revolution being imported along with Nicky and the hated Alix.

Within the family, it was generally acknowledged that this was May's revenge for all the times Alix had made her feel the inferiority of her morganatic status, but the price Nicky, Alix and their five children paid was rather higher than May had intended. As all the world knows, they were brutally murdered. And Georgie, who thereafter blamed Lloyd George for the outcome, labelling him a 'murderer', was clearly guilt-ridden, for he knew better than anyone else that it was he who had instructed his Prime Minister to withdraw the offer of sanctuary, so ultimate responsibility lay with him. Nor would George V have been blind to the reality that it was his wife who had precipitated this tragedy. But kings seldom berate themselves or their spouses when they can shift blame elsewhere, to hapless politicians who are simply complying with their instructions.

The cold inhumanity which allowed May to settle childhood slights so disproportionately was apparent to her relations even when she was a young woman. George's paternal aunt, the German Empress Frederick (Queen Victoria's eldest, namesake daughter who was Kaiser Wilhelm II's mother), observing her with her children, wrote that she was 'very cold and stiff and very unmaternal.'[21] This viewpoint was shared by her eldest son David, who wrote after he had become the Duke of Windsor that she had 'ice in her veins'. He did acknowledge, however, that he loved her, and her letters and actions, some of which will be revealed later on in this book for the first time, indicate that in her frosty way she also loved him. Though never so much that she would ever put her child before her Sovereign, not even when right and Christian charity demanded it.

Being reared with such emotionally barren parents had an effect on both David and Bertie. But when they were young, their difficulties with their parents were exacerbated by their nurse, who was a seriously disturbed woman with a pathological love of David but a callous antipathy towards Bertie. She had a trick to ensure that the Duke and Duchess of York, as

George and Mary were then known, would curtail the visits which took place most afternoons around tea time. As the children were standing outside the door to whichever room their parents were in, she would pinch them, so that they were crying by the time they reached their parents. Because the aloof and unmaternal Mary could not abide crying children, and the authoritarian George regarded tears as bad behaviour, this was an ideal way of ensuring that the boys grew up having no relationship of any substance with their parents.

Bad as this was, in the nursery this demented woman, who reigned supreme, showered love upon David while ignoring Bertie utterly. Nothing Bertie said or did was rewarded, while everything David did, was. She was never too preoccupied to listen to David, never so unoccupied that she could give Bertie her ear. So antipathetic was she towards the poor child that she never bothered to feed him properly, while David of course was fed royally. The result was that Bertie had serious digestive problems and a speech impediment, both of which would stay with him in varying degrees for the rest of his life.

Fortunately for both boys, this woman had a complete breakdown. She was replaced by Mrs. Brill, who soon discovered what had been happening in the nursery. By this time the damage had been done and Bertie was, justifiably, a nervous wreck who, in his eagerness to please, alienated. He twitched, blinked compulsively, drooled incessantly, and could never get a sentence out without tripping over most of its words. One would imagine that someone would have taken pity on the little boy and realised that many of his problems were a direct result of the abuse to which he had been subjected. But no one seems to have made the connection, and his behaviour was marked down as natural failings which must be eradicated. After all, he was a prince, and princes must be brought up to conform to the mould of appearing to be socially superior beings. So he was made to know in no uncertain terms that he would simply have to conform to the stereotype.

One of the few innate problems which Bertie had, and which would compound the characteristics of traumatisation which he had already manifested, was that he was left-handed. This emerged when he was old enough to begin lessons with his mother's old governess, Madame Bricka, who now joined Mrs. Brill in the nursery. But this only became a real problem when he was six, and he and David were deemed to be old enough to leave the care of the women and be turned over to a tutor named Mr. Hansell and a valet named Frederick Finch. Left-handedness then being seen as a moral failing with overtones of maladjustment and rebelliousness as well as imbecility and nonconformity, Mr. Hansell drummed it into Bertie on a daily basis that he must use only his right hand. This caused Bertie's stutter to worsen dramatically, which only had the effect of increasing the pressure upon him, for Mr. Hansell now had yet another failing with which to castigate him. The schoolroom became a torture chamber where he was subjected on a daily basis to a never-ending series of reminders as to how inadequate he was. Only too soon, Mr. Hansell was complaining about Bertie's lack of concentration and the uncontrollable rages to which he was becoming increasingly prone as the frustrations built up within him. But there was no respite for Bertie, not even when he went to bed. He was badly knock-kneed, so the monarch's doctor, Sir Francis Laking, Bt., GCVO, KCB, MD, fitted him with specially constructed splints, which he had to wear most days and every night. These were wretchedly uncomfortable, and one cannot help but be moved by the plight of this good-natured and stoical little boy, who had the pluck to write his mother, 'I am sitting in an armchair with my legs in the new splints. I have got an invalid table, which is splendid for reading but rather awkward for writing at present. I expect I shall get used to it.'[22]

But not even someone as stoical and eager-to-please as Bertie could come to terms with the unremitting pressure which increased each day with the tutor's demands and his inability to fulfil them. By the time he was twelve, Bertie's response to any failure was so heartfelt that he would either sob uncontrollably whenever he made a mistake, or throw a temper tantrum. This caused his father to write to him in as understanding a manner as someone as admonitory as George V could muster. 'You must really give up losing your temper when you make a mistake in a sum. We all make mistakes sometimes, remember you are now nearly 12 years old & ought no longer to behave like a little child of 6.'[23]

Life might well have become intolerable for a child who suffered as much as Bertie did on a daily basis, but for two reasons. The first was that he was confident of the love of his parents. Notwithstanding their aloofness and innately forbidding characters, they were both fundamentally decent people who did care about the welfare of their children. Somehow, they managed to communicate the love they felt for them, and while David would grow up to have an antipathetic relationship with his father, though not with his mother, Bertie never did. He was always clear in his mind and in his actions where his parents were concerned: he loved them and wanted their approval.

The second reason which made his fate tolerable was the loving indulgence he received from his grandparents, who were Prince and Princess of Wales until becoming King Edward VII and Queen Alexandra in 1901. Young Bertie had been named after his grandfather, who in turn was known as Bertie, as he too had been named in honour of his father, Queen Victoria's beloved Prince Consort: Prince Albert of Saxe-Coburg-Gotha. The elder Bertie and Alexandra were very fond of children. Although George V would say that he had been terrified of his father and expected his children to be commensurately terrified of him, he seems to have been the only sibling who felt like that, and by the time his children were born, both his father and 'Motherdear', as he and all his siblings called their indulgent mother, were archetypal grandparents who enjoyed having their grandchildren to stay, and spoilt them thoroughly while they were under their care. They encouraged the grandchildren to tear about the house 'romping', and encouraged them to mingle and show off in front of their adult friends. This degree of licence and encouragement was almost too much for their five York grandchildren, suppressed and restricted as they were on a daily basis at home. All of them were prone to overexcitement, but none more so than Bertie. Sometimes he would have to be sent off to bed to calm down, but the morrow always brought fresh freedom, new delights, more joyousness and excitement in adult approbation.

In their own way, Edward VII and Alexandra gave Bertie a much needed glimpse of what family life could be like, within the bosom of a less judgemental and regimented family than his own. This not only provided the boy with much-needed positive reinforcement, but also gave him an insight into how enjoyable family life could be. Old Princess Louise, Duchess of Argyll used to say that she was sure that Bertie fell in love as much with Elizabeth's family as with her. This is a judgement with which many a psychologist would concur, for it was only when Bertie went to stay at Glamis, and discovered how similarly rambunctious to his own grandparents the Strathmore family was, that he started to think in terms of her as a possible wife for himself.

If Bertie and his siblings had no real scope for the pleasures of family life except when they were with their grandparents, each of them nevertheless did have staff who provided them with some of the emotional sustenance all children need. In her acclaimed 1986 biography *Queen Elizabeth: A Life of the Queen Mother*, Penelope Mortimer made the point that 'the handsome, stalwart, muscular' Finch was the nearest thing either Bertie or David had to a parent, and both boys were devoted to him. His duties included waking them up in the morning, hearing their prayers, bathing them, dressing them, and tucking them into bed last thing at night. During the day he took care of their clothes when he was not taking care of their needs. Nevertheless, it was clear to everyone, Bertie included, that David was his favourite. Indeed, Finch went on to serve him in adult life firstly as his valet and latterly as his butler when he became Prince of Wales.

It would have defied the laws of natural justice for Bertie to lack any virtues whatsoever, but his were all hidden, like the strength of character which adversity was forming. Few of the adults surrounding him were aware of any redeeming features, but one redoubtable woman early on came to develop a sneaking suspicion that he might be more worthy than most people suspected. This was Mabell Airlie, his mother's lady-in-waiting and Cecilia Strathmore's good friend and neighbour in Scotland. She was one of the few adults to treat him kindly. In return, he developed a marked veneration of her. In *Thatched with Gold*, her memoirs, she recounts how he waylaid her at Easter 1902 with a card he had made for her. Intending to present it to her, he lost his nerve, so silently thrust it into her hand before darting off silently. 'When I succeeded later in gaining his confidence he talked to me quite normally, without stammering, and then I found that far from being backward he was an intelligent child with more force of character than anyone suspected in those days.' She also thought that the card was well and imaginatively made, indicating yet again that Bertie was not the imbecile he was generally regarded as being.

When King Edward VII died in 1910, Bertie was fourteen and a half years old. Although visits to his grandmother Queen Alexandra continued, they were not as much fun as they had been when Grandpapa England had been alive. But he was still able to bask in his grandmother's affection. This was just as well, for the course of his life had gone from grim to grimmer. Notwithstanding that he suffered from severe seasickness, tradition decreed that both the heir and the spare should enter the Royal Navy. He was also pathologically shy with the inevitable tongue-tied handicap of all stutterers, so a less suitable environment could not be imagined than being on a ship full of sailors, with their robust practices and rough ways. However, no sooner did he turn thirteen than he was made to sit the entrance examinations to the Royal Naval College for Cadets at Osborne House, Queen Victoria's Italianate pleasure palace on the Isle of Wight which the Prince Consort had designed for her, and which had been the scene of some of the happiest days of her life. Edward VII, however, had no affection for the place, and no sooner did he succeed to the throne than he turned it over to the nation.

Bertie did not have many memories of Osborne House as a family home, but even if he had had, his stint in this former royal residence would have remained the painful experience it was. When he started there in January 1909, David was in his final term, but this was scant comfort to the dreadfully homesick and nervous younger brother. The rules forbade communication between the older and newer cadets, and as a result the tongue-tied, painfully shy Bertie was left to fend for himself.

Bertie's constitution came to his rescue, just as it would time and again in the future whenever the pressure became unbearable. (This propensity to being rescued by ill health was something he shared with Elizabeth, who displayed a similar tendency all her life.) He came down with whooping cough six months into his naval course, and, in a reminder of his basic insignificance, was not treated by the chief medical officer the way David would have been, but by an assistant, Surgeon-Lieutenant Louis Greig. This would prove to be a happy coincidence, for this was the start of a long and rewarding relationship between the young and needy prince and the older and sensible man who would become like a beloved, relatively young uncle-cum-mentor.

Even though Bertie was of little consequence as a mere second son, he was nevertheless a member of the Royal Family, and once he was back on his feet, the doctors decided to err on the side of caution and prescribe a long period of rest. He was sent to an estate ten miles from Balmoral in the Scottish Highlands with the loyal Finch and Mr. Watt, a tutor. Without the relentless pressure which had so far characterised his miserable life, his health improved, as did his stammer. He fished and shot and stalked and walked. As he enjoyed the serenity of country life and a pressure-free existence, he even stopped drooling, a disconcerting nervous trait which was partly responsible for people believing him to be 'backward' or simple-minded. Soon he was so fit and well that his other nervous habits such as twitching and squinting all but disappeared, and the true personality of this abused prince became visible for the first time in his life. He even stopped flying into rages the way he had done all his life.

With recovery, however, came a return to the life he loathed, and he was compelled to return to the navy. It was only a matter of time before the pressure of this unsuitable way of life brought back all his nervous ailments as well as his perpetual seasickness. But Bertie was developing an indomitable aspect to his character, and no matter how much he was beaten down, he refused to be beaten. He knew his father, by now King George V, wanted him to remain in the navy, so stay in the navy he would. Although illnesses such as measles did occasionally provide him with a welcome respite, as soon as he was fit for service he willingly returned to this hated way of life, not because he was a sucker for punishment, but because he felt it his duty to fulfil his parents' expectations irrespective of his personal persuasions.

For four long years, Bertie endured an existence he found unendurable. But ill health was hovering in the background, waiting to come to his rescue. This it did three weeks after the declaration of war on Elizabeth's fourteenth birthday, 4th August, 1914. His ship, the *Rohilla*, had to return to port in

Aberdeen to discharge the prince who was doubled over with crippling stomach pains. Diagnosed as suffering from appendicitis, a condition which had nearly killed his grandfather Edward VII in 1902 and had caused the postponement of his Coronation, Bertie was operated upon and prescribed the standard rest period of three months. Just as he was due to return to sea, he developed yet more crippling stomach pains, which seem to have been anxiety-induced. These kicked off a two-year period of illness and recovery, during which time he was posted to the Admiralty with a desk job. Bertie was intensely sportive and physically robust (another of the far-from-apparent traits he shared with Elizabeth), but his doctors denied him the physical release exercise would have brought him. He wasn't even allowed to do the calisthenics which he loved, for his father's advisors were eager for him to become fit again for naval service, lest he be seen as a shirker.

This was at a time when there was a tremendous build-up of anti-German feeling in the United Kingdom. The Royal Family, with its German origins and German relations, many of whom were anglicised but nevertheless German by birth or name, became increasingly sensitive to the invidiousness of their unEnglishness. One of the first heads to roll was that of Prince Louis of Battenberg (Prince Philip's maternal grandfather), who was hounded out of office as First Sea Lord by a vicious campaign of denigration. Married to George V's first cousin and the Empress Alexandra of Russia's eldest sister Princess Victoria of Hesse, not even the King could save his position, and his fate became a stark warning which George V and his advisors heeded.

After nearly two years of stomach problems, Bertie was finally judged to be well enough to return to sea. But he saw little active service on HMS *Collingwood*, for he was confined to the infirmary with acute depression. Nevertheless, he made sure that he left his sick-bed to man his post at the top of a turret for the Battle of Jutland, and in so doing showed that, whatever else he lacked, it was not courage. After that battle, he returned to the sick-bay, where he was once more confined for some months, until he was put ashore with a diagnosis of a duodenal ulcer. He was sent to Windsor Castle to recuperate, and as soon as he was fit enough to return to sea, he did so.

There was something almost inevitable about the denouement. No sooner did the bowels of the ship engulf Bertie than illness did as well. Finally, as 1917 headed towards its bloody conclusion, even he realised that no amount of willingness to please his father would result in his becoming one of those fit sailors Elizabeth Bowes Lyon was so obsessed with from the safety of her parents' houses. Finally throwing in the towel, he wrote George V from his sick-bed asking to be relieved of his duties at sea. That November, he was operated upon for ulcers, and in February 1918 the decision was finally taken to keep him on dry land. He was appointed Officer in Charge of Boys at the Royal Naval Air Service's training establishment at Cranwell, which would turn out to be a propitious decision.

Aeroplanes were then a new phenomenon. They were often shaky contraptions held together with little more than string, so flying was a dangerous occupation. So unsafe was it that the wives of many an aviator developed a lifelong terror of flight. One who did was the young Wallis Warfield Spencer, whose first husband was an airman. Bertie, however, had no terror of the skies the way his future sister-in-law did. Indeed, he seems to have had no terror of anything except falling short in the eyes of his father and mother.

His health continued to remain uncertain, as it would throughout the remainder of his life. But he now had his own doctor-in-residence, for Louis Greig had been relieved of his post as second surgeon of the *Malaya* in 1917 and appointed to Bertie's permanent staff. This was another inspired appointment, and would work in favour of both men, for each had qualities and gifts which would ultimately enhance the other's life. Indeed, the Greig family would go from strength to strength as a result of Louis's role in Bertie's life, and his grandson Geordie Greig is now one of England's most eminent print medium executives, having for many years been the editor of Society bible *Tatler* magazine before becoming editor of the London *Evening Standard* newspaper.

One of the first, and most sensible, things Louis did was to lift the interdict on physical exercise. He saw that it was not only medically unsound, but counterproductive. An excellent rugby union and tennis player, he shared Bertie's love and need for sport, and it was only a matter of time before doctor and patient were hunting, fishing, shooting, stalking, and playing tennis to their hearts' content. So good were they that they even won the RAF Doubles Competition at Wimbledon.

After the Royal Naval Air Service was amalgamated with the Royal Flying Corps to create the Royal Air Force on 1st April, 1918, Bertie was appointed a squadron leader (Officer Commanding No 4 Squadron of the Boys' Wing) at Cranwell, where he remained until August 1918. Louis Greig transferred from the navy to the air force at the same time and was appointed Bertie's equerry. Ultimately, he would rise to the rank of wing commander.

In the closing weeks of the war, Bertie served on the staff of the RAF's Independent Air Force at its headquarters in Nancy, France. Following the disbanding of the Independent Air Force after the Armistice on 11th November, 1918, he remained on the Continent as an RAF staff officer, which is how he came to meet James Stuart. One of Bertie's first duties as a royal prince and serving officer in peacetime was to represent his father and accompany King Albert I and Queen Elisabeth of the Belgians on their victorious ride back into their capital. They had been forced to flee Brussels by the Germans earlier in the war when much of Belgium was overrun. The Belgians had had an even worse war than the English, and George V was keen to show solidarity with his fellow monarch and cousin, both being members of the House of Saxe-Coburg and Gotha despite the English name change to Windsor the year before. (Queen Victoria's uncle Leopold of Saxe-Coburg and Gotha had been nominated King of the Belgians on 21st July, 1831, following Belgium's independence from the Netherlands.) James Stuart informs us in his autobiography that he and Bertie 'had a great deal of fun', for Brussels still had fine restaurants and a vivid nightlife which neither war nor peace had dented. James and Bertie being equally fun-loving (another trait shared with Elizabeth), both young men cut a swathe through Brussels until their sojourn came to an end.

Returning to England in time for the Christmas celebrations, Bertie attended a ball and met the woman he would fall in love with: Sheila Loughborough. She was a good friend of Freda Dudley Ward, wife of the Liberal MP for Southampton, William Dudley Ward, with whom Bertie's brother David had fallen deeply in love since meeting her earlier that year. In her memoirs, which have not been published and therefore remain inaccessible to the world at large, Sheila tells how she and her friend frequently danced with the two brothers at balls, 'which annoyed the dowagers. However, we didn't care. We knew no party was complete without us – and them.'[24]

By one of those curious twists of fate which show how coincidence can affect the future in the most unpredictable ways, my late mother-in-law Louise, Duchess of Argyll, had a longstanding affair with Prince Dimitri of Russia, the man whom Sheila married as her third husband in 1954, after she had divorced Lord Loughborough in 1926 and was widowed by Sir John Milbanke, 11th Bt., in 1942. My mother-in-law hoped to marry this urbane and handsome son of the Grand Duchess Xenia when she and the 11th duke were divorced, but by the time their marriage was dissolved in 1951, the affair had run its course. But this was not the end of the matter. Big Ian, as my father-in-law was known within the family, alleged that both his sons were the progeny of other men, and that his younger son Colin was actually Dimitri's natural son. This caused a lawsuit known as the Argyll Bastardy Case in the 1950s. The result of all of this interweaving of the families' destinies is that I was privy to all sorts of information that one would otherwise not have had access to. It deeply affected my father-in-law's subsequent wife, the legendary Margaret, Duchess of Argyll, and his eldest child and only daughter, Lady Jeanne Campbell, who was eighteen years older than my husband and already a young woman at the time of the gruesome machinations.

Interestingly, in her memoirs Sheila paints a picture of Elizabeth that is at odds with the propaganda spread once she became Duchess of York. She calls into question the level of Elizabeth's desirability by recounting an occasion at a ball when she and Bertie were dancing. She noticed 'a young girl standing alone by the doorway with no partner and felt sorry for her. I asked somebody who she was and they told me she was a debutante called Elizabeth Bowes Lyon.'[25] This suggests that Elizabeth was significantly less popular than she was later alleged to be, notwithstanding that she was undoubtedly regarded as desirable within her own narrow circle of friends.

Bertie's affair with Sheila was in full flow by the time he was sent in January 1919 to Trinity College, Cambridge, along with his younger brother Henry and Louis Greig, to study history, economics and civics for a year. Not for him anything so pedestrian as attending lectures or sharing dormitories, however. His tutors came to the house which the Palace had taken for the brothers and their staff, and when Bertie wasn't studying, he was undertaking the royal duties which now formed a part of his new, civilian, life.

The world which Bertie was being prepared to enter no longer possessed the secure structure that the pre-1914 one had done. Not only had many of the monarchies been swept away, but those that remained were acutely aware that they too could suffer the same fate unless they espoused popular and populist policies. Social unrest and the possibility of revolution from the Bolsheviks were not idle threats, especially when Rosa Luxembourg and other revolutionaries nearly toppled the newly-created Weimar Republic in Germany and the Hungarian state was in danger of falling to a Red regime.

By then the British monarch and his government had already woken up to the necessity of dealing with the new political forces which the Great War had unleashed. Not the least of these was the Labour Party, which had grown in two decades, from a negligible organisation commonly regarded as more a nuisance than a threat to the Establishment, into the largest opposition party, following the Khaki Election called by Lloyd George at the end of 1918.

In furtherance of the objective of realigning the monarchy with these new political forces, George V's Private Secretary, Lord Stamfordham, recommended that the Crown reposition itself as a 'living power for good'. Hitherto, it had been the bastion for the Great and the Good.

After much deliberation, the King and his advisors agreed that the Royal Family would reach out to the new powers-that-be in the country by taking a pro-active interest in the way of life of the workers, whom the Labour

Party represented in Parliament. David was sent to Canada, on the first of a series of prolonged tours of the Empire which would result in his being the most extensively travelled Prince of Wales of all time. These were intended to strengthen the ties between the many British overseas territories and the Crown, and they would succeed in doing so.

Meanwhile, his sister Mary started to undertake extensive royal engagements, usually associated with charities or other good works. Bertie's brief was to establish links between the mainland working classes and the Crown through contacts with industry. This was a radical step for a monarchy to take, but also an inspired one, and it shows how prescient George V and his advisors were in riding the crest of the new wave of populism via the working classes.

By a timely coincidence, the Revd. Robert Hyde was seeking royal patronage for an organisation which he had set up in 1918 to improve the working conditions of the lower orders through industry. Scores of businesses, also alert to the threat of a Bolshevik takeover in the event that the working classes' demands were, if not met, then at least listened to, were involved, and though right-wing elements in the Establishment thought the whole venture a dangerous experiment which would only encourage Bolshevism, The Boys' Welfare Association was deemed to be a Godsend by more moderate political entities. These included the Monarchy and Government, but significantly not the aristocracy or the bourgeoisie.

Although royals traditionally did not become patrons of fledgling organisations, preferring to wait until these had proven track records as solidly and fruitfully established successes whose benefits would enhance the prestige of their patrons by association, the Palace and Government were aware that this was no time for dallying. The threat of revolution was too real, the need to palliate the restive too great. So rather than wait until The Boys' Welfare Association emerged as a success, Bertie was named president without further ado.

This proved to be yet another of the inspired appointments which were now coming Bertie's way. Its success would owe much to the ostensible inadequacies of the man. Positively synergistic in marrying such superficially incompatible opposites as an apparently privileged prince and the deprived working classes, the choice of this victim of an oppressive childhood, who could and did empathise with the many forms of deprivation he encountered as he set about fulfilling the functions of president of The Boys' Welfare Association, was just one of the unexpected bonuses of the appointment.

Yet the harbingers, unrecognised at the time, were good from the moment Bertie opened his mouth and stammered out his consent, with the proviso that he would fulfil the role only if 'there's no damn red carpet about it.'[26] This comment was more than just a promising sign. It was almost a guarantee of success, for an unprepossessing and unpretentious prince who was willing to roll up his sleeves figuratively, and muck in with the downtrodden without the flummery that usually accompanied royalty, was striking just the right note for a position which had such crucially important political overtones.

The success of the appointment was apparent within a few short months. With its down-to-earth and charmingly intense but diffident royal patron, as well as the backing of the Palace and Government behind it, the Association now grew so rapidly in both accomplishments and influence that its name was quickly changed to the more politically impressive Industrial Welfare Society. Its work, however, remained the same. This was sterling, and Bertie was not only willing, but eager, to do what he could to assist a group of people whose plight he clearly identified with on an emotional level. As he clambered over construction sites, down mineshafts and into the driver's seat of a tramcar, his basic good sense shone through in a way that no one but Mabell Airlie had perceived in 1902, when he had sought to give her the Easter present he had made for her. As he asked sensible questions (such as where were the lavatories or lunch rooms for the men to eat) and gained telling answers (usually to the effect that there were none), he was gaining invaluable knowledge which he could take back to the Palace so that George V and his Government could really learn what conditions on the ground were like for workers, and what needed to be done.

Only too soon, Bertie could see that people were starting to respect him. This was a new experience for him, and galvanised him to further action. Before too long he was even receiving praise in the popular press for the unpretentious manner and solid good sense he displayed as he went about his unglamorous but politically sensitive work. On the back of this, he came up with the idea of starting boys' camps for students from all walks of life to get together and learn about one another. Inevitably for someone as sportive as Bertie, physical activities, including the calisthenics of which he was so fond, rather than book learning or intellectual activities, formed a large part of a process that had never been tried before. To ensure the success of his camps, Bertie not only oversaw their organisation, but also attended as many of them as he could.

But Bertie was not all work and no play. There was Sheila. There were the balls and dances and parties and levees and nightclubs which he and his brothers attended, usually with Sheila and Freda Dudley Ward, though they also mixed with many of the daughters of the peerage. Most of these young women and their mothers were eager for the royal brothers to cast an eye in their direction. And annoyed when they did not. As Bertie put it, they were constantly being spied upon at balls and parties, and their actions, no matter how innocent, were reported back with the worst possible interpretation to their parents.[27]

Inevitably, George V got wind of the affairs his two elder sons were conducting so publicly with married women, but he waited until April 1920 to confront Bertie about his. By this time David was away in Australia and New Zealand, on the second of the many imperial tours he was obliged to make representing his father all over the Empire. In attendance upon him was his cousin, Lord Louis Mountbatten, who left a vivid account of the deep depressions to which the lovesick Prince of Wales was prone.

Knowing that his brother would sympathise with his predicament, Bertie wrote to David that their father 'is going to make me Duke of York on his birthday provided that he hears nothing more about Sheila and me!!!'[28] Although he bemoaned his father's interference and fulminated against him, swearing that Sheila was 'the one & only person who means anything to me',[29] when push came to shove, he chose the approbation of his parents over love.

There can be little doubt that the divorces, annulments and 'inappropriate' marriages within George V's own family undermined whatever resolve Bertie had to resist his father's opposition to a union with Sheila. The Hesse Royal Family was closely related to the British Royal Family. Although they had been deposed recently, and could no longer provide brides for British princes, they nevertheless remained one of the world's most prestigious royal families. George V's aunt Alice had been Grand Duchess of Hesse until she died of diphtheria in 1878. Her widower, the Grand Duke Louis IV of Hesse, was not only the father of the last Russian Empress, Alexandra Feodorovna, but also the nephew of Tsar Alexander II's first wife, Marie Feodorovna, who had been born Princess Marie of Hesse. Six years after the death of Alice, the Grand Duke had married Alexandrina Hutten-Tsapska, the ex-wife of Alexander Kolemin, the Russian *chargé d'affaires* to his court at Darmstadt. The hue and cry from the British, Russian and German Royal Families were so deafening – Alice's eldest sister was then the German Crown Princess Victoria – and the threat to his young, unmarried children's future so great (no royal marriages of any consequence unless you get rid of *the common adulteress),* that he annulled the marriage within a year.

Although this sacrifice spared his children the ignominy of humble marriages, it did nothing for their marital track record. His son and heir Ernst Ludwig (Ernie) entered into a disastrous union with his first cousin Princess Victoria Melita (Ducky) of Edinburgh and Coburg (whose father Alfred, Duke of Coburg and Edinburgh had died the week of Elizabeth's birth from throat cancer) two years after succeeding to the grand ducal throne. This was at the insistence of their mutual grandmother, Queen Victoria, who was firmly convinced that her son Alfred and her daughter Alice's children were well suited because they were both artistic and party-loving. Ernie was not only homosexual, but possibly worse from Ducky's point of view, a conscientious ruler, while she was a spoilt brat who had a heightened taste for fun but not for royal duties. For instance, at official functions she would speak only to those people who interested her, ignoring everyone else irrespective of their importance to the grand duchy and its interests. She was also (irretrievably, it would turn out) in love with her maternal first cousin, Grand Duke Kirill of Russia. But she had been unable to marry him because the Russian Orthodox Church forbade marriages between first cousins (her mother the former Grand Duchess Maria Alexandrovna was the sister of his father Grand Duke Vladimir Alexandrovitch), so the Hesse marriage had seemed like a good way of settling the marital needs of these two cousins for whom marital happiness was an impossibility. They did produce a daughter Elisabeth (known as Ella) in 1895, but the relationship quickly degenerated into squabbles over her failure to perform her public duties, and within an uncomfortably short time Ducky was throwing her tea trays, ornaments, and anything else that came to hand, at her husband.[30]

Once Queen Victoria died, however, Ducky did divorce Ernie. She and Kirill married without the permission of the Tsar, for which they were banished from Russia and he lost his place in the line of succession and was deprived of the rank of Imperial Highness. Only when fate intervened following a rash of deaths in the Romanov family were they allowed back into Russia.

It is interesting to note the different conclusions that Bertie and David drew from the marital ups and downs of their Hesse relations, and indeed the many other relations who had married 'inappropriately', including their father's Russian first cousins. The Tsar's youngest brother, Grand Duke Michael, had eloped in 1908 with the twice divorced Natalia Wulfert, who had given birth to their son before she was divorced from her second husband. To remove all doubts about the child's paternity, her second divorce was backdated to precede the birth of Count George Romanovsky-Brasov, as the boy was styled with the Tsar's reluctant collusion. Nicholas II also allowed their sister, Grand Duchess Olga, to divorce her homosexual husband the Duke of Oldenburg and to marry the untitled commoner Nikolai Kulikovsky in 1916.

Even before the war, there had been the feeling that times were changing and royalty should be allowed to marry for love, rather than forced into making dynastic unions which covered up homosexuality and bastardy, while furthering geopolitical objectives. Even divorce no longer seemed to be an insurmountable obstacle, as the marriages of cousins Ernie, Ducky, Olga and Michael had shown. As the Great War had proven, the old-fashioned precepts for royal marriages had not prevented brother fighting sister, uncle nephew, and cousin cousin, even when they were responsible for a lifetime of personal misery. The post-war attitude was that pretty much anyone ought to be an acceptable royal marital prospect as long as he or she was well-bred and socially acceptable.

Both David and Bertie had fallen in love with married women without thinking that by doing so they were jeopardising their positions or welcoming heartbreak into their lives. Plainly, neither brother envisaged that divorce would be a major obstacle to a potential union with their *inamoratas*, especially when so many of their cousins had married after divorces.

Bertie, however, read the sub-text of his parents' objections to Sheila more accurately than David. Confronted with the choice of continuing a relationship with a woman of whom his parents disapproved, and sacrificing such worldly advantages as an elevation to a royal dukedom and its attendant advantages, or of persisting in a love affair with God-knows-what-outcome, he sacrificed his love for worldly advancement and his parents' approbation. This showed that whatever else Bertie was, he was ultimately a team player who would never go against his parents' wishes.

Despite having gained in stature and confidence by way of his enhanced reputation through his industrial activities, the Duke of York was still, beneath it all, the same old Bertie who had persisted in the navy for years, despite the damage a seafaring life had caused to his health and well-being. He did bemoan his fate to David, writing 'Oh! If only one could live one's own life occasionally,'[31] but he nevertheless made sure that he and Sheila were definitively if amicably finished.

Nor was Bertie the only person to enjoy a reward for the way he and Sheila ended their love affair. She was shown royal favour sufficiently overtly for the whole of Society to know that she remained *persona grata*. Although her husband was a renowned alcoholic and gambler who 'enjoyed himself rather more than anyone else' and was content to go 'his own way', as Prince Serge Obolensky put it in his memoirs,[32] Sheila remained popular with everyone, especially the men. She had a number of high-profile romances, including with Serge Obolensky and the silent film star Rudolf Valentino. She divorced Loughborough in 1926 three years before his death; married Sir John Milbanke, 11th baronet, in 1928, and was so socially acceptable despite having been divorced, that after she was widowed in 1947, she opened up Milbanke Travel in Fortnum & Mason, where a steady stream of aristocrats were her customers. In 1954 she was welcomed with open arms into the Russian Imperial Family by the last Tsar's sister Grand Duchess Xenia, when her son Dimitri wanted to marry her. As the Grand Duchess used to live in a royal grace-and-favour residence, Frogmore House on the Windsor estate, and was a great friend of her cousin King George VI and his wife Elizabeth, there can be no doubt that 'The Darling', as Sheila was known, remained in favour with the British Royal Family throughout her life.

And Bertie's reward was a real step up in the world. With the dukedom of York came his own Household and the funding for it. This meant that he now had his own 'rooms' like all the other senior members of the Royal Family. No longer would he be a visitor in his parents' houses. He had his own 'place'. And his own staff too. Louis Greig was appointed his Comptroller, and James Stuart, who had helped him set Brussels alight, his equerry. Queen Mary even dropped a broad hint that possibly it was time for him to consider matrimony with some suitable 'gel'. Or, to quote Bertie writing to David, 'You wouldn't think it possible but Mama actually talked about marriage to me the other day!!!!!!!'[33]

David, meanwhile, also had marriage on his mind. He was busy writing letters from the Antipodes to Freda Dudley Ward, professing undying love and proposing marriage to her.

For many years, it has been supposed that these letters were lost. In fact, they are very much in the possession of Freda's granddaughters' family. Her granddaughter Emma, Lady Temple, the daughter of Freda's younger daughter Claire Angela Louise (Angie) Dudley Ward and Major-General Sir Robert Laycock, herself told me that the family has 'half of all the letters the Prince of Wales wrote her.' After explaining how the other half had left their possession, she said that they were 'very adolescent in tone' and 'really rather dull. Full of soppy, lovey dovey protestations of undying love and how he couldn't live without her. He'd sometimes write four and five times a day. He was constantly proposing marriage to her.' Her reaction? 'She'd always avoid the issue. As far as she was concerned, the whole thing was a non-starter.'

Although Freda might not have wanted to swap her Liberal Member of Parliament for the Prince of Wales, marriage was definitely in the air. This was as it should be, because matrimony was then a serious calling which well-bred young people were not permitted to defer unless there was a very, very sound reason indeed. Such as lack of money. The marital bed was not only for pleasure, but even more importantly, for the perpetuation and enhancement of the family's status. The main measure of a young woman's success had always been the speed with which she got married following her debut at seventeen or eighteen. As all the *dramatis personae* in this royal drama were in their twenties, and some were even batting thirty, Queen Mary had been well within her rights as a mother to focus her second son's attention upon his duty. For, make no mistake about it, it was the duty of all princes to marry. The same applied to young ladies and gentlemen of rank.

Although times have changed somewhat, even in my youth, in the late 1960s and early 1970s, girls who were not married by their mid-twenties were viewed as failures, while those who swanned down the aisle at eighteen or nineteen were regarded as having achieved the ultimate. And if a girl, no matter how pretty or popular, turned thirty without a wedding band on her left hand, everyone wanted to know what was wrong with her. I even advised a famous socialite who had been engaged six times but had always broken off her engagements in the quest for Mr/Lord Perfect, to marry the man she subsequently did, because 'you need the stamp of approval that only marriage brings. You've reached the age where it is better to be married and divorced than to have never been married at all.' Agreeing with my assessment, she married, had a beautiful daughter, and is now divorced. But mercifully free of the stigma that spinsterhood would have brought in its wake.

To an extent, her dilemma was one with which Elizabeth Bowes Lyon would have identified, if only partially. Though Elizabeth knew that any marriage she entered into would have to be for a lifetime, she too was particular. Whether this was because she was after love or advantage is open to interpretation. It depends on whether you accept the viewpoint of a Stephen Tennant and a Duke of Windsor on one hand, or panegyricists like Lady Cynthia Asquith and Lord Gorrel on the other. Whatever her motives, however, the effect was that she either would not or could not close the deal, to employ the vernacular.

It is likely that Elizabeth herself did not know whether she would have the *opportunity* to marry for love or advantage. Several people who were in a position to know, such as Elizabeth's niece Lady Mary Clayton, have all said that James Stuart was the 'love of her life'. But in November 1920, when Bertie first dropped in uninvited on Elizabeth in London, his equerry was having a torrid affair with Mollie Lascelles.

Elizabeth's predicament was nothing new to womanhood. Most of us have at some time in our lives been in a similar position, with the man on whom we are keen distracted elsewhere, while the one on whom we are not, is attracted. Her actions show that she did what any other girl in her shoes would have done. She tried to entice James in every way she could, including by encouraging Bertie's attentions in a bid to reconfirm her attractiveness to the real object of her desires. Plainly she was hoping to make James jealous,[34] and while she did succeed in maintaining the lukewarm temperature of his interest sufficiently for him to continue visiting her occasionally and giving her the odd dance at balls, she was not successful in supplanting Mollie. But her ploy succeeded well enough for Bertie to arrange for that notorious lion-hunter Maggie Greville to ask her to the dinner she was hosting for him the night after his twenty-fifth birthday on 14th December, 1920.

It says much about Elizabeth's character that she enjoyed herself thoroughly, as she wrote and told Bertie. Indeed, she and Mrs. Greville took to each other the way a duck takes to water. This was the beginning of a friendship which would result in Elizabeth spending her honeymoon at Mrs. Greville's Surrey house, and ended only when the older woman died in 1942.

Because Maggie Greville had such a close friendship with Elizabeth, it is worth looking at the sort of person she was. Harold Nicholson called her that 'fat slug filled with venom', while Cecil Beaton described her as a 'galumphing, greedy, snobbish old toad who watered her chops at the sight of royalty.' She was universally loathed in Society, though it says little for the many socialites and eminences whom she entertained that they beat a path to her door despite the way they felt about her. This was largely because she was a lavish hostess who ensured that her every gathering possessed a sprinkling of royalty and the grandest names in the land to accompany the finest wines and most exquisite cuisine, so even her detractors failed to resist the benefits of an association with her.

She lived in some splendour at Polesden Lacey in Surrey. Once the home of the 19th century author and MP Richard Brindsley Sheridan, by the time Elizabeth and Bertie spent their honeymoon there it bore scant resemblance to the 19th century edifice which had once stood on the site. In 1921, Maggie Greville rebuilt the house so that it was the last word in Edwardian splendour. It contained such new-fangled luxuries as en suite bathrooms and central heating, and possessed the 'air of the Ritz', to quote Margaret, Duchess of Argyll. Indeed it was known to possess all the conveniences of a five-star hotel, and people fell over themselves to stay there, even though they were usually rude about their hostess afterwards. And often during the visit, as my stepmother-in-law observed, pointing out that such conduct might have been inexcusable generally, but was considered both acceptable and understandable because everyone acknowledged that Maggie Greville was 'dreadful'.

Dreadful or not, she possessed an indomitable character and this, together with her antecedents, was the secret of her tremendous worldly success. Born Margaret Helen Anderson in 1863, she was the natural daughter of

William McEwan, a multimillionaire brewer and art collector, and his housekeeper, Helen Anderson. Because Mrs. Anderson was married to one William Anderson, Maggie was technically legitimate. She was raised to be a lady, though being a known 'jacket' was an unavoidable preventative to success in the circles to which they aspired. Despite her father's millions, this remained the case until her mother had the good fortune to be widowed when Maggie was in her early twenties. William McEwan then married his housekeeper/mistress in 1885, and now that there was a 'legitimate' link between the vastly rich brewer and his former housekeeper's daughter, the door to acceptability cracked open a smidgen.

Doubtless it would have stayed right where it was, had William McEwan not kicked it open with the force that his money, personality, and perspicacity provided. Knowing that the only way he and his family could appease their – really Maggie's – hunger for social recognition was by throwing his money around, he started to do precisely that. First, he got himself elected the Liberal Member of Parliament for Edinburgh Central. (This was a time when elections were bought rather than won.) Then he managed, with the offer of a vast dowry, to marry off the fat and unappealing Maggie to the Hon. Ronald Henry Fulke Greville, son and heir of the 2nd Lord Greville and the 4th Duke of Montrose's daughter, Lady Beatrice Violet Graham. Although the Grevilles were only collaterals of the vastly rich and very grand Earls of Warwick, owners of Shakespeare's fairest castle in the land, Warwick Castle, they were nevertheless fully-fledged aristocrats. Mr. and Mrs. William McEwan and their daughter, the Hon. Mrs. Ronald Greville, had now indubitably arrived.

William McEwan, however, was not one of the richest men in Britain by accident. He had brains and he had a talent for achievement, and he now set about elevating his family further, by funding, to the tune of £115,000, the construction of McEwan Hall at Edinburgh University. When it was completed in 1897, he was presented with an honorary doctorate and given the Freedom of the City of Edinburgh. He stood down as an MP in 1900, but was made a Privy Councillor in 1907. This gave him the right to be addressed as The Right Honourable William McEwan. He was content with this title alone, for he was offered a peerage to accompany his new appointment, but declined it. He had no sons and his only daughter would become the third Lady Greville when her husband succeeded to the barony, so a peerage of his own seemed unnecessary.

One wonders if he would have been so quick to refuse the honour which his philanthropy had earned him had he been able to look into the future. Greville died of pneumonia in 1908, before he had a chance to become a lord, and Maggie was now condemned to live out her life as a mere honourable. Although she was made a dame in 1922, thanks to the intercession of her good friend Queen Mary, this was not an aristocratic title, and she continued to be known socially by her married name.

When she died in 1942, Maggie Greville left her jewels to Elizabeth. These included a stunning Bucheron diamond and ruby tiara and necklace, and the five-strand diamond necklace, once belonging to Marie Antoinette, which was more 'important' than anything Elizabeth or any of her relations had hitherto owned personally. Mag the Hag, as she was sometimes called by her detractors, also left Princess Margaret the then generous sum of £20,000, and the exiled Queen Victoria Eugenie of Spain a much-needed £25,000.

A fortnight after Maggie Greville's party for Bertie's twenty-fifth birthday, Elizabeth found a present from Bertie under the Christmas tree. It was a token, a starter present rather than anything valuable, but its very existence lent it significance nevertheless. She promptly wrote to thank him for the little box 'a thousand times.'[35] More modest thanks, of course, wouldn't do, not when one was dealing with a prince whom one intended to keep in one's life forever, despite finding him almost repellent, as she told Helen Cecil. How else would he know how marvellous she was, how overflowing with the milk of human kindness, how worthwhile she was of an ongoing royal friendship, unless she pulled out all the stops and was full-tilt effusive?

As more than one person who knew her over the years observed privately, Elizabeth flattered not with praise, but with effusiveness, and my own personal observation of her social demeanour concurs with that. This technique, of course, was clever, very clever indeed, and very effective too, for there are few people in the world who can resist such an onslaught of ostensible positivity, especially when they want to believe that the protagonist is being sincere.

The year ended with a visit from James Stuart, who dropped in to see Elizabeth. She informed Beryl that 'he is an angel, and I should like you to see him,' indicating that whatever else she felt about poor Bertie, who spat out his words 200 to the dozen, the man who still had possession of her heart was his heartthrob equerry. Frustratingly for Elizabeth, however, he was no nearer making a declaration of intent than he had ever been, and she must have felt rather dispirited and been glad to see the back of a year that had failed to bring her the marriage she wanted: whether as Princess of Wales or Lady Elizabeth Stuart. Moreover, 1920 had seen the Strathmores' fortunes reduced. Not only had the family had to leave St. James's Square, but Claude, feeling the pinch, had also taken the unfortunate decision to dismantle Gibside House rather than let it out again. This was a real error of judgement which would cost the family a major loss down the line, for he stripped the magnificent Bowes ancestral home near Gateshead in Durham of all its treasures – even its fireplaces – shipped everything of value to Glamis, and left only a shell, which still stands in eloquent if valueless testimony to the valuable stately home it once was.

New Years often signify new starts, and so it proved in Elizabeth's case. Bertie wrote to ask if he could come and see her, so she replied, asking him to lunch at St. Paul's Walden Bury on 17th January, 1921. By this time she knew incontrovertibly that he was interested in her, and she was canny enough to ask him to lunch *à deux*. Cleverly, she wrote that 'you see my mother has been very ill, and she and I are really only having a sort of picnic down here by ourselves.'[36] After a suitable display of feminine modesty, during which she expressed being 'so afraid you would be bored to tears' by seeing her alone, when she knew only too well that that was exactly what he was angling for, she expressed her joy at the possibility of seeing him by stating that it 'would be delightful though if you are sure you wouldn't mind not having a large luncheon party' to come down to.[37]

'My brother was a nincompoop, and Elizabeth had him wrapped around her little finger,' the Duke of Windsor often said. That may have been so, but this letter nevertheless offers a vignette into why Bertie was so enchanted by her. She was enchanting, if you liked the barrage of charm with which she gunned her way through life. An arch denialist who couched her supreme confidence in a fetching show of self-denigrating modesty, even when she was giving Bertie directions she did so with all guns ablaze. 'Keep to the right all the way, till you come to a tumbledown old white gate on the left. Then go up a bumpy road full of holes, and eventually reach an even more tumbledown old house, and a tumbledown little person waiting on the doorstep – which will be ME!!!'[38]

Significantly, Elizabeth signed off formally, with the 'I am Sir, Yours sincerely, Elizabeth Lyon' that shows that they were not yet on first name terms. He was still firstly Your Royal Highness and a curtsey, followed by a plethora of Sirs but no Berties, for he had not yet invited that mark of familiarity which would indicate that she had entered the inner periphery.

Three weeks later, Elizabeth and Bertie saw each other again when she was a bridesmaid at her friend Helen Cecil's wedding to the King's Assistant Private Secretary Alec Hardinge. This was a relaxed occasion for everyone with the possible exception of Elizabeth, who had to share bridesmaids' duties with her friends Diamond Hardinge and Doris Lennox-Gordon but also her *bête noire*, Mollie Lascelles. Despite that drawback, it was a glittering affair, with the King and Queen in attendance as well as Princess

Mary and Bertie. It was on that occasion that Bertie seems to have crossed the Rubicon. Right after the wedding, he told his parents that he would like to propose to Elizabeth. Knowing that her lady-in-waiting was a close friend and neighbour of Elizabeth's mother, Queen Mary checked with Mabell Airlie, who was able to reassure both her and, even more importantly the King, that Elizabeth was not only an absolute 'angel' but also undeniably old-fashioned.

George V doubtless drank in this information as if it were Ambrosia, for he absolutely loathed anything modern. He had even ordered Queen Mary to lower her hemline when she had raised it to show a suggestion of ankle after skirts started to rise. He had also forbidden her from altering her archetypally Victorian hairstyle when she had been daring enough to leave off the tightly-curled false fringe which was so integral to the way ladies had worn their hair when Grandmama England had sat on the throne. She was just about the only woman in England who still wore the 'stays' which pinched in the waist and moulded the bosom so that she resembled a Boldini portrait.

Because one of the cornerstones of Queen Mary's beliefs was that everyone, herself included, had to follow the lead of the monarch blindly, she too was reassured by the welcome news of Elizabeth being old-fashioned. This provided a welcome postponement of the day when they might have to deal with one of those modern 'gels' who painted their faces and nails and, worse, were slim sleek models of modernity like Freda Dudley Ward and Sheila Loughborough. But what above all else made Elizabeth acceptable to Queen Mary was that she possessed royal blood. She was descended from King Robert II of Scotland, from the 11th century King of Ireland, Brian Boru, and from the first Tudor King of England, Henry VII. She was not just an aristocrat. She was an aristocrat of royal descent, which made her very nearly *one of us*.

Despite being so buttoned-up that she was an exemplar for repressiveness, Queen Mary was sensible. Now that this jewel had been dropped in her lap, she did not intend to discourage a potential union by interfering. So she delegated Mabell Airlie to act as the 'go-between'.[39]

Events were now moving rapidly. Eight days after the Hardinges' wedding, Mabell Airlie had Bertie and Elizabeth's mother for tea at her flat at 56 Ashley Gardens in the shadow of Westminster Cathedral. With green lights flashing from all quarters, Bertie proposed himself for lunch at St. Paul's Walden Bury eleven days later. Elizabeth can have had no doubt that Bertie was building up a head of steam with a self-evident objective, and she wrote to him in as skittish and kittenish a manner as she had done previously, and indeed did with all the men she flirted with. Once more assuring him that they would be lunching *à deux*, she informed him that there were no servants but the cook, so 'if you come to luncheon there will be no one to wait on us! So if you have something more amusing to do, please don't worry to come! Otherwise if you don't mind having no servants & things, do come!'[40]

Although Bertie found the mixed messages entrancing, one can well see why a more earthy and self-confident charmer, like James Stuart or David, Prince of Wales, found the whole rigmarole unsexy.

Sexy or not, Bertie declared his feelings in the way men throughout the ages always have. Although Elizabeth's various biographers have consistently claimed that this declaration was a proposal of marriage, according to the Duke of Windsor, whose account was based upon what his younger brother told him, Bertie did not actually propose. Rather, he tried to kiss Elizabeth properly, the way men kiss girls whom they fancy, but Elizabeth recoiled. This unexpected reaction threw the both of them into a maelstrom of confusion and embarrassment, he because he was terrified that he might have blotted his copy with the 'rare' and 'patrician' 'flower' he was so keen on, she because she did not want to alienate him. She wrote him a letter which makes it clear that the Duke of Windsor's version has to be the correct one, saying, 'Dear Prince Bertie, I must write one line to say how <u>dreadfully</u> sorry I am about yesterday. It makes me miserable to think of it – you have been so <u>very</u> nice about it all – please do forgive me.' She then shows how eager she is to continue the relationship. 'Anyway we can be good friends can't we? Please do look on me as one. I shall never say anything about our talks I promise you – and nobody need ever know. I thought I must write this short letter to try and tell you <u>how</u> sorry I am. Yours very sincerely, Elizabeth.'[41]

Although Claude Strathmore might have told Robert Sencourt, 'If there is one thing I have determined for my children, it is that they shall never have any post about the Court,' his wife Cecilia had entirely different objectives. 'Everyone in Scotland has always said that she was determined that Elizabeth would marry into the Royal Family. The Duke (of Windsor) said so too,' Margaret, Duchess of Argyll told me. Since she got her information directly from the former Prince of Wales and King himself, this was not idle gossip.

'Mothers like Lady Strathmore operate by stealth,' Hugo Vickers noted in his 2005 biography of Elizabeth, going on to opine that she 'was determined that Elizabeth would remain single until she accepted her royal suitor.' He makes the valid point that in 'those days parents still controlled the fate of their daughters.' What he does not say, possibly because he did not know it – or if he did, he was reluctant to jeopardise future invitations to events like the Garter Ceremony, which he likes attending every year – is that Elizabeth's objective was David, not Bertie, irrespective of what her mother's might have been.

The evidence of Elizabeth and Bertie's courtship suggests strongly that mother and daughter did indeed function as a team, though to what extent has to remain open to question. In *The Royal Marriages* (1993), I quote the Duke of Windsor saying to the author Michael Thornton, 'She conceived the idea of marrying me. I liked her. She was great fun, I did not find her in the least appealing in that way. But there was no doubt about it. It was me she wanted to marry.' He also used to call Cecilia 'that old dragon' and 'Cookie's ambitious mother', meaningfully fingering quotation marks as he mouthed the last word to imply that Lady Strathmore had not given birth to her.

The two mothers and their go-between now swung into action, Queen Mary and Mabell Airlie functioning exclusively on behalf of Bertie, irrespective of whether Cecilia was as well. At Mabell's behest, Cecilia wrote to Bertie, telling him 'how truly grieved we are that this little romance has come to an end.'[42] She then wrote to Mabell, stating 'I do hope the Queen is not very much annoyed with E. & me, altho' it wd be quite natural that she shd be, but I shd be so unhappy to cause her any worry in her strenuous life. I hope "he" will find a very nice wife, who will make him happy – as between you & me, I feel he will be "made or marred" by his wife.' She also mentioned how 'I also suggested the alternative reason he might give to his Father, in case he had not spoken about it.'[43]

Since Cecilia did not specify what that was, the reasonable assumption to make is that the two women had cooked up an alternative scenario in case George V should be outraged at Elizabeth's rebuttal of Bertie's proposition. The King was well known to take himself and his royal status extremely seriously indeed. He brooked no opposition where his perception of royal dignity was concerned, and was moreover known to have an explosive temper. The two women were therefore right to be concerned about the way he would take the news that Elizabeth had brought Bertie's horse tumbling down at the first fence. Nevertheless, events would show that George V was so painfully aware of Bertie's inadequacies that it was only after Queen Mary started to rebel at Elizabeth's treatment of their son that he objected to the wringer Elizabeth now proceeded to put the young man through.

Nor was Queen Mary put out at this juncture. She even asked Cecilia to tea at Buckingham Palace. Presumably everyone was encouraged by the fact that the not-quite-lovebirds continued to correspond with each other. Had Bertie's elder brother David been less loving and loyal, with a weaker code of honour, they might have been shuddering rather than hoping.

In May 1921, with Cecilia's likely backing, Elizabeth showed her ambitious hand when she was infiltrated, for the second time in her life, into a royal gathering to which she had no genuine right of attendance. The Prince of Wales was on one of his goodwill tours, this time in the provinces of England. In his capacity as Duke of Cornwall, he was touring the Duchy of Cornwall and was due to stay with the Keeper of his Privy Seal, the 21st Lord Clinton, for two days at his house at Bicton in Devon. Lord and Lady Clinton's daughter Fenella was married to Elizabeth's brother Jock Bowes Lyon, and the mere fact that Elizabeth was asked to come for the duration of the Prince of Wales's stay suggests a level of family complicity. This supports the Duke of Windsor's contention that Elizabeth and her mother had their cap set for him, not for Bertie. It is unlikely that the Clintons would have been asking Elizabeth to stay to entertain the elder brother a few weeks after she had spurned the supposed proposal of the younger, or indeed if they believed that Bertie was really pressing his suit. Such conduct would have been ungentlemanly and unladylike, and people like the Clintons would never have behaved in an unseemly manner where the royals were concerned, especially when Lord Clinton was assiduous in executing the duties he had 'about the Court'. The greatest fear of socially aware aristocrats like him was to be cast beyond the royal pale, and if ever anything warranted ejection, it would have been assisting the pursuit of the senior brother when the junior was known to be desperately in love with the girl in question.

Elizabeth showed that Stephen Tennant might well have had a point when he accused her of being 'hard as nails' and a 'schemer', for she was untroubled by the possible human ramifications in the event that her ambitions vis-à-vis David should be realised at Bertie's expense. According to her, it was a thoroughly enjoyable visit, and she certainly used the occasion to sparkle and sympathise as only she could. While the 'Prince was away all day working hard, & only got back at tea time – he does have a hellish life – that's the only word for it,' she and the others 'lazed about, & occasionally did a few official Prince of Wales things and had great fun.'[44]

According to David, Elizabeth again made it clear to him that the brother she was interested in was him. She said 'something to the effect that there was only one man in the world whom she liked enough to marry,' (a phrase which resonates with one she used when writing to Beryl on 2nd January, 1923) as she flashed him one of her brightest and coyest smiles and giggled deliciously, leaving him in no doubt about whom she was speaking. Decades later, he told Margaret Duchess of Argyll that he was 'so stunned' that he was rendered 'speechless'. Not because he was surprised that she was making it so obvious that she was interested in him – she had made this plain ever since they had first met – but because she ought to have known that his brother confided in him.

According to the Duke of Windsor's reasoning, she came from a close-knit family. She knew that he and his brother were close, so cannot have supposed that he was not privy to Bertie's embarrassment when she had spurned his advances. Maybe she did not think it peculiar that he would be discomfited by the woman his brother wanted making advances to him, but he put a higher premium on the loyalty he had to his brother, so moved off without responding at all. With hindsight, he would 'come to regret not having said something then and there.' At the time, however, he thought that if ever there was an occasion when a tactical retreat into silence was called for, it was this. So he ignored her approach, and in so doing, set up two undesirable scenarios for the future. The first was that Elizabeth continued to flirt with him in the hope that he would take an interest in her over and beyond that which he did, and the second was that he and the woman he married would become the targets for her 'pathological jealousy'.

A pattern was now being set to this three-cornered hat. While David tried to hang back from Elizabeth as discreetly as he could, without causing offence ('I liked her. She was wonderful company. And there was always the possibility that she might end up with Bertie if she couldn't get me'), and Elizabeth tried to bedazzle him every time their paths crossed, Bertie was 'oblivious' to Elizabeth's attempts to charm his elder brother. This was not necessarily because Bertie was a 'nincompoop' or that he trusted his brother and Elizabeth so much, though he did. Like Elizabeth, he had a jealous streak, and would later on make a huge fuss over her flirting with Kenneth (later Lord) Clark (of *Civilisation* fame). At this time, however, Bertie was distracted because he was having an affair with the musical star Evelyn Laye, having already had one with the actress Phyllis Monkman. Noel Coward claimed that he worshipped 'Boo', as she was known by one and all, 'as if she were some sort of goddess.' He found such adoration 'very peculiar' and Helen Hardinge, confirming that Bertie was 'more than a little in love with Evelyn Laye', said Elizabeth later on had an 'amused acceptance' of Bertie's adoration for the woman she called 'your girlfriend'.[45] Others who knew both women said that Elizabeth was actually 'grateful to Boo' as her very 'existence' made it possible for her to marry Bertie. And easier thereafter to settle into her royal role.

Bertie met Boo, whom I first encountered in St. George's Nursing Home in the early nineties when she was living there along with Margaret, Duchess of Argyll, in the spring of 1920, when he went to see the musical revue *Shop Girl*. She was only four weeks older than Elizabeth, and infinitely better looking. They began an affair. Doubtless mindful of how his father had interceded to end his affair with Sheila, and being aware of the constant pressure their father had been exerting upon David to 'get rid of the lacemaker's daughter', as King George V called Freda Dudley Ward, Bertie and Boo were admirably discreet. Of course, there was no question of the Duke of York marrying an actress, so each party to the affair knew that it had its limits. But they seemed to be happy with them, and would indeed behave with such exemplary discretion throughout, that there can be no doubt as to the bedrock of genuine affection underscoring their relationship.

Throughout that summer of 1921, the King and Queen might have been in the dark where their younger son's mistress was concerned, but they were not where David's was. He was creating what his father regarded as a scandal by refusing to give up Freda, so the King and Queen turned their attention to their younger, and more responsive, son, in the hope that a marriage could be 'encouraged'. Bertie and Elizabeth were still corresponding regularly. They still continued to meet at various dances or to play tennis together. Unsurprisingly, with each of them having their eyes trained elsewhere, their relationship was jogging along inconclusively.

Queen Mary, oblivious to the fact that Elizabeth had been playing a double game with her two elder sons, believed that her sole interest was in Bertie's equerry. Being a proactive character who made no bones about asking for whatever it was that took her fancy, whether it was a stranger's Fabergé egg or portrait of a preceding king or queen of England, Queen Mary decided that the time had come for decisive action. She therefore informed Mabell Airlie that she was coming to stay with her early in September. Arriving at Airlie Castle on the 5th, she ensured that Claude Strathmore and Elizabeth came over for tea – all the better to inspect the 'gel' herself and see what – if anything at all – 'could be done with her'. On the 9th, Claude had Queen Mary and Lady Airlie over for lunch. Because Cecilia was ill, Elizabeth 'filled her mother's place as hostess so charmingly that the Queen was more than ever convinced that this was "the one girl who could make Bertie happy,"' according to Mabell Airlie.[46]

Although Queen Mary then declared that 'I shall say nothing to either of them. Mothers should never meddle in their children's love affairs,' she proved herself to be as great a disclaimer and denier as Elizabeth by doing exactly the opposite. First, however, she gave them a chance to sort things out amongst themselves. This they did as inconclusively as they had hitherto done everything else. Bertie came to shoot up at Glamis on the 24th of the month. Although Queen Mary wrote to him while he was there 'sending many messages to the Strathmores and E' in the touching belief that her active encouragement would tilt things in favour of something concrete like marriage, the best the Boo-Laye-distracted Bertie could come up with was two sweet and polite missives: One to his mother with a tepid, 'The more I see of her the more I like her,'[47] and the other to Elizabeth, stating, 'I did so love my time there, & hated having to leave you all on Friday night to come South.'[48]

Elizabeth had her distraction at this point aside from David, and it was somewhat more valid. Her mother was due to have an operation for what they thought was cancer, but the problem turned out, much to everyone's relief, to be a sizeable gallstone instead. Her love for and care of her mother touched Bertie, increasing his regard for her and developing a real channel between them, which they now pursued in letters. She needed the support of everyone surrounding her for whatever was happening in her life. He, on the other hand, was heartfeltedly sympathetic, as only people who are handicapped and have really suffered can be. As she poured out her anxieties about the mother she adored, and the efforts she was trying to make to fill her shoes, he responded with such genuine sympathy that she developed a new appreciation for how supportive he could be. Not enough to shift her focus away from the top position to the secondary one, but enough to write saying, 'Thank you again for your letter, it is <u>such</u> a help to have the sympathy of one's friends on these occasions.'[49]

If either of them could have seen into the future, they would have realised that this early establishment of mutual reliance would prove to be one of the cornerstones of their marriage, and explains why it became the success it was. In the present, however, they had to content themselves with the many opportunities which Cecilia's protracted recovery was giving Bertie to show Elizabeth what a sterling character he was. Rather than improving, Cecilia developed pleurisy, and after four weeks of tending to her mother while being responsible for the running of Glamis, the strain began to tell on the young woman, so their doctor recommended that she take a break in London. Bertie of course came to see her while she was there, confiding in her about the latest treatment he was receiving for his stammer, though avoiding any mention of Boo Laye, who remained a satisfying factor in his life. Despite this, Bertie needed a wife and Elizabeth a husband, and the course of events was deepening their relationship in ways that would ensure a successful future together, though neither of them was yet aware of it.

The downside of having an equerry, as Queen Mary was beginning to observe, is that wherever the royal is, so too is the equerry. While Elizabeth was in London, she also had a visit from James Stuart. He 'turned up and insisted on taking me to Euston, where he placed me in the train & stalked off! Rather funny,' she informed Beryl,[50] leading one to conclude that the

Duke of Windsor was indeed right when he said that her primary marital objective was him, not the Earl of Moray's third son, who seemed similarly unmoved when he came up to Glamis over the new year to tell Elizabeth goodbye. He had resigned his post as equerry, having been offered a job by Sir Sidney Greville, on behalf of Lord Cowdray, 'to go into the oil business as a learner at the production end in America, with a view to promotion to higher things after I was trained.'[51]

Queen Mary's hand was all over this offer. Greville had been a courtier to her father-in-law King Edward VII, her mother-in-law Queen Alexandra, her husband King George V and her eldest son the Prince of Wales. Lady Eva Dugdale, his sister, was one of her ladies-in-waiting. James Stuart himself told Sir Anthony Nutting that Queen Mary had arranged his shipment out of the country. 'That bitch Queen Mary, that cow, she ruined my life! I was in love with the Queen Mother, and she with me, but Queen Mary wanted her for the Duke of York.'[52]

It had clearly slipped James Stuart's mind that before heading for the oil fields of Oklahoma he stopped off in Canada to visit Lady Rachel Cavendish, whose father was then the Governor-General, and whom he would marry around the time Elizabeth married Bertie. Or that he had never once made a declaration of intent to Elizabeth when he could have done so. What was preventing him from proposing to her before his departure, except his lack of interest? One suspects his powers of recall would have been different, had Elizabeth ended up a notoriety, or even just another ha'penny earl's daughter married to a well-bred backwoodsman, instead of a queen consort. But, if the true events of history are invariably rewritten by the victors in a self-serving way, is it surprising that those with bit parts in the drama obfuscate just as comprehensively?

Whether James Stuart's absence made any real difference or not, the fact remains that, once he was out of the way, prospecting for the Pearson group of companies in Oklahoma and paying court to Rachel Cavendish, one of Elizabeth's distractions had been removed. David and Boo Laye still existed, but the formidable Queen knew nothing of either of these other distractions, and, having wielded the stick, she now brought out the carrot. The engagement of Princess Mary and Viscount Lascelles having just been announced, Queen Mary devised the strategy of using the occasion to entice Elizabeth into the royal web. While aristocratic drawing rooms throughout the land were buzzing with the rumour that the King and Queen had coerced their plain daughter into accepting the proposal, which had come about as a result of the viscount accepting a wager in his club to the effect that he could not get the princess, who was known to be 'sweet' on him, to marry him, Bertie was at pains to show Elizabeth that these stories were untrue. He wrote and told her that they had 'fixed it up themselves, and are frightfully happy.'[53] Meanwhile, Queen Mary, a firm believer in the seductive powers of the royal way of life, got Princess Mary to ask Elizabeth to be one of her bridesmaids, thus giving Elizabeth, as her biographer Elizabeth Longford would later observe, 'her first glimpse of what it was like to participate in a public royal event. With her flair for happiness, she could not but find it enjoyable.'[54]

This was a shrewd move from one ham to another. Queen Mary was a true publicity junkie who would ask where the press were if she arrived for an engagement to find no cameras clicking. She appreciated the value of public attention not only in terms of what it did for keeping public interest in the monarchy alive, but she also loved it personally, the way all true hams do. Elizabeth, whose theatricality and qualities as an actress were already being commented upon – and would increase with age – was a star already in her own narrow little constellation. She was patently aiming for a more universal one than any Earl of Strathmore could provide for her.

'One thing Queen Elizabeth understood was that there is a theatrical element to being a good royal. She was a wonderful actress and she turned her royal role into something far grander and more magnificent than it would have been in the hands of a less accomplished performer,' Julian Fellowes, the well-known actor, scriptwriter and Oscar/Emmy-winning author of such productions as *Gosford Park* and *Downton Abbey*, told me.

By introducing Elizabeth to the seductive lure of public approbation; by giving her a taste of the tremendous inflow of adulation which royals receive on public occasions, especially celebratory ones like weddings, Queen Mary was effectively saying, 'Here is the role of a lifetime if you want it.' What she didn't know was that Elizabeth had actually set her heart on a bigger role than Duchess of York. And the Prince of Wales's reluctance to elevate her to that position would prove to be an ongoing problem for the coming year.

Elizabeth and her mother will have been mindful of what an honour being asked to be a bridesmaid was, and how this one event would enhance Elizabeth and the family's prestige.

Between the invitation and the wedding itself, Queen Mary showed how interested she was, despite her disclaimers to the contrary, in the progress of her son's romance. She wrote to Bertie saying that she 'was longing to hear how Elizabeth had behaved' at the Atherstone Hunt Ball, which she had attended with him. Coming straight to the point, she asked her son 'whether she is beginning to thaw or not!'[55]

If Elizabeth was frozen where romance was concerned, she was not dispassionate otherwise. She was intensely good company largely because she had a flair for the dramatic as well as a good sense of humour, and she had the self-possession that all born actresses have naturally. Although she was a bag of nerves before the wedding – she had found it difficult to walk slowly up the aisle in high heels at the rehearsal – once the show had commenced, she found the experience itself intoxicating. She also thoroughly enjoyed the wedding breakfast at Buckingham Palace afterwards, relishing the pomp and circumstance of it all.

It is no exaggeration to say she had found her element, though not necessarily the vehicle to take her into it permanently. When Bertie did propose a week to the day after his sister's wedding, she was so taken aback – there had been no warning – that she blurted out that she couldn't possibly consider such a thing at this time. By his own account, he was, not surprisingly, 'depressed'[56] while she was as eager as ever to maintain her position inside the hallowed circle, writing, 'I do hope we can go on being friends, as it would be too sad if a happening like this should come between our friendship, and I don't see why it should, do you?'[57] Such *sang froid* takes nerves of steel, veins of ice, and a heart of stone – three traits which Elizabeth would be accused, time and time again, of possessing throughout her long life, though in fairness she was also capable of great kindness and there was no better friend to have if her interests coincided with yours.

When Queen Mary heard that her machinations had come to naught, she put a brave face on things and wrote to Cecilia saying that she and George V were 'much disappointed that the little "romance" has come to an end as we should so much have liked the connection with your family. My son feels very sad about it but he is quite good and sensible and they are to remain friends. I hope you and E. will not reproach yourselves in any way, no one can help their feelings & it was far better to be honest.' She signed off 'With my love to you and E. and many regrets.'[58]

During this period, Elizabeth was still corresponding with James Stuart as well as flashing David green lights whenever her path crossed his. This presented the heir to the throne with an ever-increasing quandary. How could he deflect the interest of the young woman his brother hoped to make his duchess, without spurning her rudely and causing offence in the process? He later said that he handled the situation by remaining 'actively passive' each time she made a remark he regarded as untoward, which might well have been the best way of dealing with such a tricky situation, but seems to have allowed her to continue to dream of future success in landing him.

In his 2005 Elizabeth biography, Hugo Vickers recounts the theory, which I first advanced in print in *The Royal Marriages* in 1993, that the reason why

Elizabeth was 'reluctant to accept the Duke of York' was that she preferred 'the Prince of Wales, a more glamorous prospect than his shy brother.' He states, 'There is some evidence for this. Even late in 1922, Elizabeth was still resisting the Duke, while in October there came an opportunity to test her chances with the Prince of Wales.'[59] This was at the coming out dance of the Earl and Countess of Pembroke's daughter Lady Patricia Herbert at Wilton House in Wiltshire. Amongst the houseguests were Elizabeth, her friend Rachel Cavendish, whose romance with James Stuart was going from strength to strength, Prince Serge Obolensky, who was 'friendly' – to use the old-fashioned term – with Sheila Loughborough, Elizabeth's childhood friend Lord David Cecil, and the Duke and Duchess of Sutherland. David had taken a hunting box at Easton Grey at nearby Malmesbury, and motored over with some friends for the dance. He fulfilled his duty to the daughter of the house, dancing with her, then was observed sitting out some of the dances with Elizabeth while the both of them laughed their heads off.[60] 'Such was the scene that there was every reason to suppose that romance might be in the air,' Vickers wrote.[61]

Undoubtedly, Elizabeth was tenacious, as her subsequent conduct throughout a long public life demonstrated. She was also canny, not much given to confidences where her innermost feelings and ambitions lay. The mere fact that she kept on stringing Bertie along, while playing for time with James Stuart and David, says that she was 'keeping her options' open until she got a better offer than Bertie was making her. Nevertheless, she continued to see her royal duke; continued to correspond with him; and continued to dance with him at the balls they attended, while he discreetly relieved his frustration with Boo Laye. This was a matter of indifference to Elizabeth, for she knew that the actress was no threat to her. He could never marry her, and all she needed to do was maintain their 'friendship' to keep him 'on the boil' in case she couldn't get the man she wanted, and had to settle for second best instead. Until such time as matters clarified themselves, life was for living, and Elizabeth continued to avail herself of the merry-go-round of social activities which made up the daily routine of an aristocrat's life: the balls, dances, and country house weekends. The riding, hunting, fishing, shooting. Royal Ascot, Henley, and the myriad other activities of the sybaritic existence she and her friends led.

In autumn, Queen Mary got wind of the fact that Elizabeth was stringing Bertie along, and doing so so cleverly that she was keeping his hopes up while dashing his expectations. She wrote him a kindly letter, praising him, and he, moved by her sentiments, replied that 'you have made me very happy telling me what you have, and I greatly appreciate it.'[62] She had heard that, far from keeping their distance the way they had promised to do, Elizabeth and her parents had been actively soliciting his company, entertaining Bertie to luncheon and to shooting weekends. Worse still, she was used to flirting with him so outrageously at the many dances and balls they were both asked to, that no other girl of suitable rank felt able to display any interest whatsoever in him. Matters came to a head at Maggie Greville's dinner dance on 13th December, when Elizabeth and Bertie had made such a spectacle of themselves that there was now open speculation as to how much longer the King and Queen would allow the public humiliation of their second son.

This situation was infuriating to Mary both as a mother and as a queen. Elizabeth was making a fool of her son publicly. Worse still, she was cleverly blocking all other prospects for Bertie. So she interceded once again, this time instructing Mabell Airlie to tell Cecilia that Elizabeth should not attend the Pytchley Ball 'as it is perhaps wiser for the sake of the young man as your letter written early in this year made it clear that nothing further could come of the friendship, to the parents' very deep regret.'[63]

There is no doubt that Queen Mary's intervention was decisive in drawing the merry dance which Elizabeth was embarked upon with the lovelorn Bertie to a close. No one can say with certainty whether Cecilia was colluding with her daughter. In his Elizabeth biography, Hugo Vickers, who did have good sources and clearly knew a lot more than he let on, suggests through the 2nd Viscount Stuart of Findhorn that Cecilia, being a friend of James Stuart's mother Lady Moray as well as of Rachel Cavendish's mother the Duchess of Devonshire, had had a hand in keeping Elizabeth's coast free for Bertie. Elizabeth's real sticking point, however, seems not to have been James Stuart, or even Bertie himself, but his position as the second son. 'She was ambitious,' the Duke of Windsor said. 'She wanted to marry me, not because she was in love with me or I with her, but because I was the Prince of Wales and would one day be King.' Indeed, he would later write to his mother complaining about his brother's 'ambitious wife', so there is little doubt as to the sincerity of his sentiments.

Queen Mary's 'request' that Elizabeth forgo the ball was a terrible warning to both mother and daughter. It was what Queen Mary herself would have called a 'shot across the bow'. Elizabeth's likely fate, if she tried to continue toying with this royal duke, was that his mother, their queen, would ensure that Elizabeth was ostracised. She would either receive no desirable invitations or, if she did, Queen Mary herself would intervene to ensure that Elizabeth was pressurised into forgoing them. Both women knew that queens had the power to throttle any socialite's social life. All Queen Mary needed to do was spread the word through her ladies-in-waiting and friends that the Strathmores and their daughter were now *personae non gratae*, for everyone to give them a wide berth. To women as socially ambitious as Cecilia and Elizabeth, this was a fate worse than death. It was a living death, and one, moreover, which would be observed by the whole of the world they really cared about: Society.

As Adolf Hitler would discover to his cost – calling Elizabeth the 'most dangerous woman in the world' – Elizabeth was not only clever, but also resourceful and indomitable. Faced with the prospect of a future without any royal prince in it, or indeed even much of a social life, she set about retrieving her situation. She had played for time. She had lost. Without social invitations and royal approval, there was no possibility of marrying David and becoming the Princess of Wales. Her route to royalty lay through the eye of one needle and one needle alone, and if she didn't move with haste, even that narrow access might be permanently blocked up. There was only one way to achieve her, and possibly her mother's, ambitions. She had to get the prince who was in love with her to propose again. And she had to accept him this time.

How Elizabeth set about it is instructive. She would have made a good assistant to Machiavelli. Her letters and conduct show why the Duke of Windsor called her 'second to none in intrigue since that other Monster of Glamis, Lady Macbeth.' She now set about retrieving the situation she had been creating for the last two years with all the skill she had deployed to keep Bertie at bay. She wrote him a letter on Christmas Day, playing upon his sympathetic streak and the love he had for her, while instilling a hope that she patently wished would result in another proposal of marriage. After telling him that she would respect his parents' wishes not to attend the ball, as she understood their point of view, she denied the undeniable and said that she had never intended to behave badly towards him. 'You know that, don't you?' she asked, her plaintiveness screaming from the page as she switched to praise: 'I think it is so nice of you to be such a wonderful friend to me, and I don't want you to regret it ever.' Showing the degree of self-confidence which made her irresistible to weaker personalities than her own, she then swung things in her favour by subtly criticising King George V and Queen Mary, accusing them of interfering in her life and Bertie's, despite the fact that the only thing which was bringing Bertie's torment to a conclusion was his parents' intervention through his mother. 'It is all very sad, and must be so annoying to you. We've had such fun these last few weeks,' she wrote before issuing the *coup de grâce* by appealing to his masculinity. Lapsing into the poor-little-me feminine role, she apologised for boring him with 'such a rambling and ill-expressed letter, but I feel I must tell you what I am going to do. Please tell me, have I done right? Yours in perplexity, Elizabeth.'[64]

Elizabeth had had Bertie wrapped around her little finger for the last two years. She would keep him there, as his brother David and other members of his family would subsequently say, for the remainder of his life. There is little doubt that she knew exactly what she was doing, and what the effect would be. As a classical illustration of the art of manipulating a man who loves you and whom you wish to push in a certain direction, this extremely well-expressed and to-the-point missive cannot be exceeded. And of course, it had the desired effect, as she doubtless knew it would. They had both been asked to the Countess of Leicester's dance at Holkham Hall three nights later. They knew it, but the King and Queen did not, so they were able to link up there and discuss his parents' opposition to the continuance of their relationship.

It takes little imagination, when reading the letters they now wrote to each other, to discern how Elizabeth was playing on Bertie's feelings and failings the way Gidon Kremer plays his Stradivarius. Before going to bed that night at nearby Sandringham, he wrote her, 'It is the limit the way other people mix themselves in things which do not concern them,' little realising that his parents' interference was the only thing that would drive Elizabeth into accepting him as a husband.[65]

He also suggested that Elizabeth visit Mabell Airlie 'and tell her exactly what great friends we are & I will do the same.'[66]

Reading between the lines, it is likely that Cecilia's great friend Mabell Airlie knew that, if she could be a successful matchmaker, all would end well with the King and Queen. Which indeed turned out to be the case.

The night after Bertie's return to London from Sandringham on 2nd January, 1923, he went on a double date with Elizabeth. His new equerry Captain Giles Sebright, whom the *Edinburgh Gazette* would subsequently list as being served with a bankruptcy notice on 12th March, 1926, and Lady Anne Cameron completed the quartet. After dining at Claridge's, they went to the theatre, before returning to the Mayfair hotel to dance. Elizabeth's wiles clearly paid dividends, because he proposed to her for the second time in their relationship before they left the hotel that night.

Time and again throughout her life, Elizabeth would display a talent for prevarication and procrastination. As her niece Margaret Rhodes observes in her memoir, *The Final Curtsey*, Elizabeth could not be hurried. Whether it was the threat of bombs raining down on them during an air raid at Windsor Castle, or something more mundane, such as accepting a proposal she had been angling for, she functioned at her own sweet pace. No one and nothing were permitted to alter that pace.

This stillness was both extremely passively aggressive and effective, for it forced everyone and everything to adjust their tempo to hers. In so doing, she silently asserted that their will was subservient to hers. This gave her a tremendous subliminal advantage in her negotiations with others, for, whether they were aware of it or not, once they had adjusted their speed to hers, they were actually declaring that they had surrendered their will to hers.

The truth of this is shown in the way Elizabeth reacted to the proposal she had encouraged Bertie to make. Having spent the last two years running rings around him, she was not about to accept it speedily. If she did so, she could lose advantages which tardiness might throw up. So she wrote him one of those marvellously manipulative, charm-imbued letters which were her specialty:

'It is so angelic of you to allow me plenty of time to think it over – I really do need it, as it takes so long to ponder these things, & this is so very important for us both. If in the end I come to the conclusion that it will be alright, well & good, but Prince Bertie, if I feel that I can't (& I will not marry you unless I am quite certain, for your own sake) then I shall go away & try not to see you again.'[67]

While Elizabeth was ostensibly pondering Bertie's proposal, a very peculiar thing happened. She had gone down to 'George' Gage's house at Firle Place for the Lewes Hunt Ball. Someone brought down the London evening papers and there, in the *Daily Star*, was an article announcing, 'Scottish Bride for Prince of Wales; Heir to the throne to wed Peer's daughter; an Official Announcement imminent…' for the engagement of David to 'the daughter of a well-known Scottish peer, who is the owner of castles both north and south of the Tweed.' This description fit Elizabeth and Elizabeth alone. 'We all bowed and bobbed and teased her, calling her "Ma'am". I am not sure that she enjoyed it. It couldn't be true, but how delighted everyone would be! She certainly has something on her mind,' Chips Channon recorded in his diary for 5th January, 1923.

If Elizabeth's diary is anything to go by, she herself was unmoved by the story, and had 'Great fun' at the Lewes Hunt Ball. She 'danced till 4 am, was home by 4:30 to eat biscuits and drink sherry, and retired at 5 am.'[68]

The existence of the article, written as it was at that time, and covering the ground it did, leads to the inescapable suspicion that Elizabeth herself had a hand in planting it. There were only three people who supposedly knew of Bertie's proposal. It would have been preposterous as well as self-defeating for either Bertie or Mabell Airlie to leak such a story. While Bertie did indeed confide in his brothers, the likelihood of any of them leaking it is even more remote. Certainly the last thing David wanted was to have his name publicly linked with the girl he had done his level best to escape from ever since he had met her, and who was now considering his brother's proposal of marriage.

Can Elizabeth have been naïve enough to suppose that a story linking her name to David's would manifest in the realisation of her secret dream? She certainly knew that Queen Mary had been engaged to King George V's older brother, the Duke of Clarence and Avondale, and had been 'reassigned' to the Duke of York after Clarence's unexpected and premature death on 14th January, 1892. Can she have really hoped that this story could have snowballed into the King and Queen strong-arming David into marrying her, to rescue her reputation now that they had been publicly linked, the way they were supposed to have coerced Princess Mary into marrying Lord Lascelles?

Elizabeth would later on show a disturbing propensity for intrigue, and for covering her tracks so well that she should have been called a phantom operative. Her brother David was as inclined to the covert as she was, and, in the absence of knowing when exactly he started acting in tandem with her, it would be folly to rule him out as an assistant in this instance. Moreover, at this point, she was neither the sophisticated nor worldly operator she would be by the time she reached her thirties.

Having had forty years' experience of how newspapers work, there is little doubt in my mind that there was one and only one possible source of the story. That was Elizabeth or someone acting on her behalf. Stories, especially ones as specific, timely and well-informed as the *Daily Star*'s, do not fall into newspapers' laps like manna from heaven. To paraphrase Freud, there are few coincidences in the newspaper world, but if Elizabeth was hoping to shift the focus away from Bertie onto David, this cack-handed story was doomed to failure. David himself was not prepared to become a feature in the public embarrassment of his beloved younger brother, or to permit Elizabeth's ambitions of a marriage with him to continue unimpeded, and, with his approval, the Royal Household issued a public denial which was rather more excoriating than denials of this sort usually were:

'A few days ago the *Daily Star* announced the forthcoming engagement of the Prince of Wales to an Italian Princess. Today the same journal states on what is claimed to be unquestionable authority that the formal announcement of His Royal Highness's engagement to a daughter of a Scottish peer will be made within the next two or three months. We are officially authorised to say that this report is as devoid of foundation as was the previous.'

Although the *Daily Star* story undoubtedly failed to fulfil the purpose of linking Elizabeth and David, it cannot be accounted a failure if there was another objective, as there might well have been. Elizabeth was only too aware that the King and Queen were moving to ostracise her, so the report, of an impending announcement of a marriage between Elizabeth and *any* member of the Royal Family, might have been a way of ratifying her suitability for royal rank. Even those with no gift for intrigue would have seen that one cannot leak a story that is correct in all respects without suspicion devolving upon one as the source. So replacing Bertie with David was an inspired way of covering her tracks, while achieving her true objective.

If the ratification of Elizabeth's suitability for a royal marriage was indeed the objective of the story, it was successful: eminently so. And it came not a moment too soon, for George V and Queen Mary were now thoroughly fed up with Elizabeth's antics and did not hesitate to say so. Writing to Mabell Airlie at the height of these dramas on 9th January, Mary thanked her lady-in-waiting for her intercession 'in this tiresome matter. The King and I quite understand from yr and Com: Greig's letters what is going on [i.e. Elizabeth pondering yet another of Bertie's proposals of marriage]. I confess now we hope nothing will come of it as we both feel ruffled at E's behaviour.'[69]

There, in black and white, is the incontrovertible proof that neither the King nor Queen any longer wanted Elizabeth to marry into their family.

There is little doubt that Mabell Airlie will have taken this dispiriting news back to Cecilia Strathmore, who will have understood, even if Elizabeth did not (which I am confident she did), that she was now being rendered unsuitable, due to her behaviour, for any royal marriage whatsoever. The window of opportunity which she had had for the last few years was now closing rapidly, and would soon lock altogether. When it did, it would never re-open. That was the royal way, and everyone concerned knew it.

Bertie now stepped in before the window slammed shut altogether. Shouldering as much of the blame as he could manage, he wrote to his mother, who was staying at Sandringham, apologising for having left her and his father with the impression that things had ended between Elizabeth and himself. Of course he knew only too well through Mabell Airlie and Louis Greig that both his parents were fully aware that things had not ended between them. He informed her that since November there had been a 'distinct change' in the way Elizabeth had been responding to him. He said that he had been pursuing this new dimension quietly and she had been responsive and charming 'in every way'. In other words, she had finally 'thawed', to use Queen Mary's word. At least enough for him to have confidence that she was viewing him as a man and not just as a friend. He recounted how he had proposed again, and how she had asked for time to give him a considered response. He asked for Queen Mary's permission to go to St. Paul's Walden Bury to hear the 'definite answer one way or the other' on Saturday which he was expecting, and expressed the confidence 'that you and Papa will give me your blessing if this all comes out right & I shall be very happy.' He said how aware he was that the endeavour had taken a very long time but felt sure he had taken the right approach in playing 'the waiting game' because did not believe Elizabeth's response would have been in the affirmative 'had I pressed her for an answer before now.'[70]

Having used his pen to keep the window from slamming shut with royal finality, at six that evening, Bertie drove the short distance from Buckingham Palace to Bruton Street in fashionable Mayfair, where Elizabeth and her parents had settled into a house more to her taste than their Eaton Square rental. She was also demonstrating how prescient Queen Mary had been in supposing that Elizabeth could be seduced by the royal show at the time of Princess Mary's wedding, for she was availing herself of all the opportunities her new-found celebrity afforded, and had spent the afternoon being 'photographed for Vogue'.[71] It is likely that she entertained Bertie, as they 'motored down to St. Paul's Walden'[72] with witty and amusing stories about her day at *Vogue*. Her letters show that she had a positive gift for making the most dull occasions amusing, and that this alchemical gift extended to boosting her stock under the guise of modest self-denigration.

The official version of the Elizabeth/Bertie saga is that she found it difficult to choose between her suitors, 'not because she was by nature flirtatious, but on the contrary, because she felt that marriage was desperately important and irrevocable,' as Lady Cynthia Colville put it with Elizabeth's express approval on page 128 of *Crowded Life*. Another string to the official bow, frequently promulgated by the many authors who wrote about her during her lifetime, was that Elizabeth was so high-minded and morally pure that she could not possibly contemplate matrimony with any man except one who brought similar spotlessness to their union. All this cant might have been necessary to cover up her delays and the ambitions behind them, as well as Bertie's perfectly normal experience with other women, but it did not alter the record. Elizabeth's diary and the Glamis archives tell their own story, and it is not one which enhances Elizabeth's reputation for softness and sweetness. On the other hand, it does show how confident she was. Tantalising Bertie for as long as she possibly could, safe in the knowledge that she would suffer no adverse consequences, she persisted even at this late stage in keeping him waiting for an answer when it was obvious that she knew what the answer was going to be. This was a subtle form of cruelty, a characteristic of hers to which writers such as Sally Innes have previously alluded. Yet there is no doubt from an examination of her correspondence and actions, both before and after this period, that she knew that she would accept him. Indeed, that she had angled assiduously to get them to the very point they were now at. Rather than show some empathy and release him from the misery of uncertainty, however, she demonstrated why her brother-in-law David would say that 'she had ice in her veins' or friends like Stephen Tennant would accuse her of being cold, hard and unfeeling beneath the charm and bonhomie.

The record shows that on the Saturday morning of 13th January, 1923, Elizabeth arose at the customarily late hour she invariably kept. After breakfasting at 10:30, she and Bertie went for a walk. They had lunch together, then joined her father to saw wood, which the poor prince, still on tenterhooks, 'sawed hard.'[73] Proving the maxim that life at country houses revolves around food, they came back inside for tea. After tea they talked 'for hours', and, after stating that she had 'decided to wait a little', expressed the 'hope I am not behaving badly' when she was far too intelligent to suppose that she was doing anything else. But Elizabeth was a natural dominatrix, a narcissist who required adoration and got a real buzz out of people prostrating themselves before her, to paraphrase the Duke of Windsor's opinion of his sister-in-law's character. And she had found herself an ideal submissive in Bertie. He was hungry for the love of a woman whom he could worship but who would push him away the way his mother had always done. Although the Duke of Windsor would not spot the similarity between his psychological make-up and that of his brother, it was obvious, listening to stories about their respective marriages, that both men on one level replicated with their wives the cold and emotionally-distant but nevertheless supportive relationship they had with their mother. And, of course, Elizabeth was hardly going to deprive herself of the pleasure, or Bertie of the pain, of cutting short the waiting game, the way any woman with true empathy for a man she loved would have done. So he went to bed having to spend yet another night ruminating on the possibility that she might, even at this late stage, refuse him.

Sunday might have been a day of rest, but not for the anxious prince, whom Elizabeth could not, would not, let off the hook she had pinned him upon. After breakfast she and Bertie sat and talked till half past twelve. One shudders to think how much she was enjoying this exercise, and how anxious he was as she then suggested a walk in the 'enchanted wood.' They returned in time for lunch, after which there was another 'long walk' followed by 'long talks after tea & dinner'. We know that he spent the whole time imploring her to marry him, and she spent the whole time forcing him to beg, because her mother has left an account of how Elizabeth had Bertie proposing 'continuously until Sunday night, when she said Yes at 11.30!!' 'Now she is absolutely happy – & he is radiant.'[74]

The following morning an ecstatic Bertie drove the woman he had so long waited for back to London. After dropping her home and returning to his rooms at the Palace, he picked her up again to take her to lunch with his sister Mary and her viscount at their London house, Chesterfield House in Mayfair. David dropped in to congratulate them and took Elizabeth back home while Bertie and Louis Greig drove to Sandringham to inform his parents. That night George V wrote in his diary, 'Bertie with Greig arrived after tea and informed us that he was engaged to Elizabeth Bowes Lyon, to which we gladly gave our consent. I trust they will be very happy.'

The Making of a Star

Chapter Five

No sooner was the engagement announced on 15th January, 1923, than the press congregated outside the Strathmore London house at 17 Bruton Street. Elizabeth now did something that horrified her future in-laws. She invited into the house and granted anodyne but chatty interviews, along the lines of Prince-Bertie-(that's-what everyone-calls-him-you-know)-is-wonderful-and-everyone-has-been-so-kind-to-me, to two Scottish journalists, one of whom was from the *Glasgow Herald*, the other from the Glamis local *Dundee Advertiser,* and to a third and rather more important English journalist: Charles Graves of the London *Evening News*. A gentleman by birth, his brother was the eminent author Robert Graves of *I, Claudius* and *Claudius the God* fame, and it is worth noting that her father himself provided a letter of introduction to his daughter when Graves first called at St. Paul's Walden Bury.

During the interviews, Elizabeth was refreshingly open, her down-to-earth delight in her engagement uncensored by reserve or pretentiousness. The two Scotsmen and Graves were completely charmed and left with the impression that she was a wonderful girl and would make a great addition to the Royal Family.

The following morning a jubilant Elizabeth read the 'Great headlines' and 'lots of rot',[1] chief of which was the *Dundee Advertiser* claim that in Forfarshire 'the news will contain little of the element of surprise', though they also made the sensible observation that the 'Duke, if nobody else, has reason to thank his stars that the war has been fought. Otherwise a dread convention of pre-war Royalty might have sent him to meet his fate in Germany instead of Strathmore.'

Although the Scots had to wait until the following day for the stories they filed to come off the presses, Charles Graves had the advantage of working for an evening newspaper. He rushed back to the Fleet Street offices of the *Evening News*, wrote up the story of this 'charming picture of English girlhood' whose eyes were 'alight with happiness' as 'she sat at a table stacked with congratulatory telegrams,' and the editor plastered this panegyric to Elizabeth's many qualities over the front pages of that very afternoon's newspaper.

This was a scoop of no mean order, heightened by Elizabeth's tantalising hint that she had refused Bertie's earlier proposals. Graves would later claim in his memoirs that the Palace tried to get her to retract the contents of the interview. It is to her credit that she refused to behave in such a dishonourable manner, though there is also the dimension that by providing such personal details, she was boosting her stock in the eyes of the world at the expense of Bertie's. Whether through honour or simple self-promoting vanity, the fact is that her refusal to succumb to Palace pressure was a wise move on her part, for she was laying down her marker with them: don't try to push me around, for you won't succeed.

Unsurprisingly, all the following morning's newspapers repeated the contents of the Graves interview as if it had been their own scoop. This had a snowball effect, with the result that Elizabeth was now much bigger news than she would have been had she been just another inaccessible fiancée. Overnight, she had become a celebrated personality.

This was hardly surprising. Never before had an actual or potential member of the Royal Family given a newspaper interview. By breaking new ground, Elizabeth not only showed how much she enjoyed the publicity that would hereafter be a feature of her life as a royal, but the positive press her actions resulted in would, many years later, be used as a recommendation for royals becoming more accessible to the press.

Contemporaneously, however, Elizabeth's accessibility was unprecedented. The reaction at Buckingham Palace was horror that anyone associated with the Royal Family would actually do something as *infra dig* as give interviews to the press of their own free will. Queen Mary herself was sufficiently annoyed to write in her diary how 'tiresome the newspaper people have been interviewing E., such a shame,'[2] and promptly got on to Mabell Airlie, who got on to Cecilia Strathmore, who got on to Elizabeth, that it was simply not done to blab to the press. Hereafter, she must abide by the royal rule of keeping her trap tightly shut.

For all the hullabaloo that the *Evening News* interview caused – the Scottish interviews, coming as they did the morning after the afternoon before, got lost in the shuffle, at least insofar as the Palace and Royal Family were concerned

– Elizabeth's interview with Charles Graves was the making of her where the press and public were concerned. This was because at that time few people in public life, and no royals, were portrayed as human beings, with personal attributes with which the readers of newspapers could identify. Whether they were charming, or well-intentioned, or charitable or even indiscreet, as she had been, was simply never commented upon. The fruit of their endeavours was the sole focus of the stories written about them, unless of course the rags were writing about scandals, in which case the focus shifted to their failings. These were usually on so much larger a scale than a humble clerk or omnibus driver could aspire to, that even then there was no identification with the subject of a story.

But the reports about Elizabeth, who was shown to possess human and appealing attributes, and to be refreshingly open about how much she was enjoying all the attention coming her way now that she was engaged to a royal duke – just as most of the readers would have felt – were exceptional and effective in projecting the image she would thereafter have: as a lovely, endearing, charming, agreeable, sweet-natured and real human being. This was a tremendous advantage, for people identify with public figures who have been humanised. If those figures are clever at playing up to their perceived image, such as Elizabeth would thereafter show that she was, they become immensely popular repositories for public affection. And they remain popular repositories as long as they maintain the façade, as Elizabeth and her successor in the affection stakes, Diana, Princess of Wales, did.

On the other hand, if a public figure has been dehumanised, even if it is through admiration because of outstanding beauty or some other rare attribute which takes her out of the human realm, the public does not identify with her. No matter how much she is revered, she is never beloved. Greta Garbo was the ideal example. Despite being the most celebrated movie star in the world, the public didn't mind seeing her suffer and die in her films. On the other hand, they would not accept a sad fate for lesser stars like June Allyson or Debbie Reynolds. This was because they were public sweethearts while Garbo, with her dehumanising ethereality and outstanding beauty, was too extraordinary to be anyone's sweetheart. And when her glittering career came to a premature end, there was far less sympathy shown for her than there would ordinarily have been for another star of her magnitude.

Fortunately for Elizabeth, her looks were more akin to Allyson and Reynolds than the extraordinary Garbo. Although at twenty-two she was pretty in a modest sort of way, she was ordinarily rather than outstandingly attractive. Bertie complemented her by being physically attractive in an equally representative manner, and since the public did not know anything about his disabilities, which knowledge would have helped to humanise him, by virtue of being a typical prince whose personal traits were a mystery to the public he would continue to remain something of a cardboard cut-out figure, whose primary purpose seemed to be as a foil for his charming and only-too-human wife.

Elizabeth must have been disappointed to learn that she was being silenced at the very beginning of her reign as the public's darling. Shawcross states in the official biography that 'Elizabeth herself, to judge from her diary, was both thrilled and appalled by the public interest.' As anyone who has been at the centre of a press storm will confirm – and I speak from personal as well as family experience – it is indeed nerve-wracking. So it is not the tremulousness that Elizabeth expressed which is the key to her deepest sentiments, but her plain joyousness once she became the cynosure of all eyes.

Although Elizabeth would not have known it at the time, Queen Mary also did her a favour by muzzling her. Silence really is golden if you want to retain the affections of an adoring public as you function in a royal or high-profile political role. Jackie Onassis herself told me that she had used Elizabeth's silence as a pattern for how best to maintain her own public image, and since this is a case of one of the 20th century's greatest public figures doffing her hat to another – and since Elizabeth would never have remained silent had wordlessness not been foisted upon her by Queen Mary – credit should be given where it is due for the formulation of an accidental but infallible technique.

Despite being condemned to speechlessness, Elizabeth was instantaneously such a figure of public interest that the press now followed her every move. Being the born actress that she was, she mimed what she could no longer convey verbally. Not for her any of the restraint and concealment of emotion which born royals were inculcated with from birth. She had been raised with the belief that she was a marvellous person for a variety of reasons, and she hammed it up as she proved that she was so effervescent, charming and outgoing, with a ready laugh and genuine wit, that her very companionability was a boon to any company she found herself in. She turned every task, no matter how mundane, like planting a tree, into an occasion of great fun, as her niece Margaret Rhodes observed in her memoirs, and as she injected some much-needed levity into the stultifying gloom that characterised life in the Court of George V, the press lapped up her antics.

Elizabeth could hardly have remained the luminary the press acknowledged she was if she had subsumed her wonderful personality beneath a mask of regal dignity. She understood that the only way she could remain the star she already was, was to show the public – *her* public – what a wonderful personality she had. In so doing, she would not only remain true to herself, and would not only bring enjoyment into her own life and that of others whose paths crossed hers, but would also retain the popularity which already mattered greatly to her.

Luckily for Elizabeth, she had Bertie's support. As Princess Louise, Duchess of Argyll would subsequently observe, one of the reasons why Bertie had been so keen to marry Elizabeth was that she and her family possessed a genuine and exceptional *joie de vivre*. This made being around them a real pleasure. As far as Bertie was concerned, if she brought joy into their public duties as well as their private lives, that was something to be encouraged, not discouraged.

Luckily for both Elizabeth and Bertie, King George V felt the same way. Despite being something of a martinet who was so obsessed with the detail of royalty that he scanned the newspapers and newsreels for photographs of his sons getting even trivia wrong on public occasions – which of course he then scolded them about, usually in writing so that a record exists – he was not immune to feminine wiles.

The King had a whole different side to his character than the one he projected as the irascible, duty-obsessed slaughterer of game and other animals, to include anyone who opposed his rigid concepts of what monarchy was all about. If the eminent author and commentator A.N. Wilson is to be believed, George V had an active sex life which did not include anything as overt as a mistress. Rather, he believed in safety in numbers and the discretion of professional ladies of the night. Although he had his favourites, no one was allowed to become so close that they would threaten the edifice of respectability which he had constructed around himself and his wife. In his own way, he was a devoted husband, even though a dullard who must have suffered from an undiagnosed personality disorder along the lines of Asperger's Syndrome or Obsessive Compulsiveness. He was rigid to the point of obsessiveness. He was pathologically punctual, and had to have his days mapped out to the last minute in a cycle of never-ending repetitiousness, which he might have found reassuring but everyone else, his children especially, found mind-numbingly dull, as their diaries confirm. He surrounded himself with the same faces day in, day out, year in, year out. He barked orders or talked at people rather than having conversations with them. One only needs to look at his childlike scrawl to see that he was neither intellectually gifted nor educationally capable. Nevertheless, he was conscientious in everything he did. Irrespective of whether he was indulging in his favourite pastime of shooting birds out of the sky, or tending to his stamp collection, which he did whenever the weather was too inclement for him to be outside (it is now one of the two or three most valuable stamp collections in the world, so his heirs have benefitted from it), or even dealing with his ministers of government and assisting them in flooding the House of Lords with so many new peers that they could implement a policy he personally disagreed with, George V fulfilled his responsibilities with exactitude. Even in his marital arrangements, his punctiliousness was more reminiscent of the bourgeoisie than the aristocracy or royalty. He and Mary slept together every night in the same bed, which was a highly unusual arrangement for a king and queen. The only other royal couple who also slept together as religiously as George and Mary was Louis XIV of France and his unfortunate queen, Maria Theresa of Spain. She had had to bear the public indignity of a succession of mistresses being paraded under her nose in front of the whole French court, including the exotic Athénaïs de Rochechouart de Mortemart. While Louis spent his afternoons in the company of the Marquise de Montespan, Queen Maria Theresa comforted herself with the knowledge that her husband would return to the marital bed each night, and would remain there until the morrow, again in emulation of the middle rather than the upper classes. Although Queen Mary had a similar consolation, she was spared the indignity of anyone knowing about George's private interests. But these showed that the King had a need for the feminine, and this clearly went beyond the merely sexual, for Elizabeth was quickly able to wrap him around her little finger the way she had already wrapped Bertie.

Her technique for winning over her future father-in-law was the same one she used on everyone else. She simply turned the full fusillade of her charms upon him. I remember observing Elizabeth doing the same thing to an old codger in the 1970s. By then she was in her seventies, so infinitely less appealing than she would have been at twenty-two. Nevertheless, it was a performance to behold. She was as flirtatious as any young woman confident in her allure. Without exactly fluttering her eyelashes, she batted them seductively. Although she sat up ramrod straight, she would sometimes withdraw provocatively with a gay laugh, her hands fluttering over her bosom, her head tilted to one side as if to say, 'You fascinate me.' A subtle study in perpetual motion, she would then change the pace, seductively leaning in as she adjusted the tilt of her head and the expression on her face. Those facial expressions, believe me, were artistry personified. She possessed the gift of articulating emotion in the subtlest of ways. Although the whole performance was ladled with a trowel, each aspect of it, her facial expressions especially were studies in suggestion as opposed to exaggeration. It was easy to see why she captivated men, because she had clearly set out to become the evocation of feminine allure.

Although such allure can be learnt, what cannot is the desire to employ it. Brooke Astor used to recount the story of a gala she attended at which the octogenarian Elizabeth was also a guest. As the evening dragged on and on, Elizabeth became bored and restless. She indicated that she wanted to leave. This would have been a 'social disaster' for the organisers, who appealed to the equally ancient and flirtatious Mrs. Astor to recommend a way of averting this shame. 'Have a few of the men take her for a stroll in the grounds,' she suggested. 'Well, they did that and the Queen Mum *loved* it and stayed the whole time. She wanted *attention*. And the attention of *men*. As soon as those men talked to her, took her for a walk, paid attention to her, the Queen Mum was happy.' And stayed to the very end of the evening.

Elizabeth 'used to flirt shamelessly with the old curmudgeon,' the Duke of Windsor told Freda Dudley Ward when he was the Prince of Wales and she his *maîtresse en titre,* explaining how Elizabeth had George V eating out of the palm of her hand. But she did not limit her charm offensive to her future father-in-law. She also turned her guns on Queen Mary and all the other members of the Royal Family, many of whom she met for the first time when she went to Sandringham on the Saturday following the announcement of her engagement.

Before Elizabeth had even arrived for this first visit to Sandringham, everyone could see the tremendous impact her charms were making. Two days before her arrival, she had posed for photographers. The press were hungry to feed the public new glimpses of the latest media star, and she in turn was eager to show the public what a delightful addition to the dour Royal Family this duchess-to-be was. This time, though, she had remained silent, in keeping with the Palace dictum that she could pose all she wanted, as long as she didn't speak. Naturally, all the following day's papers had been full of photographs of the 'smiling' royal fiancée, with adulatory comments which would ultimately prove to be far more effective in turning her into a mythical public figure than anything she herself could have come up with.

Elizabeth was due to leave for the weekend for Sandringham from Liverpool Street Station in the City of London with Bertie and her parents the Saturday after the announcement of her engagement. She arrived with her fiancé in his car, her parents following behind in a Daimler. Much to her delight, there were '[v]ast crowds there, & hundreds of photographers,' all of whom were rewarded with pictures of the smiling bride-to-be and her radiantly happy royal duke.[3]

If Elizabeth can have had any reservations about the choice she had made – there is no evidence to suggest that she ever possessed any – the wealth of attention which was now flooding her way must have washed them away. 'She loved attention and had to be the centre of attention at all times,' a variety of people including the Duke of Windsor, Margaret Duchess of Argyll and even her own daughter Princess Margaret said over the years. She also loved luxury, as all her biographers and many other people have confirmed. As she was led, with her royal duke and parents, to a special carriage that had been attached to the 11:50 train, she must have realised how sensible she had been to settle for second best. She would never be Princess of Wales and was not slated ever to be Queen of England, but she would hereafter have all her other ambitions fulfilled. Their very own carriage was then the ultimate in luxuriousness as a mode of travel, so different from the *Flying Scotsman* she and the other members of the Strathmore family were accustomed to. Only immensely rich families like the Buchanan-Jardines, who were successive Tai-Pans of the great Hong Kong trading company Jardine-Matheson along with their Keswick cousins, or senior royals such as she was due to become, travelled in such style. The King and Queen had laid on this treat for their future daughter-in-law and her parents, and as the party settled back in the well-upholstered seats, which were infinitely superior to anything First Class on the *Flying Scotsman* had to offer, they were also served a full luncheon by liveried footmen on proper plates. Although Elizabeth was not yet the sybarite she would subsequently become, this introduction to the luxuries which accompanied her new station in life must have been a welcome confirmation of the rightness of the decision she had made.

There is little doubt that Elizabeth was determined, before the train even pulled into the little station at Wolferton, which served the Sandringham Estate, that she would charm Bertie's parents the way she had been charming the press and public. She knew that she had very nearly scuppered her chances of marrying either David or Bertie. Queen Mary herself had said that neither she nor the King wanted a connection with Elizabeth, whose behaviour she had deplored. Of course, Elizabeth also knew that the King and Queen wanted their son's happiness, and that they had already reversed their interdict regarding her acceptability, otherwise they would not have given their consent to the marriage. But she had blotted her copy and she knew it.

She also knew just how to retrieve the situation. As Elizabeth would later say on many an occasion, 'My father-in-law's children were afraid of him, but I never was.' She now demonstrated to what extent she possessed fearless self-confidence. Rather than being daunted by an event that would have terrified or at least inhibited most people, even those with considerably more sophistication and experience than she possessed, Elizabeth 'came through with flying colours' what to anyone else would have been 'an ordeal not to be underestimated', to quote George VI's official biographer John Wheeler-Bennett[4] whose information came directly from Elizabeth herself.

The alacrity with which she charmed her future parents-in-law bears examination, because it provides an insight into the fundamentals of Elizabeth's character and personality. Not only did she possess self-confidence to an almost unimaginable extent. She also had a cool, detached serenity that allowed her to remain unruffled when everyone else around her was losing his or her nerve. These two characteristics, combined with her determination to prevail by winning the approbation of those she set out to conquer, made her 'irresistible'. That word was often used to describe her and, as it is one which adversaries like the Duke of Windsor and stalwarts like her niece Margaret Rhodes all used, we can conclude that hers was indeed such a potent personality that it was all but impossible to withstand.

Elizabeth proved the veracity of that statement before the end of her first day at Sandringham. Having arrived with Bertie, Claude and Cecilia at York House, the modestly-sized villa on the Sandringham Estate where George and Mary lived while his mother occupied the Big House nearby, she set out to win over everyone by being as charming and delightful as she could possibly be. This she did by being 'engaging and natural', as Queen Mary noted in her diary.[5] Both she and her husband wrote about how charming Elizabeth was, and George V went even further, recording that 'Bertie is a very lucky fellow,' and Elizabeth 'pretty.'[6]

The key to Elizabeth's desire to charm her parents-in-law-to-be lies in her upbringing. She was the product of a happy, harmonious family. She was also very spoilt. Emotionally reliant on her family – her mother especially – to an extent that only a cosseted, indulged child can be, she wanted as well as needed parental approval. Now that she was going to become the King and Queen's daughter-in-law, she aimed to replicate as closely as possible the harmonious relations she had had with her own parents. This was an ambitious as well as a tall order, but it was a lot shorter than anyone realised. Both the King and Queen were hungry for some external force to break the deadly, unremitting grind of royal family life: George because he had reached the stage where a delightful and amusing daughter-in-law would divert him and add much-needed levity to a stolid Court, and Mary because she had herself once been a lively and outgoing girl like Elizabeth. She had had to submerge her personality in her dull husband's, but the Mary of old still existed. She greatly appreciated Elizabeth's affectionate companionship, as she would tell many people, including her aunt by marriage Princess Louise, Duchess of Argyll, and her sister-in-law Princess Alice, Countess of Athlone. Later on, after the Abdication as well as before it, she would develop a healthy scepticism about certain aspects of her daughter-in-law's personality, in particular her intransigence and capacity for intrigue, but at this juncture both Mary and George took Elizabeth at face value. And liked what they saw.

On this, Elizabeth's first day at Sandringham, the King and Queen whisked their houseguests off for tea at the Big House, as Sandringham House was called. This was the start of an unforgettable few days in which Elizabeth and her parents would meet many of the world's most important royalties, as royals were then known. For people as socially ambitious as Elizabeth and Cecilia, this must have been like a dream come true, for these royalties would all soon become Elizabeth's relations. The experience must have been akin to a devout Christian waking up and discovering that he or she had become a part of Jesus and Mary's family.

The first personage they met was their hostess, Queen Alexandra, the King's mother. Virtually deaf, she found following conversations difficult, so articulated with sweeping 'Danish gestures', to quote Elizabeth. One of the most celebrated public figures of her age, Alexandra was revered for her beauty ('she was still beautiful', Elizabeth told Prince Charles in her old age) and elegance (upon which Elizabeth remained silent: their taste was diametrically opposite). She was also much admired for the élan with which she had handled her lecherous husband's many affairs. More important from Elizabeth's point of view, she would also prove to be an ideal role model of how an emotionally-needy woman could garner all the benefits of being an ostensibly loving and devoted wife and mother, while at the same time ensuring that her family did exactly what she pleased.

Thirteen years after being widowed, Alexandra still lived in the Big House. She saw no reason to vacate the vast and mostly-unused edifice for the smaller confines of York House, even though her son had a wife, six (then five after the death of Prince John in 1919) children, and a much larger Household as reigning sovereign of the world's greatest empire. Meanwhile, she, a mere dowager queen, lived in semi-solitary splendour with her ever-present bachelor Comptroller, Sir Dighton Probyn VC, her maid of honour, Charlotte Knollys, and her spinster daughter, Princess Victoria. And would continue to do so for the remainder of her life.

'Motherdear', as her children called her, was an exemplar of how a woman can use 'love' to maintain her power within the family circle. All her children did her bidding. Her daughter Victoria, whom Elizabeth was meeting properly for the first time – they had not really met at Princess Mary's wedding – was curious to see her future niece by marriage, and since she was tucked up in her sick-bed, Elizabeth was taken upstairs to meet this prematurely-aged fifty-five-year-old spinster. Her bitterness at having been condemned to a life of limbo as her mother's lifelong companion, when she could have been married, was evident to all.

However, she was George V's favourite sibling, and, as such, a power to be reckoned with. An 'absolute bitch' whose favourite pastime was to get her nephews in trouble with their father, according to the Duke of Windsor, she delighted in ruining everyone's good time. Once, on a boating holiday off the Italian coast, she deliberately thwarted Queen Mary's desire to explore the ruins at Pompeii, knowing that there would never be another chance. The only person she did not try to make as miserable as she herself was, was her brother. A philistine like her, he frequently joined her in mocking Queen Mary's artistic sensibilities; an exercise they found funny.

Waiting to welcome as well as to inspect Elizabeth was a veritable clutch of royal relations, all of whom spent a great deal of time at Sandringham, and would hereafter feature in her life to a lesser or greater extent, depending on how close in age they were to her. There was Queen Alexandra's lookalike but slightly less pretty sister Dagmar, better known as the Dowager Empress Marie Feodorovna of Russia, whose daughter, Grand Duchess Xenia, would become a great friend of Elizabeth's as well as a neighbour, when she was given Frogmore House on the Windsor Estate as a grace and favour house. And later on, when Xenia's son Prince Andrew's first wife was dying of cancer, Elizabeth would drop in on her most days. 'She really was very kind to her and to my father,' his daughter, Princess Olga, told me.

Although there was nothing wrong with the Dowager Empress Marie's hearing, she was nevertheless an even greater figure of pathos than her sister Alexandra. Indeed, in 1923 she was regarded as possibly the most tragic royal figure in existence. This was largely because of the tremendous reversal of fortune she had suffered in 1917. Overnight, she had gone from being the premiere lady of one of the greatest empires on earth (dowager empresses ranked before empress consorts in Russia) to virtually penniless. She was now dependent upon the favours of her sister, Alexandra, and her nephew, King Christian X of Denmark. He used to be annoyed by her lack of financial responsibility, and often sent servants to turn off the electric lights she kept ablaze in her section of the palace in Copenhagen. Once, to defy him, she had all the lights turned on, mindless of the tremendous expense electricity then was. She cannot have considered the penury of her nephew, relative to the vast wealth that the Romanovs had had in her day, but she was so elegant and gracious and glamorous that only those picking up the bills minded her antics. Minnie, as she was known in the family, occupied a world where unpleasant realities were dismissed, notwithstanding the fact that she had been politically astute and had warned her son against the influence of his wife Alexandra and Rasputin. She resolutely refused to accept that Nicholas II and his family had been executed by the Bolsheviks at Ekaterinburg, though she was more willing to accept that her younger son, the Grand Duke Michael, had been murdered. Possibly this was because he had not been Tsar, and the murder of a grand duke was so much more acceptable than regicide.

At this juncture, it is important to draw the reader's attention to an important distinction that has now arisen. In royal circles, sovereignty conferred literally sacred status upon its holders. While the death of any child might be sad, the death of a sovereign was something altogether more significant. This was, and is, a distinction that seems not to have received acknowledgement in the world at large. Yet it is fundamental in royal circles, and accounts for much that might seem inexplicable, even heartless.

Whatever her reasons for finding her son Michael's death easier to accept than Nicholas's, the Dowager Empress's antipathy to the Grand Duke's morganatic wife and son was inflexible. She never once received either Madame Brasova or Count George Brasov, even though he was a handsome and personable young man living in London while she was there. Since Elizabeth would later emulate such inhumane intransigence, it is worth noting the examples she found to lead the way. Also that Marie Feodorovna's haughty disdain of her daughter-in-law and grandson was not regarded in royal circles as regrettable, but admirable.

If the tragic glamour of the Dowager Empress appealed to Elizabeth's sense of the dramatic, so too did the two Cossack bodyguards who never left her side and slept outside her door every night, wherever she was, in rotating twelve-hour shifts.

Devoid of tragedy, but nevertheless glamorous, was another star of the royal constellation assembled to inspect Bertie's new fiancée. This was Queen Alexandra's youngest daughter, Queen Maud of Norway, a stylish woman who married an insignificant Danish prince named Carl for love, and then had the good fortune to become a queen when he was elected King Haakon VII of Norway in 1905. As athletic as Elizabeth and Bertie, Maud was an expert skier, whose figure remained perfect until her dying day in 1938. In 2005 there was an exhibition of her clothes at the Victoria and Albert Museum in London, which hinted at why such a sophisticate as Maud would have found Norway dull. She spent as much of her time as she could in England, at Appleton House, whose accessibility to Sandringham allowed her to use her childhood home as if it were still her own. Maud had a fascinating personal history which will have reverberated with Elizabeth and still reverberates politically in Norway even today, though that aspect of the tale is best covered elsewhere.

Rather less glamorous but with no skeletons in her closet was yet another royal relation, Maud's eldest sister, the splendidly-named Princess Royal, Princess Louise, Duchess of Fife. Born in 1867 as the third child of the then Prince of Wales and Alexandra, she was unfortunate enough to inherit the looks of her father rather than her mother. Queen Alexandra was not keen for her children to leave the nest, so Louise, who was named after her paternal aunt and godmother Princess Louise, Duchess of Argyll, was encouraged to solve her marital problems in the same way her namesake godmother had done, namely by marrying a British nobleman instead of a Continental royal. In 1889 she married the 6th Earl Fife, a minor peer with a touch of royal blood through his maternal great-grandmother, Lady Elizabeth FitzClarence, an illegitimate daughter of King William IV. He was raised to a dukedom by Queen Victoria two days after the marriage, and Louise and the most junior duke in the United Kingdom peerage moved to Scotland, where they lived lives of stultifying dullness. They produced a stillborn son and two daughters, the Ladies Alexandra and Maud Duff, and four years after Edward VII's accession to the throne he created her the Princess Royal, a title that had fallen vacant in 1901 following his eldest aunt Vicky, Empress Frederick of Germany's horrifically painful death from cancer, which had metastasised from the breast to the spine. Louise now possessed the highest dignity a royal female could have in the United Kingdom, except being a queen in her own right, and, to reflect her new position's importance, her father raised her two daughters to the rank of princess with the style of highness. They ranked immediately after all members of the British Royal Family bearing the style of royal highness, and were thereafter known as Their Highnesses Princesses Alexandra and Maud of Fife until their marriages.

The fate of these two princesses showed Elizabeth what could, and could not be done, for her relations when Bertie ascended the throne. Princess Alexandra married her mother's first cousin, Prince Arthur of Connaught, only son and heir of Queen Victoria's third son the Duke of Connaught, in October 1913. She was already Duchess of Fife in her own right, having inherited that title from her father. His death had been the result of a truly dramatic experience. The family had been shipwrecked off the coast of Morocco in late 1911. The Duke of Fife got a chill from the sea, which is rather colder than one might imagine even in summer, as anyone who has been to Morocco can attest to. This turned to pleurisy and pneumonia, and he expired in Egypt early in the new year. An altogether more attractive woman than her younger sister Maud, Princess Alexandra became a Royal Highness upon her marriage. Thereafter, she carried out official engagements on behalf of her uncle, George V, and afterwards her first cousins Edward VIII and George VI. Being one of the most senior adult members of the Royal Family in line of succession to the throne, she served as a Counsellor of State between 1937 and 1945. At the time of Elizabeth's first visit to Sandringham, she and Arthur were away in South Africa, where he had been Governor-General since succeeding the 1st Earl Buxton in 1920. He and Alexandra would remain there until 1924, when they were followed by Queen Mary's brother the former Prince Alexander of Teck, demoted to Earl of Athlone in 1917, and his wife and cousin, Princess Alice of Albany.

At the time of Elizabeth's visit to Sandringham for tea, Princess Maud was staying there with her grandmother and mother. Both mother and daughter were renowned bores who could clear a room simply by entering it. Nevertheless, Elizabeth made sure to charm both princesses too.

Later that year, on 13th November, Maud would suffer a demotion of some scope when she wed Lord Carnegie, eldest son of the 10th Earl of Southesk. Her uncle George V instructed her to desist from using her royal titles, as he did not approve of his father's actions in having raised his two nieces to the style, rank and dignity of princesses. Because Maud undertook no royal duties, this demotion was able to be passed off as modesty, but hereafter she ceased being styled as Her Highness Princess Maud of Fife and became known as plain old Lady Carnegie, and, towards the end of her life, the Countess of Southesk. She did, however, officially retain her royal titles and rank, and acted as a Counsellor of State between 1942 and 1945, in particular during George VI's absence in Africa in 1943.

Her position and that of her sister rankled to such an extent that the King's Private Secretary, Sir Alan 'Tommy' Lascelles, went to the lengths of having the criteria, by which Counsellors of State were chosen, changed with the complicity of Bertie, who by then was King George VI. As Bertie did nothing without first consulting Elizabeth, she plainly approved, and was even accused of having mooted the change in criteria for Counsellors of State to keep the reins of power more firmly under the control of those she controlled.

Lascelles' diary entry for 13th November, 1945, includes the paragraph, 'To the House of Lords to see Addison. I told him my idea for solving the problem of a Council of State, should the King and Queen and Princess Elizabeth ever go to one of the Dominions. As things are at present, the government of the Empire would be left in the hands of Princess Mary, George and Gerald Lascelles, and Princess Arthur of Connaught and Lady

Southesk – which is absurd.'

The law then required the five most senior adult heirs-in-line to the throne to be appointed Counsellors of State in the absence of the monarch. Although Lascelles was actually the cousin of George, Viscount Lascelles and his younger brother Gerald through their mother Princess Mary's husband Henry, 6th Earl of Harewood, power seems to beat blood in every contest. As Diana, Princess of Wales and Sarah, Duchess of York discovered in 1992, when their respective brother-in-law and first-cousin-once-removed, Sir Robert Fellowes, then Queen Elizabeth II's Private Secretary, isolated them to preserve the monarchy's greater interests, there is no one quicker to wield the axe against a member of the Royal Family than a relation whose links to that family are professional rather than marital.

Nowhere in Lascelles' diaries (*King's Counsellor – Abdication and War: The Diaries of Sir Alan Lascelles*, edited by Duff Hart-Davis) is there the suggestion that he exceeded the remit of his position as Private Secretary and ever sought to influence unduly or push around King George VI and Queen Elizabeth during *their* reign. On the other hand, those diaries, and Sir Winston Churchill's amongst others, do show that the King never made a step without consulting his Queen. Indeed, she sat in on many of George VI's wartime meetings with his Prime Minister. Her political sagacity was much commented upon, and anyone who wanted the King to do something he was reluctant to, only needed to get Elizabeth's approval for all objections to disappear magically.

The effect of changing the law to prevent the five most senior heirs to the throne over the age of twenty-one was that a constitutional safeguard against increasing the power of the monarch and his advisors was being removed. Hitherto, the accepted wisdom had been that these five adults would naturally perform in the best interests of the monarchy, by virtue of their very closeness to the throne. Until 1945, these royal figures had always behaved responsibly, and there was no reason to suppose that the King's sister, her sons, and their cousins would suddenly begin to do otherwise. However, if the law were changed and they lost their right to be Counsellors of State, the monarch and those closest to him could keep greater control of the reins even when they were out of the country.

All this tinkering with tradition to ensure that the Royal Family as a whole lost influence while the occupants of the throne and their advisors enhanced theirs, was very much in the future as Elizabeth sat down for tea with that lexicon of royal luminaries that Saturday afternoon in January 1923. She charmed them all to such an extent that Queen Mary was able to record how her contribution had turned what would doubtless have been just another dull royal occasion into 'a very happy cheerful party'.[7]

Afterwards, Elizabeth, Bertie, and the two sets of parents returned to York House, where the newly-weds-to-be spent a quiet time reading and replying to the tsunami of correspondence which was engulfing them.

No Sunday morning at Sandringham, then or now, has ever been complete without a trip to church, so after breakfast the following morning, the whole family congregated for the service in a ritual which Elizabeth would maintain for the remaining eight decades of her life. There were now even more royalties present than there had been at tea the afternoon before. Swelling the ranks was Queen Olga of the Hellenes, the widow of the Greek King George I, brother of Queen Alexandra and the Dowager Empress. He had been elected to the throne of Greece at the tender age of seventeen, while still Prince William of Denmark. The second son of the heir to the Danish throne, he actually became a king eight months before his father in 1863. Four years later, he went to Russia to see his sister Minnie, who had married the Tsarevitch the year before. While there, he fell in love with the sixteen-year-old Grand Duchess Olga Constantinovna and married her on 27th October. Theirs was a genuine love match. They had eight children, and their ancestors would figure prominently in Elizabeth's later life, especially their son Andrew's only son, Prince Philip of Greece.

Olga and King George I of the Hellenes were genuinely popular in Greece, but her life too had been touched by tragedy, and Elizabeth was both charming and *sympathique* when she met her. George I had been assassinated with a stab in the back in Salonika a few months short of the golden jubilee of his reign. Their eldest son had succeeded to the throne as King Constantine I, but had the misfortune to be married to Kaiser Wilhelm II's sister Sophie. The French and English, desperate to inveigle Greece into the Great War, undertook a shameless campaign against the King and Queen, who were sensibly intent on keeping Greece neutral. He was forced to leave his country in 1917 along with the Crown Prince, and his second son Alexander was declared king. Married to a Greek national named Aspasia Manos, by whom he had a daughter, Princess Alexandra of Greece who became the last Queen of Yugoslavia, he was bitten by a monkey and died of blood poisoning in 1920. His father then returned from exile to resume the throne following a plebiscite, but in 1922, Constantine I was hounded off the throne yet again, this time in favour of his eldest son, who at the time of the Sandringham church service was reigning as King George II of the Hellenes. This would prove to be an only-too-brief reign, for he too was hounded out of the country in October of 1923, and deposed in 1924, following which the Royal Family went into exile for over a decade.

With Olga at church at Sandringham was her second son, King George II's namesake uncle, Prince George of Greece. Prince and Princess George of Greece were arguably the most colourful royal couple alive at that time. She was the former Princess Marie Bonaparte, one of the world's greatest heiresses. She was also one of royalty's greatest characters. Her demeanour pointed the way for many a royal to live life on their own terms, while paying lip service to regal convention. One of only two female psychoanalysts trained by Sigmund Freud – the other was his daughter Anna – her specialty was female sexuality. In pursuit of the elusive orgasm, she had her clitoris surgically repositioned three times. Her mother had been one of the richest royals of their day, at a time when royalty made Croesus look poor. She was the former Marie Blanc, only child and heiress of Francois Blanc, the so-called Magician of Monte Carlo who owned 97% of the casino consortium, the Société des Bains de Mer et du Cercle des Étrangers. He was also Monaco's principal real estate developer. Princess George's father, Prince Roland Bonaparte, was equally exotic, though rather poorer, which was anything but penniless. Indeed, so rich was he that he waived his property rights upon marriage. He was the grandson of Napoleon's younger brother Lucien, who had spent much of the Imperial Age in exile, some in England, estranged from his elder brother, whose political objectives were contrary to his beliefs.

This branch of the Greek Royal Family possessed the knack of accommodating paradox, for Princess George's lover throughout the war had been the French Prime Minister Aristide Briand, whose intrigues, more than anything else, were responsible for the deposition of George's elder brother Constantine. There was a belief, within the Greek family, that Marie had been a Frenchwoman first and a Greek national second, but she nevertheless remained a member of the Greek Royal Family, and would continue to do so for the remainder of her long life. This was fortunate, for the family would soon have desperate need of her money when the monarchy was abolished in 1924.

Elizabeth was welcomed that first weekend with open arms by the Royal Family and its many sprigs and twigs. Nevertheless, there was an element of being thrown in at the deep end at the same time, but this unsettled her no more than the 'ordeal' of coping with George V had done. Although she had the born actress's predisposition to nervousness before any new show, self-doubt was as alien to her as self-confidence was to Bertie. She was, quite simply, impervious, her self-confidence unshakeable. Yet this did not come without a cost. As she herself wrote, although the royals had 'all been so <u>very</u> kind & charming,' by the end of her stay she was 'feeling <u>utterly</u>

exhausted.'[8]

Her efforts, however, had not been in vain. Queen Mary wrote to Bertie, 'You ask what Papa & I think of Elizabeth, well we are simply enchanted with her & think her too dear & attractive for words & you have made a wonderful choice.' Militating strongly in Elizabeth's favour was the old-fashioned King's appreciation of her old-fashioned presentation: 'so unlike some of the modern girls',[9] showing that Mabell Airlie had been perceptive when she originally recommended Elizabeth's suitability. Her aura as an old-fashioned girl harkening back to the past, who was out of step with modern ways, was a considerable advantage.

On the Monday, Elizabeth returned to London in the same private carriage with Bertie and her parents. While Elizabeth went to tea at his sister Mary's house, Cecilia, whose confidence seems to have been as great as Elizabeth's, immediately set about planning the wedding. She ordered the cake from Gunters and promised them the order for the refreshments. The implication, that they should do so for a knock-down price, is obvious. She then informed Queen Mary that she and Claude proposed renting a large house in London to entertain the guests, at which point Queen Mary took steps to scupper her plans.

Royal weddings since the end of the war had been vehicles for involving the populace in the lives of their Royal Family. To an extent, this was a politically based policy, an attempt to make the monarchy more popular through greater accessibility. With some justice, the bugbear of Bolshevism was never far from the mind of the King and the Prime Minister. The wedding of a second son might not be as important as that of the heir to the throne, but it was nevertheless an occasion to be exploited, so the decision was taken to hold it at Westminster Abbey, in full view of the public, the way Princess Patricia of Connaught's had been in 1919 and Princess Mary's the year before. Prior to those two weddings, officially sanctioned royal marriages had always been celebrated in the privacy of St. George's Chapel, Windsor Castle, the way Victoria and Albert's or Edward VII and Alexandra of Denmark's had been, or at the Chapel Royal in St. James's Palace, where George V and Mary had themselves been married.

The Lord Chamberlain, the Earl of Cromer, now wrote to The Keeper of the Privy Purse, Sir Frederick Ponsonby, whose office would be paying for the wedding, informing him that the Strathmores' idea of a wedding arranged by them must be 'put aside, as The King and Queen decided that A Royal Wedding should follows its usual course.' Cecilia was quickly learning that she might be the central figure in her daughter's life, and that that daughter might be the central figure in the second son of the King's, but she had nevertheless been marginalised. All her plans and requests would have to pass through their hands. Thereafter, Cecilia liaised with the Palace, sending endless requests for additional guests to be added to her list, rightly seeking to include as many people from her world as she could. This was proving to be something of an uphill struggle for all concerned, as the wedding was significantly smaller than Princess Mary's had been. George V had taken the decision that there should not be the same number of guests or viewing stands. Bertie was a mere second son, while Mary had been his only daughter and therefore entitled to a bigger show.

Nevertheless, a royal wedding was a royal wedding, and in the run up to it, there was mounting excitement the way there always is with royal weddings. Elizabeth was often on show, and she mimed her way through photo opportunity after photo opportunity, wasting no opportunity for display, not even upon her return from her first weekend at Sandringham, when she and Bertie had been confronted at Liverpool Street Station by a solid phalanx of photographers. Elizabeth, who did everything in slow motion, as her niece Margaret Rhodes confirms in her memoir *The Final Curtsey*, proceeded to slowly but surely give the photographers as many pictures of herself smiling radiantly as they could possibly need.

In the three months between the announcement of the engagement and the wedding, which was slated for the end of April, Elizabeth had many opportunities to let the world know, in slow-motion, what a wonderful personality she possessed. As she chose her wedding cake at McVitie & Price in Edinburgh, she was captured by the photographers who were on hand to record this historic moment, smiling beatifically. When she opened a fund-raising sale for the National Orthopaedic Hospital, this smiling Scottish lass was a veritable picture of happiness and good-naturedness. She might not have been slim, sleek and stylish like Freda Dudley Ward, who was still declining the marriage proposals Elizabeth had so wanted to receive from Bertie's glamorous brother David, but she could smile better and longer than any 'lacemaker's daughter', as she proved when she attended a reception at her mother's kinswoman the Duchess of Portland's reception for the benefit of Nottingham's lacemaking industry. Any doubts about the equanimity of her personality should have been dissipated by the rapturous smile she maintained during the several hours of loyal addresses that a variety of convocations addressed to her future father-in-law as a result of his second son's engagement to her. She might not have been a born princess, nor been beautiful and sleek like Sheila Loughborough or even Phyllis Monkman and Boo Laye, but the perpetually smiling countenance conveyed the unmistakable message that she was a joy to have around.

And that, ultimately, was more important than all the slenderness, chic and modernity of the new breed of woman.

Behind the scenes, Elizabeth also found time to gloat over the way things had turned out. Her hesitant, vacillating beau James Stuart dropped in to see her shortly after arriving back from the United States early that February. He had already written her a letter of congratulation, but she dismissed him in her diary with the withering comment: 'He is just the same – Very slow!'[10] This one comment gives the lie to the fiction that their relationship was anywhere near as committed or intense as he and even she later claimed it had been. But it does confirm how very backward he had been in coming forward, at least with her.

Elizabeth was an unusual combination of dispassionate, almost authorial observation, and romantic sentimentality. Her stock in trade was love, and now that she had committed to Bertie, she had to commit herself to loving him as well. The extent to which the headiness of royalty supplemented the affection she would have possessed for him, had he not been a prince, is self-evident from the way the relationship had developed. But now that she had cast her lot in with him, she was determined to make the relationship work as a love match. She was clear-sighted enough to see that it could work effectively on no other basis, and, to her credit, she was as intent on a happy family life as he was.

Fortunately for biographers, royalty was often apart, and when they were, they wrote letters. They also had the quaint practice of passing written messages back and forth between themselves even while staying in the same palace. So there is a paper trail to point the way to the truth. A psychologist would make much of the letter Elizabeth wrote Bertie shortly after their return from their first weekend at Sandringham. He was in Glasgow for two days of official visits and though she started off her letter convincingly, 'My dear Darling, I am just writing you a very little letter. I shall be thinking about you when you get this, & hoping that everything will go off wonderfully well. I am quite sure it will.' She then gave the game away. In a classical denialist ploy, she protested too much while trying to convince him of the sincerity of her feelings, saying, 'Also, I might add that I do love you Bertie, & feel certain that I shall more & more.'[11] The word 'do' was underlined not once or twice but a multitude of times, underscoring the insincerity yet, paradoxically, showing both her energy and commitment. And while Bertie might not have realised it, any psychologist worth his salt would have known that if you tell someone something often enough, you start to believe it yourself, as she herself was aware of, hence her confidence in stating that with time she would actually develop more love for him. Practice making perfect didn't alter the fact, however, that at the core of her affection for him lay calculation and self-interest, rather than natural attraction.

Doubtless the process of self-hypnosis upon which Elizabeth was now embarked will have been fostered by the excitement surrounding her conversion from earl's daughter into royal highness-to-be. Chief amongst the joys of her elevation was the matrimonial home which she and Bertie were now given. White Lodge had been Queen Mary's childhood home. Located in the middle of Richmond Park on the outskirts of London, it was, as its name implied, a small rather than a large house. To Queen Mary, however, it possessed sanctified status because her parents, Princess Mary Adelaide of Cambridge and the Duke of Teck, had lived there following their morganatic marriage. It had been lived in since 1909 by Lord Farquhar, a friend of the King and Queen, but he relinquished the lease so that Bertie and Elizabeth could have it.

'We went all over the house. Charming place,' Elizabeth confessed to her diary on 23rd January, 1923.[12] Two days later, she wrote in rather more effusive terms to Queen Mary, 'I was simply enchanted by it all. There is nowhere I should like to live in more, and I have fallen in love with it.'[13]

Queen Mary, whose taste was legendary, now made the mistake of trying to be helpful. Both Bertie and Elizabeth found this intrusive, though only his spirits were dampened, for she remained as resolutely cheerful as ever. 'Don't worry about White Lodge and furniture,' she wrote him on 13th March, 1923. 'I am quite certain we shall make it enchanting – you and I; so please don't fuss yourself, little darling.'[14] Her use of the word 'little' reveals that they had already lapsed into the roles they would have throughout their lives: Elizabeth the dominant but loving nanny, Bertie an emotionally-needy little boy who had to be reassured and soothed while bossed around under the guise of loving kindness.

Queen Mary's assistance, however, seems to have been exactly what it appeared to be. She was not imposing her taste upon her son and his bride-to-be, as is proven by the fact that Elizabeth and Cecilia went to choose chintzes for White Lodge on 11th April. This assignment was sandwiched between yet more photographs being taken of her, this time for the *Graphic* magazine.

Boasts are often concealed as complaints, and Elizabeth had now started to complain about how onerous all the press attention was. Her true sentiments can be gleaned from the glee with which she went before each and every camera, declining no invitation, no matter how obscure the publication. She had not yet started to say, as she later on would, that everything she wanted to do she did from 'duty', while anything she did not want to do had to be consigned to the garbage bin because it did not measure up to her high standards of probity. But she was already well on the road to the hypocrisy which George VI's first cousin George (7th Earl of) Harewood would later accuse her of possessing in such splendiferous measure.

On 10th April, Bertie accompanied Elizabeth to the wedding of the girl whose brother she might well have married had he lived. Charlie Settrington's sister Doris Lennox-Gordon married Clare Vyner at Chichester Cathedral. Happiness was now so intrinsically a part of Elizabeth's public image that *The Lady* (19th April, 1923) reported her as being 'in a happy shade of brown', as if any such thing existed. The press, naturally, were out in force, and the smiling Elizabeth received even more attention than the bride herself.

Her attire was by her favourite designer, Madame Handley Seymour, who would remain a firm favourite of hers for the following twelve years, until she dropped in on David and Wallis and overheard her stylish American sister-in-law-to-be mimicking her for being so dowdy. This outfit was one of those curious concoctions which allowed the public to identify with Elizabeth in all her non-threatening and endearing approachability. It was just the sort of thing a housekeeper, taking a stab at elegance, would have worn if she had had the means to do so: a shapeless brown coat trimmed with fur, over a dowdy dress, and topped off with an unsightly hat with a cluster of roses at the side, that had been stuck on her head at what she hoped would be a dashing angle, but somehow didn't quite make the grade. In the process, this frightful garb, and all the others like it which became Elizabeth's hallmark, further enhanced her popularity. Not only did she not look like a model, she did not even look elegant, though she did come across as trying very hard to please. She was curiously representative of what a docker's daughter would look like if their roles had been reversed.

Elizabeth's couturier had a dire reputation amongst well-dressed sophisticates. Margaret, Duchess of Argyll, who was one of the most stylish and celebrated beauties of her day, and a fixture on the Best Dressed List who put several designers on the map, including Norman Hartnell and Hardy Amies, once told me, 'Handley Seymour was hopeless. She only dressed dowagers and dullards.'

But where did Elizabeth get her appalling taste in clothes? An inspection of photographs of her and her mother demonstrate that Cecilia was her role model. Lady Strathmore was as overtly overly-feminine as Elizabeth. She had a disconcerting habit of wearing feathers and furs while all around her everyone else was dressed in tweed. This frou-frou stab at glamour had its charm, for both women were attractive in an oddball way, but neither could have been accused of dressing with elegance.

As the date of the wedding approached, Elizabeth could be found at Madame Handley Seymour's salon having fittings not only for her wedding dress, which was another study in dowdiness, but also for other frocks for her trousseau.

Meanwhile, there was much speculation, privately and publicly, as to what Elizabeth would be known as following her marriage. George V's Private Secretary, Lord Stamfordham, who had been Queen Victoria's Private Secretary during the final years of her reign, believed that she would become Her Royal Highness The Duchess of York but that she would not be a princess. The Home Secretary consulted the legal experts and informed him that she would indeed become a princess as well as a Royal Highness, because she would acquire her husband's rank, styles and titles in their entirety. She would therefore be known as Her Royal Highness The Duchess of York but in reality she would actually become Her Royal Highness The Princess Albert, Duchess of York, as well as possessing all the subsidiary titles which Bertie held. This was because the wife of a British citizen acquired his rank if hers was inferior to his.

Elizabeth was now well on the way to becoming the superstar she would be for the remainder of her life. People who think that it was all a happy accident, or that she did not put hard graft into her public persona, should reflect upon the fact that the consciousness with which she went about enacting her role was one of the main reasons for her outstanding success as a public figure. To deny the existence of her effort is to negate the characteristics it took successfully to pull off such a feat. The courage it took to project this constantly smiling and lovingly approachable persona might be lost on an age that is unaware of how unusual her tactics were in 1923, but those were days when the only acceptable public face for a member of the upper classes was one of distance and reserve. Elizabeth's presentation of herself as a smiling, endearing, jolly human being was not merely daring: it was ground-breaking. Nor did it require only courage to pull it off successfully. It also needed a degree of self-control that was almost frightening in its extent. No public figure prior to her had ever projected such accessibility and affability by smiling with the constancy and consistency that she did. A trawl through the back catalogue of photographs shows that very few photographs exist of her when she was *not* smiling. As someone who has been in the public eye, albeit in a far more limited way, for over forty years, I can say that it is not only unnatural, but also requires the sort of self-monitoring that few people are capable of. Or indeed want to apply. Just think of being on show for four hours, and then imagine beaming for the full length of that time. Remember, if you stop and frown or grimace, an onlooker might snap a photograph of you projecting an aspect of your personality you do not wish to convey. So you suppress that side of your personality for the duration. I submit the number of people who are motivated and able to carry out the exercise, on even one occasion, is limited. And those who are prepared to do so for a lifetime are virtually non-existent. Yet Elizabeth elected to do so of her own free will, and did so so successfully that she ended up being one of the most popular figures on the world stage. Such tenacity was admirable, irrespective of whether one agrees with the purpose of it or not.

The Smiling Duchess

Chapter Six

The wedding was due to take place on Thursday, 26th April, 1923. On Friday, 20th April, Elizabeth's trousseau was shown to the press. They were so dumbstruck by the dullness of the offerings that even *The Times*, that paean of praise to the Establishment, damned with faint praise, merely commenting on the 'simplicity' of the dresses and listing the colours, each one duller than the one before: beige, navy, black, mauve and white, with a dash of silver and pink to enliven the otherwise funereal aspect.

The following day, Elizabeth had lunch at Buck House, as she had now started calling Buckingham Palace, in keeping with the tradition of all those on the inner royal circle. There, George and Mary presented her with some of the considerable haul she would receive as the daughter-in-law of the world's premier monarch now that the Tsar of All the Russias and the Hapsburg Emperor had ceased to exist. From the King she got a tiara and full diamond and turquoise suite, while the Queen came up with a diamond and pearl necklace and bracelet. Bertie also gave her a diamond and pearl necklace, with a matching pendant. (Pearls were then the most desirable stones on earth.) Meanwhile, in the State Rooms at Buckingham Palace the bulk of the presents, which had been flooding in from all over the world, were put on display in large glass cases, rather like the sort seen in stores, waiting for the guests who had been asked to receptions over a three-day period to view them.

After lunch, Queen Mary and her daughter drove over to Bruton Street to inspect some of the non-royal offerings which the Strathmore family was being allowed to exhibit at its London house. These included the trousseau which had received such lacklustre commentary from *The Times*, and presents such as Claude's diamond tiara and a rope necklace of diamonds and pearls, as well as Cecilia's diamond and pearl necklace and bracelet.

The exchange of presents and viewings complete, Elizabeth was driven down to St. Paul's Walden Bury, where she spent Sunday resting. Like most brides, her mood was bittersweet. Her diary records a combination of sadness and expectancy as she contemplated leaving her happy home for the glories of the royal way of life.

Monday afternoon saw Elizabeth and Bertie and all the bridesmaids at the Abbey for a rehearsal, after which she went home to dine with her parents. With dinner out of the way, Elizabeth, Claude and Cecilia made the short journey back to Buck House, for the first of the large receptions which the King and Queen were hosting to celebrate the marriage. This one was for 800 guests, the 'whole of what is called the "world" was there in its best frocks',[1] as H.H. Asquith, the former Prime Minister, noted. He also provided us with an insight into how quickly Elizabeth's reputation was spreading: the 'bride, everyone says, is full of charm.'[2]

The Royal Family and its advisors were using the wedding as a public relations vehicle in much the same way they had used Princess Mary's the year before and Princess Patricia of Connaught's in 1919, and would thereafter use all such occasions. The reception of the night before was simply the first of three large-scale entertainments, each of which was given massive coverage and did much to popularise the Royal Family even further. The following afternoon, Elizabeth was back at the palace for a massive tea party for over a thousand members of the Royal Household staff as well as the Strathmore family retainers. To her credit, Cecilia had beavered away ensuring that as many of these workers as she could inveigle, from all her husband's far-flung properties, were in attendance.

Upon returning home at six o'clock, Elizabeth discovered that Rachel Cavendish had accepted James Stuart's proposal. Tellingly, she evinced no jealousy then or at any time in the future. As she would later display pathological jealousy of Wallis, her reactions should be used as a gauge as to what her deepest feelings were. In fact, she, Bertie and ten other friends organised an impromptu celebration of her 'slow' beau's engagement. They started the evening with dinner at Claridge's, where they all had a jolly time. From there, they went the few hundred yards to the Hippodrome, one of the most fashionable nightclubs, and, when they wanted a change of pace, they moved on to another fashionable dancing club, the Berkeley. The royal bride-to-be and her fiancé as well as her one-time love interest and his fiancée, who was one of her closest friends, all danced the night away. Elizabeth did not get to bed till 3:30 am. 'I was in good form,' she stated, and all the evidence suggests that that was because she was going to have the glorious future she and her mother had aspired to, rather than the pedestrian life that lay before this duke's daughter, who was unfortunate enough to be marrying the divinely attractive but nevertheless socially insignificant third and 'slow' son of a mere earl.[3]

The following morning Elizabeth was up at ten with what can only have been a hangover. A troll through her diary shows that she was already partial to drinking, ending days and nights of conspicuous alcoholic consumption with sherry at three in the morning. Although she awoke 'feeling very ill!'[4] she could not dally in bed, but had to get up and take part in the celebrations for her forthcoming nuptials. So she got herself together and had lunch, after which Bertie drove her to the palace, where large crowds had been congregating each day to catch a glimpse of the many glamorous public figures who were attending all the receptions. That afternoon there was another one, this time for the many people who could not be asked to the wedding itself, but who by rights expected to be part of it.

Elizabeth was quickly learning that being a royal might ensure that you were the centre of attention at all – or at any rate, most – times – but that you also had to jump through hoops. Fortunately, she was the sort of personality who enjoyed performing up to the expectations of others, and who moreover enjoyed projecting that enjoyment for all to see. This trait would prove to be invaluable in her new life, where royal duties are frequently nothing but social interchanges taking place in semi-public or public situations. As she shook hundreds of hands and beamed her beatific smile at each person she met, she was starting the way she intended to continue: with healthy relish. Rewarding though it was, both to herself and the recipients of her delightedness, being on display was also exhausting, and she left Buck House for the last time as a single woman, happy to be returning to Bruton Street. There she had a quiet evening with her parents and brothers: 'I adore them,' she recorded in her diary, and was in bed at the relatively early hour of eleven.[5]

By her own account, Elizabeth awoke bright and early (for her) 'at 8.30. Up by 10. Put on my wedding dress, aided by Suzanne & Catherine. It looked lovely.'[6] Royal weddings, like all large-scale public spectacles, are synchronised to within a second. The first to arrive were the ordinary guests, followed by the more extraordinary guests, all of whom had been allotted times of arrival. These included the present Prime Minister and his two predecessors, as well as eminent politicians such as Winston Churchill and Sir Oswald Mosley, a cousin of Cecilia's, and diplomats such as Duff Cooper with his wife, the former Lady Diana Manners.

Only after the Great and the Good had been seated did the families of the bride and groom arrive. Each had to be on time. Their arrival was staggered according to precedence, and the Strathmores, being non-royal, had to arrive first, for at royal events the first in rank is always last, and vice versa. Next came the members of the Royal Family, again in reverse order of precedence. There were nearly a score of them in attendance, including the 'old biddies' from the 'aunt heap' at Kensington Palace such as Princess Louise, Duchess of Argyll, her sister Princess Helena, Princess Christian of Schleswig-Holstein, and her daughters Their (not Royal) Highnesses Princesses Marie Louise and Helena Victoria. At exactly eleven o'clock Queen Alexandra set out from Marlborough House, the magnificent palace on the Mall opposite St. James's Palace which had been built by the first Duchess of Marlborough and which Elizabeth would covet and seek to move into when she was widowed. A minute later, the gates at Buckingham Palace swung open and the King and Queen left in the State Coach flanked by the Sovereign's Escort of the Household Cavalry. Twelve minutes later, the bridegroom and his elder brother departed in another of the ornate carriages, cavalry clattering beside and behind them in a spectacle reminiscent of the pre-war finery that had sustained the European monarchies now washed away.

While David and Bertie's coach was leaving the ornate gates of the palace, a short distance away in Mayfair, the simple front door of 17 Bruton Street swung open and Elizabeth, in a concoction that only Madame Handley Seymour could have devised, emerged with her father. Surrounding the state landau that would take the Thane of Glamis and his scion to the Abbey was a pack of press photographers, and four mounted policemen who would provide an equestrian escort for this commoner who would soon become royal. For one of the few times in her life, Elizabeth was not beaming beatifically. She had the merest suggestion of a smile, as if she were hugging to herself some delicious secret that she did not wish to impart to others. She looked almost feline, although once she was in the carriage and the crowds started to cheer her, she broke out into her customary smile and waved enthusiastically. Later, she would claim to have been both touched and amazed by the response, which of course delighted her. If ever anyone deserved the fate that awaited her, it was Elizabeth.

While she was en route to the Abbey, the royals were taking their places in ascending order of importance. After the more minor members of the family had been led to their seats, Princess Mary, her earl, and younger brother Prince George started up the aisle. They were followed by Queen Alexandra and her sister, the Dowager Empress, then the King (in a uniform of an Admiral of the Fleet) and Queen Mary, a stately relic of the Edwardian era in a stunning aquamarine and silver long dress with a matching turban, her false silver fringe a visible reminder of her husband's taste for the old-fashioned.

Standing at the altar was Bertie, resplendent in the dress uniform of the Royal Air Force. Across his chest was the Garter Riband with Star as well as the Star of the Order of the Thistle, the Scottish equivalent of the Order of the Garter to which he had been raised by his father in honour of Elizabeth's Scottish origins. Flanking him were his two supporters, for royals did not then have best men, but rather two royalties who filled the post. The joke in royal circles was that these were often absolute necessities, for how else could a poor bridegroom get through the trauma of marrying some ghastly princess, except by being propped up by his two supporters?

This was fortunately one instance where the bridegroom was anything but reluctant to wed, and his brothers David and Harry, resplendent in their respective uniforms – the Prince of Wales in the dress uniform of the Grenadier Guards, and Prince Henry in the uniform of the 10th Hussars – were there purely to fulfil tradition.

The weather had been typical for an English late April day. There were showers followed by breaks in the clouds and brilliant sunshine, leading H.H. Asquith to observe that the tens of thousands of people lining the route must all have been soaked to the skin. But the rain held off while Claude and Elizabeth negotiated their way from Bruton Street to Parliament Square, and as soon as their landau pulled up in front of the Abbey, the clouds parted and the sun shone brightly.

The bride and her father alighted to robust but respectful cheers from the assembled crowd. While her bizarre outfit pleased her, even Hugo Vickers felt compelled to point out how 'the overall effect compared badly to Princess Mary's and looks decidedly dated to the modern eye.' It evidently looked no more stylish in 1923, but the slightly shambolic and old-fashioned way she dressed appealed to her father-in-law and his humbler subjects, so she was onto a winner even as she was losing the style stakes.

Elizabeth, it seemed, found it impossible to put a foot wrong, even when she was doing so. She was one of those fortunate people who have a deft touch and the ability to pull victory out of the jaws of every defeat. A case in point is what happened as soon as the bridal procession formed inside the Abbey. One of the clergymen in front of her fainted. While the bridal party was reforming, she took advantage of the hiatus to rush to the west end of the nave and lay her bouquet of white roses on the Tomb of the Unknown Warrior. This unidentified British soldier, whose body had been found on a European battlefield, was buried on the second anniversary of the end of the Great War as a symbol of all the other unknown British soldiers who had fallen in that, and other, wars. This gesture was so original, so unexpected, and so touching that it further endeared Elizabeth to the swelling ranks of her known and unknown admirers, though Princess Louise, Duchess of Argyll would later claim that this single action put her on notice that Elizabeth was someone to watch.

Watching Elizabeth with admiration rather than suspicion as she walked slowly up the aisle, the speed and high heels no longer giving her trouble the way they had at Princess Mary's wedding rehearsal, was Bertie. *The Times* reported that he had 'shining eyes and a look of happiness' and that he and Elizabeth 'seemed to think of no one but each other', though it also managed to damn her taste in clothes yet again by alluding to 'her lovely old fashioned dress'.

The Archbishop of Canterbury, Randall Davidson, officiated along with his successor the Archbishop of York, Cosmo Gordon Lang; the Dean of Westminster, Bishop Herbert Edward Ryle; and, in deference to the bride, the Primus of the Scottish Episcopal Church, Bishop Walter John Forbes Robberds.

Elizabeth had a genuinely thoughtful streak in her nature. When this combined with the tact that was another of her virtues, and was deployed as she sought to obtain the good opinion of others by showing them how wonderful she was, she made simple choices that sometimes turned out to have unexpected boons. Out of deference to the duke she was marrying, Elizabeth had asked the Archbishop of York to give the address. Not only did he prove inspiring, saying how they should resolve to live a noble married life, and aim to realise the 'great ambition to make this one life now given to you something rich and true and beautiful,' he also mixed high-flown ideals with Establishment pragmatism. This struck a chord with Elizabeth, who also shared a similar mixture. Like birds of a feather flocking together, the ambitious and uncharitable churchman and the superficially sweet but otherwise 'hard as nails' new royal had already forged a bond which would stand both of them in good stead in the years to come, especially during the Abdication Crisis, when they proved to be an unstoppable double act.

It is arguable whether Edward VIII would have been shoved off his throne with the ease he was, had Cosmo Gordon Lang not been made Archbishop of Canterbury in 1928 and proved to be as implacable an opponent of the modernising king, and as stalwart a supporter of the amenably old-fashioned Duke and Duchess of York, as he was.

After the church service, which followed the pattern adopted by all subsequent royal marriages, including that of Prince William and Catherine Middleton, Their Royal Highnesses The Duke and Duchess of York were driven back to Buckingham Palace in an open carriage. If such a thing were possible, Bertie was even more radiant than Elizabeth, who was herself the veritable picture of joyousness. Whatever her original aims and feelings, she had embraced her destiny with admirable wholeheartedness, demonstrating that no matter how self-interested she was, once she had struck a deal, she fulfilled her end of it to the letter. This signified an honourable as well as a decent sense of obligation, and if she were cheating anyone in this marital transaction, it was herself rather than her new husband.

Once the newlyweds and other royals had returned to the palace, the crowds, numbering tens if not hundreds of thousands, were allowed to swarm into the Mall. They vociferously demanded that the bride and groom appear on the balcony, and there is footage of Elizabeth and Bertie emerging at 1:15 pm with King George V and Queen Mary. The born royals can be seen hanging back, veritable pictures of emotionally-repressed modesty, while a jubilant Elizabeth theatrically rotates her right arm in what would hereafter be known as the Elizabeth wave, her face wreathed in smiles as she joyously mouths 'thank you' to the crowd time and again.

After the wedding breakfast, which was a small affair for sixty of the bride and groom's relations, Elizabeth changed out of her 'lovely old-fashioned dress' into another of Madame Handley Seymour's frightful frocks. Suitably attired to continue solidifying the bond she had already established with the adoring crowd, Bertie and Elizabeth entered the open carriage which would take them through the streets of London to Waterloo Station. While he waved perfunctorily and grimaced shyly, the born charmer smiled and rotated her hand as if she were unscrewing a light bulb all the way to the station, where they boarded 'a special to Bookham', as Elizabeth recorded in her diary.[7] For the first though by no means last time in her life, the luxury-loving Elizabeth was being treated to an even greater perk of royalty than a mere private carriage. They now had a special train all to themselves, excepting of course the staff that were on hand to serve them. It was taking them to the station nearest Polesden Lacey, the sumptuous Regency house constructed in 1821 by Thomas Cubitt which Mrs. Greville had had redesigned by the London and Paris Ritz Hotel's architects, Mewes and Davis, in 1921.

In effect, Elizabeth was going home, for Maggie Greville had cleverly cultivated her ties with the Royal Family by writing to King George V in 1914 to express a wish to leave the house and its contents to one of his sons. She claimed she was doing so as a gesture of appreciation for his father King Edward VII's kindness to her when her husband had died in 1908. Quite what this kindness was, no one could discern, but when they are being offered great legacies, royalty troubles itself no more with such trivia than the man in the street would. George therefore accepted the offering with alacrity, nominating Bertie as the recipient on the grounds that David, as Prince of Wales and Duke of Cornwall, would have no need of it. Thereafter, Mrs. Greville became a close friend of the Royal Family, and of course she expressed a continuing interest in her heir Bertie, who could be found at her entertainments with chronic frequency, inflating her social stock and his financial prospects.

Although Lady Leslie, the sister of Winston Churchill's American mother Lady Randolph Churchill and the long-time mistress of George V's uncle the Duke of Connaught, stated, 'I would rather have an open sewer in my drawing room than Maggie Greville,'[8] Elizabeth and Bertie, as heirs to one of the most treasure-packed houses in England, had no such reservations. They absolutely adored the open-handed battleaxe, who showered them with gifts and hospitality. Maggie Greville had even offered to buy all their linen as a wedding present (a considerable expenditure when you consider that each sheet, pillowcase, towel, table napkin, tablecloth and place mat would have to be embroidered in the royal cypher and their intertwined initials).

And Polesden Lacey, which would one day be theirs, was undeniably the last word in luxuriousness, far better than any hotel and far more lavishly appointed than even the grandest of stately homes. At Glamis, St. Paul's Walden Bury, even Buck House, one had to cross corridors to use bathrooms, while in their home-to-be there were seven bedrooms with en suite bathrooms. One had to freeze away from lighted fires in winter in their other houses, castles and palaces, but at Polesden Lacey the whole place was centrally heated. Although all their other residences might have appeared impressive, they were definitely not the first, much less the last, word in comfort. Quite unlike Polesden Lacey.

Needless to say, Elizabeth loved Polesden Lacey, as her diary entries confirm. It's just as well that her introduction to married life took place in such sumptuous surroundings as the palatial estate she expected would one day be hers. Hopefully these surroundings and her new rank provided some comfort for the task which now confronted her. One has to sympathise with any young woman who had shied away from the carnal side of life the way Elizabeth had, finding herself in the situation where she could no longer avoid confrontation with matrimony's inevitable carnality.

Although nowadays intimacy is still no great joy to women who are left cold by sex, in 1923 the whole endeavour would have had another layer of horror altogether. Most girls walked up the aisle as virgins. Sex was not discussed the way it is today. There would have been no one to share her reservations with, unless she unburdened herself to her mother, who was plainly of a more passionate nature, as is evinced by the number of children she had and the joyously intimate relationship she had with Elizabeth's father.

I am old enough to remember tales of grandmothers and great-aunts preparing their daughters for the surprises that lurked beneath the sheets. The gist was: if you like it, fine. If you don't, you'll just have to grit your teeth until you get used to it. And if you still don't like it then, just remember it's a wife's duty to satisfy her husband's carnal needs. So whether you want to say no or not, you absolutely have to keep on saying yes, at least until you've had a few children. At which point you can then withdraw your favours.

Doubtless, Elizabeth will have been told something along the same lines by her mother, or whichever older woman she spoke to, for marriage in the upper classes was more about the perpetuation of the family name, and the maintenance of a worldly position, than about sexual satisfaction. And if you were of a religious bent, you could not even seek your pleasures elsewhere the way the less religious could.

Grooms, on the other hand, approached the marriage bed from an entirely different perspective. Unless they were marrying purely for advantage, they will have spent months, sometimes years, suppressing the ardour they felt for the object of their desire. Although gentlemen were reared not to treat ladies like sluts – namely that they should not make too many sexual demands upon them – men will be men. Sometimes they were so sexually besotted with their wives they could not contain themselves. One only needs to read Queen Marie of Romania's autobiography to learn just how distasteful such ardour could be to a bride who was not yet used to lovemaking, or who might be sexually motivated, as Marie was, only to discover that she did not care for intimacy with the man she had married.

Elizabeth, it must be remembered, had already indicated to her friend Helen Hardinge that she did not find Bertie physically attractive. Whether one can go from finding someone 'almost repellent', as she said she found Bertie, to appealing, is a moot point. The way she set about reeling him in, when she realised that George and Mary no longer wanted her for a daughter-in-law, suggests that she was calculating and ambitious rather than genuinely attracted. All Bertie's loving devotion over the years had not moved her until self-interest did, so it is safe to assume that such affection as she had for him did not extend to the physical.

Sex, however, was a part of every marital deal. It was also the ace to play to keep a husband amenable, at least until the wife had increased her power elsewhere in the matrimonial domain. Denying a man his rights – and they were rights – was unthinkable, at least in the early days of any marriage. While Elizabeth did not allow the ordinary borders that define others' behaviour to confine hers, she was nevertheless conventional. She lived up to expectations. She was no rebel, nor was she innovative in overturning the accepted order, despite being innovative in her interpersonal relations and the furtherance of her ambitions.

Elizabeth therefore surrendered to Bertie on the first night, and did so with good grace. We know this because he wrote and told Louis Greig, 'Everything was plain sailing, which was a relief. You know what I mean. I was very good!'

Plainly all those torrid sessions with Phyllis Monkman, Sheila Loughborough and Boo Laye had stood Bertie in good stead, but what he regarded as being good was very likely the antithesis of what she did. One would have to have a heart of stone not to be moved by the idea of Bertie trying to prolong lovemaking in the hope that he would excite the ethereal Elizabeth, while she was most likely imitating Mrs. Stanley Baldwin. Edward VIII and George VI's Prime Minister's wife had famously declared, 'I lie back and think of England' in the hope that her lack of enthusiasm would induce her husband to reduce her torment, at least to the three minutes that Napoleon allegedly took to slake his lust with Josephine. One can only hope that Bertie did the same, though there is evidence to suggest that he did not. Like all the Windsors, he was intensely sexual, and has never been accused of having been a poor lover.

Elizabeth, however, was no cheat. She gave others what was their due, at least when she wanted them to think highly of her, or wished to cultivate an ongoing relationship with them. All the evidence suggests that she and Bertie's sexual relationship was normal in all respects at this juncture. As they pottered about Polesden Lacey, or played golf or gramophone records, or sat and read the newspapers, they were creating a way of life that suited them both. Elizabeth was lazy, as her old friend Arthur Penn would later state, and could happily do nothing for days on end. She was perfectly happy to bask in the adoring prince she had married, while the more industrious Bertie enjoyed relaxing with the woman he adored and loved nothing more than just worshipping her. In so doing, he was fulfilling the deep-seated need of the neglected, emotionally-abused child who had been raised in a regimented environment with a cold mother, but who needed above all to love a woman in a cosy domestic environment.

Cecilia wrote a very revealing letter to Elizabeth at this time. 'I won't say what it means to me to give you up to Bertie – but I think you know that you are by far (underlined twice) the most precious of all my children, & always will be. I do love Bertie – & think very highly of his character, but above everything else I love his really worshipping you.'9

For her part, Elizabeth showed where her priorities lay when she wrote to her mother the day after her wedding. 'I could not say anything to you about how utterly miserable I was at leaving you and Mike & David & father. I could not ever have said it to you – but you know I love you more than anybody in the world mother, and you do know it, don't you?'[10]

Such an intense love was unusual, though less so in aristocratic than bourgeois circles, for in the former marriages were not usually based upon love, but upon advantage. Wives therefore looked to their mothers, children and relations rather than to their husbands for emotional support, though the same was not true of men. A husband like Bertie, who had married for love, had a heightened expectancy of emotional support from his wife, but even men who had not married for love expected their wives to be supportive in all ways. This was a part of normal wifely duty, and Elizabeth's new father-in-law showed to what extent he expected Elizabeth to be supportive of his emotionally-needy son when he wrote Bertie saying, 'Elizabeth will be a splendid partner in your work & share with you & help you in all you have to do.'[11] The fact that she would live up to all his expectations, and doubtless exceeded many of them as well, gives us an invaluable insight into her character as well as her *modus operandi*.

First, however, Elizabeth had to find a way to keep herself happy. She was happy by nature. Bertie had been attracted to her primarily because this was her natural state of being. She was patently highly motivated to remain happy. How she would remain so now that she had married a man who was as troubled as Bertie, who moreover was someone she had not been naturally attracted to, remained to be seen. Putting aside the sexual question, all his devotion could not obscure the fact that he was a difficult and volatile personality with a host of nervous problems which cannot have been easy to deal with.

The technique she had already devised, as her diary entries show, was to soothe him the way an indulgent parent soothes an incorrigible child. Although she was by nature a serene individual whom no one could ruffle or rush, this mode of conduct called for a level of emotional detachment that was possible only with great love or none at all. Since her own diary entries establish that such love as she was now professing was a very recent thing, the only reasonable conclusion to arrive at is that Elizabeth was still not in love with Bertie, nor would she ever be. While she might well have been moved to a degree of genuine affection by his abject worship of her, all indications are that she was still fundamentally detached from him emotionally, and would indeed remain so for the duration of their married life.

On the other hand, Elizabeth was an authoritarian personality with a need to dominate. Even her niece Margaret Rhodes confirmed that she was irresistible whenever she wanted something. There was simply no way anyone could avoid fulfilling her blandishments. Although she sought to hide her strength of purpose behind a veneer of feminine sweetness, even she admitted that she was the steel hand in the velvet glove. An even more accurate way of describing her unique combination of sweetness and steeliness was coined by the photographer and royal acolyte Cecil Beaton, an old friend of hers who described her as 'the Steel Marshmallow' because she was a 'marshmallow made on a welding machine'.[12]

Elizabeth's was also a jealous and possessive personality which required adoration from a variety of sources. 'She controlled my brother absolutely,' the Duke of Windsor told the Duchess of Argyll, 'and had done so even before their marriage. She had to be in control of everyone (who mattered to her) at all times.'

Elizabeth was also one of those characters who sail on a sea of emotion. Although she herself possessed *sang froid*, she fed off the emotions of others. Whether they were strangers, friends or family did not matter. She had to be surrounded by approval and approbation, and those in her life who were supposed to be serving her had to fulfil her wishes to the letter. I remember the milliner Frederick Fox, who used to make hats for her, once crippling me with an imitation of a fitting he had had with Elizabeth at Clarence House. 'This is so lovely, Mr. Fox,' she said sweetly, her face wreathed in smiles as she gazed at the reflection of herself and his hat in the mirror. 'So beautiful. You do things so magnificently.' She then frowned very slightly, swept her right hand up from her side to the brim of the hat, and in a semi-evocation of the Elizabeth wave, allowed her hand to flutter artfully. She looked at him quizzically, as if to say, 'What do you think?' Beaming him another of her famous smiles, she said, 'Do you think perhaps...' This, he knew, was his cue to say, 'I see exactly what you mean, Ma'am. Yes, yes, yes. Of course. A few more feathers (she could never get enough feathers) will finish it off so much better.' 'Ah, Mr. Fox, you are so clever,' she smiled sweetly. 'You've found the solution. How very, very clever of you. I'd never have thought of that myself,' when of course she had thought precisely that and had orchestrated the whole scene so that she would get exactly what she wanted – feathers, of course, being only a part of it. 'She got her own way by suggestion. There was nothing direct about her. It was all done with immense charm, but you knew better than to oppose her wishes,' Freddie said.

Elizabeth's diary gives a clue to the fact that, one week into the marriage, she was already moving to exert an even greater hold over the adoring

Bertie that she already had. She was intent on laying down her marker as the central, in fact the only, source of influence in his life save his parents. Up to this point, his central source of support had been his mentor and Comptroller, Commander Louis Greig. Theirs had been a rich and fulfilling friendship, and Greig still had a great deal of influence. In what might seem to be unseemly haste, Elizabeth now sought to minimise his influence in her husband's life by challenging the Comptroller's opinion. The subject cannot have been of any importance, and her diary gives no indication of what it was, but it is most likely that she was trying to unpick some arrangement with regard to an engagement that Greig had previously made, or to influence one which was about to be made. No other explanation makes sense for her diary entry, which states that she 'argued in vain' with Greig. Whatever it was that she was trying to influence or unpick, he was having none of it – nor should he, for he had certain duties as Comptroller which prevented him from accommodating the caprices of an interfering spouse.

As Elizabeth would utilise a similar *modus operandi* nearly two decades later when she set about ousting Sir Alan Lascelles as Bertie's Private Secretary, it is interesting to note how young she was when she first employed this technique. A technique, incidentally, which Diana, Princess of Wales replicated almost to the letter when she decided to rid herself of her first Private Secretary, Oliver Everett, in the early days of her marriage to Prince Charles.

Despite appearing to be so calm and serene, Elizabeth had 'a terrible temper' according to the Duke of Windsor. She also had the ability to whip herself and others up into paroxysms of emotion about what was effectively nothing. Having sown the wind, she then sat back to reap the benefits of the whirlwind. 'I'm never wrong, as you know,' Elizabeth once wrote and informed Lieutenant-Colonel Edward FitzGerald Campbell[13] and though she might have been jesting, there is little doubt that this was one of those instances when jest was merely masking the true word. 'She truly believed she was never wrong. Self-doubt was alien to her,' Colin Glenconner told me. 'She made it obvious that if she thought it, whatever it was, it had to be right. She was capable of the most appalling cruelties, which she felt entitled to act upon, because in her sanctimonious world-view, anything she thought or did was beyond reproach.'

Whatever it was that Elizabeth used to set herself off against Louis Greig, 'once she had the bit between her teeth, there was no stopping her,' the Duke of Windsor told the Duchess of Argyll. This seems to have been the case seven days after her wedding. Possibly she wanted a diversion away from Bertie, whose clinging obsessiveness where she was concerned can have been no easier to cope with than the Duchess of Windsor would one day find the Duke's. Or possibly she saw the benefits of killing two birds with one stone. On the one hand she could satisfy her need for drama and in so doing satisfy the markedly, albeit passively aggressive, streak she had beneath the sugar, and on the other she could satisfy her quest for absolute control over her fate and Bertie's. Her diary for this period shows that, even before the wedding, she had been telling Bertie to 'stand up for' himself; not to allow anyone to 'bully' him, and not to permit others (namely his parents and Greig) to take advantage of his good nature.

Elizabeth had whipped herself up into enough of a frenzy to convince Bertie that they had to interrupt their time alone together at Polesden Lacey with a trip to London. First the honeymooners called in at Bruton Street, where they had lunch and she 'talked very hard'[14] with Cecilia and her brothers Mike and David. If Elizabeth acted true to her proclivity to enlist supporters in her dramas, the talking hard involved getting the others to accept and encourage her in her point of view. Her family had always been unusually supportive of one another, and now that she was royal, she was accorded an even greater degree of indulgence than the already extreme extent which had hitherto been a feature of her extraordinarily agreeable family. Not only could Elizabeth do no wrong; none of the others seemed to be capable of such a failing either. It was more than a mutual admiration club. They were a mutually worshipful family whose faculties of criticism were never deployed against one another.

After lunch, Elizabeth and Bertie drove to Buck House where she 'argued in vain'[15] with Greig. Her diary implies that Greig won this round, but if he thought he was in the clear, his problems with Elizabeth were just starting. The Duke of Windsor and Colin Glenconner both said that she would never give in in any argument. She was always right and had to be acknowledged to be in the right, irrespective of whether the matter was trivial or important. There was no winning an argument with her, for even if it was broken off and you thought that that was the end of the matter, it never was. Sometimes she would wait for years to revisit the issue. She had to have her own way, and 'when she did not get it, she would nurse a white-hot fury for years on end,' according to Colin Glenconner, whose primary source, aside from his own observations of Elizabeth in action, was her daughter Princess Margaret.

Power struggles with Greig were not the only struggles Elizabeth was having, however. She and Bertie returned to Polesden Lacey for the final weekend of their stay there. The marital bed was still beckoning, which cannot have been a comfortable feature of her new life, though she had not yet found a way to get rid of that problem. On the following Monday morning, she and Bertie finally ended their stay at the palatial residence they still thought would be their future country house, though by the time Maggie Greville died in 1942 they were King and Queen and they did not need it any more. And canny old Maggie Greville, whose manipulative skills had catapulted her from illegitimate ignominy into the first rank of royal circles, understood that she had got all the mileage she needed to out of her dear 'friends' Bertie and Elizabeth. So Dame Margaret Greville left Polesden Lacey to the National Trust, with a generous endowment, rather than leave it, as she ought to have done, had she been sincere in her original desire to leave it to a needy royal, to Princess Margaret. And if ever a royal needed such a house, it was Princess Margaret. Her father had died before she was of an age to be given her own house, and, as Colin Glenconner said, there was never any prospect of 'that dreadful old biddy Queen Elizabeth giving the daughter of whom she was jealous anything that made her life easier or independent.'

The best laid plans, however, can come a cropper no matter how canny one is. Magggie Greville can have had no idea that by leaving Polesden Lacey to the National Trust she would not be perpetuating her name in the glorious manner she presumably sought, but was actually assuring her notoriety throughout the ages. The Polesden Lacey website contained, when I looked at it, a shocking number of unflattering comments about Mrs. Greville. Her secrets and shames, not to mention her foibles, were repeated with what to me was distasteful glee, and I would have been left with the impression of what a ghastly worm their benefactress was, had I not already known it. Nevertheless, one could not help but feel that no one is so ghastly that she should be submitted to such exposure by the recipients of her largesse, and I sincerely hope that those comments will be removed upon publication of this book, if they have not been beforehand.

Although Maggie Greville's manipulative skills would backfire so spectacularly after her death, Elizabeth's would prove to be in a different category altogether. Not only would she die covered in glory, but she lived with the same mantle. This is because she was always careful to present a sweet facade to everyone with whom she was not quarrelling. Even Greig did not yet realise that by crossing swords with her, and by refusing to back down, he had chopped the ground from under his own feet. His days as Comptroller were now numbered.

Because Elizabeth played a long as well as a short-term game, and refused to allow any of the many enmities she would cultivate over the years to disturb her, she invariably left the scene of any battle with her smile following shortly. So it proved this first week of her reign as Duchess of York. She and

Bertie went back to Bruton Street, where she did not allow her setback with Greig to ruin the good time she had that evening. Bertie's brother David, who now thought of her as a close friend and loving sister-in-law, joined them, her brother Mike, and her parents for what she described as 'a very gay dinner.' This was followed by one of her favourite pastimes, when they all 'sang at the piano afterwards.'[16]

Since the announcement of her engagement, Elizabeth's relations with the brother-in-law who would be the next King of England had gone from strength to strength. 'My brother and I were especially close, and she fitted right in,' the Duke of Windsor later reminisced to many different people, including the Duchess of Argyll. 'She was a breath of fresh air. So gay and full of fun. Such excellent company. After the rigidity of my father's Court, where everything was planned down to the last minute, it was sheer heaven having someone we could relax and laugh with.'

But all good things must come to an end, and after their jolly sing-along, Bertie and Elizabeth drove to Euston Station to catch the 11 pm sleeper to Scotland for the second leg of their honeymoon. This was being spent at Glamis.

They arrived at the local station at ten o'clock the following morning to see it filled with well-wishers. After graciously acknowledging the various Girl Guides, Boy Scouts, and other schoolchildren who comprised a part of the enthusiastic whole, Elizabeth repaired to the castle with her new husband. There, they had been allocated a suite of rooms on the first floor which her parents had prepared especially for them in the oldest section. Thereafter, this sitting room, dressing room, bedroom and en suite bathroom, which had been installed for them out of an old dressing room, would be reserved for their exclusive use. There were Chippendale chairs covered in petit-point which Cecilia herself had worked, 18th century tapestries, and an antique four poster bed fringed with the names of all the Strathmore children, including the deceased Violet, Alec and Fergus embroidered on it. Last thing at night, first thing in the morning, Bertie would be reminded of the fact that he had married into a loving family.

Life at Glamis followed the pattern it always had. The family still spent as much time out of doors as it could, and Elizabeth and Bertie joined the others in the long walks which she would always love so much. The fact that this was through the snow, sleet and hail made no difference. One of the endearing things about Elizabeth was that, in her day-to-day life, she preferred old clothes to new, and didn't much care whether she was bedraggled or not. Many men, Bertie included, found this almost masculine approach to her appearance appealing, especially as it was combined with otherwise overtly feminine behaviour.

Elizabeth now developed a hacking cough, but she did not allow it to interfere with her good time. There were still jolly dinners followed by the inevitable sing-alongs around the piano. She and Bertie saw friends and relations and entertained as much as they were entertained. Naturally, they dropped in at nearby Cortachy Castle for lunch with the Ogilvies and Mabell Airlie, whose help, in bringing the marriage about, had been so invaluable.

That night, Elizabeth and Bertie said goodbye to everyone at Glamis, before being taken to the station, where she was again delighted to see that another crowd of well-wishers had assembled to bid them goodbye. Unlike many of the royals, or indeed many a movie star today, she positively thrilled at the sight of any group of people who had gathered to see her, and invariably showed her appreciation with relish. In so doing, she popularised not only herself but also the institution of monarchy.

Penelope Mortimer was only one of Elizabeth's many biographers who have made the point that illness always came to her rescue whenever she was confronted by a task or situation she did not wish to fulfil. Elizabeth had been coughing throughout her stay in Scotland, and now her cough had worsened. No sooner did the newlyweds arrive at Bruton Street on the morning of Friday 18th May, than the doctor came to examine Elizabeth. He diagnosed a simple cough and prescribed cough mixture, which would suppress the cough and allow Elizabeth to resume such duties as she was already shying away from. Bertie would confide in his brother that Elizabeth's cough had put a real damper on the physical side of things. Being a considerate fellow, however, he had not expected Elizabeth to hack her way through the thing he was 'very good' at, and had even spent nights in the dressing room at Glamis rather than burden the sickly Elizabeth with his presence in the marital bed.

Elizabeth, however, was always well enough to be up and about during the day. Following the doctor's visit, she partook of a full day in London. Only at the end of it did she drive down to Frogmore House with Bertie. George V had offered it as temporary accommodation for the newlyweds until White Lodge was ready to be moved into, so that they could have their own establishment without having to worry about other members of the family looking on as they adjusted to married life. Situated in the Home Park at Windsor, this elegant 17th century house set in its own thirty-three acres of beautiful gardens had been occupied first by Queen Victoria's daughter Helena, Princess Christian and her family, then by Bertie's parents and their six children during the reign of his grandfather Edward VII, and whatever Queen Mary's failings, no one could accuse her of lacking style and taste. Something of an expert on art and antiques, all the houses she had ever lived in were testaments to her verve as well as her acquisitiveness. She was notorious for visiting people and demanding to be given something she had admired, with the result that over the years she had acquired a massive collection of the finest of everything. By this time, though, the aristocracy had cottoned on to her and used to hide away their treasures before she came to visit, so she had had to resort to bartering for bargains with her exiled relations or shops.

Frogmore House might have had only one bathroom on the ground floor, inadequate lighting (which would not have mattered to a scion of Glamis, which had no electricity until 1929), and no central heating system, but it had vast rooms sumptuously decorated in the finest antiques. Elizabeth loved it. Although Frogmore House had been the setting for some of the misery which the young Bertie had had to endure, as Penelope Mortimer observes in her biography, 'The further he got from his childhood, the more golden it seemed. The schoolroom was just the same, even the ink stains on the table. This is where he and David and sister Mary drilled with midget bayonets, that's the statue of great-great-Grandpa – we had a footman called Smithson who looked just like him, and (they are now in the dining room) I'll never forget when poor old Hua took his first mouthful of tadpoles on toast, we'd caught them in the lake and got the kitchen to serve them up – he thought they were frog's legs, we nearly died laughing. Smiling, exclaiming, asking questions, taking it all in for future reference, Elizabeth was the perfect companion.'[17]

Elizabeth was not a Scot and Bertie a royal for nothing. And as they settled in happily, the cold was providing her with a merciful boon. She needed her cough to get worse rather than better if illness were to keep on sparing her from invasive duties. Although she claimed that her cough was 'very uncomfortable', she was nevertheless not about to permit a bit, or even a lot, of discomfort to affect her pleasures. As her chief pleasure, aside from basking in the glow of a loving family, was a grand social life, she made no concession to illness when she was out of bed. So she and Bertie had David to dinner on the Tuesday evening, and when he suggested that they go to the Embassy Club for a spot of dancing, 'we dashed up to London in his car, & joined Paul's party there.'

Paul, of course, was Prince Paul of Serbia, and his guests show to what extent Elizabeth and her circle accepted bed-hopping. Chief amongst the guests were David's mistress Freda Dudley Ward and Sheila Loughborough, who was still in love with Prince Serge Obolensky, though he needed money more than lust or even love, and was there with the heiress he would marry the following year, Alice Astor. They would produce a daughter, the present Princess Guiray, who would tell me many years later that she was not sure she was in fact an Obolensky at all, as her mother Alice was having an affair at the time of her conception. Not that that affected her relations with her legal father, or indeed her legitimacy, for she was born Princess Sylvia Obolensky. Also there was 'Bobbety' (Viscount) Cranborne (later 5th Marquess of Salisbury), Elizabeth's good friend, whose sense of tolerance never precluded him from mixing with adulterers so long as they were socially desirable, though these same principles forbade him from exercising a similar tolerance when Princess Margaret wanted to marry a divorced man and it was in his interest to oppose that union.

Since Bobbety would later on play a crucial part at Elizabeth's behest in derailing her daughter's life, this might be a propitious moment to point out how he was untroubled by the fact that he had extended the double standard even further, for the Prime Minister in whose Cabinet he served was himself a divorced man. Sir Anthony Eden (later 1st Earl of Avon) had even remarried, his second wife being Sir Winston Churchill's niece Clarissa. But there seemed nothing hypocritical to Bobbety in such dualism, and indeed he and Elizabeth would remain strong admirers of each other. Which was hardly surprising, for she was, according to Bertie's first cousin George Harewood, someone who saw no conflict in using high moral precepts to annihilate her enemies while excusing her friends and birth family for even greater lapses.

Hypocrites or not, the merry band of bed-hoppers had a wonderful evening, and though Elizabeth recorded that she 'coughed a great deal'[18] at the Embassy Club, this did not prevent her from dancing 'hard till 2.30. David sent us back in his car. Very tired & enjoyed it awfully.'[19]

Fortunately for her, Elizabeth's cough did not get better, and when the doctor came by on Friday, he diagnosed whooping cough. Because this was highly contagious, there was now no way Bertie could come near her. 'You can imagine how very disappointed we both are about it,'[20] Bertie wrote to Queen Mary, not yet realising that the whole purpose of the illness was to keep him away from her, though he would appreciate it soon enough. Rather more presciently, he reflected 'it is so unromantic to catch whooping cough on your honeymoon.'[21]

The question, as Penelope Mortimer and others have asked over the years, is: where did Elizabeth catch whooping cough? No one with whom she came into contact had it. There was none of it about. No one she was with, over the three weeks she had been hacking her way through her honeymoon and grand social life, had caught it from her. Moreover, whooping cough has a characteristic sound, as I and anyone else who has had a child with it can attest to. It sounds nothing like any other cough, hence why it is called 'whooping'. All the evidence therefore suggests that whatever Elizabeth had, it was not whooping cough, but something more fundamental.

Irrespective of what she was suffering from, Elizabeth had found her merciful release. She could continue to be a good and loving wife from the comfort of a solely-occupied marital bed, if such a proposition is not too much of an oxymoron.

Nine days later, Elizabeth and Bertie left Frogmore House, where the Grand Duchess Xenia would take up sometime residence, and headed for the suburban reaches of Richmond. White Lodge was finally complete, Queen Mary having gladly stepped into the breach while the supposedly highly-contagious Elizabeth remained in her sick-bed.

With her propensity towards exaggeration, control and convenience, there was never any real prospect of Elizabeth liking a house that was on the outskirts of London. This, remember, was the individual who had turned her nose up at living in Eaton Square because it was across the park from Mayfair. To live in suburbia was therefore anathema to her, and she soon started to carp about how awful and inconvenient White Lodge was. Of course, she was much too tactful to do so to her parents-in-law, so, while professing to love the house to the King and Queen, she was already decrying her lot to Cecilia. It had 'eighteen reception rooms, only one of which was large enough to receive in, and their warren of bedrooms, only one of which was large enough for the ducal bed.'[22] Quite where Bertie's dressing room was, she does not particularise, but one hopes it was not too far from the conjugal bedroom, otherwise he would have seldom seen her once darkness had fallen. She was still not fully recovered from her whooping cough, which seemed to be taking an inordinate length of time to clear up.

A month after the newlyweds had moved in, Queen Mary came down from London to see how they were settling in. Her resentment crackling across the page, Elizabeth underlined in her diary how they 'went all over the house till 5.15.'[23] This woman who never thought anything of walking for hours on end, and would stand in the pouring rain for extended periods while she fly-fished at nearly a hundred, and never felt ill enough to forgo the pleasures of the dance floor, even managed to moan about how she was 'exhausted about the legs'[24] from the two-hour tour. One gets the sense that had Mary not been a queen, Elizabeth would already have had her in her sights, the way she had Louis Greig. But the one thing Elizabeth always had was a fine appreciation of whom it was safe to target, and whom it was tactically advantageous to cultivate. So she wrote her mother-in-law effusive letters about how much she loved her new home, while bemoaning to Cecilia how hideous she found it, her bedroom included.

Bertie, Prince Charles, even the Duke of Windsor, have attested to what a 'born home-maker' Elizabeth was. She had the ability to add a picture or two, a vase of flowers, a throw over a sofa, and move around a few pieces of furniture and, in so doing, turn a domestic desert into a homely oasis. This she had done with White Lodge, and Queen Mary, whose taste, though different, was also superb, congratulated her on how charming she had made her old family home look.

But White Lodge had one drawback which no amount of fine furniture or tapestry covers could conceal. It was several miles outside of London. Moreover, the route to and from town was edged with unfashionable areas. Although the traffic was not so bad then as it is now, it nevertheless was a journey which she could have well done without. George and Mary had allocated a suite of rooms at Buckingham Palace which Bertie and Elizabeth could use whenever they wanted, but this London apartment had no appeal for her either. She wanted her own house in London, and already had her eye trained on one of the palatial residences in Carlton House Terrace, where the great Victorian Prime Minister, William Gladstone, had lived. These were owned by the Crown Estate, but none was available, and Bertie moreover was not yet so much under her influence that he would actually fly in the face of his parents and move out of a house they had just moved into. So Elizabeth was forced to bide her time.

Meanwhile, her popularity was increasing. Days after she had moved into White Lodge, on 9th June, 1923, Queen Victoria's daughter Helena, Princess Christian died in London. Aunt Lenchen had blotted her copy with Queen Mary, whose memory was as elephantine as Elizabeth's, in 1891, at the time of Mary's engagement to George V's older brother, Prince Albert Victor (Eddy), Duke of Clarence and Avondale. Lenchen was furious that her mother Queen Victoria favoured a match between their cousin Princess Mary Adelaide's morganatic daughter May, as Mary was then known, rather than her own royal daughter Princess Helena Victoria of Schleswig-Holstein-Sonderburg-Augustenburg. The fact that May was prettier, wittier and brighter than Lenchen's Thora (sometimes called 'Snipe' because of the sharpness of her features), did not figure in her reckoning, any more than Eddy being known to be highly emotionally charged, and fixated upon the physical attractiveness of any woman who would be his wife. His two previous marital prospects had both been royal beauties, Princess Alix of Hesse, who subsequently became the last Tsarina of Russia, and Princess Hélène of Orléans, a great-granddaughter of the last French King who eventually became the Duchess of Aosta.

Whether George V's aunt Helena had been in favour or out, she had still been a royal princess, so Court mourning was declared. Everyone had to dress in black and avoid going to parties, which would have been a real sacrifice for Elizabeth, had she not been able to put up her friends in the rabbit-warren of tiny bedrooms that White Lodge possessed.

Princess Christian had been popular, with a particular interest in nursing homes (to this day Princess Christian Nursing Homes are dotted around the British Isles), and now that she was dead, her charities thrashed about looking for a royal replacement. Most directed their gaze towards the Smiling Duchess, as Elizabeth was already starting to be called. But she, being inexperienced and eager to have as purely private a life as possible – in other words, to do as little work as she could get away with – did not avail herself of the opportunities presented to her. Later though, once this natural performer understood how much she enjoyed the royal stage and all the positive feedback it brought her, she would actively seek out royal engagements the way Queen Mary, another ham, did.

No matter how much she shied away from working, Elizabeth was now a royal, and the business of royalty was to perform official functions. She therefore needed a lady-in-waiting. Although she would later on appoint friends and relations as ladies-in-waiting, at this point she and anyone she would have wished for the post were too inexperienced, so Queen Mary chose Lady Katharine Meade. Twenty-nine years older than Elizabeth, this daughter of the 4th Earl of Clanwilliam had been the longstanding lady-in-waiting to Queen Victoria's daughter-in-law the Duchess of Albany. The former Waldeck Pyrmont princess had been a beautiful young woman who was widowed in her twenties when Prince Leopold died of haemophilia. Her daughter, Princess Alice, presently away in South Africa as the Governor-General's consort, was married to Queen Mary's brother Alexander, while her son was the ultimately tragic Prince Charles Edward who had been stripped of his English dukedom of Albany in 1917 and deposed as Duke of Coburg when Germany became a republic in 1918. Later, at the end of the Second World War, he would endure an even worse fate, when he was detained by the authorities because he had been the president of the German Red Cross during the war. With Queen Mary's approval but against the wishes of Elizabeth, whom Bertie ignored on this occasion, Princess Alice and Lord Athlone were allowed to travel to Germany to plead her brother's cause with the Allied authorities. Although they refused to release him, and he was heavily fined by a Denazification Court and almost bankrupted, at least he was not imprisoned.

All of this was mercifully still in the future as Elizabeth adjusted to the honour of having such an eminent personage as Lady Katharine parachuted into her life as teacher and door-keeper. The one thing authoritarian personalities cannot stand, however, is authorities appointed over them. She would last only three years before Elizabeth managed to force her out with a combination of studied politeness and chilled charm. In the meantime, Elizabeth recorded in her diary that Lady Katharine was 'quite nice'. Coming from someone whose idea of euphemism was to describe the most mundane events as 'absolutely <u>wonderful</u>,' this level of enthusiasm was akin to *The Times* describing her trousseau as simple. Nor are the parallels between Elizabeth's diplomacy and *The Times'* misplaced. Both entities played by rules which dictated that what they wrote would ultimately be read by strangers (royal diaries invariably entering the archives for historical inspection). So she was really damning with apathetic praise.

Once Elizabeth had her lady-in-waiting, she was ready for official engagements. Her first as Duchess of York was with her husband on 30th June at the Royal Air Force Pageant at Hendon. Sitting down watching an air show after meeting and greeting a line of dignitaries was not exactly hard work for anyone, but for someone like Elizabeth, who was a born actress, it was a positive pleasure. She charmed everyone, and Bertie, in awe of the spectacle of his wife actually enjoying what he dreaded, commented on how much he admired her ability to bring such zest and joy to even mundane activities like speaking to the mayor. 'She is marvellous the way she talks to old mayors & the like at shows, & she never looks tired even after the longest of days,' he wrote and told David.[25]

A few days later, Elizabeth and Bertie joined his parents for their annual Scottish Court at the Palace of Holyroodhouse. After driving through the streets of Edinburgh to tumultuous acclaim, she wrote her friend D'Arcy Osborne and told him how she was loving every minute of her time in her home country. Waxing enthusiastic, she indulged her strong streak of theatrical expressionism, commenting that her countrymen were 'so romantic & sentimental & generous & proud that they have to hide it all under a mask of reserve & hardness, & they seem to take in people very successfully!!'[26] Had she omitted the word reserve, she might well have been speaking about herself.

Throughout her five-day stay in Scotland, Elizabeth lapped up every bit of the approbation with which the Scots, justly proud of having one of their own married into the Royal Family, showered her. Naturally, the press commented on how charmingly she conducted herself, and one Dunfermline reporter actually remarked on what an aptitude she had with the crowds. Which, indeed, she did.

The greatest stars are born, not made, and Elizabeth was already well on the way to the superstardom which would make her a longer-term luminary than even the longest-reigning movie star or popular entertainer who has ever lived. Arguably, she was the greatest luminary of the 20th century. Certainly, she was the longest-lasting one. While her longevity had something to do with this, so too did her determination to remain a figure of admiration. And fun. For without her genuine love of fun, it is unlikely that she would have retained the affection and admiration of the public the way she did. Largely, this was because Elizabeth loved having a good time at the same time as she loved being loved. Being as well brought-up as she had been, she could couch the vainer, less appealing aspects of her personality in a carapace of misleading attractiveness. Later on, she would be frank about the fact that her public face was a performance. She would say things like, 'Let the performance commence,' as she was about to enter a room. This has been confirmed by many different sources, including her niece Margaret Rhodes. To see a public figure of her grandeur actually enjoying herself made those she was meeting feel good too, and, as her performance never sank into unseemliness or obvious neediness, and did not veer into the undignified, she was the living evocation of how perfectly suited her personality was to her public role.

One of the reasons why Elizabeth achieved the outstanding success she did was that she was remarkably consistent. She did not vary her intensity despite the size of her stage. She was as comfortable and in-character in front of tens of thousands as she was in front of a handful of people. Whether you were a stranger or a friend, she remained herself – or at least, the marvellous, personable, fun-loving individual she wanted to project, which undoubtedly was a part though not the whole of the picture.

Although there is no doubt that the performance got more polished as Elizabeth grew more experienced, the evidence suggests that she was already a fully-blown charmer long before she even met Bertie. If Princess Louise, Duchess of Argyll was correct in her observations and opinions – she actually thought Elizabeth was a self-promoting actress whose charm concealed a lack of sincerity – the Smiling Duchess treated her personal life as just another stage upon which to enact the marvels of her personality. Princess Louise's opinion was one which other royals such as Princess Mary would ultimately come to share. 'I do wish she'd stop smiling so much,' Bertie's sister complained on many an occasion. Later on Mary would also show how witty she was beneath her dour facade when she alluded to the Cheshire cat who could never stop smiling and said, 'A bit more Scotland and a bit less Cheshire cat would be so much more appropriate.' She thought all that smiling was unnecessary and undignified and conveyed insincerity and regrettable over-eagerness to please, rather than charm.

Others, however, were of a different opinion. Indeed, the vast majority of the people who came across Elizabeth never questioned her sincerity. They were simply delighted that she made such an effort. Sincere or not, it flattered them to know that someone of her eminence could go to such lengths to show her delight in meeting them, in enjoying the activities that involved them.

That first July after her marriage, however, Elizabeth's obvious charm was not yet the suspect thing it later became. After she had finished lavishing it on her countrymen, she returned to London with Bertie. There Society was treated to it as the new royal duchess threw herself into enjoying herself and her elevated status while smiling her way through one function after another. The Season was in full swing. If the old adage was true, and everyone loved a lord, how much more did they adore royal charmers? Both she and Bertie therefore slotted right back into the rhythm of what would become the norm for them: lives of popularity and pleasure spent playing sport, dining with friends and relations, dancing (at the conventional mixture of private dances and balls and private clubs such as the Embassy), with the occasional official engagement thrown in to leaven the loaf.

At this stage, and indeed afterwards by choice throughout much of her married life, Elizabeth preferred joint official engagements with Bertie. They were a good double act, but more importantly, each one's presence provided something that nurtured the other. In her case, it was her élan, her verve, her sense of fun, while in his it was that he was the perfect, admiring foil who never ceased to let her know how marvellous he thought she was. She also liked being needed, and he needed her. So she used his perceived need of her to limit the number of solo engagements she was expected to undertake.

The work-shy but attention-loving Elizabeth was able to get away with this sleight of hand because the Royal Family was then substantially larger than it is now. The courtiers who normally plan royal diaries knew how emotionally fragile Bertie was, so they allowed Elizabeth to skive away from many of the solo engagements which she would otherwise have been expected to undertake under the pretence of saving herself for Bertie. But an examination of the sizeable number of official duties which he undertook on his own shows that it was Elizabeth rather than Bertie who was not prepared to function independently. Nor would she do so until she had no choice. Namely when widowhood intervened.

Despite Elizabeth's reluctance to perform without Bertie, her position as royal duchess meant that she did have to fulfil the occasional solo engagement whether she wanted to or not. Her first one actually took place on the afternoon of 19th July, 1923. It followed a joint morning engagement when she and Bertie visited a holiday camp for a thousand slum children from London in Epping Forest. She inspected a new ward at the Cheyne Hospital for handicapped and incurable children in Chelsea, of which her grandmother-in-law Queen Alexandra was president.

Interestingly, the one segment of the populace Elizabeth was never accused of overwhelming with her charm was children. She seems to have lacked the warmth that children pick up on and respond to instinctively. Although charm can substitute for warmth with adults, it seldom does with children.

Even if Elizabeth did not possess the warmth that children respond to, that does not mean she was unkind. Indeed, she could be capable of genuine, unsolicited kindness, usually towards people with whom she had formed relationships, even across the class divide. A case in point was Sergeant Ernest Pearce. She had struck up a friendship with him when he was a convalescent at Glamis in 1915. Since then, they had corresponded, and when he wrote to tell her that he was having trouble feeding his family because he was being prevented by strikers from going to work, she enclosed £10 for him in a letter. This was a considerable amount of money at a time when domestics earned less than £1 a week, and he was able to write her back telling her how he had used her present to buy his children new clothes and shoes and had fed them 'the best Sunday dinner'.[27]

Yet for all Elizabeth's kindness there was also the iciness which Queen Mary had detected, however unconsciously, when she enquired of Bertie whether Elizabeth had started to 'thaw'. Although Bertie undoubtedly said nothing to his parents about the sexual side of his relationship with Elizabeth, he did confide in his brother David that he was finding it difficult to re-establish the intimacy they had had before she had developed 'whooping cough'. Although the younger brother danced around the issue, the elder one was made to understand that Elizabeth was withholding her favours. They were so happy out of bed, however, that he had every confidence that matters would right themselves and he could once again show her how 'good' he was.

Time would tell whether his hopes were justified or forlorn.

Motherhood and Its Perks

Chapter Seven

Only someone as lacking in self-doubt as Elizabeth could have settled into her new role as seamlessly as she did. Within months of her marriage, she had not only devised a public power base as the popular and Smiling Duchess, but was well on the way towards shoring up her private power base too. How she set about doing so is telling.

During Elizabeth's first summer as a royal, she laid down many precedents which she would hereafter use. Never one to squander an opportunity when it presented itself, she had a knack for paving the way with a minimum of fuss and a maximum of effect.

The first opportunity to come her way fell into her lap on her twenty-third birthday on 4th August. Her good friend Paul of Serbia announced his engagement to Princess Olga of Greece, the namesake granddaughter of the Dowager Queen of the Hellenes, who was Queen Alexandra's sister-in-law and whom Elizabeth had met during her first Sandringham weekend. Eleven years later, Olga's beautiful sister Marina would marry Bertie's brother Prince George, Duke of Kent, and in so doing, strengthen the links between the two families.

Although Elizabeth had declined to attend the wedding of her good friend Rachel Cavendish to her erstwhile beau James Stuart that same day, she voiced her pleasure in the engagement of Paul and Olga and let Louis Greig know how much she would like to attend her friend's wedding if such a thing were possible.

Days later, Elizabeth and Bertie left for Scotland, where they divided their time between Glamis and Balmoral. Prior to Elizabeth's entry into the Royal Family, and even after it, anyone who married into the family was absorbed into it so fully that they seldom spent much time with their own family. To an extent, the only person who had managed to eke out some independence had been Princess Louise, Duchess of Argyll, but that was because Queen Victoria had told her daughter that her husband was 'as good as a king in his own country, and might well have been King of Scotland had I not been its queen' when Princess Louise complained about having to spend time with the Campbell family up at Rosneath and Inveraray Castle, the two Campbell ancestral homes in Scotland which she found as dull as Balmoral.

Bertie having married Elizabeth in part because of her vibrant family life, he was not about to forgo the pleasure of staying with the Strathmores, so rather than head for Balmoral, they visited Glamis first. His brother David even came to stay, thrilled to escape from the regimentation of his parents' own castle, which then had a reputation for deadly dullness exceeding anything Diana could complain about sixty years later.

Too soon for any of them, the demands of royalty kicked in and they had to leave the pleasures of Glamis for the pain of Balmoral. As the Duke of Windsor put it, his father's life was a 'masterpiece in the art of well-ordered, unostentatious, elegant living.' In other words, it was rigid to the point of stultification, dull beyond compare, and formal to the extent of strangulation. Life revolved around food and sport, but without the joyousness of Glamis. Every night the King dined in full white tie, as he did wherever he was, and even when they were alone, Queen Mary had to wear her tiara. After dinner, she would withdraw with the ladies trailing behind her, each one curtseying to the King resplendent in his chair as they passed him. He would be waiting to smoke one of the many cigars and cigarettes he got through every day, for he was, like his father before him and his sons after, a chain-smoker. As the dining room filled up with smoke, the King would pass the port with the men and set the world to rights for a prescribed number of minutes. With the precision of one of the clocks which were everywhere in his many houses, he would rise when the alarm clock in his head went off, and, with the men following, make his way to re-join the ladies in the drawing room. Invariably, he found Queen Mary sitting on her own sofa, a lady or two chatting with her, in keeping with the custom laid down some time before that one or two ladies at a time should be brought up to sit with her until she got bored. Then, she would indicate graciously and regally but unmistakeably, that the audience was over, at which point her lady-in-waiting, who was hovering for the signal, would replace the dismissed with another tranche of ladies. Unlike George V, Queen Mary bored easily, or, as Hugo Vickers put it, she was only interested in people who could provide her with information she found interesting. Dinners were therefore always large enough to provide her with an inexhaustible supply of after-dinner conversation.

Fortunately for Elizabeth, the more Mama and Papa, as she now called the King and Queen, saw of her, the more they liked her. With her sparkling wit and confident, open, and almost but never overtly irreverent personality, she 'managed to keep the King in a good temper which was the main thing & very few people can do least of all his sons.'[1] After this visit, George V told Bertie that the 'better I know & the more I see of your dear little wife the more charming I think she is.'[2] Queen Mary echoed these sentiments, stating 'the more I see of her the more I love her, we are indeed lucky to have got such a charming daughter in law & you such a delightful wife.'[3] 'Everyone,' George V declared, 'fell in love with her here,'[4] but neither George nor Mary was quite as deceived, as those words might suggest, about the steeliness of the material from which the candy floss had been forged.

The proof of their awareness is contained in the King's own words and arose out of the way Elizabeth used her first major trip abroad as an excuse to sabotage Bertie's relationship with Louis Greig.

Both George and Mary had enormous respect for the doctor who had mentored their shy, diffident son. The fact that they had promoted him to Comptroller (head) of Bertie's Household was a testament to the respect they possessed. Under Greig's ministrations, Bertie had changed from being a withdrawn, nervous wreck who dribbled and drooled and appeared to be a simpleton into a more outgoing, confident, and friendly individual. George V had a genuine affinity with Greig, largely because they were both direct, bluff individuals who came straight to the point, though Greig's charming and outgoing personality was doubtless also a factor in facilitating a harmonious relationship with his irascible sovereign. Even Queen Mary, normally so glacial, visibly unfurled around Greig. Possibly this was because he had such an attractive personality – warm, outgoing, confident – though the fact that he was an attractive man physically cannot have done any harm either. He had the body of the accomplished athlete he was. He had captained the Scottish rugby team for three years, was an ace tennis player, and a good, all-round sportsman. This blend of physical and moral appeal was heightened by his sense of fun and the irreverent approach he had to life and George V's descriptive nickname for Greig says it all: The Tonic.

Over the fourteen years of Greig and Bertie's relationship, George and Mary had grown so fond of this Glasgow merchant's son that they even asked him to spend Christmas with them at Sandringham. Such an invitation not only confirms the regard they had for the man, but also shows how much they enjoyed his company. Although George V's children might not have realised it, the King did actually like people who were good company. This would prove to be one of the holds Elizabeth had over him, and it was also a reason for having Greig around.

It was Greig's job as Comptroller of the York Household to field all invitations. He was also the person who would suggest invitations on behalf of the Yorks, for instance, to the Foreign Office if they wished to go on a foreign trip. He was in fact the conduit through which just about everything got done.

The wedding of Prince Paul of Serbia was due to take place in Belgrade the day after the christening of the only son of King Alexander and Queen Marie of the Serbs, Croats and Slovenes (as the kingdom would remain until its name was officially changed in 1929 to Yugoslavia). Bertie and Elizabeth had been asked to be godfather and godmother to the infant Crown Prince, and since Elizabeth was known to be a particularly close friend of Prince Paul, and had expressed a desire to attend his wedding, and since Queen Marie's mother was a member of the British Royal Family, it made sense for the Yorks to be the royals who would represent the British monarchy at both these events.

There were geopolitical implications to any official visit a member of the British Royal Family made to the Balkans. Known as the powder-keg of Europe – the Great War had started as a result of Serbia – no visit could proceed without the approval of the Foreign Office. Careful consideration would have to be given to the foreign policy implications of members of the British Royal Family showing what was tantamount to support for the newly-formed Triune Monarchy, as the Kingdom of the Serbs, Croats and Slovenes was also known after its creation in 1919. Although this kingdom was not particularly problematic, the Greek situation was unstable and there was the possibility of Britain becoming inadvertently sucked into any future degeneration of political stability in the Balkans owing to the Triune Kingdom's links with Greece, and Britain's own links with the three Balkan states of Greece, Romania and the Triune Kingdom. Queen Marie's sister was Queen Elisabeth of the Hellenes, as the Greek queen was officially styled, and their mother was a British princess, the former Princess Marie of Edinburgh who was, arguably, the most celebrated woman in the world: Queen Marie of Romania. Known within the family as Missy, she had been the most beautiful princess in Europe and she and George V had been in love. They were first cousins, the son and daughter of Queen Victoria's two eldest sons, Bertie the Prince of Wales who became King Edward VII, and Alfred the Duke of Edinburgh who became Duke of Coburg. Both fathers and their joint grandmother Queen Victoria heartily approved of the match, which would see the beautiful and vivacious Missy (whose personality, ironically, had much in common with Elizabeth's) a Queen of England one day now that George had succeeded his late brother Eddy as heir to the throne.

But both mothers were rabidly against the marriage. Alexandra hated the Germans because Germany had annexed her father the King of Denmark's duchies of Schleswig and Holstein. Missy's father, though still Duke of Edinburgh, was now the reigning Duke of Coburg, and therefore a German Head of State within the German Empire. German militarism under Kaiser Wilhelm II being a constant concern to the British and the Danes, Alexandra was also not prepared to have as a daughter-in-law any princess whose father would have to take Germany's side in any future conflict – even though the father was her own husband's brother.

If it is possible, Missy's mother, the former Grand Duchess Marie Alexandrovna of Russia, was even more hostile to the marriage. Although her marriage had been a love match and she had come to England full of hope for the future, she had ended up loathing the country and its people. She was of the firm view that the British were petty pedants. She much preferred the Germans, and happily departed for Coburg when her husband was offered the duchy. Partly this was because she became increasingly disillusioned with Alfred, a weak man who had turned to the bottle, but an even larger element, if her diaries and those of her children are to be believed, was Queen Victoria's refusal to allow this only daughter of Tsar Alexander II precedence over her sister-in-law, Princess Alexandra of Denmark, by then the Princess of Wales. Maria Alexandrovna had never before played second fiddle to anyone, and the idea of doing so to a mere Danish princess was humiliating in the extreme. Alexandra's father was known as one of the poorest monarchs in Europe, while her father was the richest in Christendom. Even her title became a sticking point. Marie Alexandrovna wished to be known as Her Imperial Highness The Duchess of Edinburgh, but Queen Victoria, mindful of her own dignity and the implications of Imperials claiming themselves to be superior to Royals, insisted that she could not ignore the Royal appellation. So she tried to call herself Her Imperial and Royal Highness The Duchess of Edinburgh. As this still conveyed the superiority of imperial rank, Victoria demanded that she be known as Her Royal and Imperial Highness The Duchess of Edinburgh. Feeling demeaned and unsupported by her husband, who plainly could not do anything to assist her, Maria Alexandrovna had let in the rot which would blight her marriage and ruin any chance she had of happiness in her new country.

Faced with the implacable hostility of the two mothers, the betrothal was called off and Maria Alexandrovna quickly thrashed about for a replacement who could also make her daughter a queen. She alighted upon a German princeling of the House of Hohenzollern-Sigmaringen whose uncle, King

Carol I of Romania, had named him Crown Prince. The seventeen-year-old Marie was quickly married off to her third cousin, Crown Prince Ferdinand of Romania, while George soon afterwards married his late brother's fiancée, Princess May of Teck.

Although Ferdinand and Marie's marriage had not been personally fulfilling, they were regarded, inside and outside of royal circles, as one of the great double-acts of their age. While he was solid and reserved, she was even more flamboyant than Elizabeth could ever hope to be. Every bit as vivacious, witty and fun-loving, she was also a great beauty and the greatest royal superstar of her time. Even more wily and politically astute than Elizabeth, who would have to observe the diminution of her husband's empire, Marie instead increased her kingdom significantly by pitching up at the Paris Peace Talks after the First World War and refusing to leave until her husband's kingdom had been allowed to incorporate and annex large sections of its neighbours' territories. Like Elizabeth, she came alive not only with people but in front of a camera, and like Elizabeth she shied away from the pleasures of the marriage bed. However, unlike Elizabeth, who had yet shown no interest in other men, Marie had produced several children whose paternity was as suspect as Elizabeth's own maternity. Marie herself had blurted out to King Carol I that her third child, and namesake daughter Marie (Mignon), was not her husband's but her cousin Grand Duke Boris Vladimirovitch of Russia's. Her next child, and second son, Nicholas, was commonly supposed to be the progeny of her lover William Waldorf Astor, even though in later life he so closely resembled the Hohenzollerns that there is some doubt as to whether he was indeed an Astor. Her last two children's natural father, however, was her long-term lover Prince Barbu Stirbey, though, in keeping with the principle of presumption of legitimacy, they were members of the House of Hohenzollern and known as Princess Ileana and Prince Mircea of Romania.

Ferdinand and Missy of Romania were due to attend the christening of their grandson Peter in Belgrade, so if Bertie and Elizabeth were permitted by the Foreign Office to attend, they would not only be going on an exotic trip, but they would also be meeting the fabled Queen Marie of Romania, whom Elizabeth did not know. For someone who loved stardom and intrigue as much as Elizabeth did, this would have been a treat and then some.

After weeks of deliberations, the Foreign Secretary, Marquess Curzon of Kedleston, decided that the trip could go ahead. The reason he gave was that it would be an invaluable way of showing British support for the Triune Kingdom. Whether such support was either necessary or desirable was immaterial. What counted was that the Foreign Secretary had come up with a lofty reason to justify the royal couple making a trip, at public expense, which Elizabeth wanted to embark upon.

George V telegraphed the good news to Bertie at Holwick Lodge, one of the Bowes Lyon properties in Durham where he was staying with Elizabeth. Her influence upon him can already be discerned by the way he reacted to what should have been welcome news. Where formerly he would have been obliging, even if it was a trip he had not wished to make, now he reacted with fury at the lateness of the permission. He wrote a blistering letter to Louis Greig, complaining that 'Curzon should be drowned for giving me such short notice. I have written to him for his reasons & also asked to see him before leaving.'[5] He signed off with the demand that his wife be accorded all the care and consideration which she was demanding behind the scenes: 'He must know that things are different now.'[6]

Plainly, Elizabeth's injunctions to Bertie, many of which are dotted throughout her letters and diaries at this time, that he should not allow himself to be pushed around or bullied, had started to bear fruit. And on her behalf no less. For while he would always remain remarkably accommodating where he himself was concerned, this was the beginning of a pattern where her cares and attitudes were concerned. He entered the fray, fists flying, decrying whatever perceived injustice had been done, or vociferously asserting whatever perceived standard must be maintained, while she stayed in the background, having put him up to the job, her proverbial smile fixedly in place as ever.

Even at this early stage of her royal life, Elizabeth's demeanour shows how remarkably controlling and aggressive she was beneath the sweet exterior. But you had to know her very well, or have access to her diaries and letters as well as inspecting her actions carefully, to see beneath the surface, for she loved casting herself in the role of innocent protector of rights – her own or other peoples' did not matter. The Earl of Harewood would later say that no one played the 'sanctimonious' card with greater skill than she did.

But that was not the only game she was playing at this time. Indeed, as she set about ordering yet more dire dresses from Madame Handley Seymour for her first official trip abroad, the fuss she had caused Bertie to create through Greig with Lord Curzon and the Foreign Office seems to have been a power ploy. What she had done, and would continue to do on many another occasions in the future, was throw her weight around with endless demands and create an atmosphere of such fractiousness that the courtier at the centre of the havoc would either surrender his will to hers or then throw in the towel. Her true purpose seems to have been to establish absolute ascendency over Bertie's office. Greig must either bow to her will and fulfil all her requirements and demands, no matter how petty or unreasonable they were, or she would then make life so unpleasant for him that he would want to leave his job.

But if Elizabeth thought everyone was blind to her tactics, she was wrong, as King George V's comments make clear.

Once Elizabeth had fomented enough of a maelstrom of discontent to motivate Bertie to function as her protector, it was a simple enough matter to switch the target from the Foreign Secretary to his Comptroller. She was not comfortable around Louis Greig. He had not been as understanding towards her as she would have liked. He was not giving her her due. Like Curzon, he was not sufficiently mindful of the fact that Bertie was now a married man and her feelings had to be considered as well as his interests. One needs little imagination to see how this scenario would play out, especially when Elizabeth convinced Bertie not to take his Comptroller along to Belgrade, but to choose instead his former Private Secretary and equerry, Lieutenant Colonel Sir Ronald Waterhouse. Because he was not friendly with him, and did not even have any real liking for him, this choice was particularly insulting to the Comptroller he was leaving behind.

By Greig's own admission, he was extremely hurt when he was overlooked. This showed him that remaining on Bertie's staff would become an increasingly thankless task. Bertie was plainly in thrall to his headstrong and wily wife, and if the relationship between duke and mentor was to be preserved, it would be best done at a distance.

While Greig was left in England to reel from the shock of being left behind by the man he viewed almost as a beloved nephew or much younger brother, Bertie and Elizabeth set out for Paris, where they were due to pick up the Simplon Express to Belgrade. With them were Waterhouse, Elizabeth's lady-in-waiting Katharine Meade, two valets and two maids, including Catherine Maclean, who had helped to dress her for her wedding. They were also accompanied by Arthur Ferguson, a newspaper photographer from Personality Press.

Elizabeth thoroughly enjoyed her first official trip abroad, even if she was eclipsed at every turn by the flamboyant Queen Marie of Romania. However, she was not yet used to being the star turn at royal events. Whenever she was with her parents-in-law, protocol dictated that she play second fiddle to them, and on this occasion it was appropriate that Queen Marie of Romania would sparkle more brightly than this twenty-three-year-old earl's daughter who was relatively new to the royal scene. What helped Elizabeth to enjoy herself was the combination of splendid formality and relaxed informality. Although everything was as sumptuous as in England – if anything, there was even more gold braid and gold leaf in evidence than in England – everything was late. This meant that for the first time in her life, she was on time. She actually found that everything 'is very funny here, just like a musical comedy!'[7] which contains just enough of the mocking disdain, which Lady Gladwyn, wife of the future British Ambassador to Paris, would later on complain about, to show that even as she was confessing to enjoying herself, there was already an element of *hauteur* in her appreciation.

On the evening of the Yorks' arrival, there was a dinner at the palace. The following day the christening of the Crown Prince took place. The Patriarch of the Serbian Orthodox Church dropped the baby in the font, and Bertie had to fish out the mewling infant before he drowned. As Orthodox baptisms require complete submersion, this was a very real prospect. Following the successful conclusion of this ceremony, there was the inevitable balcony scene in which all the visiting and resident royals took part, including Elizabeth. She treated the citizens of Belgrade to the Elizabeth wave both then and also later that afternoon, when Paul and Olga drove them around the city.

The following morning, Elizabeth watched her friend marry her future sister-in-law's sister. Never one to hide her light under a bushel, Elizabeth recorded how Paul 'was enchanted at having us there, & otherwise he had no real friends.'[8] We have to take her word for it, but it does seem surprising that Bertie, who barely knew him, and she, who did know him well and was an old friend, would be his only friends, but Elizabeth was always prone to laying claim to being special, even as she took care to present herself as being a veritable picture of sweet modesty.

She and Bertie were due to leave for the three-day journey back to London early the following morning, but their departure had to be formally acknowledged, so the decision had been taken to have the leave-taking ceremony the evening before. They would then steam out of the train station in the royal train and spend the night in their own sleeping compartment in a special siding. After dinner with the Royal Family, King Alexander accompanied them to the station. Elizabeth's account is interesting, not only for what she intended to tell us, but for what she did not. 'So we went through all the *usual* pomp & a guard of honour, looking exactly like the male chorus of a revue, & a band, & rows of ladies with bouquets, & kisses all round, & then we steamed triumphantly out of the station, for about 20 yards, where we stopped all night! It was so funny, because it was all a sham, & they knew it too! You have no idea how odd they are.'[9]

What is revealing here is Elizabeth's choice of words. If you did not know that she had been royal for less than six months, and had never before actually taken part in anything of this nature, you would have thought that all this talk of 'the usual pomp' meant that she was an old, jaded hand at this royalty business, while describing the assembled soldiers in their ceremonial attire as 'the male chorus of a revue' was mockery bordering on bitchiness. And somewhat misplaced bitchiness at that, unless she was blind to the guards outside of Buckingham Palace where she had her suite of rooms, and in Whitehall, which she passed several times a week as she was chauffeured back and forth from the private dancing clubs where she cavorted with such frequency.

But Elizabeth seldom ended anything on a sour note, even when she had someone in her sights, which she did not in this instance. So, having conveyed the desired amount of disdain to show that she was unimpressed with all that truly captivated her, she ended on an upbeat note, conceding that they were 'so nice.' They all certainly thought that she was too, or so, at any rate, Bertie believed. He informed George V that 'they were all enchanted with Elizabeth.'[10]

The enchanted web which Bertie seemed, with some justice, to believe that Elizabeth was able to weave upon others the way she had upon him, stood her in good stead when they returned to London. One person who was disenchanted, however, was Louis Greig. He had come to the conclusion that Elizabeth's existence was making his job impossible. Hers was too overwhelming and divisive a presence, and though he had hoped that with time he might be able to find a way of accommodating Bertie's wily and controlling wife while working with the man of whom he was so fond, he had used their time abroad to come to the conclusion that there was no likelihood of the situation improving. On the contrary, with each passing day it would degenerate.

The dilemma facing Greig was one which the Duke of Windsor would later describe. Elizabeth was so adept at conveying hostility even as she was smiling at you and pretending to be 'sugar itself'[11] that you were left virtually defenceless. On the other hand, she conveyed her feelings of aggression so capably, that you could hardly ignore the potent message. 'My nincompoop of a brother could never see through her,' David said, quite forgetting that it was only after she had turned against him that he began to see through her as well.

And if you accused her of aggression, or even just voiced the opinion that she was manipulating behind the scenes, she would deny it and accuse you of victimising her, as she later did with her friend Helen Hardinge after she had orchestrated Alec Hardinge's removal as King George VI's Private Secretary in 1943 – then had the gall to tell Helen Hardinge that she was 'angry' with her for 'believing' such rumours, despite a wealth of documentary evidence to show that Lady Hardinge was right and she was lying.

Greig, however, could see through Elizabeth. He was not prepared to tolerate a situation which had become as untenable as it was invidious. So he tendered his resignation when Bertie returned from Belgrade. He was not surprised that Bertie accepted it; for he could see that the kindly but needy prince had found someone he needed even more than he needed him. To his credit, he was fond enough of Bertie to be glad that he had a wife he could be as involved with as Elizabeth, though of course he would not have been human had he not regretted that Elizabeth's egotism and 'virulent jealousy', as the Duke of Windsor put it, precluded her from allowing others who were close to Bertie to remain features of any consequence in his life.

Bertie now wrote to his parents to inform them of what had happened. He claimed that the decision was mutual. 'I feel that now I am married it is better to have a change as things have not been working too smoothly and we both feel the time has come.'[12] Both King and Queen demanded that Bertie rescind his acceptance of Greig's resignation. George V actually went so far as to lay the blame fairly and squarely at the feet of 'the little Duchess' and made it clear he would not tolerate a decent and loyal servant being treated so abominably. Bertie, of course, denied that Elizabeth was responsible, but neither George nor Mary was fooled. This time they both waded in, pointing out how marvellous Greig had been to Bertie, and effectively telling their son that he was an ingrate to treat someone who had done so much for him so badly, all because his spoilt, manipulative brat of a wife wanted to wield the power that her new position afforded her, though of course they didn't put it quite like that. But the meaning was nevertheless clear to anyone who wished to see it.

Although Bertie wavered, Greig did not. He could see that delaying the inevitable made it no less so. If he didn't leave this time, there would be another time. And no matter how bad things were now, they were nowhere near as bad as they would be next time around. Greig was quite right in discerning that Elizabeth was as implacable as she was intransigent. As far as she was concerned, she was the only person in Bertie's life who should have any influence over him. As Shawcross put it in a masterpiece of euphemism in the official biography, 'His departure was perhaps inevitable once the Duke had a wife who was not only anxious but also well able to offer him even greater support and encouragement.' So, when the King and Queen interceded and asked him to stay, Greig explained to them that he thought the best way of preserving his relationship with Bertie lay in leaving his employ. An agreement was then struck whereby Greig would remain as

Bertie's Comptroller until 28th February 1924. This would give everyone time for the dust to settle and for Greig to find other work. Rather than return to medicine, he joined the stockbroking firm of his wife Phyllis's family, J & A Scrimgeour. George V's diary blames Elizabeth and Elizabeth alone for what had happened, and the King made as public a protest as he could, by appointing Louis Greig a Gentleman Usher in Ordinary on 1st March, 1924.

Elizabeth then did something she would do time and again in the future. Once Greig had departed and she became aware that the story had got out about how she had orchestrated his departure, she wrote him a sweet letter denying any involvement and expressing her and Bertie's gratitude for all Greig had done for him. This was a canny move. She knew only too well that all royal correspondence enters the Royal Archives. There was no better way for a denialist to deny involvement in something she was up to her neck in. Thereafter the record would show that she had been innocent of any wrongdoing, as well as grateful. Bertie, however, had written Greig a letter of appreciation on 29th February, the day after his departure. In this, he expressed gratitude, appreciation and implied regret. After asserting that a 'parting between friends is always a painful ordeal, but a parting between us, I hope, is an impossibility,' he then left the door open for a personal relationship by stating, 'I hope and trust we shall always be the best of friends and that we shall see something of each other in the days to come.'[13]

In the years to come, the two men did remain friends. They visited each other, though such visits seldom involved Elizabeth.

Lessons, once learnt, are not necessarily remembered. Although the King and Queen now knew exactly how deadly Elizabeth could be beneath all those smiles and 'saccharine', to quote the Duke of Windsor, and although George V would not have occasion in the future to recall Elizabeth's manipulative skills, Queen Mary certainly would. Unfortunately for her and the rest of the Royal Family, it would be many years after she should have been applying the lessons she had just learnt, that she finally woke up to just how conniving her daughter-in-law could be. And worse, how ruthless she was when she wanted to get rid of someone. Elizabeth did not factor that individual's rights into the equation, nor consider whether those rights were proportionately more important than her desires. What Elizabeth wanted, Elizabeth had to get and, since she wanted as pleasant and agreeable and fun-filled a life as she could engineer, there was no room for the accommodation less pleasure-loving and more flexible personalities would have tolerated. You either worshipped at her feet, or you were out.

By the time Queen Mary fully realised the full extent of Elizabeth's proclivities, however, it was too late to repair the damage she had wrought within the Royal Family. Much misery might have been averted had the old lady remembered the lessons of the Greig incident. Regrettably, queens are no more adept at remembering the lessons they should have remembered than us more ordinary mortals.

Greig's departure, moreover, was not the only scheme Elizabeth had on the boil at this time. She was intent on leaving White Lodge. With that in mind, she had delegated the outgoing Comptroller to negotiate with the Ministry of Works to find her another house. On 13th January, 1924, she recorded in her diary her 'terrific disappointment' when he telephoned to tell her that the refurbishments to the house had been too expensive for the Government to consider providing her with another house. There were also other considerations. Aside from no suitable replacement being available, a political crisis was brewing which was more important than satisfying her caprices. On 22nd January, 1924, the Conservative Prime Minister Stanley Baldwin resigned, to be replaced by the first ever Labour Prime Minister, Ramsay MacDonald. Now more than ever, Elizabeth would simply have to tolerate living in suburbia. The prospect of a left-leaning Government condoning the expenditure of more public monies on yet another property so that she could be housed in one of the palatial Crown Estate residences she coveted was even more unlikely than the already dim prospect it had been under the Conservatives.

Terrifically disappointed though she was, Elizabeth had some consolation. Bertie had rented them a country house at Guildsborough in Northamptonshire for the winter. While he hunted, she relaxed. In the official biography, Shawcross obtusely confirms the Duke of Windsor's claim that she had a 'terrible temper' and often 'had a go at' Bertie. He says, 'She liked him to hunt but she was aware of the dangers and got nervous – and sometimes cross – if he returned late from the field.' In fact, she was already practised at 'flying at him over the slightest thing' if he deviated even one iota from an agreed plan, though she preferred to think that she was teaching him to have consideration for her wishes and feelings rather than being a demanding termagant.

As Elizabeth's chief complaint at this time was the misery living in suburbia was causing her, one needs little imagination to conjure up how she nagged the happily henpecked Bertie on a daily basis to get them out of Richmond – usually done in the sweetest tone and under the guise of communicating the feelings which he would thereafter, and for the rest of their lives together, have to put before everything else, even if she occasionally lost her rag and 'flew at him' too.

Bertie, however, was highly motivated to fulfil the demands of the demanding woman he had married. Indeed, there is much to be said for the fact that both he and David would not have been as fulfilled in their marriages, had their wives been less demanding. Both Elizabeth and Wallis were, on some level, substitutes for the aloof and demanding mother Queen Mary had been. In adulthood, they were living out their childish needs for the mother who had eluded them. Since they had never been able to please Queen Mary in childhood, they had married substitutes whose demands must be as extensive and never-ending as their mother's had been, and indeed continued to be, for Mary put royal duty above all else and was self-abnegating to an unusual degree. The key to the success of their marriages was therefore the motivation both men had happily to fulfil the demands of their demanding, mother-substitute wives. Arguably, neither man would have been as obsessed with either woman had she been less demanding or even displayed initial interest in him. It was this very lack of genuine interest which made her so compelling. And each man would have lost interest in his wife had she ceased to fulfil his need to avoid failure by fulfilling her demands. In other words, marital success could only be achieved by the never-ending self-abnegating fulfilment of their demands. As time would show, this would prove to be no problem for either woman, as both Elizabeth and Wallis were selfish, self-centred, pleasure-loving sybarites.

So vociferous did Elizabeth become in her demands to be freed from the shackles of White Lodge, that Bertie got his sister Mary and her husband Viscount Lascelles to come to their rescue and lend them Chesterfield House for the summer.

Now that June saw Elizabeth back in Mayfair, her complaints ceased. She and Bertie once more had the means to go out to nightclubs as many times a week as she liked without the necessity of taking a twenty-minute car journey back to Richmond, or worse, spending the night in their apartment at Buck House. She was uncomfortably aware that it was easy for the courtiers to keep track of their movements and report back to the Monarch that she frequently did not get to bed before three o'clock in the morning, or rise before eleven, and while George V did not actually expect her to do much work, he did expect her to limit her social activities to places he deemed to be acceptable.

This expectation was a concern to Elizabeth. Earlier that year, while Greig was still Comptroller, George V had heard that she and Bertie had been seen at the *louche* cabaret revue, Midnight Follies. This was housed in the nightclub at the Hotel Metropole, which offered a cabaret of scantily-clad entertainers. When George found out about his son and daughter-in-law going there, he instructed Greig to issue a stern rebuke. Elizabeth promptly wrote her father-in-law one of her letters which were kissed with genius. 'I am so sorry about this, as I hate to think of you being annoyed with us, or worried in any way,' she started, before denying the undeniable and claiming 'it really is a most respectable place. I promise you we would not go anywhere that we ought not to.'[14] Having made it clear to him that any further objections on his part would be unreasonable, she continued to go to the Midnight Follies, and just about every other place of entertainment that her circle of sybarites patronised, though she was plainly taking care not to fly too openly in his face, hence the need to avoid sleeping at the palace.

Although June and July were months which Elizabeth and her circle always spent in the south – the London Season being the focal point, albeit with frequent trips to country houses within easy reach of the capital – in August and September the north beckoned. But, now that she was royal, the world, as opposed to just the British aristocracy, was her stage; and Elizabeth was not about to forgo the perks that her new position offered. Remember, in those days travel was far rarer and more exotic an activity than it is now. Even aristocrats viewed a 'trip' of any description as a big deal. While Elizabeth had been to Paris once or twice prior to her marriage, now that she was a royal duchess, the world was her oyster. And she was one pearl who intended to avail herself of every opportunity she had – or could create.

This second summer of her royal existence, Elizabeth set off for Scotland in the knowledge that her desire to travel to a distant venue, which none of her friends had yet visited, was being fulfilled. Bertie, who echoed everything Elizabeth said, had willingly become her mouthpiece once the idea of going to East Africa had been suggested to her. He claimed to the powers-that-be who arranged royal tours that they needed a holiday after an exhausting year and a half of married life. The only way the public purse would pay for this private jaunt was if they tacked on the occasional official engagement to the itinerary. While Bertie already did a relatively modest amount of official engagements at home, by any reckoning Elizabeth's contribution was meagre, so whatever the cause of the need for a break, exhaustion from work had nothing to do with it, though of course exhaustion from play was another matter entirely. All those nights out floating on a sea of booze until 3 am and 'early' mornings when she rose an hour before midday, would have exhausted even someone with a less stalwart constitution than Elizabeth.

While the trip was being planned, the Yorks went to Glamis, where she contrived to spend more time than at 'so boring' Balmoral.[15] While he shot and stalked, she walked, wrote letters and lazed around. Hers was hardly an arduous life, except in Bertie's eyes, though she already had him convinced that so rare a creature as she was should never be pressurised into too much activity, unless of course, such activity entailed enjoying her full and fun-filled social life, in which case she could be relied upon to rise to the challenge with all the good humour that was at her disposal.

According to Elizabeth, Winston Churchill was instrumental in convincing her that East Africa was a place she absolutely had to see. 'I remember sitting next to him at dinner just after we were married and he said, "Now look here, you're a young couple. You ought to go and have a look at the world. I should go to East Africa. It's got a great future, that country (sic)."' When Elizabeth leapt at the suggestion, he contacted the Colonial Secretary, J.H. Thomas, who organised a full-scale colonial tour as an excuse for them to have their much-needed break from the heavy socialising they were doing in the United Kingdom.

Since safaris pretending to be royal tours are always much of a muchness, there is little merit in recounting in depth the perfunctory things they did or the many places they went, though Elizabeth herself was captivated by the sight of 'Cain's tomb, & the place where the Queen of Sheba embarked, & the Water Tanks made by King Solomon' in Aden.'[16] Having left London on 1st December, 1924, they arrived in Mombasa in Kenya on 22nd December. No trip would have been complete without a spot of dancing, so when they were in Nairobi they made sure that they were taken to the Muthaiga Club, the most fashionable nightclub south of the Sahara, where they danced the night away.

For the next several months, they were on safari. They saw rhinoceros, spotted lions, looked for buffalo. She 'shot birds as big as capercailzie (the word which had got her accused of being a show-off all those years before at school) for the pot, and then I shot buck, and by great flukes managed to kill and not wound, and then I shot a rhinoceros which nearly broke my heart.'[17] Having yet again ended another inconsistent account of heartlessness on a sweet note – were the buck and other animals not equally worthy of consideration, or did only a huge death count for anything? – Elizabeth readied herself to make a tearful departure from the 'country' she had come to love.

Prior to doing so, however, she managed to write a letter to the brother-in-law with whom she appeared to be in total sympathy. 'Darling David, I know now your feelings of relief and freedom when you get away from England on your own – away from all the petty little annoyances and restrictions that drive one crazy. It's marvellous, isn't it?'[18] She then continued, 'I hope your affairs are going well, and that neither your heart nor your staff are giving you cause to worry. Those two seem to give you most trouble in life, and also of course you are <u>very very</u> naughty, but delicious,'[19] making it clear that she had no reservations whatsoever about condoning his affairs with married women. She even complained about having to return home because 'I hate being under the eye of a narrow- minded autocrat,'[20] aligning herself firmly on the side of the future king against the present one. In the process, she was creating a sympathetic bond between them because of the petty restrictions which their respective staffs, on behalf of his father, visited upon them in their everyday lives. Though Elizabeth's minor restrictions – unless you counted living at White Lodge – did not compare with David's, involving as they did constant criticism from his father while he toured the world on his behalf and endured daily reprimands about such trivia as wearing trousers with turn-ups, drinking cocktails, and having week-ends, by linking herself with him she was not only showing sympathy but cleverly – and unjustifiably – laying claim to similar victimhood.

Quite how George V would have felt, had he known that the daughter-in-law who was invariably so charming to him while professing undying love and admiration, regarded him as a 'narrow-minded autocrat', is open to question. But this one letter alone gives the lie to Elizabeth's later posturings, when expediency made it convenient for her to hurl brickbats at her brother-in-law and the love of his life from behind a wall of lofty moral precepts, that her objections to Wallis were based upon her status as an adulteress.

Should there be any doubt as to the position Elizabeth took at that time regarding David, Captain Roy (Samaki) Salmon, one of the white hunters who acted as their guide during the second of their safaris, this time through Uganda, wrote that she 'says David (the Prince of Wales) is a perfect dear & a great pal of hers & the strongest man in the way of endurance in England.'[21] In other words, he was more hardworking and self-sacrificing than anyone else in the kingdom. This hardly accords with her later claims that he was irresponsible and lazy, and indeed his track record of fulfilling his duties was exemplary. No other royal had more extensive engagements, and he was already the most widely travelled royal of all time, crisscrossing the world on behalf of his parents time and again.

All good things, regrettably, have to come to an end, and so it proved with Elizabeth and Bertie's four-month 'break'. Having steamed down the Nile, on 6th April they disembarked from their steamer, the *Nasr*, at Kosti. They boarded a train, and after a diversion to see the newly-built Sennar Dam across the Blue Nile, ended up at Khartoum. After two days in the Sudanese capital they boarded another train, this time for Port Sudan, where they boarded the SS *Maloja* for the journey back home. Elizabeth would later on say how 'wonderful' the trip was and it was the '(b)est bit of one's life.'[22]

The day after Bertie and Elizabeth returned to London, David left for another of his long tours, this time western and southern Africa as well as South America. Bertie told him that neither he nor Elizabeth was glad to be back from their travels. 'We miss you terribly, of course, & there is an awful blank in London of something missing, & that blank is you.'[23] According to Shawcross, they 'missed calling on him at lunchtime at St. James's Palace for a cocktail, they missed evenings out at slightly risqué clubs with him, and they missed being able to share complaints about life with him.' Chief amongst these, of course, were the complaints about the 'autocrat' whom Elizabeth would then convert into a veritable picture of regal benevolence and kindly dutifulness once it suited her purposes. It is hardly surprising, when seeing the written proof of Elizabeth's true feelings, why the Duke of Windsor became so enraged with her later on.

Now that Bertie and Elizabeth were back, the questions as to when she might be producing an heir started to be asked with greater intensity than they had hitherto been. Everyone knew that it was the duty of all royal brides to produce heirs to the throne. Although no one at this juncture expected that Elizabeth would be producing an heir who would actually end up sitting on the throne – David, after all, was a healthy young man and well known to be libidinous – she nevertheless had a duty to provide spares for the heirs whom David would one day father.

The only difficulty was that it is not a straightforward matter to produce a legitimate baby if you are reluctant to sleep with your husband. And if Bertie's confidences to David can be relied upon, conjugal relations, which had only been intermittently re-established after the honeymoon, had petered out into real but asexual affection. Whether Elizabeth found the whole process of sex distasteful, or simply sex with Bertie, was not a question anyone was asking at this juncture, though the question would arise later.

Being a healthy young man with what used to be called 'needs', Bertie had resumed his relationship with Boo Laye. He confided this fact to David, who subsequently told Margaret, Duchess of Argyll amongst many others, and she, amongst others, told me. Indeed, it would be through her that I met Boo Laye many, many years later.

No one frowned upon their 'friendship', as it was sometimes called. And confirmation of its existence came from such varied but reliable sources that it is unlikely that it was misleading. For instance, Elizabeth's good friend Helen Hardinge told the author Michael Thornton that Bertie 'was rather more than a little in love with Evelyn Laye' until he died. Elizabeth's Private Secretary and equerry for forty years during her widowhood, Sir Martin Gilliat, confirmed that Elizabeth had always been aware of Bertie's feelings for Boo Laye and even used to refer to her as Bertie's 'girlfriend'. Since Elizabeth was virulently jealous except where Bertie's 'confidantes' (as such ladies used to be known in preference to harsher terms like mistress or lover), were concerned, one can only conclude that she was happy for others to fulfil that aspect of the wifely role, as long as Bertie looked to her for everything else – which he did.

The Royal Family was as sophisticated as the aristocracy when it came to accommodating personal preferences, especially those of a sexual nature. There was nothing unusual about a wife disliking the marriage bed, though there was something unusual about one refusing to fulfil her conjugal duties the way Elizabeth was doing. Bertie, however, had married for love, and he remained absolutely committed to their union. This of course gave her a tremendous advantage over a wife whose husband did not love her, for Bertie would never force himself upon her the way many other men did when claiming what was theirs by right (both legally and morally at that time).

Indeed, the most famous divorce case of the Victorian age, which had taken place within living memory, involved connections of Bertie's as well as this author's, and it was an awful warning to everyone in royal and aristocratic circles as to the dreadful fate that befell those who did not respect the need to keep marital relations civilised. It too, ironically, involved a couple who had been a love match. Bertie's great-aunt Princess Louise, Duchess of Argyll's brother-in-law, Lord Colin Campbell, had married the brilliant and ravishingly beautiful Gertrude Blood despite opposition from both families. When she discovered that he had infected her with syphilis, she undertook a cure which she believed had worked. Knowing that he remained infected, she refused to resume conjugal relations. At this point, his love proved rather weaker than Bertie's. He demanded restitution of conjugal rights. When she refused, his insistence became so great (in other words, he had indicated that he would rape her if she continued to resist, though the crime of rape did not then exist within marriage), that she applied to the court for a legal separation. This was the start of the longest, costliest, and most scandalous divorce ever to take place in England. Lord Colin Campbell tried to have his wife imprisoned in Paris. He also countersued in England, citing adultery on Gertrude's part with four separate men. Queen Victoria herself was outraged on behalf of the unfortunate Gertrude Campbell, but that did not stop Society closing its ranks against both the victim and her tormentor. Ultimately, honour of a dubious sort was decreed to have been served when both Colin and Gertrude's suits were thrown out. They remained married until his death. She died at the relatively early age of fifty-three in 1911, the former fencing champion and athlete reduced to a cripple in a wheelchair because of the syphilis she had not been cured of.

If Bertie was more accommodating of his wife's desires than Colin Campbell had been, the Campbell divorce had nevertheless been a sensation which everyone in royal and aristocratic circles remembered as a dreadful warning of what could happen when understanding broke down. The prospect of such a rancorous marital breakdown occurring within the Royal Family itself was unthinkable, so when marriages proved to be less than ideal, a *rapprochement* was invariably sought to keep relations civilised. In Bertie and Elizabeth's case, however, there was still genuine affection between the young couple. They were indubitably happy. And, despite the lack of conjugal relations, they were closer than most other couples and clearly well suited in every other respect.

However, they needed to produce an heir. If Elizabeth would not allow Bertie to impregnate her naturally, they had to find the means of impregnating her unnaturally. There was no question of Elizabeth going to one of the Harley Street miracle workers who had supplied heirs to titles like the earldom of Carnarvon. This baby had to be genuinely legitimate. Nor was there any possibility of what we can call a 'Strathmore solution' being resorted to. Ever since Mary of Modena had unfairly been accused of substituting a stillborn or female baby with the genuinely royal James, Prince of Wales, all royal births were witnessed by officials so that there could be no substitution.

There was only one course of action. Artificial insemination had the merit of accommodating both Bertie's and Elizabeth's needs, insofar as the conception of a legitimate heir to the throne was concerned. Moreover, the Royal Family had form with artificial insemination. Bertie's aunt Queen Maud of Norway had used this method to conceive his first cousin, the former Prince Alexander Edward Christian Frederik of Denmark.

For many years the tale had been told in aristocratic drawing rooms of how the childless Princess Carl of Denmark, as Maud was then styled, had contrived to conceive even though her husband, Queen Alexandra's nephew, was sterile. In October 1902, she had left her home in Denmark and slipped incognito into England, where she was secretly hospitalised under the care of her father Edward VII's Physician-in-Ordinary, Sir Francis Laking, 1st Baronet. He artificially inseminated her, using the sperm of his son and heir, Guy Francis Laking, and nine months later, on 2nd July, 1903, she produced her one and only child, Prince Alexander of Denmark. Known to history as Crown Prince (later King) Olav of Norway, following his father's election to the Norwegian throne in 1905, King Olav V bore a striking, almost uncanny, resemblance to Sir Guy Laking, 2nd Baronet.

For many decades, this story remained just another rumour within royal circles until the publication of the second volume of the officially sanctioned biography of King Haakon VII (as Prince Carl of Denmark had become when he was elevated to the throne of Norway) and Queen Maud by the respected Norwegian biographer Tor Bormann-Larsen in October 2004. Although he does not name Sir Guy as the father, he implies that he is. What he does do, however, is assert that Olav cannot have been Haakon VII's natural son. The dates do not match. Husband and wife met only once in a ten-month period and that meeting could not have resulted in conception.

Following publication of the book, the Norwegian Palace took the unusual step of advising their Parliament of its contents. It also continued to invite the author to events.

Although the Norwegian Royal Family and Parliament have successfully circumnavigated any possible problems that might have arisen out of the natural paternity of their elected king's heir, the only meaningful parallel between Maud's predicament and Elizabeth's was that the former wanted a child but was married to a man who could not provide her with one, while the latter needed a child from a man who presumably could provide her with one. But Elizabeth was not prepared to open herself up to the activity involved to conceive. Although the root causes of the problems were therefore radically different, the solution was identical.

There was no prospect of Elizabeth going to Sir Francis Laking, however. He had died in 1914. So she went to one of the finest physicians of the age: Dr. Walter Jagger. He inseminated her with Bertie's sperm, and she did indeed become pregnant in July 1925, a few months after her return from East Africa.

It is worth noting at this stage how prevalent this version of events has always been in aristocratic and royal circles. When I mentioned to Donald Douglas, the actor/partner of Emma, Lady Temple (Freda Dudley Ward's granddaughter) that I was writing this book, the first question he asked me was, 'Are you going to say how the Queen and Princess Margaret were conceived?'

The sources for the births of both princesses were legion, and included the Duke of Windsor, Margaret, Duchess of Argyll, Lord Beaverbrook through his granddaughter Lady Jean Campbell, and last but not least, the Marquesa de Casa Maury, as Freda Dudley Ward became when she divorced her Liberal MP husband and remarried. Nor can anyone be accused of gossiping. It was an open secret in the circles in which Elizabeth and Bertie mixed that theirs was a *marriage blanche*, but a very happy one nevertheless.

Elizabeth was only two months pregnant and not showing when David returned from his six-month tour of half the world. He was accorded a hero's welcome, his trip accounted a great success by all. The Government and several senior members of the Royal Family, including his father and mother, were on hand at Victoria Station to greet him. En route to the palace with his father and brothers, he was cheered robustly by crowds, who surged forward when he entered the palace and came out on the balcony for what was now almost the inevitable balcony scene. Elizabeth, who drove back to the palace with Queen Mary, claimed to be as happy as Bertie to have the brother-in-law she 'adored' back.

A few weeks later, on 20th November, the crowds gathered for an altogether sadder reason. Queen Alexandra died, aged eighty, of a heart attack at Sandringham. The first port of call for 'Darling Motherdear… was the little church where she had worshipped for 62 years.'[24] The following day her body was taken to Westminster Abbey for her funeral service, following which she was interred beside King Edward VII in St. George's Chapel, Windsor.

With the death of the dowager queen, Elizabeth was now the second lady in the land. Her position had already been much enhanced the previous month, when Bertie had told his parents that she was expecting a child. 'It is most necessary that E. should take the greatest care of her precious self,' Queen Mary, now suitably aligned with Elizabeth's concept of herself, wrote to Bertie on 20th October, 1925. 'It is a great joy to Papa & me to feel that we may look forward to a direct descendant in the male line of our family & the country will be delighted when they are allowed to know.'[25]

Elizabeth did not hesitate to take advantage of these means to achieve all the ends she had hitherto been unable to. She immediately used her pregnancy as an excuse for not going to Sandringham except on rare occasions. She also used it as the reason to move out of White Lodge, which was closed down for the winter, and to move into Curzon House on Curzon Street in Mayfair, which Bertie rented for them.

Elizabeth's ability to surmount health challenges, however, was as multifarious then as it would prove to be throughout her life. Because she already loved all the accolades and feedback fulfilling official engagements brought her, she found the strength to high-tail it across London to Hackney, where she opened their Maternity and Child Welfare Centre, a residence for nurses at the Hackney District Nursing Association, and, since she was already in the area, called in on the headquarters of the British Legion. Hackney and Richmond are more or less the same distance from Mayfair, but Cheltenham, which is much further from London than either Richmond or Sandringham, also saw Elizabeth nobly rise to the occasion when she visited the County of Gloucester Nursing Association's bazaar. If she was maddeningly inconsistent, her tactics were nevertheless sound, for she always managed to get her own way, and to do so in such a way that there could be no backlash against her. She did, however, manage the journey from Mayfair to Sandringham for Christmas, which she spent with the Royal Family.

Early in the new year, Elizabeth was making plans for the birth. Chief amongst these was to line up the maternity nurse she wanted. Maternity nurses usually stayed for the first month or six weeks following a birth. They took the burden of an infant off a new mother at the same time as teaching her how to cope with the baby. Like all Society women, Elizabeth would never have coped without a maternity nurse, for even more so then than now, women of a certain social rank left the majority of the tasks in dealing with an infant up to the maternity nurse in the first instance, and the baby's nurse (nanny) thereafter. Elizabeth had chosen someone she knew well. Annie (Nannie B) Beevers, a widow in her mid-fifties who had previously tended to her sisters May and Rose, was her choice, and once she booked her, she could sit back and relax in the knowledge that once Baby came, it, and she, would be well cared for.

The only problem at this time was that the lease on Curzon Street was about to expire. Never too ill to do anything she wanted, Elizabeth eagerly inspected a house in ultra-fashionable Grosvenor Square with Bertie, and agreed that they should take it. They would now be in Mayfair for the whole of the summer. However, the lease arrangements could not be satisfactorily agreed, so, rather than return to White Lodge or find another house, Elizabeth cannily opted for seeking refuge with her parents at 17 Bruton Street. This put covert pressure on the Crown Estate to find her another property, for it would be decidedly unseemly for a new royal mother, whose child would be third in line to the throne, to have nowhere to live. The impending birth had caused her stock to rise dramatically, and on the back of that, her desire to live in London instead of suburban Richmond would just have to be accommodated. White Lodge was already history, even if no one else but the expectant mother knew it.

Elizabeth was being tended by two of the most eminent medical men of her day: her obstetric miracle-worker Dr. Walter Jagger (1871–1929) and the obstetric surgeon Sir Henry Simson (1872–1939). When they realised that the baby was in the breech position, they called in Sir George Blacker (1865–1948), an obstetric specialist from University College Hospital, London. Following a consultation, the three doctors decided to move forward the due date from the end of the month to the earliest feasible date.

In keeping with the accepted custom of the time, there was no question of Elizabeth having the baby anywhere but in a private house. Hospitals were then places for the sick, usually lower class at that, and birth, though a dangerous occupation, was regarded as the supreme testament to good health. Even though the doctors knew that the baby was in the breech position and there was every likelihood that they would have to perform a Caesarean unless it could be turned successfully during labour, the birth was nevertheless scheduled to take place at 17 Bruton Street, her parents' London house. This decision alone makes an utter nonsense of Elizabeth's later claims about her own birth, with her fanciful tales of horse-drawn ambulances and taxis thrown in for diversionary measure.

Labour was induced on 20th April, 2011, and the Home Secretary, an eminent solicitor by the name of Sir William Joynson-Hicks, Bt. (and later 1st Viscount Brentford), duly arrived to stand guard, as required by law when a child in direct line of succession to the throne was being born, to prevent substitution. When it became apparent that the baby could not be turned, Sir Henry made the Caesarean incision and Dr. Jagger pulled out the future Queen Elizabeth II at exactly 2:40 am on 21st April, 1926.

The baby, who remained unnamed for nearly a week, could not have come at a more anxious time. Revolution was a word on the tip of many a tongue. The Trades Unions Congress had called a general strike for 3rd May in sympathy with the plight of the miners, whose wages and hours had been cut at a time when the country was booming. Once more, Bolshevism and the terrors of a red menace were sweeping the nation, with the upper classes in dread of what might happen if the crisis could not be contained, and the lower classes in expectation of a better way of life if such a happy eventuality should occur.

While the nation trembled at the prospect of grinding to a halt, or worse, Elizabeth and Bertie focused on choosing a name for their baby. For nearly a week they went over this all-important matter. To those who knew Elizabeth well, it was hardly surprising that the first name chosen would be her own, while Bertie, ever the adoring husband, now a besotted father, would have acted out of character had he not regarded Elizabeth as the best of all choices. The second and third names were somewhat trickier. The choice of Alexandra, for the recently-deceased dowager queen, to follow Elizabeth seemed peculiar to some, especially when it was followed by Mary in honour of the queen consort. Princess Louise, Duchess of Argyll, would later state that the elder members of the family, including Queen Mary and her sister-in-law Princess Alice, Countess of Athlone (Princess Louise's niece as well as neighbour), found the sequence jarring, and believed that this was a subtle way of Elizabeth both honouring and denigrating her mother-in-law at the same time. The more expected running order was Elizabeth Mary Alexandra.

Possibly there was nothing ominous about the sequence. The new parents might just have preferred Alexandra to Mary, but to the elder members of the family, it did raise questions as well as suspicions. Not that anyone acted upon them, for the Royal Family, like many other families, especially large families, was well used to accommodating conflict in its ranks. Its desired way of coping was pretending that such issues did not exist. And Elizabeth might well have meant nothing by her choices. But the mere fact that questions were being raised indicates that the elder members of the family were now alert to the possibility that there was more to dear sweet Elizabeth than met the eye.

Knowing that the King would have to agree to any choice he and Elizabeth had made, because royal children cannot be named without the consent of the monarch, Bertie wrote to tell his father his and Elizabeth's decision on 27th April. Since the King and Queen were already aware that Elizabeth was the guiding light in that relationship, they were not blind to the choices owing more to her than to him. The defensive tone of Bertie's letter also encouraged rather than dispelled the suspicion that he had some awareness of the potential for embarrassment, even refusal, for he wrote, 'We are so anxious for her first name to be Elizabeth as it is such a nice name & there has been no one of that name in your family for a long time. Elizabeth of York sounds so nice too.'[26]

It is hardly surprising, when reading this letter, that Queen Mary, Princess Alice, Princess Louise and others felt that the choices were Elizabeth's rather than Bertie's. One can almost hear her voice behind his pen. The use of the word *your* instead of *our* to describe his and his father's family – the same family – was itself a giveaway, but despite the misgivings, Elizabeth had yet again shown how adept she was at getting her own way. The King agreed to her choice of names, and the future Queen Elizabeth II was duly registered as Her Royal Highness Princess Elizabeth Alexandra Mary of York.

The following week, the United Kingdom ground to a halt with the onset of the General Strike of 1926. Hyde Park was turned into a milk depot and the Government formed an Organisation for the Maintenance of Supplies to move food between places. The drivers ferrying food back and forth were primarily upper-class and middle-class men. Public transport also ground to a halt, until a variety of noble and bourgeois drivers started to man the buses and trains. Because those amateur services were skeletal, people mostly hitched rides, often with strangers, walked, or cycled to and from work. Otherwise people stayed at home.

To ensure that public order was maintained, special constables were created willy-nilly. Many a duke and earl donned the uniform of these special policemen, and the doormen at the Pall Mall gentlemen's clubs such as White's or Boodle's soon got used to doffing their hats at noblemen dressed in working-class gear as they showed up at these exclusive venues for lunch or tea, before returning to duty keeping the public peace.

Although the supporters of the strike divided along class lines, there was remarkably little bitterness. There was a football match in Plymouth between the police and the strikers which the King used as an example of why the politicians should not make excessive demands or use excessive force to break the strike.

George V had returned to London as soon as the strike started, and remained at Buckingham Palace, for its duration, urging caution against the more extreme solutions being cooked up by the more reactionary elements in the Government. He was adamant that no attempt should be made to sequester trades unions' funds, which he warned would be inflammatory and turn what had hitherto been a peaceful strike into a conflagration. He regarded the desire of the Chancellor of the Exchequer, Winston Churchill, to call in the army to safeguard the constitution as 'imprudent'.[27] Although he was more appreciative of the *Daily Mail*'s initiative in keeping its readership informed by printing its papers in Paris then flying them over to London, while most other newspapers ceased to function, his primary purpose was to calm all sides so that order could be restored with the minimum of mishap. This was monarchy at its finest, along the lines of his first cousin the Danish King announcing that he was king of all Danes, Communists included, and after nine days the General Strike was called off when divisions arose between the Trades Unions Congress and the Miners' Union. Although not everyone returned to work immediately, within weeks even the dock and transport workers and the printers were back at work, along with the newspapers, though it would be another six months before all the miners returned to the mines.

Once the strike was over, the healing began. The skilful way the King had negotiated such dangerous political shoals meant that the monarchy had not been damaged, and the Royal Family, ever keen to promote the people's affection for itself, enlisted the Smiling Duchess to pose for photographs with her baby. Unsurprisingly, mother and daughter were taken up in force by the press. A new wave of popularity for Elizabeth had begun, this time as the young matriarch.

For the first two months of Little Elizabeth's life (she would become 'Lilibet' because she could not pronounce her name, but for the sake of ease will hereafter be referred to by that nickname), Nannie B occupied a room adjoining Baby's in the nursery at 17 Bruton Street. When she was over a month old, Clara (Alah) Knight joined the household, Elizabeth's sister having graciously surrendered her. Hereafter, both Elizabeth and Lilibet were set up, the former released from all but the most pleasurable of maternal duties; the latter because she was given a level of care which she would thereafter claim was superb. Indeed, so satisfied was Lilibet with her nurse that she would ensure that her firstborn was tended to by Alah as well.

Elizabeth took full advantage of having a baby. In keeping with upper-class traditions, she tended Lilibet only minimally, but her arrival was a useful excuse to escape from such work as she did not wish to undertake. Although she would virtually retire from all but the most pleasurable of official engagements now that she was a mother with a child, she was far from idle. When she was not posing for photographs with the baby to boost the monarchy, she was as active socially as she had ever been. She was out and about, often with her mother, choosing fabric to cover furniture and make curtains. This superb homemaker's active demands for a suitable London residence for her husband, her child, and herself, coupled with her passive resistance in refusing to return to White Lodge, which remained closed down, had finally borne fruit. The Marquess of Northampton surrendered the lease on his townhouse at No. 145 Piccadilly, a Crown Estate property, and Bertie in turn swapped his on White Lodge for a new one on the mammoth Mayfair residence which was a five-minute walk from Buckingham Palace and only three minutes from the Ritz Hotel.

Overlooking Green Park near Hyde Park Corner, this was just the sort of house Elizabeth had always aspired to. It was large, sumptuous and grand, with some twenty-five bedrooms, several reception rooms, and a large if dark entrance hall. It also had a large communal garden in the back which it shared with the neighbouring houses. This was at least as good as, if not better than, 20 St. James's Square, and infinitely superior to 17 Bruton Street. Elizabeth was right where she had always wanted to be.

The Fairest of Us All

Chapter Eight

Having given birth to an heir to the throne, Elizabeth's position was not only enhanced generally, with the world at large, but particularly, with the Royal Family itself. Like all dominating personalities, she knew just how to eke out the advantage this gave her, to further enhance her position and in so doing, increase her power in what was tantamount to a circular motion.

As far as Elizabeth was concerned, Lilibet was *her* baby, not anyone else's, and no one, but no one, would be allowed to interfere with what *she* wanted for *her* baby. If it were possible, the already supremely self-confident Elizabeth's confidence had been boosted to an even greater level. It would remain there for the remainder of her life, unopposed by any of the people who could, and maybe even should, have reeled her back in occasionally.

The first means of assertion was to go against tradition and impose her own choice of clergyman for the christening of the baby, which was due to take place at Buckingham Palace in the private chapel on 29th May. The Archbishop of Canterbury would have been the normal choice, but if she had acceded to that, she would have missed this golden opportunity to assert herself, which could, of course, be done only at the expense of others. So, under the guise of consideration, she opted for Cosmo Lang, trotting out the excuse that since they were the York family and he was the Archbishop of York, he was a better option. She also chose both her parents and her sister May to be godparents, while Bertie chose his parents, his sister Mary, and his great-uncle the Duke of Connaught. Since it was normal for royal babies to have a plethora of royal godparents, Lilibet was already being deprived of the many other royal relations who could, and quite possibly should, have been named as godparents. Europe, after all, still had a host of monarchs and crown princes; many of them close friends and relations of the British Royal

Family. It would have been tactically preferable for the baby to have at least one or two foreign kings or queens or their heirs, such as the Belgians, Romanians, Danes, Swedes or Norwegians, as godparents. The message Elizabeth was conveying was that her family was every bit as important as the various royal families. While this was understandable on one level, on another it was impractical, almost delusional, for in a royal world a half-royal child already had a handicap, and exacerbating that was hardly the way to increase its future prospects. As might well have become apparent if David had produced children and Lilibet had remained Princess Elizabeth of York.

Following the christening, Elizabeth drove home the point that Bertie had been absorbed into her world even more than she had been into his – the perks of royalty excluded, obviously. Mother, father and baby remained ensconced in her parents' relatively small house at 17 Bruton Street, rather than taking up residence in either of the royal properties to which the Duke and Duchess were entitled, where space was no problem. But Elizabeth was determined not to return to White Lodge or to use Buckingham Palace, so she and the ever-obliging Bertie continued to stay with her parents. Although this too struck a discordant note with the older members of the Royal Family, neither she nor Bertie was sufficiently important in the royal scheme of things for anyone to do anything about it, except raise an eyebrow and remark about the extraordinary turn events had taken. Meanwhile, the Yorks remained living *en famille* with the Strathmores until it was time to depart from London for the summer. Then they headed up to Glamis.

Having already fired a few generalised warning shots across the royal bow, Elizabeth now fired one directly at her mother-in-law. Although the queen had only limited power within the Royal Family – she invariably deferred to her husband and King – she was nevertheless The Queen and a figure of veneration inside and outside of royal circles. This meant that the competitive and jealously possessive, but nevertheless non-argumentative and apparently pliable Elizabeth, had to find some means of communicating to Mary that she was the primary fount of power within her own particular unit of the family. So she took steps to prevent the queen from seeing her granddaughter. In another of his masterpieces of understatement, Shawcross confirms in the official biography how 'Queen Mary was anxious that Princess Elizabeth should visit Balmoral too, but this the Duchess parried, writing to her mother-in-law, "I am longing for you to see her. She has grown so round and pink [and] merry. The country air suits her marvellously well I am glad to say. I would have so loved to bring her up, but I am sure you will agree that so many changes is [sic] not a good thing." When the Yorks made their own trip to Balmoral at the end of September, they left the baby with the Duchess's mother at Glamis.'[1]

Although Elizabeth's overtly disobliging stance was a new feature in her relationship with Queen Mary, it was one which would continue until the old queen's death. Her attitude could not have been clearer. No matter how much saccharine she poured over the chalice, the poisonous fact was that she was not prepared to consider Queen Mary's thoughts, ideas, or feelings when opposing them could somehow score her an advantage in the power games she was playing. While this frustrated the old lady and made her unhappy, there was little she could do about it unless she was prepared to threaten the civility and superficial harmony that existed between them. This she would never do overtly, though there would be times in the future when she would work behind the scenes to counter Elizabeth. This was especially true in the future where Lilibet's education was concerned, for Elizabeth tried to replicate her mother Cecilia's happenstance position in which good manners and femininity should be regarded as acceptable substitutes for knowledge. Queen Mary and Lilibet's governess, Marion (Crawfie) Crawford, seeing how disastrous such ignorance would be in a queen regnant, joined forces and, using subterfuge, did their utmost to redress the balance. Though their successes were more limited than they would have liked, and certainly not as much as Princess Margaret claimed either she or her sister needed, the net result of their efforts was that Lilibet would nevertheless receive tutoring from such experts as masters from Eton who, left up to Elizabeth, would never have crossed the river from that College to Windsor Castle.

Having made the point that she was the only person who had the right to dictate what her daughter could and could not do – a revolutionary concept in royal families, in which the will of the king or queen is usually deemed to be of supreme importance – and having got away with it, Elizabeth was now set for the next phase of her determination. The Australian Prime Minister, Stanley Bruce, had invited the King to send one of his sons out to Australia early in 1927 to officially open the new federal Parliament in the capital, Canberra. David had made an extensive Australasian tour in 1920, and it appears from the way things developed that Bruce was hoping that he would return. Bertie, however, proposed himself to the Dominions Secretary, Leo Amery, articulating how much he had enjoyed his East African sojourn. Of course there was no doubt that Bertie would never have made such a suggestion without Elizabeth's consent or approval, and, as we have seen, she had been the prime mover in the East African safari, so it is likely that she was behind this endeavour as well. George V, however, was not eager for his stuttering son to go on a full-scale official tour – East Africa had been only a vacation passing itself off as semi-official – because he would have to make speeches and might make a fool of himself, or worse, the monarchy, in front of the whole Empire. Nor was Bruce eager for Bertie's participation. The whole purpose of the tour was to spread gold dust everywhere. There would be precious little magic in a tour centred on a prince who couldn't get out three words without tripping over them. But Bertie, with his newly-stiffened backbone, was adamant. He, i.e. Elizabeth, and maybe even he, wanted to go.

According to Shawcross, 'Elizabeth was dismayed by this prospect.' Not only would she have to leave Lilibet behind for the six months' duration, but she would also have to support her stuttering husband.

With the passage of time and the death of all the participants, it is difficult to say whether Elizabeth really was as dismayed as Shawcross believes. All the evidence suggests that Bertie seldom did anything, no matter how trivial, without her consent and approval, and bowed to her will in all major decisions. While this might have been one of those rare occasions upon which he did not factor her desires into the equation, the evidence suggests otherwise.

Moreover, in refutation of Elizabeth's ostensible dismay, by the time the tour was mooted she was already leaving Lilibet for fairly lengthy periods while she and Bertie went to stay with friends. Of course, she was not being a negligent mother in her own eyes. She was being a good mother. Baby must not have her routine disturbed. Even though one set of whitewashed nursery walls in one stately home was pretty indistinguishable from another even by the most perceptive of adults, much less a baby of a few months old, and even though taking Alah and Baby along would hardly have inconvenienced their hosts, Elizabeth was far too well-mannered ever to make such a suggestion, notwithstanding that many another mother would have done so. Instead, she nobly sacrificed her time with Baby, while she and Bertie resumed their round of fun-filled stately visits.

Although days and weeks were not months, one cannot avoid the suspicion that the actress within Elizabeth was already eager to gain new rounds of applause as she visited new scenes and conquered new audiences with her delightful charm. How likely was it that Bertie would have been pushing for a tour of six months' duration if Elizabeth had not wanted it? Such conduct is entirely contrary to everything anyone has ever known about him. On the other hand, the disclaiming Duchess denying what her true desires were, while nobly professing dismay about leaving her baby behind, and thereby garnering extra admiration for the dutifulness with which she went about her self-sacrificing life, is very much in keeping with Elizabeth's *modus operandi*.

Whatever her motives, Elizabeth swung into operation as soon as George V agreed that his second son and daughter-in-law could go on this latest journey. By the time it was over, they would have spent a full year out of the four years they had been married outside the country.

Preparations now had to be made. Naturally, the first place Elizabeth headed to was Madame Handley Seymour's, where she ordered a whole raft of yet more frightful frocks. She also managed to choose one unsightly hat after another from Mayfair milliners, proving just how antithetical her style was compared with her brother-in-law David's women. Despite this, hers was a winning style, if only amongst the unstylish, which, in those days, consisted of the largest percentage of the female population.

Kitting herself out in bizarre fashion, however, would not guarantee the success of the tour. George V had already made it plain that he did not consider Bertie a suitable representative of the Crown owing to his speech defect. Unless something could be done to alleviate his stammer, he would be an embarrassment and the tour a failure. Elizabeth, who was never one to shy away from a challenge, took matters in her own hands. She set about finding a speech therapist, much against Bertie's wishes, for he had tried several, and all had ended disappointingly. This is where Elizabeth's glorious indomitability now came into its own.

Quite how she got Boo Laye involved has been lost in the sands of time. What is known is that she and Bertie had remained on good terms with Boo both privately and publicly, to such an extent that in the first year of marriage she had accompanied Bertie to two of Boo's shows, *The Merry Widow* and *Madame de Pompadour*. Michael Thornton tells how Elizabeth would announce, 'Bertie, there's your girlfriend,' when Boo came on stage. It was his view that Elizabeth was never jealous of Boo, but grateful for her discretion, which was so exemplary that she, Boo, would scratch out any mention of her relationship with Bertie out of deference to his wife, even as both women were approaching their centennials. There is a classic photograph of the two of them, taken in 1960, beaming away at each other, and though both were accomplished actresses who might well have been indulging in hypocritical repartee for the benefit of the camera, there seems to have been a genuine regard between them. Boo herself said that she thought that Bertie had married the right woman, because only Elizabeth had the strength of character and the confidence to bring him out the way she did. Although Boo would never confirm whether she and Bertie had resumed their relationship after his marriage, the Duke of Windsor confirmed that they had, though whether it continued once Boo got married is unknown.

By the time Elizabeth had picked up the cudgel on Bertie's behalf to find a cure for his stammer, Boo was recently married to the actor Sonnie Hale. Whatever the nature of her relationship with Bertie at that juncture, she was still sufficiently friendly with both the Yorks to recommend Lionel Logue, the Australian speech therapist whom she knew through theatrical circles and whose relationship with Bertie was so ably depicted in the Oscar-winning film, *The King's Speech*.

Once Boo had made her recommendation, Bertie's Private Secretary, Patrick Hodgson, became involved. After he had checked Logue out and found out that he was not a rogue, he made an appointment for Bertie. Elizabeth accompanied him. From the outset, Logue and Bertie and Elizabeth hit it off. They worked as a team, with Elizabeth involved in aspects of Bertie's regimen. She often accompanied Bertie to Harley Street or the Logue flat in South Kensington. She would sit on her husband to aid his breathing exercises, and was assiduous in encouraging him at every step of the way. Logue himself said both Elizabeth and Bertie were commendably open to his help, though Bertie was 'the pluckiest and most determined patient I ever had'.[2]

As willing as Bertie was to help himself, however, the reality is that no one had been able to help him before Elizabeth came on the scene and shored up his self-belief with some of that indomitable spirit which was such a characteristic of her personality. It is doubtful that Logue's technique would have succeeded to the extent that it did had Elizabeth not been functioning in tandem with him to open Bertie up to the possibility that he could help himself. And help himself he did, with a discernible improvement that was both dramatic and almost instantaneous.

Behind the scenes, however, Logue was not the only person assisting Bertie. Though he was undeniably the primary instrument, Boo Laye also used to have Bertie come to her rehearsal studio in the West End. There, the newly-married singing star and her erstwhile lover would go over his breathing exercises. Their sessions would end with them singing duets of her hit songs like *I'll See you Again* and *Love is a Song (But Two Must Sing It)*.[3]

Elizabeth plainly knew about these sessions, which could not have continued without her consent. It is interesting in the light of how jealous she could be about some people, women especially, though men as well, that she never once in nearly eighty years evinced any jealousy of 'Bertie's girlfriend'.

By the time Christmas rolled around that year, profound change was underfoot not only in the Yorks' lives but also in the Royal Family's. Elizabeth was putting the finishing touches on 145 Piccadilly, which would be her new home for the next decade. Queen Mary was full of helpful advice, such as how she could achieve what she wanted in the way of borrowing pictures and furniture from the royal collections through the simple expedient of keeping King George V, who should have been consulted, out of the loop. Although Bertie was not yet articulate, his fluency was considerably greater than it had been a few short weeks before. And George V and Mary had finally been able to move out of York Cottage into the Big House at Sandringham. This year the festivities would therefore be celebrated in the comfort of Sandringham House, rather than the cramped quarters of the incommodious villa which had housed the King and Queen for the first sixteen years of their reign.

For Elizabeth, however, no royal house occupied by anyone but herself had more appeal than a house belonging to her own family, so, once the Christmas celebrations were over, she and Bertie headed for St. Paul's Walden Bury to stay with her parents for the new year. Without a doubt, the Strathmore household was more fun than Sandringham, but there was also an additional reason for heading to Hertfordshire. Elizabeth had decreed that Lilibet would be put in the care of her mother for much of the duration of their tour abroad. While there is little doubt that Cecilia Strathmore was a more maternal woman than Queen Mary, it was nevertheless surprising that this non-royal royal duchess would leave her royal child with its non-royal grandmother while the royal grandmother was given short shrift. This, of course, excited much comment in the Royal Family, with Princess Louise, Duchess of Argyll, wondering aloud how Queen Victoria would have reacted to such a slight. Queen Mary, however, 'rose above it', quite possibly with a combination of relief and frustration, for she was unused to anyone but her Georgie ignoring her wishes and imposing theirs upon her. On 5th January, 1927, Elizabeth wrote that 'the Queen wants to have her for at least three out of the six months', but in the event, it was her mother who had the lion's share of Baby.

Bertie and Elizabeth left London on 9th January. Accompanying them were the 10th Earl of Cavan as Chief of Staff; his wife Joan as one of Elizabeth's two ladies-in-waiting; Patrick Hodgson the Private Secretary; two equerries in the shape of Colin Buist (who would remain a friend of theirs and play a slight but important role in the Abdication Crisis) and Major Terence (later 1st Baron) Nugent; Harry (later Sir) Butterbee as political secretary; Surgeon Commander H.E.Y. White; the usual complement of dressers, and last but not least, the second lady-in-waiting, the Hon. Mrs. Little Gilmour. Victoria 'Tortor' Gilmour, daughter of Viscount Chelsea and granddaughter of the 5th Earl Cadogan, was married to John Little Gilmour, son and heir of a baronet. She was scatty but great fun and would become a lifelong friend of Elizabeth's. She was also the mother of Sir Ian (later Lord) Gilmour, 3rd Bt., the eminent Tory politician in the Thatcher Government whom the Prime

Minister dismissed as 'wet' because of his liberal conservative policies. Although John and Tortor, who became Lady Victoria when her father succeeded to the earldom, were divorced in 1928, Elizabeth saw no reason why divorce should prevent her friend from continuing in the royal circle, which was either commendably tolerant or archly hypocritical, depending on who was doing the talking.

The Australian tour of 1927, like all other royal tours, turned out to be a great success. Bertie's earnestness and eagerness to please won him many admirers, and he was even able to speak with minimal interruptions owing to the new regimen which Logue had devised and he and Elizabeth had been practising with relish. Yet again, she seduced everyone with whom she came into contact with her charm, grace and friendliness. Her gaiety was infectious and people loved meeting a royal who patently enjoyed meeting them. This was yet another illustration of how happily her personal traits, both virtues and failings, coincided to create the ideal public figure, and of course Bertie's letters back home were full of pride and praise, stating time and again how everyone was in love with the woman with whom he was entranced.

Once more Elizabeth's genius for the right sort of publicity resulted in invaluable column inches. A typical example of this was the report in *The Dispatch* of how Elizabeth convinced Bertie to make an impromptu stop at the Anzac Memorial Hospital at Albany. Australia had suffered tremendous casualties during the Great War, especially at Gallipoli, and Bertie, far more regimented and unimaginative than his wife, wanted to adhere to the timetable. But 'it is with a tremble of the voice and a glistening of the eye that the little Royal Lady, having the true heart of a woman and the gracious grandeur of a queen, begs her lord to accede to the request', and, reminiscent of her gesture in laying her wedding bouquet on the Tomb of the Unknown Warrior in Westminster Abbey, she rose to the occasion with a splendour that only another instinctive crowd-pleaser like Queen Marie of Romania could have done.

Success breeds success and confidence increases confidence. By the end of the tour the Governor of South Australia, Sir Tom Bridges, was able to write a glowing tribute to King George V about how 'His Royal Highness has touched people profoundly by his youth, his simplicity and his natural bearing, while the Duchess has had a tremendous ovation and leaves us with the responsibility of having a continent in love with her'.[4] The political secretary echoed these enthusiastic sentiments, telling George V's Private Secretary, Lord Stamfordham, that 'there can be no doubt that the Australian Tour has been a great success and done a great deal of good. A nail has been driven into the coffin of Bolshevism, which will securely hold it down,

I trust, for some time to come'.[5] Bertie himself gave credit where it was truly due, telling his father how grateful he was to Logue for all the tools he had given him to conquer his speech impediment. He also paid tribute to his main helpmate: 'I could never have done the tour without her help; that I know, & I am so thankful she came too.'[6] Elizabeth had made herself indispensable to Bertie and, in so doing, she had carved out a position of such power in the family that her parents-in-law were – if not exactly happy, then certainly more than willing – to overlook the downside that accompanied the upside of her extraordinarily assertive personality.

On 27th June, 1927, the *Renown,* which had been away from home for six months, steamed into Portsmouth Harbour with the royal party. Meanwhile, in London, Lilibet and Alah had just moved into 145 Piccadilly. The house was full of flowers which, at Queen Mary's behest, she and Cecilia had dotted throughout as a welcome. On the quayside was a welcoming committee headed by Bertie's three brothers: David, Harry and George. After the usual kisses, handshakes and salutes, they repaired to the special train which was to take them to Victoria Station. There, George V would be waiting to greet them, with Queen Mary and the Strathmores as well as the families of the other members of the royal party. He had warned his son that there must be no public embracing, and to remember to raise his hat to his mother when kissing her. Cecilia was accompanied by ten members of her family, while Tortor's two daughters and their nanny were much in evidence, as well as sundry other relations of the various royal party members. No sooner did the train doors open than flashbulbs popped as everyone fell into everyone else's arms except George V and Bertie, who remembered to conduct himself with regal dignity towards his parents, if not his in-laws, whom he embraced wholeheartedly.

Afterwards, Bertie and Elizabeth climbed into an open carriage for the journey back to the palace via the circuitous route down Whitehall and up the Mall. The assembled crowds cheered themselves hoarse and both royal duke and duchess beamed delightedly at this, their most pronounced success to date. Once inside Buck House, they were reunited with the baby daughter they had not seen for six months. Afterwards, the whole family, Baby included, went out onto the balcony for the obligatory communion with the applauding masses. The 'ever smiling Duchess', as the *Daily Mirror* called her, won all hearts when, *The Times* reported, she 'brought the Princess forward' twice, 'her face radiant with smiles'.

No diva likes surrendering centre stage, and Elizabeth was no exception. Once she was back in Britain she came down to earth with a thud, or, as Shawcross puts it so diplomatically in the official biography, 'On her return from her long voyage, the Duchess felt a conflict of emotions'. According to him, the reunion with Lilibet was counterbalanced by her loss of 'the intimate intensity which she and her husband had shared throughout their voyage. The tour had been gruelling, but it was their own tour; their days were often exhausting, but they and they alone were the principals; they were far from parental supervision, and everything they did was new, exciting and shared. Back in London they had to play their supporting roles in formal Court rituals in which they were only pieces in an elaborate jigsaw, presided over by the King, who could be kind but was often critical and irritable.'[7]

Elizabeth, however, had a greater than normal capacity for happiness. She understood that life is not ideal and it is up to each of us to come to terms with our situation in such a way that we are as happy in it as we can possibly be. This attitude was not only commendable, but also fundamental in the life she had chosen for herself. While she would have been happier remaining the centre of attention, even when she was playing a subsidiary role in the greatest of all royal productions on the world stage, this was still a lot better than her allotment would have been had she not married Bertie. Being one of those people who also insisted upon being successful no matter what, she adjusted her ambitions, settled for the best she could achieve at that moment in time, and, picking back up the still-enviable threads that the subsidiary role of Duchess of York brought in its wake, was soon happily enjoying her life. But the tour had given her a glimpse of what royal superstardom in a primary position was all about. This would have ominous repercussions for the whole Royal Family and the Monarchy itself in the future, but for the moment the 'Other Lady Macbeth', as the Duke of Windsor sometimes referred to Elizabeth later on, lapsed back into the character of the sweet, happy, obliging Duchess of York who spread joy wherever she went.

In his superbly balanced biography of Queen Elizabeth II, Ben Pimlott makes the point that the 'half-royal' York family lived 'half-royal lives' the whole time they were in residence at 145 Piccadilly. There is much merit to this point of view. Neither Bertie nor Elizabeth had particularly taxing public lives. Neither of their workloads increased dramatically between the years 1927 and 1936. Lilibet too led a half-royal life with her parents until Bertie acceded to the throne when she was ten years old. With no expectation of succeeding to the throne, the Yorks led regular upper-class lives that were virtually indistinguishable from their non-royal friends, except for the occasional royal engagement which they, and still mostly he, undertook.

The young Lilibet had a greater degree of freedom than she would have had, had she been perceived as being a monarch-in-waiting. Bertie, of course, deferred to Elizabeth in child-rearing as in everything else. The regimen she set for her young daughter was very similar to the one Cecilia had set for her. 145 Piccadilly had a back garden which it shared with the other residents of the street. As these were all well-to-do or aristocratic, their children were deemed to be acceptable playmates for the young princess, who would be taken outside by Alah as much as the weather allowed. There were many happy occasions there or in the park, where Alah and her charge would meet other nurses and their charges.

As the baby grew into a toddler, then a little girl, there was no question of her being sent to kindergarten or, indeed, to anything akin to a school. Although Bertie's younger brothers Harry and George had gone to school, neither of the Yorks had done so and Elizabeth, moreover, held to her mother's view that young ladies should not have their minds cluttered up with too much knowledge of a bookish nature. So Lilibet really received no education of any substance until Marion Crawford joined the York household in autumn 1933, after which there was a constant struggle between mother and governess, and grandmother with governess against mother, who, of course, brooked no more opposition to her wishes in this matter than she customarily did where anything else was concerned.

As far as Elizabeth was concerned, the main thing was that Lilibet be well-behaved and well-mannered, with a pleasing personality and a fitting sense of her place in the scheme of things. Elizabeth was very aware of being a very special person with very special standards, and if she had anything to do with it, her daughter would be too. Although she did not resort to homilies with the frequency that her mother had done, she did not need to. Elizabeth was an altogether more inflexible individual than Cecilia. The regimen she set was infinitely less easy to breach, and Lilibet's governess Crawfie recounted in her memoirs how the young princess was so anxious never to get anything wrong that she would get out of her bed at night to check that her shoes were in a straight row just the way her mother wanted them to be.

Despite the extreme level of obedience which Elizabeth required and which underlay the superficially jolly atmosphere at 145 Piccadilly, as far as royal establishments went it approached a greater level of normality than most others. This was because it was not divorced from everyday life the way so many other royal or hyper-aristocratic households were. Fortunately for everyone, Elizabeth was a fun-loving dictator who wanted to be surrounded by happy, albeit accommodating, people. As long as things were going her way, and her wishes were being adhered to, she could be surprisingly easy-going as well as a delight to be around. Of course, if things were not going her way, there would be 'all hell to pay', to quote the Duke of Windsor.[8] But since she was a consistent rather than a capricious personality – and consistently intransigent unless checked by powers greater than herself – those in her orbit knew what the ground rules were, and took care to adhere to them. Failing to do so was never looked upon kindly by the authoritarian duchess who seemed to regard herself as the ultimate arbiter of everything.

In pursuit of the normal aristocratic lifestyle of weeks in town and weekends (or hunting periods) in the country, Bertie took a lease on Naseby Hall in Northamptonshire. They now had a country house to repair to when they were not visiting friends and relations. Although Elizabeth found the Northamptonshire countryside bleak and ugly, she liked the wind ripping tiles off the roof and used to go for long walks while Bertie went hunting. Ever the country girl, she would dress in old clothes and made sure that Lilibet spent as much time out of doors as she herself had done as a little girl.

By the beginning of 1929, the Yorks had established a gentle and pleasurable way of life which was an enviable combination of happy domesticity and grandiose socialising. The post-war boom was in full swing, with Wall Street achieving such heights that John D. Rockefeller, the richest man in the world, was questioning how sustainable the market was when even his shoe-shine boy was asking him for advice on stocks. But this jeremiad was the exception rather than the rule, and as Bertie and Elizabeth set out for Norway to attend the wedding of Crown Prince Olav to Princess Marthe of Sweden, it looked as if the good times had a long way to roll before they would come to a halt. Bertie was Olav's best man. In the full-dress uniform of a naval officer, Bertie accompanied his first cousin from the royal palace to the Church of Our Saviour, while Elizabeth, having no starring role in this production, had to make do with Prince George of Greece. By this time, the prince and his Bonaparte heiress wife were playing host to his exiled nephew Prince Philip's family at St. Cloud in France, for the Greek monarchy had once more been abolished. However, most of the Greek royals were there, as well as representatives of all the other European royal families, both reigning and exiled, the two magnets for international families like royalty being weddings and funerals.

Naturally, Maud relayed how well her nephew and his wife had done to her sister-in-law, telling Queen Mary how much she and Haakon and everyone else 'loved having dear Bertie' while '(e)veryone of course lost their hearts to Elizabeth, she was so sweet to all'.[9]

Whether that comment about Elizabeth was praise or code is open to question. Already certain members of the Royal Family were remarking on how aggressively charming she was to all and sundry – but how ruthlessly self-willed. There is little likelihood that Queen Maud will not have known by this time how guarded Queen Mary already was about Elizabeth. And how defenceless she was to counter the charm offensive. It is therefore entirely possible that the two queens were communicating in keeping with the longstanding tradition of damning with too much praise. They will have both known that anything they wrote would be open to inspection in the future. They therefore had to be careful what they said. However, in civilised circles it has always been acceptable to over-egg the pudding. This is a very convenient way of letting someone know exactly how dreadful you think someone else is, while at the same time avoiding falling into the traps of indiscretion and hypocrisy. In my private life, I myself resort to this technique all the time. Indeed, it is one of the most effective ways of communicating, for there is no downside and you actually haven't said what everyone knows you've just communicated.

Irrespective of whether the Norwegian queen was singing Elizabeth's praises or damning her, the wedding itself now fixed Bertie and Elizabeth's minds on their dynastic duty in a way weddings often do. As Prince Olav's very existence proved, the fact of an heir was infinitely more important than the means by which it had come about. Whether Elizabeth reflected on the parallels between her own situation and Queen Maud's is open to speculation, but these were rather more limited than they might have appeared to be on the surface. Although both women had become pregnant as a result of artificial insemination, Olav was only technically legitimate, while there was no question about Lilibet's legitimacy. Already the little girl was a dead ringer for Queen Mary. This physical resemblance would continue to strengthen throughout her lifetime, as indeed would the many character traits she shared with her paternal grandmother. This led to the conclusion that the Teck side of her genetic code was particularly strong. That is not to say that Lilibet was not being influenced by her mother, for she was, and often positively too. But one only needs to look at photographs of Queen Elizabeth II, Queen Elizabeth The Queen Mother, and Queen Mary to see how little the present queen of England looks like her mother; how much like her grandmother; and how she has always performed her role as Queen in the dutiful and intelligent mode of her grandmother, rather than in keeping with the pleasure-loving, fun-seeking demeanour to which her mother was prone.

Although Bertie and Elizabeth enjoyed Olav's wedding, royal weddings are not only about pleasure. They are also affairs of state whose primary purpose is perpetuation of the line. Procreation was therefore in the air, and neither Bertie nor Elizabeth was immune to the atmosphere. Upon returning to England, they started to discuss the possibility of having another child. This was obviously not as straightforward for a couple in a *marriage blanche* as it would have been had theirs been a *marriage rouge*. What complicated matters somewhat was that Dr. Walter Janner died around this time. So Elizabeth sought the assistance of Sir Henry Simson, the eminent obstetrician who had performed her Caesarean. Married to the well-known actress Lena Ashwell, this tall, good-looking man had been attached to the Soho Hospital for Women as well as the West London Hospital, where he would remain for the remainder of his professional life. Born in India and educated in Edinburgh, he also became the Dean of the West London Post-Graduate College, so he was just the sort of person who would appeal to Elizabeth, who liked everyone with whom she was closely involved to be like her: at the top of their game.

With Sir Henry's assistance, by the end of the year, Elizabeth was pregnant. Once more, there was no doubt that Bertie was the baby's father.

By Elizabeth's own admission, when she was with child she found the taste and smell of alcohol revolting. The harm alcohol did to foetuses was not then known, and Elizabeth was already a stalwart drinker who could match most men, so it is just as well that nature protected her unborn children from a level of consumption which the medical profession would now regard as dangerous. She also claimed that she only wanted to retreat into her own cocoon while pregnant. Possibly this made it easier for her to leave Lilibet with her grandparents at Sandringham, for when she and Bertie departed after spending Christmas 1929 there, Baby remained behind.

King George V and Queen Mary were enthusiastic grandparents, and though Elizabeth tried her utmost to keep the reins in her own or her mother's hands, there were times when even she had to relent and allow the King and Queen a chance with their grandchild. Gradually Lilibet and her paternal grandparents were developing a bond which would become more pronounced with the passage of time, and would outstrip that which she had with her maternal grandparents. This was entirely due to the King and Queen using majesty to counteract Elizabeth's attempts to make Lilibet more Bowes Lyon than Windsor. And after George V died in 1936 and Cecilia two years later, it became almost natural for Lilibet to incline more towards her remaining grandmother than her grandfather.

Nevertheless, natural affinity and shared destinies also helped tilt things in Queen Mary's favour. The evidence of diary entries, letters and statements from those who knew all the parties, such as Princess Alice, Countess of Athlone, confirm that Lilibet and Queen Mary had a profound understanding. The old Queen, who had reverence for the role of sovereign, went out of her way to ensure that she influenced her granddaughter positively, especially once it became apparent that the girl might end up the queen regnant. This was not done through vanity alone, though there might well have been that element. Even Shawcross acknowledges in the official biography that the relationship between Queen Mary and Elizabeth was more strained than their superficially affectionate correspondence indicated. The fact is, Mary had a withering contempt for Elizabeth's intellectual viewpoint and lack of actual gravitas beneath the wily Machiavellianism. She also despised Elizabeth's flamboyant lack of modesty as she went about her official duties, and ensured that Lilibet understood that real Queens are modest and sincere rather than insincere players to the gallery, and that style was no substitute for substance.[10]

After leaving Sandringham that Christmas of 1929, Bertie's stay in London was short. He was scheduled to attend the wedding on 8th January, 1930, of the Italian Crown Prince Umberto, who was known in Italy by his formal title of Prince of Piedmont. This scion of the House of Savoy, which had produced several consorts for the Kings and Dauphins of France over the centuries, was marrying one of Bertie's cousins. Princess Marie José of Belgium was the strikingly attractive daughter of King Albert I and Queen Elisabeth of the Belgians, behind whom Bertie had ridden in their triumphal re-entry to their capital following the Great War.

Once she became a member of the Royal Family, Elizabeth embraced royalty with all the passion of a convert, though paradoxically she would do her utmost to ensure that her daughters married British aristocrats. Nevertheless, once she was royal, she embraced both the reigning and the deposed royals, many of whom crossed the Rubicon during her long life, to her ample bosom. King Umberto's cousin the Duke of Aosta, another descendant of Queen Victoria, once told me that he 'adored' Queen Elizabeth, who was 'wonderfully hospitable' to him whenever their paths crossed. This was long after the Italian monarchy had been abolished. Tellingly, Elizabeth proved to be less hospitable to King Umberto himself, possibly because she enjoyed the admiration of junior royals while senior ones like Umberto were less deferential. Indeed, in royal circles an ex-king like Umberto was considered Elizabeth's equal. To paraphrase Gertrude Stein, 'A king is a king is a king. And a queen is his equal but never his superior.'

Margaret, Duchess of Argyll knew King Umberto well. She thought he was charming, agreeable, and more importantly, one of the most decent people you could hope to meet. He was also a gentleman who preferred the company of other gentlemen. Queen Marie José used to say that the marriage had never been happy, the implication being that it could never have been for obvious reasons. Nevertheless, when it was arranged, there was no other Catholic crown prince available and no one knew that in less than two decades the splendid House of Savoy would be driven into exile. Admittedly Spain was still a monarchy headed by His Most Catholic Majesty King Alfonso XIII. His consort, Queen Victoria Eugenia, was yet another sprig of the pre-Windsor House of Saxe-Coburg-Gotha by way of Battenberg. But no one in their right mind would have hoped for an alliance with the Spanish Royal Family when the Italian crown prince was available. Firstly, the heir to the Spanish throne, the Principe de Asturias, was far from ideal matrimonial material. Although only a year younger than Marie José, he was a haemophiliac. The brother immediately younger than him was a deaf mute, and it was a well-known fact that the Spanish king loathed his queen, blaming her for having introduced haemophilia into their family. This, of course, was despite the fact that when Alfonso had fallen in love with King George V's first cousin Princess Ena of Battenberg, as she was then known, while on a State Visit to England, the point had been made to him that her brother Leopold (Lord Leopold Mountbatten after 1917) was haemophilic (he would bleed to death aged thirty-two in 1922 during an operation at Kensington Palace), and her grandmother Queen Victoria was the most noted carrier of the disease ever to have lived. Putting aside the risk to health marrying into the Spanish Royal Family could cause, the country was also politically unstable. By 1930, Diego Primo de Rivera was its dictator and the Spanish monarchy was hanging on by a thread – one which would be snipped the following year, when the king was driven into exile in Rome. As with Umberto and Marie José, once Alfonso and Ena had no throne to bind them together, they too separated, the king remaining in Rome at the Grand Hotel while his queen went to Switzerland with her brood of six surviving children, three of whom were disabled.

Undoubtedly Bertie would have been in better humour had Elizabeth accompanied him for the Roman wedding in 1930. In her absence, however, he could find nothing right about the event, its arrangements, or even the people, notwithstanding the fact that Rome is one vast aesthetic paradise that appeals even to philistines. His letters home were one long moan, which must have been something of a comfort to the wife who loved being needed as much as he loved needing her.

When Bertie returned to England, he and Elizabeth picked back up the threads of their life together. As her pregnancy progressed, she withdrew from public life altogether, though of course not from her private social life. Unsurprisingly, her pregnancy excited a certain amount of talk in stately drawing rooms. This was because Elizabeth's repudiation of carnality was well known – as indeed was Bertie's slavishness in executing her wishes at all turns. The consequence of such an attitude had to be the preclusion of his insisting upon his conjugal rights the way so many other husbands would have done. These two facts ensured that speculation about how she was able to become pregnant at all was widespread. The very idea of Bertie foisting himself upon Elizabeth occurred to no one, largely because the dynamics in the Yorks' relationship were so obvious for all to see that people inferred, rightly as it turned out, that if nature could not take its course, something else had obviously done so. Artificial insemination then being the hot ticket in Society when heirs were necessary and nature was disobliging, it is hardly surprising that just about everyone in the grandest social circles was talking about the method to which the Yorks had resorted for the duchess to become pregnant for a second time.

Although Bertie had told David, and David had told Freda, about the technique used to create this second miracle baby, there is no evidence to suggest that any of these individuals spread the story at this juncture. Later, of course, would be another matter, but by then the way the girls had been conceived was already so well known within the social circles in which the Yorks and Windsors moved, that repetition might have lent verification, but it was not the point of origin.

The baby was due in August 1930. Elizabeth, in yet another of the assertive displays to which she was already prone, had decided that she wanted this child born in the land of her paternal ancestors. So in mid-July she, Bertie, Lilibet and Alah headed up to Glamis with Nannie B, who was going to be the maternity nurse yet again. There they settled down to await the birth. They were soon joined by Sir Henry Simson and Frank Neon Reynolds, a thirty-five-year-old obstetrician and gynaecologist, who, Shawcross informs us, was 'conscious of the honour of attending upon the Duchess.' The honour soon palled. The skies opened up and stayed open. Had Elizabeth's waters been as accommodating as the Scottish cloudbursts, Dr. Reynolds might not have started to bemoan his lot, but the baby soon showed the assembled company that she was sufficiently like her mother to be tardy, and 'as the waiting extended, he became nervous about his patients back in London'.

Reynolds has left us with his impressions of both Elizabeth and Bertie. He thought she had a 'lovely expression' for she was unfailingly sweet and smiling with him, as she was with most other people whose paths crossed hers. Bertie he found somewhat less agreeable, and remarked that his conduct was so awkward 'it makes one wonder if one is being backward and gauche, but it seems it is the same with everybody'.[12]

To ensure that the baby would arrive in keeping with the law of the land, Sir Henry sent for the Home Secretary, John Robert Clynes. This former president of the National Union of General and Municipal Workers reflected the change that had taken place in British politics. The year before, Ramsay

MacDonald had become the left-wing Labour Prime Minister of Britain for the second time since the war. He arrived the day after Elizabeth's thirtieth birthday on 4th August, and stayed with Mabell Airlie at Airlie Castle.

By this time, Elizabeth had realised the mistake she had made in choosing to have the baby in Scotland. Never one to deprive herself of her creature comforts, and with the canny eye of a Scotswoman for the benefit any deal ought to be bringing her, she explained that a birth in the capital was 'much more agreeable for both of us I think, as when one is in the country one misses all the lovely flowers and cadeaux (presents) for the baby, & little excitements like that!!'[13] To drive home her point, she used not one but two exclamation marks. Soon her letters were revealing rather more than just regret. Irritation intermingling with disdain, she wrote Queen Mary telling her how she was being given 'all sorts of horrid drinks, so as not to keep these foolish people waiting', and ended up by unfairly accusing them of hounding her because 'here they are all waiting & hovering like vultures! I shall be very glad when they are gone.'[14] Quite what Dr. Reynolds would have thought of the sweet duchess with the lovely expression if he had known that she thought he was a foolish vulture who was feeding her vile drinks to speed up the birth is open to question. Fortunately he, like so many others whose paths crossed Elizabeth's, never saw the woman behind the façade, which was just as well. Otherwise her powers of attraction, and the good they did for the cause of monarchy, would have been sorely reduced.

For the next two weeks everyone, including the press who were camped out in the village, waited while Princess Margaret took her own sweet time in coming. Everyone, that is, but Bertie, who stomped the fields shooting game. On the Glorious Twelfth he managed to annihilate enough grouse to feed everyone at Glamis that very evening.

On the afternoon of 21st August, Elizabeth finally went into labour. Six hours later, yet another girl arrived. In royal and aristocratic circles, male heirs have always been preferable to female. To paraphrase Oscar Wilde, one girl might have been a happy accident, but two daughters were an accidental misfortune. Queen Mary expressed her disappointment forthrightly, but the irascible King, who was always lambasting his sons for offences more imagined than real, managed to come up with a reason why the daughter-in-law with whom he was somewhat beguiled even as he saw through her wiles, decided that maybe another granddaughter wasn't such a bad thing after all. He and the Queen would be able to play with her longer than they would a grandson, and in any event, Bertie and Elizabeth were young. There was plenty of time for them to produce a son.

Although these were happy times for the York family, they were less so for the country and indeed the world at large. Following the Wall Street Crash of the year before, the economies of all the leading nations had wobbled. Although the Great Depression had not yet begun in earnest, by the beginning of 1931 unemployment had risen in the United Kingdom, and even the Royal Family were constrained to apply economies. Bertie gave up his hunters, partly because it was desirable for the Royal Family to be seen to be making such cutbacks, but largely because Elizabeth had gradually worked herself up into such a lather about the possible consequences of an accident, that he preferred to sacrifice one of his favourite pastimes than subject her to further anxiety. Without the need for a hunting lodge, there was no longer an excuse for renting that particular house in the country, so he did not renew the lease on Naseby Hall and they were once again reduced to being a one-house family. Early in 1931, King George V came to the rescue and offered Bertie and Elizabeth the use of Royal Lodge in Windsor Great Park.

Royal Lodge had been the country retreat of King George IV when he was Prince Regent. Rather than live with his mother Queen Charlotte and unmarried sisters at Windsor Castle, where his father King George III was incarcerated, George IV, whose architectural taste was second to none amongst English sovereigns, expanded the country 'cottage' until it was a gracious country house. Even after he succeeded to the throne in 1820, he continued residing there in preference to the nearby castle. After his death in 1830, much of the house was demolished. What remained was used primarily by members of the Royal Household, until Bertie's father offered him its use in 1931.

Queen Mary was not enthusiastic. She thought Royal Lodge too small for the family and feared that it would be too expensive to run, especially as how the garden was large and would cost a lot to keep up. She encouraged Bertie and Elizabeth to turn it down, but their taste was radically different from the majestic Queen's. One of their more endearing qualities was a love of cosy domesticity and a commensurate love of beautiful gardens. Both of them realised that Royal Lodge would be ideal for them, and Bertie suggested to his father that he pay the £5,000 renovation costs out of his own pocket rather than tax the Privy Purse at this sensitive time. George V agreed, they were granted a lease on the property, and immediately set to work on turning what they called 'their real home'.[15]

Once they had decided to take on Royal Lodge, Queen Mary threw herself into the task of helping them in any way she could. Yet again her actions demonstrated that there was nothing petty about her desire to enhance their lives. She did her utmost to secure good furnishings and chattels for them, patently not minding that they had made a choice with which she had initially disagreed. Her attitude was not only commendable, but rather rare, though whether it was born of pragmatism or nobility or a combination of the two is open to question. What is not, however, is the willingness she showed to be helpful.

Thanks in part to Queen Mary's assistance, within a few months the house had been turned from an unwanted series of unloved rooms into a desirable residence. It became and would remain Elizabeth's 'real home', as she called it, for the remainder of her life.

Royal Lodge's refurbishment should have alerted everyone to the fact that Elizabeth had decided that she would not be having any more children. No one, however, seems to have noticed that the paucity of bedrooms might be indicative of a reluctance on her part to produce more progeny.

What was already apparent, however, was how quickly she was running to fat. She had always loved her food. Now she started to 'gorge on chocolates', to quote the Duke of Windsor. Nor were chocolates her only indulgence. She ate massive breakfasts and huge lunches, which barely seemed to sustain her till tea time. She was renowned for demolishing tea tables stacked high with a concoction of bakers' delights, piling her plate with sandwiches, cakes, scones, jams and biscuits. These seemed barely able to sustain her until dinner, when she would hoover up each and every course as if she had never seen food before. This was reminiscent of the way she used to gorge herself on cake and bread when she was a little girl. While she had been pleasingly plump then, she was becoming something of a pudding now, such looks as she had once had disappearing as her girth expanded and her face swelled, not only because of the food she was consuming, but also her generous intake of alcoholic sustenance.

Princess Louise, Duchess of Argyll, openly enquired if Elizabeth was deliberately trying to make herself unattractive so that Bertie would never be tempted to require her conjugal favours. This said more about the aged man-eater, whose conquests had included her own brother-in-law Prince Henry (Liko) of Battenberg, than it did about Elizabeth, whose aim was hardly likely to be deflecting the sexual attentions of a man already under true subservience. Her motivation was more than likely a quest for satisfaction of senses that mattered to her, rather than compensating for the absence of satisfaction of those that did not.

And what most definitely did not matter to her was what seemed to matter to everyone else except Bertie: the need for a son. As far as she was concerned, the monarchy would just have to rub along without a male heir from her. Her reasoning seems to have been simple: why put herself to all that bother when David would eventually marry and produce his own heirs?

By this time, David's private life was as much an open secret in Society as the Yorks'. Freda Dudley Ward's granddaughter, Lady Temple, told me, 'The Prince of Wales and my grandmother did not have an exclusive relationship. He had other girlfriends and she had other boyfriends.' In the early days of the relationship, David had indeed been so besotted with Freda that he was 'always proposing marriage'. By the mid-1920s, however, the feverish quality which is contained in his earlier letters to Freda had cooled into something which was still loving, still carnal, still devoted, but more accepting of the fact that the relationship would never lead to marriage.

This acceptance allowed both David and Freda to pursue elsewhere other relationships which might, in turn, lead to matrimony. The fact that each was serious about finding a marital partner is obvious from their behaviour. The year after Princess Margaret's birth, Freda divorced her husband. Although she would not remarry until 1937, at which time she became the Marquesa de Casa Maury, the mere fact that she was making herself available for the eventuality of marriage was an open declaration of intent.

From David's point of view, he too wanted to marry. His relationship with Freda might have changed into something that did not include a future union, but this did not preclude him from continuing it. Nor from looking elsewhere for a woman whom he could love and, hopefully, eventually marry. By his own admission, he did not consider divorce a preventative. At the end of the 1920s, Western society had changed so much that everywhere divorce was becoming more and more acceptable. Contrary to popular belief, divorced individuals were already being received at Court, as indeed was David's latest love interest, the first of his American divorcées, and the one with whom Elizabeth enjoyed cordial relations: Thelma, Viscountess Furness. The identical twin sister of Gloria Vanderbilt senior, mother of the celebrated American socialite/artist/designer Gloria Vanderbilt junior, and grandmother of the CNN telejournalist, Anderson Cooper, she was one half of the most famous twins on earth.

Cecil Beaton has left a wonderful description of Thelma and Gloria, who were 'as alike as two magnolias and with their marble complexions, raven tresses and flowing dresses, with their slight lisps and foreign accents, they diffuse an Ouida atmosphere of hothouse elegance and lacy femininity.' Born Thelma (pronounced Tel-ma in the Spanish fashion) and Mercedes Morgan at the Hotel National in Lucerne, Switzerland in 1904, their father, Henry Hays Morgan, was the American Consul-General in Brussels, and their half-Chilean, half-Irish American mother Laura Delphine Kilpatrick a descendant of the royal house of Navarre through her maternal grandmother Luisa Fernandez de Valdivieso. The 'Magnificent Morgans', as the identical twins and their elder sister Consuelo were known in the Society columns, were three of the most feted and glamorous socialites of their age. It is difficult with hindsight to say who was the most fabulous, for they were all strikingly beautiful and led lives that read like movie scripts.

Thelma eloped in Washington D.C. on 16th January, 1922, at the age of seventeen with John Vail Converse, the grandson of Thomas N. Vail, founder and former president of the iconic AT&T (American Telephone and Telegraph Company). He was his bride's senior by a decade and had already been married and divorced once before. Although they were divorced after three years, the failure of that marriage seems not to have put Thelma off older men, for within a year, on 27th June, 1926, she married another multi-millionaire as his second wife. This time her husband was the widowed Marmaduke, 2nd Baron and 1st Viscount Furness, who was two decades her senior. He was also tremendously rich, and, more to the point, new money to boot.

The grandson of a Liverpool docker whose elder son founded the shipping wholesale provision merchants, Thomas Furness and Company, Marmaduke's father Christopher (the 1st baron) had spotted the potential for owning, rather than merely stocking, a merchant fleet while working for his elder brother. He therefore bought several steam vessels from the local Hartlepool, County Durham shipbuilder William Gray, while working with Thomas. Five years later, in 1882, the business was so successful that the brothers split it in two, with Thomas Furness and Company provisioning ships, while Christopher Furness and Company not only owned its own fleet of carriers, but also went on to become one of greatest shipping lines in the British Empire. By 1891 he had expanded further, amalgamating with Edward Withy and Company to form Furness, Withy and Company. This company continued as one of the largest employers in the area for nearly a hundred more years.

By the time Thelma Morgan Converse married Marmaduke Furness, he was not only the head of one of the world's great shipping lines, but also a gentleman of the first order who did not allow his plebeian antecedents to detract from his appeal. At first the marriage was happy, certainly happy enough for Thelma to produce a son, the Hon. William Anthony (Tony) Furness, on 31st March, 1929. Although this boy would succeed to his father's title on 6th October, 1940, he was actually only the second son. His elder half-brother, the Hon. Christopher Furness, however, died a hero's death at Arras in France earlier that year, and was awarded the Victoria Cross for bravery. Despite her son Tony's peerage being a source of some pride for Thelma, the marital history of her family seems to have had an adverse effect upon him. He became a devout Roman Catholic, and a Knight of the

Sovereign Order of Malta who never married. Despite being celibate, he was no stuffed shirt. He was a well-known 'angel' who backed many hit movies and plays, including *Easy Rider*. When he passed away in 1995, the title died with him.

Fatefully, for the Furness marriage if not the entertainment Thelma would thereafter provide the world, her path crossed the Prince of Wales's at the Leicestershire Agricultural Show, held at Leicester on 14th June, 1929. Lord and Lady Furness had a splendid house at nearby Melton Mowbray. By Thelma's own account, this was not the first time she had met David. That had been in 1926 at a ball at Londonderry House. This time, however, something between them clicked. Soon he was asking her out for dinner and, before long, paying her such serious court that she went on a safari with him to Nairobi in Kenya early in 1930. According to her, 'This was our Eden, and we were alone in it. His arms about me were the only reality; his words of love my only bridge to life. Borne along on the mounting tide of his ardour, I felt myself being inexorably swept from the accustomed moorings of caution. Each night I felt more completely possessed by our love, carried ever more swiftly into uncharted seas of feeling, content to let the Prince chart the course, heedless of where the voyage would end.'[16]

So began the affair that would ruin Thelma's marriage and lead inexorably though circuitously to the Abdication Crisis of 1936. When David returned to England in April, Thelma became the regular hostess of his weekend house parties at Fort Belvedere, the bijoux-like castellated folly near Windsor Castle which was his retreat and would remain so even after he became King. He was an avid host and gardener, who enjoyed nothing better than leaving his friends to enjoy themselves while he and a few of the men went off to plant flowers, clear bush, and weed. These were interests he shared with his brother Bertie and sister-in-law Elizabeth, whose own interest had been handed down through her mother, another avid hostess and gardener.

While Thelma was playing chatelaine at Fort Belvedere, she had the constant support of her elder sister. Consuelo had divorced her first husband, Comte de Maupas du Juglart, and married Pennsylvania railroad and banking heir Benjamin Thaw Jr. on 4th June, 1924. He was a career diplomat who had been secretary at the American Legations in Belgium and Chile before being posted in the same capacity to the American Embassy in London in 1930. Theirs was a happy marriage and it is fair to say that they were at the very pinnacle of American Society wherever they went. To the ignorant, being Mrs. Thaw might have seemed a step down after being a countess, but to the cognoscenti, the name Thaw reeked of old money and lots of it. While the family did not have as high a public profile as the Carnegies, the Whitneys or the Fricks, they were connected to them, and every bit as grand. Several of the women had married into the aristocracy, including Alice Thaw, who became the Countess of Yarmouth when she married the 6th Marquess of Hertford's heir in 1903.

Also frequently in evidence was Thelma's fabled twin Mercedes, who had changed her name to Gloria 'after years in America when the girls at the Sacred Heart Convent shortened it to "Mercy" and I did not like it, that I changed it to Gloria'.[17] The twenty-six-year-old Gloria Vanderbilt was the most feted widow on earth. No name, except the Prince of Wales, evoked greater glamour or splendour than Vanderbilt. Combined with Gloria's beauty and style, it was a potent mixture which would ultimately have disastrous and unpredictable repercussions for those most closely connected to her. But when Thelma's affair with David began, Gloria was still an archetypal figure of approbation.

Unlike Thelma, who had eloped with her first husband, Gloria had married the hugely eligible Reginald (Reggie) Claypoole Vanderbilt on 6th March, 1923, with their father's blessing. Though he was divorced and a forty-two-year-old alcoholic, Reggie was nevertheless the son of Cornelius Vanderbilt II and the grandson of William Henry Vanderbilt, the richest man in the world at the time of his death in 1885, when he left the then unimaginably vast fortune of $194,000,000. Nor was the family name synonymous with wealth alone. Reggie's cousin Consuelo Vanderbilt, the greatest heiress of the Gilded Age, had married the 9th Duke of Marlborough, and their son Burt was then the Marquess of Blandford and heir to Blenheim Palace and all the other Churchill possessions entailed upon the dukedom. Although that marriage had ended in divorce in 1921, the mixture of great wealth and aristocracy had so raised the profile of both the Vanderbilt and Marlborough families that nothing could eclipse them. At least until the Duke's first cousin Winston Churchill became the most respected man in the Free World following his appointment as Prime Minister during the Second World War.

Eleven months after marrying into this pre-eminent family, Gloria gave birth to Little Gloria on 20th February, 1924. Just over a year and a half later, on 4th September, 1925, Reggie died of an oesophagal haemorrhage which was a direct consequence of his alcoholism. Because Laura Morgan had led the twins to believe that they were born in 1905 instead of 1904, both Glorias were deemed to be minors. Big Gloria, however, had been left Little Gloria's guardian as well as custodian of her daughter's trust fund. As Gloria herself wrote in her 1936 memoir *Without Prejudice* (E.P. Dutton), 'Had I not thought myself a minor at this time…there would have been no necessity for a guardian for myself…[or] for a legal guardian for my child's person…

On this untruth – irrevocable and irremediable – hinged the currents of my child's life and my own.'

Although Gloria did not say it, other fates hinged on that lie. Those of Thelma, David, and the woman who their sister Consuelo brought into all their lives: Wallis Simpson, though the fallout would involve others further down the line, such as Little Gloria.

In some ways, the Magnificent Morgans were a potentative mixture. Each sister's success paved the way for her siblings' further elevation, which would result in their three stunning matrimonial unions.

Once Gloria was widowed, she embarked upon a lifestyle that was then virtually unheard of. Commuting between New York and England, France and Switzerland with Little Gloria and the baby's nurse, Mrs. Emma Sullivan Kelslich, who had taken care of her since she was two weeks old but would turn out to be a less than devoted employee, Big Gloria looked as if she had the world at her feet and that she would continue to ride from height to ever greater height. It was almost inevitable that she would captivate a prince, and the press certainly expected her to end up marrying into the aristocracy.

Gloria duly met Bertie and David's second cousin Prince Gottfried of Hohenlohe-Langenburg in spring 1927. Queen Marie of Romania, who had had a long affair with William Waldorf Astor and was still friendly with many of the American expatriates who converged on London each year, pushed for a marriage between the rich widow and her sister Alexandra of Edinburgh and Coburg's eldest son. By October 1927 news of the unofficial engagement had leaked out.

Then the relationship hit an insurmountable problem. Gottfried was the heir to the Hohenlohe-Langenburg fiefdom in the former Kingdom of Württemberg, whence Queen Mary's paternal ancestors originated. His constant presence was required, for the abolition of the German monarchies eight years before had not erased royalty's duties to their heritage. Gloria herself explained the dilemma well, while giving one of those embarkation interviews which were so characteristic of that age: 'I have just returned from a most delightful visit with the prince's family. They are most charming, but we disagree on one important point. They insist that the prince and his bride should live at the castle in Wurtemberg (sic), but I speak not one word of German, and besides I love Paris and America. So it will be impossible for us to set a date for the wedding until I return to New York in January.'[18]

For another year, it looked as if the relationship would end in marriage. Gloria agreed to live three months of the year in Berlin, while Gottfried claimed he too liked Paris and New York and was prepared to lead the peripatetic life of idle internationals. However, Fürst and Fürstin zu Hohenlohe-Langenburg were adamant that their heir remember his duties and be a constant and visible presence in his territories. By March of 1929 the press were reporting that the engagement was at an end and the world's most glamorous widow was being pursued by another European nobleman. After much toing and froing, the engagement was called off. Two years later, while Thelma's relationship with David was going from strength to strength and it looked as if she might outstrip her twin and become a royal highness rather than a mere serene highness, Gottfried married David's cousin, Princess Margarita of Greece. She was one of Prince Philip of Greece's older sisters and as such became another of Lilibet's sisters-in-law.

Freed from the need to live in a country she had no desire to, Gloria's personal life continued as glamorously and exotically as it had been. Indeed, it soon took a turn upwards when Thelma became David's primary girlfriend. All three sisters were often with the Prince of Wales in London or at Fort Belvedere. Not unnaturally, Lord Furness was hardly pleased with the way David had hijacked his wife. The heedless abandonment displayed by the Prince of Wales as he ardently pursued the young wife and mother was noticed by one and all. 'When he was in love, no one was more in love than him,' said Margaret, Duchess of Argyll, who became the wife of the handsome American golfer Charles Sweeny in 1933 and, as such, a member of the colony of rich, fashionable expatriate Americans in London of which the Magnificent Morgans were an integral part.

Within a year of David and Thelma meeting for that second time at Leicester, 'everyone' in fashionable social circles in Britain, America and Europe knew about the romance. This lack of discretion, allied to David's intensity and Thelma's reckless responsiveness, made Marmaduke understand that there was no point in continuing with a marriage which would turn him into a laughing stock unless it was terminated. Although he was gentleman enough to abide by the convention that a lady must never be seen to be the guilty party in a divorce, he was man enough to require an end to a union that had degenerated into farce. The alternative, that he avail himself of the 'honour' of laying down his wife for royalty, had no appeal for him. He was too rich, too successful, and too eminent to need such a complication when all he had ever wanted was a happy marriage, so in 1933 he and Thelma were divorced. In August that year he married the Australian-born Enid Lindemann, widow of Brigadier General Frederick Cavendish and of Roderick Cameron, and finally achieved what he had wanted all along. His final viscountess proved to be unlucky for a third time, however, when Marmaduke Furness died at the relatively young age of fifty-six in 1940. Nor would her luck turn. In early 1943 she married the 6th Earl of Kenmare, who was better known as

Valentine, Viscount Castlerosse. A director of the Beaverbrook papers, the *Daily Express*, the *Sunday Express* and the *Evening Standard,* he wrote a popular column called 'Londoner's Log' and was a highly successful front-man for the William Hickey gossip column.

The divorce of Marmaduke and Thelma freed her to marry the Prince of Wales, if marriage was what either of them wanted. It has commonly been supposed that marriage was not an option, but this is not true. Although David did not propose as compulsively as he had with Freda in the early days of their romance, they did discuss getting married. As usual, David was the party doing most of the running. Thelma was genuinely in love with him, and would actually remain so, to some extent, till her dying day. My late friend Dominick Dunne recounted in *Fatal Charms and the Mansions of Limbo* (Ballantine, 1999) her niece Gloria Vanderbilt's recollection of how the proof of this statement surfaced: 'She dropped dead on Seventy-third and Lexington on her way to see the doctor. In her bag was this miniature teddy bear that the Prince of Wales had given her, years before, when she came to be with my mother at the custody trial, and it was worn down to the nub.'

Thelma was an altogether softer individual than the woman who would replace her in David's affections and this could be why David's relationship with her ultimately failed, while his with Wallis succeeded. Wallis was far more like Elizabeth than their superficial differences implied. A man who wants to be a supplicant with his wife rather than an equal or dominant partner will ultimately miss the challenge of a softer personality, while thrilling to that of someone colder and harsher. This seems the likely reason why David eventually replaced Thelma with Wallis. But it says much for the strength of their relationship that he knew Wallis for three years before he even considered her as anything but what used to be called a 'social acquaintance'. In all that time, he and Thelma were devoted to each other, their long-term goal being marriage when the opportunity presented itself.[19]

Playing the waiting game until the moment was right was sensible, as David's successor as Prince of Wales would prove when he utilised the same tactic of waiting until the moment was propitious for marrying his long-term mistress, Camilla Parker Bowles. David had an identical goal and similar expectations of success.

This is not fanciful speculation. Not only does Thelma covertly hint at it in her memoirs, but Margaret, Duchess of Argyll, who knew all the participants in the drama well, confirmed to me that David and Thelma were planning to marry as soon as they could.

Another corroborative source was (the 1st) Lord Beaverbrook, who confided all in his favourite grandchild, my sister-in-law Lady Jeanne (Jean) Campbell. He played a prominent part in the Abdication Crisis, and indeed wrote a book about it. He had to be careful what he said. He and Elizabeth disliked each other intensely, and he used to say privately that David was right to call her the Monster of Glamis, for she could have taught Lady Macbeth a thing or two about how to intrigue successfully. He even remarked that Lady Macbeth at least had the decency to wash her hands constantly in an attempt to remove the stains upon them, while Elizabeth was of the firm view that anything and everything she did was right, irrespective of how wrong it was. Since he was not the only person to make this observation, one can rely upon it rather more than if it had been exclusive to him.

Being the proprietor of one of the most successful and influential newspaper companies in the country, Lord Beaverbrook was privy to all sorts of information that was not always available to others. He himself would readily acknowledge that not all his sources were admirable, but knowledge was power and 'The Beaver', as he was known, enjoyed the power his position gave him. He told his granddaughter Lady Jean Campbell that he had long known that David was hoping to marry Thelma, but the person who provided him with incontrovertible proof was his columnist Valentine Castlerosse. Castlerosse's wife Enid, Marmaduke Furness's widow, had told him that David himself had told Lord Furness that he need have no fear of what would become of Thelma if he divorced her. He, David, would marry her. Although this might seem like tame stuff nowadays, in the middle of the last century it was dynamite. The divorce laws specifically excluded collusion, and Lord and Lady Furness as well as the Prince of Wales would have been implicated in a serious legal problem had this conversation become public knowledge. That, together with Elizabeth's continuing influence in Establishment circles, compelled The Beaver to be discreet, at least publicly.

From a practical point of view, Thelma could not have come on the royal scene at a worse time. King George V's health was precarious. A heavy smoker who had unwittingly ruined his health with that habit, he very nearly died in November 1928 after catching a '(f)everish cold'[20] laying a wreath at the Cenotaph on Remembrance Sunday. Within ten days this had developed into a streptococcal chest infection, then septicaemia. In those pre-antibiotic days, people often died because of far less severe infections, and Lord Dawson of Penn, George V's physician, immediately appreciated the severity of his patient's condition. All the children were notified. Bertie rushed over to Sandringham from Naseby, while Elizabeth came from London. Princess Mary wrote on 6th December to tell David that their sister-in-law, whose calm and sympathetic demeanour was just what one needed in a crisis, was 'a great comfort to us'.[21] Meanwhile, David was making his way from Kenya, where he had been on safari with the Earl of Winchilsea's white-hunter brother, the Hon. Denys Finch Hatton, whose affair with Karen Blixen (Isak Dinesen) would be turned into the hit movie *Out of Africa*.

When David received the news from his Private Secretary, Alan (Tommy) Lascelles, that the Prime Minister had sent a coded cable to say that the British people would be shocked if he did not return home to stand vigil, his reply was a study in scepticism. 'I don't believe a word of it. It's just some election dodge of old Baldwin's.'[22] Certainly the Prime Minister's political position was insecure enough for him to be unseated shortly thereafter, and Baldwin was known to be even wilier than most politicians, so David's viewpoint was reasonable. But Tommy Lascelles did not like his master, and never missed an opportunity to condemn him even when he was being sensible. His diary states that he responded angrily (and rather officiously), 'Sir, the King of England is dying, and if that means nothing to you, it means a great deal to us.'[23]

Shawcross repeats in the official biography how 'the Prince apparently looked at him, said nothing, left the room and spent the rest of the evening getting to bed with the wife of a local British official. He told a friend it was the best thing to do after a shock. Once he was convinced of the gravity of his father's condition – and the fact that he might soon be king himself – the Prince made his way home as swiftly as possible by land and by sea.'[24]

David arrived in London on 11th December to see his father close to death. By the 12th he was unconscious and declining rapidly. Lord Dawson realised that he would lose his patient if he did not locate the source of the primary infection, which was immediately behind the diaphragm. With nothing to lose and everything to gain, he probed until he located the site. Having done so, he inserted a needle into it and withdrew over a pint of pus. Later that night, the remainder of the pus was drained away following the removal of a rib to gain access.

Although this procedure saved George V's life, his recovery was slow and patchy. It was another month before Queen Mary was able to record in her diary on 6th January that her husband was now strong enough to have the first conversation with her for six weeks. And it was another month before he was well enough to be sent away to convalesce. The place chosen was Bognor, the quaint little seaside resort on the south coast which would shortly glory in the addition of Regis as a token of the King's gratitude for what he believed was the place which had helped to save his life. In March Elizabeth allowed Lilibet to join her grandparents for a bucket and spades holiday while she and Bertie headed for Norway for Crown Prince Olav's wedding.

All in all, George V's recovery took six months. However, he never regained his former vigour and looked much older than his sixty-three years. This was because he continued to smoke heavily, not that he or anyone else realised the dangers of that habit. But it was obvious to all that he would die sooner rather than later, and this put an additional pressure upon David. In all likelihood, he would accede to the throne in the not too distant future. When that would be, of course, no one actually knew. It made planning impossible, especially after he fell in love with Thelma later that year.

In the absence of possessing the knowledge required to make a firm plan, David and Thelma did what most other people would do. They made none. This does not mean that they did not consider their future; simply that they could not map it out as clearly as they would have liked. But time appeared to be on their side. When she became a free woman in 1933, he was still in his thirties and she in her twenties. She had already had one child, so there was no doubt about her fertility. Since it was a relatively common phenomenon for women in those days to have babies even in their late forties and early fifties – albeit after having spent a lifetime producing earlier offspring – there was no need to suppose that Thelma would not be fecund in her thirties. Elizabeth, after all, had recently given birth to a baby at thirty, and no one regarded her as being too old to fulfil her duty and produce another two, three or even four children. David's own mother hadn't been married until she was twenty-seven. She gave birth to six children in a little over a decade, having her last son, Prince John, when she was approaching forty.

David and Thelma had already settled into an agreeable pattern of happy domesticity. Although they ran separate establishments in London, they were constantly together and he frequently left her house in the early hours of the morning. On weekends, they effectively lived together at the Fort. All the young royals liked Thelma and she liked them. The Yorks were especially close to her. They were constantly at the Fort, or she and David at nearby Royal Lodge. Even Shawcross admits that the 'Yorks liked Thelma and the two couples often spent time together, particularly over weekends at Fort Belvedere or Royal Lodge.' Theirs was such an easy relationship that both couples were on dropping-in terms, which meant that they did not need an invitation to call on each other. This indicates a degree of intimacy that is astonishing, especially for royalty, who even then liked scheduling visits rather than resorting to the peradventurousness of the impromptu.

Much cant has been written over the years about Elizabeth's moral strictures, which were so high-flown that she could never tolerate sin of any kind, much less adultery. But a simple examination of how she dealt with David's affairs with both Freda and Thelma proves what utter rubbish this supposed repugnance for adultery was. Not only did she condone both romances, but she also actively assisted her brother-in-law with them. In the official biography, Shawcross, in yet another of his masterpieces of understatement, tells how she had become such a close friend and confidante of Bertie's brothers that they turned to her for advice. Since David's significant relationships were invariably with married women, and George's were with boys as well as girls, one has a difficult time squaring the circle of someone who could never condone immorality, but who assisted her brothers-in-law in breaking the Ten Commandments and other Biblical injunctions as well.

Although Shawcross is careful not to tell us the full extent of Elizabeth's complicity – something, incidentally, which I do not condemn – the fact is, she actively colluded as a co-conspirator in David's two romances. I know this from Freda Dudley Ward herself. Margaret, Duchess of Argyll was a close friend of hers, and my step-mother-in-law introduced me to the aged *grande dame* towards the end of her life for a royal book I was supposed to write, but never did – though later on I used the insights she gave me in another royal book I wrote in 1993.[25] According to Freda, Elizabeth could not have been nicer or kinder to her throughout the many years of her affair with David. Even after it came to an end, with Thelma's advent, Elizabeth continued to embrace her with the warmth, kindness and hospitality she had invariably shown her while she was David's 'favourite', as she was known in Society.

Margaret Argyll confirmed to me that Elizabeth was the same with Thelma. Not that we actually need external corroboration of that fact, for Thelma provides it in decorous but unmistakable fashion in *Double Exposure*, the memoir she and her twin Gloria Vanderbilt wrote in 1958. She recounts weekends at the Fort, with her as hostess and Elizabeth and Bertie as enthusiastic guests, or at Royal Lodge, with the roles reversed. There was, for instance, the memorable occasion when Virginia Water froze over and they went skating on the pond. Thelma and Elizabeth were novices, so they hung on to the back of kitchen chairs while the men whizzed by. Thelma tells us she and Elizabeth were 'in gales of laughter'. There was also the time Bertie questioned whether David's new plastic records could actually live up to their promise. '"Come on, David, let's see if these are really unbreakable as the label says," Bertie cried. While the brothers roared with laughter, the Duke had us ducking and dodging like rabbits. Unfortunately the records didn't break, and the game went on until we all fled inside. They followed us in and continued their sport in the drawing room until one of the Prince's most treasured lamps was bowled over by a direct hit...'

There were many such weekends filled with the sort of ribald high jinks that appealed to Elizabeth and Bertie, who had adopted her family's predilection to mud fights and other forms of fun which might not seem all that amusing to people past a certain age, but would nevertheless remain a source of delight to her even in her old age. There were also more sedate pleasures, such as dining well, drinking plentifully, and gossiping, for Elizabeth loved a good gossip, as most people who enjoy other people do.

It is no wonder that Thelma was able to conclude, 'If ever I had to live in a bungalow in a small town, this is the woman I would most like to have as a next-door neighbour to gossip with while hanging out the washing in our backyards.'

Compulsion and Abdication

Chapter Nine

There was a third woman at that skating party at Virginia Water. Her name was Wallis Simpson, but she was regarded by the others as a figure of scant profundity: window-dressing rather than someone central to the scenario. She regarded herself in the same light, for she had come along with her husband Ernest Simpson to fill out yet another one of David and Thelma's house parties, which were always heavily weighted with Americans.

This was not only because Thelma was American, though of course that played a part. The Prince of Wales was an overt modernist who admired anything that was progressive. This meant that he was impressed with American get-up-and-go. Of how that emerging power had a can-do attitude to all aspects of life, unlike the ethos of his own country, where cautiousness and restrictiveness frequently functioned as a brake on progress.

The Duke of Windsor is on record as having said that he wanted to modernise the system. Margaret, Duchess of Argyll confirmed to me that, prior to his accession to the throne, David often bemoaned the strictures which he felt were preventing the national system from modernising and, in so doing, improving the lot of everyone, from the common man to the Royal Family. He felt that much of what he called 'princing' and 'kinging' were wastes of time and resources, and is even quoted in the Shawcross book stating that royal tours as they stood were a waste. Although he blamed the politicians for keeping the nation back, he did not spare his father and the Court from the part he believed they played. He felt they were partly responsible for the frustrating lack of progress the country was making, with their obsession with tradition and the 'old ways'. He was always talking about how he would sweep away the old fuddy-duddies and their ossifying practices when his day came, which, as everyone expected, would be sooner rather than later.

As can be imagined, his words did not fall on deaf ears.

Unfortunately for him, David did not reserve his future political plans for those who sympathised with his objectives and attitudes. He made his intentions clear to people like Lieutenant-Commander Colin Buist, who was a fully-paid-up member of the ossifiers. This former naval classmate of his brother Bertie at Dartmouth and Osborne had gone on to become the Duke of York's equerry. He and his wife Gladys were by this time close friends of both the Yorks, so Buist was a conduit to what was effectively an opposing camp, although David still had no idea that such a thing existed.

Had David just stopped to think, however, he would have realised that he was building up trouble for himself. Elizabeth had no appetite for modernism and would soon see, if she could not already do so, just how quaint and ridiculous she would look in this new world once David had acceded to the throne and swept away the antiquated practices which still proliferated at the Court of George V. As nothing mattered to Elizabeth more than how the world at large perceived her, and there was no possibility of updating her 'act' when to do so would mean changing the self which she and her legion of admirers regarded as the pinnacle of human perfection, David was inadvertently inviting the sister-in-law of whom he was so fond to join the Fifth Column.

Patently, no one had ever told the next King of England that forewarned is forearmed. He prided himself on his frankness, as any examination of his correspondence shows. Time and again he informs people that he has a reputation for frankness, which indeed he did. However, there were occasions when even someone as powerful as a present or future King of England needed to tread carefully, otherwise he would inadvertently make so many potential enemies that he would have undermined the security of his tenure upon the throne before he even sat upon it.

It was into this maelstrom of looming trouble that Wallis Simpson stepped. It has to be said, trouble was often her close companion from the moment of her conception, possibly even before it. Born on 19th June, 1896, in Square Cottage at the Monterey Inn Hotel directly opposite the Monterey Country Club in Blue Ridge Summit, Pennsylvania, where grand southerners summered, Bessie Wallis Warfield was the only child of Teackle Wallis Warfield and Alice Montague. Even before she was born, controversy dogged her. The union of her parents was opposed by both families, not because they were socially unsuited, but because her father was a consumptive. According to the Maryland Historical Society, the Warfields were 'old, old Baltimore' while the Montagues were 'one of the first families of Virginia'. T. Wallis, as her father was known, seems to have been a magnet for young women despite his health, and it is likely that Alice Montague became pregnant. The young couple was married on 19th November, 1895, and exactly seven months later, the future Duchess of Windsor entered the world without any suspicion of being premature.

Wallis, however, would never remember her father. He died of tuberculosis four days short of his first wedding anniversary, on 15th November, 1896. Thereafter, Wallis and her mother endured the fate of poor relations. For the first six years of her life, they lived with her paternal bachelor uncle, Solomon Davies Warfield. The founder and president of the Continental Trust Company, he lived in a comfortable four-storey house with his widowed mother at 34 East Preston Street. But in 1901 her mother's elder sister Bessie, after whom she had been named, was widowed when her husband T. Buchanan Merryman died, and the following year Alice and Wallis moved in with her into her comfortable four-bedroomed house at 9 West Chase Street, Baltimore. They stayed there for another year or two before moving into an apartment of their own, then a house, which was modest compared with her relations' houses.

In 1908, Wallis's fortunes changed when her mother married John Freeman Rasin, the son of a prominent member of the Democratic Party. A further improvement occurred between 1912 and 1914, when her Uncle Sol paid for her to be sent to Oldfields School, the most prestigious (and expensive) school in Maryland. Wallis quickly became friends with Renee du Pont, whose father Senator T. Coleman du Pont was a scion of the immensely rich du Pont family, and Mary Kirk, whose family owned Kirk Silverware. The latter young woman would play a prominent, some would say fateful, part in Wallis's life, and for a while they were the closest of friends. Indeed, had Mary Kirk not existed, there might have been no abdication at all.

Like Elizabeth, Wallis was a charismatic figure in youth as well as in old age. She was intelligent, well dressed and energetic as well as vivacious. In his 2005 book *Mrs Simpson* (Pan Books), Charles Higham quotes one of her school friends stating, 'She was bright, brighter than all of us.' She was also determined, as this same schoolmate confirmed. 'She made up her mind to go to the head of the class, and she did.'

Like Elizabeth and all her other contemporaries, Wallis's future life would be predicated upon the man she married. If she married well, she would have a good life. If she did not, she would not. By the time Wallis was old enough to leave school and 'come out', she was already known as a flirt. One only needs to cast one's mind back to Cecilia telling Elizabeth that she needed to be more flirtatious to appreciate how important it was for any girl to utilise her feminine wiles. Competition in the marriage market was stiff and a girl's whole future lay with her ability to attract the right sort of husband. There was no disgrace in doing so.

In April 1916, the year before the United States entered the Great War, Wallis, who was searching for a husband as all her contemporaries all over the world were, went to visit her cousin Corinne Mustin in Pensacola, Florida. Situated there was one of the main US naval bases for pilots. It was while she was there that Wallis met Earl Winfield (Win) Spencer, Jr, a handsome naval pilot. Proverbially tall, dark and handsome, he was also an alcoholic, though she did not yet know this. But he was from a good family, despite not being rich. While the Warfield and Montague families found him acceptable, she could hardly have been accused of fortune-hunting. In fact, at this point in her life, Wallis seems to have been her mother's daughter in more ways than one, for Alice's first marriage had clearly also been the conquest of heart over wallet. On 8th November, 1896, at the Christ Episcopal Church in Baltimore, Wallis (who had long since foresworn the Bessie part of her name) Warfield married the man she loved and became Mrs. Earl Winfield Spencer, Jr.

The marriage was doomed from the start because of Win Spencer's drinking. He was not only a menacing drunk, but also a reckless one. He drank even before flying and once crashed into the sea. Although he escaped with only minor injuries, this, together with the two fatal crashes Wallis had previously witnessed, were enough to put her in a permanent state of anxiety. Thereafter, she had a terror of flying which she never lost. Even as an old lady, she could count on her fingers the number of times she had been in an aeroplane.

Win was also prone to violent rages. Once, he locked her into a bathroom and refused to let her out. But Wallis was feisty as well as practical. This marriage *had* to work. So she followed her errant husband to San Diego when he was appointed first commanding officer of the Naval Air Station North Island training base in Coronado.

This posting lasted for four years. Towards the end of it, Wallis and Win separated for four months. This was the first of many separations followed by reconciliations. They reunited, however, in spring 1921, when he was posted to Washington. Although Wallis would later state that she was hoping that a change of scenery would bring about a change of Win's habits, it did not. So this reconciliation was short-lived.

By the time Win was posted to the Far East as commander of the Campagna in 1922, he and Wallis had separated again and she was romantically involved with Don Felipe Espil, the six-foot tall, dapper First Secretary at the Argentine Embassy. By her own account, Wallis had fallen totally in love with the worldly, sophisticated thirty-five-year-old diplomat. 'He was intelligent, ambitious, subtle, gracious, in many respects the most fascinating man I have ever met,' she said, claiming that he 'acted as both teacher and model in the art of living.'[1] She was also hoping he would marry her, but he had other ideas. The fact that she would be a divorcée if she became free to marry him cannot have been the objection, for he would subsequently marry another American *divorcée*, Courtney Letts Borden, a Senator's daughter who had grown up in Washington and whose previous husband had been John Borden of the socially prominent Chicago family. This family was far more politically prominent than the Warfields or Montagues could ever aspire to being. Ellen Borden, for instance, would marry the former Governor of Illinois and two-time Democratic presidential candidate Adlai Stephenson II, whose namesake grandfather was himself a statesman of some stature, having served as the Vice-President of the United States of America between 1893 and 1897. Either Felipe Espil did not love Wallis enough to marry her, or he felt she had too little to offer in worldly terms.

Whatever his reason, in January 1924, with few other options than to reconcile with her drunken husband, Wallis crossed the Atlantic where she 'took in' Paris with her recently-widowed cousin Corinne Mustin before boarding a troop carrier, the USS Chaumont, for the trip east to Hong Kong. Husband and wife were reunited for an even shorter reconciliation than the last one.

As anyone with any imagination will appreciate, living with a violent alcoholic is no picnic, but at that time, wives had little option but to remain shackled to their husbands, even when they proved to be as unsatisfactory as Win Spencer. So Wallis hung in there until her health gave out. Only then did she leave him, at which point she faced the inevitable. The marriage was unsustainable.

This was a daunting prospect for any young woman of good family, for divorcées had fewer options open to them the poorer they were. And Wallis had no money of her own. But another of the characteristics she shared with Elizabeth was gumption. Not to mention the pragmatism of the practical sybarite. Her old friend Katherine Moore Bigelow had recently married Herman Rogers and was living in Peking, so Wallis decided to accept Katherine's invitation to stay with them and see something of China, rather than rush back to the United States, where a life of uncertainty awaited her yet again. Using the Rogers' house as a base, Wallis did travel elsewhere, but her base remained the highly respectable residence of Mr. and Mrs. Herman Rogers.

According to Mrs. Milton E. Miles, whose husband was a brother officer of Win Spencer's, it was while Wallis was in Peking that she met Galeazzo, Count Ciano. Not yet married to Edda Mussolini, the handsome Italian aristocrat began an affair with the newly-separated American. Unfortunately, this resulted in her becoming pregnant. Because there was no possibility of their marrying, or of Win Spencer accepting the child as his own, Wallis had little choice but to have an abortion. This was botched and she was thereafter unable to conceive.

Although Edda Ciano would later deny that there was any truth to this story, there was little motivation for Mrs. Miles to have lied, especially as how Wallis was well known to be the innocent victim of an alcoholic husband. On the other hand, Countess Ciano had good reason for denying that her executed husband had compelled the Duchess of Windsor to have an abortion which had rendered her barren thereafter. While there is no longer any way of proving what did or did not happen, Margaret, Duchess of Argyll told me that the word, in the circles in which the Windsors mixed, was that it was true.

If the story has one merit, it is to provide refutation of the claim that Wallis was a hermaphrodite. According to this rumour, she suffered from Androgen Insensitivity Syndrome. Patently, the pedlars of this alternative tale have never bothered to research that condition. They assert that because Wallis had some masculine features – a strong jaw, large hands and a big head – her physiognomy is proof that she was a biological male, whose genitalia was feminised before birth owing to androgen insensitivity. What they have patently failed to appreciate is that individuals who suffer from this condition are invariably more, rather than less, feminine than their biologically female counterparts. Had Wallis suffered from what used to be known as Adreno-Genital Syndrome, she would have had a smaller head, smaller hands, and a weaker jawline than she did. What they employ as corroboration of her hermaphroditism, therefore, is actually incontrovertible proof that she could not have suffered from the ascribed condition, for she was simply too masculine in appearance to have been intolerant of the male hormone androgen.

This story has become widespread since it was first aired in the late 1980s. In his entertaining memoirs, *Redeeming Features,* Nicky Haslam informs his readers that corroboration for the tale as told by him was inadvertently provided through Wallis's maid. His account involves Wallis spotting her panties with urine, which he concludes must be verification of the rumours, as the location of the spots was towards the front of her crotch. There is some merit to his account, though Nicky leapt to the wrong conclusion. Doubtless this was through a combination of ignorance of the physiognomy of Androgen Insensitive females as well as of ordinary females. He is a gentleman who prefers the company of other gentlemen, so his ignorance of the female body is hardly surprising. But the urinary tract of AIS and XX females is in the same place. AIS females do not have penises, so Nicky's belief, that Wallis's urinary spotting was confirmation of her hermaphroditism, is somewhat wide of the mark.

Yet there is little doubt in my mind that his account of Wallis's maid's indiscretions is accurate, because I witnessed an exchange between Margaret Argyll and her maid Edith Springett in the mid-seventies which involved Wallis and her maid.

I was visiting my step-mother-in-law at her house at 48 Upper Grosvenor Street, which had been 'done up' by Syrie Maugham. It was directly opposite the American Embassy. Margaret had called for Springett, who was duly shown by the butler into the drawing room. She reprimanded Springett for returning her silk panties in an unacceptable condition. Springett, who was very partial to a tincture of whiskey, responded aggressively, informing Margaret that 'old slappers' like her couldn't expect all traces of their urine to be removed from their underwear, and if she'd wanted clean underwear at her late stage of life, she shouldn't have been 'putting it about' the way she used to. With a face like thunder, Margaret barked, 'Springett, that's quite enough. You may go now.' But Springett wasn't about to be dismissed without the final word. As she was stomping out of the white-on-white room, she turned and said to me, 'At least this Grace leaks from only one hole. Unlike that other old slapper, the Duchess of Windsor, who leaks from both.' I didn't know whether to laugh or wince, but saw my opportunity to lessen Margaret's obvious embarrassment by imputing the maid's word. So I said in as dignified a manner as possible, 'Now, Springett, how could you possibly know that?' A look of triumph came over her countenance as she proudly informed me, 'The Duchess's maid told me herself, My Lady. She said that the Duchess dribbles urine at night when she's the worse for wear. And day and night, her piles leave their mark.'

Of course, tact precluded me from acting as if one word of what Springett had said could possibly be true. To have accepted her comments about Wallis would have meant accepting them about the step-mother-in-law of whom I was fond, so I condoled with Margaret about yet another drunken outburst from her recalcitrant maid. But I could tell that Margaret knew as well as I did that every word of what Springett had said about Wallis was true. Which made me even more intent on abiding by my grandmother and mother's stricture against allowing maids to wash our underwear, and I can say in absolute honesty that no one has ever washed a pair of my panties since childhood. Would be that Margaret and Wallis had had similarly wise mothers and grandmothers.

If further refutation of the canard about Wallis's biological status is required, she was operated upon for uterine fibroids in 1951. It is not possible to suffer from Androgen Insensitivity Syndrome and have a uterus. Her doctor, Jean Thin, also confirmed that her genitalia were normal. While AIS females have the appearance of normal genitalia externally, their vaginas are seldom fully developed. As Wallis's was, the body of evidence tilts very much in favour of the Duchess of Windsor having been a normal, XX female.

Innuendo often clings to women of great sexual allure, and whatever else Wallis's failings were, lack of sex appeal was not amongst them. She spent over a year in China, leading a life that was as socially correct and morally acceptable as any of Elizabeth's, Bertie's, David's, Thelma's or Freda's friends. Largely because the world seemed a much bigger place in the 1920s and 1930s than it does in our global age, and China, with its competing warlords, deposed Emperor and international cities, was the ultimate exotic location, this period of Wallis's life would provide her detractors with rich hunting grounds. They would make the most damaging claims about her, chief of which were contained in the so-called 'China Dossier'. This matter, however, is best dealt with elsewhere, showing as it does the lengths to which certain members of the British Establishment were prepared to go to plant false stories about the 'interloper' they were intent on ridding themselves of.

By September 1925, Wallis and Win were back in the United States, though still living apart. Shortly after her arrival home, she met the very married Ernest Aldrich Simpson and his wife Dorothea through her old school friend Mark Kirk, by then Mrs. Jacques Achille Louis Raffray. In *The Heart Has Its Reasons,* Wallis stated that he was attracted to her and she to him, before describing him in these terms: 'Reserved in manner, yet with a gift of quiet wit, always well dressed, a good dancer, fond of the theatre, and obviously well read, he impressed me as an unusually well-balanced man. I had acquired a taste for the cosmopolitan mind, and Ernest obviously had one.'[2]

No one describes better what happened next than the soon-to-be discarded Mrs. Ernest Simpson. Wallis possessed 'enough of "what it takes" to steal a man',[3] and was a predator who 'moved in and helped herself to my house and my clothes and, finally, to everything.'[4]

Wallis and Ernest were soon embarked upon a passionate romance. Once she saw that it would last, she took steps to free herself so she could marry him. Both sides of her family were aghast, for divorce was less acceptable in the staid circles the Warfields and Montagues moved in than in the freewheeling circles occupied by the Magnificent Morgans. Or indeed the Simpsons, for Dorothy Parsons Dechert had been a Massachusetts *divorcée* when Ernest had married her in 1923. Aunt Bessie Merryman told Wallis, 'The Montague women do not get divorced,' while Uncle Sol Warfield pointed out that there had never been a divorce in the Warfield family and warned her, 'I won't let you bring this disgrace upon us. What will the people of Baltimore think?'

Wallis would pay a high price for failing to heed the warning. On 24th October, 1927, after she had filed for divorce in anticipation of becoming the second Mrs. Simpson, but before it came through on 10th December, 1927, Uncle Sol died. He had not only been a rich man, but an eminent one. And one to whom reputation mattered. His major accomplishment, aside from the accumulation of a considerable fortune, was to extend the Seaboard Air Line Railway into South Florida and also to connect the east and west coasts of that state. To this day, Amtrak use the rail links established by S. Davis Warfield, as he was known in the business community. Rather than leave the niece, who was more like a daughter to him, a proportionate share of his $5,000,000 estate, and in so doing assure her financial future, he demonstrated his disapproval of her conduct in the most potent way possible. She was left a derisory $15,000 trust fund and the right to occupy a room in the home for aged and indigent gentlewomen which was to be established out of the bequest he made for Baltimore ladies who had fallen upon hard times, but had not fallen, like Wallis, from a state of respectable grace.

Six weeks later, the girl who could have been a major heiress had she delayed her desire to marry an already-married man, was free to marry her lover. Ernest, however, was not all he seemed to be. True, he was comfortably off, being a partner and son of one of the co-founders of the international ship-broking firm Simpson, Spence and Young. True, his mother Charlotte was the daughter of Royal Aldrich Gaines, and the name Aldrich then as now signified the upper echelons of American Society. True, he had been born in New York and educated at The Hill School and Harvard. His father was undeniably the well-known British-born shipbroker Ernest Louis Simpson, and gentlemanliness clung to both father and son like a cloak drenched in claret. Ernest had definitely crossed the Atlantic during the First World War and become a captain in the prestigious Coldstream Guards, one of the Household Divisions charged with guarding the person of the Monarch. What was less well-known – in fact, was totally unknown – was that Ernest Simpson senior had been born Ernest Solomon. In a world of Gentiles, he was a Jew passing himself off as a WASP at a time when only WASPs were accepted in the social and professional circles in which he moved.

While both Ernest and his sister Maud knew of their Jewish roots, it is open to question whether Wallis did. There is an utter lack of evidence either way. If she was *au fait* with the secret, she was as careful as Ernest to keep quiet about it. Indeed, it is unlikely that the family's secret would ever have got out had Maud Kerr-Smiley not informed Ernest's son, Ernest Child Simpson, of their Jewish heritage following his father's death from throat cancer in 1958. 'I believe Maud wanted to spite her younger brother. But suddenly I felt I belonged somewhere. I had always felt neither fully English nor American, but I could become Israeli. I changed my name to what I thought was the family surname and went to live in Israel,' the newly-minted Ahron Solomons said.[5]

While there is little doubt that Wallis was not anti-Semitic, she was socially ambitious. As indeed was Ernest Simpson. By his son's own account, all he ever wanted was to be accepted as an English gentleman. And Wallis, it seems, was better able to share the life he wanted for himself than Dorothea. Whether Ernest felt any compunction about leaving his wife and little daughter Audrey for Wallis has never been determined, but even if he had done so, once Wallis was disinherited, no gentleman would have left a lady in the lurch following such a reversal of fortune on his account. So he and Dorothea were divorced early in 1928, and he moved back to London, to work in the London offices of Simpson, Spence and Young.

At the end of May, Wallis arrived in London, taking a *pied-à-terre* in Stanmore Court. On 21st July, 1928, her future seemed assured when she became Mrs. Ernest Aldrich Simpson at the Chelsea Register Office.

The Simpsons' first matrimonial home was a furnished house in the then ultra-fashionable district of Mayfair, at 12 Upper Berkeley Street. They took a year's lease from Lady Chesham, and had four servants. When this expired, they moved to a spacious three-bedroomed flat at 5 Bryanston Court, Bryanston Square, in the less appealing but nevertheless acceptable district of Bayswater. Syrie Maugham, the ex-wife of the then immensely popular author W. Somerset Maugham, and the most desirable interior designer of her day, helped Wallis to furnish it in the latest, snappiest style.

Now that Ernest and his new wife were living in London, they needed a social life. There was no necessity for them to look further than his elder sister Maud. Married to Peter Kerr-Smiley, the Unionist MP for North Antrim between 1910 and 1922 and second son of Sir Hugh Smiley, 1st Bt, the Kerr-Smileys, as they started styling themselves in 1905, were at the very heart of chic London Society. Indeed, it was at a party that Peter and Maud Kerr-Smiley gave at their grand and sumptuous house at 31 Belgrave Square that Freda Dudley Ward first met the Prince of Wales.

Strictly speaking, Freda had not been a party guest. An air-raid siren had rung, signalling a Zeppelin raid at the precise moment that she and her Latin American escort for the evening, 'Buster' Dominguez, were crossing the square. They rushed to the nearest point of shelter, which happened to be the portico of the Kerr-Smileys' house. They asked the butler for permission to stay there just as Maud Kerr-Smiley and her guests, who included the Prince of Wales, were making their way downstairs to seek shelter in the basement. Seeing that they were a lady and gentleman, she asked them in, and the rest, as the proverbial saying goes, is history.

Proverbial sayings seem particularly appropriate at this juncture. Lightning was about to strike again as a result of another introduction made by Maud Kerr-Smiley. This time, though, the effect of the bolt was less instantaneous than it had been when David was rocked to his core by the *coup de foudre* with Freda Dudley Ward, even if in the end the delayed effect would create a constitutional crisis. Without Maud Kerr-Smiley's introduction to Consuelo Thaw, the eldest of the Magnificent Morgans would never have been able to introduce Wallis to her younger sister Thelma with the telling and truthful phrase, 'Mrs. Simpson is fun. You will like her.'[6] Thelma and Consuelo would never have brought Wallis into their orbit, central to which was the Prince of Wales. And because Wallis's relationship with David was the antithesis of a *coup de foudre* – such attraction as there was took years to develop – it is unlikely that she would ever have had the opportunity to get to know him well enough for him to discover her hidden depths, and then fall in love with her.

Wallis first met David in the drawing room of Thelma and Marmaduke's hunting lodge, Burrough Court, at Melton Mowbray, in November 1930. Originally, she had not been on the guest list at all. Consuelo had to drop out at the last minute and suggested that Thelma ask Ernest and Wallis as replacements for her and Benny Thaw. Not surprisingly, the socially ambitious Simpsons leapt at the opportunity, not that either of them could imagine where it would all end. Despite nursing a heavy cold, Wallis gladly hopped on a train to Leicestershire, practising her curtsey with Ernest in their first-class compartment for much of the way. When they arrived, she not only had a chance to use it on David, but also on his youngest brother George.

Wallis was thirty-four and 'rather plain, almost like a governess,' Margaret, Duchess of Argyll reminisced to me years later about this latest addition to the American expatriate community in London. 'She was always great fun, but nothing to write home about (visually). At least not at first. She was quick on the uptake. She smartened up her act almost overnight and became **so** *soignée*. When I stop to think of the Wallis I first met and the chic, stylish woman who dominated the Best Dressed List with people like me and Babe Paley, it's almost as if one were speaking about two different women.'

At this first meeting with her future husband, Wallis made no visible impression upon either prince. Nevertheless, David, ever the romantic, would later claim that she made an indelible impression upon him at luncheon the following day. She was seated beside him and he brought up the subject of central heating. According to his memoirs, 'Mrs. Simpson did not miss the great boon her country had conferred upon the world. On the contrary, she liked our cold houses. A mocking look came into her eyes. "I am sorry, Sir," she said "but you have disappointed me." "In what way?" "Every American woman who comes to your country is always asked the same question. I had hoped for something more original from the Prince of Wales."'[7]

Thelma dismissed this version of events, observing, with some justice, 'it would have been not only bad taste but bad manners. At that moment Wallis Simpson was as nervous and as impressed as any woman would have been on first meeting the Prince of Wales.'[8]

Although Wallis could hardly have contradicted her husband publicly, when it came time for her reminiscences, she inclined towards Thelma's interpretation. After fudging the issue by saying that she couldn't 'imagine how the subject ever came up', she stated, 'The truth is I was petrified.'[9] She also admitted thinking, as she left Burrough Court the following day, 'I had already dismissed from mind the possibility of our ever meeting again.'[10]

Wallis was right to expect little or nothing from what had been an encounter with no obvious significance. Six months later, when she met David again, this time in Thelma's London house at 21 Grosvenor Square to celebrate his return from his South American tour, 'As he passed close by his glance happened to fall upon me. He then nudged Thelma, who was standing beside him, and seemed to be asking in a whisper, "Haven't I met that lady before?" In any event he presently came over to where Ernest and I were standing to say, "How nice to see you again. I remember our meeting at Melton."'[11]

Her next encounter was more propitious. On 10th June, 1931, Wallis achieved the apogee of her ambitions by being presented at Court. Although she had missed out on the first presentation young ladies had when they made their debut as single women, now that she was married she was eligible for the second presentation. Being divorced was no bar for her any more than it had been for Thelma or any of the myriad other *divorcées* who dropped deep curtsies to King George V and Queen Mary. All they had to do was satisfy the Lord Chamberlain's Office that they had not been the guilty party.

Virtually everything Wallis wore to Buckingham Palace was borrowed from the two Morgan sisters. Consuelo provided the simple but stunning white silk, bias-cut evening dress which was the height of fashion, and showed off her slender figure to perfection, while Thelma contributed the train, feathers and fan which were requisites for any presentation of married women.

Wallis was presented by Mildred Anderson, an American who had married an Englishman and was a member of the American expatriate community which had become so fashionable now that David was known to favour Americans. According to her future husband, Wallis dropped a dignified and graceful curtsey to the King and Queen, who were flanked by him and his eighty-one-year-old great-uncle. This was Queen Victoria's only surviving son, the Duke of Connaught, another lover of Americans, his long-term mistress being Lady Leslie, born Leonie Jerome and sister to Winston Churchill's beautiful mother Lady Randolph Churchill, who had herself been a girlfriend of King Edward VII when he was the Prince of Wales.

As the Royal Family were proceeding through the Apartments of State after the Presentation, Wallis overheard David say to the aged Duke, 'Uncle Arthur, something ought to be done about the lights. They make all the women look ghastly.'[12]

This comment provided the first indisputable opportunity for Wallis to show the asperity which would ultimately so captivate the prince. She was at a cocktail party at Thelma's shortly afterwards, and David came up to her and said how much he had liked her gown. '"But Sir," I responded with a straight face, "I understood that you thought we all looked ghastly." He was startled. Then he smiled, "I had no idea my voice carried so far."'[13]

Although Wallis's tartness definitely appealed to David, they did not see each other for another seven months. Then in mid-January 1932 she received a letter from him asking Ernest and herself for the next but one weekend at Fort Belvedere. Thelma, of course, was the hostess and Thelma, of course, had suggested Wallis and Ernest as guests, but correct form meant that the invitation could not come from her, but had to come from him.

Wallis was transfixed, as Elizabeth had been, by her first glimpse of royalty at home. What astonished her more than anything, however, was the sheer simplicity, indeed ordinariness, of it all. The men cleared bush, the women sat around gossiping. The most noteworthy thing was that David did needlepoint, just like his mother and Elizabeth's.

There was a gap of eight months before Wallis and Ernest received another invitation to the Fort. They went for tea, followed by another weekend. Wallis was such fun and Ernest so easy-going and interesting without being pushy that, in the new year, they were asked back four times within three months. By June of 1933 the committed lovers were sufficiently friendly with the Simpsons for David to host a dinner party at Quaglino's, the chic

Mayfair restaurant, in celebration of Wallis's thirty-seventh birthday. She reciprocated by giving a dinner at 5 Bryanston Court, Bayswater in honour of her host, who was of course accompanied by the lady in his life, Thelma.

Like Elizabeth, Wallis had an eye for detail and a gift for saying and doing just the thing that would appeal to the person she was trying to impress. Her choice of menu could not have been bettered. She served the prince who admired all things American an all-American feast: black bean soup to start, followed by a fish course of grilled lobster, a meat course of southern-style fried chicken, and a dessert of raspberry soufflé.

Just as Elizabeth's ability as a hostess had impressed Queen Mary and Bertie, Wallis's stock rose in David's eyes as she comported herself with consummate grace and ease. Despite this, his gaze remained firmly fixed on Thelma, who herself was a gracious hostess.

Wallis would later confess to having had doubts 'about the durability of his interest in either Ernest or me', but as 1933 progressed they became 'permanent fixtures at the Fort weekends. The association imperceptibly but swiftly passed from an acquaintanceship to a friendship.'[14]

By this time, Wallis and Elizabeth knew each other well enough to have forged a pleasant if insubstantial relationship. The Yorks customarily dropped in at the Fort over the weekend, and David would take his guests over to Royal Lodge for tea, drinks, or just a short visit. He was a particularly devoted uncle to Lilibet and little Margaret Rose, who was already a beautiful little girl and as much a scamp as her mother had been at the same age. When he was not with the adults, he would be with his nieces. The two households were so intertwined that they frequently ate together, played together, laughed together, even skated together.

Wallis would later tell friends, including Margaret, Duchess of Argyll, that she and her future sister-in-law had a perfectly cordial albeit impersonal relationship at this stage. However, she did not particularly warm to the Duchess of York, whom she found 'pretentious, precious, and frankly ridiculous'. Nor was she alone in this opinion.

Elizabeth pointedly would not or could not drop her act of royal duchess. She refused to become just another member of even this intimate group, and got backs up left, right and centre with her posturing and attitudinising. She always held herself aloof from any group that was not her own, and of course when she was surrounded by her own group, there was no doubt as to who the leader was.

There was a swimming pool at the Fort. David, his younger brother George, who was a frequent houseguest, and all the other houseguests, including Thelma, Lord and Lady Louis Mountbatten and the Simpsons, would spend large tranches of time when the weather was good sitting around the pool in their swimming trunks. Elizabeth, however, would always be dressed in a frock and hat. It wasn't the dress that was the problem, for she was already very plump and allowances were made for the possibility that she might be embarrassed to reveal her figure in front of gatherings where everyone else was slender. The hat, however, jarred. Even when she was *en famille*, Elizabeth was so self-consciously regal, so pointedly acting out the royal role, so intent on reminding everyone who she was, that she made herself a laughing stock with her brother-in-law's friends. Although people liked her, they found her constant posing too much to take.

This was a criticism which would echo throughout the corridors of power time and time again. Even Eleanor Roosevelt would feel compelled to question why Elizabeth always had to be so self-consciously regal, though the American First Lady was more concerned about the effect such perpetual role-playing had upon her psyche, than critical of her pretentiousness.

None of these critics seems to have understood that Elizabeth was a born actress, who brought to life the Shakespearean theory that 'all the world's a stage' and she was perfectly happy to 'strut and fret' upon hers for as many hours as there were in the day. Insofar as she was concerned, she was the living embodiment of the virtues she aspired to. There was no distinction, in her attitude and presumably in her mind, between her identity and the character she was portraying. She was the act.

In *Elizabeth The Queen Mother,* Hugo Vickers quotes people implying that there was a void at Elizabeth's core. When she was not acting, there seemed to be no one there. They thought this sad, but whether Elizabeth herself did is open to question. If there really was an element of emptiness there, and her whole life had been a quest to fill or at least compensate for it, she had been manifestly successful, and deserves commendation for having been so.

Not that those close to her necessarily felt like that. Queen Mary and Princess Louise, Duchess of Argyll were only two of the older royals who were wary of Elizabeth. Although no one was yet afraid of her, as many people close to her would become before the decade was over, she actually had few admirers in smart circles. That is not to say that people disliked her. She was charming and agreeable and made a point of endearing herself to everyone, but few, outside of her little band of admirers and the general public, actually looked up to her. She was too studiedly Her Royal Highness The Duchess of York for starters. Although she softened the more discomfiting aspects of her disquieting presentation with charming agreeability, most of David's friends, who were the most desirable social group in the kingdom and indeed the world, tolerated her with affection rather than admiration.

Largely, this was because Elizabeth often stuck out like a sore thumb. They were all hyper-sophisticates; she was not. They were all sleek and glamorous; she was not. They were creatures of their time; she was not. They enjoyed being themselves, while, if observations are accurate, Elizabeth did not have a self to be when she wasn't acting. They were alive to the new ideas and ideals, in which background and privilege had their place, but should not exclude accomplishment and merit, and certainly did not mean that the old guard was better than newcomers simply because they had been around longer. This openness was antipathetic to Elizabeth and her cronies, who firmly believed that God intended them to remain rich men in their castles, while poor men must abide by the ordained order and remain housed, albeit kindly, at the gate, whence they should and would serve their betters with reverence, grateful for the *noblesse oblige* that had been shown to them by their kindly patrician masters.

Even though Elizabeth did not fit in, she was nevertheless excellent company. Like Wallis, she was fun. Like Wallis, she had a snappy sense of humour. She too liked a good laugh. She also enjoyed nothing better than a party, and loved bedecking herself in furs and jewels and what she thought of as glamorous clothes, even if everyone else in the group thought that her taste was frightful.

Despite the underlying lack of admiration for Elizabeth, she was nevertheless an integral part of the Royal Family and her brother-in-law David's circle. However, while he and Thelma, she and Bertie, Wallis and Ernest, Consuelo and Benny, and their many friends enjoyed carefree weekends at the Fort, with forays to and from Royal Lodge, the Great Depression was biting all over the world. Banks were closing everywhere. People could not get jobs even when they wanted them. Poverty and hardship were rife. Hitler was appointed Chancellor of Germany at the beginning of this momentous year of 1933. The Reichstag was set on fire by the Nazis, and the Oxford Union declared that it would not fight for King and Country should the world's elite take the nation into another war. There was widespread sympathy for Germany, which had been virtually destroyed by the reparations laid down by the Treaty of Versailles, and as hunger and deprivation bit across the land of the victors of the Great War, the harsh and unfair way in which Germany – and innocent Germans – had been treated, was being acknowledged.

It would be churlish and unfair to deny that the Royal Family was not distressed by what was happening in the world at large. Bertie and David both rolled up their sleeves and tried to help the lot of the common man, undertaking increased engagements which brought them into contact with the working classes. Elizabeth also did her bit, though bit is the operative word.

While she expressed sympathy for the common man, hard work had never been her forte, and she still kept her official engagements to a minimum. Despite this, she was superb when she was cast in the role of lady bountiful. She made all the right sounds, leaving her audience filled with admiration for her big-heartedness and sensitivity. Undeniably, she did have a broad streak of sentimentality in her nature, and like many overt sentimentalists, she was moved, if only superficially, by anything dramatic. Since suffering is always powerfully dramatic, and since she possessed the gift of appearing to be affected even if its reach was only momentary, the recipients of her largesse were always left with the feeling that the Duchess of York cared about them.

To read the Countess of Longford's panegyric entitled *Elizabeth R*, which was written with the Queen Mother's co-operation, all these events paled into insignificance because '1933 was the year of the corgi'. Elizabeth was a dog lover, as indeed were Wallis and David, whose pugs would become the children they never had. Both women appreciated the many benefits that canines could bring, not the least of which is unconditional love. Both had always had dogs; now Elizabeth introduced the breed which would hereafter become synonymous with the British Royal Family when a corgi named Dookie was delivered to Royal Lodge.

In her insightful biography, Penelope Mortimer observes, 'The animal, unfortunately, emulated the less pleasing aspects of the royal temperament. Members of the Household gallantly hid their bleeding hands while passing the time of day with the Princesses; the staff went in constant fear of hydrophobia. This angry animal was soon joined by Jane, Mimsy, Stiffy, Scrummy and Choo Choo. The last four were not corgis. They were golden retrievers and a Tibetan lion dog.'[15]

Wallis, meanwhile, had to make do with a single cairn terrier.

Life did not look up for the world at large in 1934, nor for Thelma and her identical twin, Gloria Vanderbilt. But the new year definitely heralded an improvement in Wallis Simpson's lot. Gloria's misfortune and Thelma's loyalty would provide her with an opportunity, and she took it with an alacrity that showed that while she and Elizabeth would eventually become sisters-in-law, under the skin, they were sisters.

The year had begun badly for the most glamorous widow on earth. Big Gloria's mother and Little Gloria's adored nanny Emma (Dodo) Keislich had joined forces to prevent Mrs. Vanderbilt from disrupting their lives by travelling with Little Gloria to the extent that she did. Most of the participants, in what *Time* Magazine described as 'the world's greatest scandal', would later agree that Laura Kilpatrick Morgan, who had been divorced from the girls' father in 1927, was a seriously unstable woman. And Dodo, like many a nanny before her and since, felt that she, rather than the child's mother, should be calling the shots. So mother and carer, who had been undermining Big Gloria in Little Gloria's eyes for years, cooked up a scheme with Little Gloria's aunt, Gertrude Vanderbilt Whitney, to wrest control of Little Gloria from her mother.

In June 1932, Little Gloria had had her tonsils removed and Big Gloria had agreed that her daughter could recuperate for the summer at her sister-in-law's house in Old Westbury, Long Island, while Big Gloria was in Europe. Gertrude then informed Surrogate Judge Foley that her niece was living with her. This was a shrewd move, for Big Gloria had relatively little money of her own, and needed the income provided for her through the trust to maintain her lifestyle. He ordered that Big Gloria's allowance from the trust fund, which was worth $5,000,000, be cut from $48,000 per annum to $9,000.

It is worth noting that $5,000,000 was exactly the same sum Wallis's Uncle Sol had failed to leave to her. This shows the extent of Wallis's loss, for Little Gloria was regarded as one of America's great heiresses, despite having only a half-share of the trust fund. Her elder half-sister, Cathleen Vanderbilt, the daughter of her father's first wife Cathleen Neilson, had the other half. It is tempting to wonder whether the objections to Wallis, which arose because she was perceived by Elizabeth and the English Establishment as a common adventuress, would have been viable had she been seen to be the aristocratic American heiress she would have been had she inherited Uncle Sol's millions.

Wallis, however, would prove not to be the only person unfairly judged. Surrogate Judge Foley's decision to reduce Big Gloria's allowance from her late husband's trust fund meant that Big Gloria had overnight ceased to be a woman of means. Her then lover, movie magnate A.C. Blumenthal, therefore introduced her to a lawyer named Nathan Burkan, with a view to gaining restitution of her daughter and income. He discovered that Big Gloria had never been her daughter's guardian, owing to the erroneous supposition that Big Gloria had herself been a minor at the time of Reggie Vanderbilt's death. Why Laura Kilpatrick Morgan had lied, and persisted in the lie, that the twins had been born one year after they were, will never be known, but, as Big Gloria stated in her memoirs, her fate and that of her daughter hinged upon this deception.

Meanwhile, Gertrude was refusing to hand back Little Gloria, who had been effectively kidnapped from her mother's house by Dodo when Big Gloria had reclaimed her. Gertrude moreover refused to allow her sister-in-law to visit Little Gloria unless someone was there to prevent her from removing the child from her precincts. The only way that this outrageous situation could be brought to a halt was for Big Gloria to be appointed her daughter's legal guardian, which she ought to have been and would have been without recourse to the courts, had her mother not lied about her age. Nathan Burkan therefore applied to the court for Mrs. Vanderbilt to be appointed guardian.

Laura Kilpatrick Morgan's response was to lodge an objection, stating that her daughter was an unfit mother. According to Mrs. Morgan, Gloria led a decadent, immoral life and was both a negligent mother and damaging influence upon her child.

What became the most sensational custody case of all time, Vanderbilt vs. Whitney, now started to wend its sleazy way through the courts. The truth, which would only emerge much later, was that Little Gloria was well tended by Dodo. She was no more and no less neglected by her mother than most of her peers were by theirs. And though the level of involvement between Society ladies and their children fell far short of what contemporary society now regards as acceptable, Little Gloria was given all the care and attention any child needs to flourish by the person who was charged with her care: Dodo. Of course, the nanny's desire to usurp the role of mother from Big Gloria, and in so doing gain even greater control over Little Gloria, was not in either the child's or the mother's short- or long-term interest. And, as things would turn out, not in Dodo's either, though she couldn't have known that when she joined forces with Laura Morgan to betray her mistress.

The grandmother's desire to grandstand as the saviour of her famous granddaughter at the expense of her even more famous daughter, in what seemed to most onlookers was an aging egotist's malice against her successful offspring, was hardly commendable either. Even Gertrude's presumed interest in her niece's welfare was more apparent than real. She would lose all interest in Little Gloria and neglect her as soon as she was awarded custody, which was even more unconscionable than any of the alleged acts of neglect Big Gloria was accused of. At least Little Gloria's mother had always left her daughter in the charge of a beloved nanny, while Gertrude did not even do that. A consequence of Dodo's treachery was that she was herself excluded from Little Gloria's life, so everyone in this American version of a Greek tragedy lost out, with the exception of Gertrude Vanderbilt Whitney, whose time was absorbed by her career as an artist and the Whitney Museum of American Art, which she had founded in 1931.

Although the Matter of Vanderbilt, which was dubbed the Trial of the Century, would not begin until 1st October, 1934, by January of that year the legal teams were gearing up for the coming fight. Feeling in need of her twin's support, Gloria asked Thelma to join her in California. Thelma agreed to do so, and informed David on 12th January that she would be away for five to six weeks. According to Thelma, 'his face took on a look of resignation, as if to imply that although this was not to his liking, he would do nothing that might interfere with my pleasure'. Days later she was having lunch with Wallis at the Ritz when her friend observed, 'Oh, Thelma, the little man is going to be so lonely.'

'Well, dear,' Thelma replied, 'you look after him for me while I'm away. See that he does not get into any mischief.'[16]

On 20th January, Thelma sailed for New York after David threw a farewell dinner for her at the Fort. Everything between the lovers was as good as it had always been, and she had no inkling that she was about to be supplanted in his affections.

But events were gathering pace. The Simpsons spent the following weekend at the Fort, as David told Thelma when he telephoned her shortly after her arrival in New York. Proving how conscientious she was at honouring her promise to take care of her absent friend's boyfriend, Wallis then asked David to join Ernest and herself for dinner at Bryanston Court. He must have been enjoying the care she was taking of him thoroughly, for he broke new ground a few days later when he telephoned her directly for the first time ever. Could she and Ernest join his party for a dinner he was hosting at the Dorchester on the following Tuesday?

Thelma had been gone exactly ten days when the dinner, which would prove to be something of a turning point in Wallis and David's relationship, took place. They were alone at the table, the others having gone to dance. David started talking about his aspirations for the future of the monarchy. This was heady stuff for anyone. Here was the future King of England telling her how he planned to reign once he ascended the throne. Wallis was transfixed, which he must have misinterpreted as boredom, because he suddenly stopped talking. 'But I am boring you,' he said apologetically. 'On the contrary. I couldn't be more interested. Please, please go on,' she responded. He then crossed some sort of emotional bridge, for he said, more apocryphally than factually, 'Wallis, you're the only woman who's ever been interested in my job.'[17]

That statement was untrue. Although there is scant evidence of Thelma's direct involvement in David's working life, much evidence exists of Freda's over the sixteen years since they had met. Indeed, she had only recently helped him set up the Feathers Clubs Association, a charity to assist the unemployed, and their correspondence proves that she played an active role in encouraging and assisting him in his work.

David, however, was one of those emotionally needy individuals whose impulses override the more rational elements of their personality. Like many extremely dependent people, his feelings in the present wiped out those of the past, and once he made an emotional connection, the impulse was overpowering. There might even have been an additional but unconscious thrill enabling this process, for, while Freda and Thelma were strong personalities, neither of them was dominating like Wallis. Also, she had one attribute that both of them lacked. She was not in awe of royalty. To her, David was just a man, albeit one with more than his fair share of desirable trappings. While both Freda and Thelma had a reverence for royalty and treated him accordingly, Wallis did not. She was polite and gracious, but there was something in her demeanour which made him discern that she viewed him as just another human being. This he found intoxicating, indeed liberating, for he had finally found someone who viewed him as a person and not as a prince.

From that dinner party at the Dorchester until Thelma's return, David and the Simpsons were together with a constancy that denoted more than just casual interest. In fact, he was so frequently around that Ernest felt compelled to make a waspish comment, which Wallis dismissed out of hand. She still could not believe that the Prince of Wales, the world's most desirable bachelor, was genuinely and irrevocably intrigued by her.

This insecurity did not stop her from encouraging him. As she herself frequently admitted, both in print and in private, she was flattered by his interest and responded positively. But she didn't really believe that things would take the turn they did.

Thelma, meanwhile, was enjoying her American sojourn and doing her level best to lift the spirits of her twin. After two months abroad, she boarded the German liner, the Bremen, for the return trip home. On board was the Aga Khan's elder son, Prince Aly Khan. Although only twenty-three, this future husband of Hollywood movie queen Rita Hayworth already enjoyed a reputation as irresistible. One of his notable conquests had been Margaret, Duchess of Argyll, who met him at her presentation as a debutante at Buckingham Palace. According to her, 'I made a very slow curtsey in order to give myself time to take a good look at the Royal party. As I was rising, my attention was suddenly caught by an incredibly handsome young man standing behind the Queen. He was dressed in a white knee-length Indian tunic with a high military collar and a white turban glittering with an emerald the size of a large bird's egg. For a split second our eyes met before I had to turn and walk away from the throne. I wondered who he could possibly be. The next night I met him at Brook House at a ball given by Lord and Lady Louis Mountbatten. He was introduced to me formally as Prince Aly Khan. He was then nearly nineteen, dark haired, with magnificent brown eyes.

We danced every dance together that evening. It was love at first sight.'[18] He proposed marriage, Margaret accepted, but her father, the industrialist George Whigham, refused to give his permission on racial grounds. Since then, Aly Khan had been cutting a very sexy swathe through the drawing rooms and boudoirs of the world's most desirable women, as if to say to their fathers, 'You might not want me to marry your daughters, but you can't keep me out of their beds.'

Thelma was a prize that any swordsman would relish. At the time, not only was she beautiful and elegant and witty, but she was also the Prince of Wales's girlfriend. There were few better feathers for a playboy to stick in his cap, and Aly Khan proceeded to flood her stateroom with red roses. Before the ship had even docked, word had spread back to England of the attention he was paying her.

This can hardly have done her cause with David any good. Thelma would later say that he was an inadequate lover who suffered from premature ejaculation, and that his penis was extremely small. While he was indeed of slight build generally, Freda Dudley Ward assured me that he was 'normal in every way'. His penis was not excessively small, nor did he ejaculate prematurely, and Thelma's comments possess an element of the vengeance of a woman scorned.

Be that as it may, there is no doubt that David was in an altogether humbler league as a lover than Aly Khan. Someone who had a romance with Aly Khan, but asked that I never reveal her identity, told me that he was the most amazing lover. 'He could make love all night. They said he had learnt secret, Eastern ways of keeping control of himself. I never asked him if that was true, but there was no other man like him. He was a true sensualist. He made love like no one else. To be in bed with him was to be transported to heaven.'

Few men would wish to be pitted against such a god of love, and David was no exception. By the time he and Thelma met up at her town house in Regent's Park for dinner on the evening of Thursday, 22nd March, 1934, the Prince of Wales was decidedly sulky. 'I hear Aly Khan has been very attentive to you,' Thelma recounted him saying. 'Are you jealous, darling?' she responded,[19] hoping for rather more than the icy silence which thereafter emanated from him.

If the homecoming had not been a success, she had hopes for the future. She was due to go down to the Fort for the weekend, but while there, she noticed that, though he was 'formally cordial, [he] was personally distant. He seemed to want to avoid me. I knew that something was wrong. But what? What had happened in those short weeks while I was away?'[20] What, indeed, aside from Aly Khan.

Thelma turned to Wallis, hoping that she could provide an explanation. 'But the only answer I got to my questions was the saccharine assurance, "Darling, you know the little man loves you very much. The little man was just lost without you."'

While they were having this conversation, Wallis's maid interrupted to inform her mistress that she was wanted on the telephone. Wallis reminded her that she had asked not to be disturbed, and the woman let the cat out of the bag by informing her that His Royal Highness was on the line. Thelma could overhear Wallis informing David that she was there, but he did not ask to speak to her. This was strange indeed. And ominous to boot. But Thelma tried to contain her suspicions in the hope that matters would rectify themselves.

Easter was the following weekend. If Thelma had dreams of restoring her relationship with David to what it had been prior to her departure for America, they were dashed as she went down to the Fort for the weekend and observed her friend and her lover's level of intimacy. They 'seemed to have little private jokes. Once he picked up a piece of salad with his fingers; Wallis playfully slapped his hand. I, so over-protective of heaven knows what, caught her eye and shook my head at her. She knew as well as everybody else that the Prince could be very friendly, but no matter how friendly, he never permitted familiarity.

'Wallis looked straight back at me. And then and there I knew the "reason" was Wallis. In a line that has gone down as an all-time classic, she said, "I knew then that she had looked after him exceedingly well. That one cold, defiant glance had told me the entire story."'[21]

After dinner, Thelma, who had a cold, retired for the night. Before turning in, David came up to check on her. '"Darling," I asked bluntly, "is it Wallis?"

'The Prince's features froze. "Don't be silly," he said crisply. Then he walked out of the room, closing the door quietly behind him. I knew better. I left the Fort the following morning.'

This was the end of Thelma's relationship with David. She never went back to the Fort or St. James's Palace. She never once saw or heard from him again. It was as if she did not exist, and indeed, when he came to write *A King's Story*, he omitted to mention her name. Even worse, David then required his equerry, Brigadier-General G. Trotter, whom he had asked to befriend Thelma, to drop her. When he refused to do so, he was eased out of his post.

Next up was Freda. Her elder daughter Penelope had been gravely ill and she was so distracted by this fact that she did not notice for some weeks that she had not heard from David. When she eventually surfaced, she telephoned St. James's Palace, where she was something of a favourite with the switchboard operators. 'I have something so terrible to tell you that I don't know how to say it. I have orders not to put you through,'[22] the clearly upset telephonist informed her.

Freda's response was dignified beyond compare. She continued to be the chairman of the Feathers Clubs Association for the next three decades, her presence a visible reminder of the injustice of David's comment to Wallis that she was the only woman who had ever displayed any interest in his work. She granted no interviews to the press, wrote no memoirs, but Lady Donaldson is wrong to allege, as she did in *Edward VIII*, that she burnt all her correspondence. Her daughter Angela's descendants still have their half of all the letters, as her granddaughter Emma Temple confirmed to me.

If Thelma did not deserve to be treated the way she was, neither did Freda. David excised her equally absolutely in his memoirs, as if by doing so he could rearrange the past. No one any longer knows if he tried to force his brother George and his cousin Lord Louis Mountbatten to drop Freda the way he had tried to force Brigadier-General Trotter to cut Thelma. If he did, he was no more successful with them than he was with his equerry. No matter what, George remained Freda's friend till his dying day, as did Lord Louis. He had a great deal of respect for the woman his cousin had wanted to marry, and said, 'There was something religious, almost holy, about his love for her. She was the only woman he ever loved that way. She deserved it.'[23]

Deserve it she did. Lady Temple told me, 'She seldom spoke about him.' And when her good friend Margaret, Duchess of Argyll arranged for me to speak to her prior to her death in 1983, she was at pains to confirm that he had always been a perfectly normal man, and all the claims that have proliferated to the contrary, were untrue. It was clear to me that she had residual affection for the man he had once been, and had forgiven him for the way he had discarded her. She understood him, and appreciated that once he was in the grip of the compulsion which Wallis had engendered, he was helpless to perform otherwise. To her credit, she also had only kind words for Wallis, whom she felt had not had an enviable lot in life. She left me with the impression that she thought the outcome had been tragic and unforeseen, and kindness and gentle acceptance were more appropriate than the vile sensationalism which had resulted from the debacle.

And what was Elizabeth's reaction to David's excision of the two women who had been such integral parts of their common circle? Whenever she saw either of them, she was as pleasant as ever. But she made no attempt to maintain either friendship now that they were beyond the central orbit. She would also behave the same way when Prince Paul of Yugoslavia, as Prince Paul of Serbia had become in 1929, was exiled. When you were in, you were in. But when you were out, you were out. And though 'sugar would flow,' as Wallis put it, 'the sweetness was meaningless.' The ultimate tactician always positioned herself to bat on the winning team.

Nevertheless, Elizabeth's sweetness, whether heartfelt or otherwise, could touch its recipients. It did when Thelma accompanied her son Anthony, the 2nd Viscount Furness, to Buckingham Palace where Bertie was awarding his late half-brother Christopher the Victoria Cross for valour in the field.[24] She greatly appreciated the kindness with which King George VI spoke to her, and was moved to receive a friendly message from Queen Elizabeth.

Such thoughtfulness, even if it was superficial, meant a lot to people, which is one of the reasons why Elizabeth became such a successful queen. She understood that a small gesture on her part could make a big difference to others, and, if her motivation was egotistical rather than sincere, it mattered little to the recipient, who was simply grateful that someone in such an eminent position had bothered to think about them at all.

Such hypocrisy, if hypocrisy it was, would have served David better than the frankness which sometimes came across as callousness. His extraordinary dismissal of Thelma and Freda did neither himself nor Wallis any favours. And of course, because this latest American love was a relatively obscure entity whose provenance was known to few outside her own, narrow, Baltimore circle, much of the blame was ascribed to her.

This was hardly fair, for David was well known to be a compulsive personality whose impulses got the better of him. His cousin Prince Christopher of Greece is on record as having found him 'impulsive'[25] and Margaret, Duchess of Argyll also told me that he was. Although I did not know him well, I knew him well enough to observe that he was indeed impulsive. And, like Bertie, he was always eager to go just that extra mile to fulfil the wishes, real or perceived, of the woman in his life.

Wallis would not have been human if she had not been uncomfortable having Thelma around. The successor is notoriously discomfited by the presence of her predecessor, especially when she has poached the man. While there was therefore some justification for David, and indeed Wallis, to put a degree of distance between themselves and Thelma, there was no necessity to do it so totally. David was the Prince of Wales and should have known how to behave both as a gentleman and a prince. He had an obligation to display a level of nobility irrespective of his or anyone else's personal feelings. And Thelma was a great as well as a famous lady. If she was being cast out, it should not have happened as publicly and humiliatingly as it did. She had given up her husband for the Prince of Wales. The least he could do was repay the favour by maintaining a semblance of a relationship socially, if only to preserve her position in the world at large.

If David's actions where Thelma was concerned had some justification, albeit little excuse, with regards to Freda, they had none whatsoever. Cutting her out with the finality and discourtesy he did was both gutless and ignoble. His behaviour was inexcusable, and no one made any excuses for him, then or afterwards. Many people, seeking to maintain the respect they wished to possess for him, blamed Wallis. No one will ever now know whether she had a hand in Freda's exclusion or not, but even if she had, no man worth his salt would have behaved as he did. It is a precept of nobility that one does what is right, even when it is inconvenient, and that one does not do wrong, even when it is tempting.

The Duke of Windsor I met struck me as someone who was so desperately in thrall to his duchess that there was no room left in his life for anyone else. The expression 'hooked on her' could have been invented for him. He was like a junkie shooting up smack; she was his heroin. In my opinion, once he decided that she was the woman for him, his psyche left room for no one else, and that, rather than Wallis's discomfort in having around the friend she had betrayed, lay at the crux of this matter.

Yet the Duchess of Windsor I observed seemed to be altogether more grounded than her husband. She came across as someone who had come to terms with his excessive devotion, but basically did not like it. There was a palpable air of having resigned herself to her lot, which was being saddled with this perennial child.

People who knew the couple well, such as Margaret, Duchess of Argyll and Diana, Lady Mosley, maintained that she did love him, but there was no doubt that the greater love was on his side. He was plainly obsessed with her, while she was merely tolerant of his obsession, and did not return it. For instance, if you were at dinner with them, he could not pay attention to anyone for longer than two minutes before his glance would stray in her direction. If he happened to catch her eye, she would acknowledge it lovingly, but you could see that what everyone said was true: he worshipped her, while she had grown to be sincerely fond of him. But the weight of such obsessive love was a burden she bore decently, even though she did confess to her best friends how difficult it was to cope with. She was also mindful of how it had derailed her life and, in her eyes at least, caused mayhem. Circumstances and her conscience had forced her to live out a life she would never have chosen for herself, and she was a devoted wife, but one who often commented on how 'difficult it is to live out a great romance. Day after day.

Year after year.'[26]

The way David had gone about cutting out Thelma and Freda created an immediate groundswell of disapproval that opened up far more overt opposition to Wallis than would otherwise have occurred. He had, figuratively, given people the knife with which to stab her. 'Everyone knew that he had replaced Thelma with Wallis,' Margaret, Duchess of Argyll remembered. 'And everyone preferred Thelma to Wallis. They did because she was softer and fitted in better. Although Wallis's edges would be smoothed off over the years, in the early days she was very, very American. She came across as harsh and abrasive. She could be sassy in the way only Americans can be, which was very entertaining if you understood what she was about. But if you did not – and many of the English in those days had not travelled much beyond France or Italy – America was a whole different world to them – and she came across as a brash, wisecracking smart-aleck.'[27] This, of course, is precisely what appealed to David, but it got up the backs of the less sophisticated courtiers, chief amongst which were the ossifiers.

There was also another dimension to the reservations that the courtiers, who wanted to freeze the monarchy, and their positions with it, had about Wallis. They believed the Morgans were grander than the Warfields. The Furnesses had definitely been several cuts above the Simpsons, and Elizabeth and her circle of friends decided that Wallis was nothing but a 'common American' who had managed to get her claws into the Prince of Wales. Had they bothered to investigate, they would have discovered that her family was every bit as good and most likely rather better than the Morgans.

It is interesting to suppose how differently Wallis would have been perceived had she inherited all or even just a decent cut of Uncle Sol's $5,000,000 estate. As it was, however, no one in England even knew of her uncle's fortune.

As Wallis's star rose in David's constellation, Elizabeth took steps to put some distance between herself and her brother-in-law's new favourite. Privately, the Duchess of Windsor used to say that a large part of her motivation in doing so was that she objected to Wallis treating her as just another human being. There is doubtless some merit to this observation, for Elizabeth was only comfortable around people who were deferential towards her. If they were, she could be charm itself. But if they were not, she would withdraw with *froideur* and try to find some moral or noble justification for her attitude, which was really the manifestation of a spoilt egotist.

Although both David and Wallis noticed that Elizabeth was seldom around, they were so caught up in the excitement of their burgeoning relationship that neither one paid it much mind. By summer, they were so solidly an item that he took her away on a cruise in Lord Moyne's yacht, the *Rosaura,* and to Biarritz in south-western France, while Ernest was conveniently away on business in America. Wallis's constant presence presented no one but Elizabeth with a quandary. Everyone remained cordial towards her, including Prince George, who lived with his brother at St. James's Palace during the week, and often stayed with him at the Fort on weekends, when he was not off visiting friends or relations elsewhere.

The year before, King Gustav V of Sweden had tried to arrange a marriage between David and his granddaughter Ingrid, but David, who already had plans to marry Thelma when he could, was unresponsive to the idea. His youngest brother George was mooted as a suitable replacement, which did not appeal to the Swedish king, who felt that Ingrid's qualities warranted a throne. Rather than settle for the fourth son of the King of England, he looked to the crown of Denmark, which Ingrid would indeed one day wear upon her head.

The brothers' aunt Victoria, 'that absolute bitch' or 'bitch of the first order', as David used to refer to her, now entered the melee. She was of the firm conviction that Princess Marina of Greece was ideal for David. To the extent that Marina was beautiful, *soignée*, sophisticated and social, she was indeed the sort of woman that David found appealing. Princess Victoria also decided that another Greek princess, Marina's first cousin Irene, was perfect for George, but her nephew and uncle's granddaughter had other ideas. George and Marina hit it off well and decided to marry. Their engagement was announced on 28th August, 1934, while David and Wallis were disporting themselves in the resort which the author Irene Nemirovsky denounced as being full of rich charlatans, despite having residents such as my future parents-in-law, the 11th Duke and Duchess of Argyll. This left Irene out in the cold, but she would soon marry Crown Prince Umberto of Italy's cousin and heir, the Duke of Aosta.

Six weeks later, on 12th October, Prince George was created Duke of Kent, Earl of St. Andrews and Baron Downpatrick, the received wisdom being that royal princes must become royal dukes before their marriages. Some of the courtiers, knowing of the new duke's past, were convinced that it was a marriage of convenience. George was renowned in Court circles to have been catholic in his sexual tastes. He had had flagrant affairs with Noel Coward and 'Chips' Channon, the black cabaret singer Florence Mills, the singing star Jessie Matthews, the author/socialite Barbara Cartland, who would later claim that her daughter Raine (Diana, Princess of Wales's step-mother) might well have been his child, and the Maharanee of Cooch Behar. George was also rumoured to have had more discreet liaisons with his cousin

Prince Louis Ferdinand of Prussia and Elizabeth's distant cousin, Anthony Blunt, who would later become Surveyor of the Queen's Pictures and be stripped of his knighthood when he was exposed as a Soviet spy.

In 1926, George had been involved in a *ménage à trois* with Alice 'Kiki' Gwynne Preston, a well-born American just like Wallis who was coincidentally Little Gloria Vanderbilt's cousin, and Jorge Ferrara, the bisexual son of the Argentine Ambassador to the Court of St. James's. She became pregnant and gave birth to a son, who was adopted by the American publisher Cass Canfield. Named Michael Temple Canfield, he became the first husband of Jacqueline Kennedy Onassis's younger sister Lee Bouvier. The Duke of Windsor was convinced that the young man was his nephew,[28] and equally confident that Kiki Preston, who was known as 'The Girl with the Silver Syringe' because she was openly addicted to drugs, was responsible for George becoming hooked on morphine and cocaine. The brothers devised their own cure, with George going cold turkey at York House in St. James's Palace, while David sat with him and tended him. Whatever David's faults, he was a kind and generous brother.

Although George was not born to sit upon a throne, that did not stop the handsome young man from aspiring to one. He had tried to pay court to Princess Juliana of the Netherlands, knowing that she would one day be that country's monarch, but she spurned his advances in favour of the singularly masculine Prince Bernhardt of Lippe-Bisterfeld. George was no more successful in acquiring another crown when it was offered to him, Poland having decided that it wished to revert to monarchy. He was made to turn the offer down by the British Government, which feared that having a British prince occupy the throne of Poland might result in the British Empire being sucked into a future war. This is ironic in the light of the trigger for World War II, and begs the question whether Stalin would have been so quick to gobble up that state at the end of the Second World War, if an English prince had been wearing the Polish crown.

If the ossifiers doubted the sincerity of George's love for Marina, his good friend Freda Dudley Ward did not. He had confided in her that he was in love with the delectable Marina.[29] His pride in his fiancée was apparent in the letter he wrote to his old friend and brother-in-law-to-be, Prince Paul of Yugoslavia, on 20th September, 1934. Prior to seeing Marina, everyone in Britain had been expecting 'a dowdy princess, such as unfortunately my family are', but, when they beheld 'this lovely chic creature, they could hardly believe it & even the men were interested & shouted "Don't change – don't let them change you."'[30]

Chief amongst the enthusiasts was that prime appreciator of feminine flesh:

King George V. Queen Mary had tried to warn Marina against appearing before her future father-in-law with blood-red nails. 'I'm afraid the King doesn't like painted nails. Can you do something about it?' To which Marina had archly riposted, 'Your George may not, but mine does.'[31]

Although the King could not abide painted nails any more than unpunctuality, he willingly overlooked, just as he had done with Elizabeth's tardiness, the flashes of red originating from the hands Marina used so elegantly while talking.

George had chosen as strong a woman as of both his brothers. She also enjoyed being the centre of attention and within days of arriving in England was as much a star-turn as Elizabeth had been when she had arrived on the royal scene eleven years before. This she would remain till her dying day. Despite being the most junior-ranking royal duchess in the United Kingdom, she was indisputably accepted nationwide as the most stylish, elegant and beautiful member of the Royal Family.

Proud as George was of his fiancée, he was not blind to her one drawback. He did not share David and Bertie's desire to be dominated by a woman, and confessed to Lady Alexa Bertie[32] that his one reservation about Marina was that she might be 'too bossy'. Although his personality prevented her from ruling the roost the way Elizabeth and Wallis did, she soon found she needed every bit of her backbone to contend with one particular member of the Royal Family. This individual would remain her nemesis for the remainder of her life, and her name was Elizabeth, Duchess of York.

This I know through several sources, one of which was Margaret, Duchess of Argyll, who was also a friend of Princess Marina's. Hugo Vickers patently possessed similar information, for he observes in his biography of Elizabeth that the 'only member of the Royal Family not wholly entranced was the Duchess of York.'[33] That was putting it mildly. Her nose was massively out of joint at the arrival of a beautiful, slender, stylish and genuinely royal competitor. 'Her jealousy was pathetic,' the Duke of Windsor would later comment.[34] He stated that her hostility and enviousness kept on popping through the veneer of saccharine which was the chief attribute of her charm, and she effectively made something of a spectacle of herself as her famous self-possession for once deserted her.

If Elizabeth's attitude was not commendable, it was at least understandable. Until Marina's arrival in London on 16th September, 1934, the Duchess of York had been the public's darling as a result of her charm and her two daughters, who, along with the Hollywood child actress Shirley Temple, were the three most famous children on earth. Overnight, Marina had displaced her.

To add salt to the wound, Marina was visibly unimpressed by Elizabeth's now-unreliable charm. She made it clear that she did not like her and that she found her future sister-in-law affected, pretentious and insincere. She could hardly believe that anyone who cared about their appearance, as Elizabeth did when on show, could dress as badly as she did. As she got to know her better and saw how Elizabeth cloaked herself in the mantle of regal dignity even when it was inappropriate to do so, she decreed that Elizabeth did not know how royalty should behave. This was targeting Elizabeth in an area where she had no defences, for Marina was the daughter of a Greek and Danish prince and a Russian grand duchess, while Elizabeth was at best the daughter of a backwoods earl. Marina made several choice comments on the subject, some of which have been quoted by other authors, though others have not. Amongst the quoted ones are that Elizabeth was 'that common little Scottish girl',[35] and 'was not even mediatised'.[36] This was an allusion to the ruling families of Europe who had lost their (usually tiny) states after the Napoleonic Wars, but had retained their royal status at the Congress of Vienna in 1815. They effectively became second-class royals, fit only for supplementing breeding stock when the reigning families needed an external boost, but otherwise excluded from the royal way of life.

Both these comments got back to Elizabeth, as well as a few others which have never been quoted before. These included the corker, which Marina shared with George's favourite great-aunt, who would become something of a favourite of hers as well, namely Princess Louise, Duchess of Argyll (who had never been able to abide Elizabeth either): 'She isn't even Part 3.' This was an allusion to that bible of royalty and the upper aristocracy, the *Almanach de Gotha,* which was published in three parts: Part 1 being the genealogy of the royal and imperial families of Europe; Part 2, the mediatised families; and Part 3, the non-royal ducal and princely houses of Europe such as the Youssoupoff princes and the ducal families of Argyll and Buccleuch, whose duchess would one day be her old competitor for James Stuart's hand, Mollie Lascelles.

One needs little imagination to perceive how rattled and irate Elizabeth was in the run-up to the wedding. Not only was this beautiful princess pouring scorn on her humble antecedents, but every day when she opened up the papers, they were full of Marina, Marina, Marina. Where she had once reigned supreme, largely through her pedestrian charms, the Greek princess was now doing so in three areas she could not hope to compete with: royal lineage, physical beauty, and sleek stylishness.

Two nights before the wedding, which was due to be held at Westminster Abbey on Thursday, 29th November, 1934, the King and Queen gave a ball

for eight hundred at Buckingham Palace. Elizabeth, of course, was there with Bertie. She was sidelined as she had never been since joining the Royal Family. And, to her horror, not only by Marina, but by that other sleek *styliste* whom her other brother-in-law had introduced into the royal circle: Wallis.

Ernest and Wallis Simpson had been asked to the ball. According to the diarist Marie Belloc Lowndes, when George V saw that David had proposed them for the guest list, 'the King had drawn a line through the name. The Prince hearing of this went to his parents and said that if he were not allowed to invite these friends of his, he would not go to the ball. He pointed out that the Simpsons were remarkably nice Americans, that it was important England and America should be on cordial terms, and that he himself had been most kindly entertained by the Simpsons. His parents gave way and the Simpsons duly came to the ball.'[37]

Wallis wore 'the most striking gown in the room', according to Marina's brother-in-law and Elizabeth's old friend, Prince Paul of Yugoslavia.[38] Purple lame with a vivid chartreuse sash around her slender waist and a matching bolero, Wallis and Marina, in a stunning white evening dress which showed off her figure to advantage, were the cynosure of all eyes. 'They were like two fine racehorses surrounded by a stable of carthorses,' the Duke of Windsor would later say, and he certainly appeared eager to show Wallis off. Leaving Ernest to cool his heels on the periphery, where an ever-attentive Bertie hovered over the deflated Elizabeth, plain and plump in yet another of those horrors from Madame Handley Seymour, this time in putrid pink, David used his foremost position as Prince of Wales to ensure that Wallis shared the limelight with Marina.

Knowing that nothing would pave the way for Wallis's acceptance by everyone else better than a personal introduction to his parents, he escorted her up to where the King and Queen were standing. Presenting his latest love with the anodyne words, 'I want to introduce a great friend of mine,'[39] George V and Queen Mary were able to take a good look at the woman their son was in love with as she dropped a graceful and well-executed curtsey to them. According to Queen Mary, she 'had shaken hands with her without thinking much about it,'[40] which shows that at this juncture there was no real opposition to Wallis, even if there was no enthusiasm for her either.

But if Queen Mary wasn't thinking much about Wallis, Elizabeth was. One does not need to be a psychologist to see that anyone who liked attention as much as Elizabeth was hardly likely to view the dilution of her ascendency without some resentment. How she now reacted to Wallis, whom she had not seen since Thelma's departure from the scene, says it all. When David took Wallis over to say hello to his brother and sister-in-law, she reacted with

icy rudeness. Up to this point, their exchanges had always been cordial, if impersonal. Now, Wallis detected a decidedly personal *froideur*.

In her autobiography, Wallis hinted at this, but gently, as she did not want to give Elizabeth yet another dagger with which to stab her. David was hoping that the breach with the other members of the Royal Family could be healed, as his niece had recently ascended the throne and a new reign might mean a new day for him. Rather than overtly make the point that Elizabeth had previously been cordial, but was now the antithesis, Wallis instead obtusely prevailed upon knowledge of their previous contact which few readers or reporters had, and said that, for the first time, she noticed the 'almost startling blueness' of Elizabeth's eyes as she frostily cast them over her body in a look of icy and disapproving appraisal. To those in the know, what Wallis was saying was that Elizabeth was so enraged to find herself sharing the limelight with not one but two other women, that she was shooting daggers at Wallis through those eyes, which had turned bluer with envy, before coolly eyeing her slender body in its stunning attire in a look of reproach which said, 'You should not be wearing something so attention-grabbing. Since I can't, no one else should. I therefore decree that it is not done.' Without saying a word, therefore, Elizabeth had conveyed her hostility, disapproval, and opposition.

Wallis, however, was no more intimidated by Elizabeth than Marina had been. If anything, she was in an even stronger position than the Greek princess. George was the mere sixth in line to the throne, while David was the undoubted next king. Wallis would later say that she wasn't at all bothered by Elizabeth's preposterous behaviour. Hers was the stronger position, at least on the face of it, because David was the Prince of Wales while Bertie was only the Duke of York. Neither she nor David was about to let the self-important Elizabeth spoil their night, which was, as far as David was concerned, as much Wallis's coming-out as his beloved, as it was George and Marina's wedding ball.

With that in mind, David kept on showing Wallis off. The Kings and Queens of Denmark and Norway were there along with the entire Greek Royal Family and a host of other European royals. David presented Wallis to as many of his far-flung relations as he could, all of whom got the message.

In his memoirs, Prince Christopher of Greece confirms this. He recounts how David 'laid a hand on my arm in his impulsive way: "Christo, come with me."' He wanted to introduce his cousin to Mrs. Simpson. But his cousin had never heard of her, so asked, "'Who is Mrs. Simpson?" "An American," then he smiled. "She's wonderful," he added. The two words told me everything. It was as though he had said: "She is the only woman in the world."'[41]

It is not credible that cousins like Christopher of Greece could pick up in a two-minute exchange the depth of feeling that David possessed for Wallis, and Elizabeth, who was far more intelligent than most of her peers, had not already done so. Though she would later affect ignorance of the depth of feeling which was already apparent to others, including George the newly-created Duke of Kent, a simple testament to her perspicacity and insightfulness gives the lie to her disclaimer. The author and diplomat (later Sir) Harold Nicolson, *Chargé d'Affaires* at the British Embassy in Berlin and subsequently the official biographer of George V, wrote a letter to his wife Vita Sackville-West on 8th April, in 1929. He was not only full of praise for Elizabeth's charm, which he 'could not exaggerate. It was overwhelming,' but also her intelligence. '(S)he and Cyril Connolly are the only two people who have spoken intelligently about the "landscape" element in [his book] Some People. She said, "You choose your colours so carefully; that bit about the Palace in Madrid was done in grey and chalk-white; the Constantinople bits in blue and green; the desert bits in blue and orange."'[42]

It is inconceivable that someone who was astute enough to pick up obtuse literary devices which only one other person had ever done – the well-known writer Cyril Connolly – could have been dim enough to miss the threat that Wallis posed to her own regal hegemony now that this other American had supplanted Thelma as the primary figure in the Prince of Wales's life. Even ignoramuses knew that one Prince of Wales was worth five Dukes of York in Court circles, irrespective of the personal attributes of the holders of their respective titles. And this Prince of Wales was the most glamorous man on earth, while this Duke of York was regarded by all but those who knew him well as little better than a bumbling simpleton.

Elizabeth's reaction to the dilemma facing her shows what superb instincts she possessed. Hereafter, until she was sitting on the queen consort's throne, she displayed a canny mixture of reservation intermingled with correct but almost overtly insincere charm. In so doing, she demonstrated a politician's, or a trapeze artist's, gift for a finely balanced act which would serve her well no matter what the future held.

As 1934 ended and 1935 dawned, it looked as if Elizabeth would indeed be condemned to play the tertiary role which even Shawcross noted, upon her return from her first African tour, was decidedly less to her taste than starring as the centre of attention. There is little doubt that she was chafing under the demotion imposed upon her from all quarters. It was bad enough that she and Queen Mary had to act out a loving relationship which was anything but. Good politics alone dictated that she show respect to her Queen, who moreover was a figure of great reverence to all, including her own mother and Bertie. Whether she knew that the old Queen feared her, worried that the intransigent and emotional Elizabeth would limit her contact with her adored granddaughter Lilibet if she dared oppose her openly, no one will ever know. But Queen Mary's sister-in-law, Princess Alice, Countess of Athlone, told the Revd. Philip Hart that that was indeed Queen Mary's motivation for never openly opposing Elizabeth.

To now have to put up with the insufferable lack of reverence which both Marina and Wallis were showing was too much for a woman who lived by and would die for her dignity the way Elizabeth did. Yet she had little choice but to rub along with both Marina and Wallis, so she did so with the patience of a panther hunting antelope.

As the months passed and it looked as if the status quo would never change in her favour, Elizabeth once more started to drop in at the Fort, and to have David's house guests over the way she and Bertie used to in Thelma's day. To all concerned, it looked as if a new norm, similar to the old one, was being established. The better Wallis got to know Elizabeth, however, the less she liked her.[43] Time seemed to be on her side, not Elizabeth's, for King George V was clearly ailing and it was obvious he did not have long to live.

On 6th May, 1935, the King celebrated the silver jubilee of his accession to the throne. Because of the Depression, the celebrations were muted, in that there were few grand balls and lavish entertainments, though there were inexpensive functions such as street fetes, thanksgiving services, and drives through the streets. To his consternation, the obviously-declining King was accorded a hero's welcome wherever he went. When he and Queen Mary proceeded through the streets of London for the official celebrations, he was so taken back by the adulation of the crowds that he said, with tears in his eyes, if his aunt Princess Louise, Duchess of Argyll is to be believed, 'I believe they really do like me.'[44] Dull and modest though George V had been, he had been a dutiful, committed king, and the people had indeed taken him to their hearts over the years. Now that they could see that he was fading before their very eyes, they communicated their appreciation for his worthy, decent, unsnobbish, unglamorous but endearing style of kingship in the way that mattered to him the most, and he would die a happy man within the year, confident that he had succeeded in the task for which his elder brother Eddy, Duke of Clarence and Avondale, and not he, had been born and bred.

It was against this backdrop of anticipation that Elizabeth had to cut her cloth as she fashioned the cloak of accommodation which would preserve her against the elements while she coped with Wallis and, to a lesser extent, Marina. She was functioning from a position of weakness, while Wallis was doing so from one of strength, as David would be king only too soon.

She therefore tried to normalise relations insofar as her personality would allow her to, but she had waited too long. By opening up the void the way she had done, Elizabeth had given people around David, who thought her precious and preposterous, the opportunity to bring their so-far-suppressed reservations about her character to the fore. Once people's opinions had taken wing, there was no forcing them back into the cage. Elizabeth had now become a figure of fun, but not the sort of fun she wanted to be, rather the sort she dreaded being. Although she enjoyed mocking people, as the British Ambassadress in Paris Lady Gladwyn would later remark upon with open disapproval, Elizabeth took her regal status too seriously to find mockery of her sacred person acceptable. Now, however, whenever her name came up, everyone would laugh about her demeanour, her style of dressing, even the way she stood, splaying their feet as if they were ducks. Wallis would sometimes entertain guests by mimicking 'the Dowdy Duchess', which she now took to calling her. 'She was really very funny,' Margaret, Duchess of Argyll told me. 'She had the voice, hand movements, facial expressions, even the fluttering of the eyelids down just pat.' It was only a matter of time before word got back to Elizabeth, or worse, she found out for herself.

In *Royal Feud,* Michael Thornton recounts a scene which took place around this time, when the Yorks dropped in unexpectedly at the Fort. (That in itself shows that they were on rather more cordial terms with David than some historians would now like to believe.) Ella Hogg, wife of Brigadier Oliver Hogg, who would go on to be the Director of Technical & Military Administration in the Ministry of Supply during World War II, was one of the guests present. Wallis, who 'considered the Duchess of York's too goody-goodiness to be false and artificial and it was that sort of imitation,' was holding forth when 'Elizabeth walked into the drawing room…'[45]

One needs little imagination to envisage how humiliated Elizabeth would have been. Mrs. Hogg would later on say that 'from the moment of overhearing, the Duchess of York became her implacable enemy.'[46]

While there is some merit to Mrs. Hogg's assertion, it needs to be leavened with the fact that Elizabeth was already Wallis's natural enemy, just as she was Marina's. Tellingly, she would not be her other sister-in-law's, for Lady Alice Montagu-Douglas-Scott, who became Prince Harry's wife and Her Royal Highness The Duchess of Gloucester later that year, though attractive and elegant, shied away from the limelight. Because she had no desire to shine, Elizabeth did not target her the way she did the other brothers' women, and it is likely that no matter who David married, Elizabeth would have had her within her sights as long as the woman in question liked the limelight and was unwilling to kowtow to her the way both Thelma and Freda had done. It really was a matter of the walk possessing only enough room for one cock. Who would be left to crow was then unknown, but time, which then seemed so adverse to Elizabeth, would tell another story.

Shawcross quite rightly states in the official biography, 'By 1935 it was clear to his family and close friends that the Prince was in thrall to Mrs. Simpson. There was private speculation at the time – and much more later – that her hold was at least partly sexual.' What he did not say, and might well have been ignorant of, was that Elizabeth herself was the source of those rumours. And she spread them in an attempt to see off Wallis.

Quite when Elizabeth conceived the idea that she could put the skids under David's relationship with Wallis by imputing her morally will never be known, but she implemented the plan in 1935. It was certainly a clever idea, and would prove to be very effective. Being a canny operator who always played her cards close to her chest, she seldom left any trace of any part she played in a scheme. Only if one accidentally happened upon evidence, or knew enough to stand back and amass sufficient details, would a picture of circumstantial evidence emerge. The matter of the China Dossier, however, is one of the few times that she slipped up, the part she played falling in the hands of someone who would become an adversary.

This, unfortunately for Elizabeth, is what now happened. Lord Beaverbrook became privy to her machinations. Thereafter, as he told his granddaughter Lady Jean Campbell, he was antipathetic towards her. He regarded her as vengeful, unscrupulous and ruthless, and she would return his antipathy in spades when she discovered that he was privy to what she had orchestrated.

During the Second World War, when Britain's back was to the wall and there was every chance that we would lose the war, Elizabeth tried to block his appointment as the Minister for Aircraft Production and Minister of Supply, despite the fact that he was clearly the best man for the job. The Prime Minister, Winston Churchill, who was a good friend of Max Beaverbrook and had also played a part in the Abdication Crisis and knew just how clean The Beaver's hands were, was not about to let Elizabeth, by then Queen, deprive the nation of one of its most competent businessmen just because of a personal feud. He demanded King George VI let the appointment stand, and Bertie, for one of the few times in his life, allowed someone to prevail against the will of his vengeful and dominating spouse.

Elizabeth put her plan into operation in 1935. She used Helen Hardinge, who was still beguiled by the wiles of her old friend, as the vehicle, confiding how worried she was that David was being led astray by Wallis. She claimed that someone had told her that that Wallis's hold over her brother-in-law was sexual, and derived from 'secret practices' she had learnt in a brothel in China. If only Papa's Assistant Private Secretary, Helen's husband Alec Hardinge, could investigate and gather the proof through the Empire's overseas contacts, she felt sure that King George V would be in a position to demand that David discard her. Which, of course, David would do once he realised that his girlfriend was no better than a common prostitute.

So began the Saga of the China Dossier. Investigations were duly made of Wallis's sojourn in that country by men on the ground. A report was compiled that was heavy on impertinent questions and vague suppositions, but offered absolutely no findings whatsoever of a visit to a brothel or any other actual wrongdoing. Nor was there substantiation of the acquisition of knowledge of secret sexual practices then known only to Chinese whores. Indeed, the very idea that an American lady would have been consorting with this category of native, to learn the tricks of their trade, showed a disturbing disconnection with the realities of what American women were then about. They were far more racist than their British counterparts, who were nevertheless dyed-in-the-wool white supremacists, as indeed Elizabeth and Wallis both were and would remain throughout their long lives. This slur on Wallis's integrity also showed how ready Elizabeth was to use the sexual purity which her disinterest in the carnal provided her with, to hop on her high horse and flog to death the reputation and prospects of a woman whose sexual conduct might have been more overt than the sexless Elizabeth's, but was no worse than the majority of Elizabeth's friends and relations or indeed most other women who enjoyed the carnal side of life. Ignoring the Biblical injunction against bearing false witness, Elizabeth had demonstrated, as The Beaver and indeed Bertie's nephew George Harewood would observe, that her Christian scruples served her rather better than she served them.

The absence of tangible proof of any wrongdoing on Wallis's part, however, did not prevent the very existence of the China Dossier from inflicting the grossest damage upon her reputation. As Elizabeth had doubtless foreseen, officialdom would feel that the very fact that questions had been raised about the Prince of Wales's lady being in a brothel in China rendered Wallis unsuitable for any position in his life. It wasn't even a question of where there is smoke, there is fire. Once the questions had been asked, irrespective of the outcome of the enquiry – which was inconclusive but, no surprise to anyone who knows how officialdom works, did not absolve Wallis despite there being no evidence to support the questions – the damage was irreparable.

In a cynical ploy, the ossifiers, many of whom were Elizabeth's closest friends, now ensured that they spread the damage as far and as wide as they could with a whispering campaign, so that Wallis's reputation would be destroyed not only within the portals of officialdom, but also the drawings rooms of the land. Not since the so-called Comtesse de la Motte-Valois had concocted equally preposterous accusations against Marie Antoinette, which brought about the highly-damaging Affair of the Diamond Necklace scandal, had a supposedly well-born woman with links to a Royal Family come up with such an imaginatively destructive tale. While Wallis would fare better than the beheaded queen, her reputation never quite recovered either.

Tellingly, the Dossier was never used by George V to pressurise David into giving up Wallis. Although he regarded her as 'unsuitable as a friend, disreputable as a mistress, unthinkable as Queen of England,'[47] he took no steps to actually use the contents of the China Dossier, doubtless because he could see that they were a damp if stinking squib. This did not prevent him from lambasting his son to all and sundry. He told his second cousin once removed, Count Albert von Mensdorff-Pouilly-Dietrichstein, 'He has not a single friend who is a gentleman. He does not see any decent society.' When this second son of the Prince Dietrichstein von Nicholsburg pointed out that David had many notable attributes, George V said, 'That is the pity. If he were a fool, we would not mind. I hardly ever see him and do not know what he is doing.'[48] He also told Lady Algernon Gordon-Lennox just a few weeks before his death, by which time he knew the end was near, 'I pray to God that my eldest son will never marry and have children, and that nothing will come between Bertie and Lilibet and the throne.'[49]

Yet George V had only himself to blame. David had been in love with Lady Rosemary Leveson-Gower and wished to marry her in 1918. There is little doubt that she would have accepted his proposal had she not learnt that King George V disapproved of the match. His objections were not directed against her personally, or her lineage, which was one of the most splendid in the land – they were also one of the richest families – but because of her mother and her uncle. Millicent, Duchess of Sutherland had been as great a beauty as her daughter but, after her husband died in 1913, she remarried Brigadier-General Percy Desmond FitzGerald. This marriage quickly fell apart and they separated. Although they were not yet divorced, Millicent was known to have a new lover whom she wished to marry, so there was every likelihood that they would be divorced soon, as indeed they were the following year. Worse from George V's point of view, however, was the lifestyle of her brother, the 5th Earl of Rosslyn, who was Sheila Loughborough's father-in-law. At the time of David's proposal, he had been married and divorced twice. He had also been bankrupted twice, despite having inherited a vast fortune which he had gambled away. He was famous for being the man about whom the 1892 hit song, *The Man Who Broke the Bank of Monte Carlo*, had been written. He was also a notorious drunkard who was frequently removed from establishments in the prone position. As George V was already concerned about the amount of liquor his three eldest sons consumed, and was frequently embarrassed by his first cousin Princess Marie Louise's tendency to reel in public after a few too many drinks, he felt the Royal Family could do without any more soaks.

He therefore informed David of the grounds for his objection to Rosemary becoming the Princess of Wales, leaving the young man in the impossible situation of having proposed marriage to a girl with whom he was in love and who had eminently fulfilled all the qualifications imposed upon him following the recent ruling of the Privy Council regarding royal marriages to non-royal aristocrats. As soon as Rosemary, who had not yet accepted the proposal but was about to do so, found out, her attitude towards David changed immediately. If her family wasn't good enough for his, there was no question of her marrying him. A few weeks later, he met Freda Dudley Ward, and the following year Rosemary married David's best friend, Eric, Viscount Ednam, the Earl of Dudley's heir. She produced three sons and died on 21st July, 1930, when the plane she was flying in broke up in mid-air and plummeted to the ground near the village green of Meopham, Kent. Her husband Eric remained David's best friend and was one of the few people who remained loyal to him after the abdication.

If George V did not rue the day that he had objected to the beautiful Rosemary Ednam, he should have done so. As Helen Hardinge so succinctly put it in her memoirs, 'One can forever wonder how the history of our Monarchy in the twentieth century and after would have turned out, if the Prince of Wales had had his way in those early days.'[50]

Although as 1935 drew to a close the gossip in Court circles was that the King now felt that Wallis would be David's destruction, there is no real evidence that this was anything but another slur being spread by Elizabeth and her ossifying cronies. He is meant to have told Stanley Baldwin that 'the boy' would destroy himself 'within a year' of his death, but whether he actually made such an accurate prediction or Baldwin simply self-servingly made it up to add ballast to his own role in the Abdication Crisis, is open to question.

Nevertheless, matters were gathering momentum. Although David would not learn of the China Dossier's existence until the Abdication Crisis, when Lord Beaverbrook told him that Elizabeth and her friends, who included Helen and Alec Hardinge, had been industrious in rolling that particular snowball down the slopes of Society, it was now gathering such pace that it had eradicated all vestiges of Wallis's acceptability as his consort in the eyes of those who had heard about it. The main sources all had one thing in common, Elizabeth, thereby providing independent corroboration of Max Beaverbrook's claims about her being the source of it.

Philip Ziegler states on page 236 of *King Edward VIII: The Official Biography,* which was published by Knopf in 1991 with the co-operation of the Royal Family, that Queen Mary was told that Wallis had control of David because she had released him from an undefined sexual dysfunction through practices learnt in a Chinese brothel. Although he does not state who told her, I can.[51] It was Cosmo Gordon Lang, the erstwhile Archbishop of York whom Elizabeth had so cleverly cultivated even before her marriage, knowing that one day he would become Archbishop of Canterbury, so her friendship with him would provide her with even greater influence for its having started before he had become the Anglican Church's leading prelate. Like many another authoritarian personality, Elizabeth had a positive gift for spotting whom she should align herself with, and when Lang became Archbishop of Canterbury in 1928, he was ideally placed to be of help to her in ways which neither of them could yet imagine, but which she, with her superb instincts, will have already discerned might be useful in the future. After all, the one thing ambitious people need is friends in high places.

The way Elizabeth flattered Lang gives an insight into how she functioned. Once he was Archbishop of Canterbury, she discarded all the objections she had once deployed against his predecessor, to enable Lang to marry her and christen her elder daughter. For instance, when Princess Margaret was born, Elizabeth decided that she wanted him to come up to Glamis to baptise her. Suddenly, all her injunctions against Archbishops of Canterbury performing ceremonies, which were more appropriately performed by the Archbishop of York for the family of the Duke and Duchess of York, went out the window. Showing herself to be a past mistress of flexibility where her standards were concerned, now that the man she had cultivated, in the expectation that he would one day be the Primate of All England, did in fact occupy that august office, only he could christen her baby daughter. When the Court prevented him from doing so on the grounds that the Church of Scotland would object to the leading prelate of the Church of England coming up to their country to fulfil a function which was more properly theirs, Elizabeth demonstrated how resourceful and determined she was, by having Lang bless the infant Margaret at Glamis, then baptise her at Buckingham Palace two months later.

Now, five years later, he was up in Scotland to perform another task for the duchess of whom he was so fond. He was at Balmoral conveying her Christian and royal concerns about the American woman, whose technique for holding her beloved brother-in-law David in thrall, had been acquired in a Chinese brothel. Having heard these rumours from no less a personage that the Archbishop of Canterbury, it is hardly surprising that George V did not regard Wallis as suitable to be his heir's friend, mistress or wife.

To further demonstrate how all roads led back to Elizabeth, even the Archbishop of Canterbury's chaplain, Dr. Alan Campbell Don, waded in, both privately and publicly, stating that he suspected that David was 'sexually abnormal which may account for the hold Mrs. S. has over him.'[52] Such conduct begs the question: what were the leading Christians in England doing, ignoring Biblical injunctions against scandalmongering and false witness? Or did they believe, as appears to be the case, that they were fighting the good fight because they thought that their source was unimpeachable?

Whatever their belief, the whole cabal surrounding Elizabeth was hard at work. Even the head of the Metropolitan Special Branch, charged with the protection of the Royal Family, now got in on the act. In 2003 state papers from the National Archives (PRO MEPO 10/35) were released confirming that on 3rd July, 1935, Superintendent A. Canning told the Metropolitan Police Commissioner, Sir Philip Game, that Wallis was also having an affair with Gus Marcus Trundle, an employee of the Ford Motor Company. This was untrue, and when this accusation was made public it was dismissed by Captain Val Bailey, who knew Trundle well and whose mother had had an affair with the gentleman in question.

By the autumn, it was obvious that the King was fading fast. Then his favourite sister, the spinster Princess Victoria whose life had been ruined by Queen Alexandra's selfish insistence on her remaining her unmarried companion, died on 3rd December. George was grief-stricken. He cancelled his public appearances, including his attendance at the State Opening of Parliament, and went into a major slump. He would never be seen in public again.

That Christmas, Elizabeth stayed at Royal Lodge with Bertie. Illness had come to her rescue, the way it always did when there was something unpleasant from which to escape. Lilibet and Margaret Rose and Alah nevertheless went to stay with the dying King and Queen at Sandringham. So too did Elizabeth's brother David and his wife, Rachel Spender-Clay, a niece of Viscount Astor, whom he had married in 1929.

As January progressed, the King faded rapidly. On 20th January, he held his last Council of State. That same day, the Archbishop of Canterbury's chaplain, Dr. Alan Campbell Don, reported upon a rumour doing the rounds of the anti-Wales, pro-York lobby: 'That the P. of W. would like to make way for the Duke of York and his charming Duchess I do not doubt, but that there is truth to the rumour [that David wanted to renounce his right to the throne or marry a Catholic and thereby preclude his accession to the throne] I refuse to believe. The next few hours may enlighten us.'[53]

At 9:25 p.m. that same evening, the King's physician issued a bulletin stating: 'The King's life is moving peacefully to its close.' Lord Dawson of Penn was able to do so as authoritatively as he did because he himself administered the injection which ensured that George V would meet his Maker. To quote from his diary, 'I therefore decided to determine the end and injected morphia gr.3/4 and shortly afterwards cocaine gr.1 into the distended jugular vein.' Notwithstanding that the King had survived a similarly-serious illness at the end of the last decade, and might well do so again if given the chance, slim though it was, he had taken the decision to end his monarch's life **because he wanted him to die in time for the morning edition of The Times!** In furtherance of his objective, this doctor even telephoned his wife and instructed her to alert the editor, George Geoffrey Dawson, who was a close friend of the Prime Minister, Stanley Baldwin, and promoted his policies in *The Thunderer*, as his paper was known. Timing things with the professional competence for which he was admired, Dawson duly administered the fatal injection, and the King died at five minutes to midnight.

When I first reported the fact of King George V's killing in *The Royal Marriages* (St. Martin's Press) in 1993, my remarks were greeted with disbelief in some quarters. By May 29th of the following year, however, J.H.R. Ramsay was writing in the *British Medical Journal* that it was his opinion that Lord Dawson had wanted the King to die sooner rather than later as a harmonious sequitur to his earlier bulletin, and to permit him to return earlier to his busy London practice. He did not accept the description of the death as 'a facet of euthanasia or so-called mercy killing' as it was now being called in some quarters, and considered it 'convenience killing' whose cause lay in Dawson being 'guilty of the besetting sin of doctors and that is arrogance.' He neglected to mention two other sins: greed and vanity.

Dawson planned to publish his memoirs, which he couldn't very well do while the King was still alive. By killing him, he would cover himself in glory and attract even more patients than he already had.

In his 2005 biography *Elizabeth The Queen Mother,* Hugo Vickers touched upon this ignoble set of motives for the way the King's physician had dispatched him: ' It would also have helped sell the memoirs that Dawson fully intended to sell,' he wrote.

As soon as George V was declared dead, Queen Mary took the hand of her eldest son, and, paying obeisance to the new King, who had suddenly become a figure of reverence in her eyes, she kissed his hand. When Lilibet succeeded to the throne in 1952, she would make a similarly reverential gesture.

One of David's first acts as king was to include Bertie, who was now heir presumptive, and Elizabeth, in the prayers said in churches throughout the land during services. Aside from himself, people would now pray for 'our gracious Queen Mary, Albert, Duke of York, the Duchess of York, and all the Royal Family.'

That David could be extremely thoughtful and loyal had never been in question. Another of his ideas was to stand vigil with his three brothers when their father's coffin had been removed to the Chapel Royal, St. James's Palace. This so touched Queen Mary that he had a picture painted of the occasion, which he gave to her and which remained one of her most reassured possessions for the remainder of her life.

Giving an insight into his priorities, another of David's first acts was to have the Sandringham clocks revert to standard time. Throughout his father's reign, much to his annoyance – and it has to be said, of many others as well, including Elizabeth and the Private Secretaries – the clocks had been half an hour fast. Despite their previous objections to this quaint practice, the ossifiers were immediately up in arms about David puncturing this bubble of unreality. They ignored the anomaly, that there was nothing unreasonable in realigning Sandringham time with everywhere else, as they went about fomenting opposition to their new king. One cannot help but feel that had anyone else but David done this, they would have been praising rather than criticising him, but they had formed themselves into a pack of critics who were baying for his blood, and until they got it, they would not desist.

This pack consisted entirely of Elizabeth's cronies, and they had started the new reign the way they would continue throughout it. Normally, monarchists regard the holder of the crown as almost sacrosanct. Courtiers, especially, will usually go to great lengths to compensate for or explain away the failings of their monarch. They had certainly done so with all King Edward VIII's predecessors. Within living memory, Queen Victoria, King Edward VII, and George V had all had their foibles, eccentricities and inconsistencies accommodated and covered up. But then, none of them had declared his or her intention of altering the monarchy and, in so doing, reducing the influence and job security of the courtiers who 'ran the show'.

By this time, the cabal was already so deeply entrenched and so sanctimoniously confident of their right to decry the new king that their carping was literally boundless. Presumably, its primary objective was to whip the new king into line so that he would behave as they wanted, rather than vice versa, as he had made clear over the years would happen when he came to the throne. To demonstrate their level of pettiness, Helen Hardinge even felt able to criticise the degree of grief shown by David at the time of his father's death, deeming it excessive and therefore inappropriate. Clearly, no aspect of Edward VIII's person or personality was off-limits to these detractors. No matter how justified, reasonable, excusable, admirable, understandable or noble his behaviour was, they would pick, pick, pick, hound, hound, hound, carp, carp, carp, surrounding him with a miasma of destructive criticism. Nor did they desist until they had seen him off the throne.

Although there is no conclusive evidence to suggest that his removal as king was their objective, sufficient exists that they set out to make his life so uncomfortable, that there might well have been an underlying if unstated hope, that they would either break him or hound him off the throne, and replace him with their good friend Elizabeth's malleable spouse.

Nor is this mere speculation. As early as 29th April, 1929, Time Magazine was reporting that David was expressing the view that he might renounce his rights to the throne. According to the magazine's report, David teased his sister-in-law, calling her 'Queen Elizabeth'. It questioned whether 'she did not sometimes wonder how much truth there is in the story that he once said he would renounce his rights upon the death of George V – which would make her nickname come true.'

The Duke of Windsor would later say, after Lord Beaverbrook brought the existence of this story to his attention at the time of the Abdication Crisis, that he had never ever expressed the intention, to Elizabeth or anyone else, of renouncing the throne until he first uttered those words to his Prime Minister, Stanley Baldwin, in late 1936. He admitted that he did sometimes tease his sister-in-law and call her Queen Elizabeth, in much the same way that her family had called her Princess Elizabeth when she was little. He had done so because she would behave in such a regal way that her conduct begged for some light-hearted relief. It had all been, he thought, good, clean, innocent fun, though in the light of subsequent events, he could not help wondering if he had not planted a seed in her fruitful and imaginative mind, which had germinated under the power of her ambition.

As Max Beaverbrook rightly pointed out to David, a story of this nature does not drop into the lap of a publication. It is planted by someone. Both men believed Alec Hardinge was the source of the story. They surmised that he had whispered it to one of the correspondents who were frequently crossing paths with his. At the time of publication in 1929, he was contemplating resigning his position as Assistant Private Secretary to the Prince of Wales. He had already informed David on more than one occasion that he did not regard his character or beliefs as appropriate for a Prince of Wales or King of England, which, in my view, is what makes David's appointment of him as Private Secretary naïve to the point of recklessness when he acceded to the throne. Anyone who was less trusting than he would have seen that the keeper to your gate cannot be someone who wants others to possess your treasure, but he, regrettably, was congenitally incapable of imagining the worst of others. Even when they had pointed out to him that they reviled him, as Hardinge had done prior to resigning in 1929.

Within days of David's accession, the briefing in the press against the new king had begun. Since the information being imparted can only have come from the king's office, suspicion naturally had to devolve upon his Private Secretaries. No one else in the office would have the motive, opportunity, or indeed the gall to be dripping poison in journalists' ears. As early as 25th January, 1936, Charles A. Selden was able to write in the *New York Times* that Britain, i.e. the Establishment, i.e. David's Household, was 'anxious about the new monarch.' He was too radical and unconventional; he lacked friends amongst the politicians; he was too outspoken in denouncing the poor living conditions of subjects such as the miners – some of whom were literally starving, not that this was mentioned – and such concern was not a virtue, but a failing; and, last but not least, he lacked a wife. These failings were contrasted with Bertie's virtues, which of course could not be listed, as he possessed not one which David lacked. Nevertheless, he was already being promoted as the preferred alternative: 'There has never been a breath of scandal about him or his family. As far as the public knows neither he nor his wife ever made a single false step to impair their usefulness or popularity.' The implication, that the new king was scandal-ridden, could not have been more untrue. He had succeeded upon a wave of overwhelming popular support, and there had been no public scandal. That, of course, from the point of view of Hardinge and the other ossifiers, was something to overlook and rectify by planting stories in the newspapers.

There is little doubt that that the *New York Times* story was only the first of many acts of betrayal perpetuated by Hardinge and the other ossifiers. Before the year was out, they had leaked like such sieves that Lord Beaverbrook was able to provide King Edward VIII with chapter and verse about the way they had been dripping poison to the press. His own publications included.

Perfidious Albion has not enjoyed a reputation for treachery and hypocrisy for hundreds of years without some cause. Within days of that well-placed banana skin, the New York Times London correspondent, Frederick T. Birchall, was being fed yet more disingenuous information, calculated to denigrate the new monarch in the eyes of the average American. Knowing how unpopular Nazism and left-wing politics were in the United States of America – both were popular in the United Kingdom at that time – King

Edward VIII's own courtiers leaked the story that the new king had, during his very first State reception, provided a warm welcome to the German Foreign Minister, Baron Constantin von Neurath (who would subsequently be tried at Nuremburg for war crimes and imprisoned in Spandau Prison until 1954), and the German Ambassador, Leopold von Hoesch. The report claimed Germany had been feeling 'isolated and friendless, and here unexpectedly a new and powerful friend may have come into her orbit'.

This was nothing but a low blow. Aside from the fact that many of the ossifiers, such as Hardinge, Elizabeth, and Lord Halifax, were dyed-in-the-wool appeasers, there was nothing exceptional about a monarch greeting warmly the representatives of a foreign power, especially a former enemy. Diplomacy required such conduct. Anything else would have been unprofessional, and would have opened up Edward VIII to the just criticism that he was not behaving with the rectitude and dignity required of a sovereign.

Nor was this the only nail being hammered into the coffin of David's reputation in the *New York Times*. Birchall's information was that the new king was 'more Left and less Conservative in his predilections than any British monarch within living memory'. Undoubtedly, whoever was undermining David's reputation possessed skill. The two political bugbears which would thereafter haunt the Duke of Windsor for the remainder of his life – pro-Nazism and paradoxically, irresponsible liberalism – were getting their first airing less than two weeks after he had become King.

Meanwhile, as David settled into kingship, he discovered that his father had not left him any money. Believing that he would have accumulated sufficient funds whilst the Prince of Wales and Duke of Cornwall from the Duchy of Cornwall's overflowing coffers, George V had left the major portion of his vast fortune to his other children.

In fact, David had not built up a particularly large nest egg, and was upset by his father's actions. He would tell friends that he regarded this as yet another act of animus to add to the many derogations that George V had inflicted upon him over the years, and when Margaret, Duchess of Argyll commented upon the lack of mementos and photographs of his father in his Bois de Boulogne house, the Duke of Windsor explained that being left out of the will had been the final straw. Rene Silvin also noted that when he used to visit the Duchess of Windsor the Bois de Boulogne residence contained a plethora of reminders of Queen Mary, but nowhere at all was there any evidence that King George V had even existed.

Faced with relative penury, but required to maintain a position as the world's premier monarch, David made economies where he could. Balmoral and

Sandringham were his private properties, and he was therefore personally responsible for their upkeep. So he decided to trim what fat he could from the running costs. Unfortunately, one of the ways chosen was to make staff cuts. This, of course, had a backlash, as the country was still in the grips of the economic doldrums. People complained to Bertie and Elizabeth and the Private Secretaries, and while there is little doubt that both the Yorks did what they could to place people elsewhere, there is also no question that Elizabeth, Hardinge and Lascelles used the King's need to make economies to further undermine him in the eyes of everyone they could. Drawing rooms all over the land were now abuzz with how callous and careless the new king was about anything or anyone except Mrs. Simpson. What no one, except the very sources of the story knew, was that David simply did not have the money to maintain his father's lifestyle.

By March, the courtiers were telling all who would listen that King Edward VIII was dreadful, unfit to rule, and it was such a pity that the Duke and Duchess of York were not on the throne. Margaret, Duchess of Argyll was only one of the people who heard this and were horrified by this campaign of denigration. Nothing puts it more succinctly, or confirms the source of it more absolutely, than Helen Hardinge's diary entry for 12th March, in which she confirms that there was 'nothing but ghastly conversation of how awful the new king is'[54] whenever her husband and the other courtiers got together.

This, of course, was not a statement which she took care to broadcast when she came to write her memoirs, but it exists, bold as brass, in black and white, incontrovertible proof of a campaign that should never have taken place, but which had both a successful and tragic outcome.

While the Hardinges, Elizabeth and her other ossifying cronies were destroying David's reputation amongst the Establishment with this campaign of denigration, she and Bertie were richer than they had ever been, thanks to George V's bequest. Not that Bertie, who had a reputation for parsimony, was about to push his hand in his own pocket and give money to any of the many people who were now jobless. In fairness to him, though, he did not betray his brother by denigrating him publicly, the way Elizabeth and their friends were doing, despite his being critical of David's cost-cutting actions to Elizabeth and the other critics, as various diary entries and letters confirm.

As David picked up the cudgels of kingship, surrounded on all sides by critics who were more loyal to their own and Elizabeth's interests than to their king's, he believed that something approaching normality had returned to the relationship with his brother and sister-in-law. The visits between the Fort and Royal Lodge had resumed, albeit less frequently than they had once been. Nevertheless, a new sense of harmony and cordiality existed, or so he believed. One Sunday afternoon he took Wallis over to Royal Lodge to show Bertie and Elizabeth the new Buick he had bought. Crawfie left a priceless account of this incident in her memoirs, the gist of which was that Wallis listened while David and Elizabeth conducted a conversation with the odd word thrown in by Bertie. 'She was a smart, attractive woman, already middle-aged, but with that immediate friendliness American women have. She appeared to be entirely at her ease; if anything, rather too much so.'[55] The girls were brought in to say hello, and the visit passed off with superficial amity, though the governess could tell that Elizabeth was uneasy, not because of what she said, but what she left unsaid. Afterwards, she acted as if it had not taken place at all, rather than being her normally effusive self.

By this time, the stately homes of England were afire with stories about David and Wallis. He was covering her in jewels. She was being pushed forward as the power behind the throne. You didn't stand a chance with him unless you took her up. So great hostesses like Lady Cunard and Lady Colefax, and socialites like Chips Channon, duly promoted Wallis and themselves at the same time, as indeed did many of the people who would later claim to have had little or nothing to do with her. The Duke and Duchess of Marlborough entertained her at Blenheim Palace. The Duke and Duchess of Kent played host to her at their new country house. Philip Sassoon had her to stay at Trent Park. She was seen with Lord and Lady Sackvillle at Knole, their magnificent palace in Kent. The Earls of Granard, Dudley and Portarlington also had her for visits, for, as Cecil Beaton observed, 'Even the old Edwardians receive her, if she happens to be free to accept their invitations.'[56]

One would have to possess a heart of stone not to shudder on Elizabeth's behalf. Circumstances had forced her into a back seat and already she was being treated by all and sundry, except her little band of followers, as if she was no longer the second lady in the land, but rather as someone of the third rank, which of course is precisely what she would literally become unless a way could be found to get rid of Wallis.

Meanwhile, Wallis had asked Mary Kirk Raffray to come and stay with her. She felt the need of a friend, and Mary had not only been to school with her, but had even been a bridesmaid at her first wedding. Also, it would be nice to have someone around with whom Ernest got along. David made such claims on her attentions that her husband was often sidelined. Because Wallis genuinely loved Ernest, as the letters she wrote to him after they had separated and were married to their subsequent spouses confirm, she was at pains to see him comfortably occupied elsewhere. She had clearly forgotten what she had done to Thelma, for she was furious and outraged when she discovered that throwing Ernest and Mary together had provided the same result for them as had happened with David and herself. As she complained about how Mary had betrayed her trust, she not only had to cope with a full-blown love affair, but worse, Mary and Ernest wanted to get married.

'Wallis had always viewed Ernest as her ultimate protection,' Margaret, Duchess of Argyll explained. 'As long as she was married to him, the King could not marry her. She never wanted to marry him, you see. She wanted to remain his mistress. He was *awfully* demanding. Not the sort of man any woman in her right mind wanted to have around for twenty four hours a day. As long as she remained married and he remained King, she had the best of both worlds. We all know how she ended up with the worst of all worlds.'

It has often been alleged that Wallis took steps to secure a divorce so that she could marry the King. That is not so. According to Margaret, Duchess of Argyll, who knew all the parties involved and remained lifelong friends with both the Windsors, Ernest is the one who wanted the divorce. He wanted to marry Mary. She was also married, and she too asked her husband for a divorce.

From Wallis's point of view, her husband's romance could not have come at a worst time. David was not even crowned yet. He was hardly established on the throne. Everything was so new that she was nervous lest the pace of change was overwhelming.

Despite this reservation, these were also heady days and Wallis blossomed with all the attention and adulation she was receiving. Being the King's beloved was a wonderful thing, and she enjoyed it.

In May, David informed her that he was having the Prime Minister for dinner and wanted her to attend. 'Then he paused, and after a moment, with his most Prince Charming smile added, "It's got to be done. Sooner or later my Prime Minister must meet my future wife."

'"David," I exclaimed, "you mustn't talk that way. The idea is impossible. They'd never let you."

'"I'm well aware of all that," he said almost gaily, "but rest assured, I will manage it somehow."'[57]

What David did not appreciate was that Wallis did not want to marry him. Nor did she want to divorce Ernest, of whom she remained fond and whom she would gladly have reconciled with, had he not been intent on marrying Mary. 'She regarded Mary as a Judas and never spoke to her again,' Margaret, Duchess of Argyll told me.

The dinner duly took place on 27th May. Because it was so important, it was laden with heavy hitters and supporters. The guests included David's cousin Lord Louis Mountbatten and his wife Edwina; his father's Private

Secretary and Lady Wigram; the Secretary for War and Lady Diana Cooper; Lady Cunard; Admiral of the Fleet Sir Ernie and Lady Chatfield; his equerry the Hon. Piers (Joey) Legh and his wife Sarah; and Lucy Baldwin, who has gone down in history with her remark that she 'lay back and thought of England' when her husband partook of his conjugal rights. It was, by all accounts, a roaring success. Baldwin 'did recognise that Mrs. Simpson's influence on the King was not without its good side,' and 'discounted the wilder tales.'[58] His 'personal impression of her was not unfavourable and he was not disposed to interfere,' according to Lord Donaldson, the friend of the Yorks who had encouraged Bertie to propose to Elizabeth, who unsurprisingly added for good measure, 'I did not share SB's favourable impression of Mrs. Simpson.'[59] He was hardly likely to, considering his closeness to Elizabeth, whose views were well known to all within her circle. All of them were now openly asserting that she and Bertie would be far more suitable on the throne than David, with his fancy American woman whose hold on him had been secured in the brothels of China.

Six weeks later David hosted a second dinner party at York House, the purpose of which was similar to the first. By introducing his future wife to the Great and the Good, he was hoping that they would form a favourable impression of her, so that when the time came for him to announce their marriage, she would be a known and accepted entity.

Once again, Wallis helped David to plan the dinner party and, superficially at least, everything went like clockwork. Beneath the surface, however, things were far from smooth. Although a few on the guest list were neutral, most of them were ossifiers of the first order who were already natural enemies (or sufficiently closely linked to those who were), to be of little help to David and Wallis. The principal guests were Bertie and Elizabeth. The former Viceroy of India and Lady Willingdon were there. So too were the Under-Secretary of State for Foreign Affairs and the Countess Stanhope; the Countess of Oxford and Asquith, whose late husband had been the wartime Prime Minister; the First Lord of the Admiralty and Lady Maud Hoare; the Under-Secretary of State for Air, Sir Philip Sassoon; the Government Chief Whip, Captain David Margesson; the Receiver-General of the Duchy of Cornwall, Sir Edward and Lady Peacock; yet again Duff Cooper and his wife Lady Diana; Lady Colefax, and Alec and Helen Hardinge.

Too many of the guests had links, some more tenuous than others, to Elizabeth. The Strathmores had over the years entertained and been entertained by the Willingdons, who had known Elizabeth from her youth. They were great admirers of hers. Margot Asquith had been born a Tennant and as such was related to Lord Glenconner who had been Elizabeth's suitor. The Hardinges of course were very close friends of hers and were busy undermining the King, and had been doing so on Elizabeth's behalf from as early as 1929. The Hoares were also cronies of the Strathmores, and great admirers of Elizabeth, who was a figure of almost reverence with many of this set, owing largely to her success in having scaled the heights by becoming royal.

Paradoxically, while revering Elizabeth for having joined the most exclusive club in the world, many of these people had mixed feelings about the royals themselves, whose positions they revered even as they looked down upon them as individuals for being so 'different' from them. As far as they were concerned, what made Bertie so desirable was that he displayed a marked lack of individuality. Of all the royal princes and princesses, he was the least like a royal. Indeed, since his marriage to Elizabeth, he had become virtually indistinguishable from any of her many aristocratic friends. He had successfully 'gone native', a testament to Elizabeth's ability to lead him around by the nose. For the opposite reason, they disliked David, who was decidedly royal and displayed no tendency to 'jumping ship and going native' the way his brother had done.

That summer of 1936, the ossifiers were able to see just how different life would be under Edward VIII if he were allowed to remain on the throne. David had chartered Lady Yule's motorised yacht, the *Nahlin*. With his equerry Major John Aird, Wallis, the Duff Coopers, Lord Sefton, the Buists, Lord and Lady Brownlow, Mrs. Josephine (Foxy) Gwynne, Lord Beaverbrook's sister-in-law Helen Fitzgerald, Herman and Katherine Rogers, the Duke of Kent's equerry Humphrey Butler and his wife 'Poots', his former Private Secretary Sir Godfrey Thomas and Assistant Private Secretary 'Tommy' Lascelles, and Wallis of course, he was being shadowed by two Royal Navy destroyers, the *Grafton* and the *Glowworm*. The royal boats cruised around the Greek islands and the Dalmatian coast. The party took side trips to such places as Yugoslavia, Turkey, Bulgaria and Austria, while the world's press followed them and reported on the great love affair between the King and his American inamorata.

Elizabeth and Bertie, meanwhile, were up at Birkhall, which David had let them have. The Archbishop of Canterbury, according to Hugo Vickers, 'was pointedly not invited to Balmoral this year,' and '(a)ware of this, the Duchess of York asked him to Birkhall for a night in September.' The 'invitation caused the King great annoyance. He chose not to see it was an act of courtesy to a prelate and friend, but as an attempt to establish a rival court.'[60] In that, if in so little else, David was prescient, for that is precisely what Elizabeth and the ossifiers were in the process of setting up.

Nevertheless, Balmoral without the monarch was like a mannequin without a head. Only when David arrived in Scotland on 19th September did the castle come alive. David pulled out all the stops to have both an eminent and an entertaining group for what would be Wallis's first (and last, though no one knew it then) summer at his private castle in the Highlands. Guests included the Dukes and Duchesses of Kent, Sutherland, Marlborough and Buccleuch (Elizabeth's old adversary Mollie Lascelles, whose sister-in-law was now Elizabeth's sister-in-law Alice, Duchess of Gloucester). The Earl and Countess of Rosebery were there, as well as Lord and Lady Louis Mountbatten, who remained close friends of the King and his inamorata. The Colin Buists, who had been cruising with the King and appeared to be his friends, though they were actually friends of the Yorks and therefore in the enemy camp, were also there, being as charming and duplicitous as ever.

Wallis was due to arrive on 23rd September. Some months before, the King had been asked to open the Aberdeen Royal Infirmary. He had declined to do so on the grounds that he was in mourning (Court mourning only ended on 20th October), so the Yorks, who were equally in mourning but prepared to interrupt their holidays, agreed to fill in for him. While they were fulfilling this duty, David was across town, at the train station, picking up Wallis. The following day, the Scottish papers printed photographs of the two couples side by side: the Yorks hard at work, the King and his friend hard at play. As Michael Thornton so aptly puts it in *Royal Feud*, 'With the Aberdeen incident, the King had caused widespread offence and had alienated the Scottish middle classes.'

But had David been discourteous, or had he been set up? Lord Beaverbrook would later claim to his granddaughter that his newspapers, as well as the others, had all been tipped off that the King would be picking up his friends at the precise moment that the Yorks were fulfilling a duty which they had volunteered to do after he had declined it. It is unlikely, indeed unthinkable, that Bertie would have had a hand in such treachery, but The Beaver always believed that Elizabeth and Alec Hardinge had cooked up this little pot of poison with which to kill off David's reputation north of the border. Since it is not only unlikely, but almost beyond imagination, that a photographer would unknowingly have been hanging around outside a remote train station on the off-chance that someone of importance might arrive at a time that had been purposely chosen because it was so obscure, his suspicions seem well founded. Either that, or the gods were as eager for Elizabeth and her cohorts to prevail as they themselves were, and were smiling upon them to an extent that even believers in fairy tales would find hard to accept.

The publication of these photographs the day after Wallis's arrival set the tone for the remainder of her visit. Beneath the surface, there was constant carping and criticism of her and the King. Soon even the castle staff had joined in as members of the Royal Household took the time and trouble to question them as to whether they were happy with the new changes. This, of course, was a green light for them to complain, and complain they did. To a very receptive audience, which took care to detail such complaints as the fact that David and Wallis taught them to make *American-style sandwiches* and such atrocities as *hot dogs and hamburgers*. These requests have always been held up as outrages against the British way of life, impositions which required the staff to undertake extraordinary acts of labour which tradition had not prepared them for, but which were fortunately redressed when the King was exiled and the kitchen staff could return to cooking roast beef and Yorkshire pudding. The only difficulty with this criticism is that it does not stand up to reason, for it is infinitely easier, and less time-consuming, to make hot dogs, hamburgers and sandwiches of any description, than it is to prepare and cook roast beef and Yorkshire pudding or any of the other traditional English dishes which the cooks were supposedly so eager to return to preparing.

Even the way David and Wallis dressed became a club with which to beat them. Notwithstanding that the Duchess of Buccleuch stated that the King was invariably dressed in a kilt unless stalking, and photographs show Wallis exquisitely dressed at all times, Marie Belloc Lowndes heard from the ossifiers that Wallis and David put on shorts one day when the weather was good. This and other modes of behaviour such as asking for American-style sandwiches were deemed by Elizabeth's cronies to be solecisms which could not be allowed to continue. So various members of the Royal Household, especially Alec and Helen Hardinge, took Wallis aside 'to try to explain how certain things would not be acceptable', as Helen Hardinge recounted in her memoirs.[61] When these 'quiet talks' did not have the desired effect, Wallis was 'told that it was simply impossible for her to succeed Queen Mary as Queen. But such warnings did not seem to penetrate her mind. For anyone to step into Queen Mary's shoes was really a very difficult exercise; for her, it was an impossibility.'[62]

It seems not to have struck Helen Hardinge, her husband, or any of the other courtiers who were servants of the Crown, that it was actually one hell of an impertinence for them to be dictating terms as to whom they deemed acceptable as a consort of the King. The law of the land was clear on the point. He had the right to prevent other royals from marrying. No one had a reciprocal right where he was concerned. By Helen's own account, however, King Edward VIII's servants were pulling his girlfriend to one side to inform her that they did not find her acceptable. As if they had the right to do so. And all because she was doing things like wearing shorts with the King and teaching the kitchen staff how to make American-style sandwiches. The extent of their arrogance and entitlement was truly astonishing.

They also criticised Wallis for acting as the official hostess. Since the bachelor owner of any house has the right to nominate whomever he pleases to act as his official hostess, David would have been well within his rights even if he had done so. The fact that he was the King-Emperor gave him even more authority to do so. There would have been nothing untoward had he done so. However, he did not. There was an independent witness, moreover, who gave the lie to this version of events, which became yet another cudgel to batter the reputation of the King and his beloved. This was Mollie Buccleuch, sister-in-law to Her Royal Highness The Duchess of Gloucester and arch-adversary of Elizabeth ever since she had slept with James Stuart. In a letter she wrote to Michael Thornton on 3rd June, 1983, she stated that she 'saw no signs of Mrs. Simpson acting as official hostess.'

Tellingly, the one incident which is meant to have catapulted Elizabeth into open enmity with Wallis is not even mentioned in Helen Hardinge's diary, notwithstanding that she was present for the latter part of the evening, being an after-dinner guest. According to the ossified version, which Elizabeth herself disseminated far and wide, on the evening of Saturday, 26th September, the King had a dinner party to which the Yorks had been asked. According to the twaddle which they purveyed and which was swallowed only by the gullible or imbecilic, Elizabeth had not wanted to attend, because she disapproved of the conduct of her host and his paramour, whose behaviour did not accord with her high standards. Bertie, however, had insisted that she attend. Being a dutiful and obedient wife (presumably under the thumb of her dominating spouse), and moreover a wonderful human being who always thought of everyone before herself, and knowing that Princess Marina was six months pregnant with the future Princess Alexandra and could not be disturbed – and would of course have promptly gone into labour had her dear, dear sister-in-law Elizabeth (whom she could not stand) absented herself from the castle – Elizabeth make the supreme sacrifice. Dripping diamonds from the top of her head to the ample bosom which seemed in imminent danger of jumping off her chest, she entered the drawing room of Balmoral Castle. Wallis, doing what Thelma had done on countless occasions to high praise from all quarters, stepped forth to say hello. Elizabeth, however, was outraged, positively outraged, to be greeted by a woman who was in the process of being divorced, and one moreover who did things like wear shorts in castles when she should be wearing woollen suits, pearls, and hats, the way

Elizabeth always did, even around swimming pools while everyone else was in swimsuits. So, with her nose pointed firmly in the air, her eyes blazing yet again, she cut Wallis dead and sailed past declaring, to all and sundry but no one in particular, 'I came to dine with the King.'

It is open to question whether this event ever took place at all. What is not open to question is how Elizabeth, 'whose imagination frequently ran riot,' to quote the Duke of Windsor, justified her supposed conduct. She made Bertie leave early, and allowed Professor Robert Sencourt to impart the information to his readers, in a book she co-operated with, that that the reason why she behaved as she did was that she is a 'very religious woman' and when 'Mrs. Simpson received her' her moral sensibilities were so outraged that she 'left as soon as she conveniently could.'[63] So now we know as a fact that the tooth fairy is not only alive, well and kicking, but also a hypocrite to boot.

What gives the lie away is Helen Hardinge's diary. She was fixated with reporting even the most trivial of imagined infractions of courtly behaviour. She would not have failed to record such a pronounced act of hostility against Wallis if it had indeed taken place. There is no doubt that such an event would have caused a flurry of chatter, yet she omitted to mention it at all in her diary. This leads to the conclusion that it was invented afterwards by Elizabeth, and her merry band of followers simply remained silent about her invention, which was yet another nail that Elizabeth was hammering in Wallis's coffin while boosting herself in the eyes of the world.

By the time Wallis and the King left Balmoral on 30th September, never to return, his position was already more significantly undermined than either of them could have imagined. It was about to be undermined even further. On 14th October, the Hardinges, at Elizabeth's behest, got in touch with one of Queen Mary's Household at Marlborough House, to warn '"caution needed over which invitations the Queen should accept at Buckingham Palace." For we know that if she were exposed to an "accidental" meeting with Mrs. Simpson, it would cause her already trying position to become even more painful.'[64]

The following day, Alec Hardinge used an innocent call from The Press Association to ignite the fuse of the bomb which the ossifiers hoped would blast Wallis right out of everyone's life: possibly taking David as well. He alleged that the reporter informed him that Wallis's divorce was due to be heard at the Ipswich Assizes on 27th October, a fact he claimed not to have known before. Since he was not incompetent, that was akin to stating that Pope had never heard about the Feast of the Assumption. He now wrote to the Prime Minister asking Baldwin 'to see the King and ask if these proceedings could not be stopped, for the danger in which they placed him was becoming every day greater.'

Baldwin quite rightly did not wish to interfere with something which was not his concern, but Hardinge eventually convinced him to do so. He therefore asked for an audience with the King, who saw him on Tuesday, 20th October at the Fort.

For an hour the two men danced around the issue, until Baldwin baldly asked, 'Must the case really go on?'

'I have no right to interfere in the affairs of an individual. It would be wrong of me to attempt to influence Mrs. Simpson just because she happens to be a friend of the King's,' David explained.[65]

What he did not say, and the others might well have not known, was that Wallis had not been the prime mover in the divorce. It had been Ernest, who was now readying himself to marry Mary Kirk Raffray.

When Baldwin reported the inconsequential outcome to Edward VIII's Private Secretary, Hardinge took it upon himself to call upon the Duke and Duchess of York in an official capacity and warn them that the possibility existed that King Edward VIII might abdicate. Up to now, no one – that is, neither the King nor the Prime Minister – had even thought of abdication as a possibility. The word had not been mentioned by either of them, so it is suspicious that Hardinge was introducing the concept. Bertie was aghast and Elizabeth, who was playing the innocent as capably as she had always done, affected incredulousness. This she quickly replaced with righteous indignation, dramatically bemoaning the fact that Bertie might be forced to become king – the inevitable consequence of which, of course, would be that she would become Queen Elizabeth and possess the very moniker that she and Hardinge had most likely first floated as an idea in Time Magazine seven years before. Her old trick, of denying that which she yearned for, was once more to the fore.

At 2.17 p.m. on Tuesday, 27th October, Sir John Hawkes heard the matter of Simpson vs. Simpson. Wallis was granted a decree nisi after evidence to the effect that Ernest had spent the night at the Hotel de Paris at Bray with Mrs. E.H. (Buttercup) Kennedy. A week later, on 3rd November, Edward VIII comported himself magnificently at his first and last State Opening of Parliament.

Behind the scenes, however, Alec Hardinge and the other ossifiers were whipping up a frenzy, making contact with the Government and inciting it to resign if the King should seek to marry Mrs. Simpson. The proof of this scheming is contained in Helen Hardinge's diary. Even though there had been no discussions about the question of the King's marriage raised between him and his Government, and even though Hardinge had no authority to raise it with them without his employer's knowledge, consent and approval, his wife was able to write that he had taken it upon himself to do so. 'Government are not prepared to carry on,' his wife recorded.[66]

Meanwhile, even the most senior courtiers were hedging their bets lest Hardinge and company fail to execute their *coup d'état*. Chips Channon recorded a meeting at the opera between the Earl of Cromer, the Lord Chamberlain, which is the most senior position at Court, with his wife, and Wallis. 'The Cromers, suave aristocrats, were obsequious, and Honor (Channon's wife Lady Honor Guinness) remarked that they did everything except curtsey. Poor Wallis, the cynosure of all eyes, she can do no right. All her tact, sweetness and charm – are they enough?'

In Queen Mary's eyes, such virtues might not have been enough, but Wallis's ability to control David's drinking was. She told Sir Robert Bruce Lockhart on 13th November that '"the one thing I have always feared for David is drink. I was afraid it would ruin him or make him a laughing-stock." And she has been a sane influence in that respect. And that is important.'[67]

That same day, Hardinge sprang the trap he had set. He wrote to the King, who returned to the Fort having spent the previous two days with the Home Fleet at Portland, to inform him that the press would most likely cease to maintain the silence they had so far kept concerning his friendship with Wallis. He recommended that Wallis go abroad immediately.

This was the *coup de grâce*, concocted by a clever and knowledgeable individual with insight into David's character. The Duke of Windsor always said that he had no doubt that the idea originated with Elizabeth. All the indications are that he was correct. If he and Wallis could be separated, there was every likelihood that he would flounder and replace her with someone else the way he had replaced Thelma when she had left him alone.

Although Wallis was in favour of going abroad, David would not hear of it. 'You'll do no such thing. I won't have it. This letter is impertinence.'[68]

It was indeed an impertinence. The way even the upper echelons of the Establishment were now treating Wallis is an indication of how readily she would have been accepted by most people, had the ossifiers not managed to hound Edward VIII off his throne. That very night, Chips Channon recorded an incident in his diary which took place at the Yugoslav Embassy. The Regent (Elizabeth and David's old friend Prince Paul) with his wife Olga, brother-in-law Prince George (the Duke of Kent) and cousin the Infanta Beatrice (Queen Marie of Romania's sister) were filing down to dinner following a charity concert. Madame Grouitch, their hostess, 'suddenly spied Mrs. Simpson, and seizing her, dragged her, in spite of her protests, before the photographers, and then pushed her into the Royal supper room.' In confirmation of the fact that Wallis was not the pushy American adventuress which Elizabeth and her friends were portraying her as being, Chips Channon observed, 'It is this sort of behaviour which causes Wallis such trouble and she, poor woman, was indignant.'[69]

By this time, Lord Beaverbrook had enlightened David of the roles played by Hardinge and Elizabeth, the prime fomenters of the opposition to Wallis. He therefore took the sensible precaution of hereafter avoiding any dealings through his Private Secretary, who was now overtly conspiring against his boss and king, and actively encouraging the Prime Minister to seek a meeting with the Monarch in an attempt to force the issue and have Wallis sent abroad. Edward VIII therefore appointed Walter Monckton, a lawyer who had been Attorney-General to the Duchy of Cornwall since 1932 (later 1st Viscount Monckton of Brenchley) as his advisor. It was through him that all subsequent negotiations were conducted.

The King now made one of the fatal misjudgements which would result in the loss of his throne, but which it is likely Elizabeth, who knew him well, was aware his impatient and impulsive nature would make inevitable. Rather than abide by Winston Churchill's advice, which was to play a waiting game – time was on his side, for once he was crowned king, there was little the Government could do to prevent him from marrying whom he pleased – he committed the cardinal error of agreeing to meet Baldwin at Buckingham Palace on 16th November. In fact, Baldwin had no right to bring up the subject of his wife. But that did not stop Baldwin, who had been briefed by Hardinge, from doing so. And Edward VIII fell right into the trap. He informed him that he intended to marry Wallis. The following day, he also informed Bertie of his intention.

Now began the incredible toing and froing as to whether Wallis would become Queen, Duchess of Edinburgh, Duchess of Lancaster, or something else. Being King-Emperor, Edward VIII had no limits upon his choice of bride, save that she could not be Roman Catholic, for that was specifically forbidden under the Act of Settlement of 1688. He needed no one's permission, and no one had the right to object to any choice he made.

Michael Thornton, who interviewed the Duke and Duchess of Windsor and knew Margaret Argyll well, wrote in *Royal Feud,* 'After the blistering snub delivered by the Duchess of York to Wallis at Balmoral, the two women had not met again, and would not do so for more than thirty years, but Wallis had become increasingly aware that Elizabeth was the major obstacle to her ambitions.'[70] This is a fair assessment of the situation. And, Elizabeth being Elizabeth, as soon as the temperature rose, so too did hers. Once more she took to her bed, illness rescuing her from the unpleasantness her intrigues had created. It also had the merit of providing her with the perfect cover, for she was thereafter able to claim, rather disingenuously, that she could not have had anything to do with what was going on, because she was ill. In fact, all she was missing was the inevitable *dénouement* which her actions, calculations and cohorts were bringing to fruition.

On 23rd November, Elizabeth wrote to Helen Hardinge from 145 Piccadilly, 'I would love to see you, because there is nobody I can talk to & I know that you understand the horrible complications of the situation.'[71] Indeed, she did, being one of Elizabeth's main cohorts.

Despite knowing by now of the intrigues of his courtiers and sister-in-law, David naïvely believed that the honourable course was for him to acquire the blessing of his many governments. Notwithstanding that no other king had ever done so before, on 25th November he asked the Prime Minister to sound out the Government and Dominions as to their views. This was the second fatal error he was making. While Helen Hardinge was visiting her supposedly sick friend at 145 Piccadilly – 'Go out to see the Duchess of York who is an angel as usual'[72], Baldwin was framing the questions in such a way that he elicited the responses he wanted:

(1) The King should marry Mrs. Simpson and she should be recognised as Queen.
(2) The King should marry Mrs. Simpson and she should not become Queen.
(3) The King should abdicate in favour of the Duke of York.

Before the answers were in, Alec Hardinge made a mistake which Elizabeth would use as the excuse to cost him his job. The 6th Viscount Hardinge of Lahore told me, before I wrote *Royal Marriages* in 1993, that his father had informed him that Alec had mooted the question as to whether the Duke of Kent might not be a more favourable option for king than the Duke of York. He was aware that, in many quarters, Bertie was perceived as being little better than an imbecile. Harry, the brother next in line, was no more prepossessing or intelligent. The only other attractive brother, aside from David, was George. Could a case be made for taking two unprecedented steps at once, or would the whole fabric be torn asunder by this double whammy? According to Charles Hardinge, he had raised the question not so much because he believed skipping the first two heirs in line was a desirable option, but rather as a precaution against later accusations of not being thorough. However, Elizabeth later used this as her justification for demanding that Bertie dismiss him. Although he declined to do so outright, Elizabeth thereafter created so much trouble and made Alec's life so difficult that it became impossible for him to do his job properly, and he felt compelled to offer his resignation. He did not expect the King to accept it, but thought if he tendered it, Bertie would see to what lengths his troublemaking wife had driven him. No one was more shocked than he by the alacrity with which Bertie accepted his resignation.

Even Shawcross is compelled to report in the official biography, 'Many members of the Household believed that the Queen had played a large part in Hardinge's removal.'[73] Anthony Eden's Private Secretary, Oliver Harvey, recorded that 'the strong, sensible, progressive minded Private Secretary' had been forced to resign 'by the Queen who was determined to get him out.'[74] And there we have the real crux of the matter. Hardinge was too strong and too progressive for Elizabeth's taste, and once he had served his purpose and been the Trojan horse which let in the foot soldiers to hack David's throne from beneath him, he became expendable.

The Hardinges, however, had a wealth of contacts, most of whom liked them. They were informed that Elizabeth had been the prime mover behind the scenes. This came as no shock to them, for they knew for themselves how ably she had manipulated events in the run up to the Abdication. Bertie had been quite happy to keep him *in situ,* fully appreciating that it had been his duty as Private Secretary to consider all the options and variables, but Elizabeth had used this as an excuse to push, and push and push, causing havoc the way she had done with Louis Greig, until Alec had felt that he had no choice but to resign.

Helen, knowing only too well how she and Alec had co-operated with Elizabeth in trying to drive Wallis out of the country – little realising that they were driving the King out as well (or so at any rate was their version of events) – felt so betrayed by the woman she had regarded as her close friend that she wrote her a letter of subtle recrimination. Once more Shawcross bears quoting. 'She said that she had been told by trustworthy people that the Queen had been trying to get rid of her husband for a long time.'[75] Playing upon her old friendship with Elizabeth to protect her family's position – she knew only too well what happened to people when they crossed Elizabeth – she wrote, 'I do not know whether it is true or not – but if by any chance it should be – Your Majesty only had to send for me and tell me what you thought.'[76]

Elizabeth responded to this letter with the same remarkable degree of disingenuousness which she had shown every other time she had been caught out. She sent for Helen, who recorded in her diary, 'Went to see the Queen. She's very angry with me for believing they could have ill wished Alec.'[77]

Appreciating that failure to play along with the fiction would result in untold damage being wrought to her family and herself by the vengeful Queen, who could never forgive people when they crossed her, Helen acted as if she had bought the lie. But she had not. Aware though that her whole family's future depended on her acting as if all was all right, she pretended to do so. Then put in just enough revealing information in her memoirs for those with sharp enough eyes or ears to pick up on the fact that Elizabeth was not the sweet, kind, wonderful person she wanted everyone to believe she was.

Alec's downfall was in the future, however, as the Abdication Crisis developed momentum. He and Helen and Elizabeth had conspired well in laying the ground to force out Wallis, and possibly David as well. He had fed Baldwin the information which the Prime Minister had needed to act, and both men had performed ably and in tandem, their objective identical: the removal of Wallis and, unless he became more malleable, the King.

As both Private Secretary and Prime Minister had envisaged, once the Government and the Dominions realised that they had choices which covered everything from Queen Wallis to ex-King David, there was little enthusiasm for Wallis as queen or morganatic consort. Unless David surrendered the woman he loved on the altar of their demands, he would have to go.

Meanwhile, Wallis's house was being attacked. David therefore ordered her to leave the country, largely, she believed, because as long as she was around, she would be a restraining influence upon him. He therefore instructed his friend and equerry Perry (Lord) Brownlow to spirit her out of the country. They drove down to Herman and Katherine Rogers's house in Cannes, where she would seek refuge for the next six months.

Matters now reached their climax. Confronted with the option of abdicating or giving up Wallis, on 8th December David decided to abdicate. He had his brother Bertie over for dinner with Walter Monckton at Fort Belvedere, where they discussed his decision to abdicate. The following day the Instrument of Abdication was drawn up, and signed on the morning of 10th December at the Fort by David and his three brothers.

Afterwards, David and Bertie had a talk. According to the Duke of Windsor's account, Bertie happily agreed that there would be 'no trouble' over Wallis's rank, style and title, which would proceed, in settled practice, from his own. Although he would cease to be King Edward VIII once the Abdication came into effect, he still remained His Royal Highness The Prince Edward of the United Kingdom of Great Britain and Northern Ireland. Bertie informed him that his first act as king would be to create his beloved brother, who was sacrificing so much for love, a duke as well. They then agreed that he would go into exile for a year to give Bertie time to establish himself as king, after which David and Wallis would return and assume the positions of the youngest son and his consort. His status as youngest son was a given fact, because by renouncing the throne, he had renounced the

Elizabeth Bowes Lyon was a much-wanted child, beautiful and angelic looking but called Merry Mischief by her family for good reason. (Portrait by Francisco Torrone in the collection of E. Charles Hanna, Esq)

Glamis Castle, Elizabeth's ancestral home, is literally the stuff of legend, and even figures in Shakespeare's *Macbeth*.

Elizabeth and her younger brother
the Hon. David Bowes Lyon
were two peas of one pod, and
known as the Two Benjamins.
They shared many character
traits, not the least of which were
theatricality and a gift for intrigue.

St. Paul's Walden Bury
in Hertfordshire was
Elizabeth's childhood home
until her grandfather died
and her father succeeded
to the earldom and the
splendours of Glamis Castle.

Although Elizabeth wanted to marry the glamorous Prince of Wales rather than his younger brother the Duke of York, she nevertheless took to royal life the way a great actress takes to the stage and would thereafter become the most enduring media superstar of the 20th century.

Elizabeth and her mother achieved their ambitions for royal status in 1923 when she married the Duke of York (central figure), second son of King George V and Queen Mary (right), seen here at Buckingham Palace with her parents, the 14th Earl and Countess of Strathmore (left).

Elizabeth's charm and approachability won her popularity among the press and public but critics in the Royal Family. Here she is at the Cenotaph on 11th November 1925 with (left to right) Princess Helena Victoria, Duchess of York, Princess Beatrice, Princess Louise, Duchess of Argyll, Queen Mary and Queen Victoria Eugenia of Spain. (The Royal Collection © 2011 Her Majesty Queen Elizabeth II)

Motherhood increased Elizabeth's power within the Royal Family exponentially, but like her peers she left the day-to-day child-rearing to her daughters' nanny and their governess, Marion Crawford, seen here with Princess Elizabeth (Lilibet) and Princess Margaret Rose of York (Margot).

The marriage of Elizabeth's youngest brother-in-law Prince George, Duke of Kent to the beautiful Princess Marina of Greece in 1934 infuriated the competitive Elizabeth, who now had to share the stage with a younger, better looking and more stylish princess who looked down upon her.

Elizabeth was great friends with the Prince of Wales's celebrated married mistress Thelma, Viscountess Furness, seen here with her even more famous identical twin sister Gloria Vanderbilt. The Vanderbilt custody battle of 1934 was the 'greatest scandal of the time' according to *Time Magazine,* and created the opening for Wallis Simpson to replace Thelma as *maîtresse en titre.*

The Abdication of King Edward VIII resulted in Elizabeth being crowned queen in May 1937. In the official Coronation photograph she appears with (left to right) the Princess Royal, the Duchess and Duke of Gloucester, Queen Mary, King George VI, the Duke and Duchess of Kent, Queen Maud of Norway, and in the foreground Princess Elizabeth and Princess Margaret.

An oil sketch of the State Portrait of King George VI by Gerald Kelly, from the private collection of the author. Elizabeth so enjoyed the artist's company that she not only housed him for years, but prominently displayed another of his oil sketches for the same portrait at Clarence House. (David Chambers)

The displaced Edward VIII became Duke of Windsor and married Wallis Simpson the month after the scheduled date for his aborted Coronation. He never forgave Elizabeth for the part she played in his dethronement.

Even in old age the Duchess of Windsor retained the chic and sleek look which her husband admired and earned her a permanent place on the World's Best Dressed List.
(René Silvin)

Above: Elizabeth overheard Wallis mockingly refer to her as the Dowdy Duchess. This fed her animosity but did wonders for her attire, as she called in the great English couturier Norman Hartnell (seen here after his knighthood) who turned her into a style icon.

Left: Hartnell credited King George VI with instructing him to base the glamorisation of Elizabeth on the Winterhalter portraits of the beautiful 19th century Empresses, Elisabeth of Austria and Eugenie of the French.

Above: The 'Special Relationship' between Britain and the United States of America was developed by King George VI and President Franklin Delano Roosevelt as a 'bulwark against Fascism' following the 1939 State Visit, when the King and Queen stayed with the Presidential couple at the White House and the Roosevelt family estate in Hyde Park, where they were photographed, (left to right) Eleanor Roosevelt, the King, Sara Roosevelt, Elizabeth, the President.

Britain declared war on Germany over Poland, and played host to the Polish Government-in-Exile and its Prime Minister, General Wladyslaw Sikorski, seen here (left) with King George VI and Queen Elizabeth during the war.

The Royal Family based itself at Windsor Castle for the duration of the war, and used to go over to Royal Lodge, their country house in Windsor Great Park, for a sense of normality. Here 'We Four' as Elizabeth and George VI referred to their family, are having tea, (left to right) King George VI, Princess Elizabeth, Princess Margaret, Queen Elizabeth.

Elizabeth wanted her daughter to marry a British aristocrat and drew up a list of the First Eleven, but Princess Elizabeth wanted a real man and chose her third cousin Prince Philip of Greece, who had the looks of a Greek God and a personality to match. (David Chambers)

A sketch of 'The Hun', as Elizabeth called her son-in-law, in his 1953 Coronation robes. (David Chambers)

Above: Widowed at 51, Elizabeth bought the only property she would ever own, the Castle of Mey, for the princely sum of £100.

Left: The first crisis of the new queen's reign was her sister Margaret's desire to marry the divorced Comptroller of her mother's Household, Group Captain Peter Townsend, who was photographed standing (central figure) behind Princess Margaret, sitting to the left of Queen Elizabeth II (forefront right). Forefront left are the Duchess and Duke of Gloucester, their aunt and uncle. Elizabeth's lack of support poisoned Margaret's attitude towards her.

Above: The role of grandmother caused Elizabeth fewer problems than that of mother. In particular, she adored her eldest grandchild Prince Charles of Edinburgh, later Duke of Cornwall and the present Prince of Wales, who returned her feelings in full.

Left: The power struggles between Elizabeth and her son-in-law Philip were evident by the time of Princess Anne's birth. The godparents were all Mountbattens except for Elizabeth's nephew the Rev. the Hon. Andrew Elphinstone. Photographed at the christening at Buckingham Palace are (left to right sitting) Princess Alice, Countess of Athlone representing the primary godmother Princess Andrew of Greece (Philip's mother), Princess Elizabeth with Princess Anne, Queen Elizabeth, and (left to right standing) godparents Earl Mountbatten of Burma, The Hereditary Princess of Hohenlohe-Langenburg (Philip's sister Margarita), and Andrew Elphinstone.

Above: As she aged, Elizabeth remained as vain as she had always been.

Below Left: Elizabeth was delighted when Princess Margaret married photographer Antony Armstrong-Jones in 1960. He was just the sort of man she wanted for her daughter, though the marriage ended in bitterness and further dented the mother-daughter relationship.

Below Right: Elizabeth's signature of Elizabeth R (for Regina) from the guest book at Caymanas Park, Jamaica, 1965.

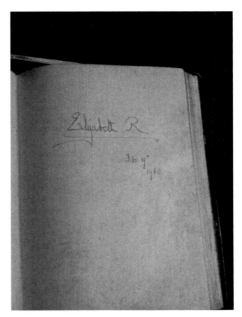

Elizabeth's hostility towards the Duke of Windsor remained intractable, even as he was dying. Nevertheless, Queen Elizabeth II, Prince Philip and Prince Charles visited him a few days before he died, and are photographed with Wallis, chic as ever. (René Silvin)

Someone who knew and was friendly in varying degrees with Elizabeth, Princess Marina, and the Duke and Duchess of Windsor was the fabled Margaret, Duchess of Argyll, photographed at the England Ball, 1976, with Lady Colin Campbell. (David Chambers)

Elizabeth heartily approved of Lady Diana Spencer as a bride for Prince Charles and encouraged the match, though when the marriage turned sour she developed a real antipathy towards Diana.

The centenarian Elizabeth photographed with (left to right) Prince William, Prince Charles, and Prince Harry.

rights of any children he might have to its succession. However, he had not renounced his royal status, nor could he, being the son, grandson, great-grandson, and great-great-grandson of sovereigns. On the other hand, his two youngest brothers retained their rights of succession, as did any issue they might produce, so he had to rank after them. Being royal, however, he had to rank before all aristocrats and commoners.

The brothers also agreed that David, who was the least well off of all his siblings owing to the fact that his father had cut him out of his will, would turn over his life interest in Sandringham and Balmoral to Bertie, in return for a specified sum and an income for life.

Elizabeth, who would shortly become the very Queen Elizabeth David used to tease her about becoming, wrote David a sweet letter from her sick-bed. Amongst the many lovely sentiments she expressed were, 'God bless you from my heart. We are all overcome with misery, and can only pray that you will find happiness in your new life. I often think of the old days, and how you helped Bertie and I (sic) in the first years of our marriage – I shall always mention you in my prayers.'

All the other members of the Royal Family wrote David wishing him well.

The following day, Friday 11ᵗʰ December, 1936, at 1.52 p.m., King Edward VIII's own royal assent was given in the House of Lords to His Majesty's Declaration of Abdication Act. David had ceased to be King-Emperor and Bertie was now King George VI. Elizabeth was Queen Elizabeth.

That evening, David went over for dinner at Royal Lodge for what would turn out to be the last time, though he had no means of knowing it. He believed that 'everything was settled' between him and his brother, his new king, who played host to him, their mother, his siblings the Dukes of Gloucester and Kent and Princess Mary, as well as his uncle the Earl of Athlone and his wife Princess Alice. 'That last family dinner was too awful. Thank goodness I had flu and couldn't go,' Elizabeth told a non-royal friend, in yet another of the inconsistencies for which she was notorious, for she persistently maintained that she never spoke about the Royal Family to anyone outside of the Royal Family, despite doing so with consistent alacrity. In his Elizabeth biography, Hugo Vickers put Elizabeth's self-serving avoidance well: 'It was a convenient time to be ill. She was able to escape a lot of Germanic emotion between mother, son, and brothers.' None of whom yet realised that David's abdication would most likely have never come to pass, had Elizabeth not been orchestrating it with her friends behind the scenes.

The question which has always preoccupied people in royal circles is: was Elizabeth really as involved as some, including the Duke of Windsor, thought, or was she more of an innocent bystander who had the good fortune to have her heart's desire come true?

In *Elizabeth The Queen Mother*, Hugo Vickers quotes Lord Charteris of Amisfield, Queen Elizabeth II's then Private Secretary, telling him in 1977, "'It is hard to believe that Queen Elizabeth did not want to be Queen in 1936, but in my reading of history she did not. She was happy to be the Duchess of York with her two young children. He paused; "That's not to say that she would not be extremely reluctant not to be Queen now….'"

Martin Charteris used to be my neighbour and we used to have occasional chats. He told me more or less the same thing, but when I asked him if he could rule out the possibility that she might have advertently or inadvertently given succour to the forces which brought about the Abdication, he said, 'No. I couldn't rule it out.'

The 6th Viscount Hardinge of Lahore also told me his father had stated that Helen and Alec Hardinge had informed him (the 5th Viscount) the Abdication could never have transpired without Elizabeth supporting the courtiers behind the scenes. She was the driving force behind it, and Alec had come to realise how dreadfully she had used him. His only consolation was that he felt that George VI had made a better king than Edward VIII would have done. That, of course, might have been mere self-consolation, for few men of honour can stare themselves in the mirror day after day realising that they have been used by a clever and ambitious woman to replace one good king with another equally good one.

Yet Edward VIII's beliefs and style were far more in keeping with those of our age. Had he been given a fair chance, the British Empire might not have gone into the terminal decline it did as soon as his brother succeeded him. For the fact is, King George VI oversaw the immediate and precipitate decline of the British Empire's fortunes. He oversaw the beginning of the dismantling of the Empire, which continued under his daughter, and might well have been averted had a more progressive king been on the throne. And a progressive king with an American queen might well have been just the antidote to much of the antipathy which saw nationalists like Gandhi and Jinnah prevail.

Even Frances Donaldson, Edward VIII's biographer who was firmly in the Elizabeth camp, made the acerbic observation, 'She cannot have been entirely cold to her opportunity' to become queen. Lady Donaldson was making this statement while Elizabeth was still alive, yet she came as close as anyone ever has to asserting that Elizabeth was ambitious, opportunistic, and, seeing her chance to be queen, seized it.

The Duke of Windsor, who arguably knew Elizabeth better than anyone else, having wallowed in her sugar before he had to endure her bile, condemned her ambition to his mother in letters which are in the royal archives, as well as to his many friends. Margaret, Duchess of Argyll told me that he was firmly convinced that she had 'orchestrated the whole thing' and had done such a clever job that there were few remaining traces. 'She set the ball in motion, knowing very well that once it gathered momentum, it would attract all sorts of reactionaries who couldn't wait to be rid of me. They remained in place for the remainder of my brother's reign. Fundamentally, he was a decent man, but where she was concerned, he was a nincompoop of the first order,' the Duke of Windsor said.

And what of the notorious China Dossier? According to Lady Jean Campbell, Lord Beaverbrook claimed that David got ahold of it and is supposed to have destroyed it himself. Whether he was able to destroy the original, or a copy existed which has survived, is not something which Max Beaverbrook conveyed to his granddaughter. But that is the main reason why David froze his Private Secretary Alec Hardinge out of negotiations in the run-up to his abdication. That and his machinations with Stanley Baldwin. Such treachery could not be condoned, nor could it be publicly acknowledged, but privately the Duke of Windsor told all who would listen that the Hardinges were Judases who had got their just desserts.

Over the years, there has been a body of opinion that David had wanted to abdicate his rights of succession to the throne while still Prince of Wales. Shawcross makes the extraordinary claim in the official biography that, 'There were those who came to believe that, even before the death of his father, the Prince had already decided to renounce his right to the succession and abscond with Mrs. Simpson. That was certainly the opinion of two of King George V's Private Secretaries, Alan Lascelles and Alec Hardinge.' In fact, although Lascelles had been appointed as George V's Assistant Private Secretary in November 1935, he only took up his appointment on 16th January, 1936. He travelled to Sandringham by train with Bertie, and would not see the King once before his death four days later. He was therefore not in a position to make any of the observations to which he retroactively laid claims. He was simply not a party to any of the happenings.

Moreover, Lascelles did not like David and considered him unfit to be king. He had been his Assistant Private Secretary between 1921 and 1929, but he had resigned because of personality clashes with the Prince, whose lifestyle he deplored. It reflects well upon David's character, albeit somewhat more adversely upon his prescience, that he kept Lascelles in the influential post of Assistant Private Secretary when he succeeded his father.

Alec Hardinge's word should also be treated with caution. Number two in George V's office to Lord Wigram, who kept out of the intrigues surrounding

Wallis Simpson, David promoted him to Private Secretary as soon as he succeeded to the throne. He had hoped that his own Private Secretary since 1919, Sir Godfrey Thomas, 10th Bt, would remain in the post, but Thomas had had enough of dealing with his headstrong boss and preferred to retire. David then promoted Alec Hardinge, not realising the deep involvement he already had in Elizabeth's machinations to push Wallis out of the royal scene. Only later that year, when Lord Beaverbrook entered the picture, would he see what had happened, by which time much of the damage, though not all, had already been done.

Max Beaverbrook's contribution aside, it should be clear to all who have read his widow Helen's memoirs that Alec Hardinge was an overbearing reactionary who had an unseemly relish for intrigue. Even without Lord Beaverbroook's verification of the fundamental part he played in betraying David, perceptive readers will find their eyebrows shooting up towards the ceiling at some of the double-dealing and self-righteous posturing which one is supposed to believe denotes noble principles.

If Sir Owen Morshead, the librarian at Windsor Castle between 1926 and 1958, is to be believed, even Bertie was at pains, once he had been handed the crown he had never sought, to explain away his possession of it. Once he was king, he alleged that David had not really wanted to be king. Bertie claimed that 'he had never meant to take it on…You see Papa's death fell wrongly for his plans…It would have been easy, comparatively, to chuck it while he was P. of Wales; he would have had a rough crossing with Papa, but he would have faced up to that.'[78] Clearly there was an element of embarrassment here. Even Shawcross casts doubt upon Bertie's interpretation, stating in the official biography that 'the new King George VI…(was) perhaps relying more than he realised upon hindsight.' In other words, he had made the whole thing up.

Wishful thinking would be a more accurate, if trenchant, description of Bertie's desire to rewrite history so that he could lay the blame at the doorstep of the brother who had only ever been supportive of him, but whose crown he now wore in large measure because of the machinations of his wife.

And what of the Duke of Windsor's version of events? In exile he constantly said that the revisionists were rewriting history. Of course, he had been well educated, so he knew that the victor always imposes his interpretation upon events. What he had not reckoned on when he abdicated, however, was that his renunciation of the throne would be used to turn him into a pariah. Nor had he expected to be cast in the role of adversary of his brother and the other members of the Royal Family. He had struck an agreement with Bertie that he would return after a year abroad and fulfil the role of a younger son.

It was this agreement, which Elizabeth would ensure was never honoured, that was now being used by the revisionists to pillory and discredit him, by claiming that he had contemplated renouncing his rights of succession before his accession. He had never had any such plans, and there was, he would point out, not one piece of paper to prove the contention. The only people who made these claims, which he denied conclusively, were those who had been a party to the Abdication, or who had profited by it. Why, he would ask, did he tell people of his plans for the monarchy prior to his accession to the throne, if he planned to renounce his rights? And why, once he was king, was he posing for his State portrait, in his Coronation robes, if he planned to abdicate?

On the other hand, there was a 'trail of barely visible slime' going all the way back to 1929 which showed that Elizabeth and her backers had been mooting the possibility of Bertie and herself replacing David on the throne.

Res ipsa loquitur.

The Warrior Queen

Chapter Ten

Irrespective of whether Elizabeth set out to be queen or not, once she was, she displayed a relish for the role which people like her sister-in-law, Princess Mary, found distasteful. 'Her delight was too evident,' Princess Mary's son George later said. 'She looked like the proverbial cat that had got the cream.' He said his mother used to say, 'I do wish she'd at least make an effort to conceal her delight. All that smiling simply won't do.' She also asked, 'Is she a Cheshire cat or a Scots' lassie? A bit more of the dour Scot would be preferable to all that skinning of the teeth.'

Princess Mary, who had been Princess Royal since 1931 following the death of her aunt Princess Louise, Duchess of Fife, had a point. There is a famous photograph of Elizabeth on a train taken as she heads towards Sandringham, shortly after the Abdication. There is no mistaking the beatific joy that jumps out at the viewer. Her Majesty The Queen-Empress is ecstatic. That one photograph alone would give the lie to any claims she would thereafter make that she had been reluctant to take on the role, though her letters of the period also show a readiness that all her obfuscation could not mask. Although she dressed things up as willingness to do her duty, there is no escaping the eagerness with which she embraced her new role. The day after David sailed into exile on the *Fury*, Elizabeth was writing to her dear friend Cosmo Lang, Archbishop of Canterbury, 'I can hardly now believe that we have been called to this tremendous task, and (I am writing to you quite intimately) the curious thing is we are not afraid. I feel that God has enabled us to face the situation calmly.' Since Bertie was known to be terrified, she can only have been employing the royal we, and ended the letter with just that touch of charming triumphalism which always sent a thrilling shiver down the spines of her victorious supporters, 'I sign myself for the first time, & with great affection Elizabeth R.'[1]

She had indeed arrived.

Lang's response was to lambast David publicly, commenting how 'strange and sad (it) is that he should have sought his happiness in a manner inconsistent with the Christian principles of marriage, and within a social circle whose standards and whose way of life are alien to all the best instincts and traditions of his people.'

The public response was immediate. Lambeth Palace was inundated with letters condemning the Archbishop from a host of furious subjects, whose tenor is best summarised by the following doggerel which became instantaneously popular:

My Lord Archbishop what a scold you are;

And when your man is down how bold you are;

In Christian charity how scant you are;

Oh, Old Lang Swine, how full of Cantuar.

The former King Edward VIII's many outraged supporters, of course, did not know that the new queen was in sympathy with the hypocritical Archbishop, but many aristocrats did, and this made the Archbishop's cant all the more odious. Where the maintenance of Christian principles concerning marriage was concerned, the new king and queen's social circle was just as guilty as David's of tolerating adultery. And there was much talk in royal circles that the former Duke and Duchess of York were both engaged in friendships with the opposite sex that were either adulterous, or then gave the impression of being so. Bertie was well known to have had two separate extra-marital relationships since his marriage, one with Boo Laye, the other with Elizabeth's good friend and lady-in-waiting Lady Maureen Stanley. The normally rabidly jealous Elizabeth's acceptance of both women had caused talk, the gist of which was that she was grateful for others who were more willing than she was to fulfil her conjugal obligations. And by this time, Elizabeth herself was suspected of having an inappropriately amorous relationship with the handsome heir to the Coats & Clark thread fortune.

Kenneth Clark was a well-known ladies' man in the mould of James Stuart. He had been the Director of the National Gallery since 1933, and the Surveyor of the King's Pictures since 1934. In that capacity, he used to advise Elizabeth on her acquisition of pictures by such modern British masters as Augustus John and Philip Wilson Steer. They were constantly shooting off on viewing expeditions together, which gave them opportunity if that is what they wanted. Although Elizabeth was always mildly flirtatious with most men, her conduct with Clark was such that Mayfair drawing rooms were buzzing with talk that she, who had so far been perceived as being cold to the pleasures of the flesh, had finally taken a lover. It is unlikely that Bertie would have knighted Clark had he already been aware of the rumours about him and Elizabeth, but he created him a Knight Commander of the Bath in 1938. Later on, Lilibet would appoint the man whom many thought of as her mother's lover Companion of Honour in 1959, and he was made a life peer in 1969. By that time, Lord Clark of Saltwood was well on his way to becoming an international television star as the presenter of the lively and erudite television show, *Civilisation*.

Clark had nothing but scorn for Bertie, whom he called 'a very stupid man'.[2] He could be wildly indiscreet about his relationship with Elizabeth, and used to say that the marriage was no love match, at least not from her side of the fence. He told all and sundry that he and Elizabeth 'were a bit in love with each other', and used to entertain listeners with how Bertie would get jealous and make scenes. There were two notable scenes, one at Windsor Castle, the other at Buckingham Palace, and, although he did not specifically say that he and Elizabeth had been lovers, his son Alan Clark M.P. did from time to time. He would refer to the Queen Mother as his father's 'girlfriend' and on one memorable occasion even joked that she 'might have been my step-mother, had the timing been right.'

Whether Elizabeth actually broke her marriage vows, or merely indulged in harmless flirtations, is open to conjecture. What is not, however, is that Alec Hardinge was quite wrong to allege that there had been talk about the Duke of Windsor and Wallis, but none about Bertie and Elizabeth. And the Archbishop of Canterbury had been equally wrong to assert that their circle was less *louche* than David's. They were both tolerant of homosexuality to a remarkable degree at a time when most other people were not. While the former King Edward VIII was markedly tetchy about being in the presence of overt homosexuals – the Woolworth's heir Jimmy Donohue would later be an exception to that rule – neither Bertie nor Elizabeth suffered from such misgivings. Indeed, she surrounded herself with gays, and her own brother David was 'rampantly homosexual', to quote his friend Burnet Pavitt. As homosexuality was then illegal as well as an infraction of Church rules, while adultery possessed only the latter disadvantage, a true Christian would have praised them for refraining from casting the first stone, though of course that would have defeated the very purpose of his cant, which was to elevate his cronies the new King and Queen at the expense of the preceding monarch, whom he disliked fulsomely.

And how did Elizabeth react to this barrage of hypocritical bile? She wrote to her friend Victor Cazalet commending the scolding Archbishop, stating, 'I think the nation vaguely <u>felt</u> it, but <u>he</u> put the issue clearly and as no one else had the right to do. Nowadays we are inclined to be too vague about the things that matter, and I think it well that for once someone should speak out in plain and direct words, what after all was the truth.'[3]

Since the letters of vituperation Lang was receiving from the outraged nation outstripped by far the few ones of support he received, one wonders just what nation Elizabeth was speaking on behalf of. It certainly was not the great British nation, so must have been her evocation of it. This is but the first of many occasions when Elizabeth's ego would ally itself with her prejudices to enable her to associate herself with a body of people who did not exist, save in her own imagination.

Bertie's innate connection to reality, however, provided him with a more accurate barometer of what the public might, and might not, really feel. Far less dynamic and proactive than his wife, whose streak of sybaritic laziness was always replaced with consummate energy whenever the demands of ambition or stardom required her to step onto the stage and shine brightly – or to protect her access to that treasured platform – he was riven with self-doubt and wondered whether the people would ever 'take to him' the way they had taken to David.

Although Elizabeth too was worried that the public would not take to her as the Queen, as an inspection of her diary and correspondence confirms, David had not been out of the country for more than eight days before she was laying the ground to make his exile permanent. Owen Morshead, the librarian at Windsor Castle, is on record as stating on 20th December, 1936, that she expressed to him the view that 'it would be dangerous to have such a powerful personality, so magnetic, hanging about…'[4] She even threw out the lasso to Queen Mary, writing to thank her for her 'unfailing sympathy & understanding through those first bewildering days when we were still stunned by the shock of David's going,' before issuing the *coup de grâce*: 'It was so wonderful having the old family atmosphere again. I feel sure that it is our great strength in these difficult times.'[5] This was a clever move, for she was suggesting to the old lady that now that David was out of the way, and good riddance to him and his newfangled ideas and plans, the old ways, and old days, had returned, thanks to Bertie and herself. And Queen Mary, who was utterly traumatised by the Abdication, and longed for nothing more than a re-establishment of *any* semblance of order, of which the most desirable would be the old, was seduced without even realising it at that time, though later on she would come to see Elizabeth's ploys for what they were.

In the 1970s, Queen Mary's sister-in-law Princess Alice, Countess of Athlone would tell the Revd. Philip Hart that it had taken the old lady many years to discern how ably Elizabeth had used her as a battering ram with which to alienate David from his family and to destroy his ability to return to his homeland.

At the time of the Abdication, Elizabeth had played upon Queen Mary's sentiments and prejudices to garner her support for excluding David and Wallis from returning to live in England. Elizabeth was almost hysterical in asserting that Wallis would leave David as soon as she became Her Royal Highness The Duchess of Windsor. She painted lurid pictures for the benefit of the dowager queen – and anyone else who would listen – of the sexual technician whose skills had been honed in the bordellos of Peking, abandoning the former king and cavorting upon the world stage as she practised her vile skills upon other, equally gullible but richer, victims. The Royal Family, she warned, would become an international laughing stock unless Wallis was stopped and prevented from becoming a member of the British Royal Family.

According to Queen Mary, Elizabeth in full flow was 'irresistible' – something that every other detractor and admirer has said, including her own niece Margaret Rhodes. She deployed her charisma, confidence, energy, passion and imaginative potency to devastating effect, whipping up all around her with visions of the devastation that would proceed from Wallis being allowed anywhere near any of them.

Because Elizabeth lacked the mechanism which most other conscionable people possess – the ability to question whether one is right or wrong – while possessing in such rich measure the belief that she was never wrong and must therefore always be right, the new Queen was able to sow panic in the Royal Family. According to Queen Mary, it was Elizabeth who overrode Bertie's intention to honour the agreements he had struck with David. She argued that David had concealed assets to diddle Bertie out of money in their dealings over Sandringham and Balmoral. This was untrue, but even if it had been true, David's assets had no bearing upon the final calculation, which was the value of David's life tenancy interest in both properties. She demanded that Bertie did not allow David to make a fool of himself and the rest of the Royal Family over Wallis. Since Letters Patent had not been issued regarding his new title, Duke of Windsor, Bertie, she argued, could and must deprive Wallis of the right to be called Her Royal Highness by limiting the right to do so to David alone.

As Princess Alice pointed out to the Revd. Philip Hart, the nuance of depriving David's wife of her entitlement to Royal Highness would never have occurred to any born royal, for they all believed that any wife of David's would inevitably have to take his rank. Elizabeth, however, remembered the toing and froing about the possibilities of her rank, style and title being different from Bertie's prior to her marriage. She now insisted that Bertie could issue Letters Patent limiting the dignity of Royal Highness to David alone, and when he said that it would be neither correct nor legal to prevent a Royal Highness's wife from assuming her husband's rank 'in full measure', she countered with words to the effect, 'You are the King. You can do anything you want. And if it's not legally enforceable, do you contemplate for one moment that any court in the land will rule against you, should David be mad enough to sue?'

According to Queen Mary, Bertie did not give up without a struggle. The battle between husband and wife, the former intent on honouring his commitment to his brother, the latter determined on humiliating the woman who had prevailed where she had failed – though of course she hid behind a smokescreen of noble principles – was protracted, though without bitterness, for Elizabeth was much too clever to attack Bertie directly. She hid behind supposedly protective principles.

There was much else to occupy Bertie and Elizabeth as well, for he did nothing without consulting her, but the question of depriving David's future wife of royal rank seems to have been Elizabeth's main preoccupation during the first months of her husband's reign. While they were preparing for their coronation, which would take place on the same day in May which had been assigned for David's, she was like a dog with a bone. She was far too skilled at handling Bertie to allow herself to lose his admiration with cack-handedness, however, so Elizabeth would tread carefully, always hiding the mean streak, that had been evident since childhood, behind the high moral principles and avowed sweetness that deceived so many.

While Elizabeth's admirers and detractors can argue endlessly about whether her motives were noble or malicious, both have to agree that she was an able tactician. Moreover, she knew her man. She would wear him down with time by being as persistent and tenacious as only she could be. However, on this one issue, Bertie was proving to be eminently resistant to her persuasiveness. No amount of dire warnings about how the 'whore' would destroy the whole Royal Family could induce him to break his word to his brother. She must have realised that the only way she could prevail was by coming up with some precept that would allow him to believe he was doing the right thing by breaking his word, for, at the ninety-ninth hour, shortly before the Letters Patent were due to be issued, she mooted the inspired concept that, if the marriage between David and Wallis lasted, Bertie could always issue an amendment to the Letters Patent elevating her to the rank of Royal Highness, while if he failed to do so and she left David, he, Bertie, would be responsible for the ridiculous figure of Wallis floating around the world as Her Royal Highness Mrs. Married-For-The-Fourth-Time.

According to Elizabeth's line of reasoning, in breaking his word to the brother who had only ever been a tower of supportiveness to him for four decades, he would not be betraying him, but protecting him against the wiles of a harlot. This rationale got through to Bertie, though even he could see that David was hardly likely to be pleased. 'What a nice wedding present that will be,' Bertie remarked as he agreed to the unconstitutional and unlawful action, knowing how gutted his brother would be when he heard the news. Which he received just before his wedding on 3rd June, 1937.

Ironically, David used the identical words to describe his brother's betrayal of their agreement. He nevertheless retained the hope that it would be a temporary reversal. He clearly did not know his sister-in-law Elizabeth as well as he thought he did, if he could have entertained such optimism.

While it has always been accepted amongst people in legal circles that Bertie had no right to deprive David's wife of her royal rank, what of Elizabeth's claim, which Michael Thornton first informed the world about in *Royal Feud*, that Wallis could not be deprived of the rank of royal highness once it had been granted? Did her claim have any merit whatsoever? It did not. This was another of the wildly inconsistent propositions which Elizabeth was prone to advancing whenever it suited her purposes. One only needs to harken back to the divorces of Diana Wales and Sarah York to see what utter balderdash Elizabeth's hypothesis was. Under English Common Law, the monarch does *not* have the right to deprive a woman of her husband's rank, either before, during, or after marriage when it ends in divorce. (Annulments are different, but their consequences devolve from the nullification of an event which is deemed to have never occurred; not from anything the Crown does.)

Although Their Royal Highnesses The Princess of Wales and The Duchess of York became Diana, Princess of Wales and Sarah, Duchess of York after their divorces, contrary to popular belief, the Queen did not deprive Diana or Sarah of their honorifics of Royal Highness. This was done automatically, under Common Law. It has always been settled practice under English Common Law that a *divorcée* retains the right to use her former husband's name and title, but that she loses the honorific that accompanies it. For instance, when my parents-in-law were divorced, my mother-in-law ceased to be Her Grace The Duchess of Argyll, but remained a duchess as well as being able to call herself Duchess of Argyll. Scottish law accords with English law on this point, though the former affords women additional rights, for it is impossible north of the border to deprive a woman of a superior rank once she has acquired it. That is irrespective of whether she has acquired it by birth or marriage. For that reason, Diana, Princess of Wales would have retained the right to call herself Diana, Duchess of Rothesay even if she had married Dodi Fayed, just as how Christine, Lady de la Rue is styled as such, despite being the widow of Sir Eric de la Rue and her subsequent husband, David Liddell Grainger, whose first wife was, coincidentally, Princess Alice and the Earl of Athlone's granddaughter. Although she is also Mrs. David Liddell Grainger, until such time as she remarries, unless she marries another baronet or peer, she remains Christine, Lady de la Rue.

Although such niceties will have been known to a Scot like Elizabeth, she had pushed Bertie into doing something he did not want to, and agreed to only when he was convinced that he was acting in the best interests of David and the Monarchy.

At first, Queen Mary was also in favour of depriving Wallis of her legal entitlement. According to Princess Alice, Queen Mary genuinely loved David, but was deeply cut up by the Abdication. She did not mind so much if she stopped 'the adventuress', as she called Wallis, from prevailing, even if it resulted in temporarily estranging David from the family. George was actually her favourite child, though David ran a close second, but she was prepared to make the sacrifice, or at least adopt a wait-and-see attitude to the forthcoming marriage.

Princess Alice explained Queen Mary's feelings regarding her children. She loved George and David best because those two princes were bright and entertaining and erudite and sophisticated – qualities Queen Mary had once had, and valued always. But where David was concerned, his mother's feelings were complex. They had always been coloured by the fact that he was Prince of Wales and destined to be king. To Queen Mary, no greater role existed on this earth than King of England. It was a matter of reverence. The poor little morganatic serene highness who had never imagined, when she was being belittled at Darmstadt by the future Tsarina Alexandra because she was only par-royal, that she would one day become not only properly royal, but also a queen-empress and mother of the future King of England, had never lost her awe for royalty and all it represented. Even though she found it impossible to understand how her own son could give up the most prized role in the world for the love of a mere woman, she also appreciated that her own grandfather might well have renounced his rights of succession to the throne of Württemberg if he had been unable to marry her grandmother morganatically. And, closer to home, was a relatively unknown act of renunciation which had only been narrowly averted, involving her first fiancé, her late husband's elder brother Eddy.

Prior to being engaged to Mary, the Duke of Clarence and Avondale had fallen in love with the Catholic Princess Hélène d'Orléans, daughter of the Comte de Paris and a great-granddaughter of the last King of the French, Louis Philippe. She accepted his proposal of marriage, which Queen Victoria consented to, only after Eddy threatened to renounce his rights of succession and Hélène had agreed to convert to the Church of England. Her father, however, was adamant that not even the throne of England could induce him to accept his daughter's desertion of her faith. When she went to Rome to ask Pope Leo XIII to intercede on her behalf, and he confirmed her father's judgement, the couple split up.

Because of her own personal involvement with unequal marriages and the prospect of other renunciations, Queen Mary's attitude was more complex than has hitherto been acknowledged. Nevertheless, she was grief-stricken. Elizabeth herself recognised this, and wrote to her friend Victor Cazalet that the Abdication 'very nearly killed poor Queen Mary, there is indeed such a thing as a broken heart and hers nearly collapsed.'[6]

Elizabeth, of course, had then proceeded to take full advantage of the Dowager Queen's emotional state to drive a wedge between mother and son, just as she was driving a wedge between Bertie and David. That, however, did not stop Queen Mary from continuing to love the son whose conduct, in surrendering the greatest role in life, for the love of 'that common adventuress', as Elizabeth customarily referred to Wallis when not calling her a 'whore' or the 'lowest of the low', she found inexplicable.

It would take years for the dust to settle sufficiently for Queen Mary to become clear-sighted enough to discern what Elizabeth had been up to, and how she had allowed herself to be influenced and manipulated by her daughter-in-law. By then she was without either of the two sons she loved the most. That was not to say that the old Queen was not fond of Bertie and Harry, but she lacked the affinity with them that she had with David and George. She felt the estrangement from David acutely, especially after George was killed in a plane crash in 1943.

The Second World War, moreover, had frozen her options, even though by the end of it she could see through Elizabeth's modus operandi. According to the Revd. Philip Hart's account of what Princess Alice told him, Queen Mary had hoped that peacetime would bring about the opportunity for reconciliation. She hoped that David would be able to return to live in England and that the arrangement made between the brothers at the time of the Abdication would result in his being re-incorporated into the royal fold with the status of the youngest brother. She had tried time and again to get Bertie to soften Elizabeth's stance, but her son's consort had claimed that David's presence would undermine Bertie's authority. By this time,

Queen Mary could see that this was cant. Bertie and Elizabeth had become so popular as a result of the courage and indomitability they had shown during the war, that no one could seriously believe that David's return would undermine Bertie's position. Tellingly, even Bertie agreed with his mother on this point, but Elizabeth was as implacable as only she could be.

There might well have been practical as well as personal considerations motivating Elizabeth which neither Queen Mary nor Bertie will have wanted to confront. By now Elizabeth knew only too well that David and Wallis had spread the circumstances of her birth far and wide. She patently did not see that having them back within the royal fold would have functioned as a refutation rather than a confirmation of the rumours, and was possibly worried that they would give even greater coinage to the story than they had hitherto done, were they back in England. There might well have also been the actress's reluctance to share centre-stage with another competitor. Elizabeth still had to cope with the beautiful Princess Marina, an ever-present foil in the background functioning as a nuisance reminder of the disparity between the queen consort's highly eccentric style and the true elegance of the genuine royal. And her intransigence might have come down to something as simple as this: Elizabeth liked her own way, and the surest way of having it where David and Wallis was concerned was to perpetuate the banishment. Having them around would have represented defeat to her, and defeat was not a word in her vocabulary.

So Queen Mary waited until Bertie died before making her first independent move. As soon as she knew that David was coming to England for the funeral, she wrote to Elizabeth 'to beg & beseech of you & the girls to see him & to bury the hatchet after 15 whole years.' She wanted David back in England, with Wallis, whom she had taken to sending fond messages to in her letters to her son. She observed to Elizabeth that 'in the old days the 2 brothers were devoted to each other before that dreadful rift came. I feel grieved to have to add this extra burden on you 3 just at this moment but what can I do...' Then, in a masterful ploy that had all the hallmarks of Elizabeth at her manipulative best, Queen Mary, who regarded Elizabeth as one of the most hard-hearted individuals it had ever been her displeasure to come across, continued, 'I feel that you are so kind hearted that you will help me over what is to me a most worrying moment in the midst of the misery & suffering we are going through just now.'[7]

Faced with such a bald request so ably put, Elizabeth had no choice but to accommodate her mother-in-law, if only superficially. So she arranged to receive David in the presence of Lilibet, her husband Philip, and Margaret for tea on 13th February, 1952. Ten days later, Queen Mary wrote to her brother

Alexander and his wife Princess Alice with more naïveté than prescience, 'So that feud is over I hope, a great relief to me.'[8]

It was not, nor would it end until the Duke of Windsor's death. He too clearly had hopes that the rift would now be healed, and wrote to Elizabeth after the tea requesting another meeting. 'I can well understand your not wanting to be bothered by people at this terribly sad moment in your life. But I would very much like to have a talk with you alone before I return to America.'[9] If he expected that Elizabeth would defrost sufficiently to receive the woman who had married the man she had herself wanted to marry, he had misread his intransigent sister-in-law's character yet again. The many acts of friendship which he had shown her, and she him, while she was the Duchess of York and he Prince of Wales and King Edward VIII, meant nothing to her. Although she received him, she would never soften. He was out, and out he would stay.

David's account of the meetings is interesting. The wounds inflicted upon him had cut deeply, not only because he regarded them as unwarranted, but also because they had contravened his agreements with Bertie. He made no attempt to conceal his bitterness. He called Elizabeth and his mother 'ice-veined bitches',[10] little realising that the latter had bitter regrets about the way she had behaved towards him, and was taking steps behind the scenes to alter the scenario. But communicativeness had never been Queen Mary's strong point, and he observed that 'Mama as hard as nails but failing. When Queens fail they make less sense than others in the same state.'[11] He also stated how 'Cookie listened without comment and closed on the note that it was nice to be able to talk about Bertie with somebody who had known him so well' during his *tête-à-tête* with her. He told Wallis that 'Cookie was as sugar as I've told you,' highlighting the heartlessness beneath the mantle of hypocritical sweetness.[12]

Although David and Wallis hoped that his niece's reign would shepherd in a new age for them, they were bound to be disappointed, for, though Elizabeth had scant control over her daughters in the areas of their lives which excluded her, in those that included her, she was as determinedly authoritarian as she had always been.

This tough streak had its merits, especially in her early days as Queen. Having acquired a crown through the most dubious of means, she orchestrated a needless campaign of attrition against everyone who had had anything to do with either the Duke of Windsor or Wallis, ostensibly to 'protect the monarchy' but really to protect herself. By now she knew that all of David and Wallis's friends were aware of her parentage, so this was really a useful way of protecting herself while pretending to function for the good of the monarchy. In this, she had Queen Mary's backing as well as Bertie's. Lord Brownlow was dismissed from his post of equerry without even being notified or thanked, as was customary – and mere good manners – simply because he had followed his previous master's order to accompany Wallis to the South of France. Lady Colefax and Lady Cunard found all doors at Court closed to them, though George refused his brother's order to drop his friend, and pointedly continued to see her. Nor would Lady Cunard's reign as a leading hostess be over. During the Second World War, she lived at the Dorchester and held nightly dinner parties attended by all the Great and the Good, from the American Special Representative Averell Harriman and Winston Churchill's daughter-in-law Pam Digby Churchill to Lord Beaverbrook. Of all the Windsors' friends and associates, only Duff and Diana Cooper remained acceptable to Elizabeth. Those in the know believed it was because Elizabeth had a natural affinity with someone whose parentage was as open to question as her own.

By the time Elizabeth and Bertie had moved out of 145 Piccadilly into Buckingham Palace, the doors of their new residence had shut so firmly on the old order that it was as if David had never existed. Indeed, his stall as a Knight of the Thistle was removed. To date he is the only knight who was not expelled, whose emblems of office were eradicated. Such erasure was symptomatic of what the future held for him, for this monarchy was ruled by a queen whose self-belief was so absolute that she was genuinely convinced that anything and everything she did was Godly. This gave her the most tremendous licence to do precisely as she pleased, but fortunately for her husband, the monarchy, and the British people, she was strongly motivated to be regarded as the finest queen in Christendom. This desire, as well as her sincere belief that she and God were always on the same side, provided an element of protection against the wilder abuses many other equally ambitious political figures have possessed over the millennia. In the very act of courting popularity, she limited the scope within which she could function. Seldom has vanity had such a positive effect upon the political landscape, but, in ensuring that nothing and no one would ever dent her popularity, Elizabeth's vanity provided a most effective check.

Nevertheless, once Bertie was on the throne, Alec Hardinge and Tommy Lascelles began to see dimensions to Elizabeth and the new King which they had not perceived before. They were astonished at Bertie's complete ignorance of even the most basic Constitutional issues, though gratified by the way he always listened to them. He was far less wilful than his elder brother, who had wanted to let in that dangerous element called change. As Hugo Vickers rightly observes in his biography of Elizabeth, 'the new court was a throwback to that of George V, yet the austerity of that bearded monarch and his stately consort was now replaced by a kinder, younger, simpler, more smiling pair. If the new King was not a sparkling conversationalist, he was a sincere and dutiful man, and any lulls in the conversation were easily filled by Queen Elizabeth, who, despite her angelic smile, was more than capable of a remark that proved sharper on reflection than it seemed at the time of delivery.'[13]

Bertie's sincerity and malleability were not in doubt, but the Private Secretaries, who had naïvely believed that by substituting a malleable king for a wilful one they would have their own way, soon discovered that they were not the powers behind the throne. Elizabeth was. Much to the annoyance of both Alec Hardinge, and, later on Tommy Lascelles when Elizabeth had manoeuvred him into prime position, Bertie, though a good listener, was congenitally incapable of providing an opinion without reference to his steely wife. His refrain at all times was: 'I will just keep these papers, and let you know what I think in the morning.'[14] This, both Private Secretaries knew, meant that they would be presented with Elizabeth's opinion the following morning.

This did not make for an easy decision-making process, and when Winston Churchill became Prime Minister in 1940, and it became imperative that quick decisions be reached, he cut out the needless circuity by resorting to the expediency of meeting the King over lunch at Buckingham Palace in the presence of the Queen. Although she maintained the pretence of being the sweet and dutiful little woman who was merely following the lead of her dynamic husband, she was soon speaking on behalf of Bertie, expressing 'his' views while he sat nearby letting her do so. As far as Churchill was concerned, this was just as well, for while he appreciated Bertie's decency, constancy and quiet courage, what he admired was Elizabeth's intelligence, spunk, sagacity and perspicacity. He told his cousin, Lady Sarah Spencer-Churchill, that Elizabeth was 'a brilliant tactician; a superb queen; and one of the wiliest individuals he had ever encountered. She was magnificent if she was on your side, but you definitely did not want her as your enemy. Hitler was right to call her the most dangerous woman in the world. She was splendid. Deadly too.'

This was high praise indeed from another wily old fox. Elizabeth's primary virtues, aside from the candy-floss coating which deceived so many people into thinking she was a sweet and delicate flower of womanhood, were harsh, and as the 1930s grew to a close, it became apparent that the world was heading towards another conflagration. All over the civilised world, appeasement of Germany was viewed as the most sensible political recourse.

The British Prime Minister who had succeeded Stanley (1st Earl) Baldwin (of Bewdley) in 1937, Neville Chamberlain, was an enthusiastic appeaser, who has gone down in history as a figure of mockery because of the Munich Agreement in October 1938, when the Great Powers of Britain, France, Italy and Germany agreed to hand over the Czech Sudetenland to Germany without even consulting their ally Czechoslovakia. As this territory contained the largest armaments manufacturer in the world, and was so hilly that a German attack would have had little effect, this was an act of folly arising from the craven abandonment of an ally who had been able and willing to fight, and, if allowed to, might well have stopped Hitler in his tracks. In 1938, however, everyone wanted peace, and Elizabeth and Bertie, who were also enthusiastic appeasers, even went to the lengths of celebrating the abandonment of their Czech ally by unprecedentedly sharing the balcony of Buckingham Palace with the Prime Minister, when he returned from that notorious meeting with Hitler waving a piece of paper, which he confidently asserted assured the world 'peace in our time'.

Although there were few politicians of any note anywhere in the Western world who were not enthusiastic appeasers, with the exception of Winston Churchill, the Anschluss, which had occurred on 12th March of that year when the German Army had marched into Austria and annexed that state, and the dismantling of Czechoslovakia, put the world on notice that German ambitions might well be a threat to world peace. When the Wehrmacht occupied the remaining rump of Czechoslovakia on 16th March, 1939, Hitler's pretence, that he had only wanted the amalgamation of German-speaking territories with Germany, was revealed as the fallacy it was.

The British Government now swung into action to solidify its alliances even more intensively than it had hitherto been doing. Not that it had been slothful behind the scenes. There had been a State Visit of the King and Queen to France in July, 1938. This – or at any rate Elizabeth's part in it – had nearly had to be cancelled, for her mother died at 38 Cumberland Mansions, Bryanston Street, round the corner from Wallis's old marital home with Ernest, at 2 a.m. on 23rd June.

Because Cecilia Strathmore was not royal, there was no Court mourning, but Elizabeth and Bertie nevertheless went into mourning. The possibility of cancelling the State Visit was discussed, but Elizabeth, who had always said that the death of her mother would destroy her, dug deep within herself now that she was Queen and came up with the resources to counter her grief. Princess Louise, Duchess of Argyll, who was no fan of hers, would tell Princess Marina, Prince George, and the Argyll family that she would have been surprised indeed if Elizabeth had allowed anything but her own death to stand in her way as she soaked up all the attention and adulation a State Visit was guaranteed to bring. She also acerbically remarked that she had never before seen anyone so absolutely deploy the role of queen to erase most, if not all, human feeling from her heart. While this might well have been a jaundiced view, there was nevertheless an element of justice to it. The fact remained that majesty had so overtaken Elizabeth's personality that there was no room for deep human feeling beneath the charming shell.

Irrespective of whether Elizabeth's motive was to soak up the delights of being centre-stage or to fulfil her duty on the State Visit to Paris, or a combination of the two, she decided to proceed with it. This meant that every one of her costumes had to be changed now that she was in mourning, for these had been constructed in colour, and mourning forbade the use of colours. Mercifully, one benefit of hearing Wallis mock her as the 'Dowdy Duchess' had been her abandonment of Madame Handley Seymour. Out went the dire costumes and in came Norman Hartnell and his elegant creations. Everything he had designed for Elizabeth in colour now had to be hastily remade in white. The other mourning colours, black and purple, were deemed to be inappropriate for such an important visit to the fashion capital of the world.

This was an inspired choice and it was made by Hartnell himself after conferring with Elizabeth, who was wise enough to accept his guidance. I knew him slightly before his death in 1979, for Margaret, Duchess of Argyll had been one of his early clients and he always credited her with helping to put him on the map. She introduced me to him. He thought dressing the Royal Family had been both an honour and a pleasure. Bertie was another he credited with having enhanced his career. It was he who had come up with the idea of what would subsequently become the Elizabeth 'look'. He had shown Sir Norman, as Hartnell became in 1977, on a visit to Buckingham Palace the Winterhalter portraits of Empress Elisabeth of Austria and Empress Eugénie of the French, resplendent in ultra-feminine dresses with vast hooped skirts and yards and yards of tulle. His Majesty had decreed that this was how he wanted his wife to look. By a happy coincidence, the most popular film of all time, *Gone With The Wind*, was launched the following year and Vivien Leigh, looking just as if she had stepped out of a Winterhalter portrait, became the world's most glamorous film star as well as the woman everyone wanted to look like. And Elizabeth, though considerably plainer and fatter, had foreshadowed this look on her State Visit to Paris the year before.

Bertie and Hartnell between them had turned the Dowdy Duchess into something of a style icon. Paris went crazy over the Elizabeth look, which was ultra-feminine and exceedingly glamorous. It was also the perfect camouflage for less-then-ideal figures, while maximising the assets of a Venus. Since Elizabeth was most definitely not the latter, but a dumpy, podgy woman with a vast bust, rotund legs, and a bottom the size of the English Channel, she was giving hope to women of similar dimensions all over the world. The fashion message was: if she can look this good, so can I. All I need is a good dressmaker.

Elizabeth, of course, had an ace couturier in Norman Hartnell. She also had all the trappings to enhance the look. Aside from magnificent jewels, some of which Maggie Greville had already handed over to her, others of which she now had access to as the Queen Consort, she also had *accoutrements* which were open to few others. For instance, Hartnell relined a parasol, which had belonged to Catherine the Great, in lace and tulle to match one of Elizabeth's formal day dresses. When she unfurled it, to shade her perfect complexion from the sun, she also initiated a surge in the sale of an item that had gone out of fashion.

Although Elizabeth's wardrobe came in for favourable commentary, one thing that did not was her personal hygiene. She and Bertie were staying on the Quai d'Orsay. William C. Bullitt, the American Ambassador, was able to inform President Franklin Delano Roosevelt[15] that, notwithstanding President Albert Lebrun going to the trouble and expense of installing 'two superb bathrooms containing mosaic tubs with gold faucets which, during the stay of Their Royal Majesties, were never once used.'

Ablutions aside, the trip was a success in more ways than one. Not only did it spread goodwill with a much-needed ally against Germany, but it also catapulted Elizabeth onto another level of stardom altogether. Not only was her popularity widened, but she was perceived internationally, for the first time since Bertie's accession, as someone who suited a crown. The *arriviste* had well and truly arrived, much to her and Bertie's relief. Not to mention the relief of all those ossifier cronies who had done so much to assist her in her trajectory upwards onto the throne.

While Elizabeth was in Paris, an intriguing scenario unfolded which gave rise to the rumour that she had taken a French politician as a lover. Elizabeth went to Lanvin, then as now one of the leading couture houses in the world, for fittings for dresses which were being made for her. Percy Savage, the Australian couturier who used to work there, informed me, 'Everyone was convinced that she was having an affair with Leon Blum, the former Prime Minister of France. He used to meet her while she was having her fittings. There she would be, in her underwear, flirting outrageously in French – she spoke excellent French – while the muslin was being fitted. (Dresses were first made in muslin, then when that version fit to perfection, it was dismantled and used as a pattern from which the fabric was cut and the real dress constructed.)

'The fitters were well used to the protocol. Couturiers' ateliers were one of the main venues for ladies to meet their lovers. When the fitting was over, the fitter would leave the couple alone. They would be in one of the special fitting rooms, which were decked out with a chaise longue and was really a knocking shop more than a fitting room. The decorum, with which things were handled, was always exquisite. The fitter might say something like, "Oh, I am so thirsty I must go and have a coffee. Would Madame mind if I leave her alone for a half an hour?" And Madame would say, "My dear, you've been working so hard that I think you ought to take an hour," or, "Don't be too long, the chauffeur is picking me up at four thirty," or some such thing. It was all very elegantly done in code.

'You see, husbands never suspected that their wives would betray them during a fitting. Unless, of course, the lover happened to be someone else's husband, in which case he would realise the danger of letting his wife go to fittings on her own. You could always tell which husbands had had an affair gratis the couturier's fitting room. Those were the men who always accompanied their wives to fittings. They weren't being attentive. They were policing them, to prevent them from getting up to what the husbands themselves had got up to with other men's wives.

'The staff at Lanvin used to say that Elizabeth always made sure that she and Monsieur Blum had very lengthy sessions indeed.'

Like his colleagues at Lanvin, Percy Savage was convinced that Elizabeth and Leon Blum were lovers. I am not so sure. She and Bertie functioned as a unit. Even though they were both committed appeasers in 1938, they cannot have been blind to the danger that a resurgent Germany represented to British interests. Although Bertie was not anti-German, the same could not be said of his consort, who would have been strongly motivated to do anything she could to block German hegemony at every turn. Despite speaking excellent German as a result of Käthe Kübler's lessons – Elizabeth spoke it even better than French, according to everyone who knew her well – she was openly and rabidly anti-German, to such an extent that her other biographers have all touched upon this feature of her personality. She customarily referred to Germans as the Boche, felt that they had murdered her brother, and often advanced the viewpoint that they were a pestilence. While Bertie's prejudices were modified by his predominantly German heritage, Elizabeth, who was a very good hater indeed when her passions were engaged, had no German blood and functioned as if her hatred of the Germans would eradicate the

Germanic aspects of her husband and children's heritage. Paradoxically, this would indeed prove to be the case, at least insofar as the rebranding of the Royal Family as utterly British, instead of predominantly Germanic, was concerned. It is unlikely, though, that this happy consequence was anything but an accidental by-product of her genuine loathing of the Germans, which has been so well established that it needs no further reiteration.

Elizabeth's feelings regarding the German character aside, she believed herself to be a compassionate and big-hearted human being and was frequently moved to tears, and sometimes action, by the human condition. By 1938, no one with pretentions to humanity could have failed to be outraged by how the German Government had been dehumanising whole swathes of their own populace. As there is no doubt that Elizabeth did have a compassionate streak in her nature, and enjoyed bestowing sympathy to underdogs with almost as much relish as she aligned herself with top dogs, there is every reason to suppose that she too was outraged by the way the German Government had, since 1933, been euthanising retarded children and incurable adults; locking up homosexuals, Jehovah's Witnesses, Seventh Day Adventists, and Gypsies; and had enacted a series of race laws which prevented Jews from working at certain professions or attending certain educational fora, culminating in the Nuremberg Laws of 1935 which stripped Jews of German citizenship and the right to marry Aryans. Käthe Kübler, with whom Elizabeth was still in contact after all these years, was Jewish, and she had appealed to her former pupil for help, so Elizabeth's interest in what was happening in Germany would have been both personal as well as generalised.

Leon Blum, who had been Prime Minister of France twice between 4th June, 1936, and 10th April, 1938, was also Jewish. He too had a personal as well as a general interest in what the Nazis were up to across his northern border. He was the leader of the socialist party, SFIO, and editor of the party's newspaper *Le Populaire* as well as a contributor to the popular daily, *L'Humanitie*. It is entirely within the realms of possibility that someone as politically savvy as Elizabeth would have chosen just the sort of place no one would ever have suspected her of using, to meet with the most prominent Jew in France, as they exchanged political information that might be invaluable to both their countries, but which it was not safe to send through diplomatic or governmental channels. What better place to meet than in the fitting rooms of Lanvin, where no one would ever know the true purpose of the visits, and any onlooker would be deceived into thinking that they were engaged in love rather than political talk?

This, of course, is mere speculation. Elizabeth might well have done as Percy Savage and all the others at Lanvin, who were convinced that

Elizabeth and Blum were engaging in romantic assignations, believed. But it would be irresponsible not to propound an alternative theory for her conduct, especially as how her propensity for intrigue, and the skill and imagination with which she executed it, make it more than likely that she was indeed up to something, and that that might well have been political manoeuvring.

Blum, after all, was twenty-eight years older than Elizabeth, and the antithesis of the sort of man she had always gravitated towards. Although a celebrated ladies' man, he was pasty and scholarly-looking, as opposed to the dashing, handsome, ultra-muscular specimens of masculinity she liked. Kenneth Clark and James Stuart are only two examples that spring to mind, aside from the many nameless working-class hunks she used to drool over whilst a teenager. Though one cannot deny that it is within the realms of possibility that she did fall under the master's spell, it seems more likely that she was taking full advantage of a venue for covert operations of a non-sexual sort.

Whatever the reason for Elizabeth's meetings with Blum, she and Bertie departed from Paris with their prestige boosted immeasurably. She had even managed to live down the reputation for what Hugo Vickers justly called her 'distinct mousiness'.[16]

The following year, she and Bertie's reputation received an even greater boost when they toured Canada and the United States in May and June. They arrived in Canada at Wolf's Cove on the St. Lawrence Seaway on board the Canadian Pacific liner *Empress of Australia* days late, the ship having been forced to halt because it was enveloped by thick fog in an ice field, the like of which had not been seen since the *Titanic* had sunk in the approximate area twenty-seven years and one month before.

Their Majesties were well served by their Governor General, Lord Tweedsmuir, who was better known as John Buchan, the author of the bestseller *The Thirty-Nine Steps*, and by the Prime Minister, Mackenzie King, who had planned a cross-country tour which was the ideal mixture of grandeur and simplicity. Both Bertie and Elizabeth surpassed everyone's expectations, the former with his earnest sense of duty, the latter with her overwhelming charm and wardrobe of Hartnell dresses that came in for praise in Canada, even if the American press were dismissing her as too plump and dowdy to embody anyone's idea of what a queen should look like. Despite this disparagement, Buchan's writer's eye noted that there was far more to Elizabeth than the rather unappealing figure without pulchritude that the American press thought of her as being, while making no bones about the fact that they would have preferred sleek and chic Queen Wallis. Tommy Lascelles, who had substituted for Alec Hardinge as Private Secretary in the first of what would prove to be many displacements until Elizabeth managed to shove her former ally out of his post, wrote to tell his wife Joan on 31ˢᵗ May, 'So far, this tour is a roaring success…we must have seen well over a million people in Montreal alone.' Buchan gave credit to Elizabeth. She had 'a perfect genius for the right kind of publicity,' he observed, commenting on how the 'unrehearsed episodes here were marvellous.'[17] Whether she was plunging into a crowd of thousands to chat to some Scotsman, stretching out her hand to take one that was proffered in a sea of faces, or deliberately setting out to charm anti-British French-Canadians who proceeded to fall like nine-pins for her irresistible charm offensive, Elizabeth's sparkling, charismatic personality seduced one and all. As she and Bertie crisscrossed the country by the inevitable special train, she proved herself to be an indefatigable performer, taking care to present herself to onlookers, whether few or plenty, at the many stops it made, sometimes in the middle of nowhere. This was both public relations and political magic, and by the time she and Bertie boarded the train to Washington to meet President and Mrs. Franklin Delano Roosevelt, she had seduced the whole Canadian nation as absolutely as she had seduced Bertie. Everyone was so heady with the success of it all that King George VI, who was never known to move without conferring with his wife and true sovereign, knighted his replacement Private Secretary on the train. This sent an unmistakable message to Alec Hardinge in England.

The royal train arrived at Washington D.C.'s Union Station at 11 a.m. on Thursday, 8ᵗʰ June, 1939. No one expected the American public to embrace to its bosom either of the 'pygmies', as the American Secretary of the Interior, Harold Ickes, referred to Bertie and Elizabeth.[18] Nor were the weather conditions favourable. The capital was in the grip of a heatwave. Some days the temperature was 97°F in the shade. The humidity was almost, but not quite, as overpowering as Elizabeth's charm and self-control, which extended even to her sweat glands. While others sweated like pigs, she appeared to be cool, calm, and collected. Possibly her innate inability to proceed at anything but a snail's pace was indicative of a super-slow metabolism, and this had a positive effect upon her appearance, but she nevertheless felt the heat, writing to tell Queen Mary, it 'was ghastly. It is very damp heat, & one could hardly breathe.'[19]

The royal couple were met by the presidential couple, who drove with them to the White House, where they were being housed. Eleanor Roosevelt, no slouch where public relations were concerned, noticed how '(s)he had the most gracious manner and bowed right and left with interest, actually looking at the people in the crowd so that I am sure many of them felt that her bow was for them personally.'

The First Lady was a forthright, conscionable patrician with a deep, rather than superficial, concern for the welfare of people generally, and American womanhood in particular. Ugly rather than plain, with an even dowdier figure than Elizabeth's but with no pretentions to glamour, she had respect for her guest's acting abilities but nevertheless harboured reservations about her character. She found her act 'perfect as a Queen, gracious, informed, saying the right thing & kind,' but condemned her lack of genuine naturalness when she criticised her for being 'a little self-consciously regal.' She also acidly commented, 'Turning on graciousness like a tap is bound to affect one in time!' and showed her disapproval of Elizabeth's chilling obsession with perpetual performance by calling her a phoney in the most elegant way possible: 'I do not see how it is possible to remain so perfectly in character all the time.'[20]

Although both women were consummate professionals, and a measure of respect for a public role well acquitted existed between them, Elizabeth was not the sort of person the First Lady felt comfortable around. Moreover, Mrs. Roosevelt had been annoyed even before her guests' arrival by the demands of the royal couple which, she had been reliably informed, were really Elizabeth's. Some of them had caused offence, while others just irritation. For instance, while Tommy Lascelles was in Washington doing the pre-visit recce (reconnoitre) before the royal visit, he noticed that the dining chairs used by the presidential couple were different from the chairs used by their guests. Once this was reported back to Buckingham Palace, the demand was made for the King and Queen to sit upon chairs that were identical to the unique pair which the President and First Lady used. When he was informed that such a request could not be accommodated – its insensitivity was abhorrent to the Americans, if only because Roosevelt's chair was designed to mask his paraplegic status following an earlier bout of polio – endless other demands flooded into the White House demanding the fulfilment of the Queen's ever-lengthening list of expectations. Mrs. Roosevelt finally lost all patience when the demand was made that messengers – and chairs for them to sit upon – be posted outside the passage that connected the King and the Queen's bedrooms. This last requirement was one too many for Mrs. Roosevelt, who condemned it as 'seeming foolish to me, since the rooms were just across the hall from each other.' Had she lived in England and been privy to the gossip, that Bertie had not been granted Elizabeth's favours for many a year, 'the need for messengers might have become more understandable.'[21]

Nor were these silly demands the only thing that had put the presidential couple on their guard. Their Ambassador in Paris, William Bullitt, had warned them following Bertie and Elizabeth's Paris visit that 'the little King is beginning to feel his oats, but still remains a rather frightened boy,' while the 'little Queen', though 'a nice girl' was reminiscent of one of the female caddies who carried his golf clubs at Pitlochry in Scotland. He believed the Roosevelts would like Elizabeth 'in spite of the fact that her sister-in-law, the Princess Royal, goes about England talking about her "cheap public smile."'[22]

In the event, Elizabeth was a great success publicly, albeit less so privately with the Roosevelts. Bertie, however, compensated for any lack of regard they had for his wife, for they found him decent, sincere, and delightful, and were impressed by his simplicity and eagerness to learn. The respect that the President and his powerful wife had for Bertie would stand England in good stead during the war, and by its end, such reservations as Mrs. Roosevelt had about Elizabeth's personal sincerity had been supplanted by respect for the indomitability of her spirit. She may not have been comfortable with her one-on-one, but that is not to denigrate the genuine regard she came to have for the warrior queen whose public relations skills had done so much to keep up England's spirits at a time when it was 'the first line of America's defence against Fascism,' as President Roosevelt put it.

After Washington, Bertie and Elizabeth headed for New York, where the Governor, Herbert Lehman, and the Mayor, Fiorella La Guardia, accompanied them as they were treated to a ticker tape parade, akin to that which Queen Marie of Romania had been given some years before. Bertie and Elizabeth once more showed themselves eager to please, and please they did, so that by the time they had repaired upstate for a private visit to the presidential couple's Hyde Park Estate in Dutchess County, his mother Sara Roosevelt was able to see that her son and the English King had laid the foundations for what they hoped would be a democratic bulwark against Fascism.

Although the Americans would doubtless have preferred Queen Wallis to Queen Elizabeth, by the time Bertie and Elizabeth arrived back in England for that last summer of peace before the outbreak of World War II, they were both able to say, in fairness, that the Canadian and American visits had 'made' them. They had finally become prestigious international figures, rather than the interloping king and queen they had hitherto been perceived as being in many quarters. Hereafter, there could be no rational justification for the exclusion of David and Wallis, not that that would stop Elizabeth, because no sooner had war been declared than she was manoeuvring behind the scenes to keep David from occupying a post of any significance.

Britain declared war on Germany at 11 a.m. on Sunday, 3rd September, 1939. The day before, the British Government had issued an ultimatum demanding that Hitler's troops withdraw from Poland, which they had invaded the previous day. When this was ignored, Neville Chamberlain, the Prime Minister who had so confidently waved the piece of paper that guaranteed peace in our time, announced to the British people that the nation was now at war. A few hours later, France also declared war on Germany. World War II, which would prove to be Elizabeth and England's finest hour, had begun.

After the building of sandbanks in front of buildings, the issuing of gas masks and the evacuation of children from the cities, an eerie calm settled over Europe. Despite being at war, there was no fighting. The Phoney War, as this phase was called, had begun. Everything changed in the early hours of 10th May, when the Wehrmacht thundered into Belgium, Luxembourg and the Netherlands. The French Army, believing that the Maginot Line was impregnable, rushed to defend their ally Belgium. In so doing, they left vast swathes of their country exposed. This the German Army took full advantage of as it poured through the supposedly impenetrable Ardennes Forest into France, beginning what would prove to be the swift capitulation of all four states. Norway soon fell too, along with Neville Chamberlain, who tendered his resignation to King George VI on the evening of 10th May, 1940. He recommended that Winston Churchill be called upon to form a government.

Churchill had been one of David's most avid supporters, and neither Bertie nor Elizabeth was keen for him to become Prime Minister. However, the monarch was obliged under the British Constitution to take the advice of his ministers, and Bertie put aside whatever misgivings he and Elizabeth had and called for Churchill.

Although there was mutual suspicion of both sides, the dual monarchs, as Elizabeth and Bertie were in reality, and their Prime Minister soon developed a healthy respect for one another. This was hardly surprising, for both Churchill and Elizabeth had strong romantic streaks in their nature. Although these were tempered with aggressive ruthlessness and a highly imaginative take on life which would have seemed quixotic under normal circumstances, these were extraordinary times, and they called for extraordinary measures from extraordinary leaders. In their separate ways, Elizabeth and Churchill were the ideal wartime team, and Bertie's more plodding but more earthed approach was just the ballast the balloon needed as it took off on its journey towards victory.

Not that victory seemed likely in May of 1940. Although the Belgian King, Leopold III, was refusing to leave his overrun country, Queen Wilhelmina of the Netherlands, who had disliked the British ever since they had annexed the Dutch republics of the Transvaal and the Orange Free State during the Boer War, found herself unintentionally being forced to seek refuge in England. She managed to get to the Hook of Holland with her family and government as the Germans were swarming into her capital and boarded a British destroyer, HMS *Hereward,* which was to take them to Zeeland where she would spearhead the resistance against the invader. But the province was overrun before they reached it, so the *Hereward* steamed towards the eastern English seaport of Harwich instead.

Bertie and Elizabeth were as surprised as anyone else to have these royal refugees arrive so precipitously, but protocol required that they put the royal party up at Buckingham Palace. This they did until the end of the month, when Wilhelmina moved into a house in Eaton Square, the very address Elizabeth had thought too humble for Lady Elizabeth Bowes Lyon when her parents had moved there after vacating 20 St. James's Square. The rest of the Dutch Royal Family went to Canada, where they resided for the duration of the war. Meanwhile, Wilhelmina stayed in London, broadcasting to the Dutch Resistance and heading up a Government-in-Exile which was vociferously anti-Nazi.

Less than two weeks after Wilhelmina moved to Eaton Square, the Norwegian Royal Family arrived in London after two months on the run in their own country. King Haakon VII and Crown Prince Olav were put up at Buckingham Palace. This was hardly comfortable, as the place was covered in dust-sheets; had blacked out windows; and was run on a skeleton staff. Exactly two weeks after their arrival, Elizabeth was writing to Queen Mary on 24th May complaining in her pseudo-saccharine way that 'tho' we love having them, it is rather a bore never to be alone.'[23] Queen Mary and her son-in-law Lord Harewood came to the rescue of her unfortunate Norwegian relations, who rented his Green Street house before Elizabeth buried them underneath her sugary and selfish insincerity.

Possibly Elizabeth might have been more generous-spirited if Queen Maud had still been alive, but she had died the year before, six days short of her sixty-ninth birthday. The cause of death was given out as heart failure following an operation in which it was discovered that she had inoperable cancer. Rather than let nature run its course and treat her palliatively, Lord Dawson of Penn, her late father's doctor who had despatched him with fatal doses of morphia and cocaine, once more took matters into his own hands. Without the knowledge, consent or approval of anyone in the family, or the patient herself, Dawson administered a lethal injection. He then informed her doctors in Norway, 'When reading this account, you will agree that the Queen's sudden death was a relief and which saved her from these last painful stages of the disease both you and I know only too well.' It was with some justice that J.H.R. Ramsay would later on write in the *British Medical Journal*, 'There is no reason to think that King George V was the only patient he treated this way.' As Maud's demise proves, he was not, and Dawson's reputation for despatching inconvenient or chronically ill patients was so well known within the medical Establishment that Dawson's medical colleagues in the Royal Household composed the following doggerel:

Lord Dawson of Penn

Has killed lots of men;

So that's why we sing

God save the King.

Fortunately for her, the next royal to seek shelter at Buckingham Palace in 1940 had nothing wrong with her; otherwise Dawson would have succeeded where Hitler had failed. This was Grand Duchess Charlotte of Luxembourg, who had fled with her husband, mother, children, and government to France by car when the Germans invaded their country. When it became obvious that France would capitulate, they sought refuge in Portugal, and then split up, some going to the United States, others to Canada, and the Grand Duchess to England. Elizabeth seems to have been mightily relieved when this sovereign's stay proved to be more of a perch than a visit. Even in wartime, she was guarding her space jealously, and had little time for anyone outside of the narrow circle of admirers with whom she had always surrounded herself.

It is quite possible that Elizabeth's self-interested take on life was at least partially responsible for the howling success she was now making of being a wartime queen. Although things had changed slightly since Kenneth Clark had been 'shocked to see how little she…did with (the) day; she never rose before 11,'[24] she was nevertheless unstintingly supportive of Bertie in his great task of leading a war-torn nation. Despite this, not everyone in the family regarded her efforts as self-sacrificing. Princess Mary believed that 'she enjoyed wielding power, and it is no sacrifice to indulge one's pleasures.'

Be that as it may, Elizabeth was perpetually available whenever Bertie needed to refer to her, thrilling herself and all her admirers with what a wonderful wife and queen she was. Duty, however, did not prevent her from enjoying herself as much as she could. Once the war was properly underway, she showed herself to be her mother's true daughter, irrespective of whether they shared a genetic link or not, as she sandwiched duty between slatherings of pleasure. She surrounded herself with congenial company who played charades, Racing Demon and other silly games, or sang songs around the piano, while drinking like fish and generally following her fun-loving lead as she decreed that it was their duty to keep their spirits up.

By this time, Elizabeth had formed a drinking club, as Shawcross confirms in the official biography. Queen Mary had been very concerned about Bertie's drinking when he was younger, just as she had been about David's, and though the King was still hardly abstemious, he had cut way back on his consumption. Elizabeth had not. A war might have been raging in the vineyards of France, but she raided the wine cellars of her palaces and castles and floated on a sea of booze, never entirely sober, but never actually drunk either. Her appetite for drink was exceeded only by that for food. While most of the citizenry became thinner and thinner, as rationing was introduced and such staples as meat, sugar and coffee were doled out, only Queen Elizabeth and the very rich managed with each passing year to look more and more like overstuffed birds.

How they did so was an interesting reflection upon the landed way of life. People who owned great estates could shoot game, kill rabbits, jug hare, make their own bread and pastries, supplement egg rations with what their chickens laid, and gorge themselves on the produce their lands yielded before contributing the leftovers to their less fortunate brethren.

A rather less fair way of avoiding the restrictions of rationing was to take up residence in hotels like the Dorchester, the Savoy or Claridge's. Such establishments were exempt from rationing, and their restaurants did a thriving business throughout the war, according to Margaret, Duchess of Argyll, who lived at the Dorchester along with other Society figures like David's good friend Emerald Cunard.

Like Winston Churchill, Adolf Hitler, Josef Goebbels, Mussolini and Stalin, Elizabeth understood that wars could not be won without winning the hearts and minds of the people. This was where she and Churchill possessed a genius that no other wartime leader, with the possible exception of Josef Stalin, had. She went out of her way to stiffen people's spines with shows of courage and helpings of spirited rhetoric. Her fervent belief in the goodness and rightness of any cause she adopted, allied to her gift for choosing the apt phrase with which to inspire people to continue to sacrifice for the greater good, and her lust for adulation as she remained the centre of attention with as large an audience as could be arranged, created the perfect storm for what John Buchan had called her 'genius for the right kind of publicity'. Between 1939 and 1945, she made sure that she never missed an opportunity to let the British people know how much she admired them in the joint struggle that she and they were engaged in against the forces of evil. She was a personalist of the first order, and personalised everything she could, her own efforts especially. She made sure the populace knew that their feisty little queen was taking shooting lessons at Buckingham Palace so that she could repel the advancing Hun if they invaded. When the palace was bombed, she declared that she was happy it had been, for now she could look the East End of London, which had been more or less obliterated by carpet-bombing, in the face. This was only one of the inspired comments Elizabeth made. Another, which was also spread far and wide, gaining her the adulation of the people, was her retort to the Cabinet's recommendation that Lilibet and Margaret be sent to the safety of Canada, like the Dutch royal children: 'The Princesses would never leave without me, and I couldn't leave without the King, and the King will never leave.'

Princess Louise, Duchess of Argyll had regrettably died at the age of ninety-one in December 1939, otherwise she would most likely have shared the trenchant view of the other royals, both exiled and native, who questioned how Elizabeth's comment about staying in England had gained such wide coinage, if she herself had not broadcast it? The royal refugees were particularly upset because they felt that she had boosted herself at their expense. Implicit in her remark had been the criticism that they had been cowardly to flee their countries, while she was brave to stay in hers. This, they believed with some justice, was unfair, for she was the queen of an island nation whose surrounding seas protected her in a way that their lands abutting Germany's had not. But they were hardly in a position to break ranks with their host's wife, though many of them would never forgive her for what they considered to be vain indulgence at their expense.

By this time, Elizabeth was well and truly the star of the royal show. Queen Mary had been sent to stay in deepest Gloucestershire at Badminton House with her niece May and her husband, the 10th Duke of Beaufort. Queen Victoria's last surviving daughter, Princess Beatrice, was sent to live down at Brantridge Park in West Sussex, the country house of Queen Mary's brother, the Earl of Athlone, and his wife Princess Alice, her niece. Although Elizabeth's sisters-in-law, the Duchesses of Gloucester and Kent, remained active with public engagements in and near London, she managed to cleverly render them more unglamorous than herself by the simple expedient of having Bertie order them to appear in uniform at all times. The same went for that other royal clothes-horse, Lady Louis Mountbatten, whose slender figure and stylish couture clothes had to sit in her clothes cupboard for the duration of the war, while Elizabeth, and Elizabeth alone, went about her public engagements bedecked in couture suits from Norman Hartnell. These were invariably swathed in furs, offset by the inevitable three strands of pearls, spectacular diamond brooches, high heels, and stylish hats which showed off Elizabeth's ever-present smile.

When Elizabeth was asked if she did not consider it inappropriate for her to be seen in such finery at a time of such need, she anticipated Evita Peron and replied that the people who had come to see her put on their best clothes for her, so she was merely returning the compliment. According to Margaret, Duchess of Argyll, Princess Marina lit up the room with her riposte when news of Elizabeth's disingenuous disclaimer of her flagrant vanity got back to the most elegant member of the Royal Family.

While Elizabeth was smilingly keeping up spirits by picking her way over the rubble of bomb sites in elegant garb, her daughters' governess Marion Crawford was embarked upon a tremendous struggle to get her charges the most basic of educations. Ever since Elizabeth had poached this graduate of the Moray House Training College in Edinburgh from her sister Lady Rose Leveson-Gower over Easter 1933, there had been a tussle of wills over the girls' education. Elizabeth effectively wanted her daughters to possess social graces and wiles but no education of any substance. Bertie, not surprisingly, went along with whatever the oracle Elizabeth decreed. As the war progressed and the girls got older, the problems had become so acute that Queen Mary had to step into the breach. Crawfie stated that the Dowager Queen was 'a rock of strength and wisdom' in the many 'moments of doubt and difficulty' which were created by Elizabeth's obstinate and irresponsible attitude. In desperation, Queen Mary even roped in Elizabeth's old chum the Archbishop of Canterbury, to impress upon his obstinate friend how important it was that the next monarch should have an education that was something better than sub-standard.

Finally a programme was worked out. The day began at 9.15. Sometimes Crawfie was relieved by the Provost of Eton, Henry Marten, who came over to the castle to teach Lilibet such basics as a history of the explorers and their discoveries from Christopher Columbus to her contemporaries. He also taught her the history of America, while Sir Owen Morshead, Windsor's librarian, used to arrange tours of the castle for the girls, with instruction about what they were viewing. Over at St. George's Chapel, Canon Crawley undertook a similar task, none of which was exactly stretching two intelligent girls intellectually. None of this was much above the level of your basic country house tour, but at least it was better than nothing. To Princess Margaret's lifelong regret, this was about as good as their education got.

Crawfie used to keep in close touch with Queen Mary, writing her regular updates, such as the letter she wrote her on 23rd February, 1941, informing her that her granddaughters were 'happy and well, and are having knowledge poured in as fast as I can pour it in.'[25] Significantly, a copy was sent by Queen Mary to the Archbishop of Canterbury under cover of a separate letter dated 26th February, and is in the Lang Papers at the Lambeth Palace Library. It would be reassuring to conclude that all the parties were having their concerns alleviated, but this was not the case.

Elizabeth would prove to be as inflexible and intransigent over her daughters' education as she was over the Duke and Duchess of Windsor, who by this time had been posted to the backwater of Nassau, where David had been relegated to the insignificant post of Governor. At a time when Britain was fighting for its survival, Elizabeth not only tried to ensure that the former king's talents should go to waste, but had stepped up her vendetta against his wife. She had instructed Alec Hardinge to send Lord Lloyd, the Conservative Secretary of State for the Colonies, a diatribe of abuse about the duchess in the hope of blocking David's appointment as Governor, which Churchill wanted and she did not. After sanctimoniously hiding behind yet more high-flown verbiage about a woman with three-husbands-living being unsuitable to be a Governor's wife, as the people of the Empire were used to looking up to the King's representative, and Wallis's presence would therefore threaten the Church's position that family life was fundamental to the stability and happiness of the community, she accused her sister-in-law of being 'the lowest of the low.'26 In so doing, she exposed herself as being personally and maliciously motivated, notwithstanding her disclaimer that 'these words are written from the point of view of general policy – they are not personal' and her objections were 'on moral grounds, but in this world of broken promises and lowered standards, who is to keep a high standard of honour, but the British Empire?'27

Lord Lloyd told Lord Beaverbrook that he was astonished to have received such a letter from any woman, much less a queen, and took not-so-secret delight in processing the appointment, knowing it would infuriate Elizabeth. Thereafter, he could never look at her without seeing the viciousness and vengefulness that lurked beneath the supposedly sweet smile. She had, quite unnecessarily, lost another potential admirer.

Gradually, the tide of war, which had seemed to favour the Axis Powers so much in the first two years, turned, especially after Hitler committed the ultimate folly of declaring war on the United States following his Japanese ally's attack upon Pearl Harbor on the morning of 7th December, 1941. This compounded his folly earlier that same year of opening a second front, when on 22nd June he had launched Operation Barbarossa against the Soviet Union. By the summer of 1942 Hitler's Sixth Army was sweeping into Stalingrad, where it became bogged down in one of the fiercest battles of all time. Hitler had clearly forgotten that the Russian winter had destroyed Napoleon's *Grande Armée* and would destroy his too. By January 1943 he had awoken to the realities of losing his whole army. In an act of desperation, he promoted General Friedrich Paulus to the rank of Field Marshal, in an attempt to avert his surrender to the Soviets. No German Field Marshal had hitherto ever been captured or surrendered, but Paulus set a new precedent on 31st January, 1943. The fall of Stalingrad and his surrender were the decisive turning point of the war, and though it was by no means over, everyone thereafter knew that the tide was finally flowing in the Allies' favour.

Meanwhile, at Windsor Castle, the prospect of an end to the war was turned into a joke at the expense of Gerald Kelly. One of the leading painters and portraitists of his day, Kelly, who had been a Royal Academician since 1930 and was a member of the Royal Fine Arts Commission between 1938 and 1943, had been commissioned to paint the state portraits of the King and Queen before the outbreak of the war. An Old Etonian, he had been lodging at his old school and popping over to nearby Windsor Castle to work on his commissions. He had done some notable oil sketches, in the tradition of Sir Joshua Reynolds and the Russian masters, prior to embarking upon the full-scale works.

Once war was declared, Elizabeth invited him to move into the castle. This proved to be rather too much for some of the Household staff, for even Kelly's promotion to Keeper of the Royal Academy in 1943 could not dislodge him from the sanctity of his royal lodgings. As the historian Kenneth Rose recounted, 'It was said that to prolong his stay he would steal down to the studio at the dead of night to erase the previous day's work.'[28] Whether he actually did that, or merely dragged out the work to ensure safe and regal lodgings for as long as possible, Kelly was such good company, and Elizabeth so enjoyed the company of artists and other erudite people, that she colluded in the perpetuation of his stay. Only when the war ended in 1945 did he complete the state portraits, which were highly commended and resulted in the King knighting him. He went on to have an even more gilded career than the glittering one he had hitherto had, becoming president of the Royal Academy in 1949, and died covered in glory in 1972.

From Elizabeth's point of view, the Kelly experience had been a happy one on several fronts. She not only liked the man, but also his work. She hung one of the oil sketches of King George VI at Clarence House and often commented on how much she liked it. Ironically, her sketch accorded less with the final version than the one which I have in my collection, and which is shown in the photographic section of this book. From time to time friends would say, 'You're lucky Queen Elizabeth doesn't know that you have a better version of the Kelly state portrait than hers, otherwise she might do a Queen Mary and want you to give it to her.' I had no fear of that, for Elizabeth was not acquisitive the way Queen Mary had been, and in any event, there was little likelihood of her coming to my house to see the picture. But my friends, even the royal ones, also knew that I was one of the few people who would not have regarded a royal request as a command. My Gerald Kelly oil sketch of King George VI therefore remained safe and secure on my drawing room wall, where it still reposes.

Different people celebrated different aspects of the war in different ways. Elizabeth was no exception. If the historian Tariq Ali is to be believed, as Britain's wartime fortunes took a turn for the better, its queen consort rewarded herself with the ministrations of a handsome young Communist named Christopher Freeman. Born in 1921, and a member of the Communist Party since his student days at Abbotsholme School in Staffordshire (he would only resign in 1956 following the Soviet invasion of Hungary), 'Freeman's posting to Balmoral during the war was not an accident. Military intelligence didn't want too many Communists on the front and thought it would be funny to send this good-looking Leftie to guard the Royal Family.'[29] Patently, the powers-that-be did not appreciate Elizabeth's established susceptibility to handsome young men in uniform. Nor was Freeman just a pretty face. He was highly intelligent and an 'absolute charmer' and he and Elizabeth began a relationship that might, or might not, have culminated in more than flirtation, but definitely included a romantic element. Ali claims that Eric Hobsbawm, the supremely eminent historian who was made a Companion of Honour by the Queen in 1998, and is also the president of Birkbeck College, University of London, confirmed the relationship, while Freeman himself admitted it. Possibly that is why Chris Freeman then found himself posted to the front after his stint at Balmoral, whence he was exposed to all sorts of danger, but nevertheless managed to survive the war. He went on to have an outstanding academic career as the world's leading proponent of the science of innovative technology. He was the author of several scholarly works, a Professor of Science Policy, the winner of several international awards including the 2001 World Technology Award for Policy, and is credited with the creation of concepts which public policy institutions such as the Belfer Center for Science and International Affairs at Harvard's Kennedy School propound. By the time he died on 16th August, 2010, his romantic involvement with Elizabeth, for what it had been worth, was the least of his accomplishments.

If Elizabeth felt the need to reward herself with a flirtation, who could begrudge her? Her qualities had proven to be an inspiration to the nation in its hour of direst need. So she was an extremely aggressive woman beneath the benign and serene surface. So she believed, as she told her old friend Lord

David Cecil, that the traits a queen needed most were 'patience and anger'.[30] While Queen Marie of Romania, who had been an overwhelmingly successful queen consort in rather more difficult circumstances than Elizabeth, would not have agreed that anger had any place as a driving force, despite patience being an absolute necessity, she would have conceded that iron resolve was also a fundamental for success. And Elizabeth had such resolve in spades. Indeed, she was very open about it privately, even if she took care publicly to mask her dominating tendencies behind a façade of fluttering femininity. As she wrote and told her old friend Cosmo Lang, it was desirable to have 'a will of iron, which is all the equipment a lady needs! And as long as she can disguise her will, & use her eyes, then all will be well.'[31] She could also be frank about '(w)hat a lot of our life is spent in acting', as she wrote and told her friend D'Arcy Osborne. But how the Western world had profited from this acting ability in its hour of darkness.[32] Of course, not all her traits were admirable when viewed in isolation, or even when applied against personal adversaries, yet their amalgamation ensured that she was the ideal warrior Queen when Britain needed just such a feisty, indomitable, intransigent, hard-nosed toughie to inspire its King and populace.

Peace and Death

Chapter Eleven

As far as Elizabeth and the other European belligerents were concerned, World War II ended at 0241 hours on the morning of the 7th May, 1945, at the Supreme Headquarters for American and European Forces at Rheims in France, where General Alfred Jodl, Chief-of-Staff of the German Armed Forces High Command, signed documents unconditionally surrendering all German armed forces to the Allies. Because Russia had suffered greater losses than all the other nations combined, and Generalissimo Stalin was demanding that Germany surrender to his forces as well, General Wilhelm Keitel and other German representatives travelled to Berlin, where he unconditionally surrendered the following day at the former German Army Engineering School in the district of Karlshorst (the present German-Russian Museum), to the most decorated Russian commander of all time, be it Tsarist, Soviet, or Republican: Marshal Georgei Konstantinovitch Zhukov.

The terms of surrender required the German armed forces to lay down arms by 2301 hours Central European time on 8th May, which meant that there were effectively two Victory in Europe dates owing to the time difference between the states which were east of that time zone. For that reason, Britain and France and the Western European nations celebrate VE Day on 8th May, while Russia and its neighbours celebrate it on 9th May.

The end of the war in Europe was a massive relief to everyone concerned. In London a vast crowd congregated outside Buckingham Palace and shouted for Bertie and Elizabeth, safe in the knowledge that they were now amongst the most revered kings and queens of all time. Theirs had been a formidable accomplishment, and it could not have been achieved without Elizabeth's 'genius for the right kind of publicity' or the indomitability which was at the root of her appealing but ultimately ruthless personality.

Although Germany had been utterly destroyed, it was not the only nation that was on its knees by the end of the war. All over Europe there was devastation, including in England. Whole swathes of London had been reduced to rubble, as well as cities such as Coventry, but worse, there was no money for reconstruction. Although Britain had been a victor, the expense of the war meant that it was now broke. It was in relatively worse shape financially than any of its Allies, including France, which had capitulated early and rejoined the Allied cause late in the day. In so doing, France had saved itself much of the expense and devastation of the other Allies, though Churchill had ordered the scuppering of its navy following the Armistice in 1940, when the First World War hero Marshal Philippe Petain agreed to head the collaborationist Vichy state.

One of the first moves of the Gaullist peacetime French Government was to try the eighty-nine-year-old Hero of Verdun and the other members of his Government. Petain was found guilty of high treason and imprisoned for the remainder of his life, dying in 1951 on the island prison of Ile d'Yeu, where he is buried. He fared better than his Prime Minister, Pierre Laval, who was executed by firing squad on 15th October, 1945, along with other collaborationists. This taint, however, did not stop Elizabeth, once she was a merry widow, from associating with Laval's daughter, the Comtesse de Chambrun, and her husband Rene, who was a descendant of La Fayette, as well as the nephew of President Theodore Roosevelt's son-in-law Nicholas Longworth through his American mother Clara, and the president of the world-famous crystal manufacturer Baccarat. He was too appealing for Elizabeth to harbour old enmities, especially when they might affect her social life, which thereafter remained the central feature of her long life.

Although the English upper classes tried to resume their pre-war way of life after 1945, the main hue of the national landscape for the first decade was a depressing shade of grey. Staples, which had not been rationed during the war, now were, as the austerity policies bit under the Socialist Government headed by Prime Minister Clement (later 1st Earl) Attlee, who had trounced Winston Churchill at the polls during the post-war General Election of 26th July, 1945.

Within two years, Bertie's cousin Louis Mountbatten, (created 1st Viscount Mountbatten of Burma in 1946, and 1st Earl in 1947) was overseeing the dethronement of Bertie and Elizabeth as Emperor and Empress of India. He arrived in India as its last Viceroy with the brief of dismantling the British Raj. At 2345 hours on 14th August, 1947, it underwent the first of its death knells when the State of Pakistan came into existence under its first Governor-General and Speaker of the National Assembly, Mohammed

Ali Jinnah. Seventeen short minutes later, at 0012 hours in the morning of 15th August, 1947, the independent Dominion of India came into existence headed by Mountbatten as Governor-General and Jawaharlal Nehru, who was rumoured to be his wife Edwina's lover, as Prime Minister.

Nor were Bertie and Elizabeth the only monarchs who were being shorn of their crowns. Romania, Bulgaria, and Yugoslavia were now Communist states and either had lost, or would soon lose, their status as monarchies. Greece was involved in a bitter civil war, and though the royalists would prevail for the duration, by the 1970s that state had once again exiled its Royal Family and reverted to republicanism. The Albanian King reposed in exile, and though Italy might well have not voted its king out of power, the republic of Italy had nevertheless come into being. Hungary, which had technically remained monarchist under the Regency of Admiral Horthy, now became a republican satellite of the Soviet Union. Only Spain, under its *El Caudillo*, Generalissimo Francisco Franco, remained a monarchy. But this was a technicality that might or might not have relevance in the future, for its last anointed king, Alfonso XIII, had died in exile on 28th February, 1941, and his appointed heir, the Count of Barcelona, was whiling away his time in exile in Portugal along with other exiled actual or putative monarchs such as the former King Carol II of Romania and King Umberto II of Italy.

However, the worst consequence of the war, from a moral point of view, was the fate of Poland. Britain now found itself in what can be politely described as an anomalous position. It had ostensibly gone to war to preserve the independence of that state. Yet it and the other Western Allies had colluded with the Soviet Union and stood by silently while the Red Army pulverised Warsaw and other Polish territory prior to rolling in and establishing a satellite state in Poland, which ceased to be an independent country for nearly fifty years thereafter.

In England, the powers-that-be took a complacent view of Poland's fate, but across the water in Paris, where the Duke of Windsor was beginning the long years of exile now that Elizabeth had made it clear to him through intermediaries that she was not prepared to countenance his or Wallis's return to the United Kingdom, Elizabeth and Bertie's success as King and Queen seemed rather tarnished by the consequences of the policies their occupancy of the throne had allowed to prevail. The Duke himself felt that the re-drawing of the map of Europe, so that the Soviet Empire was even more powerful than it had been before the war or indeed even during Tsarist days, was a shame that should never have occurred. Britain had won the war but lost the peace.

Over the years, many historians have maintained that David was pro-Nazi, but his own comments, both public and private, belie that fact. Margaret, Duchess of Argyll, told me that he had been so horrified by the bloodbath of the First World War and what the Communists were up to in Russia, that he felt the most moral and expedient political policy in the run-up to the Second World War was for the West to stand by and let Hitler and Stalin fight against each other. Although he admired some of what the Third Reich had accomplished, such as the regeneration of the German economy, he was no apologist for the Führer. He nevertheless believed that Communism was a greater evil than Nazism, and used to make the point that the number of people killed under that form of government far exceeded the number the Fascists were responsible for.

David had trouble reconciling the tremendous loss of life and property sacrificed upon the altar of Poland's independence, only for the British Government of the day (headed, incidentally, by his old friend Winston Churchill) to hand over the very *casus belli* to a Head of State that was at least as bad, and most likely much worse, than Hitler had been. He doubted that the Nazis would ever have been able to implement the Final Solution without being at war with the countries whose opinions they cared about the most, namely the Anglo-Saxon nations, especially the British, and felt that while there would have been considerable loss of life in any war between the Third Reich and the Soviet Union, the West at least would have been spared. He went to his grave believing that, had he been on the throne, he might well have been able to avert England's participation in the Second World War.

David also expressed the view to Margaret Argyll that the Empire might also have survived in a more updated form, a sort of loose federation of nations under the Crown: a Commonwealth with teeth and greater meaning than the loose associations which came into being after the colonies were given independence in the fifties and sixties. He believed that Bertie and Elizabeth's style of monarchy had been disastrous for the continuation of the Empire, because they had harkened back to an age that had already passed and was already crying out for change when he, David, was touring the Empire in the 1920s and 1930s as Prince of Wales. The very policies which he had foreseen were required to modernise the British style of governance, and in so doing to preserve and perpetuate the Empire under more liberal and progressive political structures, were the ones the ossifiers had ensured would never come about, by shoving him off the throne with Elizabeth's connivance. He believed that, while Elizabeth had been very imaginative in acquiring power and adulation for herself, she had been bankrupt of ideas for progressing the monarchy. And Bertie, though basically a good man, was 'too much of a nincompoop' to have any imagination at all.

Last but not least, the Duke of Windsor believed that Baldwin and Elizabeth had given the Americans the chance which they had been seeking since the First World War, when the so-called Fourteen Points of President Woodrow Wilson's Doctrine had been propounded. This doctrine was supposed to assist self-determination, but its natural consequence was to undermine the European Empires and, in so doing, create a power vacuum into which the United States of America could step and increase its spheres of influence internationally. He believed that a liberal British Crown, served by a modernising British Government headed by a king with contemporary ideas which had been gained through his years of exposure to the countries in question, and with an American queen by his side, would have stymied America's ability during and after the Second World War to undermine the British Empire the way it had done. While such views are open to interpretation and certainly allow for contentiousness, time has nevertheless shown that they had more merit than they were contemporaneously accorded by the Duke of Windsor's critics.

It was therefore against a backdrop of public adulation but private recrimination, as well as with increasing economic austerity and declining national fortunes, that the British King and Queen tried to pick up the threads of their pre-war life. Bertie was mightily relieved that they could resume a more pleasurable and relaxed way of life, and that his daughters, who had been virtual prisoners at Windsor Castle during the war, now had more opportunities for 'fun'. Elizabeth, even more fun-loving than Bertie, was delighted that Lilibet and Margaret could become more active socially, and that the old Court functions and social calendar, which were now re-instituted, would provide a platform for them and herself. Once more, she would be able to preside over Royal Ascot, garden parties and Court levees and balls, in the couture garments which Norman Hartnell designed for her. Although stardom became her in all its guises, the occasions she liked best were the glamorous and aristocratic ones, rather than dramatic and plebeian ones like tramping over rubble. As she descended upon the West End for premieres in Scarlett O'Hara-type crinolined gowns that anticipated Christian Dior's New Look, twinkling like a Christmas tree in the jewels Maggie Greville had left her, or that she had access to through the royal collection, she did not forget the equal charms of private socialising. She entertained friends and relations with a luxuriousness that had been unthinkable during the war.

Insofar as the royal couple's romantic lives were concerned, each of them betrayed where his and her priorities lay with the way they conducted their peacetime relationships. Bertie and Elizabeth had a solid marriage, but it was in no way a contemporary one. They had not shared a bedroom since that disastrous foray up to Glamis on honeymoon, when Elizabeth had judged it necessary to develop the whooping cough that had struck out of nowhere. Although Chris Freeman had been posted abroad, and Kenneth Clark was diverted elsewhere with other extramarital interests, the romance of being queen superseded any romance a man could offer her. Such interest as she had in men did not extend to the sexual, though she enjoyed nothing more than flirting with men. As she resumed the pleasurable tenor of her life, there was no noticeable sense of deprivation just because all the handsome swains surrounding her were averse to carnal pleasures with females. She thoroughly enjoyed the gaiety that the mostly gay men in her life brought with them. Friends, Household and staff were mostly homosexual, and those that were not were so arch and camp it was hard to tell that they were not.

If Elizabeth was all show and no go, Bertie was a man who genuinely liked women. Now that the war was over, he turned his attention to three safely-married women. (The protocol in royal and aristocratic circles was that romantic attachments should only be formed between married men and married women.) For her part, Elizabeth proved herself to be as indulgent of Bertie's involvement with Rosemary Townsend, Magdalen Eldon and Camilla Sykes as she had been with Boo Laye and Maureen Stanley.

Each of these women had an interesting background, and each was stunningly good-looking in the mould of Sheila Loughborough. Rosemary Townsend was the daughter of a Deputy Lieutenant for Hertfordshire, Brigadier-General Hanbury Pawle, and as such, a member of the landed gentry. On 17th July, 1941, following a courtship of two weeks, she had married the tall, handsome and much-decorated Royal Air Force flying ace, Peter Townsend (who had brought down the first German bomber to crash in England since 1918), while he was recovering from injuries suffered in an aerial dogfight. They had two sons, Giles (1942) and Hugo (1945), for whom King George VI stood as godfather following Peter's posting to Buckingham Palace in 1944 under the Equerries of Honour Scheme.

Both Townsends were an instantaneous hit with the Royal Family. By 1946, Bertie was flirting openly with Rosemary, while Princess Margaret was making a more covert play for Peter. The sight of father and daughter behaving so flirtatiously with husband and wife under the benign and approving gaze of Queen Elizabeth was too much for people such as my father-in-law Ian Campbell (11th Duke of Argyll), who felt that the hypocrisy was unendurable. Of course he had a personal axe to grind, because he was forbidden from going to Royal Ascot as a result of having accepted blame in his divorce from Lord Beaverbrook's daughter, the Hon. Janet Aitken. But he was not alone in finding the whole spectacle laughable, despite it being no joke. Indeed, once Bertie was dead and Princess Margaret's romance with Group-Captain Peter Townsend became public knowledge, Elizabeth would find her complacent smile wiped right off her face.

By this time, Rosemary and Peter Townsend were divorced (1952) and she was married to John de Laszlo, the son of the famous Society portrait painter, Sir Philip de Laszlo. She divorced him in 1977 and married the 5th Marquess Camden in 1978. It was in that guise that my path crossed hers at various social events in London. She was always admired for her dignity, her refusal to accept any of the vast sums newspapers and publishers offered her for her memoirs, and the way she had refrained publicly from casting blame for the break-up of her marriage onto Princess Margaret. But everyone around Lady Camden said that it was after the teenaged Margaret went gangbusters to seduce her husband that the marriage had been brought to a shuddering halt. Rosemary's romantic attachment with Bertie had started after Margaret had turned Peter's head, and was incidental to the collapse of the Townsend marriage.

Magdalen Eldon was the wife of the 4th Earl of Eldon and the daughter of the 14th (by some reckoning 16th) Lord Lovat, Chief of the Clan Fraser. Her sister Veronica was married to Brigadier Sir Fitzroy Maclean, 1st Bt, whose sponsorship of Marshal Tito during the Second World War saw the ascendency of the Communist partisans over the royalists. She was no fan of the Duke of Windsor. Once, when he was a guest of her father at Beaufort Castle, he promised her a ride in his aeroplane, then promptly forgot about it. Thereafter, she would tell one and all that she wasn't surprised at the way things had turned out, for he had not been a reliable character. Her brother Brigadier Simon (Shimi) Fraser, 15th (17th) Lord Lovat, was famous during the Second World War for having ordered his personal piper, Bill Millin, to pipe his battalion ashore during the Normandy landings in 1944 in defiance of a specific order not to do so. The memorable photographs, which flew around the globe, did more good than harm to the war effort, and established the Frasers as stylists of the first order. He was also married to Rosamond Delves Broughton, the daughter of Sir Jock Delves Broughton, who was tried for, and acquitted of, the murder of the 22nd Earl of Erroll in Kenya in 1941. This saga was subsequently turned into a book and film, *White Mischief*. According to Veronica, whom I also knew slightly (she was a neighbour in Scotland), her brother-in-law and first cousin Lord Eldon was a great friend of and lord-in-waiting to King George VI. He had 'no ambitions other than to farm, fish, shoot, hunt and take photographs – all of which he did exceptionally well – and to live the life of a good and placid country gentleman.'[1] Magdalen's outstanding 'characteristic was her gaiety and bubbling sense of fun', and she was as dedicated to the Red Cross as Edwina Mountbatten was to St. John's Ambulance.[2]

The last of these beauties was Camilla Sykes. She was the daughter of Sir Thomas Wentworth Russell and wife of Christopher Sykes, second son of Sir (Tatton) Mark Sykes, 6th Bt, who has left his imprint on history as the co-author of the Sykes-Picot line, which divided up the Middle East at the end of the First World War. Their son Mark and his wife have shared Christmas lunch with me on more than one occasion over the years, and my children and I have also stayed at the Sykes family seat, Sledmere House, the magnificent 20th century reconstruction of the 18th century Palladian-style house which burnt down at the beginning of the last century, as guests of the famous diplomat's namesake grandson, who is styled Sir Tatton Sykes, 8th Baronet. Camilla Sykes would often dine *à deux* with the King at Buckingham Palace, with the blessing of Elizabeth.

If romance was in the air for Bertie and Margaret, marriage was on the cards for Lilibet, who was in love with Prince Philip of Greece. Queen Mary told Mabell Airlie, 'They have been in love for the last eighteen months. In fact, longer I think. I believe she fell in love with him the first time he went down to Windsor (during the war), but the King and Queen feel she is too young to be engaged yet. They want her to see more of the world before committing herself, and to meet other men. After all, she's only nineteen, and one is very impressionable at that age.'[3]

Elizabeth, however, wanted Lilibet to marry a British aristocrat. She even drew up a First Eleven list which included Mollie Buccleuch's son the Earl of Dalkeith and Charles, 10th Duke of Rutland, who would subsequently marry Margaret, Duchess of Argyll's daughter Frances. Another of the men on the list, whose members were trotted under Lilibet's nose in the hope that they would divert her attention away from the handsome Greek prince, was Porchy Porchester, the heir to the 6th Earl of Carnarvon, whose interesting background is recounted elsewhere in this book. He came closest of any of them to capturing Lilibet's discerning eye, for she was a true Hanoverian, in the tradition of her uncle David and great-great-grandmother Queen Victoria, who needed the spark of good looks and the fire of sexual potency to ignite their romantic interest.

Both Lord Porchester and Lord Carnarvon were technically legitimate, but if the 6th Earl's wife Tilly Losch was to be believed, he was sterile, and Young Porchy was the son of a butler gratis the Miracle Workers of Harley Street. Moreover, no one, not even the 6th Earl's mother Almina, knew if Big Porchy was actually the son of the 5th Earl, whose fame rested upon being the backer of the Tutankhamun Expedition. She had been having an affair with the half-European Prince Duleep Singh, a son of the last Maharajah of the Punjab, when she became pregnant. Almina herself was never sure who the child's father was, but as he grew up, he looked more like the half-Indian prince than the fully European earl, especially around the eyes. Since even Almina was only technically legitimate, Elizabeth had chosen a man for her daughter whose cupboard contained even more skeletons than her own. Almina's natural father had been the immensely rich banker Alfred de Rothschild, who made her his heiress, though her legal father was her mother's husband, Captain Frederick Wombwell.

Although such rackety lineage meant nothing to Elizabeth, with her putatively solidly working-class roots via Marguerite Rodiere, it did to Bertie. When he noticed that Lilibet was responding to Young Porchy's charms, he took steps to counter Elizabeth's encouragement of the suit by encouraging his young cousin Philip of Greece, whom he liked and approved of.

For her part, Elizabeth could not abide the tall, handsome, confident, assertive and independent Greek prince. He was too masculine, too direct, too straightforward for someone as courtly, circumlocutory and disingenuous as England's queen consort. The only son of Prince and Princess Andrew of Greece, Elizabeth used to refer to him as 'the Hun' notwithstanding that the Greek Royal Family is Danish in origin. Indeed, Queen Alexandra, who was a Danish princess, so disliked the Germans that she blocked the marriage of her son George to the Duke of Coburg's daughter Missy. She also ensured in 1917, when her son King George V was anglicising the British Royal Family by stripping its members of their German titles, that the only foreign royals not to lose their princely rank were her Danish cousins Princesses Helena Victoria and Marie Louise. Like Alexandra, they were Princesses of Schleswig-Holstein, the Danish duchies whence the Royal House took its name.

Elizabeth cared nothing for such distinctions. As far as she was concerned, the Schleswig-Holsteins were Huns, as were the Battenbergs. Her fabled sympathy deserted her where this son of Andrea, as Prince Andrew was known within the family, and the former Princess Alice of Battenberg, was concerned. The family was simply too unconventional and free-spirited for someone as conventional as Elizabeth, and the fact that they did not defer to her, the way British aristocrats did, only made matters worse. 'Secretly, she knew that many born-royals despised her,' her old beau Christopher Glenconner's heir Colin told me, recounting a funny story of how he witnessed a row between mother and daughter in which Princess Margaret silenced her mother with the withering riposte, 'Oh, do shut up. You weren't even born royal.'

Prince and Princess Andrew had separated in 1930, after Alice suffered a psychotic break, following which she was diagnosed with paranoid schizophrenia by Dr. Ernst Simmel at Tegel, Berlin. She was then committed to Dr. Ludwig Binswanger's sanatorium in Kreuzlingen, Switzerland. This was a well-respected institution with many celebrated patients, including Vaslav Nijinsky, the legendary ballet dancer who was also a patient while she was there. The fact that she was able to leave and function normally says much for the quality of treatment she received.

During the two years that Alice remained incarcerated at the sanatorium, her four daughters married German princes without their mother attending any of their weddings, while the nine-year-old Philip was sent to live in England with her two brothers, the former Princes George and Louis of Battenberg, now styled the 2nd Marquess of Milford Haven and Lord Louis Mountbatten. George had married Countess Nadejda Torby, another par-royal (her father was the Grand Duke Michael of Russia, her mother a half-royal double-morganatic scion of the royal houses of Luxembourg and Nassau) who had been accused during the infamous Vanderbilt custody trial of being Gloria Vanderbilt's lover. George would die at the relatively early age of forty-five of bone cancer, before the beginning of the Second World War, leaving the seventeen-year-old Prince Philip to the exclusive care of his younger brother Louis and his exotic, half-Jewish heiress wife, Edwina.

Elizabeth disliked the Mountbattens because they were too liberal and too unconventional for her taste. Although they had been close friends of David and Wallis, and although they had deserted them when pressed to do so by Elizabeth, Edwina Mountbatten had nevertheless scandalised Elizabeth by taking the famous black pianist Hutch and the celebrated Negro spiritualist Paul Robeson as lovers, prior to settling upon the aristocratic Indian political leader, Jawaharlal Nehru. Dickie, on the other hand, was known to like boys as well as girls, while Alice's breach with reality had involved her having sexual visions which Elizabeth found frankly frightening.

To make matters worse where the family-centred Elizabeth was concerned, when Alice was released from the sanatorium, she refused to have anything to do with any of her family for the next three years except for her mother, the former Princess Victoria of Hesse, who lived at Kensington Palace alongside her cousins the Princesses Louise, Duchess of Argyll and Beatrice. Thereafter, her connection to the rest of her royal relations was semi-detached, to say the least. In 1937, she saw her husband for the first time since 1930 when they both attended, along with Hermann Goering, the funeral of her daughter Cecilie, her son-in-law the Hereditary Grand Duke of Hesse, her grandchildren and their other grandmother, the Dowager Grand Duchess of

Hesse, who had been killed in that plane crash at Ostend when they were flying to London for the wedding of his brother Prince Ludwig to the Hon. Margaret Campbell-Geddes.

Elizabeth could hardly understand how someone as grand as Alice could then return to Athens (the monarchy had been restored in 1935) and, of her own free will, elect to live in a two-bedroomed apartment near the Benaki Museum, where she dedicated herself to the most unglamorous of unsung charity work rather than live the regal lifestyle. For someone as right-wing as Elizabeth, the idea of any lady, much less one with royal connections, abandoning the regal way of life to live as a simple individual, was inexplicable and disturbing, and Elizabeth did not like being disturbed any more than she could accommodate people who were radically different from herself.

What seems to have most disquieted Elizabeth about Alice, however, was that she was handicapped. She had been born deaf, and, though she could lip-read fluently in several languages, her unique combination of beauty, brightness, illness and deafness meant that she had rejected all the vanities that Elizabeth held so dear. During the Second World War, she willingly stayed in Greece, even after it was invaded by the Germans in 1941, and her nephew King George II had fled to Crete before being forced into exile. Her one concession to worldliness was to move out of her tiny flat into her rich, Bonaparte-connected brother-in-law Prince George's elegant three-storey house in Athens. From there, she worked tirelessly for the Red Cross, organising soup kitchens for the starving populace, and even visited Sweden – a perilous enterprise in wartime – under the pretext of seeing her sister Louise, the Crown Princess. Her real purpose was to acquire and smuggle into Greece much-needed medical supplies.

Alice had a genuine contempt for her own safety. She organised two shelters for stray and orphaned children and a nursing circuit for impoverished neighbourhoods. Her aunt Marie of Battenberg's son, Prince Victor zu Erbach-Schönberg, had been the German Ambassador to Greece until the German invasion in 1941, and it was assumed that a woman whose two sons-in-law, Prince Christoph of Hesse and Berthold, Margrave of Baden, had been top-ranking army officers, would be sympathetic to the Axis cause. However, when a German general visited her and asked her if there was anything he could do for her, she informed him, 'You can take your troops out of my country.'

By 1943, Alice was hiding a Jewish widow, Rachel Cohen, and two of her five children, from the Gestapo, who by now were crawling all over occupied Athens. But she was equally indifferent to Allied authority. Following the

Liberation of Greece, the British imposed a curfew which she broke with alacrity as she distributed food parcels to the needy. When warned that she could be killed, she replied that 'they tell me you don't hear the shot that kills you and in any case I am deaf. So, why worry about that?'

Elizabeth's disquiet where Alice was concerned was possibly born of her own family's experience with disability. There were two strains running in the Bowes Lyon family. The first was undiagnosed, and gave rise to the legend of the Monster of Glamis. According to Douglas's *Scots Peerage*, on 21st October, 1821, a son and heir was born to the 11th Earl of Strathmore's heir Thomas, Lord Glamis, and his wife, the former Charlotte Grimstead. Confusingly, Cockayne's *Complete Peerage* gave the date as three days earlier. The infant was so horrifically deformed that he was baptised Thomas and declared to have died. Because the midwife had left the baby in rude good health, rumours immediately started in the village, especially when no burial site or tombstone could be found for the putative deceased. Eleven months later, on 28th September, 1822, another son, again called Thomas, was born. He was normal and would inherit as the 12th Earl, while his older brother, who by rights should have succeeded to the earldom, was supposedly locked up in a secret, windowless room, fifteen feet long by ten feet wide. In 1969 the 16th Earl, Elizabeth's nephew Timothy, showed the author Michael Thornton where the room had been. By then it had been bricked up, but had once led off the present Charter Room.

The so-called Monster of Glamis's 'head ran straight into his shoulders and his arms and legs were toy-like while his chest (was) an enormous barrel, hairy as a doormat', showing that he had achieved puberty and was functional sexually. He lived to a ripe old age, being fed by a trustworthy keeper through an iron grille, but otherwise kept isolated from all human contact. The only other people who saw him were the incumbent earl and his heir, who was initiated into the secret on his twenty-first birthday. It was said that this was the reason why all the 19th and early 20th century earls of Strathmore possessed a taciturn streak, for the horror, once seen, was never forgotten.[4]

This story might seem implausible until one remembers the fate of Elizabeth's two nieces, Nerissa and Katherine Bowes Lyon, who suffered from the second, and diagnosed, disability to run in the Bowes Lyon family. The daughters of Elizabeth's brother Jock and the Hon. Fenella Hepburn-Stuart-Forbes-Trefusis, Nerissa was born on 18th February, 1919, (d. 1986) and Katherine on 4th July, 1926, ten weeks after her first cousin Princess Elizabeth of York. Both girls appeared to be normal at first, but, as they grew up and approached adulthood, they exhibited increasingly jerky movements.

Their mental capacities also degenerated gradually, especially their ability to communicate, and as their facial expressions and general demeanour became odder, it became impossible to ignore that there was something seriously wrong with them. On 5th August, 1941, both sisters were dispatched to the Royal Earlswood Institution for Mental Defectives in Surrey. Nerissa's medical notes state that she was an 'imbecile', and the fact that this was a preferred option conveys the severity of the condition the family was trying to hide. The sisters' sole visitor was their mother, who died on 19th July, 1966.

By this time, *Burke's Peerage,* the genealogical reference book for the British aristocracy and gentry, was purveying the misinformation that Nerissa and Katherine had died in 1940 and 1961. Harold (Brookie) Brooks-Baker, then the editor of *Burke's,* told me when the story broke in 1987 that the sisters were alive, 'It really is too much to have families lying to us about who is alive and who is dead. We rely upon them to provide accurate information to us as **a matter of honour.**' The emphasis was his, not mine.

How the story had emerged was almost as intriguing as how it was covered up. Hovering over the upper reaches of English Society in the 1970s and 1980s was an obsequious opportunist who called himself James Dorset. Although from a humble background, he had a brilliant mind and a ready wit, and, having achieved academic glory, went to work for Gabbitas Thring as a tutor to privileged children. This was a highly reputable organisation, and there came an inevitable parting of the ways, after he had used the contacts gained through tutoring to launch himself upon London Society. For James Dorset had hit upon a novel way to supplement his meagre wages. He would simply inform his students' parents that he could keep compromising information about them out of the newspapers. This was little short of blackmail, and when word spread about his activities, he simply changed his name from Stephen East to James Dorset and started covertly selling the type of stories to the press that he had previously got people to pay him to withhold. He had a perfect understanding about how Society worked as well as who was, and was not, of consequence in Society. This knowledge he had acquired through obsessive study of the reference books which list the genealogy of all the royal and aristocratic families of Europe. He used to boast that he owned every genealogical reference book ever published on the aristocratic and royal families of Europe, and had whole shelves of these works in his flat above the Scotch House in Knightsbridge. If you wanted to know anything about your family, you only needed to ask him. He could tell you to whom your third cousin twice removed was married, which was convenient, impressive, and flattering, for who can resist someone who finds one more interesting than one finds oneself? He also had a great sense of humour, was charming and entertaining, and possibly best of all, openly gay. This meant that all the ladies confided in him the way they did with their girlfriends, while all the husbands were happy to have him act as a substitute for them at the many social events they could not be bothered to accompany their wives to. It was, in short, a recipe for great success, and for a while, James Dorset went everywhere and saw everyone.

While his star was shining brightly, however, he was busy making himself money tipping off Nigel Dempster and the other gossip columnists about the secrets he became privy to on his peregrinations. He also had a roaring trade going on the Continent with the various magazines which published stories about royalty and aristocracy, selling preposterous tales, most of which he invented, though he did occasionally leaven the loaf with something that was true. It was he who ferreted out the fact that Princess Michael of Kent's father had been a member of the Nazi Party, and he who claimed credit for exposing the grim existence of Queen Elizabeth The Queen Mother's nieces, Nerissa Bowes Lyon, who had died the year before, and Katherine, who was still alive.

The totality of James Dorset's double-dealing would only emerge when he died in 1987. It has to be said, the timing of his death was finely judged. He had sold so many stories about so many people to so many different publications that the whole edifice of his carefully-constructed façade had started to tumble down. I was but one of the many people who by then was cold-shouldering him. Although for about two years prior to his Judas tip, he had been a sometime-walker of mine, our friendship thundered to a halt when he sold a story about me to Nigel Dempster. I had always had one inflexible rule: if you sell a story about me, you are out: ad infinitum. I was also fortunate that he didn't last out twelve months following that act of betrayal. He died, rather to my relief and that of just about everyone above the rank of baronet, of organ failure, which might or might not have been caused by AIDS, or hepatitis, or a combination of the two. 'English Society breathed a collective sigh of relief', one of the newspapers, who were a wealth of information about him once he had expired, observed while revealing the nefarious activities he had got up to making money through them. Nevertheless, he died on friendly terms with at least one member of the extended Royal Family, as I can attest to, for she telephoned me to ask if I believed the rumour going around town that he had been bumped off by MI5. I said I did not. He had gone from a short, rotund man five feet tall by five feet wide, to a skinny stick in six months, and if nature had not got him, it cannot have been MI5, for they were not known to publicly starve people to death.

How James Dorset came to find out about the grim fate of Nerissa and Katherine Bowes Lyon is something none of us will ever know, but once the story had been published, members of the family developed a justifiable dislike of him. Of course, the story of Nerissa and Katherine Bowes Lyon was intensely embarrassing for the Bowes Lyon family as well as the Royal Family, especially as Queen Elizabeth The Queen Mother was the president of Mencap, the charity for the mentally disabled, and had never once visited either of her nieces throughout the four decades of their incarceration, despite swanning about at Mencap events as if she cared deeply about the mentally handicapped.

Apologists stated that the reason why the girls had been locked away was to prevent their handicaps from discouraging the suitors of their two healthy sisters, Anne and Diana. However, Anne Bowes Lyon had married Viscount Anson, heir to the 4th Earl of Lichfield, on 28th April, 1938, at a time when both Nerissa and Katherine were still living with the family, so there was no question of their presence being a discouraging factor for potential suitors. And Diana did not marry until 1960, when she wed Peter Somervell. Prior to that, she led a full and active social life, the peak of which was being a bridesmaid to Lilibet when she married Prince Philip in 1947.

To disinterested spectators, it appeared as if the real reason for Nerissa and Katherine's incarceration was the Bowes Lyon family's pronounced interest in social pleasure to the exclusion of all else. This, allied to hypocrisy, was where detractors felt the truth lay. Anne's divorce in 1948 and remarriage, at the Chapel at Glamis Castle in 1950, certainly seemed to support the latter viewpoint, for Elizabeth managed to put aside her well-worn distaste for remarriage for women with living husbands, now that her own niece had bagged herself a prince. Up and down the drawing rooms of the land, Elizabeth's avowed objection to Wallis, so conveniently put aside now that her own family's advancement needed to be facilitated, evinced accusations of ambitious double-standards. The fact that Elizabeth tried to pay lip service to her professed, high-flown moral standards by avoiding the church service, cut no ice with anyone, especially as how she showed up at the wedding reception, dead on time for the first time in her life, congratulating the couple on having effected what, in her scheme of things, was adultery. She beamed from ear to ear, though there was no doubt that this time what the Princess Royal called her 'cheap smile' was utterly genuine and not the insincere prop of an accomplished performer.

Elizabeth's facilitation of her niece's remarriage did her reputation no good amongst the Great and the Good. The Duke of Windsor made sure that he spread the story far and wide about how she not only condoned the marriage, but actually moved heaven and earth so that the former Viscountess Anson could become a princess, when proposed to by his cousin Prince George of Denmark, a great-grandson of King Christian IX of Denmark and King Oscar II of Sweden and Norway. Normally, Danish princes who married commoners gave up their princely rank and became Counts of Rosenborg. Elizabeth, however, prevailed upon Bertie to convince his kinsman King Frederick IX that it would be humiliating for her if her niece were denied princely rank, and, not wishing to alienate the formidable Elizabeth, the Danish King agreed to make an exception in this instance. The *divorcée* Anne, Viscountess Anson therefore became Princess George of Denmark upon her marriage, and, even better still, was frequently styled as Princess Anne of Denmark. But Frederick felt sufficiently put out to complain about Elizabeth's hypocrisy to his cousin David, whose wife Wallis was still being denied her royal rank by Elizabeth and Bertie.

Although it would be some years before accusations of gross hypocrisy would be fairly levelled against Elizabeth yet again, once the story about Nerissa and Katherine Bowes Lyon being consigned to a mental institution was published in 1987, Elizabeth found her supposedly high standards being questioned publicly. For her and the rest of the Bowes Lyon family, the experience was mortifying. But not enough to actually visit. Katherine remained at the Royal Earlswood Hospital, as it was renamed, with no member of her family bothering to see her. Their excuse was that doing so would excite and therefore unsettle her, as if joy communicated in the environs of a mental institution is detrimental, though of course when it is conveyed in a London drawing room, at a historic house, or better still at a palace, it is something worth relishing.

The tragedy of both sisters was that they knew who they and their loved ones were. When they saw their Aunt Elizabeth or cousins Lilibet and Margaret on the television, they would curtsey and point to the television excitedly. They had difficulty communicating through the spoken word, but anyone who took the time to listen to them would get the gist of what they were trying to convey. In other words, they were handicapped, but not without cognition. One wonders how many 'normal' people would relish being consigned to a grim institution and thereafter ignored, all the while being aware that they have been abandoned, while their family has the means to have them cared for at home in more pleasant and loving surroundings.

In 1996, the Royal Earlswood Hospital was closed down and Katherine was moved to the less Dickensian Ketwin House, a care home in Surrey, where she remained until that too was closed down in 2001 as substandard.

At the time of writing, she remains in another nearby care home, tended by the staff, which says much about the level of care she has received, for she has lived long past her life expectancy. But still without any relationship with her own family.

What has hitherto never been revealed is that the sisters were diagnosed as suffering from Huntington's Chorea, as the disease was called when they were first institutionalised. Huntington's is a congenital, hereditary, incurable neurological disease. Its onset is usually later in life, between the ages of forty-four and fifty-five, but early-onset Huntington's can start at any age. Although it does not actually kill its victims, Huntington's does destroy the quality of their lives and their social and motor skills. It is one of the most tragic of neurological conditions, and certainly when the sisters were committed in 1941, there was little the medical profession could do to alleviate its symptoms.

Although many Huntington's sufferers do end up in institutions, in recent years there has been medical progress with the alleviation of symptoms. This has helped to extend the quality of their lives, though it remains one of the incurable neurological conditions that has an excessively high suicide rate, for many people, confronted with a diagnosis and knowing from previous generations the fate awaiting them, prefer to die rather than witness their own degeneration.

How do I know that the sisters had Huntington's Disease? Because one of the doctors who treated them, Dr. Etienne Dunnett, was the mother of a friend of mine who is herself an eminent member of the medical profession.

Of course, there were sound reasons for covering up such a devastating diagnosis. Most families with a strain of Huntington's opt not to reproduce. The mere fact that members of the Queen Mother's family suffered from it meant that word of it getting out could have damaged the marital prospects of the Royal Family. While many a girl might want to become a princess, few would want to run the risk of producing Huntington's princes and princesses. The dreaded spectre, of a possible heir to the throne being a Huntington's victim, was also something to be avoided at all costs.

Unsurprisingly, attempts were made to lay the blame firmly at the door of Fenella Trefusis's family. Even Shawcross implies in the official biography that the condition must have come from her line, and while that is possible, it is not certain. There were questions about Jock Bowes Lyon's own medical history which everyone wanted to avoid having to answer, if only because these made it possible that he himself had either suffered from Huntington's, or another, equally unappealing but undetermined neurological or mental condition.

Just prior to the Battle of Aubers Ridge in 1915, Jock had shot himself in his left forefinger. Although it was ruled an accident, shooting off one of your left fingers was a well-known ploy for avoiding battle. Indeed, Julian Fellowes even has a caddish servant, who wishes to be sent home from the trenches, do so in an episode of *Downton Abbey*.

Suspicions of cowardice were then one of the greatest disgraces that could befall any man, and Jock took care while being treated for his injury to play up suffering from chronic neurasthenia as well as having had a nervous breakdown in 1912. Thanks to family influence, he was removed from the front, and posted later that year to the Ministry of Munitions, then the Territorial Army in 1916. At the end of the war, he was twice threatened with courts-martial when he failed to show up as ordered for demobilisation. Once more, however, family influence preserved his and their good name.

It is worth remembering that many young men without influential families were shot at dawn for far less severe breaches of military discipline, and by the time he died in 1930, it was accepted that Jock was not mentally normal. His wartime experiences were blamed, though how his 1912 nervous breakdown could have been laid at Kaiser Wilhelm II's doorstep is anyone's guess.

To the medical teams dealing with Nerissa and Katherine Bowes Lyon, there was an element of compassion for the family's desire to keep the diagnosis secret. But there was round condemnation for the family's neglect of them. They had really been abandoned to their fate. As Etienne Dunnett stated, 'What horrified me above all else, was the complete lack of interest or care any member of the family showed those two sisters. In all the time that I saw them, I know for a fact that not one single member of the family ever came to visit, or enquired after them. It was as if they had already died and been forgotten. The family's conduct was inexcusable.'

When people compared how the Bowes Lyon family had behaved towards their own flesh and blood, and how Prince Philip's mother had treated strangers during the Second World War, they found it impossible to reconcile Elizabeth's sneering mockery of the woman she called 'the smoking nun' with the respect Alice really deserved. Nor did Elizabeth's lack of compassion for how Prince Philip had been abandoned by his father win her any plaudits. Prince 'Andrea' had lived a sybaritic existence in the South of France, bouncing from watering hole to watering hole with his mistress, while his son was sent to boarding school at Gordonstoun in Scotland, and farmed out to relations during the holidays.

Elizabeth, however, had an affinity with winners and an antipathy for losers. She regarded Andrea, who had been banished from Greece for life since the early 1920s, when he had been sentenced to death for treason on trumped-up charges, as a definite loser more worthy of contempt than compassion. When he died in Monte Carlo, Monaco on 3rd December, 1944, one suspects that she might even have been secretly pleased that she had one fewer connection to the louche Mountbattens, especially after Lilibet made it clear to her parents that no matter how many obstacles Elizabeth put in her way, she would marry the man she wanted. And the man she wanted was Prince Philip of Greece.

In summer 1946, Lilibet showed her mettle by asking Philip to spend a whole month with her at Balmoral. Princess Marina told Margaret Argyll that though Elizabeth and Lilibet's relationship remained superficially agreeable, both mother and daughter were now diametrically opposed. Elizabeth, completely ignoring the realities of her daughter's highly-charged Hanoverian sexuality, was still trotting chinless British wonders under her nose in the futile hope that she would settle for an antiseptic union rather than an impassioned one. Lilibet, meanwhile, was becoming more and more captivated by the rugged charms of the decidedly masculine Philip, who had a healthy interest in the opposite sex and a past which boded well for a martially-fulfilling future. This, to Elizabeth and her cronies, who included Tommy Lascelles and the senior courtiers, was a decided black mark. How could Lilibet even consider marrying a man who was so ruggedly masculine? It was 'common', they decreed, and embarked upon a whispering campaign doubting whether someone as potently masculine could remain faithful. Even more farcically, they wanted to know why any English princess would prefer a foreign prince to a British aristocrat. This merely demonstrated how right the Duke of Windsor and Chips Channon had been, nearly two decades before, to observe that the courtiers were a bunch of preposterous fogeys whose hold on reality was, at best, tenuous.

Lilibet, however, was not only her impassioned father's daughter, but also her regal grandmother Queen Mary's granddaughter. She could see no reason why any born princess should marry a commoner in preference to a royal prince, and was not about to view as a disadvantage something which any other Court in the world would have regarded as desirable. This experience was already instilling in her a healthy scepticism where her mother's double standards were concerned, and this helped her to hoe her own path irrespective of Elizabeth's prevarications.

The Government had decided to send the family on a tour of South Africa in 1947. This was partly to give the King, who was plainly in ill health, a break in the sunshine, and partly to lend support to the South African Prime Minister, Field Marshal Jan Smuts, whose assistance during the war had been so invaluable that Winston Churchill's Private Secretary, Sir John Colville, had proposed to King George VI that, should Churchill die during the war, Smuts be appointed British Prime Minister in his place. Unfortunately for Smuts, his support of the Imperial war effort had gone down less well in South Africa, where the Boers had never forgiven the British for seizing their republics, and the courtiers, displaying yet again a fundamental disconnection with reality, actually imagined that a royal tour would boost Smuts' popularity. He was voted out of power at the next election.

Before the Royal Family's departure, Lilibet and Philip decided that they wanted to get married, and she duly informed her parents. Elizabeth, still hoping that obfuscation would result in her daughter forgetting about Philip, got the ever-malleable Bertie to inform her that he would only consider giving his consent after their return from the South African tour.

While 'We Four' were away, and the English nation froze in one of the coldest winters on record, Dickie Mountbatten arranged for his nephew to renounce his rights to the Greek throne; to be received into the Anglican Church; and to acquire British citizenship via naturalisation. On 18th March, 1947, while Elizabeth was enjoying being centre stage on yet another of the royal tours she so enjoyed, and which she would continue to undertake well into old age, and Bertie, Lilibet and Margaret were being dutifully supporting acts to the real star of the royal show, Lieutenant Philip Mountbatten, RN, came into existence.

The College of Heralds had suggested that Philip anglicise the name of the Danish royal house and adopt Oldcastle as his surname, but Cheuter Ede, the Socialist Home Secretary, had advocated using the anglicised version of his mother's family instead. 'Mountbatten is certainly more glittering and grander than Oldcastle,' he declared.[5] This idea appealed to Philip's uncle Dickie even more than to Philip, who nevertheless opted for the Home Secretary's recommendation.

As soon as We Four returned from their tour, Lilibet took matters into her own hands. She informed her father that she was ready to marry Philip, and he gladly gave his consent, doubtless relieved that Elizabeth, who hated to be opposed in anything, had decided to put a gracious face on defeat and was skinning her teeth at Philip as if she had always wanted him to join the family.

On 19th July, 1947, the announcement that the King and Queen were delighted with the engagement of their daughter to the newly-minted Lieutenant Philip Mountbatten, RN, was announced. Life, for Elizabeth, would never be quite the same again. A real man, one with both backbone and compassion, had entered the Royal Family. With his royal blood, intelligence, liberal and modernising outlook that was curiously reminiscent of the last Prince of Wales's, and a self-belief that rivalled hers but did not tip over into delusional grandiosity the way hers did, he would prove to be a formidable opponent. Ultimately, his presence would break the stranglehold she had hitherto had on the Royal Family, though her very existence would stymie him in many of the changes he wished to undertake, especially in the early days of his wife's reign.

Lilibet and Philip, who was created His Royal Highness The Duke of Edinburgh, Earl of Merioneth and Baron Greenwich on the morning of the wedding, became husband and wife on 20th November, 1947, at Westminster Abbey. Royals, both reigning and exiled, poured into England from all quarters, including King Michael of Romania and his mother Queen Helen The Queen Mother, a Greek princess who was Philip's first cousin. The Communist Government in that Soviet satellite had expected their monarch to take this opportunity to flee, but when he returned to his country, having met and decided to marry Princess Anne of Bourbon-Parma (whose paternal aunt was the last Empress of Austria and whose mother was a Danish princess), they used this as the pretext to depose him and abolish the monarchy.

If royals elsewhere were being dethroned in the aftermath of Soviet ascendency, in England the former Greek prince was flourishing. Philip had come into the marriage with two suits (one a uniform, the other a well-worn lounge suit), savings of £6 10s 0d, his naval lieutenant's salary of some £11 per week, and a wife's supplementary allowance of £4 7s 6d. This was clearly not enough to support the heiress presumptive to the British throne, so Bertie gave the couple the use of Clarence House, a Crown property opposite St. James's Palace on the Mall, and Sunninghill Park in Windsor Great Park. He also approached Parliament to provide his daughter and son-in-law with adequate incomes, sending a message stating that he was 'relying on the liberality and affection of my faithful Commons.'[6] He was furious when the Leader of the House, Herbert Morrison, appointed a select committee which voted, by thirteen to five, to increase Lilibet's annuity to a mere £50,000 per annum, and to allocate Philip the measly sum of £10,000. This was insulting when compared with the £30,000 that had been awarded to Prince Albert at the time of his marriage to Queen Victoria over a century before, when the purchasing power of the pound had been five times higher.

Nor was the sum awarded for the refurbishment of Clarence House any more generous. Notwithstanding that Clarence House had not been lived in since the old Duke of Connaught had vacated it prior to the First World War, when he had moved to Bagshot Park near Windsor, only £50,000 was awarded for the works. Bertie's complaints to the Prime Minister, Clement Attlee, did not see an increase in the sum, though they did have the effect of making the fuss public at a time when the nation was in the grips of austerity. The notoriously tight-fisted monarch had to push his hand in his pocket and hand over £100,000 of his own money to his heiress so that she could begin married life in relative comfort.

While the refurbishments on both houses were taking place, the newlyweds lived at Buckingham Palace in their own suite of rooms. Unlike Elizabeth, who had pointedly preferred to live with her parents at Bruton Street rather than use the apartment King George V and Queen Mary had allocated her and Bertie at Buck House, Lilibet and Philip had nothing to hide and no wish to manipulate, so they came and went without finding their own suite of rooms the burden her mother had.

Then, just as it looked as if Sunninghill Park was taking shape, it burnt down. Arson was suspected, but the announcement was made that it had been an accident, despite a report concluding otherwise. Since it was deemed absolutely fundamental that the Edinburghs, as Lilibet and Philip were now known, would need a country house for weekends, Bertie had to dip his hands yet again into his tightly-sewn pockets. Windlesham Moor in Surrey near Windsor was rented for them.

If Bertie's relationship with his royal cousin and son-in-law was flourishing, the same could not be said of that with Elizabeth. Although she and Philip put a civil face on things, it was an open secret that there was little love lost between mother-in-law and son-in-law. As had happened with Wallis, two cocks in one walk were one too many. But Philip was a genuine rooster, Elizabeth only a pretend one despite being egotistical and authoritarian.

Philip also had one advantage. He was married to the future monarch, whose first loyalty was to her husband. This would prove to be a real boon to both Philip and Lilibet as she put much-needed distance between her domineering mother and herself.

Meanwhile, Philip was close to his royal cousins, who were spreading the word in royal circles that Elizabeth Bowes Lyon had encountered her Nemesis. Especially vociferous on this front was Princess Marina, who happily told Margaret Argyll and many other friends how her old adversary Elizabeth was now giving Philip the Monster of Glamis treatment, brushing past him at all turns with spikes laced with treacle, albeit to no avail. Marina's message was clear: Elizabeth had had her day. Although this would prove to be an over-optimistic assessment, from here on in the sugar-coated steel cages which Bertie had allowed her to construct for one and all, by deferring to her wishes and vendettas at virtually every turn, would become less and less confining.

One senior royal who was delighted with the way things were turning out was Queen Mary, who thoroughly approved of Philip. She loved the fact that Lilibet had married a prince as well as a man. Elizabeth's dislike of him, and his lack of fear of her, were welcome bonuses to the Dowager Queen who, even Shawcross concedes in the official biography, had a less than ideal relationship with her strong-willed and troublesome daughter-in-law beneath the patina of affectionate politeness.

Elizabeth, however, was much too canny to fall out openly with anyone it was in her interest to get along with. Just as she had always maintained civil relations with Queen Mary, even as she was obstructing her at every turn, she was already playing a clever game where Philip was concerned. Her smiles and sweetness did not deceive him or anyone else, but at least they made it possible for family life to unfold more easily than frankness and honesty would have done.

Elizabeth knew, as all opportunists do, that life, in its multiplicity, would present her with an opportunity to reassert herself and regain some of the control she had lost with his advent. Queens, as she had said, needed patience and anger if they are to prevail. And prevail she intended to do. On 14th November, 1948, Lilibet produced a son and heir, His Royal Highness Prince Charles of Edinburgh. This, it would turn out, was the opportunity Elizabeth had been waiting for, and she seized it wholeheartedly. She quickly established herself as a loving, indulgent, possessive and grasping grandmother in the mould of Queen Alexandra. However, unlike that queen, or Queen Mary, who never sought to undermine the parents' relationships with her own grandchildren, Elizabeth set out from the word go to do precisely that. And she succeeded brilliantly. By the time Charles was a baby, she had struck up a deep and lasting affinity with him which undermined the affection he had for either parent, but more especially, his father. For Elizabeth encouraged him to be as fey and hypersensitive and precious as she herself was, safe in the knowledge that if she left her mark on him, theirs would be the closer relationship and she would be driving a wedge between parents and child. This, indeed, proved to be the case, and the evidence for it exists not only in the observations of people who knew the family, such as Princess Marina, but also in the ordinary meaning of the comments Prince Charles made to his biographer Jonathan Dimbleby.

Two years after Charles's birth, Lilibet produced another grandchild. This time it was Princess Anne, and though Elizabeth saw a great deal of her, she never forged with her the special bond she had with Charles. Nor was the closeness replicated when Prince Andrew arrived on 19th February, 1960, or Prince Edward on 10th March, 1964. The future King remained the apple of her eye, inducing Princess Margaret to liken her mother's love of Charles to

Queen Mary's of Lilibet. 'Snobbery pure and simple. The only grandchild who counted was the one who would be the Sovereign.'[7]

Life was presenting Elizabeth with her golden opportunity, in the form of her first grandchild, to regain some of the influence which had slipped through her fingers, at a time when she was only too aware that her hold on power was increasingly tenuous because of Bertie's health. The first signs of trouble had actually occurred while Lilibet was pregnant with Charles. Bertie, in residence at the Palace of Holyroodhouse in Edinburgh for the Scottish Court in the summer of 1948, was out walking to Arthur's Seat with his equerry, Group Captain Peter Townsend, when his left leg became numb. 'What's wrong with my legs? They won't work properly,' he exclaimed.[8]

Although Bertie was not prone to exaggeration the way Elizabeth was, within weeks he was in constant pain. By the time he returned to London in October, his left leg was permanently numb. Elizabeth called in his medical team, who diagnosed Buerger's Disease.

Buerger's Disease is a form of arterial sclerosis caused by smoking. The arteries throughout the body constrict and the blood, which would circulate freely with wider, healthier arteries, ceases to reach the extremities. This can result in gangrene, which is what Bertie's doctors now feared. It was apparent that his left leg, in particular, was in danger of literally dying on him. Professor James Learmonth, whose chair in surgery was at the University of Edinburgh, was called in to assess the King's condition. Ironically, he was also a heavy smoker and would die from lung cancer in 1967. The decision was taken to avoid surgery if possible, so Bertie was prescribed bed rest and a series of exercises to improve the circulation, especially in the endangered leg.

Although Bertie was as punctilious in fulfilling the demands of his medical team as he had been in living up to expectations in every other area of his life, his condition did not improve. In March 1949, Learmonth therefore had to perform a lumbar sympathectomy in the hope of saving his leg. A grateful Bertie, horrified that the affected limb might have to be amputated, knighted him in his bedroom.

After this procedure, Bertie's health did improve slightly, though Chips Channon recorded in his diary that he had taken to wearing thick make-up to conceal his pallor. The author Michael Thornton also told me that he remembered seeing the King when he was a little boy, and wondering why his 'face was concealed beneath a thick mask of cosmetics.'[9]

For the next two years, a tentative sense of normality settled over Buckingham Palace. Although the King was obviously not in robust good health, his condition did not worsen. Bertie sensibly and compassionately advised Philip, who had ambitions to become a top-ranking naval officer, to develop his own interests and to pursue his own career, instead of hanging about like a gooseberry the way the courtiers, and Elizabeth, wanted him to. When Philip was appointed First Lieutenant of the destroyer HMS *Chequers*, the leader of the flotilla based in Malta, Bertie encouraged them to move there.

This the Edinburghs did on 17th October, 1949, beginning what Lilibet described as 'one of the happiest periods of my life.'[10] Philip's uncle, Dickie Mountbatten, who had surrendered his post as Governor-General of India, was posted there as well. He and Edwina lived in sumptuous splendour in Villa Guardamangia, which is where the young couple now made their home. For the first and last time in her life, Lilibet led a normal life. Although she had the occasional royal duty to perform, she was largely a young wife, her two children having been left behind in Britain with her parents, who cautioned against unsettling them with such an upheaval. Lilibet would go out wining, dining, and dancing. She sailed, swam, tanned on the beach and even had the (for her) extraordinary experience of going to a hairdresser's salon instead of having the hairdresser come to her.

In 1950, Philip was promoted as Commander of the frigate, HMS Magpie. It was his ambition to become the First Sea Lord like his grandfather, Prince Louis of Battenberg, 1st Marquess of Milford Haven, who had died when he was three months old. By the following summer, however, it was obvious that this would never happen. Bertie's health had once more declined, and Philip was recalled to Britain on 'indefinite leave' with Lilibet. 'The past eleven months have been the happiest of my sailor life,'[11] he told his crew as he took his leave of them in July 1951, his position of consort to the heiress presumptive taking precedence over his own career.

Bertie and Elizabeth had been due to embark upon a tour of Canada in September 1951. However, he had had a hacking cough since spring. An X-ray had revealed a shadow on his left lung, and a diagnosis of pneumonitis, a less severe form of pneumonia, was made. The prescribed cure was lots of bed rest and daily doses of penicillin. Nothing he or anyone else did could shift the cough, however, and by the time of Philip and Lilibet's return from Malta, the doctors were sufficiently concerned about the King's health to suggest the Edinburghs replace her parents on the North American tour.

Elizabeth loved tours, and had always viewed her and Bertie's tour of 1939 as 'the making of us'. She had been looking forward to another coup, especially as their stock was high as the Warrior King and Queen of World War Two, but she appreciated the necessity of the substitution, and stepped aside with good grace.

When Bertie caught a chill while out shooting at Balmoral on Princess Margaret's 21st birthday, his health took another turn for the worse. By 1st September, his condition had deteriorated to such an extent that Elizabeth sent for all the experts, whose numbers were swelled by a new addition, Clement Price Thomas, an oncologist who specialised in cancers of the chest. They advised that he return to London for an X-ray, and this he did on 7th September. On the 16th, Elizabeth learnt that he had cancer, and on the 23rd his diseased lung was removed. So too were the nerves of the larynx, to which the cancer had spread. The very real threat now existed that he would never speak in a normal voice again, if at all. This was a cruel twist of fate, for Bertie had always had a beautiful voice, and had worked so hard over so many years to overcome the stammer which had blighted it.

Lilibet and Philip had been due to depart for Canada on 25th September on board the liner *Empress of Britain*. There was talk of cancelling the tour, but Bertie would not hear of it on his account, so they flew across the Atlantic once they knew that his life was in no imminent danger.

This tour was, in many ways, the 'making' of Philip and Lilibet in the same way it had been of her parents. Although they had been the hot, young and glamorous royal couple before it, afterwards they were regarded as the most desirable young couple on earth. There were good reasons for this. Philip was a handsome man and Lilibet, though not photogenic, was extremely attractive in person. They were, in short, a young, good-looking, rather sexy couple, and though the sexuality on Lilibet's part was banked fires, Philip's robust masculinity roared eloquently at all times. Lilibet was even able to write to her mother about how the young women shrieked their approval when Philip passed them by, while the men shouted out, 'Good old Phil.'[12] If it was her intention to point out to her mother how wrong she had been to object to Philip, it was an attempt heartily wasted, for Elizabeth still continued to refer to her son-in-law as the Hun behind her daughter's back, as Princess Margaret would later tell friends.

Lilibet's public performance did not compare badly with her mother's. Though she definitely did not possess that special something which makes for a natural superstar, she was better looking, and even if she lacked Elizabeth's outgoing personality, she was nevertheless natural, down-to-earth and regal in the Queen Mary mould. She did not act the way Elizabeth did (which might have gone down well with the public, but had earned her an army of detractors closer to the throne). And Philip was, in many ways, the perfect foil for her, with his jocular humour, his ready, unstuffy wit, and down-to-earth manner. By the time the Edinburghs returned to the British Isles, the young Elizabeth had eclipsed the older Elizabeth as the reigning royal superstar, while girls all over the world were gagging for Philip in a way they never had for Bertie.

A woman as attention-seeking as Elizabeth can have hardly been pleased with being supplanted by her own daughter, but she was used to fighting off the competition, and she would do so with Lilibet, and later on Margaret, by the simple expedient of ignoring their successes and focusing on her own act. This ensured that when the family appeared together, she, Elizabeth, would be the focal point and not either of her daughters. Seeing her with them, as I did from time to time over the years, was a master-class in the art of one-upmanship. Neither daughter had her ease of manner. Neither was a born actress like her, though Princess Margaret had many of her mother's theatrical traits and was something of a ham as well as a trouper, who enjoyed nothing better than playing the chanteuse. But Margaret lacked her mother's innate ability to compel attention. Rather, she demanded it, which was an altogether cruder and less capable way of achieving it. And Lilibet, who has always had a justly deserved reputation for being an incredible mimic, nevertheless shared her sister's inability to compel attention. She could not switch on the klieg lights of superstardom the way her mother did.

Therefore, although Lilibet was a commanding presence when you met her, you could tell that much of this was a side effect of her majestic heritage, and not innate the way her mother's charisma was. Had Lilibet been just another noblewoman, she would have been no more charismatic than any other bright, pleasant, and attractive lady.

This, however, was not true of her mother. Elizabeth's light shone brightly from within, commanding attention, ensuring that, with the tilt of her head, the flick of her wrist, the twinkle of her eye, she would garner attention from all quarters and become the cynosure of all eyes. As I write this, I can see her being driven up the Mall late at night. I am waiting by the traffic lights at St. James's Palace when her Rolls-Royce passes by en route to nearby Clarence House. Even though there is no one else about, she is sitting up in the back seat, her spine a good few inches away from the seat, ramrod straight. The light in her car is on, so that her figure is spotlit. She is slowly looking from the left to the right, her face wreathed in a beatific smile. Although she is not waving, she might as well be, so obvious is it that she is still performing the majestic act she had been doing earlier that evening at Covent Garden. Her tiara is sparkling brilliantly, as is her necklace. The whole impression is one of a personage of immense importance who is shimmering brightly for onlookers.

This incident left me with a vague feeling of disquiet. Could Elizabeth be so in-character at all times that she remained 'on' even late at night on the off-chance that incidental passers-by might catch an accidental glimpse of her? Or was she the consummate professional? I asked a friend of mine, who was close to her Treasurer, Sir Ralph Anstruther, 7th Bt. The answers that came back were both affirmative.

By then, of course, Elizabeth had been a solo performer on the royal stage for nearly half a century. The solo part of her act had begun while Lilibet and Philip were on their Canadian tour and Bertie was recovering from his operation. Elizabeth had been fulfilling as many regal functions as she could. She had always enjoyed both the public and private faces of being a queen, and it is very unlikely that someone of her intelligence can have been blind to the fact that this period might well be her swansong as a queen consort. Bertie, it is true, was on the mend. He now spoke in a reedy, rasping voice, rather than the deeply mellifluous tone which he had previously had, but he did at least have the power of speech.

Whether the doctors told Elizabeth that Bertie was dying is open to conjecture. Certainly Princess Marina and the Duke of Windsor suspected as much. He came to London to see his brother and wrote asking his sister-in-law to see him, but she declined. So Queen Mary interceded, writing to Bertie to persuade Elizabeth to see him and 'to bury the hatchet at last, he seemed so anxious to see her again when he was here that awful week of yr illness, but E. could not face it, however perhaps now she might feel able to manage it.'[13]

Although Elizabeth adjudged herself too frail to receive her brother-in-law, she was robust enough to have Tommy Lascelles, the Private Secretary, arrange for the creation of a Council of State consisting of herself and her two daughters. This was the sort of inconsistency which inflamed the Duke of Windsor when word of it got back to him, for he quite rightly felt that a woman, who was too weak to receive him, could hardly be strong enough to assume the duties of the Crown. Her claim, that she was only trying to relieve her sick husband of onerous duties, struck even her die-hard admirers as disingenuous, for everyone who knew Elizabeth well saw that she thoroughly enjoyed the business of monarchy and gathered the reins in her own hands whenever she could.

In the midst of the King's recovery, there was a general election. On 25th October, 1951, the Conservatives, under the leadership of Winston Churchill, were returned to power. Six weeks later, on 9th December, the nation celebrated Bertie's recovery with a National Day of Thanksgiving.

Christmas that year was spent at Sandringham with Queen Mary. On 30th January, 1952, the family was back in London. They attended a performance of *South Pacific* at the Drury Lane Theatre. The following day a hatless, almost sepulchral Bertie, looking very much as if the Grim Reaper were hovering over his shoulder, was at London Airport with his consort to wave goodbye to his heiress presumptive and her husband, who were substituting for them yet again, this time on an Australasian tour that was scheduled to take in many a stop to and from their ultimate destination. Charles and Anne were again staying with their grandparents.

In February, Elizabeth and Bertie returned, with Charles and Anne, to Sandringham for the end of the shooting season in one of those special trains of which she was always so fond. The next few days were happy ones. On the morning of 5th February, Keepers' Day, Bertie was up bright and early to shoot rabbits. James Macdonald, who had been on Bertie's staff for twenty years, said he shot 'superbly' and was 'as gay and happy' as he had ever known him to be.[14] He was still full of the joys of the coming spring that evening, saying, 'Well Macdonald, we'll go after the hares again tomorrow.'[15]

While Bertie had been tramping the fields blasting rabbits, Elizabeth and Margaret had gone to nearby Ludham to see the well-known Norfolk landscape painter, Edward Seago. He took them for a spin in his cabin cruiser, which was moored at the bottom of his garden, after which they departed with a selection of his latest works. These Elizabeth showed Bertie, whom she went to see immediately upon arriving at Sandringham 'as I always do, & he was in tremendous form & looking so happy & well.'[16] They had a quiet but enjoyable supper with Princess Margaret, who was the apple of her father's eye, and at 10:30 Bertie said goodnight. He retired to the ground floor bedroom he was using instead of his old bedroom upstairs, for the stairs were an effort to be avoided even though tramping the shooting fields was not.

At midnight the night watchman noticed Bertie open the window to let in some air.

At 7:30 the following morning Macdonald brought Bertie's tea. He opened the curtains, drew Bertie's bath, and, realising that the King had not stirred, as he normally would have done, shook his shoulder gently. Bertie looked as if he were asleep, but when Macdonald touched his forehead, it was cold. Appreciating the significance of this, he sent a message to Elizabeth's dresser, so that she could be awakened and come immediately, then went himself to inform Sir Harold Campbell, Bertie's equerry. Elizabeth 'flew to his room, & thought that he was in a deep sleep, he looked so peaceful – and then I realised what had happened,' Elizabeth wrote Queen Mary later that day.[17]

Lilibet and Philip were on safari in Kenya, at Treetops, a tree house built over a watering hole, where they had been observing the animals, when they received the news of her father's death. She was now Queen. When her Private Secretary, Martin Charteris, asked her what name she wished to reign under, she replied, 'My own name of course – what else?' At that moment, Queen Elizabeth II came into being.

Back in England, the other Queen Elizabeth fully appreciated the enormity of her reversal of fortune. The fate of other dowager queens, including Queen Mary and Queen Alexandra, filled her with foreboding. Was it really her lot in life, to be put out to pasture, like an old and useless mare, at the relatively young age of fifty-one and a half, after only sixteen short years on the throne?

And Let There Be Fun

Chapter Twelve

The death of King George VI proved to be more devastating for Elizabeth than she or anyone else could have predicted. There were sound reasons for this, both personal and impersonal.

On the personal front, theirs had been, in several ways, a true and close union. While there was some dispute as to whether she had entered the marriage with sincere feelings for Bertie the man, there was no doubt of the depth and scope of her passion for the positions of Duchess of York and Queen of England, or of her desire to have a happy personal life.

Whether through sincerity or ambition, Elizabeth had set out to make herself an admirable wife, and had succeeded in such measure that Bertie was able to write their daughter, on the eve of her marriage, to say that he thought her mother the most wonderful person on earth. It doesn't matter whether Elizabeth's motivation was egotism or something more profound. You cannot involve yourself closely with another human being without developing a degree of intimacy, irrespective of whether that was your intention or not. Nor is it feasible to discount the degree of dependency even an independent opportunist develops for someone who worships at his or her feet. The appreciation the adored ultimately develops, over the years, for the adorer, may be an unexpected by-product of such unions, but that does not lessen its power.

Over the years, Elizabeth's life and fate had become so wrapped up with Bertie's that they had ended up functioning as a unit in many spheres. They were also true boon companions. Both of them were intensely sociable, and the ever-increasing splendour of their circumstances had provided them with a wealth of opportunities for enhancing their social lives. They enjoyed the good times together and supported each other during the bad. Even if a large part of Elizabeth's motivation had been self-interested vanity, the fact remains that she had been a magnificent and very effective handmaiden. Ultimately, the results, at least where Bertie was concerned, were superb, and if her motives were mixed, these did not lessen his regard for her.

That does not mean that their marriage had been quite as placid as the public believed. At close quarters, Elizabeth could be maddening. She always had to move at her own pace and would not, could not, be hastened. If you fell into line with her way of doing things, you were fine, but if you did not, there was no way of getting her to alter her conduct or attitude. Her stubbornness and utter disregard for what anyone said were legendary, as was her inability to be on time. This was the source of much conflict between the royal couple, especially as Bertie was so punctual that he had been known to stand and wait until the appointed time of arrival before departing from a train that was early.

Although Elizabeth was apparently placid by nature, he was highly volatile, and barely able to keep his temper in check at the best of times. The Court even had a word for these explosions, which they called the King's 'gnashes' as in gnashing your teeth with rage.

Elizabeth seemed to enjoy setting Bertie off. 'Her household was full of stories about the King losing his temper with her. Before they were due to go anywhere together, he would pace up and down, waiting, waiting. "Where is that fucking woman?" he once shouted, for he had the strong, earthy language of a sailor, and when he lost his temper, he used it.'[1] Sometimes, she would arrive apparently oblivious to the atmosphere she had created and, under the guise of re-introducing tranquillity, which would have prevailed had she not been late, she would mock him. On one memorable occasion, which is used in most biographies as an illustration of how the equable Elizabeth used her good humour to calm her crazed husband down, she marched up to him, took his hand, looked at his watch, and lightly said 'tick tock' until the outburst had ended.

Princess Marina, however, had an interesting take on such scenes. She expressed the view to Margaret, Duchess of Argyll that Elizabeth's lack of punctuality was 'determined. She enjoyed keeping people waiting. It was her way of telling them that she was more important than they were.'[2] For the same reason, she ground schedules to a halt, as she conveyed in deed though not word that her doings were more important than what anyone else had planned. Marina also believed that Elizabeth enjoyed showing people the control she had over the King. Causing him to lose his temper, then calming him down with what the Princess regarded as 'mockery posing as consideration' was nothing but the 'cheap ploy of an inveterate show-off.'[3]

Whether Elizabeth was passively aggressive or merely a self-indulgent exhibitionist who enjoyed playing to the gallery or a combination of the two, Bertie had never lost the touching regard he had had for her since their earliest days together. He remained deeply grateful that she had accepted him, and if theirs had not been the most fulfilling of marriages in all its aspects, which marriage was?

There is an interesting observation of their marriage made by Lady Diana Cooper to her husband Duff after seeing Bertie and Elizabeth at the theatre in 1926. 'They are such a sweet little couple and so fond of each other. They reminded me of us, sitting together in the box having private jokes, and in the interval when we were all in the room behind the box they slipped out, and I found them standing together in a dark corner of the passage talking happily as we might.'[4]

This observation is significant for two reasons. Firstly, it captures the companionable, almost conspiratorial element, of the marriage, which was one of its most notable features from beginning to end. Secondly, it was written by someone whose distaste for the carnal side of marriage rivalled Elizabeth's. Diana Cooper made no secret of actually befriending and sometimes even choosing her husband's mistresses. Once, at a luncheon party at which Diana Cooper and I were both guests, she actually went as far as to state that sexless marriages were often closer and more companionable than sexual ones, because they allowed the couple to be truly close without all the tension sex generated. She also said that Duff Cooper's death in 1954 had left a hole in her life that no one, and nothing, had been able to fill.

Although Elizabeth would be more successful in filling the gap left by Bertie's death, she too was now discovering that she missed her adorer more than she had ever believed possible. This evidently came as a shock to Elizabeth as well as to everyone around her, if only because she had coped so well with the deaths she had previously predicted would devastate her. For instance, she had always said that she had no idea how she would cope with her mother's demise, but when Cecilia died in 1938, Elizabeth herself had been surprised by how well she had managed. Her father's death at the age of eighty-nine from bronchitis on 7th November, 1944, had also left barely a mark, though she might have fared less well had she realised that the dying Claude had told Dr. Ayles, who was attending upon him at Glamis Castle, that his youngest daughter Elizabeth and youngest son David were not the children of his wife Cecilia, but the cook, Marguerite Rodiere. The dying man had been so proud of the accomplishments of his two youngest children, and of the way Cecilia had raised them, that he had finally confirmed what had only been gossip prior to his admission.

While I was writing this book, the chatelaine of one of Scotland's most beautiful historic houses, who is also one of Scotland's most established social figures, told me point blank that I would be doing everyone a disservice if I did not include the dying Earl's remarks to Dr. Ayles.

The death of a king always engenders greater excitement than the death of a commoner, but even so, the period between death and funeral is always a period of frantic activity. This provides a welcome distraction, especially if the passing is sudden, albeit not entirely unexpected. While George VI was lying in state at Westminster Hall, Elizabeth and her two daughters were diverted by the array of foreign guests who flooded into London for the funeral. So too was Queen Mary, who had now lost three sons, though Elizabeth, in her letter of condolence to her mother-in-law, forgot about the epileptic Prince John and mentioned only Bertie and George. The Court was plunged into full Mourning, which meant the cancellation of all celebrations, but that did not mean the suspension of the civilities which governed royal protocol. There were visits to be made and received; letters to be written and to receive; people to see and be seen by.

Like many another widow, Elizabeth was buoyed by the activity surrounding her until after Bertie's funeral in St. George's Chapel, Windsor Castle, on 15th February, 1952. Afterwards, however, she went into a real slump. The adored had not only lost her adorer, but the consummate performer had lost her platform.

For Elizabeth, Bertie's death therefore had not only personal but also practical ramifications. Dowager queens were expected to retire from public life. Although they were still called upon to undertake the occasional public engagement, and be seen at the occasional official event, they immediately became peripheral to the main action and performed, so to speak, from the wings, leaving centre stage to the new incumbents. Queen Alexandra and Queen Mary had both done so without any trouble, but then, neither the former Princess Alexandra of Denmark nor the former Princess May of Teck had lived for the limelight the way the former Lady Elizabeth Bowes Lyon did. Indeed, they had viewed their widowhood as an opportunity to be free of the many public demands made upon a monarch's consort. Retirement had been welcome to them, and indeed at the end of the Second World War, when Queen Mary was informed that she would have to leave the seclusion of Badminton House in Gloucestershire for the official splendours of Marlborough House in London, she had bemoaned the fact that she would have to stop being herself and become Queen Mary again.

As Eleanor Roosevelt and many others had noted, however, Elizabeth and her public role were inseparable and interchangeable. She welcomed seclusion no more than any other professional actress does the waning of the spotlight and the removal of her platform. Who would see her if she could no longer perform? Certainly she delighted in the admiration of those closest to her, but only in the way a great diva values the box-seat holders in a theatre. And audiences consist of many different categories of ticket-holder, all necessary to the constitution of the whole. Just as how stall-holders are revered by performers, so too are those who sit in the gods, and everyone in between. To deprive Elizabeth of her majestic platform would be like depriving the great Eleanora Duse or Sarah Bernhardt of their stages, hence why the latter was still playing to the galleries even after she had had a leg amputated.

Three days after Bertie's funeral, Elizabeth fired the first shot in her attempt to avoid being relegated to the shadows. She issued an articulate and moving message to the nation through Bertie's Private Secretary, Tommy Lascelles.

'I want to send this message of thanks to a great multitude of people – to you who, from all parts of the world, have been giving me your sympathy and affection throughout these dark days. I want you to know how your concern for me has upheld me in my sorrow, and how proud you have made me by your wonderful tributes to my dear husband, a great and noble King.

'No man had a deeper sense than he of duty and of service, and no one was more full of compassion for his fellow men. He loved you all, every one of you, most truly. That, you know, was what he always tried to tell you in his yearly message at Christmas; that was the pledge that he took at the most sacred moment of his Coronation fifteen years ago.

'Now I am left alone, to do what I can to honour that pledge without him. Throughout our married life we have tried, the King and I, to fulfil with all our hearts and all our strength the great task of service that was laid upon us. My own wish now is that I may be allowed to continue the work we sought to do together.'

The Duke of Windsor said that as soon as he saw Elizabeth's message, he knew that she would do everything in her power to remain centre stage. Whether Lilibet would allow it remained to be seen. Nevertheless, her statement contained a disturbing indication of her failure to understand what her role had truly been. She had only ever been the queen consort. Although she had frequently acted as if she had been the sovereign, and had indeed been handed power by her husband, she nevertheless had taken no coronation oath and made no pledge because she had not actually been the monarch. No dowager queen in history had ever been allowed to continue to fulfil her late husband's pledge, if only because the pledge was unique to him and died with him. It was not transferable, which is what Elizabeth was now trying to make it.

Although Elizabeth was trying to avoid a life in the shadows, there were practical issues to deal with, such as where she would now live. The sovereign's official London residence was Buckingham Palace, and now that she was no longer married to the King, Elizabeth would have to vacate it. Windsor Castle, Balmoral and Sandringham were also no longer her residences, and though she and the King had always retained Royal Lodge, and it would continue to be hers, she no longer had a London base. Clarence House had recently been refurbished for Lilibet and Philip, and the new Queen was suggesting that her mother move there, when she and her family moved into Buckingham Palace.

Shawcross puts Elizabeth's reaction to the loss of the status quo well: 'The prospect of leaving the Palace distressed her. On at least one occasion she collapsed in tears on discussing her inevitable move with the Queen.'[5] Not only was Elizabeth disconsolate at having to vacate the sovereign's official residence, but her sense of grandeur was affronted by where it was being suggested she move to.

Elizabeth was not a canny operator for nothing, and she now tried playing for time. Princess Marina told Margaret, Duchess of Argyll that she believed Elizabeth was hoping to delay the move until Queen Mary, who was visibly fading, had died. She had her eye on Marlborough House, which was a far more splendid residence than Clarence House and had, moreover, been the dower house of the last two dowager queens. She shrewdly appreciated that it would be much harder for her to acquire Marlborough House if Queen Mary died after she had moved into the less palatial residence, so she suggested to her daughter that she and Philip move into the Belgian Suite on the ground floor at Buck House while she would remain upstairs in her own rooms on the first floor 'and I could be quite self contained upstairs, meals etc, and you would hardly know I was there'.[6] She said she wanted to move 'without any ghastly hurry' as 'I know it took Granny some months to pack up everything & I fear I shall need some time too. But what is a few months in a lifetime anyway!'[7]

If Elizabeth was playing a waiting game in the hope that Marlborough House would fall into her lap, celerity was her hallmark as she utilised her influence with her late husband's courtiers to ensure that she perpetuated her, and their, power. New reigns usually signalled new appointments, and Lascelles can have been under no illusions that he would be replaced as the monarch's Private Secretary sooner rather than later, unless he acted quickly and effectively. He was well known to be an Elizabeth man, and have made his contempt for and disapproval of Philip too well known. Both he and

Elizabeth knew that her son-in-law would be arguing behind the scenes for his replacement, and indeed he was replaced the following year.

Bertie, however, had only been dead for two weeks before Elizabeth was informing Lascelles that she wanted to continue to act as a Counsellor of State, as she had been during the King's reign. She said, 'Naturally I would like this, as it would give me an interest, & having been one, it seems so dull to be relegated to the "no earthly use" class.'[8] This, coming from the woman who had said that the Duke of Windsor should start his own charity if he wanted to do something useful, was a bit rich, but consistency had never been Elizabeth's strong point.

On the other hand, determination was. Under the Regency Act of 1937 (amended 1943), her eligibility to act as a Counsellor of State, in the event of the Sovereign's incapacity or absence abroad, had lain in her status as the monarch's spouse. This was now Philip, who would share the honours with the four most senior adult heirs-in-line to the throne. Legislation would have to be introduced to permit Elizabeth to continue to have her hands on the reins of power, the way it had been at the beginning of Bertie's reign – at her behest.

How Elizabeth and her cronies went about securing power in the new reign was instructive. Before Lilibet had even returned to the realm, they had instituted a whispering campaign against Philip and his uncle, Lord Mountbatten, alleging that both nephew and uncle were intent on radicalising the monarchy even more dramatically than Edward VIII would have done.

Mountbatten's elder daughter Patricia, then Lady Brabourne and now the present Countess Mountbatten of Burma in her own right, said, 'My father was considered pink – very progressive. The worry was that Prince Philip would bring into Court modern ideas and make people uncomfortable.'

My father-in-law, the Hereditary Master of The Queen's Household in Scotland, confirmed to my sister-in-law Lady Jean Campbell that he was but one of the many people attached to the Court who were nobbled with alarmist stories. The message was clear. The only way to preserve the institution in its present form was to create a solid phalanx of opposition against the Mountbattens by increasing Elizabeth's powers and keeping the courtiers in place who had served the monarchy so well to date.

Philip and Lilibet now found themselves in a similar position to her uncle David when he had succeeded to the throne. Lord Beaverbrook saw this immediately, but it is doubtful that Philip did. He was a novice to intrigue, and in any event he was too straightforward and honourable a character to ever descend to the Machiavellian tactics of Elizabeth and the ossifiers. It is doubtful he even appreciated what they were up to until it was too late.

By then, 'Philip was constantly being squashed, snubbed, ticked off, rapped over the knuckles,' Patricia's husband John, the 7th Lord Brabourne, said.

Nor did the vain-glorious but essentially straightforward Dickie Mountbatten possess the acumen to notice what was afoot. Although he was politically liberal and delighted in the dynastic heights which his family had reached, his sole worldly ambition was to become First Sea Lord like his father. The idea that he wished to grasp the reins of power was frankly preposterous, as Dame Barbara Cartland confirmed over lunch at Camfield House in the 1980s when the subject arose. Although one could have dismissed her denials as loyalty (she had actually harboured hopes of marrying him and remained one of his closest friends until his assassination in 1979), not one iota of proof has ever been furnished to support the assertion that either he or Philip had the ambitions which Elizabeth and the ossifiers set about claiming they had as soon as Bertie was dead.

Nevertheless, Dickie Mountbatten's overweening dynastic pride provided the cabal with the weapon they needed to strike right at the heart of power. Within days of Lilibet's accession, he was telling anyone who would listen that the House of Mountbatten now reigned. While this was technically correct – just as how the House of Hanover had given way to the House of Saxe-Coburg-Gotha, so too had the House of Windsor to the House of Mountbatten once Lilibet married Philip and acceded to the throne – that was all Elizabeth and the ossifiers needed to hear before using it as proof that their direst fears and most far-fetched suspicions were well-founded.

An examination of the sequence of events, however, shows that Elizabeth and the ossifiers had moved long before Mountbatten had even opened up his mouth. Sir Martin Gilliat, Elizabeth's Private Secretary, would confirm that 'the manoeuvrings of a few well-placed courtiers and members of the government, who were jockeying for positions of influence over the new monarch,' placed Lilibet and Philip's marriage under a strain as soon as she succeeded to the throne.[9]

The first official ceremony of any new reign is the Accession Council. This was chosen by the ossifiers as the shot across the young couple's bow. Just before ten o'clock on the morning of 8th February, 1952, they left Clarence House and headed to adjacent St. James's Palace. They made for the main entrance of the palace, from which the Levee Room and Throne Room are accessible. No sooner did they reach the door, however, than the unimaginable happened. The officials handling the ceremony informed the new Queen that protocol forbade her husband from accompanying her. He lacked the precedence. That honour had to go to her uncle Harry, the Duke of Gloucester. Philip's access was firmly blocked and he had to gain admittance through a back door with his Private Secretary, Michael Parker.

The ossifiers continued as they had begun. On 25th February, 1952, intent on maintaining as much influence as they could, Lascelles and Elizabeth worked on Lilibet to obtain her consent to approach the Prime Minister and the Lord Chancellor about changing the law so that Elizabeth could remain a Counsellor of State. The following day Lascelles was writing to Elizabeth to inform her that the matter was in hand, and on 1st April, he was informing her that her daughter had approved a submission from the Prime Minister to include Elizabeth's name, following that of the Duke of Edinburgh, but before the four actual heirs to the throne, as a Counsellor of State.

In the official biography, Shawcross hints at the desire of the powers-that-be to remain in power. 'The Private Secretary, the Lord Chamberlain, the Keeper of the Privy Purse, the Master of the Horse, the Surveyor of the Queen's Pictures – all of these and many more wanted to serve their new monarch and wanted her to see them do so. They wanted access to the Queen, not to her husband,' he maintains, ignoring the fact that they were also Elizabeth's men; they had her ear and actually spoke with her words; and Philip had given no indication of wishing to usurp his wife's role. On the other hand, the same could not be said of Elizabeth. Even Lascelles, who was now actively colluding with her to increase her powers as a dowager, complains in his diaries that Bertie could never tell him what he thought about anything until after he had consulted Elizabeth. She had been, in everything but name, the *de facto* monarch.

Before King George VI was even warm in his grave, Elizabeth and her cronies had found a rich vein to mine by making the source of conflict the name of the dynasty. They had alighted upon a highly emotive issue, and one, moreover, which aroused prejudices which Philip would find difficult to counter. They could argue, as they did, that Windsor was a British name while Mountbatten, though anglicised, had its roots in Germany. In so doing, they played upon the Hun's supposed German antecedents, when of course the Danish Royal Family are Danes, not Germans, and Philip was no Hun. They also stated that the British people would not want their Royal Family to have a German name, certainly not so soon after the war, quite forgetting that Mountbatten was not German but English. They had taken the struggle straight to Philip and Lilibet's greatest vulnerability: that part of their ancestry which was German. Then Elizabeth demonstrated why Hitler had been right to call her the most dangerous woman in the world. She cannily got Queen Mary involved.

The old queen's sister-in-law Princess Alice, Countess of Athlone would later tell the Revd. Philip Hart that Mary herself claimed that Elizabeth had approached her to obtain her support for the name remaining Windsor, and to oppose recognition of the dynasty as Mountbatten. 'I am not sure Queen Mary realised what she was getting involved with,' the aged princess told the Anglican priest, for she had lived to see the damage these machinations wrought, while Queen Mary did not. The marriage of Lilibet and Philip might well have been a casualty, and certainly suffered strain for years thereafter as a result of this issue. Nevertheless, it has to be said that Queen Mary genuinely believed that the name should remain Windsor as it was quintessentially English. It also had the merit of being linked to none of the dynasties whence the Royal Family came.

Once Elizabeth had obtained Queen Mary's approval for the name to remain Windsor, the ossifiers got the matter raised in Cabinet, where they had some well-placed friends, chief of whom were the Prime Minister, Winston Churchill, and Bobbety, the 5th Marquess of Salisbury. He was Lord President of the Council, Leader of the House of Lords, and Secretary of State for Commonwealth Relations. Conversely, Lilibet and Philip, being the new kids on the block, had no friends whatever.

What the new Queen did have, however, was a sovereign's right. Just as how her grandfather had had the right to change his dynasty's name from Saxe-Coburg-Gotha, so too did she. She was no more bound by his ruling than he had been by any preceding monarch's. However, she was new to the throne, young, inexperienced, and fearful of making errors of judgement. Which, when you stop to consider the Duke of Windsor's fate, might have been the preservative that ensured that she kept the throne, even if her marriage underwent a degree of strain as a result of the Cabinet's recommendation, which was that the dynasty's name could not be changed to Mountbatten.

Philip's reaction was bitter. He stated that he had been treated no better than an 'amoeba' and with justice made the observation that he was the only man in the country whose children could not bear his name. The fact that Lilibet herself had never borne her family's true name of Saxe-Coburg-Gotha, but had contented herself with the fabrication of Windsor, seems to have been lost on him.

Amidst a backdrop of bitter diversionary wrangling, Elizabeth, sweet as ever on the surface, was playing her cards shrewdly. She was increasing her power while avoiding a diminution of her lifestyle. Dowager queens customarily reduced their households. She, however, had no intention of doing any such thing. As far as she was concerned, nothing could be too grand for her. She therefore hid behind her renowned sentimentality and conveyed the message that she was too tender-hearted to relieve anyone of their duties. As days became weeks, and weeks months, it became apparent that her household would remain the size of a reigning monarch's.

Nor did Elizabeth concern herself with trivialities like where the funding was coming from to maintain this lavish lifestyle. She had trained Lilibet well, and knew that in any conflict between her daughter and herself, she was liable to win. All she needed to do was hold her nerve and wait for Lilibet to crack. Which she, being a loving and dutiful daughter, would do, time and time again, but even more quickly now than in the future, for her marriage with Philip had suddenly become decidedly rocky thanks to the machinations of the ossifiers, and she needed the stability her mother appeared to offer more than ever.

This dichotomy is where the children of conniving parents often get hoisted unknowingly on unseen petards. They seek refuge at the very source of their problems. While there is some doubt as to whether Lilibet actually ever came to a full appreciation of her mother's character, there is none where Princess Margaret was concerned. Before long, she would see right through her mother. Thereafter, she could be extremely rude about her, as Lady Gladwyn observed when the two women went to stay in Paris at the British Embassy while she was the Ambassadress.

That first June of her widowhood, after Elizabeth had sown such seeds of discord, she headed up to Balmoral. She had grown used to the drama of government, and missed Bertie and all the majestic manoeuvrings which had gone along with the role of queen consort. She told Queen Mary, 'Life seems incredibly meaningless without him – I miss him every moment of the day.'[10] A week later she was at the northernmost tip of mainland Britain, staying near John O'Groats with her friends Clare and Doris Vyner. She was out driving with her hosts when she caught sight of 'this romantic looking castle down by the sea. And then the next day I discovered it was going to be pulled down. I thought that would be a terrible pity.'[11] Elizabeth, who liked nothing better than a project which required conquest, had found herself a new scheme with which to divert herself.

Barrogill Castle had been built by the 4th Earl of Caithness for his second son, and was originally named the Castle of Mey. It was the northernmost castle in the British Isles, but its history was riven with murder and strife, and the name had been changed after the Earl, who succeeded in 1789, inherited it from yet another brother who had been murdered.

The romance and drama of Barrogill appealed to Elizabeth, who decided that she must have it. She offered to buy it from the owner, Captain F.B. Imbert-Terry, but he declined to sell it to her, though he was prepared to give it to her. After an elegant quadrille of negotiations, she paid him the nominal sum of £100. It was the first, and would be the last, property she ever owned, and she soon set about restoring it with enthusiasm.

This, however, was hardly a project which would occupy all her time.

Elizabeth returned south, to Sandringham, where she reminded her daughter that Bertie had told his mother that she must continue to regard Sandringham as her own home. 'I would so love it if you would say that to me too,' she wrote Lilibet on 21st July, 1952.[12] Two days later, the dutiful daughter responded stating that 'of course' her mother must continue to treat the house as her home. Significantly, Queen Mary had not taken Bertie up on his unprompted offer. She had avoided staying at Sandringham once she was widowed except on the rarest of instances, but Elizabeth would thereafter take full advantage of the response she had elicited and continued treating the house as her own.

After her birthday, Elizabeth headed northwards in keeping with her established pattern of migration. This time, however, the trip was not particularly welcome. She had to vacate Balmoral and move into Birkhall. Notwithstanding that the latter had been her Scottish home during her supposedly happy days as the Duchess of York, when she had professed to love it and wanted no elevation beyond her then-status as a royal duchess, she now complained that it was 'cramped'[13] and 'rather awful'[14] and she would give anything to be allowed to remain in the castle. However, her antics over the Mountbatten name had not endeared her to Philip, and even if Lilibet had been inclined to allow her mother to continue in situ, the son-in-law she called the Hun behind his back was not.

Even before King George VI's death, Lilibet's marriage to Philip had reduced Elizabeth's power within the family circle. This might well have been one of the features which appealed to Lilibet about her testosterone-driven husband. Had she married one of the men Elizabeth had wanted for her, she would have remained under the thrall of her mother. However, she had opted to marry someone whose personality was even stronger than her mother's, but who had greater compassion and individualism. Because Philip had no compunction about taking on his strong-willed mother-in-law, Lilibet had obtained by virtue of his presence the dual advantages of breaking her mother's spellbinding hold over the family, while also replicating its familiar and reassuring potency with a more liberating entity. Philip respected her in a way that her mother would never have done, so his very existence was a way of escaping from her control. A measure of the power marrying Philip had given Lilibet can be seen from the comment made by Tommy Lascelles' good friend Dermot Morrah shortly after the marriage. 'I know the Prince is the one person who can bully the King and Queen when they are inclined to be stuffy.'[15] He might have added: or when she is also being the candy-coated dominatrix she can be.

Widowhood, however, had disempowered the dominating Elizabeth even more than the acquisition of a strong son-in-law. As she adjusted to her new circumstances, they had little appeal for her. She disliked the lack of stimulation that went along with a reduction in her importance and found it depressing to adjust to the downscaling required of her life as a widow. Even though she had done her level best to inflate the position of dowager, there was no escaping the fact: she was now an incidental player on the stage of monarchy.

How Elizabeth set about remedying that problem is a master-class in the art of achieving your objectives irrespective of the parameters which exist as apparent preventatives. Like most great performers, she had the ability to communicate emotion to a degree that few normal human beings possess. She now deployed this talent to garner sympathy, and through it, to change her circumstances. There is little doubt that her misery was absolute, but had it been more for the loss of a beloved husband than the loss of a beloved platform, it is likely she would not have hammed things up the way she now did.

Several people, including Princess Marina, thought that Elizabeth set out to embarrass Lilibet and the government into upgrading the position of dowager queen so that she could return to the spotlight she so relished. In their opinion, her supposed misery was an act, though I am not so sure. Having known one or two Elizabeths in my time, I have observed that their grief is as heartfelt as yours or mine, and no less painful for being selfish and shallow rather than selfless and deep. Indeed, there is even a school of thought which says that it can be more difficult for them to cope with reversals of fortune than normal people, precisely because they lack the resources that their less vain compatriots possess.

There is some evidence to support Princess Marina's contention. Elizabeth had seen the Prime Minister, Winston Churchill, at dinner at the Salisburys' on 1st August. Knowing how supportive Bobbety and Betty Salisbury would be, she had played the brave pathetic to perfection. This, however, had not elicited the response she sought, so she set about staging a new scene. When Churchill arrived at Balmoral for his annual Prime Ministerial visit, she was conspicuously morose in a wholly uncharacteristic way. Churchill had a strongly sentimental streak in his nature, and it was Lord Beaverbrook's view that Elizabeth played upon this skilfully. She got her lady-in-waiting, Lady Jean Rankin, to suggest to him that he drop in unannounced on 2nd October, knowing full well that he would be moved by the sight of the distraught widow pining for a lost and useful life. Churchill fell right into the trap, and managed to convince the grieving widow that the nation still required her shining light. She must not hide herself away in the Scottish Highlands becoming more and more depressed. She should re-join the troupe. Or, as Jean Rankin put it, 'I think he must have said things which made her realise how important it was for her to carry on, how much people wanted her to do things as she had before.'[16]

Note the words: 'to do things as she had before.' These are significant because Lady Jean was actually saying that Elizabeth had managed to get the Prime Minister to recommend that her role be upgraded so that she would in effect be accorded the stature of a second consort rather than a dowager queen. This was unprecedented, and could well have caused problems, had Lilibet been anywhere near as vain and competitive as her mother was. Churchill, after all, was advocating that Elizabeth return to the royal stage in a principal role, knowing full well that Lilibet would be obliged to accept his recommendation, for constitutional monarchs are required to accept the recommendations of their Prime Minister on matters of state policy. One can only hope that Churchill had cleared the offer with Lilibet first, otherwise he had ambushed her into sharing the glory if not the power of the throne.

As the 12th Earl of Stair's daughter observed, Elizabeth's mood lifted as soon as she heard what the Prime Minister had to say. Thereafter sadness was banished and joyousness, which was Elizabeth's natural habitat – as long as it co-existed with attention – was re-established. The superstar performer would soon be back where she had always wanted to be. Centre stage.

To accomplish this, Elizabeth had managed to uphcave a system that had been established for hundreds of years. In so doing, she had shown for the second time since the Abdication what a canny operator she was, possibly even a maverick who could overturn any established order if it stood in the way of her desires.

Even the title Elizabeth had chosen in widowhood befitted the grandiosity which was such a feature of her personality, and which she had now been given the opportunity to indulge for the remainder of her life. Two weeks after Bertie's death, she had announced that she wished in future to be known as Queen Elizabeth The Queen Mother. Although she would tell Lilibet that it was a 'horrible name',[17] one only needed to look through her correspondence, to see how often she called things she loved awful or horrible. The Duke and Duchess of Windsor seemed to be nearer the truth than their denialistic sister-in-law when they observed, 'She managed to get queen twice into one title.'[18] She could, of course, have opted for The Dowager Queen Elizabeth, 'but that would have denied her the pleasure of being queen twice over,' as her brother-in-law David drily observed. Since remaining Queen Elizabeth alone was not an option, the way Queen Mary had remained Queen Mary, if only because it would be too confusing to have Queen Elizabeth and Queen Elizabeth II floating around virtually indistinguishable, she was now doubly a queen in one name.

Just as how Stalingrad had been a turning point in the Second World War, Churchill's talk with Elizabeth proved to be the event that saw the tide flowing once more in her favour. For the first time in her life, she could create for herself the sort of life she wanted without thought of anyone else. She no longer had powerful parents-in-law to pander to, or a husband to consider as she worked her way round him to achieve whatever it was she wanted. She was a solo act, and, now that the Prime Minister had indicated that she could function once again at the level of splendour she required, she could construct a lifestyle that was wholly pleasing.

When Bertie had been alive, life had had to revolve around him. That he allowed her to do as she pleased did not alter the fact that she had had to factor him, his concerns and interests into every equation. Although he had spoken with her words, she had had to use his mouth. Now she could use her own. She did not need to think of him. She need think of herself and herself alone. And she did. Colin Glenconner told me, 'Queen Elizabeth is the most self-centred woman I have ever met.' He also used some rather choice adjectives to describe her which are best left to the imagination, though he repeated almost verbatim what Margaret, Duchess of Argyll said Princess Marina had told her: Elizabeth was a 'witch' but you were at liberty to spell that word with the second letter in the alphabet if the mood took you.

For someone who was notoriously lazy, Elizabeth was also extremely energetic when she chose to bestir herself. As she swung into action to establish herself in her new role as the second consort in the land, her ladies-in-waiting kept a journal of her activities, and would continue to do so throughout the five decades separating Bertie's death from her own. These show that her public life revolved around her charities, the army and the church, while her private life was dominated by her interest in the ballet, music, art, horse racing and entertaining.

Until Princess Margaret's marriage, mother and daughter were a frequent double act for gala events, though Elizabeth was always the central point, with Margaret relegated to the supporting role. I remember the Princess when she was young, and she was genuinely beautiful. Even so, protocol required that queens ranked before princesses, so Margaret had to follow in her mother's wake. Protocol in England also prevented single women from wearing tiaras, so Elizabeth would alight blazing from the tip of her coroneted head to the toe of her sparkling shoes like a bejewelled doll, while

Margaret had to rely solely upon her natural beauty.

'Queen Elizabeth did everything in her power to eclipse PM,' Colin Glenconner said. 'She resented her for being better looking than she had ever been, as well as for being her father's favourite. The King had adored her. Queen Elizabeth had had to put up with that while the King was alive, but she hadn't liked it. She had to be the centre of attention and if anyone stole her limelight, she resented it. PM stole **a lot** of her limelight, especially from the King, and while there was little she could do about it while he was alive, once he was dead, it was payback time.'

Because Bertie had not been told that he was dying, he had not made adequate provision for his younger daughter in his will. Had he known his days were numbered, there is little doubt that he would have ensured that she was financially secure for life. He would have taken steps to buy her a country house which was accessible to London for her to use later on as a weekend retreat, along the lines of Coppins, which Princess Victoria had lived in after her mother Queen Alexandra's death, and which she had in turn left to her nephew the Duke of Kent, whose widow Princess Marina still used as her country retreat. Bertie would also have left Margaret a significant sum of money for her to live a comfortable and self-sufficient life irrespective of whom she married. He might even have bought her a lease on a London house the way his father had done for him at 145 Piccadilly or for his brother Prince George at Belgrave Square near Buckingham Palace. Although he was tight-fisted, no one who knew him believed that Bertie intended to leave his younger daughter virtually penniless, which is what happened.

And Margaret was the only member of her immediate family who had no money. By virtue of being heiress presumptive to the throne, Lilibet had been financially secure even before her accession. And because Elizabeth was the monarch's widow, she not only inherited everything he owned personally, but also paid no tax on any of it. She was now a very rich woman in her own right, and could easily have set Princess Margaret up financially. She chose not to 'out of pure spite', according to Colin Glenconner. If that was not her motive, gross irresponsibility coupled with the most astounding lack of concern for her daughter's welfare and security can be the only reasons for her failure to make these basic provisions, especially as how they were well within her reach financially.

Despite the fact that Margaret would have needed setting up once she was married, in the early 1950s, there was nothing unusual about unmarried women of marriageable age living with their parents. Only spinsters who were securely on the shelf, such as Princesses Helena Victoria and Marie Louise, lived in their own establishments. It was therefore to be expected that a beautiful young woman like Princess Margaret would live under her mother's roof until she was married or ready for shelf-life. She therefore moved into Clarence House in May 1953 with Elizabeth, who immediately set about trying to swap it for Marlborough House. Unsuccessfully, as it would turn out.

Some years ago, one of the most senior officials of the Commonwealth Secretariat said, 'I was told that the Queen offered us Marlborough House as a way of stopping her mother's nagging. The Queen Mother was desperate to have it, but the Queen rightly understood that it would have been a very unpopular move. Can you imagine the hue and cry there would have been at a time of austerity? The Queen Mother had just spent a none-too-small fortune doing up Clarence House and would have gladly spent another one doing up Marlborough House. But the Queen wouldn't hear of it. I was told the Queen Mother was furious. Furious. But there wasn't a thing she could do about it. We're still here, and she's still there – all of two houses away from us, but in terms of grandeur, light years away.'[19]

At the time of the move into Clarence House, Margaret was romantically involved with Group Captain Peter Townsend, who was the Comptroller of her mother's Household. Colin Glenconner told me that both the King and Elizabeth had known about the romance for some time. Margaret in fact used to say that 'Papa viewed Peter as the son he had never had.' She herself told Colin that 'Papa would have arranged things so that we could have married, had he lived.' She believed at worst she would have had to wait until she was twenty-five, the age at which she no longer needed the sovereign's consent under the Royal Marriages Act of 1772 once she served notice of her intention to marry.

Townsend's presence in the life of mother and daughter papered over many of the cracks that were already beginning to exist between them. Because both women were fond of him, and he was a personable and phlegmatic figure, they formed a happy little trio, sharing lunches, teas, suppers, weekends and picnics together in a way that neither Elizabeth nor Margaret would have been inclined to do had he not been present. The harmonious atmosphere, however, concealed fissures beneath the surface, and these would come to the surface when news of the Margaret/Townsend romance erupted.

It did so at Lilibet's coronation on 2nd June, 1953. Margaret was photographed removing a bit of fluff from Townsend's coat. The gesture bespoke such intimacy that within hours the news that the Queen of England's younger sister was in love with a divorced man had circled the globe. Margaret now found herself at the centre of a constitutional storm made all the worse by the position her mother had insisted upon continuing to take with regard to the Windsors. Princess Alice, Countess of Athlone believed that Margaret was unlucky. Had Queen Mary not died on 24th March, 1953, but been alive to witness the conflagration, she would have used her considerable influence with Lilibet, who revered her grandmother, to facilitate Margaret's marriage along with the re-incorporation of the Duke of Windsor into the family fold. And since he was well known to live by the motto, 'We go nowhere unless we can enter through the front door,' Wallis would have had to come with him.[20]

But Queen Mary was dead and Colin Glenconner believed that Elizabeth was far too selfish and sanctimonious to reverse any position she adopted, especially one that would let the Duke of Windsor back into the fold. So, rather than help her daughter, Elizabeth was superficially sweet but inhumanely aloof and unhelpful beneath the surface. He also said that Princess Margaret herself came to realise that her mother had been double-dealing with her and Townsend on the one hand, and courtiers such as Tommy Lascelles and members of the Government such as Bobbety Salisbury on the other.

There is much evidence to support Princess Margaret's observation. Notwithstanding Townsend's own adultery with the Princess, he had obtained a divorce from Rosemary on the grounds of her adultery with John de Laszlo in November 1952. This cleared the way for him, as the innocent party, to remarry. He and Margaret had long been making plans along those lines, and as soon as he was a free man, he informed Tommy Lascelles, who was still Private Secretary to the monarch, that he and Margaret were deeply in love with each other and wished to get married.[21] Lascelles asked who else knew of their intentions, and he replied only the Queen and Prince Philip. He suggested they inform Queen Elizabeth The Queen Mother as soon as possible, and would later claim that they did not do so until February 1953.

This claim would be one of the many details which furnished Margaret with proof of her mother's duplicity, for in fact she had known of their intention, as had her father, even before his death. According to the Lascelles/Elizabeth version of events, the Dowager Queen then discussed the matter with her daughter the reigning Queen, after which he wrote to Elizabeth questioning if the 'Queen, Head of Church & State, & the high priestess, so to speak, of the ideal of family life – whether she should or should not be advised to allow her sister to marry a divorced man in a registry office.' These words were pure Elizabeth, as Margaret noted to Colin Glenconner. Lascelles also stated that 'it is, after all (and especially since 1936) fundamentally a State matter',[22] which was also the line Elizabeth had always taken with regard to the Abdication of the Duke of Windsor.

Elizabeth injudiciously responded to Lascelles on 12th June, 1953, 'I would like to talk to you, soon please. I have nobody I can talk to about such dreadful things.'[23] This was a mistake, because once Margaret discovered the contents of this letter, she could tell that her mother had orchestrated a meeting so she could manipulate events in person. Nor did Elizabeth resist the urge to grandstand when he went to see her. 'The Queen Mother wept when I talked to her. I have never seen her shed tears before,' Lascelles informed the Prime Minister's Private Secretary, Jock Colville.[24]

Not surprisingly, Princess Margaret hit the roof when she finally found out that the mother who was pretending to possess 'characteristic understanding', who had given no 'sign that she felt angered or outraged – or that she acquiesced' and who was 'never anything but considerate in her attitude'[25] was going behind the back of the lovers and causing trouble for them. Not only was she acting distressed when she was anything but to their faces, but she was professing ignorance of something she had known about for years and was moreover claiming to be 'quite shattered by the whole thing'.[26]

What Elizabeth had done was marshal the forces of opposition to Margaret's marriage with typical skill and cleverness. By conveying her 'distress' to Lascelles, she was tacitly stating that she would not be supporting her daughter. Margaret believed that, had Elizabeth tendered her support at this juncture, the whole course of her life would have been different, and that everyone else would have fallen into line. Instead of which, she had been encouraging Lascelles to oppose the union. According to Colin Glenconner, Margaret believed that the objections Lascelles voiced were those Elizabeth fed him. There is evidence to support this line of reasoning. Having decided that the marriage was an affair of state, Lascelles requested a meeting with the Prime Minister. This was the precise tactic Hardinge had employed with Baldwin to start the snowball of the Abdication Crisis rolling downhill. Churchill was at Chartwell, his country house in Kent, so the Private Secretary drove down there. When Churchill was informed of the possible marriage, his response had been effusive. 'What a delightful match! A lovely young royal lady married to a gallant young airman, safe from the perils and horrors of war!'[27] This was definitely not the sort of response the Private Secretary wanted, and he communicated his disapproval eloquently. It was only when Churchill realised that Lascelles was against the marriage that he fell silent, but what really made him change his tune was when his wife Clementine came out arguing strongly with Lascelles. 'Winston, if you are going to begin the Abdication all over again, I am going to leave! I shall take a flat and go and live in Brighton,' she declared, backing up Lascelles comprehensively.[28]

Churchill knew Elizabeth well. He was fully aware that any objection Lascelles voiced had her backing and would be her position. She was

Margaret's mother. Without her backing, the venture was impossible. However, he had a conscience and feelings, and did not want to stand in the way of a young couple's happiness. So he recommended that the marriage could go ahead as long as the Princess renounced her rights to the succession – something which several royals have done since then while remaining in the royal fold, including Prince Michael of Kent, the Earl of St. Andrews and Lord Nicholas Windsor.

Lascelles, however, reported back to Elizabeth that Churchill had further required Margaret to surrender her status as a royal highness and her inclusion on the Civil List.[29] These were claims which Jock Colville was at pains to deny two years later, when the whole matter came to a head. He committed pen to paper to assert that the Prime Minister 'was in reality opposed to any attempt to prevent their marrying.'[30]

Plainly, Lascelles and Elizabeth were up to their old tricks, putting words into people's mouths which they would never have uttered, as they manipulated the situation to achieve the outcome they desired.

Nor did Elizabeth want Townsend to remain her Comptroller or join the tour to Southern Rhodesia which she and Margaret were due to embark upon on 30th June. The claim has been made that Churchill himself did not deem it suitable, which could well be true, for now that the world knew that Margaret and Townsend wished to marry, his presence on the tour would have been distracting and in somewhat dubious taste. The man chosen to wield the axe, however, convinced Margaret that her mother was behind the move, which she contemporaneously regarded as being helpful, though she would later change her mind. Sir Arthur Penn, Elizabeth's Treasurer and old friend as well as one-time suitor, took Townsend to dinner on 16th June and informed him that the best option would be for him to retire gracefully from the scene for a while. Like Margaret, Townsend understood that Elizabeth herself was sending the message, and wrote her the following day to say that he would accept whatever post was offered to him. He was appointed the Air Attaché at the British Embassy in Brussels. Not yet appreciating the double game she was playing, he wrote, as if he and Margaret would be together forever, 'Your Majesty is going through so much for us and I can never thank you enough for your kindness and your help, and for the way you have stood by Princess Margaret. We will never forget how much you are thinking of the Queen too, and will always do everything we can to consider her.'[31] He was duly replaced on the tour by Patrick, the 7th Lord Plunket, who was a good friend of Margaret and Lilibet.

Patrick Plunket, whose youngest brother Shaun was an old chum of mine, would ultimately become the Deputy Master of Queen Elizabeth II's

Household'. His parents, who had died in a plane crash in America in 1938, had been close friends of Elizabeth's, an intimacy possibly fostered by the former Dorothé Lewis Barnato having been the illegitimate daughter of the 7th Marquess of Londonderry and the actress Fannie Ward, though it has to be said in her favour, she and the rest of the family remained superb friends to the three Plunket brothers.

The tour was as howling a success as all Elizabeth's tours were. Shawcross observes in the official biography that she 'had recovered much of her *joie de vivre.* Those with her remembered much laughter and high spirits on the trip. Everywhere she went she seemed to enjoy herself,' which was indeed the case. No one had a greater capacity for enjoying herself than Elizabeth, especially when she was the centre of attention, as she always was on tour.

Margaret, on the other hand, was having a dreadful time, especially after she discovered that Townsend would be sent abroad to pick up his posting before she returned home. She had been led to believe that they would have a brief reunion, and was so distressed to discover that she would not be able to see her lover for at least another year, that she took to her bed for days.

Her main ally, Winston Churchill, was also out of the picture. He had suffered a stroke prior to her departure which had affected his speech and ability to walk. It would be several months before he was fit enough to return to 10 Downing Street. In the meantime, he was down at Chartwell recovering from what the public was told was 'exhaustion'. Although he remained Prime Minister in name, in deed much of the slack had been taken up by his deputy, the Foreign Secretary Anthony Eden, a *divorcé* who was married to Churchill's niece Clarissa. Although Colville confirms that Churchill remained in favour of Margaret marrying Townsend, he was now viewed as yesterday's man, and would no longer be Prime Minister when the matter finally came to a head after Margaret's twenty-fifth birthday in August 1955.

Shortly after Elizabeth and Margaret returned to England, the older woman celebrated her birthday. Then they headed north to Scotland, where they initially stayed at Balmoral with Lilibet and her family. By Elizabeth's own account, she enjoyed 'laughing & talking & being a family which is the only thing worth living for.'[32] Then she repaired to Birkhall where she entertained the Salisburys and communicated her opposition to her daughter's marriage, so that when the time came, he could lead the attack against Margaret in the Cabinet. That, however, was a year away, but Elizabeth was adept at laying the ground. As she had proven time and again ever since she had become embroiled with the Royal Family, she played a very long game indeed, though it was one which allowed for sudden change of direction, such as when she realised that she could not achieve her ambition of becoming the Princess of Wales, so became the Duchess of York instead. Time would tell if she needed to change tack, or whether her well-laid objections would achieve their objective.

By November, mother and daughter were back in London. Lilibet and Philip departed for a five-month tour of the Commonwealth which took in Bermuda, Jamaica, Fiji, Tonga, New Zealand, Australia, Ceylon, Aden, Uganda, Malta and Gibraltar. While they were away, Elizabeth was thrilled to take care of her grandchildren. She wrote many happy letters about the whale of a time she was having with Charles and Anne, and presided over a very festive Christmas at Sandringham, which, it was clear, she continued to treat as her own home.

Meanwhile, Margaret was trying to lead the semblance of a life despite being in romantic limbo. The Margaret Set had come into being, and consisted of a merry band of privileged revellers, who included Sharman Douglas, daughter of the American Ambassador between 1947 and 1950 (and who my younger sister was named after); Lewis W. Douglas; the Earl of Dalkeith, whose parents were the 8th Duke of Buccleuch and Elizabeth's *bête noire* Molly Lascelles; the Hon. Dominic Elliot-Murray-Kynynmound, a son of the 5th Earl of Minto; Billy Wallace, son of Captain Euan Wallace MP, who would remain a lifelong friend of the Princess; and the Hon. Colin Tennant, later 3rd Lord Glenconner, whose father had been the suitor of Elizabeth's who kept the engagement ring in his pocket and failed to propose marriage.

It was a mark of her nonchalance concerning the welfare of her daughter that Elizabeth made no move to encourage a match with any of these men, though she did make it known that she would have liked Johnny Dalkeith as a son-in-law. 'Pure snobbery on her part,' Colin Glenconner believed. 'Even though she was a queen, she could never quite forget that she was this little Scottish lass. Her whole world was measured not in terms of royalty, but in terms of who did and did not count in the Anglo-Scottish aristocracy.' It was almost as if she believed that she could make them superior to foreign royalty by endowing them with greater recognition.

If Elizabeth did nothing to encourage any of those relationships, she was decidedly active when she wanted to destroy the possibility of future developments. Margaret and Colin Glenconner, who was then known as the Hon. Colin Tennant, became such good and cosy friends that he fancied he had a chance with her, should she and Peter Townsend not get married. He would ultimately even propose marriage, and always maintained that she said yes, then changed her mind. She, on the other hand, always denied that she had ever accepted him.

The truth could lie somewhere between the two versions. In the 1970s, I had a dinner party at my flat in West Eaton Place in London's Belgravia district. One of my guests was a former Tai Pan of a great Hong Kong trading company. I had very nearly married his cousin, and this almost-cousin told us that the reason why PM, as she was sometimes affectionately known, had not been allowed to marry Colin Tennant was that Elizabeth had personally intervened to prevent the marriage, because she was worried that the family, whose money had partly come from their sugar estates in the West Indies, might have 'coloured blood'.

Having been brought up in Jamaica, and known other people with a West Indian connection such as Prince George of Denmark, who was a descendant of the Empress Josephine, I picked up the theme and recounted how he often complained to me that schoolchildren in Europe were systematically taught that she had black blood. The idea of slaves and masters intermarrying during the days of slavery was beyond preposterous and denoted a level of ignorance of social morés that was almost laughable to anyone from a former slave society.

Nevertheless, there had been constant interbreeding between slave and master which had resulted in an appreciable population of fair-skinned slaves. It was my view that Elizabeth was either very ignorant of the way things were in the days of slavery, or then such 'coloured blood' as the Tennants might have had was minuscule and would have resulted from a marriage with the heiress progeny of a rich planter or trader and a 'coloured' freewoman. Such cases had existed, though they were hardly usual, and usually the issue looked fully European.

The former Tai Pan said that Elizabeth 'had been worried about throwbacks', going on to regale us with how the Queen Mother had absolutely refused to countenance a match between Colin and Margaret, notwithstanding the fact that she might well have accepted his own father as a husband had he proposed and neither prince rallied to her cause.

If Elizabeth had double standards, she also had power. While Townsend was in Brussels and Margaret at a loose end, Lilibet and Philip were abroad on their long tour of half the world, which meant that she headed up the Council of State. Her fellow Counsellors were Princess Margaret, the Duke of Gloucester, the Princess Royal and her son George, who had succeeded his father as Earl of Harewood on 24th May, 1947. As the chief Counsellor, Elizabeth was having the time of her life. She held six investitures at Buckingham Palace. She presided over seven meetings of the Privy Council to fulfil the monarch's constitutional obligations. She received countless ambassadors and high commissioners. She knighted worthies, including the heart-throb of her teenage years, George Robey, the sight of whom reminded her of her ducal beau Charlie Settrington. She gave audiences to ministers of government and twice received the Prime Minister, though Churchill would never fully recover his powers and retired shortly thereafter.

When Lilibet returned in May, Elizabeth simply substituted one primary stage for another, and set about planning yet another royal tour. This time she was going to Canada and the United States. She arrived in New York in October 1954 on board the *Queen Elizabeth*, which she had launched in 1938. After touring the United Nations and charming her way through a whole series of receptions, luncheons, dinners, and visits, President Eisenhower sent the presidential plane to bring her to Washington. She stayed at the White House with the Eisenhowers, who treated her like an old friend. She and Bertie had had many a wartime encounter with the former Supreme Commander of the Allied Forces, and the respect was mutual, even if she found their White House stuffier and more formal than the Roosevelts'. But then, the Roosevelts were patricians, just like Elizabeth, and they all had an appreciation of the relaxed approach to formality which *arrivistes* and born royals did not possess. Nevertheless, she was as roaring a success with everyone in Washington as she always was everywhere else.

Elizabeth's relationship with her younger daughter, however, was about to take a turn for the worse. Margaret turned twenty-five in August 1955 and she informed her mother that Townsend was coming over from Brussels for them to make a final decision. Although Margaret had by her own admission 'blown up at intervals when we've discussed the situation,'[33] she still did not appreciate the extent to which her mother had colluded in undermining her. This would come soon enough. On 12th October, Townsend arrived back in London. He stayed at the Lowndes Square maisonette of the Marquess of Abergavenny, whose brother Lord Rupert Nevill and sister-in-law Mickie were extremely close friends of Lilibet and Philip. That in itself was something of an indication of Lilibet's lack of active opposition to the marriage, for the Nevills would not have been putting up someone the Monarch disapproved of.

Both Townsend and Margaret, who was staying at Balmoral, were under the impression that their marriage was now almost a done deal. Nevertheless, she was concerned by the overt lack of support from her family. She 'prevailed on a friend to discuss her crisis with the Queen, but nothing came of this as the Queen was anxious that her sister must never believe that she had been forced into taking one action or another,' as Hugo Vickers so elegantly puts it in his Elizabeth biography. He euphemistically continues, 'Nor did the Queen Mother help her, since she made it a point not to interfere in the life of her daughters.' The reality is that she did not help, but she did interfere, though she did it in such a way that she left little or no trace of her actions. Their very absence, however, when taken in conjunction with the visible opponents, was enough for Princess Margaret to figure out that her mother was the chief architect of opposition to her marriage.

Matters whirled to their *dénouement* as soon as Elizabeth arrived back in London on 13th October. She buried herself in a frantic round of dinner parties, all the better to hide the interference which was lurking beneath the ostensibly sweet but apathetic exterior. Although Margaret had not yet figured out how her mother had been aiding the enemy, she was dumbstruck by her utter lack of concern for her predicament. By this time, the press were camped outside of Lowndes Square and Clarence House, following Townsend and Margaret wherever they went. There were daily updates on the saga and as many new photographs as could be snatched. The Margaret/ Townsend romance was the biggest news story of its day.

According to Hugo Vickers, 'Queen Elizabeth spent the weekend at Royal Lodge, feeling guilty that she had not done anything to help, though it was now too late. By this time mother and daughter were scarcely on speaking terms and on one occasion Princess Margaret had even thrown a book at her mother's head.'[34] In fact, it was not too late to help, though Elizabeth had marshalled the forces of opposition so effectively that it would have been a major embarrassment for her to reverse her position. As for feeling guilty, she had never felt guilty about anything in her life, for she had never admitted to herself or anyone else that she was capable of doing anything wrong. That does not mean that she did not feel awkward about her lack of help now that her daughter was beginning to figure out how she had betrayed her interests, but that is not the same thing as guilty feelings.

Elizabeth was intelligent and wily, but Margaret had inherited her mother's brains. Although she had neither the aptitude nor inclination for the game-playing that were such characteristics of the older woman's personality, she was as sharp as two pins, and inevitably, as events unfolded, she began piecing the puzzle together. She was furious to learn that Bobbety Salisbury had threatened to resign from the Government if the marriage were allowed to proceed. She knew he could never have made such a threat if he did not have her mother's backing, and 'spat bricks'[35] that Elizabeth had facilitated the advancement of her niece Anne from divorced commoner to royal princess, but could not assist her own daughter in similar circumstances. She became convinced that her mother would not have minded in the least if she were demoted from royalty to commoner, a sentiment with which Colin Glenconner concurred wholeheartedly. 'She was jealous of PM and derived no greater pleasure than seeing her struggle,' he said, recounting how his friend thereafter used to fling her mother's non-royal origins in her face every time they had a row, reminding her that 'you are not really royal at all. You weren't *born* royal. I was.'

Margaret had now decided that her mother was an 'arch-hypocrite'.[36] Meanwhile, royal engagements continued as if the participants were not the central figures in this huge, public drama. The internecine warfare between mother and daughter formed no part of the public picture, though. Only Princess Margaret's closest friends knew about it. Meanwhile, Elizabeth, Lilibet, Margaret and the other members of the Royal Family attended an unveiling of the King George VI Memorial at Carlton Gardens. The President of Portugal arrived for a State Visit and there was the customary gala for him at Buckingham Palace, where all the members of the Royal family gathered, including Margaret and Elizabeth.

The Lord Chancellor, Lord Kilmuir, was advising the Prime Minister of the legalities of altering the Royal Marriages Act of 1772 so that Margaret could renounce her rights of succession and still remain a princess on the Civil List. In so doing, Kilmuir was creating the most massive kerfuffle, talking about involving Parliament and the governments of the Commonwealth. All of this was unnecessary, as would become clear when Prince Michael of Kent was able to marry the Catholic *divorcée* Marie-Christine Troubridge without altering any law or involving any government. But there was a significant difference between Michael's and Margaret's marriages. Elizabeth was indifferent to the first, while determined to do all she could to scupper the second. And what better way to do that than have the officials throw up a load of constitutional hurdles which would have to be surmounted?

On 26th October, Margaret was left in no doubt of the opposition to her marriage within the narrow band of courtiers and powers-that-be who surrounded her mother, when she opened up *The Times* to see a vicious editorial demanding that she be made to give up her royal status if she went ahead with the marriage. She knew only too well how the Palace worked hand in glove with *The Times*, and had no doubt that the story was a plant. Lady Patricia Ramsay, the former Princess Patricia of Connaught who had given up her royal style and titles in 1919 to marry the Hon. Alexander Ramsay, sympathising with her lot, warned her that she must not, on any account, make the mistake she had done. 'It's no picnic being demoted from princess to lady,' had been the gist of her recommendation, and Margaret listened, for she had seen with her own two eyes how her artist cousin regretted the loss of her royal status.

Townsend states in his memoirs that he believed that Margaret faced a starker choice than she actually did. This means that they were being deliberately starved by the courtiers, who had a duty to keep her well informed, of the positive information that existed. This could only have been in the hope that she and Townsend would become discouraged and throw in the towel. On page 231 of *Time and Chance*, he asserts that the choice was either renunciation of the marriage or renunciation of her royal status: 'conditions which, frankly, would have ruined her.' As the official documents show, however, she no longer possessed such a narrow choice. In fact all she would have lost was her right of succession to the throne.

Lilibet already had two heirs and, being a young woman of child-breeding age, was liable to provide even more heirs to the throne (which she went on to do), so Princess Margaret would actually have been surrendering nothing of any consequence to marry Townsend.

It is of course possible that Townsend knew the full facts but had to pick his way around them when he was writing his memoirs, so that he would do no further damage to Princess Margaret or himself. It is equally possible that he genuinely did not. If that is the case, it shows how determined the ossifiers were to prevent the marriage. There is no doubt that the Government informed the courtiers of developments as they were taking place, so if the courtiers failed to inform Princess Margaret, that can only have been because someone royal in the background had let them know that it was safe not to do so. As that individual was not the Queen, it can only have been Queen Elizabeth The Queen Mother.

Margaret would later claim publicly that she and Townsend came to a joint decision not to proceed with the marriage at this stage of the proceedings. However, she confided in Colin Glenconner and other friends that it was actually he who pulled out. Whether his motivation was because he believed she would lose her royal status, or he realised that Elizabeth's lack of support would always be a drag on their marriage, he would undoubtedly have been influenced by the fate (which we shall come to shortly) that had befallen Lilibet and Margaret's governess Crawfie when she had dared to hoe a different furrow from that which Elizabeth desired. Making an adversary of the Queen Mother was not something any but the very brave did, and while he was a courageous, decorated war hero, an enemy in the sky was one thing, but one on the ground – and a palatial ground at that – was another. He might also have understood that by marrying a degraded princess, much of the glamour which had attached to her position of sister to the Queen would have disappeared, and along with it, her desirability. That left just Margaret the woman. Ned Ryan, who was a mutual friend of hers and mine, always said that fond as he was of her, she was 'extraordinarily difficult'. Even her cousin Margaret Rhodes makes the point in her memoir, *The Final Curtsey,* and it seems likely that Townsend decided not to proceed when he realised that their marriage would simply not be worth the sacrifices they would both have to make to achieve it.

Colin Glenconner also believed that Elizabeth would have taken 'malicious delight' in making life difficult for the couple if they had gone ahead, and they both realised this. While Margaret was prepared to pay the price, Townsend was not. This might seem far-fetched until one considers how Elizabeth behaved towards Margaret when her marriage to Tony Snowdon came to an end. She actively took his side even though he, rather than Margaret, was the party whose actions had brought that union to its knees. The eminent author and journalist Anne de Courcy wrote a superb biography of Snowdon[37] which creates a chilling portrait of what it was like to be married to him. As this was written with his co-operation, one must conclude that it is both a fair and true picture. No one can read it and not feel both compassion and admiration for Princess Margaret, which makes her mother's support of him all the more indefensible. However, Elizabeth liked Tony. He charmed her the way she had charmed half the world. She felt no compunction about throwing in her lot with the son-in-law she enjoyed rather than the daughter she disrespected. 'The way she treated PM was a disgrace. You wouldn't treat a dog as badly,' Colin Glenconner said of the mother/daughter relationship, cataloguing a host of slights, gratuitous cruelties, and downright heartless actions which she passed off as parental concern under the heading of 'pull yourself together'.

That, however, was in the future as Margaret was driven to Lambeth Palace on Thursday, 27th October, 1955 to see the Archbishop of Canterbury. She was enough of her mother's daughter to hide the decision not to marry beneath a carapace of face-saving principle, which, in her situation, was justified, considering the wringer she had been put through. She therefore informed him that she had decided not to marry Group Captain Peter Townsend on Christian grounds. The following day, she and Townsend spent their last weekend as a couple together with Lord and Lady Rupert Nevill at their house at Uckfield. It was, by all accounts, a happy time made all the more poignant by its bittersweet element. They had truly been a well-suited couple, far better than Margaret and Tony Snowdon. There is every likelihood that the marriage would have lasted, because there was genuine affection and respect between the two of them, and their relationship had none of the darker elements which would ultimately overwhelm the Snowdon marriage.

On Monday 31st October, Margaret's official statement was released, stating, 'Mindful of the Church's teaching that Christian marriage is indissoluble, and conscious of my duty to the Commonwealth, I will not be marrying

Group Captain Peter Townsend.'

I believe the postscript is best left to Hugo Vickers, who, in his understated way, captures the underlying heartlessness that allowed Elizabeth to ruin her daughter's greatest chance of happiness. 'That night Princess Margaret was at Clarence House, while Elizabeth was due to keep an evening engagement at the University of London. The Queen Mother set off for this, unaware or unconcerned that her daughter would be having dinner alone on a tray.'[38]

Afterwards, mother and daughter continued to live together at Clarence House. With Townsend out of the way, there was no unifying factor to paper over the cracks which had now developed into huge fissures. Mother and daughter seldom met. Margaret was out most nights with her friends, and spent most days in her room. Like Elizabeth, she was a late riser though, unlike Elizabeth, she stayed in her room as much as possible, partly to avoid having to see her mother. Inevitably, their paths would sometimes cross, and when they did, it was usually for lunch in the library or occasionally for tea, though Margaret preferred taking that with the Household. She was a popular figure in Society. Her beauty and glamour were outstanding, and, having inherited her mother's theatrical *élan,* wherever she went she created a splash. Since her early twenties she had arguably been the most desirable single woman on the planet, which seems to have given her mother none of the pleasure a proud mother would naturally possess. According to Colin Glenconner, 'They were like two ships passing in the night – preferably far enough apart to not have to dip their lights at each other.'

However, the Townsend affair had tarnished Margaret in more ways than one. Not only had it broken her heart and showed her what sort of character her mother was, but as she approached her thirties, she was starting to look like aging and rather sad goods. In 1958 she told Cecil Beaton, 'I like angry young men. They're not nearly angry enough. If they're angry, I'm furious.'[39]

One needs to be careful what one wishes for in life. Answered prayers and satisfied tastes can have unforeseen consequences, as Margaret would soon discover. Her close friend and lady-in-waiting Lady Elizabeth Cavendish introduced her to Antony Armstrong-Jones, an up-and-coming photographer who had photographed the Duke of Kent in 1956 and the Queen, Prince Philip and their children in the garden at Buckingham Palace in 1957, thereby launching himself as a royal favourite. Although short and slight, he was good-looking and charming in the Elizabeth mould, in that his superficial appeal hid conflicting depths. His mother was the formidable but ravishingly beautiful Countess of Rosse. She was a close friend of Margaret, Duchess of Argyll, and had a reputation for being the biggest social climber in the

British Isles. Her brother Oliver Messel was a talented artist and designer with whom my brother was sufficiently friendly to stay in Barbados. The Messels had scaled the social heights, proving that English Society was not anti-Semitic, for they were Jewish and well known to be.

What was less well known was that Anne had little time for her children from her first marriage to the untitled barrister Ronald Armstrong-Jones. Once she married her earl[40] and produced his heir[41] and spare[42], she treated her two lots of children as distinctly as Cinderella's step-mother had done. Unless Anne de Courcy's book is wrong, which I very much doubt, this had a marked effect upon her son Tony. It did not help that he also had polio as a child.

He was potently attractive and he and Margaret became an electrifying couple, marrying, with Lilibet's consent, in 1960. Although the wedding at Westminster Abbey was a full-scale royal production, the European royals stayed away in droves. They considered the union between a half-royal princess and a commoner photographer to be *déclassé*, but this did not matter to Elizabeth. Tony was just the sort of son-in-law she had always wanted: artistic, sensitive, charming, camp, flattering to her. They struck up a close and lifelong friendship which provided the perfect counterfoil to her relationship with her other son-in-law.

At first, the marriage was happy, but by the late 1960s it was in trouble. By the mid-1970s, it was over. Colin Glenconner then introduced Margaret to Roddy Llewellyn, with whom she began a lovely romance which turned into a touching, lasting friendship. I know this because I knew Roddy and many of the people involved, such as Sarah Ponsonby and John Rendall, who used to live together in a commune at Surrendell in Wiltshire which Princess Margaret would visit. It takes no imagination to see how horrified the hyper-conventional Elizabeth was that any daughter of hers would choose a lifestyle that embraced modernity and ordinariness (albeit of an aristocratic sort) over the arch-conservatism that was a hallmark of her thinking. Out of deference to Roddy, who is a delightful man and who proved to be a good and true friend to Princess Margaret, I will decline to mention any of the comments Elizabeth made. Suffice it to say Elizabeth's lack of comprehension for a relationship that brought her daughter comfort and joy said more about the Dowager Queen's disconnection with human feeling than the quality of her daughter's relationship with a physically attractive, fundamentally decent, and entertaining man.

By this time, PM had semi-detached herself from royal life. Her friends were people whom she liked and who liked her. Chief amongst them was Ned Ryan, another chum of mine who was delightful. A kind-hearted and very funny Irishman who had started life as a trader at Portobello Market, he became a success in business. There were two members of her set of whom I was not particularly fond, but putting those aside, Margaret had aspired to, and achieved, a circle of friends who genuinely liked her as a person, and whom she also liked. This, believe me, isn't so easy to achieve in royal circles, and it said much about her character and values. What also militated in her favour, and showed how essentially decent Princess Margaret was, was the relationship she had with her two children, David, Viscount Linley, and Lady Sarah Armstrong-Jones (now Chatto). Rather like Jackie Onassis, she proved to be an excellent mother and her children became her finest accomplishment.

Putting aside the troubled nature of Elizabeth's relationship with Margaret, the Queen Mother also made a great success of her personal life. She had a large family and many friends, and, by and large, she got along well with them. The real difference between mother and daughter was that the former never forgave anyone who crossed her and discarded those who got on her wrong side for whatever reason, while the latter did not. For instance, when Roddy Llewellyn fell in love with Tania Soskin, and informed PM that their relationship could no longer continue in its present form, she opted to make a friend of the younger woman and kept Roddy as one of her inner circle for the remainder of her life. This was not something her mother would ever have done.

Elizabeth had a well-worn track record for cutting people out of her life, which is best illustrated by the way she froze Crawfie out of the royal circle. The scheme began innocently enough. Elizabeth was on cordial terms with Bruce and Beatrice Blackmar Gould, the joint editors of the immensely popular American magazine, *Ladies' Home Journal*. They had many noteworthy contacts, such as Elizabeth's good friends Stella, Marchioness of Reading; Nancy, Viscountess Astor; and Eleanor Roosevelt, whose memoirs, *My Story*, they serialised. During the war, they had accompanied the American First Lady on her English visit, and met Queen Elizabeth at luncheon at Cliveden, the palatial Astor country seat near Windsor. With Nancy Astor's approval, they suggested to Elizabeth that she permit them to write an article about her for their series 'Women of the World', which she listened to 'with warm concentration, but with non-committal ease, explaining again and again that she would need to consult her advisors.'[43] Although Elizabeth had long since discovered the wisdom of remaining silent, so important did she regard the Goulds that she sent the King's Private Secretary, Tommy Lascelles, to the Ritz, where they were staying, to inform them that she could not partake in such an exercise as she was 'above and beyond politics'.[44]

Relations between the Goulds and Buckingham Palace remained so cordial that by 1948 the editors were suggesting a series of articles under Lilibet's by-line, written by an author of their choice. These would focus on how the Princess was being trained for the role of sovereign. The idea was espoused by such eminent personages as John Gilbert Winant, The American Ambassador to the Court of St. James's, and Brendan Bracken, the sometime Conservative Member of Parliament who was also the editor of the *Financial Times* newspaper and one of Winston Churchill's closest political colleagues and personal friends. In an act that signalled the Palace's co-operation, the project was then passed on to the Foreign Office, where the novelist, biographer and BBC Governor, Mary Agnes Hamilton, informed the Goulds that the Palace could only agree if their own writer were appointed. Tommy Lascelles, the King's Private Secretary, proposed his good friend Dermot Morrah. He accepted the assignment for the then generous sum of $2,500, and was duly sent over to the US, and commissioned to write a series of anodyne articles.

Morrah is on record stating that Elizabeth was keen that he write the articles, as was Philip, though that prince did not wish to become personally involved. With such backing, it was hardly surprising that the author found that everywhere he turned; there was 'a long list of court worthies, all of whom have been most anxious to help.'[45] The only person who 'gracefully evaded' his requests to see her was Lilibet and Margaret's former governess, Marion Crawford, who had recently retired. Not even the intervention of Queen Mary's lady-in-waiting, Lady Cynthia Colville, could budge her. Crawfie had lived as the fifth party to We Four, as Elizabeth and King George VI called the family unit, and was not prepared to do anything to jeopardise her privileged position.

Between 1933, when she joined the Royal Family, and her retirement in January 1949, Crawfie had been a fully participating member of the family unit. She was privy to the dynamics of the family and knew many if not all of their secrets. She had been like a maiden aunt to the princesses, and there are letters in the royal archives in which Elizabeth thanks Crawfie for being the trustworthy, reliable, responsible and loving presence that she had consistently been. In these, Elizabeth asserts how she could never have been able to function as effectively as she had done, without Crawfie in the background in loco parentis.

Crawfie was on cordial terms with all the members of the Royal Family's innermost circle: family, friends, and courtiers. She went to their parties, and they came to hers, especially after she married Major George Buthlay in September 1947 and moved into Nottingham Cottage, the grace and favour house she was given at Kensington Palace following her retirement on full salary in January 1949.

Buthlay has been blamed for the breakdown of Crawfie's relationship with Elizabeth. According to that version of events, he instilled dissatisfaction in his wife at the way she had been treated because she had only been given the CVO (Commander of the Victorian Order) instead of being made a Dame, and that her wedding presents from the Royal Family had not been generous enough. In fact, she received a 'complete and very beautiful' dinner service from Queen Mary, a coffee set from Lilibet, and three table lamps from the teenage Princess Margaret. Tellingly, Elizabeth gave her nothing, which indicates that there were already problems in the relationship between mistress and governess by 1947.

An examination of the documents shows that Buthlay was merely the convenient scapegoat, for nowhere is there proof that he actually set his wife up against the Royal Family, or that she acted contrary to her agreements with Elizabeth.

Moreover, Crawfie had been given a good residence within the Kensington Palace complex, opposite Prince Philip's grandmother the Dowager Marchioness of Milford Haven. She was on full pay. She had a full and active social life in Court circles and was welcome everywhere with open arms. Sir Ulick Alexander, the Keeper of the Privy Purse, had arranged for Buthlay himself to be employed by the Bank of Scotland, and the claims that he was disaffected with this and wanted to help run the royal accounts cannot be substantiated by any records or any reliable accounts.

As with the Abdication and the forcing out of Greig and Hardinge, Crawfie was being set up by Elizabeth, who invited the former governess to come to see her in February 1949 to encourage her to co-operate with the projected publicity. It is beyond dispute that Crawfie then met with Elizabeth. Crawfie left believing that Elizabeth had asked her to provide co-operation not through Morrah, but to the Goulds directly. They would appoint a ghost-writer who would tell her story about bringing up the princesses. Elizabeth would have the right to see the manuscript and change material she was not happy with.

Crawfie appointed the agents Pearn, Pollinger & Higham to represent her. While they were discussing terms with the Goulds, Elizabeth herself wrote to Crawfie on 4th April, shifting the goal posts. 'I do feel, most definitely, that you should not write and sign articles about the children, as people in positions of confidence with us must be utterly oyster, and if you, the moment you finished teaching Margaret, started writing about her and Lilibet, well, we should never feel confidence in anyone again. I know you understand this, because you have been so wonderfully discreet all the years you were with us. Also, you would lose all your friends, because such a thing has never been done or even contemplated amongst the people who serve us so loyally……..'

Aside from the threat implicit in the statement – 'you would lose all your friends' – the rest of the letter made no sense. Elizabeth's own governess Beryl Poignand had written two books on Lilibet and Margaret in the 1930s as well as several articles on the Royal Family in the 1940s. These had all been published with Elizabeth's blessing, as had Käthe Kübler's memoirs in 1937. Moreover, Elizabeth herself had encouraged Crawfie to co-operate with the Goulds. Was she now saying that Crawfie could still speak, but only if she did not profit, as she would if the articles were published under her own name? Off this line of reasoning, the issue wasn't the information Crawfie would be conveying, but whether she should receive any financial reward. Had Elizabeth tricked her into co-operating, and done so so cleverly that she had dangled the prospect of a reward, only to snatch it away?

The answer to that question came soon enough. Elizabeth's good friend Sir Arthur Penn wrote to Morrah stating that Her Majesty would prefer that Crawfie's recollections not be published under her own name, which might lead to embarrassment, but that they be incorporated into the body of the Morrah articles. Why would her recollections be embarrassing if they were produced under her own by-line, but not if produced under Morrah's? There was something almost insulting about this line of reasoning, and Crawfie chose to believe that as long as she did not go back on the February agreement the two women had struck, Elizabeth remained bound by it. On the strength of that, she entered into a contract with the Goulds on 25th May, 1949.

Thereafter, the ins and outs of the saga were typical of the convolutions Elizabeth always created whenever she wanted to get rid of someone. Having set things up so that she could claim down the line that Crawfie had let her down, she waited until *The Little Princesses* had been written before exploding. This she did when her brother David, whose very presence in itself was an indication that the two intriguing Benjamins were yet again up to no good, handed her a copy of the edited manuscript which the Goulds had sent to Nancy Astor for onward transmission to her. Patently, if Lady Astor, the Goulds or Crawfie had had any inkling that the material was incendiary, they would not have proceeded the way they had done.

Elizabeth claimed to be particularly put out by the suggestion that she and the King had not taken care to see that their daughters received an adequate education, and that Queen Mary had had to intervene to rectify the matter. This, of course, was the plain truth and well known to everyone. If she had valued education, why had Elizabeth gone to such lengths to prevent her daughters getting one? After all, she was the one who had always been adamant that she didn't want their heads turned with too much book knowledge. Why therefore object now to the revelation of a policy she had always maintained was in their best interests?

Elizabeth also claimed to be incensed that Crawfie had mentioned a harmless game of charades in which the Duchess of Kent had enacted the term Royal Flush by pulling a lavatory chain. Had she lost her fabled sense of humour, or was she clutching at straws?

She also claimed to be none too pleased that Crawfie had said that she disliked scenes. Since when had a love of harmoniousness become a flaw?

Although Crawfie had been put on notice by Elizabeth's April letter that she did not wish her reminiscences to go out under her by-line, the former governess nevertheless believed that she was living up to the spirit and letter of the agreement they had struck in February. Still, she had no wish to antagonise Elizabeth, so demanded that the Goulds incorporate all the changes the Queen Mother wished. She still did not appreciate that Elizabeth had decided to rewrite history and now chose to believe 'that Crawfie had promised not to publish under her own name. Crawfie believed that she had only promised to submit her text for approval,' as Hugo Vickers stated.

This dichotomy was typical of Elizabeth's modus operandi.

Morrah saw the problem clearly. 'The Queen has dug her toes in firmly and is not going to budge on the principle that all former royal servants are forbidden to write under their own names about the royal family. This means, I fear, that Mrs. Buthlay has blotted her copybook for good and all.'[46]

He also discerned that Elizabeth's claims about Crawfie had been fabricated, and implied as much when he wrote to Bruce Gould on 9th December, 1949: 'It's an interesting dispute about Crawfie's alleged promise to the Queen, but I'm rather glad that my interest in it need be no more than academic. The background of it is evidently two women who, after long years of association, have got on one another's nerves; and when that happens they are likely, with the most honest intentions in the world, to put opposite interpretations on the plainest documentary evidence. I'm prepared to believe that the production of the letter may settle the question for you and me and Lady Astor but don't expect it for a moment to do so for the two principals.'[47]

He was quite right, aided to his conclusion no doubt by his friend Tommy Lascelles, who had brought him on board and knew Elizabeth only too well.

That Christmas Crawfie received her usual card, sent from Malta, by Lilibet. She also heard from Queen Mary, but not a peep from Elizabeth. She was not unduly worried, and wrote to Bruce Gould on 26th December, 1949:

'I have no fear of what might be called "consequences" because I have adhered to the terms of my understanding with the Queen and if she decides to be unfriendly, or worse, she will be the loser. If any action on Her Majesty's part is brought to bear on me to my detriment, I shall not hesitate to expose it in the Press if necessary, and if an attempt should be made to eject me from this house and/or deprive me of my pension, I shall fight in Court and have the facts made public if I am driven to do so. All this is not likely to happen, however, as I have earned both house and pension, and in any case I feel that, as you have already said, the Queen will merely feel she should show a certain amount of disapproval, and the non-arrival of the usual Christmas card may be the first sign of it, absolutely childish as it is.'[48]

Plainly, Crawfie did not appreciate just how subtle and effective Elizabeth could be. She had quite forgotten stating that Elizabeth was seldom confrontational. The Dowager Queen played the long game stealthily, never taking the direct or obvious route, serenely going about her business as she shoved the stone down the ski-slope and waited until it had become a massive snowball crushing all in its path as it hurtled to its final destination. The Household had not yet got word of Elizabeth's desire that Crawfie be frozen out, so Lady Mary Alexander duly attended a cocktail party the Buthlays had at Nottingham Cottage, which had recently been provided with central heating. When she needed a car, one was provided for her. She and her husband received an invitation to a Buckingham Palace garden party in July, 1950, for her articles were being published in the *Ladies' Home Journal,* increasing their circulation by 500,000 to 2,000,000, and it would be a tactical error to fall out with Crawfie until publication had concluded.

In the meantime, Crawfie had made some $80,000 from the articles alone, and the book *The Little Princesses,* which was then published by Harcourt Brace, quickly became a worldwide bestseller, netting her another small fortune.

By the end of the year, however, Crawfie had come to realise that she was being cold-shouldered. Elizabeth's threat that she would lose her friends was becoming a reality. She no longer received invitations the way she used to, and when she issued them, hers were declined. Lord Charteris told me that she was 'shunned by everyone in the Household' for word had come down from on high, i.e. Elizabeth, that she did not consider Crawfie a suitable person for anyone in the royal circle to be associated with. Had anyone gone against this interdict, they too would have been frozen out the way Elizabeth had ensured that all the former King Edward VIII's friends and supporters had been.

Faced with this wall of silence, Crawfie bought a large house in Aberdeen in November 1950 at 60 Rubislaw Den South. She retired there with her husband, and continued to publish books and articles on the Royal Family.

There was a biography of Queen Mary in 1951; *Queen Elizabeth II* in 1952; *Happy and Glorious and Princess Margaret* in 1953. By 1955 she was a successful 'writer' even though most of her journalistic work was ghosted in the offices of the magazine *Woman's Own*, who had her under contract. However, on 16th June, 1955, *Woman's Own* published her typically romanticised but appealing account of Trooping the Colour and Royal Ascot. The only problem was, in the six weeks between the magazine going to press and publication date, there had been a national rail strike and both events had been cancelled.

Having been turned by Elizabeth into a pariah in Court circles, she was now a public laughing stock. Neither her reputation nor her social life recovered from these two debacles, and she and Buthlay lived out the remainder of his life in seclusion in Aberdeen. Thanks to the money she had made through her royal writings, she was comfortably off, and they remained devoted to each other until his death in 1977. She lingered on for another eleven somewhat sad years, during which time she made a suicide attempt. She finally died at Hawkhill House, an Aberdeen nursing home, on 11th February, 1988, shunned by the royal circles which had meant so much to her, and never once seeing or hearing from either of her charges. The press covered her lonely funeral, reporting on the lack of acknowledgement from Lilibet or Margaret as well as Elizabeth. What the press did not realise was that Elizabeth's two daughters would have been brave indeed if they had dared seek a *rapprochement* with the governess they had revered, for she had been using the word Crawfie the way others used Judas for nearly forty years. 'Doing a Crawfie' meant betraying someone, and Elizabeth would continue to use that expression for the remainder of the governess's life, though she tellingly stopped doing so once she was dead.

Elizabeth had succeeded brilliantly in eliminating Crawfie from her life, and in so doing had ensured that she would not have to share the maternal role with the woman who had helped to bring up her children and who, by her own admission, had often been their mother in deed if not in fact.

The Duke of Windsor always said that Elizabeth had got rid of Crawfie because she was 'jealous' of her daughters' relationship with their former governess and could not abide 'having to share their love with her.' While the documents do not reveal that aspect of the puzzle, they certainly do support the contention that Elizabeth was behind the scenes, manipulating Crawfie to perform as she did not initially wish to do, then, having fired her up, breaking her agreements with the governess she wanted to be rid of. One cannot help but conclude that the former King Edward VIII might well have hit this particular nail on its head.

Covered in Glory

Chapter Thirteen

The last five decades of Elizabeth's life demonstrate what a privileged individual can achieve if she turns her work into a pleasure, and her pleasures into an approximation of duty. Although she might have had a jealous and ruthless side to her character, by and large she loved life, loved being with people, and loved being loved by them. She was what her grandson Prince Charles called a 'life-enhancer', and as she entered old age, her way of life divided up into two distinct elements. When she was at home, she juggled a full schedule of public engagements with an even fuller diary of private ones. Because she enjoyed opening bazaars and speaking to old mayors, work was almost as much fun as speaking to her friends, many of whom had been in her life since her youth. When she was abroad, she was either undertaking private tours of places of interest, such as the various ones she undertook looking at the châteaux of the Loire in France, or then she was visiting former British colonies in the West Indies and Africa and dominions such as Canada, which became a great favourite of hers and played host to her on many occasions.

There is a sameness to royal engagements which is as stultifying to list as to witness, unless you are a participant in the event, in which case they develop an interest out of all proportion to their actuality. For that reason, it would be futile to enumerate the hundreds of events Elizabeth undertook each year, or the many tours she went on as she flew the flag for Britain and herself. Suffice it to say, she was as brilliant a performer as she had ever been, and even when she was a hundred years old, the comment Bertie made to his brother David on 9th August, 1925,[1] applied: 'She is marvellous the way she talks to old mayors & the like at shows, & she never looks tired even after the longest of days.'

She was always surrounded by people, both privately and publicly, and always going to the theatre, the ballet, to dinner, whether in a private or public capacity. Indeed, but for the attire and the level of fuss made, there was often little to distinguish the private from the public sides of her life.

Elizabeth's sense of fun did not diminish with age. For instance, in 1965 she went to Jamaica to collect an honorary degree from the University of the West Indies. She was accompanied to the ceremony at the Mona campus by Sir Clifford Campbell, Jamaica's first native-born Governor-General. The University's Chancellor was Princess Alice, Countess of Athlone, who used to spend every winter on that island fulfilling her duties and avoiding Kensington Palace winters. She was scheduled to hand her niece-by-marriage her degree. Just as Elizabeth was being walked up the aisle by Sir Clifford, there was a power cut. At that time, pest control was in its infancy and Jamaica had some rather impressive cockroaches. Elizabeth, however, was terrified of that insect, so she managed to turn what might have been an awkward moment into a witty one by observing, 'If the cockroaches didn't eat the electric cables, at least they spared us the sight of them.'[2]

She also charmed everyone when she visited the racecourse at Caymanas Park. This had been moved a few years before from Knusford Park in the city of Greater Kingston, and was now tucked away on one of the largest and most valuable sugarcane estates in the West Indies. She was entranced by the whole operation, and took her own sweet time inspecting everything from the course to the stables, while speaking to everyone from the grandest owners to the humblest stable hands. It almost does not need to be said that when she left, late as usual, she had everyone eating out of the palm of her hand.

The Caymanas Estate was owned by the Hamilton family, and Elizabeth had known Alec and Ian Hamilton's great-uncle, General Sir Ian Hamilton and his widow Jean, for some time. She happily joined the family for tea, and had a typically good time, being her customarily charming self as she scattered stardust from the picturesque verandah that overlooks cane fields for as far as the eye can see.

Some time later, when Ian Hamilton's wife, the celebrated portrait painter Basia Kaczmarowska Hamilton, informed her that Jean's memoirs had just been published, she asked, 'Are they indiscreet?' Upon hearing that they were not, she replied, 'What a pity.'[3] The truth was, she enjoyed gossip and grit in a way that was wholly representative of the legion of admirers who thought of her as beyond reproach, but who nevertheless delighted in the peccadilloes of other celebrities.

Even when she became a centenarian, she still possessed her wits as well as her wit. Basia Kaczmarowska Hamilton had been commissioned to paint her portrait for the Sikorski Museum in London to commemorate the role she had played during the Second World War in trying to preserve Poland's independence. To ensure punctuality, she had asked her husband to drop her off at Clarence House at the specified time. However, he was late, which of course made her late. Basia arrived in floods of tears. She explained what had happened, then, bemoaning how she had not been able to get her husband to do what she wanted, asked, 'My husband never listens to me. Did yours listen to you?' Quick as a flash and with a twinkle in her eye, Elizabeth replied, 'They never do.'[4]

Life can be very boring if you have the world at your feet and no interests. Elizabeth made sure she did not fall into the trap that stifled the lifeblood of other over-privileged icons of the 20th century such as Barbara Hutton. She not only maintained old interests, but in the second half of her life acquired new ones. Chief amongst these was racing. Although she had always liked horses, it was only in widowhood that she converted a vague interest into an abiding passion. By the mid-1960s, she was a fully-fledged racing fanatic. She attended just about every race meeting of any consequence whenever she was in England, and when she was abroad, did likewise in whatever country she happened to find herself.

In those days, many of the leading English jockeys, such as the great Lester Piggott, supplemented their earnings during the English off-season by going to places like Jamaica and the Bahamas, where they acquired mounts and considerable sums of cash which were beyond the reach of the English taxman. This was the period in which the British tax rate was amongst the highest in the world, so the practice was win-win from the point of view of the jockeys and foreign owners/trainers. The Piggotts of this world elevated the standard of racing wherever they went, while the wealth of the Indies helped them to earn much-needed income.

From the unfortunate Lester Piggott's point of view, however, it would all come to grief in 1987, when he was jailed for three years for tax evasion. Although he only spent 366 days in prison, the Queen was required to strip him of the Order of the British Empire which he had been awarded for his outstanding contribution to racing. He had been Champion Jockey eleven times.

One of the beautiful things about racing is that it protects its own. Though no one could prevent the law from taking its course, once Piggott had served his time, it was back to business as usual, and in 1990 the racing fraternity showed the regard it had for its fallen brother by instituting annual awards for outstanding jockeys. These were named The Lesters, in honour of the man who went on to become a leading trainer after he had been the leading rider.

To her credit, when The Lesters were introduced, Elizabeth was overheard telling one of the owners how pleased she was that Piggott was getting the recognition he deserved. 'Such a **pity** about the OBE, but **that** couldn't be helped,' she said.[5] The words in bold were her emphasis, not the author's. In the process, she conveyed regret for the action her daughter had been forced to take, while absolving her for having done so. It was this sort of demeanour that endeared her to people, and ensured that as she approached her nineties, she remained one of the greatest celebrities on earth – and the longest-lasting of all time.

As philosophers from Jesus Christ to Emmanuel to Kant have acknowledged, irony is one of life's cornerstones. All virtues have their negative aspects, all vices their mitigating features. One of Elizabeth's greatest traits was the very pronounced mischievous streak she had had from earliest childhood. It was both one of her more endearing attributes and a hint of less desirable traits lurking beneath the surface. Although there were times when it tipped into meanness, it more usually betokened good, clean, innocent fun. She was famous for forming conga-lines and making stuffy old generals and fusty old ladies trail behind her as they wove in and out of various rooms at Clarence House, sometimes into the garden and back again, having a better time than they could ever have imagined being capable of. She was also deliciously notorious for having William Tallon, her Page of the Backstairs, loosen the inhibitions of her guests with extremely generous helpings of alcohol. As a result, her parties usually went with a bang, and many a stuffed shirt discovered that he was more entertaining than he or anyone else had ever suspected.

Elizabeth was also known to prick the pompous and tease them deliciously. For instance, one of her guests once remarked that she was surprised that Elizabeth's luncheon table was laid with fish knives and forks. In England, there was a school of thought that these implements were non-aristocratic, or in the vernacular of snobs, 'common'. To people like these, the only way to eat fish was with two forks instead of a knife and fork. Plainly, these unfortunates were too insular to know that Continental royalty customarily use fish knives and forks, and have done so for the last two centuries. There is therefore nothing déclassé or nouveau about the practice. But it did become a rich source of amusement for Elizabeth once this snob had made the mistake of making her observation. Thereafter, each time she entertained this lady, Elizabeth served her fish and made a point of waving her fish knife and fork playfully, teasing her gently but mockingly. No one was safe from

Elizabeth's mockery; not even herself. As Hugo Vickers puts it, 'The Queen Mother enjoyed mimicking herself acting her charm.'

Mockery and teasing were the two sides of coins that sometimes diverged tellingly between fun and cruel disdain. Her 1956 visit to Paris is a case in point. Publicly, it was a massive success. Crowds ten and twenty deep lined the route between Le Bourget airport outside Paris and the British Embassy in the city, where British Ambassador Sir Gladwyn Jebb (later 1st Lord Gladwyn) and his wife Cynthia, whose great-grandfather had been the great Isambard Kingdom Brunel, hosted her. The City of Lights went mad for Elizabeth just as it had done during her pre-World War Two visit, causing the Ambassador to advise the Foreign Secretary, Selwyn Lloyd, 'There is no doubt at all in my mind that this kind of visit has a very profound and salutary political effect.'[6] Although Lady Jebb respected Elizabeth the Queen Mother, she had grave reservations about the individual behind the magnificent façade. She did not regard Elizabeth's private face with anything like the degree of approval her husband had for the public one. 'I find her a puzzling person. So sweet, so smiling, so soft, so charming, so winning, so easy and pleasant. And yet there is another side, which sometimes reveals itself, rather mocking, not very kind, not very loyal, almost unwise.'[7] Lady Jebb found it particularly distasteful that an old governess came to see Elizabeth, and that the Queen Mother mimicked her cruelly both before and after the visit, though she poured treacle over her for the duration of the time they were together. Nor did she appreciate the way Elizabeth waspishly blamed her 'silly maid' for providing her with 'tight gloves' when she took them off on the way to the airport at the end of the stay, and had to struggle to put them back on again, largely because she was most likely flushed, not only from the heat and excitement, but also from the alcohol which she had consumed in generous measure.

Elizabeth also antagonised Lady Jebb when the Ambassadress expressed the hope that they would not encounter the author André Maurois (born Émile Salomon Wilhelm Herzog) at a reception they were due to attend. His war record had been dubious, and memories were still fresh. Marshal Pétain had assisted his entry into the Académie Française in 1938, and the Jewish biographer of Disraeli, Byron and Shelley had gratefully acknowledged this debt in his 1941 autobiography *Call No Man Happy*, written from the safety of Canada, notwithstanding that the Marshal was by then the head of state of collaborationist Vichy France. Elizabeth, however, was as contrary as 'any other old soak', as the Duke of Windsor put it. Once she knew that Lady Jebb did not want them to see Maurois, she therefore insisted that she must meet up with him, and duly did so.

This mixture of rebelliousness, mischievousness, and downright cussedness might have been annoying sometimes, but at other times, it could be funny, and at yet others, a mixed bag indeed. For instance, Elizabeth once put herself in the middle of the feud between Margaret, Duchess of Argyll, and Maureen, Marchioness of Dufferin and Ava. Like many women of her generation, Elizabeth loved nothing better than the whirl and swirl of Society. She thrilled to its peaks and troughs, its ebb and flow, its friendships and enmities. Two of its most legendary figures for much of the 20th century were Margaret and Maureen. They had once been friends, but Maureen had turned against Margaret in the run-up to the infamous Argyll divorce of 1959–1963, 'when she thought I was done for socially', to quote Margaret.[8] She had even funded litigation against the Duchess, which Margaret regarded as unforgivable treachery.

Each year, Maureen used to have a large dinner party at which Elizabeth was the guest of honour. This became the vehicle for Elizabeth's mischievousness. She saw Margaret at a reception and made a beeline for her. As Margaret told it, Elizabeth said, 'I understand I will be having the pleasure of meeting your daughter-in-law at Mrs. Maude's.'[9] Mrs. Maude was Maureen, and Elizabeth was being very naughty indeed, but delightfully so, in calling her that, for though Maureen had continued to style herself Marchioness of Dufferin and Ava, she had remarried twice since her first husband's death in 1945. Her second husband had been Major Desmond Buchanan for six years, following which she had divorced him in 1954 and married His Honour Judge John Maude, to whom she remained married until his death in 1988. So technically she had been Mrs. Buchanan and Mrs. Maude as well as the Dowager Marchioness of Dufferin and Ava.

Although Margaret picked up Elizabeth's deliciously bitchy way of demoting Maureen, she was perplexed at how the Queen Mother could be telling her that she was going to be seeing her son's wife at one of Maureen's dinners. So she said, 'I cannot imagine Brian accepting an invitation from Maureen or allowing Judith (his then wife) to go on her own.' 'No, not her,' Elizabeth said. 'Your stepson Colin's wife,'[10] with which Elizabeth sashayed off, her laughter tinkling mischievously as she looked behind her shoulder as if to say, 'I would so love to stay and chat, but duty demands that I depart.'

Bright and early the following morning, I received a telephone call from the step-mother-in-law of whom I was fond. She was wavering between hurt perplexity and barely-concealed anger. How could I have 'betrayed' her by accepting an invitation from 'that bitch'? That description was fair comment, for Maureen did have a reputation along those lines, to such an extent that Cecil Beaton had observed in 1935 to hosts who were also entertaining her,

'Do you realise that you have here, in Maureen Dufferin, the biggest bitch in London?'[11]

I explained to Margaret that I had actually encountered Maureen at something a few weeks before, and she had asked me if I would like to come to her dinner for Queen Elizabeth The Queen Mother. 'I had little doubt that the only reason she asked me was to hurt you. On the few occasions that our paths have crossed, we've exchanged barely ten words, so I didn't think she was asking me for my wit,' I explained, somewhat gratified that my perceptions had proven to be accurate. 'I thanked her for her kind invitation and told her I knew I would be busy that evening. I didn't want to be rude to someone who could be my grandmother, and tell her that I could not possibly accept any invitation from her, as my relationship with you is far more important to me. But I have no doubt that she got the message loud and clear, because I declined without even bothering to consult my diary.'

'That explains it then. The bitch told Queen Elizabeth that you were going, knowing only too well that she wouldn't be able to resist the temptation to tell me. I daresay Maureen expected me to be so upset that I'd cut you dead without ever telling you why.' At that, Margaret laughed. 'That was a miscalculation, wasn't it, sweetie? I do think though that it was a bit naughty of the Queen Mother to tell me. Suppose it had been true.'

It had indeed been naughty. I could never see what she hoped to accomplish, save to keep her oar in and establish that she was a part of the dramas and conflicts that were the lifeblood of the social world. At a time when no one worked seriously the way people do nowadays, Society was full of people who had so much time on their hands that they frequently occupied themselves with creating confusion. They would then sit back and enjoy the chaos they had unleashed, sixty- and eighty-year-olds acting like six- and eight-year-olds.

Elizabeth relished being the fairy at the top of this tree. Although she had a sense of humour about it and would send herself up when the mood took her, it would be a mistake to think that she regarded her role as a joke. All the world might have been her stage, and she strutted and fretted her hour upon it with levity and jocularity, but Eleanor Roosevelt had been right to be frightened about her inability to ever drop the regal act and just be herself. Even in the privacy of her family's homes, she never ceased to act out being royal. She often entertained or visited her relations, chief of whom was her favourite sibling, David. Even with him, however, she never eased up. The wealthy Hoffman La Roche businessman, pianist and Royal Opera House board member Burnet Pavitt used to rent a house from David Bowes Lyon. In defiance of the customs of the time, this youngest son of the earl had been left St. Paul's Walden Bury and the estate by his father, who favoured his two children with Marguerite Rodiere above all the others. Burnet was a great friend of one of my son's godfathers, and was also very friendly with David and his family. He also knew George Harewood, who was one of the leading lights in the opera world, and had the highest respect for my cousin Sir Peter Jonas, who was then the Director of the English National Opera. We therefore had many points of sympathy. He told me, 'Queen Elizabeth is absolutely extraordinary. Even though they were brother and sister and as close as could be, you could never, for one second, forget that you were in the presence of a queen. I have known other queens, and they never behaved like that. With her, it was Ma'am this and Ma'am that, even from her brother. He would have to wait at the foot of the stairs when she was due to descend for dinner. She invariably kept him waiting. But he dared not go into an adjoining room. He had to be there, standing, waiting, waiting, waiting, so that when she got to the landing and looked down, she could see him hovering. She would give him a little wave and float down, all smiles, and he would kiss her, and, if you had not been staying for the weekend and were just there for dinner, he would bow and call her Ma'am before leading her in to meet the guests who would be assembled in the drawing room. The whole performance was in case someone had missed his bow in the morning, which always had to be delivered irrespective of who was and wasn't there. During conversation, he would address her as Ma'am. That always struck me as extraordinary. Significant. It would be Ma'am, even when it was just the three of us together. Quite extraordinary. And quite unlike the way other queens behaved.'[12]

Burnet Pavitt told me that those who did not do exactly as Elizabeth required were cut out of her life. Both she and David also had a love of intrigue, and were often hatching schemes together. One he featured in was the dispatching of Crawfie, though no one knows if he realised what Elizabeth was up to until Crawfie found herself frozen out of royal life. He was always loyal to his sister, however, and would never say a word against her, though he also took care to let you know that she still had him acting as her co-conspirator, in much the same way they had done as children.

One of the greatest sadnesses of Elizabeth's life would be the death of this beloved brother, who died on 13th September, 1961. He had been staying with her at Birkhall on the Balmoral Estate in Scotland, and she discovered him in bed. According to Burnet, she was more cut up by his death than she was by anyone else's, with the possible exception of King George VI's. As we have seen, her husband's death had had both personal and worldly repercussions for her, so it would have been doubly affecting irrespective of her personal feelings. Her reaction to David's death leaves us in no doubt of the great bond brother and sister shared.

As Elizabeth got older, more and more of her friends and relations died. Two who remained hale and hearty, however, were her brother-in-law David and his wife Wallis. Notwithstanding her best endeavours over the years to make them pariahs, they were, in many respects, the uncrowned king and queen of French and American Society. She might have had England, but outside of it they possessed a degree of eminence that none of her efforts had been able to dent. In 1955 President Eisenhower entertained them at the White House, showing that all the propaganda about the Windsors being pro-Nazi had not had the desired effect of excluding them from being feted by the American Government and its head, who had been the wartime Supreme Commander of Allied Forces, and therefore in a position to know as a fact that all the pro-Nazi stories had been nothing but vicious canards.

Indeed, to Americans, Wallis was *their* duchess, just as how Grace Kelly became their princess. They were justly proud of both women, who conducted themselves exemplarily. Even before Lilibet and her family were taking part in *Royal Family* in the United Kingdom in the 1960s, Wallis and David were blazing the way by being interviewed by Edward R. Morrow on *Person to Person* in the United States in 1956.

By the 1960s, however, the Duke was becoming infirm. In December 1964 the world-famous heart surgeon Michael DeBakey operated on him in Houston for an aneurysm of the abdominal aorta, and in February the following year he and his duchess were in London for Sir Stewart Duke-Elder, Surgeon-Oculist from his reign to the present queen's, to operate upon him for a detached retina in the left eye at the London Clinic. His sister Mary, the Princess Royal, was the first of his family to visit.

Mary had never become reconciled to the way he had been treated, and had even declined to attend the wedding of their niece Lilibet, pleading ill health though it was well known within the family and royal circles that she had refused to go because David had not been asked. It goes without saying that, by this time, inviting David meant having Wallis as well, for there was no question of his accepting an invitation that did not include her – unless, of course, she wished to refuse it on her own behalf.

Although the former king was subsequently invited to the weddings of his two other nieces, Princess Margaret in 1960 and Princess Alexandra of Kent in 1963, he declined both invitations, for by then he had no desire to be a part of the Royal Family.[13] Too much water had flowed under that particular bridge for him to enact a public charade of happy families, although he and Wallis did entertain Margaret and Tony Snowdon to tea at the Waldorf

Astoria when both couples were in New York. As far as he and Wallis were concerned, it was more dignified to remain apart from the official life of the Royal Family than to have partial inclusion at this late stage, though they were pleased when private contacts were made.

Princess Marina also came to visit at the London Clinic, and they were absolutely delighted when Lilibet, to whom he had been inordinately close for the first ten years of her life, dropped in to see them as well. It was good to have the fences mended, though to no one's surprise, Elizabeth remained as implacable as ever. It was as if she could forgive those who had harmed her, but not those whom she had harmed. And she had damaged no one quite so effectively as David, the brother-in-law who had ever only shown her kindness and generosity when he had been in a position to do so. Quite unlike the vitriol she had poured over him once she had wrested that power from his grasp, after which she behaved as if they had always been implacable enemies.

To the consternation of the whole Royal Family, the week after Mary visited David at the London Clinic, she dropped dead while out walking at Harewood House with her son George. Although David was too ill to attend her funeral, he and Wallis did attend her memorial service, proving how sincere he was when he used to say, 'We must never go anywhere unless we can both enter through the front door.'[14]

Thirty-one years after the Abdication, Wallis and Elizabeth's paths finally crossed again when the Windsors attended in 1967 the ceremony for the unveiling of the plaque celebrating the centenary of Queen Mary's birth. The meeting was charged with symbolism and electricity. Elizabeth arrived looking like homespun sugar, smiling sweetly to one and all, spreading insincere bonhomie like fake gold dust over those who did and did not want it, while Wallis was sleek, chic and gracious, a study in sincerity and dignity. She curtsied to the Queen but her knees locked and she straightened up rather than dipping, when Elizabeth hove into view. Though she looked correct enough while they were exchanging the pleasantries that civilised conduct requires, you could tell from her underlying look of distaste that she could not abide either Elizabeth or her hypocrisy. Afterwards, she told many friends, including Margaret, Duchess of Argyll, that she had felt defiled by the encounter with her old adversary. Elizabeth 'poured poisoned sugar' as naturally as her ambitious predecessor Lady Macbeth, but lacked the 'decency to wash her sticky fingers'.

After the ceremony, the Windsors lunched with Princess Marina at Kensington Palace, little realising that Marina would be dead within a year. She died from a brain tumour at Kensington Palace on 27th August, 1968, at the relatively young age of sixty-one. David came over for her funeral and interment at the Royal Burial Ground at Frogmore, where he is meant to have inspected his own and the Duchess's burial sites which would be nearby the widow of his favourite brother.

The private fence-mending within the family continued the following year when Lilibet invited the previous Prince of Wales and his duchess to his great-nephew Prince Charles's investiture as Prince of Wales in an arcane but beautiful ceremony devised by Tony Snowdon in Wales. As Philip Ziegler, Edward VIII's official biographer, confirms, David declined, stating that Charles would not want 'his aged great-uncle there'. In fact, as the Duke and Duchess both told Margaret, Duchess of Argyll, they had long ago taken the decision that the most dignified way to behave was to avoid all public events associated with the Royal Family, save those that involved death. Although they appreciated the efforts now being made by the younger generation, it was too late to erase the past. To do that would have been validating the wastefulness which had been imposed upon them by Elizabeth's malice and jealousy. David had only ever wanted to continue to contribute to his country the way he had been trained to do – and more importantly, wanted to do. Although he and, to a lesser extent, Wallis had found their exclusion an indignity, the main issue for them had not been a matter of status, but the waste of his talents, energies and training. He was not going to pretend that three decades of enforced inactivity had meant nothing to him.

If the Windsors were not prepared to allow the British Court to include them in its activities, they were definitely open to any signal of honour or recognition emanating from North America. In 1970 they were delighted to accept an invitation from President and Mrs. Richard M. Nixon to be guests of honour at an official dinner at the White House. David was dapper in white tie and tails and Wallis was stunning in a long white dress with a heavily jewelled band extending from her narrow waist to the base of her bosom. Although she could have worn a tiara, or any of her spectacular array of jewels, she was a study in simplicity, with no necklace, modest earrings, and white gloves concealing the rings on her fingers, though a simple, elegant diamond bangle sparkled over one glove.

By the following year, the Duke's health had declined further. A heavy smoker like his brother, father and grandfather, all of whom had died of smoking-related diseases, he went to the American Hospital in Paris, where it was suspected that he might be developing throat cancer. Wallis herself would later tell Margaret Argyll and many other friends, as well as Richard Rene Silvin, who ran the American Hospital in Paris, that she bitterly regretted not having taken her husband elsewhere once she realised that he had a problem. By the time they began intensive treatment, it was too late.

Lilibet, Philip and Charles were in Paris on an official visit from 15th to 19th May, 1972. They called in on Uncle David and Aunt Wallis, knowing full well that it was the last opportunity they had to see their dying uncle. Afterwards, Wallis joined them for a photo-call outside.

The Duke of Windsor died less than two weeks later, on 28th May, 1972, a month short of his seventy-eighth birthday. His dying words were, 'The waste.....the waste.....oh, the waste.....the waste of it all.....' He had never regretted marrying Wallis, and always said that he would marry her 'again tomorrow' if given the chance. But he had never got over the waste that Elizabeth had exacted, in his opinion, solely because he had married Wallis instead of her. 'Her malice was incalculable,' he used to say. 'Incalculable and unpredictable. Bertie and I had been such friends and I'd thought she was my friend too. Until I discovered that she was my implacable enemy. So sad. And so unnecessary.'

As had been agreed with his niece Lilibet, David's body was flown back to England. He lay in state at St. George's Chapel, Windsor, where a multitude of people, some who had known him, most who had not, came to pay their respects. Wallis was then flown to London, where she was put up at Buckingham Palace, proving that she had never really been the sticking point, as is further confirmed by Nicky Haslam, who quoted Princess Margaret in his memoirs confirming that it was David rather than Wallis who was the target of antipathy.

Wallis attended the funeral, which was held at Windsor in the presence of the whole Royal Family, including Elizabeth, who knew only too well that the one person whose presence Wallis did not want at this most painful point was hers.

To make matters worse, Elizabeth could not resist the urge to 'pour poisoned sugar' over the widow during the event. In Wallis's view, this faux sweetness was nothing more than a ploy on Elizabeth's part to enhance her reputation for kindness while knowing that by inflicting her unwanted attentions, she would actually be increasing the discomfort of the grief-stricken individual. Such cruel hypocrisy did nothing to make Wallis's task in saying goodbye to the man she had come to love any easier. 'Had she had true consideration, she would have got whooping cough or one of the other convenient illnesses she was always prey to,' Wallis told Margaret, Duchess of Argyll and several other friends. 'I could tell she was really enjoying herself. She had such a cruel streak. She could be such a monster.'[15]

Rather than stay on after the burial at Frogmore, Wallis opted to leave immediately for Paris on board an aircraft of the Queen's Flight. She had appreciated Lilibet's gesture in putting her up at Buckingham Palace, but couldn't wait to return home, where she did not have to be subjected to the 'phoney saccharine sweetness of the Monster of Glamis.'[16]

'Wallis was a wonderful woman. She made an excellent duchess and would have made a magnificent queen,' Rene Silvin told me. He knew her well because she sat on the board of the American Hospital which he ran, and was 'moral' and 'helpful'. She was also a superb tactician, and assisted him when he had trouble with some of the board members who were opposing the elimination of old privileges and antiquated practices. 'She was a very great lady, and it hurts to think of some of the injustices she suffered. But she was stalwart and had a sound character. She once said to me, "Like I was, you have been harshly criticized for doing the right thing. Do try to make such criticism strengthen you. You will always be criticized regardless of what you do, so you might as well get used to it." She was very humane and wise, and strong.'

Once Elizabeth had turned on the treacle, however, she was determined to continue pouring it over the sister-in-law whose life she had damaged. Thereafter, until Wallis's own decline into dementia six years later, Elizabeth would periodically send her flowers or offer to call upon her when she was in Paris. She would also send Christmas cards. Wallis steadfastly refused to see her, had the flowers promptly sent to hospitals, and never put out the cards. 'She's playing to the gallery,' she used to explain. 'Trying to establish herself as a kind-hearted old biddy when she is nothing but a poisonous witch who did everything in her power to destroy my husband's life. Her cruelty knew no bounds. Now she hopes that by sending a few flowers and cards and offering to visit she can eradicate decades of destruction. But she can't. She made a waste of David's life and his dying words were "the waste, the waste of it all". I would have to be as monstrous as she is to receive her. And that I am not.'[17]

The Duchess of Windsor thought that her husband's death might also have given the Queen Mother some sort of release from the frustration and jealousy that his rejection of the maiden Elizabeth, and marriage to herself, had engendered. This might have been true. The cessation of Elizabeth's venom when David died might not have been solely an act of cruelty or a ploy to shore up her reputation in the eyes of the world, though those two elements were most likely a part of the whole as well. She might well have been relieved to be free finally of the pathological rage which had resulted from his rejection of her and marriage to Wallis, and might well have been genuinely trying to sympathise with what in her mind was their joint loss, while at the same moment protecting her reputation for sweetness.

Psychologists will tell you that duality of purpose can result from conflicting and contradictory elements within the personality. There is every likelihood that Elizabeth's friendliness towards Wallis might therefore have been born of conflicting elements of widely divergent motivations which, on the face of it, were anything but straightforward.

Although the lion's share of Elizabeth's attentions ceased once Wallis was engulfed by dementia, she did from time to time enquire of the bedridden and mindless Duchess until Wallis's death in 1986. When this event occurred, Wallis's body was flown over to England and she was buried beside the Duke of Windsor in the Royal Burial Ground at Frogmore. Elizabeth, of course, was at her funeral, but the woman whose waterworks flowed for everything from one of her horses winning a race to the death of strangers shed not one tear. Indeed, she smiled benignly throughout the funeral, as if Wallis's death had released her from something as well.

To many observers, it was peculiar that a woman who had shunned the Duchess in her life could show up at her funeral as a mourner. As Margaret, Duchess of Argyll observed, 'Wallis must be spinning in her grave to know that her old adversary gave her the respect in death she could never quite manage in life.'

Wallis was interred beside David. The simple tablet still denies her the rank of Royal Highness to which the wives of all English princes are entitled, and perpetuates the fiction that she was merely 'Wallis, Duchess of Windsor'.

Nor were the Windsors' deaths the only ones that seemed to provide Elizabeth with a release from her private demons. The death of Prince Philip's mother in fact had been the first of a series of royal deaths which somehow set Elizabeth free from discomfiting emotions.

Alice, Princess Andrew of Greece had been an extraordinary woman. Not only did she lip read in English, German, French and Greek, having been deaf since birth, but she had formed a nursing order of Greek Orthodox nuns within two years of her son's marriage to the future Queen Elizabeth II. Thereafter, she was also known as Mother Superior Alice-Elizabeth – the second name in honour of her aunt, Elizabeth Feodorovna, Grand Duchess Serge of Russia (and sister of the last Tsarina), a saint of the Russian Orthodox Church, who had founded a similar order in Russia in 1909.

Alice established a home for the order in a hamlet outside Athens, and undertook two fund-raising tours of the United States in 1950 and 1952, which were successful enough to keep the order afloat. However, it would ultimately fail because of a paucity of suitable applicants.

By the time her daughter-in-law was crowned queen in 1953, Alice had renounced the fripperies of a worldly existence and attended the coronation in her grey habit. However, she was no stick-in-the-mud. As her mother, the Dowager Marchioness of Milford Haven, put it, 'What can you say of a nun who smokes and plays canasta?'[18]

In many ways, Alice was the polar opposite of her daughter-in-law's mother, Elizabeth the Queen Mother. While the former lived a life of extreme simplicity, the latter lived one of supreme lavishness. While one opted for plainness, the other strove at all times to embellish. Yet each in her own way had achieved something profound through the force of her personality and the power of her beliefs. If Alice's contribution had been smaller, that was because she was a mere princess of a minor power, and not a queen and former empress of a world power like Great Britain. Nevertheless, it was generally acknowledged, amongst people who knew both women well, that Alice's motivations and accomplishments had been purer, because they lacked the taint of self-interest which often attached itself to Elizabeth's far greater accomplishments.

There was little or no common ground between the two women, save their children's marriage and their mutual grandchildren. However, because Alice lived in Greece and Elizabeth in Britain, there was little room for antipathy. Then, in April 1967, the Colonel's Coup overthrew the democratically-elected government of Greece. The young King Constantine II spent the remainder of the year trying to find a way to rid the country of the military dictatorship, but the putsch he organised came to nought, and in December of that year he and his young queen, the former Princess Anne-Marie of Denmark, were forced into exile in Rome.

Philip and Lilibet had sensibly not waited until then to ask Alice to come and live with them at Buck House. And she, who had been hostage to so many coups and counter-coups in her adopted country for much of the century, made the decision to leave once and for all. She therefore did so shortly after the colonels seized power, spending the remaining two years of her life with her son and daughter-in-law in her own suite of rooms at the palace.

This, evidently, became a problem for Elizabeth. Princess Margaret told Colin Glenconner that her mother was 'insanely jealous' that Lilibet 'preferred' being with Alice. They had a good, easy, loving relationship, free of any of the frictions that characterised the other relationship.

Although Elizabeth was 'not a happy bunny' having Alice around, there was little she could do about it except pass acid comments about the 'chain-smoking nun' whose biggest 'affair had been with God' – an allusion to Alice's breakdown in 1930 when she is meant to have imagined herself having congress with the Lord. These remarks were frequently dressed up as sympathy or even admiration and couched with the customary coating of sugar. On reflection, though, they always had a nasty sting in the tail, such as praising Alice's otherworldliness, then tartly commenting on how 'nothing rivets the eye quite so much as a nun in grey surrounded by everyone else in hats and gloves. Such a scene stealer.'

By the time Alice came to live at Buckingham Palace, she was physically frail, largely due to the ill-effects of being a chain-smoker. Elizabeth did nothing to discourage the rumours that Alice was also suffering from senile dementia, but this was not the case. She remained lucid until the end, dying on 5th December, 1969, at Buckingham Palace. She left no possessions, having given everything away to the poor years before.

Inevitably, word of Elizabeth's relief that 'the nun who is a Hun' was no more got back to the Duke and Duchess of Windsor, just as word of her dissatisfaction at the success Alice had had during the two and a half years she lived with Lilibet and Philip at Buck House had reached them. The Duke of Windsor told Margaret, Duchess of Argyll that he was sure that Elizabeth welcomed Alice's death, because it released her from having to cope with the feelings of jealousy that her daughter Lilibet's love for Prince Philip's mother would have aroused in her self-centred mother.

Whatever the Windsors' failings, hypocrisy was not amongst them. They were refreshingly candid about how much they had enjoyed reports of Alice's success with Lilibet driving Elizabeth up the wall. Wallis admitted that they had not relished another's misfortune so much since they had heard, in December 1966, that Elizabeth had been operated on for colon cancer. 'All those chocolates have bunged up her plumbing,' Wallis had said, alluding to her sister-in-law's well-known passion for that candy. David's response had been to puff his cheeks out in emulation of Elizabeth's, and to laugh and say, 'I always warned her that too many chocolates would be her undoing.'

Although the Windsors' comments were unkind, they contained more than an element of truth. William Tallon used to say that Elizabeth liked nothing better than sitting in bed eating a whole box of chocolates, and Lady Diana Cooper stated that the Queen Mother was such a chocoholic that she would even eat Good Boy dog biscuits. As Hugo Vickers so elegantly put it, 'She had settled into a cosy existence of rich food and a certain laziness.' Aside from chocolates, '(s)he relished butterscotch, cream and butter. She punctuated the day with elevenses and afternoon tea, and she lunched and dined well.' It is hardly surprising that a diet such as hers had resulted in both obesity and cancer, but Elizabeth had good genes, and she made a complete recovery.

One must remember that Elizabeth was the sort of personality who loved her pleasures and loathed any form of discomfort. This meant that she was averse to any unpleasantness that would puncture her serene bubble. She maintained an ostrich-like serenity with determination enhanced by a steady intake of alcoholic beverages, which took the unpleasant edge off things and helped to keep her in the state of euphoria which seemed her natural habitat. Whether she was an alcoholic was a question frequently asked by people in Court circles. Certainly the Windsors believed she was; they customarily referred to her as a 'soak'.

Her drinking habits demand examination. If Elizabeth was up early, for instance to fulfil an official engagement, her staff would instruct her hosts that she should be offered a drink upon arrival. This meant that she would have her first drink at ten or eleven in the morning. She invariably had spirits before lunch followed by wine with lunch. Later on, she would have yet more spirits before dinner as *aperitifs*, followed by wine and champagne and yet stronger alcoholic drinks as *digestifs* after dinner.

Elizabeth had been floating on a sea of booze for much of her life. As Shawcross confirms in the official biography, she had even started a drinking club when she first became queen. But her alcoholic intake, though excessive if applied to the average person, can have done her no harm. She remained in robust good health for over a century, and died after eight decades spent knocking back booze with a relish that was equalled only by the amount of food she consumed.

Although Elizabeth had a reputation as a boozer, she was never drunk, though never sober either. She paced herself well enough so that she never appeared to be inebriated. She also managed to avoid damaging her health. Her intake was steady but measured, and while someone with a weaker constitution would doubtless have suffered adverse consequences from indulgence of food and drink in such vast quantities, the fact that she spent eight decades gorging herself and buried most of her contemporaries shows that she was also doing something which agreed with her.

According to any accepted medical criteria of the level of alcoholic consumption which qualifies an individual for a diagnosis of alcoholism, Elizabeth was undoubtedly an alcoholic. Whether she was an alpha or a beta alcoholic was another matter. At the very least, she was what is known as a functional alcoholic. Alcoholics are notoriously prone to using booze to blot out issues which they find unpleasant or inconvenient to deal with. They typically dampen emotions which cause them discomfort, and heighten those which provide pleasure. This Elizabeth obviously did, though whether one can adjudge such conduct a mistake if it keeps one alive, healthy and happy into one's hundred and second year is open to interpretation.

As the years passed and Elizabeth's friends and relations began dying off in ever-increasing numbers, she herself gave no intimation of age slowing her down. In 1980 she turned eighty. She was as fit as a fiddle. She still walked for miles at a stretch, rode, fished, and danced Scottish reels with a vigour that many twenty-year-olds could not manage. That she would live to celebrate another milestone, such as her eightieth birthday, was celebrated as a major event unlikely to be repeated.

There were two main aspects to the celebrations of this milestone. The first was for the family, and began with a dance at Windsor Castle shared with the two other royal octogenarians, the widowed Princess Alice, Duchess of Gloucester (who would actually outlive Elizabeth), whose husband Harry had died on 10th June, 1974, and 'Master', the 10th Duke of Beaufort, whose wife May was born Princess May of Teck and was Queen Mary's namesake niece. Present was Elizabeth's *bête noire* Mollie, by now the Dowager Duchess of Buccleuch, who was, of course, Princess Alice's sister-in-law and still only too happy to remind everyone of how she had prevailed with James Stuart while Elizabeth had not.

The public celebrations were kicked off with a Service of Thanksgiving at St. Paul's Cathedral which took place on 15th July, 1980. I can remember that there was a distinct feeling that this had better be a good show, as Elizabeth was unlikely to live to experience another quite like it. Lilibet yielded precedence to her mother so that Elizabeth could remain the centre of attention as she arrived at and left the cathedral in a procession of carriages that clattered through the streets of London as people in their thousands shouted their acclamations. The Archbishop of Canterbury made the shrewd observation that Elizabeth had 'occupied the centre of the stage since 1923 without suffering the fate which so frequently befalls the fashionable personality who is played out after ten years or so in the public eye.' She was also acclaimed in the House of Commons by politicians of all parties, though the left-winger Dennis Skinner and the republican Willie Hamilton deftly contrasted her supreme privilege with that of most other octogenarians, and in so doing showed that she might have been extraordinary, but so too had her luck and circumstances. Mrs. Thatcher, who had been elected Prime Minister the year before, did however praise her as 'a Queen who had been strong with the brave, had mourned with the sad, and had enchanted everyone by her grace and wit.' Following that, there was a garden party at Buckingham Palace, at which one guest commented on how worried she had been about Elizabeth's unsuitably light attire in the carriage procession. William Tallon recounted that her inimitable riposte was pure Elizabeth: 'I had the love of the British people to keep me warm.'

On the birthday itself, there was a fly-past from the Royal Air Force Flying School in an 'E' formation. This was followed by a ballet gala at the Royal

Opera House, Convent Garden. This was a glittering occasion outshone only by the birthday girl herself, who sparkled as only she could from the top of her head to the tip of her toes with jewels which were dim in comparison to the light shining forth from her brilliant personality. Everyone rose, as they always do, when royalty arrives. As she was taking her seat in the royal box, Sir Robert Helpmann, the famous Australian dancer exclaimed, 'What a performance!' Sir Frederick Ashton, the great choreographer of the Royal Ballet and director of opera, ballet and theatre revues, replied, 'Yes. But what a role!'

It was also a role that would need to be filled for a successive generation. If human nature compels us to think of our descendants before they are even born, no one is more preoccupied with their successors than royalty. Without that progeny, monarchy comes to an end. Hence why, by the time of Elizabeth's eightieth birthday celebrations, she and everyone else in the Royal Family were expressing concern that Prince Charles was over thirty and still not married.

Feeling the pressure from many different sources, and willing though not eager to do his duty, Charles had been considering the feasibility of a union with his cousin Amanda Knatchbull when her grandfather Lord Mountbatten, who was his mentor and was also fostering the match, was assassinated in Ireland in 1979. Charles then turned his attention to Anna Wallace, the beautiful, headstrong daughter of a Scots landowner whom he met while out hunting. She was known as 'Whiplash' because of her fiery disposition, and even though he proposed marriage to her, she dumped him at Elizabeth's eightieth birthday party because he had left her for too long to talk to Camilla Parker Bowles.

Elizabeth was close to her favourite grandchild. She was aware that Charles was depressed by the course his life had taken. Dickie Mountbatten had been his primary emotional mainstay, and it is interesting to note that Elizabeth never once tried to come between her grandson and his 'honorary grandfather', as he called Mountbatten, notwithstanding the dire prognostications she and the ossifiers had predicted, when Lilibet first ascended the throne, would result from his supposedly overweening ambition.

None of these predictions, of course, had come about, because none of them had been grounded in reality. While many of the courtiers who had assisted Elizabeth in the Stop-the-Mountbattens movement had been encouraged to resign sooner rather than later once Lilibet was securely on the throne, their actions at the time had carved out a position of some influence and considerable participation for Elizabeth, far more than any preceding dowager queen had enjoyed.

The way she handled herself, as Charles grew up and became closer and closer to her *bête noire*, leads one to conclude that the Duke of Windsor might have had a point when he said, 'Elizabeth and Dickie are two peas of one pod. Ambitious, opportunistic and vain. They could never stand each other because they are too similar, but over the years they have developed a tolerance for each other that owes everything to rampant ambition and nothing to affection.'[19]

One indisputable area of similarity they shared was their dedication to shaping the next king. Although polar opposites politically, both had a vision of monarchy that overlapped in terms of the cultivation of public opinion; the accumulation of influence through the dual bodies politic of the Establishment and the People; a veneration for the system of Monarchy; a desire to conserve (and in his case, though not hers, to update) the institutions that had made Britain great; an enjoyment of the splendours and powers of the Monarchy; and the desire to perpetuate that Institution into the distant future. Elizabeth and Dickie might have had justifiable reservations about each other's characters, but where the larger picture was concerned, they had more in common than either would have been willing to concede. And both were wily operators who understood that making a battlefield of Charles's loyalties would have initially impacted adversely upon him, and ultimately upon themselves. Since neither was prepared to take the risk of losing in the quest for the next king's soul, they tolerated each other with scrupulous but icy correctness. 'It was an open secret that they loathed each other,' Margaret, Duchess of Argyll said. 'Barbara (her best friend Dame Barbara Cartland, who was one of Mountbatten's closest friends) could be very funny about how he would have liked nothing better than to see her drop over the railings of Britannia after two too many.'

Had Mountbatten lived, it is unlikely that Elizabeth would have prevailed, to the extent that she did, in promoting Lady Diana Spencer as a prospective bride for Charles. What is certain is that Diana would not have had the superb opening line with which she captured Charles's interest. She had been staying for the weekend as a guest of Philip de Pass, a godson of Prince Philip's and the son of a distant cousin of mine, Lieutenant Commander Robert de Pass and his wife Philippa, at their house in Petworth, Sussex. The de Passes and Lilibet and Philip were good friends, so the whole house party went to watch Prince Charles and his then team, Les Diables Bleux, play polo at nearby Cowdray Park. After the game, Charles came back to the de Pass house for a barbecue.

Like many girls of her age and station, Diana had already stated that she had ambitions to become the Princess of Wales, though Prince Andrew would do as a spouse if she couldn't get the 'top job'. At the barbecue, she sensed her chance to make an impression, so she went over to Charles, who was momentarily sitting on a bale of hay looking pensive. It was well known within royal circles that he was extremely depressed about the break-up of his relationship with Anna Wallace, and that he felt Lord Mountbatten's loss acutely. Taking a seat beside him, Diana quickly displayed the sympathetic streak for which she would later win worldwide praise when the public was treated to glimpses of it.

Her move was shrewd, but Diana already understood, as few young people do, to what extent sympathy wins hearts. She had developed this trait during her years as a boarder at West Heath, which had a compulsory scheme of community visits. Diana, who was systematically bottom of her class, had even won the Leggatt Cup for Helpfulness, and since leaving school, she had capitalised upon her facility. This she did not only privately, but in her chosen career as a kindergarten teacher, where a firm and loving hand needed to be supplemented with sympathy to bring rewards.

Like Elizabeth, Diana hid an ambitious, predatory nature behind a sweet and easy countenance. Both of them had the talent of saying the right thing at the right moment to bring about the desired effect. Both of them also knew how to seize the moment. These are not virtues that can be readily taught. They are, to an extent, instinctive, and Diana, sensing her opportunity, grabbed it effectively when she sat beside Charles on that bale of hay at the de Pass house. She brought up Lord Mountbatten and said, 'When I saw you walking up the aisle at Westminster Abbey, I thought it was the most tragic thing I had ever seen. You looked so desolate and alone it made my heart bleed for you. I thought what you need is someone to understand you, to be there for you, to take care of you.'[20]

Diana herself told me that it was at that moment that her relationship with the Prince of Wales changed from a distant acquaintanceship into something more substantial. There is little doubt that this was true, though he did not thereafter do anything like the degree of chasing she would subsequently give him credit for. Had it not been for Elizabeth's active collusion behind the scenes with Diana's family, there is little doubt that nothing would have come of this start. Nevertheless, it would prove to be promising, if only because Charles needs sympathy the way a junkie needs dope.

In many ways, Diana and her family were as ambitious as Elizabeth and Cecilia Strathmore had been. However, while the Strathmore family had never been ambitious of royal links before Elizabeth and her mother forged their glorious alliance, for two hundred and fifty years the Spencers had been actively pursuing any connection of any description they could achieve with the Royal Family. In the early seventeen hundreds, Sarah, Duchess of Marlborough had even offered King George II's heir Frederick, Prince of Wales, the then astronomical sum of £100,000 (hundreds of millions in today's money) to marry her favourite granddaughter, Lady Diana Spencer. The Prime Minister refused to countenance a union which was impertinence in a day and age when aristocrats did not marry royalty. Moreover, the Spencer and Churchill peerages were both relatively recent, and the families were therefore regarded more as *arrivistes* than established aristocrats. Although very rich, they were looked down upon in terms of breeding, and since no aristocrat was good enough to be a Queen of England, it stood to reason that a parvenu one was even more unacceptable.

After this abortive stab at becoming royal, the Spencers became just the sort of royalty-obsessed, appointment-chasing family which Elizabeth's father despised. They were about the Court the way ticks are about a dog. They attached themselves both officially and unofficially. Lady Georgiana Spencer, who later became the celebrated Duchess of Devonshire and whose life was turned into the motion picture *The Duchess*, starring Keira Knightley, was a mistress of the Prince of Wales who became King George IV, and even had his illegitimate child. Diana's father was an equerry to King George VI and Queen Elizabeth II, and his mother Cynthia was a Lady of the Bedchamber to Queen Elizabeth The Queen Mother as well as an old friend.

Before Diana's advent, the family had had high hopes that something would come of Prince Charles's courtship of her eldest sister Sarah. But the eldest Spencer sister had blotted her copy irretrievably when she tried to spur the dithering Prince into greater commitment by declaring that she would never marry anyone she didn't love, irrespective of whether he was a prince or a dustman. The diffident Charles, so careful of his feelings that his great-aunt Princess Alice, Duchess of Gloucester even said that he was 'too sensitive for his own good', misunderstood the Spencerian idea of encouragement. This accorded more with Prince Philip's ideals than Charles's or Elizabeth's, and he fled in the opposite direction.

Charles had always been hypersensitive. As a little boy, his father had tried to cajole him out of the tendency, concerned that they would be building up trouble for the future unless he became more robust emotionally. But Elizabeth was always in the background, cosseting her favourite grandson and encouraging him to do likewise and indulge his feelings the way she did hers and his own, as her letters to him confirm. He would write her long and miserable missives from school, full of complaints, in the certainty that his adored grandmother would sympathise with his terrible plight.

And sympathise she invariably did, notwithstanding the fact that she had no sympathy to spare for her daughter Margaret, whose complaints were invariably more valid. 'Oh, do pull yourself together and stop being such a bore,' might have been a more adequate response to provide Charles with, but it was Margaret who always received that homily.

Meanwhile, Charles was being trained by his grandmother to develop an appreciation for strong, decisive, powerful women who hid their power behind a fusillade of flattery and charm. He would grow into a man who could only press suits with women who accepted his dithering; who cajoled him into making the leap from procrastination to tentativeness as if they were his nanny and he their adored charge. He would then bask in a degree of attention from the potent fount of femininity in a way that only a prince or a spoilt brat would regard as desirable.

To say that Elizabeth had subverted Charles's masculine power might be to overstate the case, but not by much.

Some people believed that Elizabeth indulged Charles as a way of achieving a special position in his life. He was just the sort of man she liked: artistic, effete, precious, reliant, but also athletic. She liked her men with hard shells but soft centres; the very opposite of herself. And she liked women like herself: superficially sweet, sociable, apparently malleable, but with tough cores.

In some ways, Diana was a younger, taller, prettier version of Elizabeth. The main difference between the two women would only emerge later, after Diana had become Princess of Wales. Where Elizabeth was a dedicated team player, Diana was more of an iconoclast. While Elizabeth remained loyal to the family that had elevated her, Diana did not.

Diana was, in many ways, a more disloyal and unstable version of Elizabeth. But superficially, both women were sufficiently similar to not only deceive the world as to the seamier sides of their characters, but also into the charismatic, determined, wily, charming, and captivating aspects of their personalities without questioning what lay beneath. Both were ultra-feminine, believers in the steel hand within the velvet glove, and both used their wiles with deceptive sweetness but decided determination as they fulfilled their ambition to become global superstars.

One important difference between them, which would only emerge later, once Diana and her supporters had achieved their objective and she was the Princess of Wales, was that Diana, when crossed, would howl like a banshee and shriek like the young Jamie Lee Curtis in a horror movie. Elizabeth never behaved like that, though both women were equally adept in planting invisible slime that would send their adversaries flying. Having done so, they would then deny what they had done, assuming injured expressions and hiding behind a façade of innocence that owed much to their lack of scruple and nothing to the consciences which they asserted they possessed, but which only were operational when things were going their own way. Both were public relations geniuses, as John Buchan and Sir David English, the editor of Associated Newspapers who knew Diana well, said. Both were brilliant at presenting themselves to advantage. Both were flirtatious with men and wonderful with old mayors, old ladies, young people, indeed anyone they wished to charm.

If you appreciate how similar Diana was in character, personality and disposition to Elizabeth, you begin to understand why Charles never stood a chance once his adored grandmother joined the assault to make Diana his wife. While it is possible that Diana and the Spencers might have prevailed without Elizabeth's assistance, there is little doubt that hers helped the romance to come to fruition, by providing the stamp of approval that was a huge consideration to him and the other members of the Royal Family.

Aside from his own grandmother, other influential Diana supporters surrounded the unfortunate Charles. There was Robert Fellowes, the husband of Diana's older sister Jane and her maternal grandmother Ruth, Lady Fermoy, both of whom enjoyed official positions at Court. Robert was not only the son of the Queen's Land Agent at Sandringham and, as such, a longstanding fixture in royal circles, but he was also the Queen's Assistant Private Secretary at the time Diana's relationship with Charles was beginning. He would graduate to the senior post of Private Secretary before the marriage ended. And Ruth Fermoy was not only a Woman of the Bedchamber but also another longstanding presence in royal circles. Her late husband Edmund Maurice Burke Roche, 4th Lord Fermoy, had been the much older, half-American Irish heir to the Work fortune, who had been embroiled in a legal mire that gained the sympathy of the Court between the wars. His grandfather had stipulated that his daughter's children could only inherit if they lived in the United States. After he died, they successfully challenged the will, then returned to the United Kingdom, where Lord Fermoy became sufficiently friendly with King George V for him to grant the family a lease on Park House on the Sandringham Estate. By the time the King died, Maurice and Ruth Fermoy, whom he had married in 1931, were friends of Bertie and Elizabeth's.

After Bertie's death in 1952 and Maurice's in 1955, the two women became even closer friends. One of the bonds they had was music. Elizabeth loved music, as did Ruth, whom I first met in the mid-seventies when my brother and I went to stay for the King's Lynn Festival with a family friend, the great flautist Richard Adeney. Richard later explained the bond between Elizabeth and Ruth, whom he knew very well. 'Ruth was elegant. She had impeccable manners, was very correct but was very good company nevertheless. Above all else, she was wonderfully musical. She was a fine pianist who had studied under Cortot (in itself a sign of outstanding talent) and she founded the King's Lynn Festival in 1951. I often played there. She was great chums with (the famous conductor Sir) John Barbirolli, (the conductor) Raymond Leppard, (the composer) Benjamin (later Lord) Britten and (the tenor Sir) Peter Pears. She roped the Queen Mother in to becoming its patron, and I saw her there from time to time.'

Once she was a widow, Elizabeth preferred her ladies-in-waiting to be widowed or single women. In 1956 she asked Ruth to become an Extra Woman of the Bedchamber, and when it was apparent the appointment had been a success, she made it permanent four years later.

Like Elizabeth, Ruth had origins which she kept secret. James Dorset, the genealogist whose death had been so welcomed by Society in 1987, unearthed the fact that the former Ruth Gill's great-great-grandfather Theodore Forbes had lived with a dark-skinned Indian girl by the name of Eliza Kewark while he was in India working for the East India Company. Such couplings were prevalent at that time, and though they never married, they did have issue, including a fair-skinned daughter named Katherine. She was sent to Scotland for her education. Afterwards, she married locally and the family took to explaining away her exotic ancestry by claiming she was Armenian. This was significant, because the Armenians are Caucasian while the Indians are Mongol. In other words, one racial categorisation was white, the other brown. The name Kewark itself was something of a giveaway, however. As one of the Indian princes pointed out to me, names beginning with K are anglicised versions of the Moghul Q, with which many Arabic and Moghul names begin (e.g. Qatar). Armenian names are radically different. They are usually rather long, often end in the letters 'ian', have an entirely different cadence to Moghul names – compare Kewark with Gulbenkian – and a more accurate transliteration of the name (which indicates its origins rather too clearly) is Qakh.

Just as how it was wise of Elizabeth's family to suppress any questions about her maternity, so it was with Ruth's. In a day and age when 'coloured blood', as it was then called, was regarded as a 'taint', Ruth's ancestress's Indian blood would most likely have rendered Lady Fermoy, her daughter Frances, and granddaughter Diana unsuitable for matrimony into aristocratic and royal families. The only family which was deemed suitable despite its mixed heritage was the Pushkin, whose descendants are now interwoven into several of the royal and ducal families through the partly-royal Merensky and Torby lines. Since the Gills were neither aristocratic nor morganatic, there was no likelihood of anyone regarding their 'touch of the tar brush', as it was then called, as exotic.

Some psychologists believe that an innate disadvantage can be the grain of sand that turns the human oyster into a pearl. Certainly Ruth and Elizabeth had a lot in common superficially, but it is unlikely that they ever shared confidences about their purported origins. Diana's family was also fortunate that she was safely married by the time James Dorset ferreted out her secret. Had he known beforehand, you can be sure he would have sold it the way he sold everyone else's secrets, and the marriage which everyone worked so hard to orchestrate, might not have come off.

All credit for the initial uplift of the balloon must go to Diana. After her encounter with Charles at the de Pass barbecue, she managed to get Lady Sarah Armstrong-Jones to invite her onto the royal yacht *Britannia* during Cowes Week. Although she then shared the luscious curves possessed by Charles's two established mistresses, Camilla Parker Bowes and Dale (Lady) Tryon, and exhibited them decorously with many a dive into the cold English Channel as she sought to capture the Prince of Wales's interest, nothing substantial came of this second royal encounter. So she pressed her grandmother Ruth, who would be in-waiting at Birkhall in September, to organise an invitation for her. Ruth therefore got her invited to stay on the Balmoral Estate as a guest.

It was on this occasion that Diana actually got somewhere with Charles as well as with the assembled family. She followed him around like a faithful and adoring puppy, laughing at all his jokes, evincing an interest in any subject he broached, displaying a shared love for the countryside and all its pursuits. Elizabeth, observing her friend's granddaughter, whose other grandmother Cynthia had also been a childhood friend and a Lady of the Bedchamber until her death from a brain tumour in 1972, decided that Diana was just the sort of girl she wanted for Charles. She had always preferred British aristocrats to foreign royals, and Diana had many illustrious bloodlines in her veins. Cynthia's father had been the 3rd Duke of Abercorn (whose next duke will be a descendant of the Torby/Merensky/Pushkin family), while her maternal line included the earls of Lucan and the dukes of Richmond and Gordon. Maurice Fermoy combined the Celtic greatness of the Burkes and the Roches, while Diana's father Johnnie Spencer could even be deemed technically to be the head of both the Spencer and the Churchill families if you wanted to stretch a point, which Elizabeth often did when it suited her. As such, Johnnie was the head of the Duke of Marlborough's family as well as of his own.

Although Elizabeth might have cared nothing about the lineage of foreign royals, she did care very much about her home-grown lot. Not only was Diana sweet and charming and pliable and apparently even-tempered, but she also had the sort of heritage that made Elizabeth feel right at home. There was no way Diana would ever look down on her the way Marina or some of the other royals had. Not only would Elizabeth remain ascendant, but she would also be on a par in terms of heritage, which was always a consideration when dealing with royals, most of whom thrilled to the flowing of the Emperor Charlemagne's blood in their veins, as if there were two categories of dynasties in the world: Carolingian and everything else.

Diana's stay at Birkhall was instructive of how pressure can be applied to foster unions. Following Charles around like a puppy with its master struck a positive note not only with Charles, whose tendency has always been to bask in admiration and be outraged by its absence, but with Elizabeth as well. Flattery had always been her lynchpin, irrespective of whom she was seeking to bedazzle, and just as how she expected others to overlook questions of her sincerity, she now fatally extended the same courtesy to Diana. Naturally, Diana's relations were thrilled that she and Charles were forging a bond, and did everything to encourage it, agreeing with Elizabeth's comments about how wonderful it would be if 'something came of' things.

Although Charles might have been emotionally tentative, he was a Hanoverian on his mother's side and a Schleswig-Holstein on his father's. Sexual passion, once ignited, fired his trajectory upwards in more ways than one. His valet Stephen Barry was a veritable fount of information about how he used to ferry Diana to and from Highgrove,[21] which Charles had recently bought from Viscount and Viscountess Macmillan of Ovenden. Although the house was being done up, the lovers would have picnic suppers and afterwards avail themselves of a habitable bedroom for a night of passion, which always ended at dawn. Barry would then drive Diana back to London, so that the fiction of her virginity could be maintained. They also stayed at friends' houses and with Elizabeth herself from time to time. Once more, the fiction of propriety was maintained with the courting couple being given separate but easily accessible bedrooms.

Although Diana soon had Charles hooked sexually, she still could not get him to propose marriage, so his father quite rightly stepped into the breach and reminded him that he was dealing with a suitable young lady and must either 'piss or get off the pot'. Diana would later claim that Elizabeth also had a quiet word with Charles, encouraging him in her subtle way to 'go for it' if he felt the marriage would work.[22] She evidently reminded him that Diana was 'so suitable' and they 'seemed so well suited.' According to Diana, Elizabeth was one of her 'greatest supporters' and she believed that his grandmother's encouragement had a positive effect upon Charles, especially as how she was also extremely friendly with Andrew Parker Bowles and his wife Camilla, who was well known to be Charles's *maîtresse-en-titre* along with Dale Tryon.

Ironically, only two people warned against the marriage. The Queen expressed the view that Diana did not have the right character for the role of Princess of Wales. 'She has never stuck to anything she has ever undertaken,' she shrewdly observed to her heir, while his Private Secretary, the Hon. Edward Adeane, whose father Michael (Lord Adeane) had been Lilibet's Private Secretary, also warned against Diana's character for the long haul. Neither, however, belaboured their opposition having given their viewpoint.

Before she died, Ruth Fermoy would also claim that she had warned Diana against marrying Charles, pointing out that 'they're not like us', that they 'have different senses of humour'. She is also meant to have said that she did not believe that Diana was suited for such a restrictive way of life. Whether this was said with hindsight or not is a matter for conjecture, but what is certain is that she kept her lips firmly sealed in the run-up to the marriage, and was absolutely thrilled when her granddaughter became the Princess of Wales.

The year after the marriage, both grandmothers were 'over the moon' when their respective grandchildren provided them with a great-grandson. Prince William of Wales would feature in both their lives as a source of great pride but neither materfamilias was actually close to him. There was too much of a generational gap for them to do anything but cluck from a safe distance, then drift off into the afternoon or the evening to entertain themselves and be entertained by their rich and varied social lives.

Although Elizabeth had been an involved grandmother to her six grandchildren – Prince Charles (1948), Princess Anne (1950), Prince Andrew (1960), Prince Edward (1964), Viscount Linley (1961), and Lady Sarah Armstrong-Jones (1964) – the only one with whom she had an extreme bond was Charles. All the others were no more and no less close to her than typical grandchildren are to typical grandparents. Because she loved being surrounded by her family, and enjoyed the hijinks and unsophisticated games that appeal to the childish as well as to children, and because she had an easy and tolerant manner as long as children were well-mannered, she had good relations with all her grandchildren. However, by the time her great-grandchildren came along, she was so old and set in her ways that she did not really relish the disruption of children.

Nevertheless, she did think along dynastic lines. Being a relatively rich woman, she was eager that her descendants benefit from her inevitable demise. This meant thwarting the taxman, who would otherwise swoop and swipe following a change in the late 1990s which meant that the monarch and his or her consort had to pay tax as well as inheritance duties. So Elizabeth made provision for her grandchildren, then set about running up massive debts. This was a clever move, because an indebted estate attracts far less tax than a solvent one, and by the time she died, Elizabeth was several million pounds in the red, and her grandchildren benefited from her efficient tax-planning in a way they would otherwise not have done.

Elizabeth's estate management overlapped with the failure of her three eldest grandchildren's marriages. By the time she turned ninety in 1990, everyone in royal circles knew that the marriage of the Prince and Princess of Wales was over in everything but name, and that Diana had been demanding a divorce, on and off, since 1987. Smart circles were riveted by the civilised way in which Charles and Diana had gone about leading independent lives. Each effectively lived on his and her own, with their own circle of friends and even their own lovers. By comparison, his sister Anne, by now the Princess Royal, and her husband Captain Mark Phillips, were testaments to discretion, despite his siring an outside child and she being 'supported' by the equerry who would eventually become her husband. There was much sympathy for Prince Andrew, who seemed to be the only person in fashionable circles who did not know that his marriage to the former Sarah Ferguson was stretched to breaking point, largely, it was said by his wife, by his absences on board ship due to his naval career, though the hunky and chunky figure of oil millionaire Steve Wyatt and the balding pate of financial advisor Johnny Bryan might have had more to do with it that she acknowledged.

Elizabeth's reaction to the disintegration of her grandchildren's marriages was much the same as to the collapse of her friends' marriages. She displayed remarkable equanimity, taking the view that adultery is not sexual congress between a man and a woman who are married to others, but a civilised practice best indulged in out of view of prying eyes. She was definitely not judgemental where adulterers were concerned, not if she liked them. For instance, even when Charles first married Diana and had stopped seeing Camilla, Elizabeth continued to entertain the Parker Bowleses the way she had while Charles's pre-marital affair with Mrs. Andrew Parker Bowles was taking place. She also used to entertain and be entertained by Dale Tryon, and once Dale herself told me that Elizabeth had called in for tea while a mutual friend of ours, the writer Catherine Olsen (Lady Mancham in private life) was staying with her. No one, and nothing, had ever been allowed to interfere with Elizabeth's social life, and no one, and nothing, would even at this late stage of her life.

Elizabeth also knew about Anne's affair with the Queen's equerry Commander Timothy Laurence, and took it in her stride. She was matter-of-fact when Anne and Mark Philips decided to divorce, and displayed no disapproval whatsoever when her granddaughter decided that she wished to remarry despite already 'having a living husband'. Patently, what had been no good for Wallis was fine for Anne, and when the Princess Royal married Laurence in Scotland at Crathie Kirk, the local church on the Balmoral Estate, at 3 p.m. on 12th December, 1992, Elizabeth showed her newly-found approval for divorced women remarrying by leaving the weekend guests she had previously invited to Royal Lodge, flying up to Scotland for the ceremony and reception, and returning later that evening to resume her duties as hostess. This time Elizabeth hadn't even bothered to pay lip service to her much-vaunted disapproval of divorced women remarrying while their previous spouses were still alive, the way she had done when her niece Anne, Viscountess Anson had married Prince George of Denmark. She was present in the front row as her granddaughter broke every precept she had held over the Windsors' heads.

The following morning, when I went to see Margaret, Duchess of Argyll, who was in St. George's Nursing Home along with Boo Laye and Loelia, Duchess of Westminster, she spoke for most of her contemporaries when she said, 'A *volte face* of this dimension is beyond belief. What would the Windsors say?'

By this time, Elizabeth's equanimity in breaching her moral standards for her grandchildren's benefit was well practised. In March of that year, she had been seemingly indifferent to the break-up of Prince Andrew's marriage, though she was incensed later that summer when the Balmoral house party opened up the *News of the World* to see photographs of Sarah York's toes being sucked by Johnny Bryan. She fully supported Prince Philip's viewpoint, that Sarah should be banished from royal life for such vulgar behaviour – notwithstanding the fact that the Duchess of York was already separated and therefore was technically entitled to be looking for love outside the marital boundaries.

Elizabeth, however, had always had double standards. These had served her well. They were the club with which she could beat her adversaries, and the mortar with which to press sustenance as and when it was required. Her active collusion in fostering Prince Charles's extra-marital relationships is a case in point. Once she was aware that Charles and Diana had what used to be called an 'understanding', she even went so far as to lend her grandson

Birkhall, so that he and Camilla Parker Bowles, with whom he had resumed his affair, should meet discreetly. She was equally understanding of Diana's affairs. Like everyone else in royal circles, she knew about the affair with her married bodyguard, Sergeant Barry Mannakee, if only because so much of it was conducted at Balmoral prior to his removal from the royal protection squad for 'over-familiarity'. She also was aware of Diana's involvement with James Hewitt, and approved of it. James was a well-mannered army officer, charming, discreet, masculine and athletic, just the sort of man Elizabeth herself used to rave about in the days before she got married and had to cope with the carnal side of life. Diana herself told me that she often wondered if Elizabeth didn't 'envy' her. She was not referring to the lovers she had, but to the adulation and liberty. 'She used to look at me so oddly, as if she was trying to figure out what makes me tick. She seemed fascinated with me.'

Elizabeth might well have been intrigued by the 'hornet' she had so naïvely let into the family. Until 1992, she was careful not to fall out with Diana. However, once she discovered that the Princess had colluded with the initial stages of Diana in Private, my 1992 biography which had started with Palace approval (even though Diana and I fell out over its contents and I went on to write a balanced but revealing portrait which sent shock waves through Court circles and ended up on the front pages of newspapers all over the world), and some time later with Andrew Morton's *Diana: Her True Story,* which was the fictionalised panegyric she had hoped I'd write, Elizabeth became Diana's implacable enemy.

The War of the Waleses preoccupied much of the world throughout 1992. Finally, after much toing and froing, the Queen gave her consent to Charles and Diana separating, and on 7th December Charles took the draft statement, which the Prime Minister would read to the House of Commons two days later announcing it, to Clarence House. He dined with his grandmother and left it for her, and it is now in the Clarence House Archives, along with the comment made in the Diary of the Ladies-in-Waiting for the 9th – 'A sad day for Clarence House.'

Diana's grandmother Ruth Fermoy was as perplexed by her granddaughter's behaviour as Elizabeth had been. She disapproved violently, Richard Adeney told me, and threw in her lot wholeheartedly with the Royal Family. Even when she was dying of cancer at 36 Eaton Square – she died on 6th July, 1993, – she made it clear she wished to have nothing to do with her 'faithless' granddaughter. This description would prove even more apt in 1995 when Diana gave Martin Bashir an interview for the television programme *Panorama* and tried her level best to manipulate events so that the line of succession would skip from Charles to her son William. Thereafter, until

Diana died, Elizabeth regarded her as 'treacherous' and 'beyond the pale', sentiments which were understandable in the circumstances. She was absolutely horrified that this 'slip of a girl' whose inclusion in 'her family' she had 'done so much to facilitate' could threaten to tear the whole fabric apart.

Despite the separation, Elizabeth and Lilibet had hoped, like most traditionalists, that Charles and Diana would remain married, if only because divorce might complicate matters when he succeeded to the throne and became Supreme Governor of the Church of England. Fortunately for Charles and everyone else concerned, good old Mountbatten progressiveness prevailed once the *Panorama* interview aired and the full implications of Diana's attempts to manoeuvre Charles out of the line of succession were appreciated. The Queen therefore wrote to both her son and daughter-in-law and demanded that they divorce, a course of action Elizabeth would normally have dreaded, but accepted as desirable in the circumstances. 'If Ruth had lived, how she would have kicked herself for promoting that match with the Queen Mother,' Richard Adeney observed to me.

One marriage Elizabeth had had little to do with was Andrew's to Sarah Ferguson. She was equally indifferent to its dissolution, though in favour of Sarah losing the title of Royal Highness. More than anything else, this loss illustrated just how cruel and unnecessary had been the Letters Patent of 1937 endowing the style of Royal Highness to the Duke of Windsor alone. In one fell swoop, the nonsense of Wallis divorcing David and going around calling herself Her Royal Highness Mrs. Next Husband was revealed to be nothing but cant. When Diana herself became the first Princess of Wales in history to cease being a Royal Highness the following year, that confirmed as nothing else could have done just how malicious the unlawful act of failing to recognise Wallis's right to the style of Royal Highness had been.

By the time Diana was divorced, Elizabeth viewed her with an antipathy she had previously reserved for Wallis. Princess Margaret, who had once liked Diana, had also turned against her. Mother and daughter now had a common bond.

In the last year of her life, Diana did try to mend fences with the Royal Family. She did realise that she had made egregious errors, chief of which had been in antagonising the Establishment and Royal Family with such antics as the Panorama interview and the Morton book. She even said that she wished Charles and Camilla well, which was quite a step forward, for there was already talk in fashionable circles that he had decided to marry her as soon as he could.

Diana's sudden death following that car crash in the tunnel under the Pont d'Alma in Paris on 31ˢᵗ August, 1997, derailed Charles's marital plans. All over the world people were in shock that anyone so young and vital could die so suddenly. Elizabeth, however, regarded Diana's passage as 'unfortunate for her children but otherwise a merciful release. Providential.' Although all the Royal Family took part in Diana's funeral a few days later, neither Elizabeth nor Princess Margaret bowed their heads the way the Queen did as her cortege passed by. Their reaction was far more emotional, and Margaret actually accounted them 'well rid of the troublemaker.'[23]

Death, however, had not stalked Diana alone. Margaret's health had been precarious for twenty years. She smoked and drank heavily, and eventually these played havoc with not only her beauty but also her health. In 1998 she had the first of the three strokes which would ultimately incapacitate her. After the third in 2001, she was wheelchair-bound and condemned to view the world through dark glasses. There were audible gasps of shock when William Tallon wheeled her to the gate of Clarence House for the photo-call surrounding Elizabeth's last birthday. She was clearly so much more infirm than her own mother who, at one hundred and one years old, was still ambulatory, while she was not. That last Christmas of both their lives, mother and daughter flew to Sandringham together by helicopter. It was a morose occasion, with Elizabeth in her room for much of the festivities, as she was nursing a cold, while Margaret was wheelchair-bound and struggling to keep up with what was going on around her.

Margaret returned to London by car, leaving her mother at Sandringham, where she marked the anniversary of Bertie's death on 6ᵗʰ February with a service conducted by Canon John Ovendon, the Chaplain of the Royal Chapel, and Canon George Hall in the small sitting room. She was not well enough to go out.

Three days later, Lilibet telephoned her to tell her that Margaret had passed away that morning. The previous afternoon she had suffered her final stroke and had been taken to King Edward VII Hospital in Marylebone, where she died of cardiac arrest.

Charles went to Sandringham to comfort his grandmother. She displayed yet more of that celebrated equanimity, informing him that 'Margot's death had probably been a merciful release.'[24] In that, she had been right. Princess Margaret's life had become so unbearable that she told Colin Glenconner's wife Anne, who was one of her ladies-in-waiting as well as a close friend, that 'she felt so ill that she longed to "join Papa".'[25]

Fifty years to the day after King George VI's funeral, his adored daughter's was celebrated in St. George's Chapel, Windsor. Elizabeth arrived by helicopter. A few days after Margaret's death, she had fallen and hurt her arm. This was bandaged and she ignored the doctor's advice not to attend the funeral. It was a small, quiet affair for family and friends only. In the course of her troubled life, Margaret had come to appreciate what was real and what was not. She even opted for a cardboard coffin and a cremation at the Slough Crematorium, after which her ashes were interred in the King George VI Memorial Chapel.

The great irony of Princess Margaret's life was that, having been prevented from marrying the man she was best suited for because he was divorced, she ended up marrying one who ultimately insisted upon a divorce so that he could marry his longstanding girlfriend. On 11th July, 1978, Margaret and her earl were divorced, and he married Lucy Lindsay-Hogg that December. Ironically, Elizabeth remained on excellent terms with him as her relationship with her own daughter spluttered from trough to trough under her complete lack of sympathy for or comprehension of the daughter Gore Vidal observed 'was far too intelligent for her station in life.'[26]

Ned Ryan told me he thought that the people who would 'miss PM the most are the Queen and her children.' All her life, she and Lilibet had been exceedingly close. They spoke on the telephone most days, and saw more of each other than most sisters, royal or otherwise.

Elizabeth had now outlived one of her children and most of her friends. Although she still had a spark of the vitality which had made her so potent a personality, she had been visibly declining all year. She left Margaret's funeral and took up residence in Royal Lodge for the last time.

Meanwhile, 2002 was the Golden Jubilee of Lilibet's accession to the throne. Celebrations and tours had been planned, starting with visits to Jamaica, New Zealand and Australia, and she was intent on honouring all her commitments. There was much sympathy for her, losing her sister at such a poignant time, but she was nothing if not consummately professional, and she went about her duties with a relish that was admirable in a woman half her age.

Nevertheless, as soon as the royal plane touched down at Heathrow Airport on 3rd March, Lilibet was driven straight to Royal Lodge to see her mother. She already knew that it was now only a matter of time, for Elizabeth was clearly not long for this world.

But still, the life-loving and tenacious old lady threw herself into life with what energy she had left. On 5th March, she fulfilled an annual event, holding a luncheon and lawn meet for the Eton Beagles and even talked about their next meeting. As if that were not enough, shortly afterwards she hosted her annual house party for Sandown Park's Grand Military Race Meeting. She was elated when her horse, First Love, won, little realising that it would be her last runner.

By the third week of March it was obvious that time was running out for Elizabeth. If the spirit was still willing, the flesh was weakening and the old lady, whose appetite had always been gargantuan, was barely eating. The Apothecary to the Household at Windsor, Dr. Jonathan Holliday, started to visit her frequently. Each afternoon, Windsor Castle's nursing sister Gill Frampton dropped in at Royal Lodge to change the bandages on her legs, which had been prone to sores for some time now, and to massage her. She had dispensed with all her ladies-in-waiting save for her niece Margaret Rhodes, who hopped over each day from her 'suburban lodge' which was only a few hundred yards away in Windsor Great Park.

On Palm Sunday, Canon Ovenden celebrated a service in the Saloon.

For the remainder of the week, Elizabeth, who plainly realised that she would soon be dead, said goodbye and tied up loose ends in her inimitable fashion. She asked her granddaughter Anne to take some of her horses, and rang around to various friends. Sir Michael Oswald, who had been her racing manager since 1970, said that it was obvious to him that she was saying goodbye, though she did not say so specifically. Sir Alistair Aird, her Private Secretary, felt the same thing when he dropped in on her staff on Wednesday, 27th March to wish them a happy Easter, and Elizabeth asked to see him. His account in the Royal Archives states, 'I found her in the Saloon sitting in a winged chair with her feet up and covered by a rug. I took a chair and sat immediately opposite her for her eyesight was very bad and she had very limited lateral vision. We discussed a few things and I told Queen Elizabeth whom I had seen recently – she always liked to be kept up to date with news of her Household and friends. She had a smile on her face and I suddenly had the feeling that this was the last time we would meet and that she was in her own way saying goodbye to me.'

By Good Friday Elizabeth was bedridden and unable to lift her head from the pillow. Even at this late stage, her fabled self-possession had not deserted her. Shawcross confirms in the official biography that 'she remained in complete control.'

The following morning Dr. Holliday was accompanied by the Queen's Physician, Dr. Richard Thompson. It was apparent to them that the end was very near, so Dr. Thompson alerted the Queen first then Prince Charles, who was in Klosters and distressed to realise that he would not make it back in time.

Elizabeth died at 3.15 p.m. on 30th March, 2002. Aside from the priests and medical staff, she was surrounded by her two non-royal grandchildren, David Linley and Sarah Chatto, her niece Margaret Rhodes, and her daughter

Lilibet. Her body was put into a magnificent oak coffin and taken to the Royal Chapel, where Canon Ovendon celebrated Evensong for the family as a precursor to Operation Tay Bridge, the ritual which had been decreed years before would take place once she was dead.

Elizabeth's funeral would prove to be one of the most splendid and moving ceremonial events ever seen. As Shawcross confirms in the official biography, 'she had been diligent in planning it herself and Operation Tay Bridge, as it was codenamed, was regularly updated.' Her genius for the right sort of publicity, which had served her so well in life, would also serve her well in death.

Elizabeth's coffin remained at the Royal Chapel until Tuesday, 2nd April. It was then taken to the Queen's Chapel, St. James's Palace, till Friday, 5th April, when there was a ceremonial processional to Westminster Hall. This was a magnificent spectacle. The coffin, draped in her personal standard, was placed on the same gun carriage which had borne King George VI's remains fifty years before. Shimmering at its head was the Queen Consort's Crown made for Elizabeth's coronation in 1937. The central stone was the Koh-I-Noor Diamond, given to Queen Victoria by the last Maharajah of the Punjab, Prince Duleep Singh, whose son might or might not have been the father of the 6th Earl of Carnarvon whose own official progeny, Porchy Porchester, Elizabeth had wanted for Lilibet. The Koh-I-Noor, along with the hundreds of other diamonds in the Crown, literally flashed as they caught the light while the gun carriage rumbled towards Parliament Square. There was a lone wreath which said 'In Loving Memory, Lilibet.' As the massed bands of the Scots Guards and Irish Guards played Mendelssohn's moving Funeral March, a quarter of a million onlookers watched silently as her four grandsons, her three great-grandsons Princes William and Harry and Peter Phillips, her son-in-law Prince Philip, and her granddaughter Princess Anne walked behind it. They were followed by other members of the Royal Family, the Bowes Lyon family, then her Household and Staff, after which were the Chiefs of the Defence, Air and Naval Staffs and the representatives of all the regiments with which Elizabeth had been associated, both in Britain itself and the Commonwealth.

It is a truism that no other nation on earth does ceremonial occasions like Britain. There was much public sympathy for the Queen, who had lost both her sister and mother within six weeks of each other, and when her state car pulled up at the door of Westminster Hall with her niece Lady Sarah Chatto beside her, there was an audible sucking in of compassionate breath from the crowd. After Elizabeth's coffin had been placed on a catafalque, the Royal Family bowed their heads as the Archbishop of Canterbury led prayers.

When the short service had ended, the Queen was driven back to the palace via Whitehall. The crowds broke into spontaneous applause, which rolled like waves on the sea, following her vehicle up the Mall, until it circumnavigated Queen Victoria's statue which had been sculpted by her artist daughter Princess Louise, Duchess of Argyll, and the gates of the palace opened to receive her. It was an intensely moving moment for everyone who witnessed it, demonstrating not only respect and sympathy but also affection for the Queen who was living as well as the one who had died.

From then until Elizabeth was interred, the reaction of the people confounded all expectations. Hundreds of thousands filed past the coffin, forcing the organisers to extend the viewing hours to twenty-four hours per diem. Despite the weather being atrocious, nothing deterred people from paying their respects, and the queues were so long that they snaked over the Embankment to the other side of the Thames. In a touch that was pure Elizabeth, the Women's Royal Voluntary Service, of which she had been firstly patron then latterly president, handed out plastic cups of tea to the people who spent hours queuing in the biting cold and pouring rain.

The coffin Lay-in-State until the evening of Monday, 8th April, guarded on a rota basis by officers from a variety of regiments. That last evening before the funeral, Elizabeth's four grandsons – Charles, Andrew, Edward and David Linley – stood guard over the coffin, in emulation of the Vigil of the Princes which had been the previous Prince of Wales's idea for honouring his father when King George V died, and which had excited so much criticism from Elizabeth's ossifying cronies as yet another example of King Edward VIII's inappropriate ideas.

The following morning, Elizabeth's funeral began at 11.30 a.m. sharp after the coffin was borne on a gun carriage by the King's Troop, the Royal Horse Artillery to Westminster Abbey, while two hundred pipers and drummers played 'My Home' and 'The Mist Covered Mountains' and various members of the Royal Family followed the coffin.

The funeral itself was celebratory rather than sad, as befitted a woman who had lived for nearly a hundred and two years and had, for most of them, been at the very top of her game.

Afterwards, Irish Guardsmen shouldered her coffin while the organ played Bach's Prelude and Fugue in E flat and the Abbey's muffled bells rang out as the coffin was taken outside to the hearse. All Elizabeth's regiments then played 'Oft in the Stilly Night' as it was loaded into the hearse and driven up the Mall towards Buckingham Palace. Two Spitfires and a Lancaster bomber from World War Two then flew overhead screaming out a last adieu, after which the vehicle headed towards her final resting place in St. George's

Chapel, Windsor Castle, accompanied, at his own request, by the Prince of Wales.

The route was lined with onlookers, some throwing flowers, others bowing or crossing themselves reverently, some even appropriately raising glasses to the queen who had always enjoyed a glass or three, and whose final nourishment had been raw eggs in champagne when she could no longer manage food.

Later that evening, Elizabeth was laid to rest alongside Bertie in the King George VI Memorial Chapel. Princess Margaret's ashes were also interred there. She had finally become reunited with the father she loved. Watching were Lilibet, the grandchildren, and her great-nephew Michael, the present Earl of Strathmore.

It had been an incredible life well lived and her accomplishments had been vast. If she had not been perfect, by and large she had been a force for good, and since none of us can be both perfect and human, such failings as she had cannot detract from the extraordinary human being she was.

Appendices

Appendix 1

Chapter 1 - The D'Arcy Concession

This Concession was the basis for the resentment which Iranians hold against the British and Americans to this day. Under its terms, Mozzafar ad-Din surrendered all rights to petroleum, natural gas, asphalt and mineral waxes in an area covering 1,242,000 square kilometres of his kingdom in return for £20,000 cash; a further £20,000 worth of shares in the company, and 16% of the net profits for the next sixty years. By 1908, large quantities of oil and natural gas having been discovered, D'Arcy's Concession was one of the most valuable entities on earth. And in 1909, when it became the Anglo-Persian Oil Company, it laid the foundation not only for the massive exploitation of Iran's assets, and for the enrichment of the British Empire, but also for the nourishment of the hostility which would simmer periodically for the next seven decades before erupting into the Iranian Revolution of 1979.

To this day, the West continues to deal with the adverse consequences of D'Arcy's Concession, though it has to be said, we also enjoy the many material benefits that accrued to us through the decades of exploitation.

Appendix 2

Chapter 3 – Morganatic Marriages

Morganatic marriages were a European tradition which allowed a royal personage legally to marry a non-royal, usually of aristocratic rank. The

Battenberg family would turn out to be the most successful of all the morganatic houses, in that one Battenberg became the sovereign of a state (Prince Alexander, who became Prince of Bulgaria prior to his deposition); his two brothers married royal princesses (Prince Louis to Princess Victoria of Hesse, Prince Henry to The Princess Beatrice, Queen Victoria's youngest child); and three of the daughters of the next generation, Princesses Alice, Louise, and Victoria Eugenia respectively became Princess Andrew of Greece, the Crown Princess of Sweden, and the Queen of Spain.

Another extremely successful morganatic branch was the Torby family, whose ancestors include the present head of the Mountbatten family (George, 4th Marquess of Milford Haven) and the Duchesses of Abercorn and Westminster, whose sons Earl Grosvenor and Marquess of Hamilton are the heirs to those two dukedoms. The Torby line came into existence when Grand Duke Michael of Russia married Countess Sophie von Merenberg on 10th March, 1891. Following her marriage to Tsar Nicholas II's cousin, she was made Countess Torby in her own right by the Grand Duke of Luxembourg, who knew that failure to elevate his younger brother's daughter to the peerage would result in her children with the Grand Duke being merely the Misses and Mister Romanovsky. Merenberg, being a German title from Waldeck and Pyrmont, was governed by Salic Law, so could not descend through the female line, hence the need for the Luxembourg title.

Sophie Torby herself had been the product of another of those unequal unions. Her father was Prince Nicholas of Nassau, her mother Natalia Alexandrovna Pushkina, daughter of the great Russian poet Alexander Pushkin. The fact that Pushkin was himself the grandson of a former slave from Ethiopia named Hannibal was another complication for the Tsar, who banished his cousin and, in so doing, saved the whole family's lives when the Russian Revolution consumed his and many of his relations, including his only living brother, who had also entered into a morganatic marriage.

Because morganatic marriages were not an accepted English convention, people like Count Michael Torby and his mother were accorded semi-royal status in the United Kingdom, especially after Queen Victoria allowed her daughter Beatrice to become Princess Henry of Battenberg.

Appendix 3

Chapter 4 – Great War Reparations

At the end of the First World War, the former German Empire was dealt with by the Allies under the Treaty of Versailles. The other Central Powers were dealt with separately under different treaties such as the Treaty of St. Germain-en-Laye, which was signed on 10th September, 1919, with the newly-formed Republic of Austria, and the Treaty of Trianon, signed under protest by the Regency of Hungary on 4th June, 1920. Without a doubt, Hungary was right to object to the flagrant injustice imposed upon it. It was deprived of 72% of its territory (from 325,111 square kilometres to 125,526), 64% of its population (from 20.9 to 7.6 million), with 31% of its ethnic population (3.3 out of 10.7 million Hungarians) now residing in territories that were ceded to Romania, the newly-formed Republic of Czechoslovakia, and the Kingdom of the Serbs, Croats and Slovenes, which would later on change its name to Yugoslavia. It was particularly galling to the Hungarians that the Serbs, whose Foreign Ministry had organised and assisted in the assassination of the heir to their throne at Sarajevo, should be rewarded for an act which, under any interpretation, was neither morally nor politically justifiable. Meanwhile they were penalised for a declaration of war against the Serbians which possessed far more justice than most declarations of war do, and was certainly within the bounds of international law.

Appendix 4

Chapter 4 – Royal Marriage and Divorce

One of the consequences of the death of Queen Victoria in 1901 was that her granddaughter Princess Victoria Melita of Edinburgh and Coburg (Ducky) moved to terminate her marriage to another of the Queen's grandchildren, the Grand Duke of Hesse (Ernie). The marriage had been bitterly unhappy, for two reasons. The year after her daughter Ella's birth, Ducky and Ernie had gone to Russia for the coronation of his sister Alexandra and her husband Nicholas II. There, Ducky was thrown together with Kirill Vladimirovitch, with whom she had been in love, and found herself still irresistibly drawn to him, and he to her, notwithstanding the Russian Orthodox Church's interdict against sexual relations between first cousins. Their flagrant flirting excited gossip, and this exposed the existence of problems within the marriage of Grand Ducal couple. This caused Ernie huge embarrassment and earned Ducky the undying enmity of her sister-in-law and first cousin Alexandra, but it did not stop the cousins from pursuing a romance. This would continue for the duration of her marriage.

The following year, Ducky returned to Hesse from a visit to her sister Marie, who was the Crown Princess of Romania, and had the good fortune to catch Ernie in flagrante delicto with a servant. It was no secret within the family where his interests lay, any more than those of their aunt Princess Louise, Duchess of Argyll's husband, and the myriad other closet queens who were married into the Royal Family, including their other first cousin Princess Marie Louise's husband Prince Aribert of Anhalt. By Ducky's own account, Ernie wasn't even in the closet. She is on record as having told one of her nieces he was so rampant that 'no boy was safe, from the stable hands to the kitchen help. He slept quite openly with them all.'

In a bid for her freedom – Ducky was determined to marry Kirill and if she could not do so, to become his mistress – she approached Sir George Buchanan, the British chargé d'affaires at Darmstadt, and asked him to obtain Queen Victoria's consent to a divorce.

Like many a naïve young woman, Ducky seems to have misunderstood the rationale for her marriage. Queen Victoria had orchestrated it, not because she expected her grandchildren to be happy together, but because she knew Ernie was homosexual and Ducky in love with a man she could not marry. The objections to Ducky marrying Kirill Vladimirovitch had not disappeared. If anything, they had intensified. The Russian Church had not changed its doctrine on consanguinity, nor would Alexandra ever allow her husband, the browbeaten Nicholas II, to agree to her sister-in-law marrying their first cousin, even if the objections of the Church could be engineered: an impossibility if ever there was one.

Stuck in the marriage, Ducky did manage to get pregnant once more, but the son she produced in 1901 shortly after Queen Victoria's death, at the beginning of the year, was stillborn. She promptly demanded a divorce, which the Supreme Court of Hesse granted in December of the same year. She went to live with her widowed mother in Coburg and was prepared to spend the rest of her life as Kirill's mistress, but he had a near death experience in 1905 during the Russo-Japanese War, when he was one of the few survivors of his ship, which had been blown apart and sunk. 'To those over whom the shadow of death has passed, life has a new meaning,' Kirill later wrote in his memoirs. 'It is like daylight. And I was now within visible reach of the dream of my life. Nothing could cheat me of it now. I had gone through much. Now, at last, the future lay radiant before me.' He asked for and obtained permission from the Tsar to leave Russia, joined Ducky in Coburg where she was still residing with her mother, and married her on the 8th October in Tegernsee. Since this was without the permission of Nicholas II and against the teachings of the Russian Orthodox Church, the marriage was invalid according to canon law. Kirill was promptly stripped of his military rank and all honours by the Tsar, including the title Imperial Highness, and Ducky was banned from Russia, despite being the granddaughter of Tsar

Alexander II and a first cousin of Nicholas II himself. Although he relented in 1910 and allowed his cousins to return to Russia, relations between the two couples remained frosty and never improved.

What assisted in making the marriage of Kirill and Ducky feasible, if not acceptable, was that Ernie himself had remarried in February of 1905. Making sure he did not repeat his father's error and marry a woman of inferior rank, his new wife was the suitably royal Princess Eleonore von Solms-Hohensolms-Lich. They ended up having the happy, companionable, supportive union which Queen Victoria had hoped her grandchildren would have. The new Grand Duchess did not use her husband's proclivities against him, but was admirably discreet. She was also a public spirited consort who gladly fulfilled her official role properly, and after the monarchy was abolished in 1918, she and her husband continued to enjoy the support of their former subjects. Both were granted the equivalent of state funerals when they died. She also produced two sons, one of whom married Prince Philip's sister Cecilie, the other, Elizabeth Bowes Lyon's great friend the Hon. Margaret Campbell Geddes. Even after Prince Ludwig's death in 1968, HRH Princess Margaret of Hesse and the Rhine often stayed as a houseguest of her British royal relations, and they in turn visited her at her Darmstadt palace until her own death in 1997.

Appendix 5

Chapter 4 – Loughborough Family Royal Links

Sheila Loughborough was not the only member of the Loughborough family to develop royal links which increased their prestige. Her elder son Anthony, who succeeded his grandfather as the 6th Earl of Rosslyn, married the exotically named Athenais de Rochechouart de Mortemart. Her seventeenth century namesake was Louis XIV's official mistress, the Marquise de Montespan, mother of five of his legitimised children, including the Duc du Maine, the Comte de Toulouse, Madame la Duchesse de Bourbon, and the Princesse de Conti. In aristocratic circles, you couldn't get much more splendid than that, and the grandeur has continued into the next generation. Sheila's Old Etonian half-French grandson Peter , the 7th Earl of Rosslyn, has been Head of the Royalty and Diplomatic Protection Department since 2003, and was awarded The Queen's Police Medal in the 2009 New Year's Honours List. Known as Commander Peter Loughborough, in allusion to the courtesy title he bore until his father's death in 1977, his is an influential position which shows how acceptable his family remains to this day.

Appendix 6

Chapter 8 – Italian Royal Family – Events leading to exile

Following the announcement on 24th October, 1929, of Crown Prince Umberto of Italy's engagement to the Catholic Princess Marie Jose of Belgium, whose religion forbade her English cousins from considering her a suitable bride, the heir to the Italian throne was laying a wreath at the Tomb of the Belgian Unknown Soldier at the Congreskolom in Brussels when Fernando de Rosa, a member of the Second International and as such a Communist, shouted out 'Down with Mussolini' and fired a single shot. Fortunately this did not hit its mark, for neither Umberto nor his future bride was pro-Mussolini. Indeed, in 1943, at the height of the Second World War, Marie José undertook the extraordinarily courageous and dangerous task of trying to arrange a separate peace between Italy and the United States. Her interlocutor was Monsignor Giovanni Battista Montini, a senior diplomat who later became Pope Paul VI. When nothing came of her attempt, she was bundled off to Sarre, in the Aosta Valley, with her children, where she was to remain isolated from the political life of the Royal Family until Italy was able to free itself of Axis influence.

Umberto himself was an excellent crown prince under adverse circumstances. In July 1943 King Vittorio Emanuele III had dismissed Mussolini as his Prime Minister amidst general concern from the Fascist Grand Council that Hitler had sucked Italy into an unwinnable and increasingly unpopular war. Amongst the many Fascisti who voted for Il Duce's downfall was his own son-in-law, Galeazzo, Count Ciano. Mussolini was duly arrested and imprisoned, Marshal Pietro Badoglio appointed Prime Minister in his place, and Italy then signed an armistice with the Allies on 8th September, 1943, joining as a co-belligerent against their former ally Germany. Four days later, on the orders of Hitler, Mussolini was rescued; the German puppet state of the Repubblica di Salò set up in northern Italy with Mussolini restored to power, and the monarchy abolished.

One of Mussolini's first acts upon reinstatement was to arrest Count Ciano. He ordered his execution and refused to consider the frantic pleas of his favourite child, Edda, for the life of her husband. To drive home the point that the former Italian Foreign Minister was dying a traitor's death, he was strapped into a chair to be shot, together with some of his Grand Council colleagues, from behind. Dignified to the end, however, he managed to turn the chair around just as the bullets were leaving the magazine and, in so doing, somewhat mitigated the disgrace of a traitor's death.

The newly-restored Mussolini also ordered the detention of the king, but Vittorio Emanuele proved more elusive. This, unfortunately, was not the case with his ultimately tragic daughter Mafalda or son-in-law Tsar Boris III of Bulgaria. Mafalda was in Bulgaria for the funeral of her sister Giovanna's husband following his sudden death by what has always been suspected as poisoning on Hitler's orders. According to Dr. Hans Eppinger, a German doctor who attended the courageous Tsar in his final illness, Boris had been killed with a slow-acting poison which takes effect over weeks and causes heart failure as well as large blotches on the skin.

There was no doubt that Hitler had the opportunity to have the poison administered. Boris had been summoned to see Hitler at Rastenburg on 14th August, 1943. There followed a meeting which has gone down in history as 'stormy' but was really cataclysmic. The king was refusing, and continued to refuse, to hand over any of the Jews in Bulgaria (for which he would become the first Gentile to receive the Jewish National Fund's Medal of the Legion of Honour as well as being proclaimed the saviour of 50,000 Bulgarian Jews by the United States Congress on 12th May, 1994). He also refused to declare war on the Soviet Union, though, having been forced into an alliance with Nazi Germany, he made a symbolic gesture by declaring war on Britain and the United States, neither of which country could actually be threatened by his army. It is unlikely that his relationship to the Belgian and English kings was much of a consideration politically, even though he was one of the three European monarchs who emanated from the House of Saxe-Coburg, but his sympathies were nevertheless anti-Nazi.

The fact that Boris was the only European leader to resist Hitler's order to 'transport' its Jews, and thereby saved his Jewish compatriots, indicated a strength of character which might be admirable to the reader, but was sufficient to bring about his death. His six-year-old only son succeeded him as Tsar Simeon II. His brother Prince Kiril became joint-Regent with the Prime Minister Bogdan Filov and Lieutenant-General Nikola Mihailov Mihov of the Bulgarian Army. Although the new government still managed to preserve the policies of their late Tsar, his refusal to declare war on the Soviet Union proved to be a vain sacrifice. Stalin coveted Bulgaria as one of its spheres of influence, and on 5th September, 1944, the Soviet Union declared war on that state. The Red Army invaded, and four days later there was a Red Army-backed coup d'état. The three regents were deposed along with the lawful Government; Parliament prorogued; and every member of the last three governments as well as all members of Parliament arrested. All were executed along with the country's leading journalists in February 1945.

At the time of Boris's death, Mafalda's position was even more insecure than her recently widowed sister's, for Tsarina Giovanna at least lived in a separate country from Hitler and the Red Army had not yet unleashed its hordes on Eastern or Western Europe. Mafalda, on the other hand, resided in Germany. She had been the Landgravine of Hesse-Kassel since 1925, when she married Queen Victoria's great-grandson and Kaiser Wilhelm II's nephew, Prince Philipp of Hesse. According to the biographer Jonathan Petropoulos, Philipp was most likely bisexual. Although he fathered four children with Mafalda, he was for a while a celebrated interior designer in Rome and was commonly supposed to have had an affair with the wartime poet Siegfried Sassoon. This did not prevent him from becoming an admirer of the Nazi Party, which he joined in 1930 along with his brother Christoph, whose wife Princess Sophie of Greece would become Lilibet's sister-in-law in 1947 when she married Prince Philip of Greece.

By early 1943, as the tide of the war was turning against him, Hitler became convinced that the German royals were working to undermine an Axis victory. There were, of course, always wartime anomalies where royalty was concerned, for they were the only true internationals, except for a few grand aristocratic families with branches in various countries and continents. For instance, Prince Philip of Greece was a serving officer in the English Navy, while the man after whom he had been named was a high-ranking Nazi officer and the Governor of Hesse-Nassau, but this did not necessarily suggest disloyalty. What it did encourage, however, was a quicker leap from a sinking ship of state than those with fewer links to the enemy might be tempted to make. So, in May 1943, Hitler tried to head off the potential problem of his royals trying to negotiate separate peaces through their foreign relations by issuing the Decree Concerning Internationally Connected Men. This banned all German princes from holding positions in the state, party, or armed forces.

On the day Italy signed the Armistice with the Allies, Hitler had Philipp of Hesse arrested. His four children were given sanctuary in the Vatican and Mafalda was tricked on 23rd September by SS-Hauptsturmfuhrer Karl Hass at the German High Command into presenting herself under the guise of receiving an important message from her husband. She was duly arrested, transported first to Munich, then to Berlin for questioning, before being finally interred in Buchenwald Concentration Camp. Hitler had developed a loathing for her, calling her 'the blackest carrion in the Italian royal house', and ensured that she had scant chance of surviving the war by ordering that she be housed beside a munitions factory inside the camp.

On 24th August, 1944, the Allies bombed the factory, killing four hundred outright and badly injuring several others, including Mafalda. She was buried up to her neck in debris and badly burnt on her arms. Fearing she was dying, she said to two Italian compatriots, 'Remember me not as an Italian princess, but as an Italian sister.' Although she did not die then, one of her arms became so badly infected that it had to be amputated two days later. During the operation she bled so profusely that there was no chance of saving her life and she died, without regaining consciousness, on the night of 26-27th August, 1944. In 1997 the Italian Government honoured her memory with a postage stamp bearing her image and name.

While Mafalda was being interrogated in Germany, and the British Royal Family was relieved that its many Continental cousins in Axis countries were finally aligning themselves with the cause of right, the rest of the Italian Royal Family and the lawful Italian Government took refuge in the south. It quickly became abundantly clear that Vittorio Emanuele III was so tainted by the years of association with Mussolini that he would need to step aside. Fatally, this once popular king took the decision to remain on the throne, though he did hand over his powers to his son in April 1944. When the Allies entered Rome in June, he went one step further and appointed Umberto Lieutenant-General of the Realm, which was effectively a regency. But he did not formally abdicate until 9th May, 1946. A referendum on the monarchy had been scheduled for the following month, and by then it was apparent that the only chance Italy had of remaining a monarchy was for Vittorio Emanuele to step aside formally. However, his abdication was too late. Italy was declared a republic by the narrowest of margins, amidst claims of vote-rigging by the republicans, on 12th June, 1946.

Umberto and his family went into exile the following day. At first, the family lived in Portugal, but when it became apparent that there would be no immediate recall to Italy, Queen Marie José moved to Switzerland, where she mostly lived for the remainder of her long life, though she did spend extended periods in Mexico with her daughter Princess Maria Beatrice. She died of lung cancer in 2001, while Umberto died in 1983.

Genealogical Tables

KING GEORGE III = 1761   Princess Charlotte
(1738-1820)   of Mecklenburg-Strelitz
                          (1744-1818)

The Prince Edward = 1818   Princess Victoria
Duke of Kent   widow of Emich Karl,
(1767-1820)   Prince of Leiningen
                   dau. of the Duke of
                   Saxe-Coburg-Saalfeld
                   (1786-1861)

QUEEN VICTORIA = 1840   Prince Albert of Saxe-Coburg
(1819-1901)   The Prince Consort
                        (1819-61)

The Princess Victoria   The Princess Alice   The Princess Helena
The Princess Royal   (1843-78)   (1846-1923)
(1840-1901)   = 1862   = 1866
= 1858   Ludwig IV   Prince Christian of
Emperor Frederick III   Grand Duke of Hesse   Schleswig-Holstein
Emperor of Germany   (1837-92)   (1831-1917)
(1831-88)

KING EDWARD VII   The Prince Alfred
(1841-1910)   Duke of Edinburgh
= 1863   Duke of Saxe-Coburg
Princess Alexandra   (1844-1900)   Princess
of Denmark   = 1874   Helena Victoria
(1844-1925)   Grand Duchess   (1870-1948)
                   Marie of Russia
                   (1853-1920)

Emperor Wilhelm II   Princess Victoria
Emperor of Germany   of Hesse
(1859-1941)   (1863-1950)
              [*continued*]   = 1884
                   Prince Louis
                   of Battenberg
            Marquess of Milford Haven
                   (1854-1921)

Princess Alice of Battenberg   Louis,
(1885-1969)   Admiral of the Fleet
= 1903   Earl Mountbatten of Burma
Prince Andrew of   (1900-79)
Greece & Denmark   = 1921
(1882-1944)   Hon. Edwina Ashley
                   (1901-60)

Prince Philip
of Greece & Denmark

Royal Family Tree

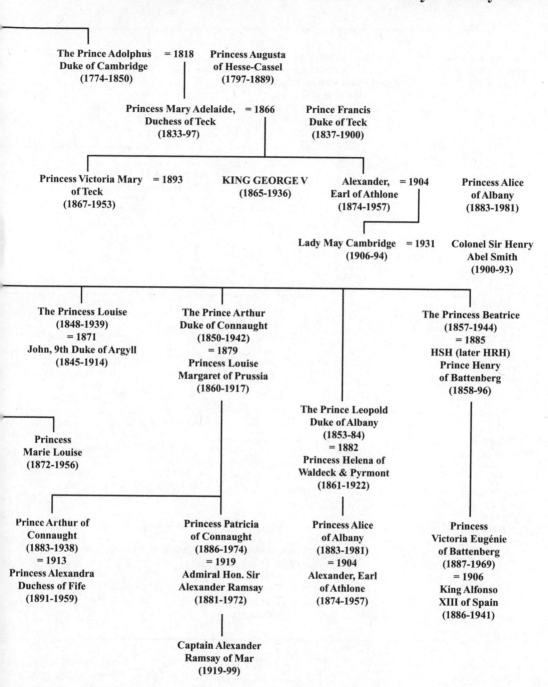

The Prince Adolphus
Duke of Cambridge
(1774-1850)
= 1818
Princess Augusta
of Hesse-Cassel
(1797-1889)

Princess Mary Adelaide,
Duchess of Teck
(1833-97)
= 1866
Prince Francis
Duke of Teck
(1837-1900)

Princess Victoria Mary
of Teck
(1867-1953)
= 1893

KING GEORGE V
(1865-1936)

Alexander,
Earl of Athlone
(1874-1957)
= 1904

Princess Alice
of Albany
(1883-1981)

Lady May Cambridge
(1906-94)
= 1931
Colonel Sir Henry
Abel Smith
(1900-93)

The Princess Louise
(1848-1939)
= 1871
John, 9th Duke of Argyll
(1845-1914)

The Prince Arthur
Duke of Connaught
(1850-1942)
= 1879
Princess Louise
Margaret of Prussia
(1860-1917)

The Princess Beatrice
(1857-1944)
= 1885
HSH (later HRH)
Prince Henry
of Battenberg
(1858-96)

Princess
Marie Louise
(1872-1956)

The Prince Leopold
Duke of Albany
(1853-84)
= 1882
Princess Helena of
Waldeck & Pyrmont
(1861-1922)

Prince Arthur of
Connaught
(1883-1938)
= 1913
Princess Alexandra
Duchess of Fife
(1891-1959)

Princess Patricia
of Connaught
(1886-1974)
= 1919
Admiral Hon. Sir
Alexander Ramsay
(1881-1972)

Princess Alice
of Albany
(1883-1981)
= 1904
Alexander, Earl
of Athlone
(1874-1957)

Princess
Victoria Eugénie
of Battenberg
(1887-1969)
= 1906
King Alfonso
XIII of Spain
(1886-1941)

Captain Alexander
Ramsay of Mar
(1919-99)

KING EDWARD VII = 1863   **Princess Alexandra of Denmark**
(1841-1910)   **(1844-1925)**

Prince Albert Victor   **KING GEORGE V**   **The Princess Louise,**
Duke of Clarence   **(1865-1936)**   **Duchess of Fife, The Princess Royal**
(1864-92)   **Princess Victoria Mary of Teck**   **(1867-1931)**
                (1867-1953)   = 1889
                                      Alexander, 1st Duke of Fife
                                      (1845-1912)

Princess Alexandra
Duchess of Fife
(1891-1959)
= 1913
Prince Arthur of Connaught
(1883-1938)

KING EDWARD VIII   **KING GEORGE VI**   **Princess Mary**
Later HRH The Duke of Windsor   **(1895-1952)**   **The Princess Royal**
(1894-1972)   = 1923   **(1897-1965**
= 1937   **LADY ELIZABETH BOWES LYON**   = 1922
Mrs Wallis Simpson   **(1900-2002)**   **Henry, 6th Earl of**
(1896-1986)   **Harewood**
                                      (1882-1947)

QUEEN   **The Princess Margaret**   **George, 7th Earl of**
ELIZABETH II   **(1930-2002)**   **Harewood**
(b. 1926)   = 1960 (div. 1978)   **(b. 1923)**
= 1947   **Antony Armstrong-Jones**   **m. twice**
Prince Philip of   **Earl of Snowdon**
Greece & Denmark   **(b. 1930)**
HRH The Duke
of Edinburgh
(b. 1921)

David, Viscount Linley   **Lady Sarah Armstrong-Jones**
(b. 1961)   **(b. 1964)**
= 1993   = 1994
Hon. Serena Stanhope   **Daniel Chatto**
(b. 1970)   **(b. 1957)**
one son, one daughter   **two sons**

The Prince Charles   **The Princess Anne**   **The Prince Andrew**
The Prince of Wales   **The Princess Royal**   **Duke of York**
(b. 1948)   **(b. 1950)**   **(b. 1960)**
= (1) 1981 (div. 1996)   = (2) 2005   = (1) 1973 (div. 1992)   = (2) 1992   = 1986 (div. 1996)
Lady Diana Spencer   **Camilla Parker Bowles**   **Captain Mark Phillips**   **Rear-Admiral**   **Sarah Ferguson**
(1961-97)   **(b. 1947)**   **(b. 1948)**   **Timothy Laurence**   **(b. 1959)**
                                                     (b. 1955)   **2 daughters**

Prince William   **Prince Harry**   **Peter Phillips**   **Zara Phillips**
of Wales   **of Wales**   **(b. 1977)**   **(b. 1981)**
(b. 1982)   **(b. 1984)**

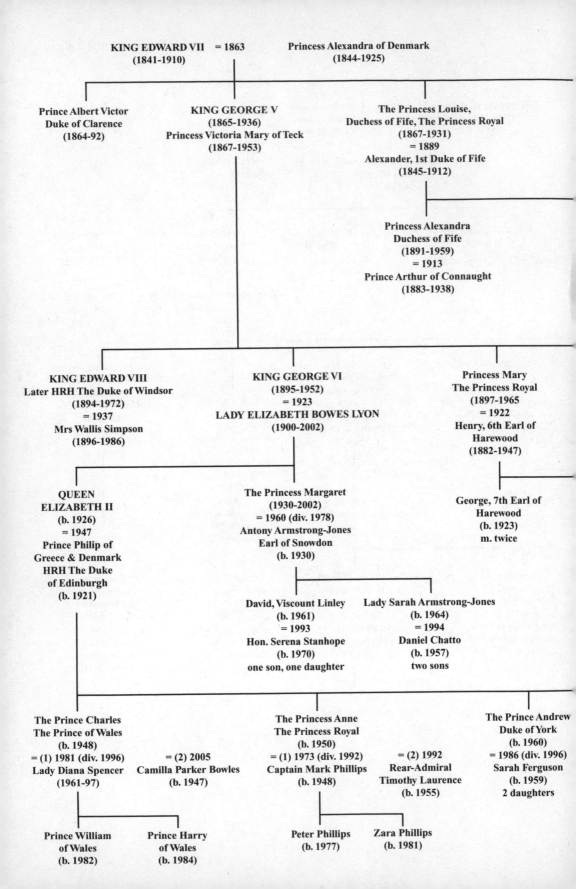

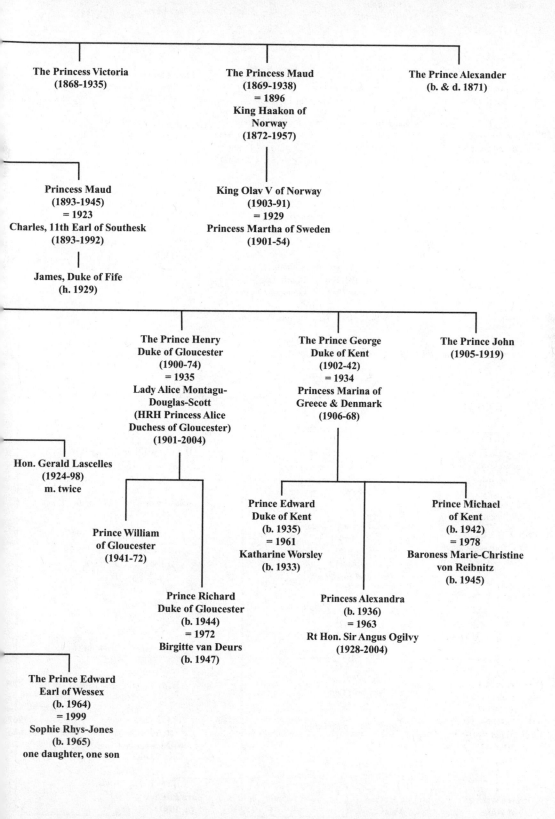

The Princess Victoria
(1868-1935)

The Princess Maud
(1869-1938)
= 1896
King Haakon of
Norway
(1872-1957)

The Prince Alexander
(b. & d. 1871)

Princess Maud
(1893-1945)
= 1923
Charles, 11th Earl of Southesk
(1893-1992)

King Olav V of Norway
(1903-91)
= 1929
Princess Martha of Sweden
(1901-54)

James, Duke of Fife
(h. 1929)

The Prince Henry
Duke of Gloucester
(1900-74)
= 1935
Lady Alice Montagu-
Douglas-Scott
(HRH Princess Alice
Duchess of Gloucester)
(1901-2004)

The Prince George
Duke of Kent
(1902-42)
= 1934
Princess Marina of
Greece & Denmark
(1906-68)

The Prince John
(1905-1919)

Hon. Gerald Lascelles
(1924-98)
m. twice

Prince Edward
Duke of Kent
(b. 1935)
= 1961
Katharine Worsley
(b. 1933)

Prince Michael
of Kent
(b. 1942)
= 1978
Baroness Marie-Christine
von Reibnitz
(b. 1945)

Prince William
of Gloucester
(1941-72)

Prince Richard
Duke of Gloucester
(b. 1944)
= 1972
Birgitte van Deurs
(b. 1947)

Princess Alexandra
(b. 1936)
= 1963
Rt Hon. Sir Angus Ogilvy
(1928-2004)

The Prince Edward
Earl of Wessex
(b. 1964)
= 1999
Sophie Rhys-Jones
(b. 1965)
one daughter, one son

Bowes Lyon

Robert I The Bruce
King of Scots
(1274-1329)
= (1) Isabella
dau. of Donald,
6th Earl of Mar

Marjorie Bruce
(d. 1316)
= 1315 Walter, 6th High Steward
of Scotland (d. 1326)

(1) 1347
Elizabeth
(d. ante 1355)
dau. of Sir
Adam Mure
of Rowallan
= King Robert II
of Scotland
(1316-1390)
= (2) Euphemia
(d. 1387),
dau. of Hugh,
4th Earl of Ross

Jean
=
Sir John Lyon
Chamberlain
of Scotland
(d. 1382?)

David, Earl Palatine
of Stratherne
(b. 1356/60, d. ante 1389)

Euphemia, Countess
Palatine of Stratherne
(b. ante 1375 - d. in or post 1434)
= 1406
Sir Patrick Graham, of Kilmont

Sir John Lyon, 2nd of Glamis
(d. ca 1435)
= Elizabeth

Patrick, 1st Lord Glamis
(d. 1459)
= Isabel dau. of Sir Walter Ogilvy

Alexander
2nd Lord Glamis
(d. 1486)
=
Agnes, dau. of
William, Lord
Crichton

John, 3rd Lord Glamis
(d. 1497)
=
Elizabeth Scrymgeour

John, 4th Lord Glamis
(d. 1500)
=
Elizabeth
dau. 2nd Lord Gray

John, 8th Lord Glamis
(d. 1578)
=
Elizabeth
widow of William Meldrum

Patrick,
9th Lord Glamis
1st Earl of Kinghorne
(1575-1615)
= 1595
Anne (d. 1618)
dau. of John, Earl of Tullibardine

George
5th Lord Glamis
(d. unmarried 1505)

John, 6th Lord Glamis
(d. 1528)

Janet
(d. 1537)
dau. of George,
Master of Angus

John, 7th Lord Glamis
(d. 1559)
=
Janet Keith
dau. of William, 4th Earl Marischal

John, 2nd Earl of Kinghorne
(1596-1646)
=
Lady Elizabeth Maule
(d. 1659)

Patrick, 3rd Earl of
Strathmore & Kinghorne
(1643-95)
= 1662
Lady Helen Middleton
(d. 1708)

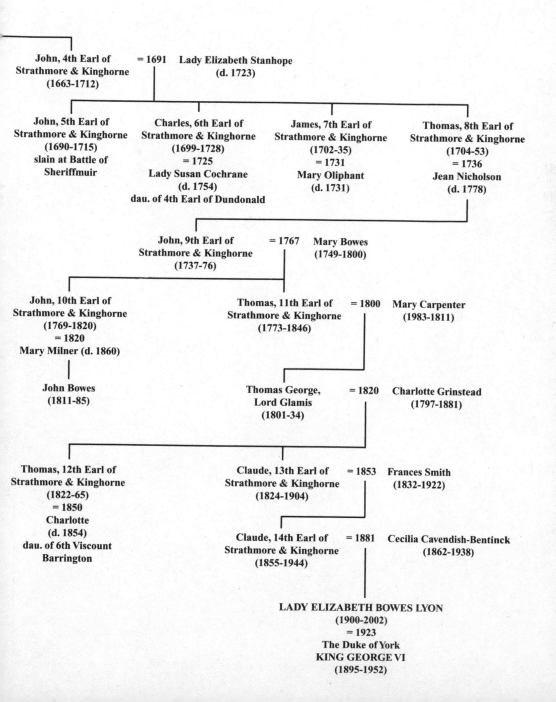

John, 4th Earl of
Strathmore & Kinghorne
(1663-1712)   = 1691   Lady Elizabeth Stanhope
(d. 1723)

John, 5th Earl of
Strathmore & Kinghorne
(1690-1715)
slain at Battle of
Sheriffmuir

Charles, 6th Earl of
Strathmore & Kinghorne
(1699-1728)
= 1725
Lady Susan Cochrane
(d. 1754)
dau. of 4th Earl of Dundonald

James, 7th Earl of
Strathmore & Kinghorne
(1702-35)
= 1731
Mary Oliphant
(d. 1731)

Thomas, 8th Earl of
Strathmore & Kinghorne
(1704-53)
= 1736
Jean Nicholson
(d. 1778)

John, 9th Earl of
Strathmore & Kinghorne
(1737-76)   = 1767   Mary Bowes
(1749-1800)

John, 10th Earl of
Strathmore & Kinghorne
(1769-1820)
= 1820
Mary Milner (d. 1860)

Thomas, 11th Earl of
Strathmore & Kinghorne
(1773-1846)   = 1800   Mary Carpenter
(1983-1811)

John Bowes
(1811-85)

Thomas George,
Lord Glamis
(1801-34)   = 1820   Charlotte Grinstead
(1797-1881)

Thomas, 12th Earl of
Strathmore & Kinghorne
(1822-65)
= 1850
Charlotte
(d. 1854)
dau. of 6th Viscount
Barrington

Claude, 13th Earl of
Strathmore & Kinghorne
(1824-1904)   = 1853   Frances Smith
(1832-1922)

Claude, 14th Earl of
Strathmore & Kinghorne
(1855-1944)   = 1881   Cecilia Cavendish-Bentinck
(1862-1938)

LADY ELIZABETH BOWES LYON
(1900-2002)
= 1923
The Duke of York
KING GEORGE VI
(1895-1952)

Selected Bibliography

Queen Elizabeth The Queen Mother: The Official Biography – William Shawcross – Macmillan – 2009

Elizabeth The Queen Mother – Hugo Vickers – Hutchinson – 2005

Queen Elizabeth The Queen Mother – Dorothy Laird – Coronet – 2005

Raymond Asquith: Life and Letters ed. John Joliffe – Collins – 1980

The Queen – Lady Cynthia Asquith – Hutchinson – 1937

The Duchess of York – Lady Cynthia Asquith – Hutchinson – 1927

Meine Schülerin – die Königin von England – Käthe Kübler - Hermann Eichblatt, Leipzig – 1937

First World War – Martin Gilbert – Henry Holt – 2004

Glamis Castle: Its Origin and History with a Brief Account of the Early Church of the Parish – Revd. John Stirton – 1938 – W. Shepherd, Forfar

Chips: The Diaries of Sir Henry Channon – Sir Henry Channon – Littlehampton Book Services – 1967

The Queen Mother: A Biography – Elizabeth Longford – Weidenfeld & Nicholson – 1981

Edward VIII: Road to Abdication – Frances Donaldson – Weidenfeld & Nicolson – 1978

The Royal Marriages – Lady Colin Campbell – St. Martin's Press – 1993

Queen Elizabeth: A Life of The Queen Mother – Penelope Mortimer – Viking – 1986 – Penguin – 1987

Selected Bibliography

Thatched with Gold: The Memoirs of Mabell, Countess of Airlie, edited Jennifer Ellis – Hutchinson & Co – 1962

A Fatal Passion: The Story of the Uncrowned Last Empress of Russia – Michael John Sullivan, Random House – 1997

Marie of Romania – Terence Elsberry – St. Martin's Press – 1972

One Man in His Time: The Memoirs of Serge Obolensky – McDowell Obolensky, NY – 1968

Within the Fringe: An Autobiography – James Stuart – Viscount Stuart of Findhorn – Bodley Head – 1967

The Final Curtsey – Margaret Rhodes – Umbria Press – 2011

Crowded Life: The Autobiography of Lady Cynthia Colville – Lady Cynthia Colville – Evans Bros. – 1963

HHA: Letters of the Earl of Oxford and Asquith to a Friend (Vol.2) – Herbert Henry Asquith, Geoffrey Bles – 1934

Louis & the Prince – Geordie Greig – Hodder & Stoughton – 1999

Haakon og Maud of Norway – Tor Bomann Larsen – I/Kongstaken – II/ Folket – Oslo: Cappelen – 2004

King George V – Kenneth Rose – Weidenfeld & Nicolson – 1983

King George VI: His Life and Reign – John Wheeler-Bennett – St. Martin's Press – 1958

The Queen: A Biography of Elizabeth II – Ben Pimlott – John Wiley & Sons – 1998

Royals and the Reich: The Princes von Hessen in Nazi Germany – Oxford University Press – 2006

Without Prejudice – Gloria Morgan Vanderbilt with Palma Payne – E P Dutton – 1936

Double Exposure: A Twin Autobiography – Gloria Morgan Vanderbilt and Thelma, Viscountess Furness – D McKay – 1958

King Edward VIII – The Official Biography – Philip Ziegler – Knopf – 1991

Mrs Simpson – Charles Higham – Pan Books – 2005

The Heart has its Reasons: The Memoirs of the Duchess of Windsor – The Duchess of Windsor – Michael Joseph – 1956

Redeeming Features – Nicholas Haslam – Random House – 2009

Who Killed Society? – Cleveland Amory – Harper & Bros – 1960

A King's Story: The Memoirs of HRH The Duke of Windsor – The Duke of Windsor – Putnam – 1951

Elizabeth R: A Biography – *Elizabeth Longford* – Orion Publishing Group – 1983

Forget Not: Her Autobiography – Margaret, Duchess of Argyll – W.H. Allen – 1975

The Windsor Story – Joseph Bryan and John Vincent Murphy – Morrow – 1979

Memoirs of HRH Prince Christopher of Greece – The Right Book Club – 1938

Grace and Favour – Loelia, Duchess of Westminster – Weidenfeld & Nicolson – 1961

The Diaries of Sir Robert Bruce Lockhart – Kenneth Young – Macmillan – Vol 1 1973 – Vol 2 – 1980

Diaries and Letters 1911–1947 – Marie Belloc Lowndes – Chatto & Windus – 1971

Harold Nicolson: Vol 1 1886–1929 – A Biography – James Lees-Milne – Chatto & Windus – 1980

Loyal to Three Kings: A Memoir of Alec Hardinge – Helen Hardinge – William Kimber – 1967

George VI – Patrick Howarth – Hutchinson – 1987

The Little Princesses – Marion Crawford – Harcourt, Brace – 1950

Self-Portrait with Friends: The selected diaries of Cecil Beaton 1926–1974 – Cecil Beaton – Weidenfeld & Nicolson – 1979

Baldwin: A Biography – Keith Middlemas and John Barnes – Weidenfeld & Nicolson – 1969

The Reign of King Edward VIII – Robert Sencourt – A. Gibbs & Phillips – 1962

A Spirit Undaunted: The Political Role of George VI – Robert Rhodes James – Little Brown – 1998

The Life and Reign of George VI – Sarah Bradford – St. Martin's Press – 1990

The Secret File of the Duke of Windsor – Michael Bloch – Bantam Press – 1988

The Secret Diary of Harold L. Ickes – Volume II: The Inside Struggle

1936–1939 – Harold L. Ickes – Simon & Schuster – 1954

Kings, Queens & Courtiers – Kenneth Rose – Weidenfeld & Nicolson – 1985

Past Forgetting – Veronica Maclean – Review – 2002

The Queen Mother's Family Story – James Wentworth Day – Robert Hale – 1967

The Prince of Wales – Jonathan Dimbleby – Little, Brown & Co. – 1994

The Light of Common Day – Lady Diana Cooper – Houghton Mifflin – 1959

The Story of My Life – Marie, Queen of Roumania – Charles Scribner's Sons – 1935

Alice: Princess Andrew of Greece – Hugo Vickers – St. Martin's Press – 2002

Royal Feud: The Queen Mother and the Duchess of Windsor – Michael Thornton – Pan Books – 1985

King's Counsellor: Abdication and War: The Diaries of Sir Alan Lascelles – ed Duff Hart-Davis – Orion – 2006

Chapter Notes

CHAPTER 1

1: Sunniside Local History Society, p2

2: *Queen Elizabeth The Queen Mother: Official Biography* – William Shawcross – Macmillan – 2009, p16

3: Ibid, p16

4: Ibid, p16

CHAPTER 2

1: *The Scotsman* – Sally Kinnes, p2 para 8 – 1 April 2002

2: Ibid

3: Ibid

4: Ibid

5: Shawcross, p25

6: *Queen Elizabeth The Queen Mother* – Dorothy Laird – Coronet – 1985, p36

7: *The Crawford Papers: The Journals of David Lindsay, Twenty-Seventh Earl of Crawford and Tenth Earl of Balcarres during the years 1892 to 1940* – edited by John Vincent – entry for 2 October 1905, p86

8: Shawcross, p26

9: *Queen Elizabeth: A Life of the Queen Mother* – Penelope Mortimer – Viking – 1986

10: *The Scotsman* – Sally Kinnes – 1 April 2002

11: Ibid

12: Queen Elizabeth (hereinafter called Elizabeth) to Archbishop of Canterbury, 23 June 1938 – Lambeth Palace Library

13: Elizabeth to Neville Chamberlain, Birkhall, 2 July 1938 – Neville Chamberlain papers, Birmingham University, NC7/4/8

14: *Sunday Telegraph* – Kenneth Rose – 1 August 1965

15: *Raymond Asquith: Life and Letters*, ed. John Joliffe – Collins – 1980, p134

16: Ibid

17: *The Queen* – Lady Cynthia Asquith – Hutchinson – 1937, p23

18: Ibid, p46–7

19: *The Duke of Windsor's War* – Michael Bloch – Weidenfeld & Nicolson – 1982

20: *The Diaries of Sir Robert Bruce Lockhart* – Kenneth Young – Macmillan – Vol 1 1973, p241

21: Ibid, p364

22: Astor Papers – MS1416/1/4/8 – Reading University

23: *The Duchess of York* – Lady Cynthia Asquith – Hutchinson – 1927, p45

24: *The Queen* – Asquith, p32

25: Mrs. Scott to Cecilia Glamis (hereinafter called Cecilia) – Glamis Archives – 10 September 1902

26: Ibid – 16 September 1902

27: Sally Kinnes – 1 April 2002

28: Ibid

29: *The Duchess of York* – Asquith, p33

30: *The Queen* – Asquith, pp22–3

31: Elizabeth – Conversations with Eric Anderson – 1994-5 – Royal Archives

32: *The Queen* – Asquith, p25

33: Laird, p40

34: *The Queen* – Asquith, p49

35: Ibid, pp45–6

36: Ibid, p56

37: Laurel Gray to Elizabeth – 1 December 1948 – Royal Archives

38: *Elizabeth of Glamis* – Terry Wolsey – Canongate – 1990, p11

39: Hon. John Bowes Lyon to Cecilia – 24 July 1911 – Glamis Archives

40: *The Queen* – Asquith, p54

41: Elizabeth – Conversations with Eric Anderson 1994-5 – Royal Archives

42: Ibid

43: *Meine Schülerin – die König von England* – Käthe Kübler – Herman Eichblatt, Leipzig, 1937, pp7–8

44: Conversations with Eric Anderson – 1994-5 – Royal Archives

CHAPTER 3

1: *The Queen* – Asquith, p59

2: Ibid, p59

3: Cecilia to B Poignand – 9 October 1914 – Glamis Archives

4: Kinnes – 1/4/02

5: B Poignand to her mother – undated – Poignand Papers

6: Ibid – 22 November 1914

7: Ibid

8: Elizabeth to B Poignand – 21 October 1917 – Glamis Archives

9: Elizabeth to B Poignand – 26 December 1914 – Glamis Archives

10: *The Queen* – Asquith, p60

11: Ibid, p67

12: Shawcross, p68

13: B Poignand to mother – 2 June 1915

14: Elizabeth to B Poignand – 9 August 1915 – Glamis Archives

15: Ibid

16: Ibid

17: Post traumatic stress disorder

18: Elizabeth to Mrs. Poignand – 23 October 1915 – Glamis Archives

19: H Ainsley to Elizabeth – 19 March 1916 – Glamis Archives

20: *Glamis Castle: Its Origin and History with a Brief Account of the Early Church of the Parish* – Revd. John Stirton – 1938 – W Shepherd, Forfar, pp36-7

21: Elizabeth to Cecilia – 25 March 1916 – Glamis Archives

22: Elizabeth to B Poignand – 26 April 1916 – Glamis Archives

23: Elizabeth to Cecilia – 25 March 1916 – Glamis Archives

24: Elizabeth to Cecilia – 28 March 1916 – Glamis Archives

25: Elizabeth to Cecilia – 4 April 1916 – Glamis Archives

26: *The Royal Marriages* – Lady Colin Campbell – 1993, p18

27: Lady Diana Cooper to author

28: Elizabeth to B Poignand – 22 September 1916 – Glamis Archives

29: Elizabeth to B Poignand – 17 September 1916 – Glamis Archives

30: Ibid

31: Cecilia to B Poignand – 22 September 1916 – Glamis Archives

32: Elizabeth to B Poignand – 5 September 1916 – Glamis Archives

33: Elizabeth to Beryl – 7 April 1916 – Glamis Archives

34: Claude, Earl of Strathmore (hereinafter called Claude) to Lady Rose Leveson-Gower – 3 May 1917 – Glamis Archives

35: Elizabeth to B Poignand – 3 May 1917 – Glamis Archives

36: Ibid

37: Elizabeth to B Poignand – 29 September 1917 – Glamis Archives

38: Elizabeth to B Poignand – 9 January 1918 – Glamis Archives

39: Ibid

40: Elizabeth to B Poignand – 5 January 1918 – Glamis Archives

41: Elizabeth to B Poignand – 7 February 1918 – Glamis Archives

42: *Elizabeth the Queen Mother* – Hugo Vickers – Arrow Books – 2006, p26

43: Elizabeth to B Poignand – 22 March 1918 – Glamis Archives

44: Elizabeth to B Poignand – 25 June 1918 – Glamis Archives

CHAPTER 4

1: Elizabeth to B Poignand – 6 April 1919 – Glamis Archives

2: Elizabeth to B Poignand – undated but late August/early September 1919 – Glamis Archives

3: Alec Hardinge to Helen Cecil, Balmoral, 14 September 1920 – Hardinge Papers, Maidstone – U2117 – C1/22

4: Elizabeth to B Poignand – estimated date 9 January 1920 – Glamis Archives

5: *Within the Fringe* – Viscount Stuart of Findhorn – The Bodley Head – 1967, p57

6: The Prince of Wales to Freda Dudley Ward, HMS *Renown*, Lyttleton, New Zealand, 22 May 1920

7: King George V to Bertie – 7 June 1920 – quoted in Wheeler-Bennett, p140

8: Ibid

9: *The Queen Mother: A Biography* – Elizabeth Longford – Weidenfeld & Nicholson 1981, p18

10: Helen Cecil to Alexander Hardinge – estimated date 18 September 1920 – Hardinge Papers, Maidstone – U2117-C2/33

11: Author's conversations with Michael Thornton and Margaret, Duchess of Argyll

12: Author's conversations (hereinafter Conversations) with Margaret, Duchess of Argyll

13: Conversations with Margaret, Duchess of Argyll

14: Helen Cecil to Alec Hardinge – estimated 18 September 1920 – Hardinge Papers, Maidstone – U2117 – C2/33

15: Elizabeth to B Poignand – estimated 18 September 1920 – Glamis Archives

16: Ibid – estimated 23 September 1920

17: Ibid

18: Lady Doris Gordon-Lennox to Elizabeth – estimated 14 October 1920 – Glamis Archives

19: Elizabeth to B Poignand – undated November 1920 – Glamis Archives

20: *The Royal Marriages* – Lady Colin Campbell – St Martin's Press – 1993, p7

21: Ibid

22: Ibid, p8

23: Ibid

24: *Waltzing Mathilda* – Lady Milbanke – unpublished – 1948, p39

25: Ibid, p40

26: Wheeler-Bennett, p164

27: Shawcross, p115

28: The Duke of York (hereinafter Bertie) to the Prince of Wales (hereinafter David) – 7 April 1920 – Royal Archives

29: Bertie to David – 13 April 1920 – Royal Archives

30: *A Fatal Passion* – Sullivan – Random House, 1997, p152

31: Bertie to David – 25 May 1920 – Royal Archives

32: *One Man in His Time* – Serge Obolensky – McDowell Obolensky – 1958

33: Bertie to David – 25 May 1920 – Royal Archives

34: Author's conversation with Charles du Cane

35: Elizabeth to Bertie – undated – Royal Archives

36: Ibid – 10 January 1921

37: Ibid

38: Ibid

39: Shawcross, p126

40: Elizabeth to Bertie – estimated 17 February 1921 – Royal Archives

41: Elizabeth to Bertie – 28 February 1921 – Royal Archives

42: Cecilia to Mabell Airlie – 5 March 1921 – British Library

43: Ibid

44: Elizabeth to B Poignand – estimated 18 May 1921 – Glamis Archives

45: *Daily Mail* – Michael Thornton – 14th August 2009

46: Airlie, p167

47: Bertie to Queen Mary – 29 September 1921 – Royal Archives

48: Bertie to Elizabeth – 2 October 1921 – Glamis Archives

49: Elizabeth to Bertie – 4 October 1921 – Glamis Archives

50: Elizabeth to B Poignand – 28 November 1921 – Glamis Archives

51: Stuart of Findhorn, p57

52: Elizabeth – Vickers, p47

53: Elizabeth to B Poignand – estimated 28 November 1921 – Glamis Archives

54: Queen Mother – Longford, p23

55: Queen Mary to Bertie – 22 January 1922 – Royal Archives

56: Bertie to Elizabeth – 8 March 1922 – Royal Archives

57: Elizabeth to Bertie – 8 March 1922 – Royal Archives

58: Queen Mary to Cecilia – 6 May 1922 – Glamis Archives

59: Elizabeth – Vickers, p57

60: *The Lady* – 2 Nov 1922

61: Elizabeth – Vickers, p58

62: Bertie to Queen Mary – 4 October 1922 – Royal Archives

63: Mabell Airlie to Cecilia – 23 December 1922 – British Library

64: Elizabeth to Bertie – 25 December 1922 – Royal Archives

65: Bertie to Elizabeth – 29 December 1922 – Royal Archives

66: Ibid

67: Elizabeth to Bertie – 4 January 1923 – Royal Archives

68: Elizabeth's Diary – 5 January 1923 – Royal Archives

69: Queen Mary to Mabell Airlie – 9 January 1923 – British Library

70: Bertie to Queen Mary – 12 January 1923 – Royal Archives

71: Elizabeth's Diary – 12 January 1923 – Royal Archives

72: Ibid

73: Elizabeth's Diary – 13 January 1923 – Royal Archives

74: Cecilia to May Elphinstone – 16 January 1923 – Royal Archives

CHAPTER 5

1: Elizabeth's Diary – 16 January 1923 – Royal Archives

2: Queen Mary to Bertie – 18 January 1923 – Royal Archives

3: Elizabeth's diary – 20 January 1923 – Royal Archives

4: Wheeler-Bennett, p15

5: Queen Mary diary – 20 January 1923 – Royal Archives

6: George V diary – 20 January 1923 – Royal Archives

7: Queen Mary diary – 20 January 1923 – Royal Archives

8: Elizabeth to B Poignand – 21 January 1923 – Glamis Archives

9: Queen Mary to Bertie – 24 January 1923 – Royal Archives

10: Elizabeth's diary – 6 February 1923 – Royal Archives

11: Elizabeth to Bertie – estimated 25 January 1923 – Royal Archives

12: Elizabeth's diary – 23 January 1923 – Royal Archives

13: Elizabeth to Queen Mary – 25 January 1923 – Royal Archives

14: Elizabeth to Bertie – estimated 13 March 1923 – Royal Archives

CHAPTER 6

1: *Letters to a Friend* – HH Asquith – Vol 2, p50-51

2: Ibid

3: Elizabeth's diary – 24 April 1923 – Royal Archives

4: Ibid – 25 April 1923 – Royal Archives

5: Ibid

6: Elizabeth's diary – 26 April 1923 – Royal Archives

7: Ibid

8: *The Royal Marriages* – Lady Colin Campbell, p25

9: Cecilia to Elizabeth – 27 April 1923 – Royal Archives

10: Elizabeth to Cecilia – estimated 27 April 1923 – Royal Archives

11: George V to Bertie – 29 April 1923 – Royal Archives

12: *Daily Mail* – Rebecca English – 8 October 2011, p37

13: Elizabeth to E Campbell – Glamis – 1 September 1913

14: Elizabeth's diary – 27-29 April, 1923 – Royal Archives

15: Ibid

16: Ibid – 7 May 1923

17: Mortimer, pp91–2

18: Elizabeth's diary – 18-22 May 1923 – Royal Archives

19: Ibid

20: Bertie to Queen Mary – 25 May 1923 – Royal Archives

21: Ibid

22: Mortimer, pp92–3

23: Elizabeth's diary – 5 July 1923 – Royal Archives

24: Ibid

25: Bertie to David – 9 August 1925 – Royal Archives

26: Elizabeth to D'Arcy Osborne – 10 July 1923 – Royal Archives

27: Ernest Pearce to Elizabeth – 1 July 1923 – Royal Archives

CHAPTER 7

1: Prince George to Elizabeth – estimated 19 September 1923 – Royal Archives

2: George V to Bertie – 20 September 1923 – Royal Archives

3: Queen Mary to Bertie – 18 September 1923 – Royal Archives

4: George V to Bertie – 20 September 1923 – Royal Archives

5: Bertie to Greig – 24 September 1923 – Royal Archives

6: Ibid

7: Elizabeth to Cecilia – 21 October 1923 – Glamis Archives

8: Elizabeth's diary – 21 October 1923 – Royal Archives

9: Elizabeth to Cecilia – 26 October 1923 – Glamis Archives

10: Bertie to George V – 26 October 1923 – Royal Archives

11: Duke of Windsor to Duchess of Argyll – Lady Colin Campbell Archives

12: Bertie to Queen Mary – 9 October 1923 – Royal Archives

13: *Louis & the Prince* – Geordie Greig – Hodder & Stoughton – 1999, p214

14: Elizabeth to George V – 14 January 1924 – Royal Archives

15: Elizabeth to Cecilia – estimated 14 September 1924 – Glamis Archives

16: Elizabeth to Cecilia – 20 December 1924 – Glamis Archives

17: Elizabeth to George V – 9 February 1925 – Royal Archives

18: Elizabeth to David – 13 January 1925 – Royal Archives

19: Ibid

20: Ibid

21: Captain Roy Salmon to Mrs. Salmon – 25 March 1925 – private collection

22: Conversations with Eric Anderson – 1994-5 – Royal Archives

23: Bertie to David – 27 May 1925 – Royal Archives

24: *George V* – Nicolson, pp529–30

25: Queen Mary to Bertie – 20 October 1925 – Royal Archives

26: Bertie to George V – 27 April 1926 – Royal Archives

27: George V – Rose, p341

CHAPTER 8

1: Shawcross, p258

2: *News Chronicle*, 13 April, 1953

3: Michael Thornton

4: Wheeler-Bennett, p230

5: Harry Batterbee to Lord Stamfordham – 26 May 1927 – Royal Archives

6: Bertie to George V – 12 June 1927 – Royal Archives

7: Shawcross, p298

8: Conversations with Duchess of Argyll

9: Queen Maud to Queen Mary – 31 March 1929 – Royal Archives

10: Revd. Philip Hart conversations with Princess Alice, Countess of Athlone

11: *Royals and the Reich: The Princes von Hessen in Nazi Germany* – Oxford University Press – 2006

12: Dr. Frank Neon Reynolds to his wife – Reynolds papers

13: Elizabeth to Queen Mary – 31 July 1930 – Royal Archives

14: Ibid – 5 August 1930 – Royal Archives

15: Wheeler-Bennett, p259

16: *Double Exposure* – Vanderbilt and Furness – D McKay – 1958, pp265–6

17: *Without Prejudice* – Vanderbilt with Wayne – E P Dutton – 1936, p31

18: *Rochester Evening Journal* – 23/1/29

19: Conversations with Duchess of Argyll

20: King George V diary – 21 November 1928 – Royal Archives

21: Queen Mary to David – 6 December 1928 – Royal Archives

22: *Edward VIII* – Ziegler, p192

23: Ibid

24: Ibid, pp192–3

25: *The Royal Marriages* – Lady Colin Campbell

CHAPTER 9

1: *The Heart has Its Reasons* – The Duchess of Windsor, p98

2: Ibid, p125

3: *Time* Magazine, 5th October 1936

4: *Who Killed Society?* – Cleveland Amory, p238

5: *Jewish Chronicle* – 18th August 2011

6: *Double Exposure*, p274

7: *A King's Story* – The Duke of Windsor, p254–5

8: *Double Exposure,* p274–5

9: *The Heart Has Its Reasons*, p171

10: Ibid

11: Ibid

12: Ibid, p175

13: Ibid

14: Ibid, pp190–1

15: Mortimer, p116

16: *Double Exposure*, p191

17: *The Heart Has Its Reasons,* p193

18: *Forget Not: Her Autobiography* – Margaret, Duchess of Argyll – W.H. Allen – 1975, pp40–1

19: *Double Exposure,* pp295–6

20: Ibid

21: *Double Exposure*, p298

22: *Edward VIII* – Frances Donaldson, p159

23: *The Windsor Story* – Bryan & Murphy, p59

24: *Double Exposure,* pp312–13

25: *Memoirs of HRH Prince Christopher of Greece,* p162

26: Conversations with Duchess of Argyll

27: Ibid

28: *Grace & Favour* – Loelia, Duchess of Westminster – Weidenfeld & Nicolson – 1961

29: *The Diaries of Sir Robert Bruce Lockhart*, ed Kenneth Young, p 309

30: Prince Paul of Yugoslavia papers – Bakhmeteff Archives, Rare Books & Manuscript Library, Columbia University, NY

31: Bruce Lockhart, p326

32: Ibid

33: Vickers, p123

34: Conversations with Duchess of Argyll

35: Mortimer, p117

36: Vickers, p123

37: *Diaries & Letters of Marie Belloc Lowndes* – Chatto & Windus – pp141–2

38: *The Heart Has Its Reasons,* p205

39: *Thatched with Gold* – Mabell Airlie, p200

40: Ibid, p200

41: Christopher of Greece, p162

42: *Harold Nicolson 1886-1929, Vol 1 A Biography* – James Lees-Milne, p365

43: Conversations with Duchess of Argyll

44: Argyll family information

45: *Royal Feud* – Michael Thornton – Pan Books – 1986, p75

46: Ibid

47: *King George V* – Rose pp391–2

48: Mensdorff Papers – 31 October 1935 – Vienna State Archives

49: *Thatched with Gold* – Airlie, p197

50: *Loyal to Three Kings* – Helen Hardinge – 1967, p66

51: Information provided by the Revd. Philip Hart who obtained it from Princess Alice, Countess of Athlone

52: *George VI* – Patrick Haworth – Hutchinson, p61

53: Alan Don Diary, 20/1/36 – Lambeth Palace Library

54: Hon. Lady Murray Papers

55: *The Little Princesses* – Marion Crawford – 1950, p72

56: *Self-Portrait with Friends* – Cecil Beaton, p47

57: *The Heart has its Reasons,* pp225–6

58: *Baldwin: A Biography* – Keith Middlemas and John Barnes, p980

59: Ibid, p981

60: Vickers, pp139–40

61: Hardinge, p114

62: Ibid

63: *The Reign of Edward VIII* – Robert Sencourt, p100

64: Hardinge, p116

65: *A King's Story* – pp317–18

66: Hardinge, p131

67: Bruce Lockhart Diaries – 1915–1938, p357

68: *The Heart has its Reasons,* p246

69: *Chips: The Diaries of Sir Henry Channon* – 13 November 1936, p80

70: Thornton, p122

71: Hon. Lady Murray Papers

72: Hardinge, p149

73: Shawcross, p573

74: *A Spirit Undaunted: The Political Role of George VI* – Robert Rhodes James, p249

75: Shawcross, p573

76: Helen Hardinge to Elizabeth – 7 July 1943 – Royal Archives

77: Helen Hardinge Diary – 7 July 1941 – Hon. Lady Murray Papers

78: Alan Morshead Note, 20 December 1936, Royal Archives

CHAPTER 10

1: Elizabeth to Cosmo Lang – 12/12/36 – Lambeth Palace Library, Lang Papers ff 181–3

2: Vickers, p203

3: *George VI* – Sarah Bradford, p300

4: Owen Morshead notes, 20 December 1936 – Royal Archives

5: Elizabeth to Queen Mary – 2 February 1937 – Royal Archives

6: Bradford, p298

7: Queen Mary to Elizabeth – 10 February 1952 – Royal Archives

8: Queen Mary to Lord Athlone and Princess Alice – 23 February 1952 – Royal Archives

9: David to Elizabeth – 18 February 1952 – Royal Archives

10: *Secret File of the Duke of Windsor* – Michael Bloch, pp264–5

11: Ibid

12: Ibid

13: Vickers, p150

14: Diaries of Sir Alan Lascelles

15: Paris, 23 March 1939 – FDR Library, Hyde Park, NY

16: Vickers, p178

17: Wheeler-Bennett, p380

18: *The Secret Diaries of Harold L. Ickes*, Vol 2, p650

19: Elizabeth to Queen Mary – 11 June 1939 – Royal Archives

20: *A Spirit Undaunted* – Robert Rhodes James – 1998, p163

21: Campbell, p40

22: Bullitt to Roosevelt – 9 May 1939

23: Elizabeth to Queen Mary – 24 May 1940 – Royal Archives

24: Mortimer, p164

25: Marion Crawford (hereinafter called Crawfie) to Queen Mary – 23 Feb 1941 – Royal Archives

26: Elizabeth to Lord Lloyd – 6 July 1940 – Lloyd Papers at the Churchill Archive Centre, Cambridge

27: Ibid

28: *Kings, Queens & Courtiers* – Rose, p151

29: Tariq Ali – *Oldie Magazine/Daily Telegraph* – Tim Walker – 18 October 2010

30: Vickers, p10

31: Elizabeth to Lang – 10 September 1930 – Lambeth Palace Library – Lang Papers

32: E to D Osborne, 13 July 1928

CHAPTER 11

1: *Past Forgetting* – Veronica Maclean,p214

2: Ibid

3: Campbell, p48

4: *The Queen Mother's Family Story* – James Wentworth Day, p133

5: Campbell, p71

6: Ibid, p76

7: Conversations with Colin Glenconner

8: Campbell, p62

9: Conversations with Michael Thornton

10: Campbell, p79–80 – Philip's Uncle Dickie Mountbatten, who had surrendered his post as Governor-General of India

11: Campbell, p80

12: Lilibet to Elizabeth – 16 October 1951 – Royal Archives

13: Queen Mary to Bertie – 17 November 1951 – Royal Archives

14: John Wheeler-Bennett interview with J. Macdonald – 20 October 1954 – Royal Archives

15: Ibid

16: Elizabeth to Lady Delia Peel – 11 February 1952 – Althorp Archives

17: Elizabeth to Queen Mary – 6 February 1952 – Royal Archives

CHAPTER 12

1: Campbell, p44

2: Conversations with Duchess of Argyll

3: Conversations with Duchess of Argyll

4: *The Light of Common Day* – Lady Diana Cooper, p73

5: Shawcross, p662

6: Elizabeth to Lilibet – undated 1952 – Royal Archives

7: Ibid

8: Elizabeth to Lascelles – 25 February 1952 – Royal Archives

9: Campbell, pp83–4

10: Elizabeth to Queen Mary – 22 June 1952 – Royal Archives

11: Conversations with Eric Anderson – 1994-5 – Royal Archives

12: Elizabeth to Lilibet – 21 July 1952 – Royal Archives

13: Elizabeth to Queen Mary – 22 August 1952 – Royal Archives

14: Elizabeth to May Elphinstone – 2 September 1952

15: Dermot Morrah to Goulds – 27 November 1948 – Manuscripts Division, Department of Rare Books and Special Collections, Princeton University Library

16: Sir Arthur Penn to Countess Spencer – 29 August 1952 – Althorp Archives

17: Elizabeth to Lilibet – 28 June 1952 – Royal Archives

18: Conversations with Duchess of Argyll

19: Author's conversation with former Deputy Secretary of the Commonwealth Secretariat

20: Information from Rene Silvin

21: *Time & Chance* – Peter Townsend, p198

22: Lascelles to Elizabeth – 11 June 1953 – Royal Archives

23: Elizabeth to Lascelles – 12 June 1953 – Royal Archives

24: *Elizabeth R* – Longford, p152

25: *Queen Mother* – Longford, p123

26: Elizabeth to Lascelles – 12 June 1953 – Royal Archives

27: Sir John Colville to Lascelles – undated 1955

28: Ibid

29: Lascelles to Elizabeth – 13 June 1953 – Royal Archives

30: Sir John Colville to Lascelles – undated 1955

31: Peter Townsend to Elizabeth – 17 June 1953 – Royal Archives

32: Elizabeth to Lilibet & Philip – 23 August 1953 – Royal Archives

33: Margaret to Elizabeth – 10 Sept 1955 – Royal Archives

34: Vickers, p363

35: Conversations with Colin Glenconner

36: Glenconner

37: *Snowdon: The Biography* – Anne de Courcy – 2008

38: Vickers, p366

39: Vickers, p435

40: Lawrence Michael Harvey Parsons, 6th Earl of Rosse (28 September 1906 – 5 July 1979)

41: Brendan Parsons, Lord Oxmantown

42: Hon. Desmond Oliver Martin Parsons

43: *American Story* – Gould and Gould, p235

44: Ibid, p236

45: Dermot Morrah to Bruce Gould – Manuscripts Division, Department of Rare Books and Special Collections, Princeton University Library – 18 February 1949

46: Ibid – 21 November 1949

47: Ibid – 9 December 1949

48: Crawfie to Bruce Gould – Manuscripts Division, Department of Rare Books and Special Collections, Princeton University Library – 26 December 1949

CHAPTER 13

1: Bertie to David – 9 August 1925 – Royal Archives

2: BK Hamilton to author

3: BK Hamilton

4: BK Hamilton

5: Conversation with Michael Ziadie

6: Sir Gladwyn Jebb to Selwyn Lloyd – 20 March 1956 – Royal Treaty Matters – National Archives

7: *The Diaries of Cynthia Gladwyn* – ed Miles Jebb, p168

8: Conversations with Duchess of Argyll

9: Ibid

10: Ibid

11: Obituary by Philip Hoare – the *Independent* – 23 May 1998

12: Conversations with Burnet Pavitt

13: Conversations with Duchess of Argyll

14: *Noblesse Oblige: The Duchess of Windsor as I Knew Her* – Richard Rene Silvin – Nike Publishing, p207

15: Conversations with Duchess of Argyll

16: Ibid

17: Ibid

18: *Alice, Princess Andrew of Greece* – Hugo Vickers – Hamish Hamilton, p336

19: Conversations with Duchess of Argyll

20: Campbell, p127

21: Interviews for *Diana in Private*

22: Diana to author

23: Conversation with Ned Ryan

24: Elizabeth to Prince Charles – 12 February 2002 – Clarence House Archives

25: Princess Margaret to Lady Glenconner – Clarence House Archives

26: *Point to Point Navigation* – Gore Vidal – Little Brown – 2006

Index